ISSUES AND READINGS IN

MANAGERIAL
FINANCE

FOURTH EDITION

ISSUES AND READINGS IN
MANAGERIAL
FINANCE

FOURTH EDITION

RAMON E. JOHNSON
University of Utah

The Dryden Press
Harcourt Brace Publishers

Fort Worth   Philadelphia   San Diego   New York   Orlando   Austin   San Antonio
Toronto   Montreal   London   Sydney   Tokyo

Acquisitions Editor	Rick Hammonds
Developmental Editor	Shana M. Lum
Project Editor	Amy Schmidt
Art Director	Jeanette Barber
Production Manager	Erin Gregg
Product Manager	Craig Johnson
Director of Editing, Design, & Production	Diane Southworth
Publisher	Elizabeth Widdicombe
Copy Editor	Donald Pharr
Compositor	Graphic Express
Text Type	10/12 Times Roman

Copyright © 1995, 1987, 1980, 1976 by The Dryden Press

Address for Editorial Correspondence
The Dryden Press, 301 Commerce Street, Suite 3700, Fort Worth, TX 76102

Address for Orders
The Dryden Press, 6277 Sea Harbor Drive, Orlando, FL 32887
1-800-782-4479, or 1-800-433-0001 (in Florida)

ISBN: 0-03-094888-6

Library of Congress Catalog Card Number: 94-71571

Printed in the United States of America

4 5 6 7 8 9 0 1 2 3 066   9 8 7 6 5 4 3 2 1

The Dryden Press
Harcourt Brace College Publishers

The Dryden Press Series in Finance

Amling and Droms
Investment Fundamentals

Berry and Young
Managing Investments: A Case Approach

Bertisch
Personal Finance

Brigham
Fundamentals of Financial Management
Seventh Edition

Brigham and Gapenski
*Cases in Financial Management:
Directed, Non-Directed, and by Request*

Brigham and Gapenski
*Cases in Financial Management:
Module A*

Brigham and Gapenski
*Cases in Financial Management:
Module B*

Brigham and Gapenski
*Cases in Financial Management:
Module C*

Brigham and Gapenski
Financial Management: Theory and Practice
Seventh Edition

Brigham and Gapenski
Intermediate Financial Management
Fourth Edition

Brigham, Gapenski, and Aberwald
Finance with Lotus 1-2-3
Second Edition

Chance
An Introduction to Derivatives
Third Edition

Clauretie and Webb
*The Theory and Practice of
Real Estate Finance*

Cooley
*Advances in Business Financial Management:
A Collection of Readings*

Cooley
Business Financial Management
Third Edition

Dickerson, Campsey, and Brigham
Introduction to Financial Management
Fourth Edition

Evans
*International Finance:
A Markets Approach*

Fama and Miller
The Theory of Finance

Gardner and Mills
*Managing Financial Institutions:
An Asset/Liability Approach*
Third Edition

Gitman and Joehnk
Personal Financial Planning
Sixth Edition

Greenbaum and Thakor
Contemporary Financial Intermediation

Harrington and Eades
Case Studies in Financial Decision Making
Third Edition

Hayes and Meerschwam
*Financial Institutions: Contemporary Cases in
the Financial Services Industry*

Hearth and Zaima
*Contemporary Investments:
Security and Portfolio Analysis*

Johnson
Issues and Readings in Managerial Finance
Fourth Edition

Kidwell, Peterson, and Blackwell
Financial Institutions, Markets, and Money
Fifth Edition

Koch
Bank Management
Third Edition

Maisel
Real Estate Finance
Second Edition

Martin, Cox, and MacMinn
The Theory of Finance:
Evidence and Applications

Mayo
Financial Institutions, Investments, and
Management: An Introduction
Fifth Edition

Mayo
Investments: An Introduction
Fourth Edition

Pettijohn
PROFIT+

Reilly
Investment Analysis and
Portfolio Management
Fourth Edition

Reilly and Norton
Investments
Fourth Edition

Sears and Trennepohl
Investment Management

Seitz and Ellison
Capital Budgeting and Long-Term
Financing Decisions
Second Edition

Siegel and Siegel
Futures Markets

Smith and Spudeck
Interest Rates:
Principles and Applications

Stickney
Financial Statement Analysis:
A Strategic Perspective
Second Edition

Weston and Brigham
Essentials of Managerial Finance
Tenth Edition

Weston and Copeland
Managerial Finance
Ninth Edition

The HB College Outline Series
Baker
Financial Management

Preface

In recent years, the world of finance has advanced exponentially in both theory and in practice. Much of this growth can be attributed to the dedication of many researchers and practitioners who have postulated the concepts that lie at the heart of financial decisions. For this edition of *Issues and Readings in Managerial Finance,* I wanted not only to pay tribute to these people and their ideas but also to make their work available to students in their studies in either advanced undergraduate- or graduate-level courses in finance.

Accordingly, I have structured the readings in the book into parts relating to the major topical areas of finance. Then, within each part, I've included one or two "classic" articles. By "classic" I mean that these articles documented the origin of a significant breakthrough in finance. In order to further clarify, advance, and update the research presented in these classic articles, I have supplemented them with tutorial reviews of current thought or practitioner articles, which put the original concepts into perspective today.

Two sources led to the genesis of the basic idea for *Issues and Readings in Managerial Finance.* The first was a presentation made by J. Fred Weston at the 1992 annual meetings of the Financial Management Association. Professor Weston constructed a history of finance ideas and issues, placing into context the people and the situations from which these ideas originated. Professor Weston has been a major participant, along with his students and peers, in the genesis and application of finance concepts. His professional life spans much of the entire period of this history.

Equally important was *Capital Ideas* by Peter Bernstein. In it, Bernstein develops a detailed history of the great ideas in finance. He also gives a highly credible account of the extent to which the practical world of finance has embraced the academic contributions of the past several decades.

In order to determine which articles to include in the book, I went through a large number of textbooks and counted the most frequently referenced articles. This research gave me my initial list of candidate articles. I then asked peers for advice and subsequently refined the list. I sent this list to a number of reviewers who made excellent recommendations. The resultant list was much too long, however, and I had to eliminate numerous articles that some users would have preferred were included. For example, the first list included Franco Modigliani and Merton Miller's 1958 and 1963 articles, and Miller's "Debt and Taxes." Only Modigliani and Miller's 1963 article, however, is contained herein in Part IV because it is the article that finalized the M&M position. Their 1963 article is followed by Stewart Myers' "The Capital Structure Puzzle" (1984); and Michael Pinegar and Lisa Wilbricht's "What Managers Think of Capital Structure Policy" (1989).

The wide range of authors, styles, and subject matter contained in the book means that some articles are more difficult than others. The tutorial pieces found in many of the parts should help students understand and apply the more difficult readings. If nothing else, I hope that all of the articles will challenge and evoke the interest of instructors and students alike.

For their suggestions regarding the various versions of the book, I am indebted to Uri Loewenstein, Ron Lease, James Schallheim, Cal Boardman, Saeed Mortazavi, Gautam Vora, Katherine Spiess, Tyler Claggett, Jr., Jerry Boswell, Daniel Pace, and Brian Belt. Of course, all errors of judgment relating to the inclusion or omission of articles are mine.

Ramon E. Johnson

Salt Lake City
September 1994

Contents

Part I   *Foundations of Financial Management*   *1*

Michael C. Jensen and William H. Meckling
Theory of the Firm: Managerial Behavior, Agency Costs, and Ownership Structure   *3*

Richard A. Lambert and David F. Larcker
Executive Compensation, Corporate Decision Making, and Shareholder Wealth: A Review of the Evidence   *53*

J. Fred Weston
A (Relatively) Brief History of Finance Ideas   *75*

Part II   *Valuation and Cost of Capital*   *107*

John Burr Williams
Evaluation by the Rule of Present Worth   *109*

Harry Markowitz
Portfolio Selection   *113*

William F. Sharpe
Capital Asset Prices: A Theory of Market Equilibrium under Conditions of Risk   *127*

Franco Modigliani and Gerald A. Pogue
An Introduction to Risk and Return: Concepts and Evidence, Part I   *145*

Franco Modigliani and Gerald A. Pogue
An Introduction to Risk and Return: Concepts and Evidence, Part II   *165*

Barr Rosenberg and Andrew Rudd
The Corporate Uses of Beta   193

Richard Roll and Stephen A. Ross
The Arbitrage Pricing Theory Approach to Strategic Portfolio Planning   209

Part III   Capital Budgeting   225

Alan C. Shapiro
Corporate Strategy and the Capital Budgeting Decision   227

David B. Hertz
Risk Analysis in Financial Investments   247

Marc Ross
Capital Budgeting Practices of Twelve Large Manufacturers   263

Samuel Weaver, Donald Peters, Roger Cason, and Joe Daleiden
Capital Budgeting   275

Samuel Weaver, Peter J. Clemmens III, Jack A. Gunn, and Bruce D. Dannenburg
Divisional Hurdle Rates and the Cost of Capital   287

Part IV   Capital Structure and Dividend Policy   297

Merton H. Miller and Franco Modigliani
Corporate Income Taxes and the Cost of Capital: A Correction   299

Stewart C. Myers
The Capital Structure Puzzle   309

J. Michael Pinegar and Lisa Wilbricht
What Managers Think of Capital Structure Theory: A Survey   327

Merton H. Miller and Franco Modigliani
Dividend Policy, Growth, and the Valuation of Shares   341

Ronald C. Lease and Uri Loewenstein
Dividend Policy: Its Impact on Firm Value   367

Part V   Long-Term Financing   389

Clifford W. Smith, Jr.
Investment Banking and the Capital Acquisition Process   391

Robert Rogowski and Eric Sorensen
The New Competitive Environment of Investment Banking:
Transactional Finance and Concession Pricing of New Issues   415

James S. Schallheim, Ramon E. Johnson, Ronald C. Lease, and John J. McConnell
The Determinants of Yields on Financial Leasing Contracts   433

John D. Finnerty
Financial Engineering in Corporate America: An Overview   453

Part VI   Short-Term Financial Management   481

Wilber G. Lewellen and Robert W. Johnson
Better Way to Monitor Accounts Receivable   483

James A. Gentry
State of the Art of Short-Run Financial Management   499

Part VII   Financial Analysis   523

Edward I. Altman
Financial Ratios, Discriminant Analysis, and the Prediction of
Corporate Bankruptcy   525

Part VIII   Special Topics   547

Eugene F. Fama
Random Walks in Stock Prices   549

Fischer Black and Myron Scholes
The Pricing of Options and Corporate Liabilities   *559*

Michael C. Jensen and Richard S. Ruback
The Market for Corporate Control: The Scientific Evidence   *575*

Bruno H. Solnik
Why Not Diversify Internationally Rather Than Domestically?   *615*

Kose John
*Managing Financial Distress and Valuing Distressed Securities:
A Survey and a Research Agenda*   *623*

part I

Foundations of Financial Management

Shareholders elect directors to represent their interests and to hire and set policy for management. Jensen and Meckling in their classic article develop the concepts of agency costs created by the separation of management and ownership. Their paper is the first in Part I.

The second article, by Lambert and Larcker, reviews the value maximizing goal and presents information on how management compensation can be designed to align the interests of managers with those of stockholders.

Rounding out Part I is a historical treatise by Fred Weston on the development of ideas in finance. This article helps all of us to understand when the great ideas were developed and by whom.

Michael C. Jensen and William H. Meckling*

Theory of the Firm: Managerial Behavior, Agency Costs, and Ownership Structure

An important issue in finance has to do with problems created when owners of firms are not the managers. Managers are agents for owners, and the challenge is making sure managers act in the interests of shareholders rather than themselves. This area of study is called agency theory; the article reprinted here is the definitive study in this area.

This paper integrates elements from the theory of agency, the theory of property rights, and the theory of finance to develop a theory of the ownership structure of the firm. We define the concept of agency costs, show its relationship to the "separation and control" issue, investigate the nature of the agency costs generated by the existence of debt and outside equity, demonstrate who bears these costs and why, and investigate the Pareto optimality of their existence. We also provide a new definition of the firm and show how our analysis of the factors influencing the creation and issuance of debt and equity claims is a special case of the supply side of the completeness of markets problem.

> The directors of such [joint-stock] companies, however, being the managers rather of other people's money than of their own, it cannot well be expected, that they should watch over it with the same anxious vigilance with which the partners in a private copartnery frequently watch over their own. Like the stewards of a rich man, they are apt to consider attention to small matters as not for their master's honour, and very easily give themselves a dispensation from having it. Negligence and profusion, therefore, must always prevail, more or less, in the management of the affairs of such a company.—Adam Smith, *The Wealth of Nations,* 1776, Cannan Edition (Modern Library, New York, 1937), p. 700.

*Associate Professor and Dean, respectively, Graduate School of Management, University of Rochester on date of publication. An earlier version of this paper was presented at the Conference on Analysis and Ideology, Interlaken, Switzerland, June 1974, sponsored by the Center for Research in Government Policy and Business at the University of Rochester, Graduate School of Management. We are indebted to F. Black, E. Fama, R. Ibbotson, W. Klein, M. Rozeff, R. Weil, O. Williamson, an anonymous referee, and to our colleagues and members of the Finance Workshop at the University of Rochester for their comments and criticisms, in particular G. Benston, M. Canes, D. Henderson, K. Leffler, J. Long, C. Smith, R. Thompson, R. Watts, and J. Zimmerman.

Source: Reprinted with permission from the *Journal of Financial Economics* (October 1976), "Theory of the Firm: Managerial Behavior, Agency Costs, and Ownership Structure" by Michael C. Jensen and William H. Meckling, pp. 305–360, Elsevier Science B.V., Amsterdam, The Netherlands. Michael C. Jensen is the Edsel Bryant Ford Professor of Business Administration at Harvard Business School. William H. Meckling is the Dean Emeritus of the William E. Simon Graduate School of Business Administration at the University of Rochester.

1. Introduction and Summary

1.1. Motivation of the Paper

In this paper we draw on recent progress in the theory of (1) property rights, (2) agency, and (3) finance to develop a theory of ownership structure[1] for the firm. In addition to tying together elements of the theory of each of these three areas, our analysis casts new light on and has implications for a variety of issues in the professional and popular literature such as the definition of the firm, the "separation of ownership and control," the "social responsibility" of business, the definition of a "corporate objective function," the determination of an optimal capital structure, the specification of the content of credit agreements, the theory of organizations, and the supply side of the completeness of markets problem.

Our theory helps explain:

1. why an entrepreneur or manager in a firm which has a mixed financial structure (containing both debt and outside equity claims) will choose a set of activities for the firm such that the total value of the firm is *less* than it would be if he were the sole owner and why this result is independent of whether the firm operates in monopolistic or competitive product or factor markets;

2. why his failure to maximize the value of the firm is perfectly consistent with efficiency;

3. why the sale of common stock is a viable source of capital even though managers do not literally maximize the value of the firm;

4. why debt was relied upon as a source of capital before debt financing offered any tax advantage relative to equity;

5. why preferred stock would be issued;

6. why accounting reports would be provided voluntarily to creditors and stockholders, and why independent auditors would be engaged by management to testify to the accuracy and correctness of such reports;

7. why lenders often place restrictions on the activities of firms to whom they lend, and why firms would themselves be led to suggest the imposition of such restrictions;

8. why some industries are characterized by owner-operated firms whose sole outside source of capital is borrowing;

9. why highly regulated industries such as public utilities or banks will have higher debt equity ratios for equivalent levels of risk than the average non-regulated firm;

10. why security analysis can be socially productive even if it does not increase portfolio returns to investors.

---

[1]We do not use the term "capital structure" because that term usually denotes the relative quantities of bonds, equity, warrants, trade credit, etc., which represent the liabilities of a firm. Our theory implies there is another important dimension to this problem—namely the relative amounts of ownership claims held by insiders (management) and outsiders (investors with no direct role in the management of the firm).

1.2. Theory of the Firm: An Empty Box?

While the literature of economics is replete with references to the "theory of the firm," the material generally subsumed under that heading is not a theory of the firm but actually a theory of markets in which firms are important actors. The firm is a "black box" operated so as to meet the relevant marginal conditions with respect to inputs and outputs, thereby maximizing profits, or more accurately, present value. Except for a few recent and tentative steps, however, we have no theory which explains how the conflicting objectives of the individual participants are brought into equilibrium so as to yield this result. The limitations of this black box view of the firm have been cited by Adam Smith and Alfred Marshall, among others. More recently, popular and professional debates over the "social responsibility" of corporations, the separation of ownership and control, and the rash of reviews of the literature on the "theory of the firm" have evidenced continuing concern with these issues.[2]

A number of major attempts have been made during recent years to construct a theory of the firm by substituting other models for profit or value maximization, each attempt motivated by a conviction that the latter is inadequate to explain managerial behavior in large corporations.[3] Some of these reformulation attempts have rejected the fundamental principle of maximizing behavior as well as rejecting the more specific profit maximizing model. We retain the notion of maximizing behavior on the part of all individuals in the analysis to follow.[4]

1.3. Property Rights

An independent stream of research with important implications for the theory of the firm has been stimulated by the pioneering work of Coase and extended by Alchian, Demsetz, and others.[5] A comprehensive survey of this literature is given by Furubotn and Pejovich (1972). While the focus of this research has been "property rights,"[6] the subject matter encompassed is far broader than that term suggests. What is important for the problems addressed here is that specification of individual rights determines how costs and rewards will be allocated among the participants in any organization. Since the specification of rights is generally effected through contracting (implicit as well as

---

[2] Reviews of this literature are given by Peterson (1965), Alchian (1965, 1968), Machlup (1967), Shubik (1970), Cyert and Hedrick (1972), Branch (1973), Preston (1975).

[3] See Williamson (1964, 1970, 1975), Marris (1964), Baumol (1959), Penrose (1958), and Cyert and March (1963). Thorough reviews of these and other contributions are given by Machlup (1961) and Alchian (1965).

 Simon (1955) developed a model of human choice incorporating information (search) and computational costs which also has important implications for the behavior of managers. Unfortunately, Simon's work has often been misinterpreted as a denial of maximizing behavior, and misused, especially in the marketing and behavioral science literature. His later use of the term "satisficing" [Simon (1959)] has undoubtedly contributed to this confusion because it suggests rejection of maximizing behavior rather than maximization subject to costs of information and of decision making.

[4] See Meckling (1976) for a discussion of the fundamental importance of the assumption of resourceful, evaluative, maximizing behavior on the part of individuals in the development of theory. Klein (1976) takes an approach similar to the one we embark on in this paper in his review of the theory of the firm and the law.

[5] See Coase (1937, 1959, 1960), Alchian (1965, 1968), Alchian and Kessel (1962), Demsetz (1967), Alchian and Demsetz (1972), Monsen and Downs (1965), Silver and Auster (1969), and McManus (1975).

[6] Property rights are of course human rights, i.e., rights which are possessed by human beings. The introduction of the wholly false distinction between property rights and human rights in many policy discussions is surely one of the all-time great semantic flimflams.

explicit), individual behavior in organizations, including the behavior of managers, will depend upon the nature of these contracts. We focus in this paper on the behavioral implications of the property rights specified in the contracts between the owners and managers of the firm.

1.4. Agency Costs

Many problems associated with the inadequacy of the current theory of the firm can also be viewed as special cases of the theory of agency relationships, in which there is a growing literature.[7] This literature has developed independently of the property rights literature, even though the problems with which it is concerned are similar; the approaches are in fact highly complementary to each other.

We define an agency relationship as a contract under which one or more persons (the principal[s]) engage another person (the agent) to perform some service on their behalf which involves delegating some decision-making authority to the agent. If both parties to the relationship are utility maximizers, there is good reason to believe that the agent will not always act in the best interests of the principal. The *principal* can limit divergences from his interest by establishing appropriate incentives for the agent and by incurring monitoring costs designed to limit the aberrant activities of the agent. In addition, in some situations it will pay the *agent* to expend resources (bonding costs) to guarantee that he will not take certain actions which would harm the principal or to ensure that the principal will be compensated if he does take such actions. However, it is generally impossible for the principal or the agent at zero cost to ensure that the agent will make optimal decisions from the principal's viewpoint. In most agency relationships the principal and the agent will incur positive monitoring and bonding costs (non-pecuniary as well as pecuniary), and in addition there will be some divergence between the agent's decisions[8] and those decisions which would maximize the welfare of the principal. The dollar equivalent of the reduction in welfare experienced by the principal due to this divergence is also a cost of the agency relationship, and we refer to this latter cost as the "residual loss." We define *agency costs* as the sum of:

1. the monitoring expenditures by the principal,[9]
2. the bonding expenditures by the agent,
3. the residual loss.

Note also that agency costs arise in any situation involving cooperative effort (such as the co-authoring of this paper) by two or more people even though there is no clear-cut principal-agent relationship. Viewed in this light, it is clear that our definition of agency costs and their importance to the theory of the firm bears a close relationship to the problem of shirking and monitoring of team production which Alchian and Demsetz (1972) raise in their paper on the theory of the firm.

Since the relationship between the stockholders and manager of a corporation fit the definition of a pure agency relationship, it should be no surprise to discover that the issues associated with the

---

[7] Cf. Berhold (1971), Ross (1973, 1974a), Wilson (1968, 1969), and Heckerman (1975).

[8] Given the optimal monitoring and bonding activities by the principal and agent

[9] As it is used in this paper, the term *monitoring* includes more than just measuring or observing the behavior of the agent. It includes efforts on the part of the principal to "control" the behavior of the agent through budget restrictions, compensation policies, operating rules, etc.

"separation of ownership and control" in the modern diffuse-ownership corporation are intimately associated with the general problem of agency. We show below that an explanation of why and how the agency costs generated by the corporate form are born leads to a theory of the ownership (or capital) structure of the firm.

Before moving on, however, it is worthwhile to point out the generality of the agency problem. The problem of inducing an "agent" to behave as if he were maximizing the "principal's" welfare is quite general. It exists in all organizations and in all cooperative efforts—at every level of management in firms,[10] in universities, in mutual companies, in cooperatives, in governmental authorities and bureaus, in unions, and in relationships normally classified as agency relationships such as are common in the performing arts and the market for real estate. The development of theories to explain the form which agency costs take in each of these situations (where the contractual relations differ significantly) and how and why they are born will lead to a rich theory of organizations, which is now lacking in economics and the social sciences generally. We confine our attention in this paper to only a small part of this general problem—the analysis of agency costs generated by the contractual arrangements between the owners and top management of the corporation.

Our approach to the agency problem here differs fundamentally from most of the existing literature. That literature focuses almost exclusively on the normative aspects of the agency relationship—that is, how to structure the contractual relation (including compensation incentives) between the principal and agent to provide appropriate incentives for the agent to make choices which will maximize the principal's welfare, given that uncertainty and imperfect monitoring exist. We focus almost entirely on the positive aspects of the theory. That is, we assume individuals solve these normative problems and given that only stocks and bonds can be issued as claims, we investigate the incentives faced by each of the parties and the elements entering into the determination of the equilibrium contractual form characterizing the relationship between the manager (i.e., agent) of the firm and the outside equity and debt holders (i.e., principals).

1.5. Some General Comments on the Definition of the Firm

Ronald Coase (1937) in his seminal paper on "The Nature of the Firm" pointed out that economics had no positive theory to determine the bounds of the firm. He characterized the bounds of the firm as that range of exchanges over which the market system was suppressed and resource allocation was accomplished instead by authority and direction. He focused on the cost of using markets to effect contracts and exchanges and argued that activities would be included within the firm whenever the costs of using markets were greater than the costs of using direct authority. Alchian and Demsetz (1972) object to the notion that activities within the firm are governed by authority, and correctly emphasize the role of contracts as a vehicle for voluntary exchange. They emphasize the

---

[10] As we show below, the existence of positive monitoring and bonding costs will result in the manager of a corporation possessing control over some resources which he can allocate (within certain constraints) to satisfy his own preferences. However, to the extent that he must obtain the cooperation of others in order to carry out his tasks (such as divisional vice presidents) and to the extent that he cannot control their behavior perfectly and costlessly, they will be able to appropriate some of these resources for their own ends. In short, there are agency costs generated at every level of the organization. Unfortunately, the analysis of these more general organizational issues is even more difficult than that of the "ownership and control" issue because the nature of the contractual obligations and rights of the parties are much more varied and generally not as well specified in explicit contractual arrangements. Nevertheless, they exist, and we believe that extensions of our analysis in these directions show promise of producing insights into a viable theory of organization.

role of monitoring in situations in which there is joint input or team production.[11] We sympathize with the importance they attach to monitoring, but we believe the emphasis which Alchian and Demsetz place on joint input production is too narrow and therefore misleading. Contractual relations are the essence of the firm, not only with employees but with suppliers, customers, creditors, etc. The problem of agency costs and monitoring exists for all of these contracts, independent of whether there is joint production in their sense; i.e., joint production can explain only a small fraction of the behavior of individuals associated with a firm. A detailed examination of these issues is left to another paper.

It is important to recognize that most organizations are simply *legal fictions*[12] *which serve as a nexus for a set of contracting relationships among individuals.* This includes firms, nonprofit institutions such as universities, hospitals and foundations, mutual organizations such as mutual savings banks, insurance companies, and cooperatives, some private clubs, and even governmental bodies such as cities, states, and the federal government, and government enterprises such as TVA, the Postal Service, and transit systems.

The private corporation or firm is simply one form of *legal fiction which serves as a nexus for contracting relationships and which is also characterized by the existence of divisible residual claims on the assets and cash flows of the organization which can generally be sold without permission of the other contracting individuals.* While this definition of the firm has little substantive content, emphasizing the essential contractual nature of firms and other organizations focuses attention on a crucial set of questions—why particular sets of contractual relations arise for various types of organizations, what the consequences of these contractual relations are, and how they are affected by changes exogenous to the organization. Viewed this way, it makes little or no sense to try to distinguish those things which are "inside" the firm (or any other organization) from those things that are "outside" of it. There is in a very real sense only a multitude of complex relationships (i.e., contracts) between the legal fiction (the firm) and the owners of labor, material, and capital inputs, and the consumers of output.[13]

Viewing the firm as the nexus of a set of contracting relationships among individuals also serves to make it clear that the personalization of the firm implied by asking questions such as "what should be the objective function of the firm" or "does the firm have a social responsibility" is seriously misleading. *The firm is not an individual.* It is a legal fiction which serves as a focus for a complex process in which the conflicting objectives of individuals (some of whom may "represent" other organizations) are brought into equilibrium within a framework of contractual relations. In this sense the "behavior" of the firm is like the behavior of a market—i.e., the outcome of a complex equilibrium process. We seldom fall into the trap of characterizing the wheat or stock mar-

---

[11] They define the classical capitalist firm as a contractual organization of inputs in which there is "(a) joint input production, (b) several input owners, (c) one party who is common to all the contracts of the joint inputs, (d) who has rights to renegotiate any input's contract independently of contracts with other input owners, (e) who holds the residual claim, and (f) who has the right to sell his contractual residual status."

[12] By *legal fiction* we mean the artificial construct under the law which allows certain organizations to be treated as individuals.

[13] For example, we ordinarily think of a product as leaving the firm at the time it is sold, but implicitly or explicitly such sales generally carry with them continuing contracts between the firm and the buyer. If the product does not perform as expected, the buyer often can and does have a right to satisfaction. Explicit evidence that such implicit contracts do exist is the practice we occasionally observe of specific provision that "all sales are final."

ket as an individual, but we often make this error by thinking about organizations as if they were persons with motivations and intentions.[14]

1.6. An Overview of the Paper

We develop the theory in stages. Sections 2 and 4 provide analyses of the agency costs of equity and debt respectively. These form the major foundation of the theory. Section 3 poses some unanswered questions regarding the existence of the corporate form of organization and examines the role of limited liability. Section 5 provides a synthesis of the basic concepts derived in sections 2–4 into a theory of the corporate ownership structure which takes account of the trade-offs available to the entrepreneur-manager between inside and outside equity and debt. Some qualifications and extensions of the analysis are discussed in section 6, and section 7 contains a brief summary and conclusions.

2. The Agency Costs of Outside Equity

2.1. Overview

In this section we analyze the effect of outside equity on agency costs by comparing the behavior of a manager when he owns 100 percent of the residual claims on a firm to his behavior when he sells off a portion of those claims to outsiders. If a wholly owned firm is managed by the owner, he will make operating decisions which maximize his utility. These decisions will involve not only the benefits he derives from pecuniary returns but also the utility generated by various non-pecuniary aspects of his entrepreneurial activities such as the physical appointments of the office, the attractiveness of the secretarial staff, the level of employee discipline, the kind and amount of charitable contributions, personal relations ("love," "respect," etc.) with employees, a larger than optimal computer to play with, purchase of production inputs from friends, etc. The optimum mix (in the absence of taxes) of the various pecuniary and non-pecuniary benefits is achieved when the marginal utility derived from an additional dollar of expenditure (measured net of any productive effects) is equal for each non-pecuniary item and equal to the marginal utility derived from an additional dollar of after-tax purchasing power (wealth).

If the owner-manager sells equity claims on the corporation which are identical to his (i.e., share proportionately in the profits of the firm and have limited liability), agency costs will be generated by the divergence between his interest and those of the outside shareholders, since he will then bear only a fraction of the costs of any non-pecuniary benefits he takes out in maximizing his own utility. If the manager owns only 95 percent of the stock, he will expend resources to the point

---

[14] This view of the firm points up the important role which the legal system and the law play in social organizations, especially, the organization of economic activity. Statutory laws set bounds on the kinds of contracts into which individuals and organizations may enter without risking criminal prosecution. The police powers of the state are available and used to enforce performance of contracts or to enforce the collection of damages for nonperformance. The courts adjudicate conflicts between contracting parties and establish precedents which form the body of common law. All of these government activities affect both the kinds of contracts executed and the extent to which contracting is relied upon. This in turn determines the usefulness, productivity, profitability, and viability of various forms of organization. Moreover, new laws as well as court decisions often can and do change the rights of contracting parties ex post, and they can and do serve as a vehicle for redistribution of wealth. An analysis of some of the implications of these facts is contained in Jensen and Meckling (1976), and we shall not pursue them here.

where the marginal utility derived from a dollar's expenditure of the firm's resources on such items equals the marginal utility of an additional 95 cents in general purchasing power (i.e., *his* share of the wealth reduction) and not one dollar. Such activities, on his part, can be limited (but probably not eliminated) by the expenditure of resources on monitoring activities by the outside stockholders. But as we show below, the owner will bear the entire wealth effects of these expected costs so long as the equity market anticipates these effects. Prospective minority shareholders will realize that the owner-manager's interests will diverge somewhat from theirs; hence the price which they will pay for shares will reflect the monitoring costs and the effect of the divergence between the manager's interest and theirs. Nevertheless, ignoring for the moment the possibility of borrowing against his wealth, the owner will find it desirable to bear these costs as long as the welfare increment he experiences from converting his claims on the firm into general purchasing power[15] is large enough to offset them.

As the owner-manager's fraction of the equity falls, his fractional claim on the outcomes falls, and this will tend to encourage him to appropriate larger amounts of the corporate resources in the form of perquisites. This also makes it desirable for the minority shareholders to expend more resources in monitoring his behavior. Thus, the wealth costs to the owner of obtaining additional cash in the equity markets rise as his fractional ownership falls.

We shall continue to characterize the agency conflict between the owner-manager and outside shareholders as deriving from the manager's tendency to appropriate perquisites out of the firm's resources for his own consumption. However, we do not mean to leave the impression that this is the only or even the most important source of conflict. Indeed, it is likely that the most important conflict arises from the fact that as the manager's ownership claim falls, his incentive to devote significant effort to creative activities such as searching out new profitable ventures falls. He may in fact avoid such ventures simply because it requires too much trouble or effort on his part to manage or to learn about new technologies. Avoidance of these personal costs and the anxieties that go with them also represents a source of on-the-job utility to him, and it can result in the value of the firm being substantially lower than it otherwise could be.

2.2. A Simple Formal Analysis of the Sources of Agency Costs of Equity and Who Bears Them

In order to develop some structure for the analysis to follow, we make two sets of assumptions. The first set (permanent assumptions) are those which shall carry through almost all of the analysis in sections 2–5. The effects of relaxing some of these are discussed in section 6. The second set (temporary assumptions) are made only for expositional purposes and are relaxed as soon as the basic points have been clarified.

Permanent Assumptions

(P.1) All taxes are zero.

(P.2) No trade credit is available.

---

[15] For use in consumption, for the diversification of his wealth, or more importantly, for the financing of "profitable" projects which he could not otherwise finance out of his personal wealth. We deal with these issues below after having developed some of the elementary analytical tools necessary to their solution.

(P.3) All outside equity shares are non-voting.

(P.4) No complex financial claims such as convertible bonds or preferred stock or warrants can be issued.

(P.5) No outside owner gains utility from ownership in a firm in any way other than through its effect on his wealth or cash flows.

(P.6) All dynamic aspects of the multiperiod nature of the problem are ignored by assuming there is only one production-financing decision to be made by the entrepreneur.

(P.7) The entrepreneur-manager's money wages are held constant throughout the analysis.

(P.8) There exists a single manager (the peak coordinator) with ownership interest in the firm.

Temporary Assumptions

(T.1) The size of the firm is fixed.

(T.2) No monitoring or bonding activities are possible.

(T.3) No debt financing through bonds, preferred stock, or personal borrowing (secured or unsecured) is possible.

(T.4) All elements of the owner-manager's decision problem involving portfolio considerations induced by the presence of uncertainty and the existence of diversifiable risk are ignored.

Define:

X = $\{\chi_1, \chi_2, \ldots, \chi_n\}$ = vector of quantities of all factors and activities within the firm from which the manager derives non-pecuniary benefits;[16] the χ_i are defined such that his marginal utility is positive for each of them;

$C(X)$ = total dollar cost of providing any given amount of these items;

$P(X)$ = total dollar value to the firm of the productive benefits of X;

$B(X) = P(X) - C(X)$ = net dollar benefit to the firm of X, ignoring any effects of X on the equilibrium wage of the manager.

Ignoring the effects of X on the manager's utility and therefore on his equilibrium wage rate, the optimum levels of the factors and activities X are defined by X^* such that

$$\frac{\partial B(X^*)}{\partial X^*} = \frac{\partial P(X^*)}{\partial X^*} - \frac{\partial C(X^*)}{\partial X^*} = 0.$$

Thus for any vector $X \geq X^*$ (i.e., where at least one element of X is greater than its corresponding element of X^*), $F \equiv B(\overline{X}^*) - B(X) > 0$ measures the dollar cost to the firm (net of any productive effects) of providing the increment $X - X^*$ of the factors and activities which generate utility to the manager. We assume henceforth that for any given level of cost to the firm, F, the vector of factors and activities on which F is spent are those, $\hat{X}$, which yield the manager maximum utility. Thus $F \equiv B(X^*) - B(\hat{X})$.

---

[16] Such as office space, air conditioning, thickness of the carpets, friendliness of employee relations.

We have thus far ignored in our discussion the fact that these expenditures on X occur through time, and therefore there are tradeoffs to be made across time as well as between alternative elements of X. Furthermore, we have ignored the fact that the future expenditures are likely to involve uncertainty (i.e., they are subject to probability distributions), and therefore some allowance must be made for their riskiness. We resolve both of these issues by defining C, P, B, and F to be the *current market values* of the sequence of probability distributions on the period by period cash flows involved.[17]

Given the definition of F as the current market value of the stream of manager's expenditures on non-pecuniary benefits, we represent the constraint which a single owner-manager faces in deciding how much non-pecuniary income he will extract from the firm by the line $\overline{V}F$ in Figure 1. This is analogous to a budget constraint. The market value of the firm is measured along the vertical axis, and the market value of the manager's stream of expenditures on non-pecuniary benefits, F, is measured along the horizontal axis. $0\overline{V}$ is the value of the firm when the amount of non-pecuniary income consumed is zero. By definition, $\overline{V}$ is the maximum market value of the cash flows generated by the firm for a given money wage for the manager when the manager's consumption of non-pecuniary benefits are zero. At this point all the factors and activities within the firm which generate utility for the manager are at the level X^* defined above. There is a different budget constraint $\overline{V}F$ for each possible scale of the firm (i.e., level of investment, I) and for alternative levels of money wage, W, for the manager. For the moment we pick an arbitrary level of investment (which we assume has already been made) and hold the scale of the firm constant at this level. We also assume that the manager's money wage is fixed at the level W^*, which represents the current market value of his wage contract[18] in the optimal compensation package, which consists of both wages, W^*, and non-pecuniary benefits, F^*. Since one dollar of current value of non-pecuniary benefits withdrawn from the firm by the manager reduces the market value of the firm by \$1, by definition, the slope of $\overline{V}F$ is −1.

The owner-manager's tastes for wealth and non-pecuniary benefits is represented in Figure 1 by a system of indifference curves, U_1, U_2, etc.[19] The indifference curves will be convex as drawn as long as the owner-manager's marginal rate of substitution between non-pecuniary benefits and wealth diminishes with increasing levels of the benefits. For the 100 percent owner-manager, this presumes that there are not perfect substitutes for these benefits available on the outside—i.e., to

---

[17] And again we assume that for any given market value of these costs, F, to the firm, the allocation across time and across alternative probability distributions is such that the manager's current expected utility is at a maximum.

[18] At this stage, when we are considering a 100 percent owner-managed firm, the notion of a "wage contract" with himself has no content. However, the 100 percent owner-managed case is only an expositional device used in passing to illustrate a number of points in the analysis, and we ask the reader to bear with us briefly while we lay out the structure for the more interesting partial ownership case where such a contract does have substance.

[19] The manager's utility function is actually defined over wealth and the future time sequence of vectors of quantities of non-pecuniary benefits, X_t. Although the setting of his problem is somewhat different, Fama (1970b, 1972) analyzes the conditions under which these preferences can be represented as a derived utility function defined as a function of the money value of the expenditures (in our notation, F) on these goods conditional on the prices of goods. Such a utility function incorporates the optimization going on in the background which defines $\hat{X}$ discussed above for a given F. In the more general case, where we allow a time series of consumption, $\hat{X}_t$, the optimization is being carried out across both time and the components of X_t for fixed F.

Figure 1

The value of the firm (V) and the level of non-pecuniary benefits consumed (F) when the fraction of outside equity is $(1 - \alpha)V$, and U_j $(j = 1, 2, 3)$ represents owner's indifference curves between wealth and non-pecuniary benefits.

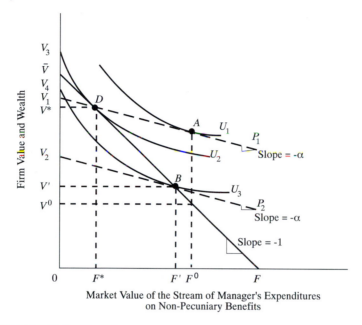

Market Value of the Stream of Manager's Expenditures
on Non-Pecuniary Benefits

some extent they are job specific. For the fractional owner-manager, this presumes the benefits cannot be turned into general purchasing power at a constant price.[20]

When the owner has 100 percent of the equity, the value of the firm will be V^* where indifference curve U_2 is tangent to VF, and the level of non-pecuniary benefits consumed is F^*. If the owner sells the entire equity but remains as manager, and if the equity buyer can, at zero cost, force the old owner (as manager) to take the same level of non-pecuniary benefits as he did as owner, then V^* is the price the new owner will be willing to pay for the entire equity.[21]

---

[20] This excludes, for instance, (a) the case where the manager is allowed to expend corporate resources on anything he pleases, in which case F would be a perfect substitute for wealth; or (b) the case where he can "steal" cash (or other marketable assets) with constant returns to scale—if he could, the indifference curves would be straight lines with slope determined by the fence commission.

[21] Point D defines the fringe benefits in the optimal pay package, since the value to the manager of the fringe benefits, F^*, is greater than the cost of providing them, as is evidenced by the fact that U_2 is steeper to the left of D than the budget constraint with slope equal to -1.

That D is indeed the optimal pay package can easily be seen in this situation since if the conditions of the sale to a new owner specified that the manager would receive no fringe benefits after the sale, he would require a payment equal to V_3 to compensate him for the sacrifice of his claims to V^* and fringe benefits amounting to F^* (the latter with total value to him

(*continued on p. 14*)

In general, however, we would not expect the new owner to be able to enforce identical behavior on the old owner at zero costs. If the old owner sells a fraction of the firm to an outsider, he, as manager, will no longer bear the full cost of any non-pecuniary benefits he consumes. Suppose the owner sells a share of the firm, $1 - \alpha$, $(0 < \alpha < 1)$, and retains for himself a share, α. If the prospective buyer believes that the owner-manager will consume the same level of non-pecuniary benefits as he did as full owner, the buyer will be willing to pay $(1 - \alpha)V^*$ for a fraction $(1 - \alpha)$ of the equity. Given that an outsider now holds a claim to $(1 - \alpha)$ of the equity, however, the *cost* to the owner-manager of consuming \$1 of non-pecuniary benefits in the firm will no longer be \$1. Instead, it will be $\alpha \times \$1$. If the prospective buyer actually paid $(1 - \alpha)V^*$ for his share of the equity and if thereafter the manager could choose whatever level of non-pecuniary benefits he liked, his budget constraint would be $V_1 P_1$ in Figure 1 and has a slope equal to $-\alpha$. Including the payment the owner receives from the buyer as part of the owner's post-sale wealth, his budget constraint, $V_1 P_1$, must pass through D, since he can if he wishes have the same wealth and level of non-pecuniary consumption he consumed as full owner.

But if the owner-manager is free to choose the level of perquisites, F, subject only to the loss in wealth he incurs as a part owner, his welfare will be maximized by increasing his consumption of non-pecuniary benefits. He will move to point A, where $V_1 P_1$ is tangent to U_1, representing a higher level of utility. The value of the firm falls from V^* to V^0, i.e., by the amount of the cost to the firm of the increased non-pecuniary expenditures, and the owner-manager's consumption of non-pecuniary benefits rises from F^* to F^0.

If the equity market is characterized by rational expectations, the buyers will be aware that the owner will increase his non-pecuniary consumption when his ownership share is reduced. If the owner's response function is known or if the equity market makes unbiased estimates of the owner's response to the changed incentives, the buyer will not pay $(1 - \alpha)V^*$ for $(1 - \alpha)$ of the equity.

Theorem: For a claim on the firm of $(1 - \alpha)$, the outsider will pay only $(1 - \alpha)$ times the value he expects the firm to have, given the induced change in the behavior of the owner-manager.

Proof. For simplicity, we ignore any element of uncertainty introduced by the lack of perfect knowledge of the owner-manager's response function. Such uncertainty will not affect the final solution if the equity market is large as long as the estimates are rational (i.e., unbiased) and the errors are independent across firms. The latter condition ensures that this risk is diversifiable, and therefore equilibrium prices will equal the expected values.

Let W represent the owner's total wealth after he has sold a claim equal to $1 - \alpha$ of the equity to an outsider. W has two components. One is the payment, S_o, made by the outsider for $1 - \alpha$ of the

---

[21] (*continued from p. 13*)

of $V_3 - V^*$). But if $F = 0$, the value of the firm is only $\overline{V}$. Therefore, if monitoring costs were zero, the sale would take place at V^* with provision for a pay package which included fringe benefits of F^* for the manager.

This discussion seems to indicate there are two values for the "firm," V_3 and V^*. This is not the case if we realize that V^* is the value of the right to be the residual claimant on the cash flows of the firm and $V_3 - V^*$ is the value of the managerial rights, i.e., the right to make the operating decisions which include access to F^*. There is at least one other right which has value which plays no formal role in the analysis as yet—the value of the control right. By *control right* we mean the right to hire and fire the manager, and we leave this issue to a future paper.

equity; the rest, S_i, is the value of the owner's (i.e., insider's) share of the firm so that W, the owner's wealth, is given by

$$W = S_o + S_i = S_o + \alpha V(F, \alpha),$$

where $V(F, \alpha)$ represents the value of the firm, given that the manager's fractional ownership share is α and that he consumes perquisites with current market value of F. Let $V_2 P_2$, with a slope of $-\alpha$, represent the trade-off the owner-manager faces between non-pecuniary benefits and his wealth after the sale. Given that the owner has decided to sell a claim $1 - \alpha$ of the firm, his welfare will be maximized when $V_2 P_2$ is tangent to some indifference curve such as U_3 in Figure 1. A price for a claim of $(1 - \alpha)$ on the firm that is satisfactory to both the buyer and the seller will require that this tangency occur along $\overline{VF}$, i.e., that the value of the firm must be V'. To show this, assume that such is not the case—that the tangency occurs to the left of the point B on the line $\overline{VF}$. Then, since the slope of $V_2 P_2$ is negative, the value of the firm will be larger than V'. The owner-manager's choice of this lower level of consumption of non-pecuniary benefits will imply a higher value both to the firm as a whole and to the fraction of the firm $(1 - \alpha)$ which the outsider has acquired; that is, $(1 - \alpha)V' > S_o$. From the owner's viewpoint, he has sold $1 - \alpha$ of the firm for less than he could have, given the (assumed) lower level of non-pecuniary benefits he enjoys. On the other hand, if the tangency point B is to the right of the line $\overline{VF}$, the owner-manager's higher consumption of non-pecuniary benefits means the value of the firm is less than V' and hence $(1 - \alpha)V(F, \alpha) < S_o = (1 - \alpha)V'$. The outside owner then has paid more for his share of the equity than it is worth. S_o will be a mutually satisfactory price if and only if $(1 - \alpha)V' = S_o$. But this means that the owner's post-sale wealth is equal to the (reduced) value of the firm V', since

$$W = S_o + \alpha V' = (1 - \alpha)V' + \alpha V' = V'.$$

The requirement that V' and F' fall on $\overline{VF}$ is thus equivalent to requiring that the value of the claim acquired by the outside buyer be equal to the amount he pays for it and conversely for the owner. *This means that the decline in the total value of the firm ($V^* - V'$) is entirely imposed on the owner-manager.* His total wealth after the sale of $(1 - \alpha)$ of the equity is V', and the decline in his wealth is $V^* - V'$.

The distance $V^* - V'$ is the reduction in the market value of the firm engendered by the agency relationship and is a measure of the "residual loss" defined earlier. In this simple example the residual loss represents the total agency costs engendered by the sale of outside equity because monitoring and bonding activities have not been allowed. The welfare loss the owner incurs is less than the residual loss by the value to him of the increase in non-pecuniary benefits $(F' - F^*)$. In Figure 1 the difference between the intercepts on the Y axis of the two indifference curves U_2 and U_3 is a measure of the owner-manager's welfare loss due to the incurrence of agency costs,[22] and he would sell such a claim only if the increment in welfare he achieves by using the cash amounting to $(1 - \alpha)V'$ for other things was worth more to him than this amount of wealth.

---

[22] The distance $V^* - V'$ is a measure of what we will define as the gross agency costs. The distance $V_3 - V_4$ is a measure of what we call net agency costs, and it is this measure of agency costs which will be minimized by the manager in the general case where we allow investment to change.

2.3. *Determination of the Optimal Scale of the Firm*

The Case of All Equity Financing.   Consider the problem faced by an entrepreneur with initial pecuniary wealth, W, and monopoly access to a project requiring investment outlay, I, subject to diminishing returns to scale in I. Figure 2 portrays the solution to the optimal scale of the firm, taking into account the agency costs associated with the existence of outside equity. The axes are as defined in Figure 1, except we now plot on the vertical axis the total wealth of the owner, i.e., his initial wealth, W, plus $V(I) - I$, the net increment in wealth he obtains from exploitation of his investment opportunities. The market value of the firm, $V = V(I, F)$, is now a function of the level of investment, I, and the current market value of the manager's expenditures of the firm's resources on non-pecuniary benefits, F. Let $\overline{V}(I)$ represent the value of the firm as a function of the level of investment when the manager's expenditures on non-pecuniary benefits, F, are zero. The schedule with intercept labeled $W + [\overline{V}(I^*) - I^*]$ and slope equal to -1 in Figure 2 represents the locus of combinations of post-investment wealth and dollar cost to the firm of non-pecuniary benefits which are available to the manager when investment is carried to the value maximizing point, I^*. At this point $\Delta\overline{V}(I) - \Delta I = 0$. If the manager's wealth were large enough to cover the investment required to reach this scale of operation, I^*, he would consume F^* in non-pecuniary benefits and have pecuniary wealth with value $W + V^* - I^*$. However, if outside financing is required to cover the investment, he will not reach this point if monitoring costs are non-zero.[23]

The expansion path $OZBC$ represents the equilibrium combinations of wealth and non-pecuniary benefits, F, which the manager could obtain if he had enough personal wealth to finance all levels of investment up to I^*. It is the locus of points such as Z and C which represents the equilibrium position for the 100-percent owner-manager at each possible level of investment, I. As I increases, we move up the expansion path to the point C, where $V(I) - I$ is at a maximum. Additional investment beyond this point reduces the net value of the firm, and as it does the equilibrium path of the manager's wealth and non-pecuniary benefits retraces (in the reverse direction) the curve $OZBC$. We draw the path as a smooth concave function only as a matter of convenience.

If the manager obtained outside financing and if there were zero costs to the agency relationship (perhaps because monitoring costs were zero), the expansion path would also be represented by $OZBC$. Therefore, this path represents what we might call the "idealized" solutions, i.e., those which would occur in the absence of agency costs.

Assume the manager has sufficient personal wealth to completely finance the firm only up to investment level I_1, which puts him at point Z. At this point $W = I_1$. To increase the size of the firm beyond this point, he must obtain outside financing to cover the additional investment required, and this means reducing his fractional ownership. When he does this, he incurs agency costs, and the lower is his ownership fraction the larger are the agency costs he incurs. However, if the investments requiring outside financing are sufficiently profitable, his welfare will continue to increase.

---

[23] I^* is the value maximizing and Pareto Optimum investment level which results from the traditional analysis of the corporate investment decision if the firm operates in perfectly competitive capital and product markets and the agency cost problems discussed here are ignored. See Debreu (1959, ch. 7), Jensen and Long (1972), Long (1972), Long (1972), Merton and Subrahmanyam (1974), Hirshleifer (1958, 1970), and Fama and Miller (1972).

Figure 2

Determination of the optimal scale of the firm in the case where no monitoring takes place. Point C denotes optimum investment, I^*, and the non-pecuniary benefits, F^*, when investment is 100 percent financed by entrepreneur. Point D denotes optimum investment, I', and non-pecuniary benefits, F, when outside equity financing is used to help finance the investment and the entrepreneur owns a fraction, α', of the firm. The distance A measures the gross agency costs.

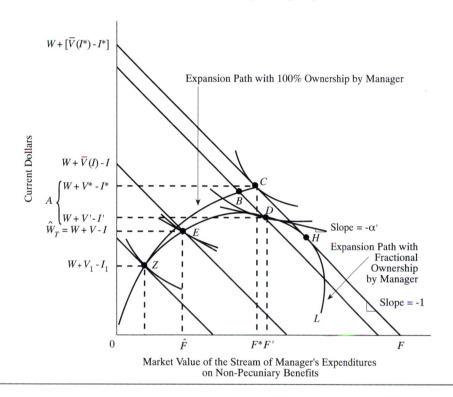

Market Value of the Stream of Manager's Expenditures on Non-Pecuniary Benefits

The expansion path $ZEDHL$ in Figure 2 portrays one possible path of the equilibrium levels of the owner's non-pecuniary benefits and wealth at each possible level of investment higher than I_1. This path is the locus of points such as E or D where (1) the manager's indifference curve is tangent to a line with slope equal to $-\alpha$ (his fractional claim on the firm at that level of investment), and (2) the tangency occurs on the "budget constraint" with slope $= -1$ for the firm value and non-pecuniary benefit tradeoff at the same level of investment.[24] As we move along $ZEDHL$, his fractional claim

[24] Each equilibrium point such as that at E is characterized by $(\hat{a}, \hat{F}, \hat{W}_T)$, where $\hat{W}_T$ is the entrepreneur's post-investment financing wealth. Such an equilibrium must satisfy each of the following four conditions:

(1) $\hat{W}_T + F = \bar{V}(I) + W - I = \bar{V}(I) - K,$

where $K \equiv I - W$ is the amount of outside financing required to make the investment I. If this condition is not satisfied, there is an uncompensated wealth transfer (in one direction or the other) between the entrepreneur and outside equity buyers.

(*continued on p. 18*)

on the firm continues to fall as he raises larger amounts of outside capital. This expansion path represents his complete opportunity set for combinations of wealth and non-pecuniary benefits, given the existence of the costs of the agency relationship with the outside equity holders. Point D, where this opportunity set is tangent to an indifference curve, represents the solution which maximizes his welfare. At this point, the level of investment is I', his fractional ownership share in the firm is α', his wealth is $W + V' - I'$, and he consumes a stream of non-pecuniary benefits with current market value of F'. The gross agency costs (denoted by A) are equal to $(V^* - I^*) - (V' - I')$. Given that no monitoring is possible, I' is the socially optimal level of investment as well as the privately optimal level.

We can characterize the optimal level of investment as that point I' which satisfies the following condition for small changes:

$$\Delta V - \Delta I + \alpha' \Delta F = 0. \tag{1}$$

$\Delta V - \Delta I$ is the change in the net market value of the firm, and $\alpha' \Delta F$ is the dollar value to the manager of the incremental fringe benefits he consumes (which cost the firm ΔF dollars).[25] Furthermore, recognizing that $V = \bar{V} - F$, where $\bar{V}$ is the value of the firm at any level of investment when $F = 0$, we can substitute into the optimum condition to get

$$(\Delta \bar{V} - \Delta I) - (1 - \alpha') \Delta F = 0 \tag{3}$$

as an alternative expression for determining the optimum level of investment.

The idealized or zero agency cost solution, I^*, is given by the condition $(\Delta \bar{V} - \Delta I) = 0$, and since ΔF is positive the actual welfare maximizing level of investment I' will be less than I^*, because $(\Delta \bar{V} - \Delta I)$ must be positive at I' if (3) is to be satisfied. Since $-\alpha'$ is the slope of the indifference curve at the optimum and therefore represents the manager's demand price for incremental non-pecuniary benefits, ΔF, we know that $\alpha' \Delta F$ is the dollar value to him of an increment of fringe benefits costing the firm ΔF dollars. The term $(1 - \alpha') \Delta F$ thus measures the dollar "loss" to the firm (and himself) of an additional ΔF dollars spent on non-pecuniary benefits. The term $\Delta \bar{V} - \Delta I$ is the gross increment in the value of the firm ignoring any changes in the consumption of non-pecuniary benefits. Thus, the manager stops increasing the size of the firm when the gross increment in value is just offset by

---

[24] *(continued from p. 17)*

(2) $U_F(\hat{W}_T, \hat{F})/U_{W_T}(\hat{W}_T, \hat{F}) = \hat{a},$

where U is the entrepreneur's utility function on wealth and perquisites, U_F and U_{W_T} are marginal utilities, and $\hat{a}$ is the manager's share of the firm.

(3) $(1 - \hat{a})V(I) = (1 - \hat{a})[\bar{V}(I) - \hat{F}] \geqq K,$

which says the funds received from outsiders are at least equal to K, the minimum required outside financing.

(4) Among all points $(\hat{a}, F, \hat{W}_T)$ satisfying conditions 1–3, (α, F, W_L) gives the manager highest utility. This implies that $(\hat{a}, \hat{F}, \hat{W}_T)$ satisfies condition (3) as an equality.

[25] *Proof.* Note that the slope of the expansion path (or locus of equilibrium points) at any point is $(\Delta V - \Delta I)/\Delta F$. At the optimum level of investment, this must be equal to the slope of the manager's indifference curve between wealth and market value of fringe benefits, F. Furthermore, in the absence of monitoring, the slope of the indifference curve, $\Delta W/\Delta F$, at the equilibrium point, D, must be equal to $-\alpha'$. Thus,

$$(\Delta V - \Delta I)/\Delta F = -\alpha' \tag{2}$$

is the condition for the optimal scale of investment, and this implies condition (1) holds for small changes at the optimum level of investment, I'.

the incremental "loss" involved in the consumption of additional fringe benefits due to his declining fractional interest in the firm.[26]

2.4. The Role of Monitoring and Bonding Activities in Reducing Agency Costs

In the above analysis we have ignored the potential for controlling the behavior of the owner-manager through monitoring and other control activities. In practice, it is usually possible by expending resources to alter the opportunity the owner-manager has for capturing non-pecuniary benefits. These methods include auditing, formal control systems, budget restrictions, and the establishment of incentive compensation systems which serve to more closely identify the manager's interests with those of the outside equity holders, etc. Figure 3 portrays the effects of monitoring and other control activities in the simple situation portrayed in Figure 1. Figures 1 and 3 are identical except for the curve BCE in Figure 3 which depicts a "budget constraint" derived when monitoring possibilities are taken into account. Without monitoring, and with outside equity of $(1 - \alpha)$, the value of the firm will be V' and non-pecuniary expenditures F'. By incurring monitoring costs, M, the equity holders can restrict the manager's consumption of perquisites to amounts less than F'. Let $F(M, \alpha)$ denote the maximum perquisites the manager can consume for alternative levels of monitoring expenditures, M, given his ownership share α. We assume that increases in monitoring reduce F, and reduce it at a decreasing rate, i.e., $\partial F/\partial M < 0$ and $\partial^2 F/\partial M^2 > 0$.

Since the current value of expected future monitoring expenditures by the outside equity holders reduces the value of any given claim on the firm to them dollar for dollar, the outside equity holders will take this into account in determining the maximum price they will pay for any given fraction of the firm's equity. Therefore, assuming positive monitoring activity, the value of the firm is given by $V = \overline{V} - F(M, \alpha) - M$, and the locus of these points for various levels of M and for a given level of α lies on the line BCE in Figure 3. The vertical difference between the $\overline{V}F$ and BCE curves is M, the current market value of the future monitoring expenditures.

If it is possible for the outside equity holders to make these monitoring expenditures and thereby impose the reductions in the owner-manager's consumption of F, he will voluntarily enter into a contract with the outside equity holders which gives them the rights to restrict his consumption of non-pecuniary items to F''. He finds this desirable because it will cause the value of the firm

---

[26] Since the manager's indifference curves are negatively sloped, we know that the optimum scale of the firm, point D, will occur in the region where the expansion path has negative slope—i.e., the market value of the firm will be declining and the *gross* agency costs, A, will be increasing, so the manager will not minimize them in making the investment decision (even though he will minimize them for any *given* level of investment). However, we define the *net* agency cost as the dollar equivalent of the welfare loss the manager experiences because of the agency relationship evaluated at $F = 0$ (the vertical distance between the intercepts on the Y axis of the two indifference curves on which points C and D lie). The optimum solution, I', does satisfy the condition that net agency costs are minimized. But this simply amounts to a restatement of the assumption that the manager maximizes his welfare.

Finally, it is possible for the solution point D to be a corner solution, and in this case the value of the firm will not be declining. Such a corner solution can occur, for instance, if the manager's marginal rate of substitution between F and wealth falls to zero fast enough as we move up the expansion path, or if the investment projects are "sufficiently" profitable. In these cases the expansion path will have a corner which lies on the maximum value budget constraint with intercept $\overline{V}(I^*) - I^*$, and the level of investment will be equal to the idealized optimum, I^*. However, the market value of the residual claims will be less than V^* because the manager's consumption of perquisites will be larger than F^*, the zero agency cost level.

Figure 3

The value of the firm (V) and level of non-pecuniary benefits (F) when outside equity is $(1 - \alpha)$, U_1, U_2, U_3 represent owner's indifference curves between wealth and non-pecuniary benefits, and monitoring (or bonding) activities impose opportunity set BCE as the trade-off constraint facing the owner.

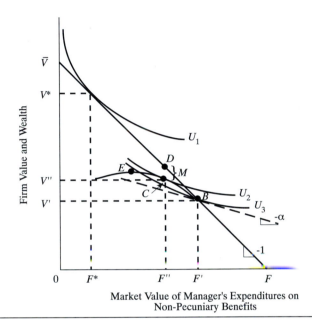

to rise to V''. Given the contract, the optimal monitoring expenditure on the part of the outsiders, M, is the amount $D - C$. The entire increase in the value of the firm that accrues will be reflected in the owner's wealth, but his welfare will be increased by less than this because he forgoes some non-pecuniary benefits he previously enjoyed.

If the equity market is competitive and makes unbiased estimates of the effects of the monitoring expenditures on F and V, potential buyers will be indifferent between the following two contracts:

(i)   Purchase of a share $(1 - \alpha)$ of the firm at a total price of $(1 - \alpha)V'$ and no rights to monitor or control the manager's consumption of perquisites.

(ii)   Purchase of a share $(1 - \alpha)$ of the firm at a total price of $(1 - \alpha)V''$ and the right to expend resources up to an amount equal to $D - C$ which will limit the owner-manager's consumption of perquisites to F.

Given contract (ii), the outside shareholders would find it desirable to monitor to the full rights of their contract because it will pay them to do so. However, if the equity market is competitive, the total benefits (net of the monitoring costs) will be capitalized into the price of the claims. Thus, not surprisingly, the owner-manager reaps all the benefits of the opportunity to write and sell the monitoring contract.[27]

An Analysis of Bonding Expenditures.   We can also see from the analysis of Figure 3 that it makes no difference who actually makes the monitoring expenditures—the owner bears the full amount of these costs as a wealth reduction in all cases. Suppose that the owner-manager could expend resources to guarantee to the outside equity holders that he would limit his activities which cost the firm F. We call these expenditures "bonding costs," and they would take such forms as contractual guarantees to have the financial accounts audited by a public account, explicit bonding against malfeasance on the part of the manager, and contractual limitations on the manager's decision-making power (which impose costs on the firm because they limit his ability to take full advantage of some profitable opportunities as well as limit his ability to harm the stockholders while making himself better off).

If the incurrence of the bonding costs were entirely under the control of the manager and if they yielded the same opportunity set BCE for him in Figure 3, he would incur them in amount $D - C$. This would limit his consumption of perquisites to F'' from F', and the solution is exactly the same as if the outside equity holders had performed the monitoring. The manager finds it in his interest to incur these costs as long as the net increments in his wealth which they generate (by reducing the agency costs and therefore increasing the value of the firm) are more valuable than the perquisites given up. This optimum occurs at point C in both cases under our assumption that the bonding expenditures yield the same opportunity set as the monitoring expenditures. In general, of course, it will pay the owner-manager to engage in bonding activities and to write contracts which allow monitoring as long as the marginal benefits of each are greater than their marginal cost.

Optimal Scale of the Firm in the Presence of Monitoring and Bonding Activities.   If we allow the outside owners to engage in (costly) monitoring activities to limit the manager's expenditures on non-pecuniary benefits and allow the manager to engage in bonding activities to guarantee to the outside owners that he will limit his consumption of F, we get an expansion path such as that illustrated in Figure 4 on which Z and G lie. We have assumed in drawing Figure 4 that the cost functions involved in monitoring and bonding are such that some positive levels of the activities are desirable, i.e., yield benefits greater than their cost. If this is not true, the expansion path generated by the expenditure of resources on these activities would lie below ZD and no such activity would take place at any level of investment. Points Z, C, and D and the two expansion paths they lie on are identical to those portrayed in Figure 2. Points Z and C lie on the 100 percent ownership

---

[27] The careful reader will note that point C will be the equilibrium point only if the contract between the manager and outside equity holders specifies with no ambiguity that they have the right to monitor to limit his consumption of perquisites to an amount no less than F''. If any ambiguity regarding these rights exists in this contract, then another source of agency costs arises which is symmetrical to our original problem. If they could do so, the outside equity holders would monitor to the point where the net value of *their* holdings, $(1 - \alpha)V - M$, was maximized, and this would occur when $(\partial V/\partial M)(1 - \alpha) - 1 = 0$, which would be at some point between points C and E in Figure 3. Point E denotes the point where the value of the firm net of the monitoring costs is at a maximum, i.e., where $\partial V/\partial M - 1 = 0$. But the manager would be worse off than in the zero monitoring solution if the point where $(1 - \alpha) V - M$ was at a maximum were to the left of the intersection between BCE and the indifference curve U_3 passing through point B (which denotes the zero monitoring level of welfare). Thus, if the manager could not eliminate enough of the ambiguity in the contract to push the equilibrium to the right of the intersection of the curve BCE with indifference curve U_3, he would not engage in any contract which allowed monitoring.

Figure 4

Determination of optimal scale of the firm, allowing for monitoring and bonding activities. Optimal monitoring costs are M'', bonding costs are b'', and the equilibrium scale of firm, manager's wealth, and consumption of non-pecuniary benefits is at point G.

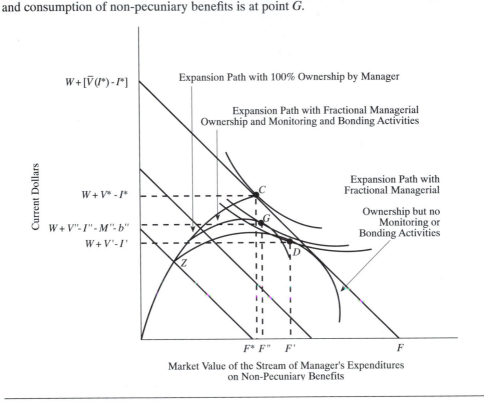

Market Value of the Stream of Manager's Expenditures on Non-Pecuniary Benefits

expansion path, and points Z and D lie on the fractional ownership, zero monitoring and bonding activity expansion path.

The path on which points Z and G lie is the one given by the locus of equilibrium points for alternative levels of investment characterized by the point labeled C in Figure 3 which denotes the optimal level of monitoring and bonding activity and resulting values of the firm and non-pecuniary benefits to the manager, given a fixed level of investment. If any monitoring or bonding is cost effective, the expansion path on which Z and G lie must be above the non-monitoring expansion path over some range. Furthermore, if it lies anywhere to the right of the indifference curve passing through point D (the zero monitoring-bonding solution), the final solution to the problem will involve positive amounts of monitoring and/or bonding activities. Based on the discussion above, we know that as long as the contracts between the manager and outsiders are unambiguous regarding the rights of the respective parties, the final solution will be at that point where the new expansion path is just tangent to the highest indifference curve. At this point the optimal level of monitoring and bonding expenditures is M'' and b'', the manager's post-investment-financing wealth is given by

$W + V'' - I'' - M'' - b''$, and his non-pecuniary benefits are F''. The total gross agency costs, A, are given by $A(M'', b'', \alpha'', I'') = (V^* - I^*) - (V'' - I'' - M'' - b'')$.

2.5. Pareto Optimality and Agency Costs in Manager-Operated Firms

In general, we expect to observe both bonding and external monitoring activities, and the incentives are such that the levels of these activities will satisfy the conditions of efficiency. They will not, however, result in the firm being run in a manner so as to maximize its value. The difference between V^*, the efficient solution under zero monitoring and bonding costs (and therefore zero agency costs), and V'', the value of the firm given positive monitoring costs, is the total gross agency costs defined earlier in the introduction. These are the costs of the "separation of ownership and control" which Adam Smith focused on in the passage quoted at the beginning of this paper and which Berle and Means (1932) popularized 157 years later. The solutions outlined above to our highly simplified problem imply that agency costs will be positive as long as monitoring costs are positive—which they certainly are.

The reduced value of the firm caused by the manager's consumption of perquisites outlined above is "non-optimal" or inefficient only in comparison to a world in which we could obtain compliance of the agent to the principal's wishes at zero cost or in comparison to a *hypothetical* world in which the agency costs were lower. But these costs (monitoring and bonding costs and "residual loss") are an unavoidable result of the agency relationship. Furthermore, since they are borne entirely by the decision maker (in this case the original owner) responsible for creating the relationship, he has the incentives to see that they are minimized (because he captures the benefits from their reduction). Furthermore, these agency costs will be incurred only if the benefits to the owner-manager from their creation are great enough to outweigh them. In our current example, these benefits arise from the availability of profitable investments requiring capital investment in excess of the original owner's personal wealth.

In conclusion, finding that agency costs are non-zero (i.e., that there are costs associated with the separation of ownership and control in the corporation) and concluding therefrom that the agency relationship is non-optimal, wasteful, or inefficient are equivalent in every sense to comparing a world in which iron ore is a scarce commodity (and therefore costly) to a world in which it is freely available at zero resource cost and concluding that the first world is "non-optimal"—a perfect example of the fallacy criticized by Coase (1964) and what Demsetz (1969) characterizes as the "Nirvana" form of analysis.[28]

2.6. Factors Affecting the Size of the Divergence from Ideal Maximization

The magnitude of the agency costs discussed above will vary from firm to firm. It will depend on the tastes of managers, the ease with which they can exercise their own preferences as opposed to

---

[28] If we could establish the existence of a feasible set of alternative institutional arrangements which would yield net benefits from the reduction of these costs, we could legitimately conclude the agency relationship engendered by the corporation was not Pareto optimal. However, we would then be left with the problem of explaining why these alternative institutional arrangements have not replaced the corporate form of organization.

value maximization in decision making, and the costs of monitoring and bonding activities.[29] The agency costs will also depend upon the cost of measuring the manager's (agent's) performance and evaluating it, the cost of devising and applying an index for compensating the manager which correlates with the owner's (principal's) welfare, and the cost of devising and enforcing specific behavioral rules or policies. Where the manager has less than a controlling interest in the firm, it will also depend upon the market for managers. Competition from other potential managers limits the costs of obtaining managerial services (including the extent to which a given manager can diverge from the idealized solution which would obtain if all monitoring and bonding costs were zero). The size of the divergence (the agency costs) will be directly related to the cost of replacing the manager. If his responsibilities require very little knowledge specialized to the firm, if it is easy to evaluate his performance, and if replacement search costs are modest, the divergence from the ideal will be relatively small and vice versa.

The divergence will also be constrained by the market for the firm itself, i.e., by capital markets. Owners always have the option of selling their firm, either as a unit or piecemeal. Owners of manager-operated firms can and do sample the capital market from time to time. If they discover that the value of the future earnings stream to others is higher than the value of the firm to them given that it is to be manager-operated, they can exercise their right to sell. It is conceivable that other owners could be more efficient at monitoring or even that a single individual with appropriate managerial talents and with sufficiently large personal wealth would elect to buy the firm. In this latter case the purchase by such a single individual would completely eliminate the agency costs. If there were a number of such potential owner-manager purchasers (all with talents and tastes identical to the current manager), the owners would receive in the sale price of the firm the full value of the residual claimant rights, including the capital value of the eliminated agency costs plus the value of the managerial rights.

Monopoly, Competition, and Managerial Behavior. It is frequently argued that the existence of competition in product (and factor) markets will constrain the behavior of managers to idealized value maximization, i.e., that monopoly in product (or monopsony in factor) markets will permit larger divergences from value maximization.[30] Our analysis does not support this hypothesis. The owners of a firm with monopoly power have the same incentives to limit divergences of the manager from value maximization (i.e., the ability to increase their wealth) as do the owners of competitive firms. Furthermore, competition in the market for managers will generally make it unnecessary for the owners to share rents with the manager. The owners of a monopoly firm need only pay the supply price for a manager.

---

[29] The monitoring and bonding costs will differ from firm to firm, depending on such things as the inherent complexity and geographical dispersion of operations and the attractiveness of perquisites available in the firm (consider the mint).

[30] "Where competitors are numerous and entry is easy, persistent departures from profit maximizing behavior inexorably leads to extinction. Economic natural selection holds the stage. In these circumstances, the behavior of the individual units that constitute the supply side of the product market is essentially routine and uninteresting and economists can confidently predict industry behavior without being explicitly concerned with the behavior of these individual units.

When the conditions of competition are relaxed, however, the opportunity set of the firm is expanded. In this case, the behavior of the firm as a distinct operating unit is of separate interest. Both for purposes of interpreting particular behavior within the firm as well as for predicting responses of the industry aggregate, it may be necessary to identify the factors that influence the firm's choices within this expanded opportunity set and embed these in a formal model." (Williamson [1964, p. 2])

Since the owner of a monopoly has the same wealth incentives to minimize managerial costs as would the owner of a competitive firm, both will undertake that level of monitoring which equates the marginal cost of monitoring to the marginal wealth increment from reduced consumption of perquisites by the manager. Thus, the existence of monopoly will not increase agency costs.

Furthermore, the existence of competition in product and factor markets will not eliminate the agency costs due to managerial control problems, as has often been asserted (cf. Friedman [1970]). If my competitors all incur agency costs equal to or greater than mine, I will not be eliminated from the market by their competition.

The existence and size of the agency costs depend on the nature of the monitoring costs, the tastes of managers for non-pecuniary benefits, and the supply of potential managers who are capable of financing the entire venture out of their personal wealth. If monitoring costs are zero, agency costs will be zero, or if there are enough 100 percent owner-managers available to own and run all the firms in an industry (competitive or not), then agency costs in that industry will also be zero.[31]

3. Some Unanswered Questions Regarding the Existence of the Corporate Form

3.1. The Question

The analysis to this point has left us with a basic puzzle: Why, given the existence of positive costs of the agency relationship, do we find the usual corporate form of organization with widely diffuse ownership so widely prevalent? If one takes seriously much of the literature regarding the "discretionary" power held by managers of large corporations, it is difficult to understand the historical fact of enormous growth in equity in such organizations, not only in the United States, but throughout the world. Paraphrasing Alchian (1968), How does it happen that millions of individuals are willing to turn over a significant fraction of their wealth to organizations run by managers who have so little interest in their welfare? What is even more remarkable, why are they willing to make these commitments purely as residual claimants, i.e., on the anticipation that managers will operate the firm so that there will be earnings which accrue to the stockholders?

There is certainly no lack of alternative ways that individuals might invest, including entirely different forms of organizations. Even if consideration is limited to corporate organizations, there are clearly alternative ways capital might be raised, e.g., through fixed claims of various sorts, bonds, notes, and mortgages. Moreover, the corporate income tax seems to favor the use of fixed claims since interest is treated as a tax-deductible expense. Those who assert that managers do not behave in the interest of stockholders have generally not addressed a very important question: Why, if non-manager-owned shares have such a serious deficiency, have they not long since been driven out by fixed claims?[32]

---

[31] Assuming there are no special tax benefits to ownership nor utility of ownership other than that derived from the direct wealth effects of ownership, such as might be true for professional sports teams, race-horse stables, and firms which carry the family name.

[32] Marris (1964, pp. 7–9) is the exception, although he argues that there exists some "maximum leverage point" beyond which the chances of "insolvency" are in some undefined sense too high.

3.2. Some Alternative Explanations of the Ownership Structure of the Firm

The Role of Limited Liability.   Manne (1967) and Alchian and Demsetz (1972) argue that one of the attractive features of the corporate form vis-a-vis individual proprietorships or partnerships is the limited liability feature of equity claims in corporations. Without this provision each and every investor purchasing one or more shares of a corporation would be potentially liable to the full extent of his personal wealth for the debts of the corporation. Few individuals would find this a desirable risk to accept, and the major benefits to be obtained from risk reduction through diversification would be to a large extent unobtainable. This argument, however, is incomplete since limited liability does not eliminate the basic risk; it merely shifts it. The argument must rest ultimately on transactions costs. If all stockholders of GM were liable for GM's debts, the maximum liability for an individual shareholder would be greater than it would be if his shares had limited liability. However, given that many other stockholders also existed and that each was liable for the unpaid claims in proportion to his ownership, it is highly unlikely that the maximum payment each would have to make would be large in the event of GM's bankruptcy since the total wealth of those stockholders would also be large. However, the existence of unlimited liability would impose incentives for each shareholder to keep track of both the liabilities of GM and the wealth of the other GM owners. It is easily conceivable that the costs of so doing would, in the aggregate, be much higher than simply paying a premium in the form of higher interest rates to the creditors of GM in return for their acceptance of a contract which grants limited liability to the shareholders. The creditors would then bear the risk of any nonpayment of debts in the event of GM's bankruptcy.

It is also not generally recognized that limited liability is merely a necessary condition for explaining the magnitude of the reliance on equities, not a sufficient condition. Ordinary debt also carries limited liability.[33] If limited liability is all that is required, why don't we observe large corporations, individually owned, with a tiny fraction of the capital supplied by the entrepreneur and the rest simply borrowed.[34] At first, this question seems silly to many people (as does the question regarding why firms would ever issue debt or preferred stock under conditions where there are no tax benefits obtained from the treatment of interest or preferred dividend payments[35]). We have

---

[33] By *limited liability,* we mean the same conditions that apply to common stock. Subordinated debt or preferred stock could be constructed which carried with it liability provisions; i.e., if the corporation's assets were insufficient at some point to pay off all prior claims (such as trade credit, accrued wages, and senior debt) and if the personal resources of the "equity" holders were also insufficient to cover these claims, the holders of this "debt" would be subject to assessments beyond the face value of their claim (assessments which might be limited or unlimited in amount).

[34] Alchian and Demsetz (1972, p. 709) argue that one can explain the existence of both bonds and stock in the ownership structure of firms as the result of differing expectations regarding the outcomes to the firm. They argue that bonds are created and sold to "pessimists" and stocks with a residual claim with no upper bound are sold to "optimists."

As long as capital markets are perfect with no taxes or transactions costs and individual investors can issue claims on distributions of outcomes on the same terms as firms, such actions on the part of firms cannot affect their values. The reason is simple. Suppose such "pessimists" did exist, yet the firm issues only equity claims. The demand for those equity claims would reflect the fact that the individual purchaser could on his own account issue "bonds" with a limited and prior claim on the distribution of outcomes on the equity which is exactly the same as that which the firm could issue. Similarly, investors could easily unlever any position by simply buying a proportional claim on both the bonds and stocks of a levered firm. Therefore, a levered firm could not sell at a different price than an unlevered firm solely because of the existence of such differential expectations. See Fama and Miller (1972, ch. 4) for an excellent exposition of these issues.

[35] Corporations did use both prior to the institution of the corporate income tax in the United States, and preferred dividends have, with minor exceptions, never been tax deductible.

found that oftentimes this question is misinterpreted to be one regarding why firms obtain capital. The issue is not why they obtain capital, but why they obtain it through the particular forms we have observed for such long periods of time. The fact is that no well-articulated answer to this question currently exists in the literature of either finance or economics.

The "Irrelevance" of Capital Structure.   In their pathbreaking article on the cost of capital, Modigliani and Miller (1958) demonstrated that in the absence of bankruptcy costs and tax subsidies on the payment of interest, the value of the firm is independent of the financial structure. They later (1963) demonstrated that the existence of tax subsidies on interest payments would cause the value of the firm to rise with the amount of debt financing by the amount of the capitalized value of the tax subsidy. But this line of argument implies that the firm should be financed almost entirely with debt. Realizing the inconsistency with observed behavior, Modigliani and Miller (1963, p. 442) comment:

> it may be useful to remind readers once again that the existence of a tax advantage for debt financing . . . does not necessarily mean that corporations should at all times seek to use the maximum amount of debt in their capital structures. . . . there are as we pointed out, limitations imposed by lenders . . . as well as many other dimensions (and kinds of costs) in real-world problems of financial strategy which are not fully comprehended within the framework of static equilibrium models, either our own or those of the traditional variety. These additional considerations, which are typically grouped under the rubric of "the need for preserving flexibility," will normally imply the maintenance by the corporation of a substantial reserve of untapped borrowing power.

Modigliani and Miller are essentially left without a theory of the determination of the optimal capital structure, and Fama and Miller (1972, p. 173), commenting on the same issue, reiterate this conclusion:

> And we must admit that at this point there is little in the way of convincing research, either theoretical or empirical, that explains the amounts of debt that firms do decide to have in their capital structure.

The Modigliani-Miller theorem is based on the assumption that the probability distribution of the cash flows to the firm is independent of the capital structure. It is now recognized that the existence of positive costs associated with bankruptcy and the presence of tax subsidies on corporate interest payments will invalidate this irrelevance theorem precisely because the probability distribution of future cash flows changes as the probability of the incurrence of the bankruptcy costs changes, i.e., as the ratio of debt to equity rises. We believe the existence of agency costs provides stronger reasons for arguing that the probability distribution of future cash flows is *not* independent of the capital or ownership structure.

While the introduction of bankruptcy costs in the presence of tax subsidies leads to a theory which defines an optimal capital structure,[36] we argue that this theory is seriously incomplete since it implies that no debt should ever be used in the absence of tax subsidies if bankruptcy costs are positive. Since we know debt was commonly used prior to the existence of the current tax subsidies on interest payments, this theory does not capture what must be some important determinants of the corporate capital structure.

---

[36] See Kraus and Litzenberger (1972) and Lloyd-Davies (1975).

In addition, neither bankruptcy costs nor the existence of tax subsidies can explain the use of preferred stock or warrants which have no tax advantages, and there is no theory which tells us anything about what determines the fraction of equity claims held by insiders as opposed to outsiders, which our analysis in section 2 indicates is so important. We return to these issues later after analyzing in detail the factors affecting the agency costs associated with debt.

4. The Agency Costs of Debt

In general, if the agency costs engendered by the existence of outside owners are positive, it will pay the absentee owner (i.e., shareholders) to sell out to an owner-manager who can avoid these costs.[37] This could be accomplished in principle by having the manager become the sole equity holder by repurchasing all of the outside equity claims with funds obtained through the issuance of limited liability debt claims and the use of his own personal wealth. This single-owner corporation would not suffer the agency costs associated with outside equity. Therefore, there must be some compelling reasons why we find the diffuse-owner corporate firm financed by equity claims so prevalent as an organizational form.

An ingenious entrepreneur eager to expand has open to him the opportunity to design a whole hierarchy of fixed claims on assets and earnings, with premiums paid for different levels of risk.[38] Why don't we observe large corporations individually owned with a tiny fraction of the capital supplied by the entrepreneur in return for 100 percent of the equity and the rest simply borrowed? We believe there are a number of reasons: (1) the incentive effects associated with highly leveraged firms, (2) the monitoring costs these incentive effects engender, and (3) bankruptcy costs. Furthermore, all of these costs are simply particular aspects of the agency costs associated with the existence of debt claims on the firm.

4.1. The Incentive Effects Associated with Debt

We don't find many large firms financed almost entirely with debt type claims (i.e., non-residual claims) because of the effect such a financial structure would have on the owner-manager's behavior. Potential creditors will not loan $100,000,000 to a firm in which the entrepreneur has an investment of $10,000. With that financial structure, the owner-manager will have a strong incentive to engage in activities (investments) which promise very high payoffs if successful, even if they have a very low probability of success. If they turn out well, he captures most of the gains; if they turn out badly, the creditors bear most of the costs.[39]

---

[37] And if there is competitive bidding for the firm from potential owner-managers, the absentee owner will capture the capitalized value of these agency costs.

[38] The spectrum of claims which firms can issue is far more diverse than is suggested by our two-way classification—fixed vs. residual. There are convertible bonds, equipment trust certificates, debentures, revenue bonds, warrants, etc. Different bond issues can contain different subordination provisions with respect to assets and interest. They can be callable or non-callable. Preferred stocks can be "preferred" in a variety of dimensions and contain a variety of subordination stipulations. In the abstract, we can imagine firms issuing claims contingent on a literally infinite variety of states of the world such as those considered in the literature on the time–state-preference models of Arrow (1964), Debreu (1959), and Hirshleifer (1970).

[39] An apt analogy is the way one would play poker on money borrowed at a fixed interest rate, with one's own liability limited to some very small stake. Fama and Miller (1972, pp. 179–80) also discuss and provide a numerical example of an investment decision which illustrates very nicely the potential inconsistency between the interests of bondholders and stockholders.

To illustrate the incentive effects associated with the existence of debt and to provide a framework within which we can discuss the effects of monitoring and bonding costs, wealth transfers, and the incidence of agency costs, we again consider a simple situation. Assume we have a manager-owned firm with no debt outstanding in a world in which there are no taxes. The firm has the opportunity to take one of two mutually exclusive equal cost investment opportunities, each of which yields a random payoff, $\tilde{X}_j$, T periods in the future ($j = 1, 2$). Production and monitoring activities take place continuously between time 0 and time T, and markets in which the claims on the firm can be traded are open continuously over this period. After time T, the firm has no productive activities, so the payoff $\tilde{X}_j$ includes the distribution of all remaining assets. For simplicity, we assume that the two distributions are log-normally distributed and have the same expected total payoff, $E(\tilde{X})$, where $\tilde{X}$ is defined as the logarithm of the final payoff. The distributions differ only by their variances with $\sigma_1^2 < \sigma_2^2$. The systematic or covariance risk of each of the distributions, β_j, in the Sharpe (1964)-Lintner (1965) capital asset pricing model is assumed to be identical. Assuming that asset prices are determined according to the capital asset pricing model, the preceding assumptions imply that the total market value of each of these distributions is identical, and we represent this value by V.

If the owner-manager has the right to decide which investment program to take and if after he decides this he has the opportunity to sell part or all of his claims on the outcomes in the form of either debt or equity, he will be indifferent between the two investments.[40]

However, if the owner has the opportunity to *first* issue debt, then to decide which of the investments to take, and then to sell all or part of his remaining equity claim on the market, he will not be indifferent between the two investments. The reason is that by promising to take the low variance project, selling bonds, and then taking the high variance project, he can transfer wealth from the (naive) bondholders to himself as equity holder.

Let X^* be the amount of the "fixed" claim in the form of a non-coupon bearing bond sold to the bondholders such that the total payoff to them, R_j ($j = 1, 2$, denotes the distribution the manager chooses), is

$$
\begin{aligned}
R_j &= X^*, \quad \text{if} \quad \tilde{X}_j \geqq X^*, \\
&= X_j, \quad \text{if} \quad \tilde{X}_j \leq X^*.
\end{aligned}
$$

Let B_1 be the current market value of bondholder claims if investment 1 is taken, and let B_2 be the current market value of bondholder claims if investment 2 is taken. Since in this example the total value of the firm, V, is independent of the investment choice and also of the financing decision, we can use the Black-Scholes (1973) option pricing model to determine the values of the debt, B_j, and equity, S_j, under each of the choices.[41]

Black and Scholes derive the solution for the value of a European call option (one which can be exercised only at the maturity date) and argue that the resulting option pricing equation can be used to determine the value of the equity claim on a levered firm. That is, the stockholders in such a firm can be viewed as holding a European call option on the total value of the firm, with exercise price equal to X^* (the face value of the debt), exercisable at the maturity date of the debt issue. More simply, the stockholders have the right to buy the firm back from the bondholders for a price of X^*

---

[40] The portfolio diversification issues facing the owner-manager are brought into the analysis in section 5 below.

[41] See Smith (1976) for a review of this option pricing literature and its applications and Galai and Masulis (1976), who apply the option pricing model to mergers and corporate investment decisions.

at time T, Merton (1973, 1974) shows that as the variance of the outcome distribution rises, the value of the stock (i.e., call option) rises, and since our two distributions differ only in their variances, $\sigma_2^2 < \sigma_1^2$, the equity value S_1 is less than S_2. This implies $B_1 > B_2$, since $B_1 = V - S_1$ and $B_2 = V - S_2$.

Now if the owner-manager could sell bonds with face value X^* under the conditions that the potential bondholders believed this to be a claim on distribution 1, he would receive a price of B_1. After selling the bonds, his equity interest in distribution 1 would have value S_1. But we know S_2 is greater than S_1, and thus the manager can make himself better off by changing the investment to take the higher variance distribution 2, thereby redistributing wealth from the bondholders to himself. All this assumes, of course, that the bondholders could not prevent him from changing the investment program. *If the bondholders cannot do so and if they perceive that the manager has the opportunity to take distribution 2, they will pay the manager only B_2 for the claim X^*, realizing that his maximizing behavior will lead him to choose distribution 2.* In this event there is no redistribution of wealth between bondholders and stockholders (and in general with rational expectations there never will be) and no welfare loss. It is easy to construct a case, however, in which these incentive effects do generate real costs.

Let cash flow distribution 2 in the previous example have an expected value, $E(X_2)$, which is lower than that of distribution 1. Then we know that $V_1 > V_2$, and if ΔV, which is given by

$$\Delta V = V_1 - V_2 = (S_1 - S_2) + (B_1 - B_2),$$

is sufficiently small relative to the reduction in the value of the bonds, the value of the stock will increase.[42] Rearranging the expression for ΔV, we see that the difference between the equity values for the two investments is given by

$$S_2 - S_1 = (B_1 - B_2) - (V_1 - V_2),$$

and the first term on the RHS, $B_1 - B_2$, is the amount of wealth "transferred" from the bondholders and $V_1 - V_2$ is the reduction in overall firm value. Since we know $B_1 > B_2$, $S_2 - S_1$ can be positive even though the reduction in the value of the firm, $V_1 - V_2$, is positive.[43] Again, the bondholders will not actually lose as long as they can accurately perceive the motivation of the equity-owning manager and his opportunity to take project 2. They will presume he will take investment 2 and hence will pay no more than B_2 for the bonds when they are issued.

---

[42] While we used the option pricing model above to motivate the discussion and provide some intuitive understanding of the incentives facing the equity holders, the option pricing solutions of Black and Scholes (1973) do not apply when incentive effects cause V to be a function of the debt/equity ratio as it is in general and in this example. Long (1974) points out this difficulty with respect to the usefulness of the model in the context of tax subsidies on interest and bankruptcy cost. The results of Merton (1974) and Galai and Masulis (1976) must be interpreted with care since the solutions are strictly incorrect in the context of tax subsidies and/or agency costs.

[43] The numerical example of Fama and Miller (1972, pp. 179–80) is a close representation of this case in a two-period state model. However, they go on to make the following statement on page 180:

> From a practical viewpoint, however, situations of potential conflict between bondholders and shareholders in the application of the market value rule are probably unimportant. In general, investment opportunities that increase a firm's market value by more than their cost both increase the value of the firm's shares and strengthen the firm's future ability to meet its current bond commitments.

The first issue regarding the importance of the conflict of interest between bondholders and stockholders is an empirical one, and the last statement is incomplete—in some circumstances the equity holders could benefit from projects whose net effect was to reduce the total value of the firm as they and we have illustrated. The issue cannot be brushed aside so easily.

In this simple example the reduced value of the firm, $V_1 - V_2$, is the agency cost engendered by the issuance of debt,[44] and it is borne by the owner-manager. If he could finance the project out of his personal wealth, he would clearly choose project 1 since its investment outlay was assumed equal to that of project 2 and its market value, V_1, was greater. This wealth loss, $V_1 - V_2$, is the "residual loss" portion of what we have defined as agency costs, and it is generated by the cooperation required to raise the funds to make the investment. Another important part of the agency costs is monitoring and bonding costs, and we now consider their role.

4.2. *The Role of Monitoring and Bonding Costs*

In principle, it would be possible for the bondholders, by the inclusion of various covenants in the indenture provisions, to limit the managerial behavior that results in reductions in the value of the bonds. Provisions which impose constraints on management's decisions regarding such things as dividends, future debt issues,[45] and maintenance of working capital are not uncommon in bond issues.[46] To completely protect the bondholders from the incentive effects, these provisions would have to be incredibly detailed and cover most operating aspects of the enterprise, including limitations on the riskiness of the projects undertaken. The costs involved in writing such provisions, the costs of enforcing them, and the reduced profitability of the firm (induced because the covenants occasionally limit management's ability to take optimal actions on certain issues) would likely be nontrivial. In fact, since management is a continuous decision-making process, it will be almost impossible to completely specify such conditions without having the bondholders actually perform the management function. All costs associated with such covenants are what we mean by monitoring costs.

The bondholders will have incentives to engage in the writing of such covenants and in monitoring the actions of the manager to the point where the "nominal" marginal cost to them of such activities is just equal to the marginal benefits they perceive from engaging in them. We use the word *nominal* here because debtholders will not in fact bear these costs. As long as they recognize their existence, they will take them into account in deciding the price they will pay for any given debt claim;[47] therefore the seller of the claim (the owner) will bear the costs just as in the equity case discussed in section 2.

In addition, the manager has incentives to take into account the costs imposed on the firm by covenants in the debt agreement which directly affect the future cash flows of the firm, since they

---

[44] Myers (1975) points out another serious incentive effect on managerial decisions of the existence of debt which does not occur in our simple single-decision world. He shows that if the firm has the option to take future investment opportunities, the existence of debt which matures after the options must be taken will cause the firm (using an equity value maximizing investment rule) to refuse to take some otherwise profitable projects because they would benefit only the bondholders and not the equity holders. This will (in the absence of tax subsidies to debt) cause the value of the firm to fall. Thus (although he doesn't use the term) these incentive effects also contribute to the agency costs of debt in a manner perfectly consistent with the examples discussed in the text.

[45] Black and Scholes (1973) discuss ways in which dividend and future financing policy can redistribute wealth between classes of claimants on the firm.

[46] Black, Miller, and Posner (1974) discuss many of these issues with particular reference to the government regulation of bank holding companies.

[47] In other words, these costs will be taken into account in determining the yield to maturity on the issue. For an examination of the effects of such enforcement costs on the nominal interest rates in the consumer small loan market, see Benston (1977).

reduce the market value of his claims. Because both the external and internal monitoring costs are imposed on the owner-manager, it is in his interest to see that the monitoring is performed in the lowest cost way. Suppose, for example, that the bondholders (or outside equity holders) would find it worthwhile to produce detailed financial statements such as those contained in the usual published accounting reports as a means of monitoring the manager. If the manager himself can produce such information at lower costs than they (perhaps because he is already collecting much of the data they desire for his own internal decision-making purposes), it would pay him to agree in advance to incur the cost of providing such reports and to have their accuracy testified to by an independent outside auditor. This is an example of what we refer to as bonding costs.[48, 49]

4.3. Bankruptcy and Reorganization Costs

We argue in section 5 that as the debt in the capital structure increases beyond some point, the marginal agency costs of debt begin to dominate the marginal agency costs of outside equity, and the re-

---

[48] To illustrate the fact that it will sometimes pay the manager to incur "bonding" costs to guarantee the bondholders that he will not deviate from his promised behavior, let us suppose that for an expenditure of b of the firm's resources he can guarantee that project 1 will be chosen. If he spends these resources and takes project 1, the value of the firm will be $V_1 - b$, and clearly as long as $(V_1 - b) > V_2$ or, alternatively, $(V_1 - V_2) > b$, he will be better off, since his wealth will be equal to the value of the firm minus the required investment, I (which we assumed for simplicity to be identical for the two projects).

On the other hand, to prove that the owner-manager prefers the lowest cost solution to the conflict, let us assume he can write a covenant into the bond issue which will allow the bondholders to prevent him from taking project 2, if they incur monitoring costs of m, where $m < b$. If he does this, his wealth will be higher by the amount $b - m$. To see this, note that if the bond market is competitive and makes unbiased estimates, potential bondholders will be indifferent between

(i) a claim X^* with no covenant (and no guarantees from management) at a price of B_2,

(ii) a claim X^* with no covenant (and guarantees from management, through bonding expenditures by the firm of b, that project 1 will be taken) at a price of B_1, and

(iii) a claim X^* with a covenant and the opportunity to spend m on monitoring (to guarantee project 1 will be taken) at a price of $B_1 - m$.

The bondholders will realize that (i) represents in fact a claim on project 2 and that (ii) and (iii) represent a claim on project 1 and are thus indifferent between the three options at the specified prices. The owner-manager, however, will not be indifferent between incurring the bonding costs, b, directly or including the covenant in the bond indenture and letting the bondholders spend m to guarantee that he take project 1. His wealth in the two cases will be given by the value of his equity plus the proceeds of the bond issue less the required investment, and if $m < b < V_1 - V_2$, then his post-investment-financing wealth, W, for the three options will be such that $W_t < W_{tt} < W_{ttt}$. Therefore, since it would increase his wealth, he would voluntarily include the covenant in the bond issue and let the bondholders monitor.

[49] We mention, without going into the problem in detail, that similar to the case in which the outside equity holders are allowed to monitor the manager-owner, the agency relationship between the bondholders and stockholders has a symmetry if the rights of the bondholders to limit actions of the manager are not perfectly spelled out. Suppose the bondholders, by spending sufficiently large amounts of resources, could force management to take actions which would transfer wealth from the equity holder to the bondholders (by taking sufficiently less risky projects). One can easily construct situations where such actions could make the bondholders better off, hurt the equity holders, and actually lower the total value of the firm. Given the nature of the debt contract, the original owner-manager might maximize his wealth in such a situation by selling off the equity and keeping the bonds as his "owner's" interest. If the nature of the bond contract is given, this may well be an inefficient solution since the total agency costs (i.e., the sum of monitoring and value loss) could easily be higher than the alternative solution. However, if the owner-manager could strictly limit the rights of the bondholders (perhaps by inclusion of a provision which expressly reserves all rights not specifically granted to the bondholder for the equity holder), he would find it in his interest to establish the efficient contractual arrangement since by minimizing the agency costs he would be maximizing his wealth. These issues involve the fundamental nature of contracts, and for now we simply assume that the rights of the "bondholders" are strictly limited and unambiguous and all rights not specifically granted them are reserved for the "stockholders," a situation descriptive of actual institutional arrangements. This allows us to avoid the incentive effects associated with "bondholders" potentially exploiting "stockholders."

sult of this is the generally observed phenomenon of the simultaneous use of both debt and outside equity. Before considering these issues, however, we consider here the third major component of the agency costs of debt, which helps to explain why debt doesn't completely dominate capital structures—the existence of bankruptcy and reorganization costs.

It is important to emphasize that bankruptcy and liquidation are very different events. The legal definition of bankruptcy is difficult to specify. In general, it occurs when the firm cannot meet a current payment on a debt obligation[50] or one or more of the other indenture provisions providing for bankruptcy is violated by the firm. In this event the stockholders have lost all claims on the firm,[51] and the remaining loss, the difference between the face value of the fixed claims and the market value of the firm, is borne by the debtholders. Liquidation of the firm's assets will occur only if the market value of the future cash flows generated by the firm is less than the opportunity cost of the assets, i.e., the sum of the values which could be realized if the assets were sold piecemeal.

If there were no costs associated with the event called bankruptcy, the total market value of the firm would not be affected by increasing the probability of its incurrence. However, it is costly, if not impossible, to write contracts representing claims on a firm which clearly delineate the rights of holders for all possible contingencies. Thus, even if there were no adverse incentive effects in expanding fixed claims relative to equity in a firm, the use of such fixed claims would be constrained by the costs inherent in defining and enforcing those claims. Firms incur obligations daily to suppliers, to employees, to different classes of investors, etc. So long as the firm is prospering, the adjudication of claims is seldom a problem. When the firm has difficulty meeting some of its obligations, however, the issue of the priority of those claims can pose serious problems. This is most obvious in the extreme case where the firm is forced into bankruptcy. If bankruptcy were costless, the reorganization would be accompanied by an adjustment of the claims of various parties, and the business could, if that proved to be in the interest of the claimants, simply go on (although perhaps under new management).[52]

In practice, bankruptcy is not costless, but generally involves an adjudication process which itself consumes a fraction of the remaining value of the assets of the firm. Thus, the cost of bankruptcy will be of concern to potential buyers of fixed claims in the firm since their existence will reduce the payoffs to them in the event of bankruptcy. These are examples of the agency costs of cooperative efforts among individuals (although in this case perhaps *non-cooperative* would be a better term). The price buyers will be willing to pay for fixed claims will thus be inversely related to the probability of the incurrence of these costs—i.e., to the probability of bankruptcy. Using a variant of the argument employed above for monitoring costs, it can be shown that the total value of the firm will fall and the owner-manager equity holder will bear the entire wealth effect of the bankruptcy

---

[50] If the firm were allowed to sell assets to meet a current debt obligation, bankruptcy would occur when the total market value of the future cash flows expected to be generated by the firm is less than the value of a current payment on a debt obligation. Many bond indentures do not, however, allow for the sale of assets to meet debt obligations.

[51] We have been told that while this is true in principle, the actual behavior of the courts appears to frequently involve the provision of some settlement to the common stockholders even when the assets of the company are not sufficient to cover the claims of the creditors.

[52] If under bankruptcy the bondholders have the right to fire the management, the management will have some incentives to avoid taking actions which increase the probability of this event (even if it is in the best interest of the equity holders) if they (the management) are earning rents or if they have human capital specialized to this firm or if they face large adjustment costs in finding new employment. A detailed examination of this issue involves the value of the control rights (the rights to hire and fire the manager), and we leave it to a subsequent paper.

costs, as long as potential bondholders make unbiased estimates of the bonds' magnitude at the time they initially purchase bonds.[53]

Empirical studies of the magnitude of bankruptcy costs are almost nonexistent. Warner (1975), in a study of 11 railroad bankruptcies between 1930 and 1955, estimates the average costs of bankruptcy[54] as a fraction of the value of the firm three years prior to bankruptcy to be 2.5 percent (with a range of 0.4 percent to 5.9 percent). The average dollar costs were $1.88 million. Both of these measures seem remarkably small and are consistent with our belief that bankruptcy costs themselves are unlikely to be the major determinant of corporate capital structures. It is also interesting to note that the annual amount of defaulted funds has fallen significantly since 1940. (See Atkinson [1967].) One possible explanation for this phenomenon is that firms are using mergers to avoid the costs of bankruptcy. This hypothesis seems even more reasonable, if, as is frequently the case, reorganization costs represent only a fraction of the costs associated with bankruptcy.

In general, the revenues or the operating costs of the firm are not independent of the probability of bankruptcy and thus the capital structure of the firm. As the probability of bankruptcy increases, both the operating costs and the revenues of the firm are adversely affected, and some of these costs can be avoided by merger. For example, a firm with a high probability of bankruptcy will also find that it must pay higher salaries to induce executives to accept the higher risk of unemployment. Furthermore, in certain kinds of durable goods industries the demand function for the firm's product will not be independent of the probability of bankruptcy. The computer industry is a good example. There, the buyer's welfare is dependent to a significant extent on the ability to maintain the equipment and on continuous hardware and software development. Furthermore, the owner of a large computer often receives benefits from the software developments of other users. Thus, if the manufacturer leaves the business or loses his software support and development experts because of financial difficulties, the value of the equipment to his users will decline. The buyers of such services have a continuing interest in the manufacturer's viability not unlike that of a bondholder, except that their benefits come in the form of continuing services at lower cost, rather than principle and interest payments. Service facilities and spare parts for automobiles and machinery are other examples.

In summary, the agency costs associated with debt[55] consist of:

1. the opportunity wealth loss caused by the impact of debt on the investment decisions of the firm,

2. the monitoring and bonding expenditures by the bondholders and the owner-manager (i.e., the firm),

3. the bankruptcy and reorganization costs.

---

[53] Kraus and Litzenberger (1972) and Lloyd-Davies (1975) demonstrate that the total value of the firm will be reduced by these costs.

[54] These include only payments to all parties for legal fees, professional services, trustees' fees, and filing fees. They do not include the costs of management time or changes in cash flows due to shifts in the firm's demand or cost functions, discussed below.

[55] Which, incidentally, exist only when the debt has some probability of default.

4.4. Why Are the Agency Costs of Debt Incurred?

We have argued that the owner-manager bears the entire wealth effects of the agency costs of debt and that he captures the gains from reducing them. Thus, the agency costs associated with the debt discussed above will tend, in the absence of other mitigating factors, to discourage the use of corporate debt. What are the factors that encourage its use?

One factor is the tax subsidy on interest payments. (This will not explain preferred stock, where dividends are not tax deductible.[56]) Modigliani and Miller (1963) originally demonstrated that the use of riskless perpetual debt will increase the total value of the firm (ignoring the agency costs) by an amount equal to τB, where τ is the marginal and average corporate tax rate and B is the market value of the debt. Fama and Miller (1972, ch. 4) demonstrate that for the case of risky debt, the value of the firm will increase by the market value of the (uncertain) tax subsidy on the interest payments. Again, these gains will accrue entirely to the equity and will provide an incentive to utilize debt to the point where the marginal wealth benefits of the tax subsidy are just equal to the marginal wealth effects of the agency costs discussed above.

However, even in the absence of these tax benefits, debt would be utilized if the ability to exploit potentially profitable investment opportunities is limited by the resources of the owner. If the owner of a project cannot raise capital, he will suffer an opportunity loss represented by the increment in value offered to him by the additional investment opportunities. Thus, even though he will bear the agency costs from selling debt, he will find it desirable to incur them to obtain additional capital as long as the marginal wealth increments from the new investments projects are greater than the marginal agency costs of debt and these agency costs are in turn less than those caused by the sale of additional equity discussed in section 2. Furthermore, this solution is optimal from the social viewpoint. However, in the absence of tax subsidies on debt, these projects must be unique to this firm,[57] or they would be taken by other competitive entrepreneurs (prehaps new ones) who possessed

---

[56] Our theory is capable of explaining why in the absence of the tax subsidy on interest payments, we would expect to find firms using both debt and preferred stocks—a problem which has long puzzled at least one of the authors. If preferred stock has all the characteristics of debt except for the fact that its holders cannot put the firm into bankruptcy in the event of non-payment of the preferred dividends, then the agency costs associated with the issuance of preferred stock will be lower than those associated with debt by the present value of the bankruptcy costs.

However, these lower agency costs of preferred stock exist only over some range if, as the amount of such stock rises, the incentive effects caused by their existence impose value reductions which are larger than that caused by debt (including the bankruptcy costs of debt). There are two reasons for this. First, the equity holders' claims can be eliminated by the debtholders in the event of bankruptcy, and second, the debtholders have the right to fire the management in the event of bankruptcy. Both of these will tend to become more important as an advantage to the issuance of debt as we compare situations with large amounts of preferred stock to equivalent situations with large amounts of debt because they will tend to reduce the incentive effects of large amounts of preferred stock.

[57] One other condition also has to hold to justify the incurrence of the costs associated with the use of debt or outside equity in our firm. If there are other individuals in the economy who have sufficiently large amounts of personal capital to finance the entire firm, our capital-constrained owner can realize the full capital value of his current and prospective projects and avoid the agency costs by simply selling the firm (i.e., the right to take these projects) to one of these individuals. He will then avoid the wealth losses associated with the agency costs caused by the sale of debt or outside equity. If no such individuals exist, it will pay him (and society) to obtain the additional capital in the debt market. This implies, incidentally, that it is somewhat misleading to speak of the owner-manager as the individual who bears the agency costs. One could argue that it is the project which bears the costs since, if it is not sufficiently profitable to cover all the costs (including the agency costs), it will not be undertaken. We continue to speak of the owner-manager bearing these costs to emphasize the more correct and important point that he has the incentive to reduce them because, if he does, his wealth will be increased.

the requisite personal wealth to fully finance the projects[58] and are therefore able to avoid the existence of debt or outside equity.

5. A Theory of the Corporate Ownership Structure

In the previous sections we discussed the nature of agency costs associated with outside claims on the firm—both debt and equity. Our purpose here is to integrate these concepts into the beginnings of a theory of the corporate ownership structure. We use the term *ownership structure* rather than *capital structure* to highlight the fact that the crucial variables to be determined are not just the relative amounts of debt and equity but also the fraction of the equity held by the manager. Thus, for a given size firm, we want a theory to determine three variables:[59]

S_i: inside equity (held by the manager),

S_o: outside equity (held by anyone outside of the firm),

B: debt (held by anyone outside of the firm).

The total market value of the equity is $S = S_i + S_o$, and the total market value of the firm is $V = S + B$. In addition, we also wish to have a theory which determines the optimal size of the firm, i.e., its level of investment.

5.1. Determination of the Optimal Ratio of Outside Equity to Debt

Consider first the determination of the optimal ratio of outside equity to debt, S_o/B. To do this, let us hold the size of the firm constant. V, the actual value of the firm for a given size, will depend on the agency costs incurred; hence we use as our index of size V^*, the value of the firm at a given scale when agency costs are zero. For the moment we also hold the amount of outside financing $(B + S_o)$ constant. Given that a specified amount of financing $(B + S_o)$ is to be obtained externally, our problem is to determine the optimal fraction $E^* \equiv S_o^*/(B + S_o)$ to be financed with equity.

We argued above that (1) as long as capital markets are efficient (i.e., characterized by rational expectations), the prices of assets such as debt and outside equity will reflect unbiased estimates of the monitoring costs and redistributions which the agency relationship will engender, and (2) the selling owner-manager will bear these agency costs. Thus, from the owner-manager's standpoint, the optimal proportion of outside funds to be obtained from equity (versus debt) *for a given level of internal equity* is that E which results in minimum total agency costs.

Figure 5 presents a breakdown of the agency costs into two separate components: Define $A_{So}(E)$ as the total agency costs (a function of E) associated with the "exploitation" of the outside equity holders by the owner-manager and $A_B(E)$ as the total agency costs associated with the presence of debt in the ownership structure. $A_T(E) = A_{So}(E) + A_B(E)$ is the total agency cost.

---

[58] We continue to ignore for the moment the additional complicating factor involved with the portfolio decisions of the owner and the implied acceptance of potentially diversifiable risk by such 100 percent owners in this example.

[59] We continue to ignore such instruments as convertible bonds and warrants.

Figure 5
Total agency costs, $A_T(E)$, as a function of the ratio of outside equity to total outside financing, $E \equiv S_o/(B + S_o)$, for a given firm size V^* and given total amounts of outside financing $(B + S_o)$. $A_{S_o}(E) \equiv$ agency costs associated with outside equity, $A_B(E) \equiv$ agency costs associated with debt, B. $A_T(E^*) =$ minimum total agency costs at optimal fraction of outside financing E^*.

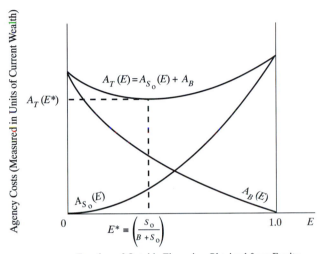

Fraction of Outside Financing Obtained from Equity

Consider the function $A_{S_o}(E)$. When $E \equiv S_o/(B + S_o)$ is zero, i.e., when there is no outside equity, the manager's incentives to exploit the outside equity is at a minimum (zero) since the changes in the value of the *total* equity are equal to the changes in *his* equity.[60] As E increases to 100 percent, his incentives to exploit the outside equity holders increase, and hence the agency costs $A_{S_o}(E)$ increase.

The agency costs associated with the existence of debt, $A_B(E)$, are composed mainly of the value reductions in the firm and monitoring costs caused by the manager's incentive to reallocate wealth from the bondholders to himself by increasing the value of his equity claim. They are at a maximum where all outside funds are obtained from debt, i.e., where $S_o = E = 0$. As the amount of debt declines to zero, these costs also go to zero because E goes to 1, his incentive to reallocate

---

[60] Note, however, that even when outsiders own none of the equity, the stockholder-manager still has some incentives to engage in activities which yield him non-pecuniary benefits but reduce the value of the firm by more than he personally values the benefits, if there is any risky debt outstanding. Any such actions he takes which reduce the value of the firm, V, tend to reduce the value of the bonds as well as the value of the equity. Although the option pricing model does not in general apply exactly to the problem of valuing the debt and equity of the firm, it can be useful in obtaining some qualitative insights into matters such as this. In the option pricing model, $\partial S/\partial V$ indicates the rate at which the stock value changes per dollar change in the value of the firm (and similarly for $\partial B/\partial V$). Both of these terms are less than unity (cf. Black and Scholes [1973]). Therefore, any action of the manager which reduces the value of the firm, V, tends to reduce the value of both the stock and the bonds, and the larger is the total debt/equity ratio, the smaller is the impact of any given change in V on the value of the equity; therefore, the lower is the cost to him of consuming non-pecuniary benefits.

wealth from the bondholders to himself falls. These incentives fall for two reasons: (1) the total amount of debt falls, and therefore it is more difficult to reallocate any given amount away from the debtholders; and (2) his share of any reallocation which is accomplished is falling since S_o is rising and therefore $S_i/(S_o + S_i)$, his share of the total equity, is falling.

The curve $A_T(E)$ represents the sum of the agency costs from various combinations of outside equity and debt financing, and as long as $A_{So}(E)$ and $A_B(E)$ are as we have drawn them, the minimum total agency cost for a given size firm and outside financing will occur at some point such as $A_T(E^*)$, with a mixture of both debt and equity.[61]

A Caveat. Before proceeding further, we point out that the issue regarding the exact shapes of the functions drawn in Figure 5 and several others discussed below are essentially an open question at this time. In the end, the shape of these functions is a question of fact and can be settled only by empirical evidence. We outline some *a priori* arguments which we believe lead to some plausible hypotheses about the behavior of the system, but confess that we are far from understanding the many conceptual subtleties of the problem. We are fairly confident of our arguments regarding the signs of the first derivatives of the functions, but the second derivatives are also important to the final solution, and much more work (both theoretical and empirical) is required before we can have much confidence regarding these parameters. We anticipate the work of others as well as our own to cast more light on these issues. Moreover, we suspect the results of such efforts will generate revisions to the details of what follows. We believe it is worthwhile to delineate the overall framework in order to demonstrate, if only in a simplified fashion, how the major pieces of the puzzle fit together into a cohesive structure.

5.2. Effects of the Scale of Outside Financing

In order to investigate the effects of increasing the amount of outside financing, $B + S_o$, and therefore reducing the amount of equity held by the manager, S_i, we continue to hold the scale of the firm, V^*, constant. Figure 6 presents a plot of the agency cost functions, $A_{So}(E)$, $A_B(E)$, and $A_T(E) = A_{So}(E) + A_B(E)$, for two different levels of outside financing. Define an index of the amount of outside financing to be

$$K = (B + S_o)/V^*,$$

and consider two different possible levels of outside financing, K_o and K_1, for a given scale of the firm such that $K_o < K_1$.

As the amount of outside equity increases, the owner's fractional claim on the firm, α, falls. He will be induced thereby to take additional non-pecuniary benefits out of the firm because his share of the cost falls. This also increases the marginal benefits from monitoring activities and therefore will tend to increase the optimal level of monitoring. Both of these factors will cause the locus of agency costs, $A_{So}(E; K)$, to shift upward as the fraction of outside financing, K, increases. This is depicted in Figure 6 by the two curves representing the agency costs of equity, one for the low level of

---

[61] This occurs, of course, not at the intersection of $A_{So}(E)$ and $A_B(E)$, but at the point where the absolute value of the slopes of the functions is equal, i.e., where $A'_{So}(E) + A'_B(E) = 0$.

Figure 6

Agency cost functions and optimal outside equity as a fraction of total outside financing, $E^*(K)$, for two different levels of outside financing, K, for a given size firm, V^*: $K_1 > K_0$.

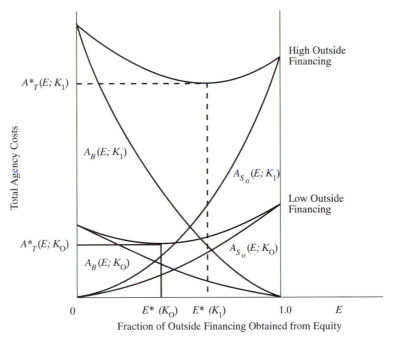

outside financing $A_{S_0}(E; K_0)$, the other for the high level of outside financing, $A_{S_0}(E; K_1)$. The locus of the latter lies above the former everywhere except at the origin, where both are 0.

The agency cost of debt will similarly rise as the amount of outside financing increases. This means that the locus of $A_B(E; K_1)$ for high outside financing, K_1, will lie above the locus of $A_B(E; K_0)$ for low outside financing, K_0, because the total amount of resources which can be reallocated from bondholders increases as the total amount of debt increases. However, since these costs are zero when the debt is zero for both K_0 and K_1, the intercepts of the $A_B(E; K)$ curves coincide at the right axis.

The net effect of the increased use of outside financing given the cost functions assumed in Figure 6 is to (1) increase the total agency costs from $A_T(E^*; K_0)$ to $A_T(E^*; K_1)$, and (2) to increase the optimal fraction of outside funds obtained from the sale of outside equity. We draw these functions for illustration only and are unwilling to speculate at this time on the exact form of $E^*(K)$ which gives the general effects of increasing outside financing on the relative quantities of debt and equity.

The locus of points $A_T(E^*; K)$ where agency costs are minimized (not drawn in Figure 6), determines $E^*(K)$, the optimal proportions of equity and debt to be used in obtaining outside funds as the fraction of outside funds, K, ranges from 0 to 100 percent. The solid line in Figure 7 is a plot of the minimum total agency costs as a function of the amount of outside financing for a firm with scale V_0^*. The dotted line shows the total agency costs for a larger firm with scale $V_1^* > V_0^*$. That is, we

Figure 8

Determination of the optimal amount of outside financing, K^*, for a given scale of firm.

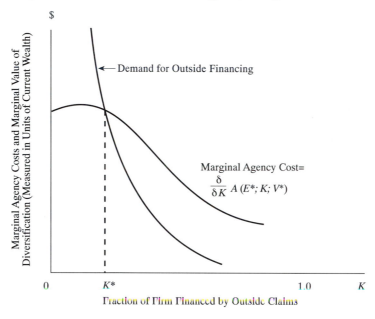

6. Qualifications and Extensions of the Analysis

6.1. Multiperiod Aspects of the Agency Problem

We have assumed throughout our analysis that we are dealing only with a single investment-financing decision by the entrepreneur and have ignored the issues associated with the incentives affecting future financing-investment decisions which might arise after the initial set of contracts are consummated between the entrepreneur-manager and outside stockholders and bondholders. These are important issues, which are left for future analysis.[64] Their solution will undoubtedly introduce some changes in the conclusions of the single-decision analysis. It seems clear, for instance, that the expectation of future sales of outside equity and debt will change the costs and benefits facing the manager in making decisions which benefit himself at the (short-run) expense of the current bondholders and stockholders. If he develops a reputation for such dealings, he can expect this to unfavorably influence the terms at which he can obtain future capital from outside sources. This will tend to increase the benefits associated with "sainthood" and will tend to reduce the size of the agency costs. Given the finite life of any individual, however, such an effect cannot reduce these costs to zero, because at some point these future costs will begin to weigh more heavily on his successors,

---

[64] The recent work of Myers (1975), which views future investment opportunities as options and investigates the incentive effects of the existence of debt in such a world where a sequence of investment decisions is made, is another important step in the investigation of the multiperiod aspects of the agency problem and the theory of the firm.

and the relative benefits to him of acting in his own best interests will rise.[65] Furthermore, it will generally be impossible for him to fully guarantee the outside interests that his successor will continue to follow his policies.

6.2. The Control Problem and Outside Owners' Agency Costs

The careful reader will notice that nowhere in the analysis thus far have we taken into account many of the details of the relationship between the part owner-manager and the outside stockholders and bondholders. In particular, we have assumed that all outside equity is nonvoting. If such equity does have voting rights, then the manager will be concerned about the effects on his long-run welfare of reducing his fractional ownership below the point where he loses effective control of the corporation—that is, below the point where it becomes possible for the outside equity holders to fire him. A complete analysis of this issue will require a careful specification of the contractual rights involved on both sides, the role of the board of directors, and the coordination (agency) costs borne by the stockholders in implementing policy changes. This latter point involves consideration of the distribution of the outside ownership claims. Simply put, forces exist to determine an equilibrium distribution of outside ownership. If the costs of reducing the dispersion of ownership are lower than the benefits to be obtained from reducing the agency costs, it will pay some individual or group of individuals to buy shares in the market to reduce the dispersion of ownership. We occasionally witness these conflicts for control, which involve outright market purchases, tender offers, and proxy fights. Further analysis of these issues is left to the future.

6.3. A Note on the Existence of Inside Debt and Some Conjectures on the Use of Convertible Financial Instruments

We have been asked [66] why debt held by the manager (i.e., "inside debt") plays no role in our analysis. We have as yet been unable to incorporate this dimension formally into our analysis in a satisfactory way. The question is a good one and suggests some potentially important extensions of the analysis. For instance, it suggests an inexpensive way for the owner-manager with both equity and debt outstanding to eliminate a large part (perhaps all) of the agency costs of debt. If he binds himself contractually to hold a fraction of the total debt equal to his fractional ownership of the total equity, he would have no incentive whatsoever to reallocate wealth from the debt holders to the stockholders. Consider the case where

$$B_i/S_i = B_o/S_o, \tag{4}$$

where S_i and S_o are defined earlier, B_i is the dollar value of the inside debt held by the owner-manager, and B_o is the debt held by outsiders. In this case, if the manager changes the investment policy of the firm to reallocate wealth between the debt and equity holders, the net effect on the total value of his holdings in the firm will be zero. Therefore, his incentives to perform such reallocations are zero.[67]

---

[65] Becker and Stigler (1972) analyze a special case of this problem involving the use of nonvested pension rights to help correct for this end-game play in the law enforcement area.

[66] By our colleague David Henderson.

[67] This also suggests that *some* outside debt holders can protect themselves from "exploitation" by the manager by purchasing a fraction of the total equity equal to their fractional ownership of the debt. All debt holders, of course, cannot do this unless the manager does so also. In addition, such an investment rule restricts the portfolio choices of investors and therefore would impose costs if followed rigidly. Thus, the agency costs will not be eliminated this way either.

Why then don't we observe practices or formal contracts which accomplish this elimination or reduction of the agency costs of debt? Maybe we do for smaller privately held firms (we haven't attempted to obtain this data), but for large, diffuse-owner corporations the practice does not seem to be common. One reason for this, we believe, is that in some respects the claim that the manager holds on the firm in the form of his wage contract has some of the characteristics of debt.[68] If true, this implies that even with zero holdings of formal debt claims, he still has positive holdings of a quasi-debt claim, and this may accomplish the satisfaction of condition (4). The problem here is that any formal analysis of this issue requires a much deeper understanding of the relationship between formal debt holdings and the wage contract; i.e., how much debt is it equivalent to?

This line of thought also suggests some other interesting issues. Suppose the implicit debt characteristics of the manager's wage contract result in a situation equivalent to

$$B_i/S_i > B_o/S_o.$$

Then he would have incentives to change the operating characteristics of the firm (i.e., reduce the variance of the outcome distribution) to transfer wealth from the stockholders to the debt holders, which is the reverse of the situation we examined in section 4. Furthermore, this seems to capture some of the concern often expressed regarding the fact that managers of large publicly held corporations seem to behave in a risk-averse way, to the detriment of the equity holders. One solution to this would be to establish incentive compensation systems for the manager or to give him stock options which in effect give him a claim on the upper tail of the outcome distribution. This also seems to be a commonly observed phenomenon.

This analysis also suggests some additional issues regarding the costs and benefits associated with the use of more complicated financial claims, such as warrants, convertible bonds, and convertible preferred stock, which we have not formally analyzed as yet. Warrants, convertible bonds, and convertible preferred stock have some of the characteristics of non-voting shares, although they can be converted into voting shares under some terms. Alchian and Demsetz (1972) provide an interesting analysis regarding the use of non-voting shares. They argue that some shareholders with strong beliefs in the talents and judgment of the manager will want to be protected against the possibility that some other shareholders will take over and limit the actions of the manager (or fire him). Given that the securities exchanges prohibit the use of non-voting shares by listed firms, the use of option-type securities might be a substitute for these claims.

In addition, warrants represent a claim on the upper tail of the distribution of outcomes, and convertible securities can be thought of as securities with non-detachable warrants. It seems that the incentive effects of warrants would tend to offset to some extent the incentive effects of the existence of risky debt because the owner-manager would be sharing with the warrant holders part of the proceeds associated with a shift in the distribution of returns. Thus, we conjecture that potential bondholders will find it attractive to have warrants attached to the risky debt of firms in which it is relatively easy to shift the distribution of outcomes to expand the upper tail of the distribution to transfer wealth from bondholders. It would also then be attractive to the owner-manager because of the reduction in the agency costs which he would bear. This argument also implies that it would make little difference if the warrants were detachable (and therefore saleable separately from the bonds)

---

[68] Consider the situation in which the bondholders have the right in the event of bankruptcy to terminate his employment and therefore to terminate the future returns to any specific human capital or rents he may be receiving.

since their mere existence would reduce the incentives of the manager (or stockholders) to increase the riskiness of the firm (and therefore increase the probability of bankruptcy). Furthermore, the addition of a conversion privilege to fixed claims such as debt or preferred stock would also tend to reduce the incentive effects of the existence of such fixed claims and therefore lower the agency costs associated with them. The theory predicts that these phenomena should be more frequently observed in cases where the incentive effects of such fixed claims are high than when they are low.

6.4. Monitoring and the Social Product of Security Analysis

One of the areas in which further analysis is likely to lead to high payoffs is that of monitoring. We currently have little which could be glorified by the title of a "Theory of Monitoring," yet this is a crucial building block of the analysis. We would expect monitoring activities to become specialized to those institutions and individuals who possess comparative advantages in these activities. One of the groups that seems to play a large role in these activities is composed of the security analysts employed by institutional investors, brokers, and investment advisory services. As well, there is the analysis performed by individual investors in the normal course of investment decision making.

A large body of evidence exists which indicates that security prices incorporate in an unbiased manner all publicly available information and much of what might be called "private information."[69] There is also a large body of evidence which indicates that the security analysis activities of mutual funds and other institutional investors are not reflected in portfolio returns; i.e., they do not increase risk-adjusted portfolio returns over a naive random selection buy and hold strategy.[70] Therefore, some have been tempted to conclude that the resources expended on such research activities to find under- or overvalued securities is a social loss. Jensen (1974) argues that this conclusion cannot be unambiguously drawn because there is a large consumption element in the demand for these services.

Furthermore, the analysis of this paper would seem to indicate that to the extent that security analysis activities reduce the agency costs associated with the separation of ownership and control, they are indeed socially productive. Moreover, if this is true, we expect the major benefits of the security analysis activity to be reflected in the higher capitalized value of the ownership claims to corporations and *not* in the period-to-period portfolio returns of the analyst. Equilibrium in the security analysis industry requires that the private returns to analysis (i.e., portfolio returns) must be just equal to the private costs of such activity,[71] and this will not reflect the social product of this activity, which will consist of larger output and higher *levels* of the capital value of ownership claims. Therefore, the argument implies that if there is a non-optimal amount of security analysis being performed, it is too much,[72] not too little (since the shareholders would be willing to pay directly to have the "optimal" monitoring performed), and we don't seem to observe such payments.

6.5. Specialization in the Use of Debt and Equity

Our previous analysis of agency costs suggests at least one other testable hypothesis: that in those industries where the incentive effects of outside equity or debt are widely different, we would expect

---

[69] See Fama (1970) for a survey of his "efficient markets" literature.

[70] See Jensen (1969) for an example of this evidence and references.

[71] Ignoring any pure consumption elements in the demand for security analysis.

[72] Again ignoring the value of the pure consumption elements in the demand for security analysis.

to see specialization in the use of the low agency cost financing arrangement. In industries where it is relatively easy for managers to lower the mean value of the outcomes of the enterprise by outright theft, special treatment of favored customers, ease of consumption of leisure on the job, and so on (for example, the bar and restaurant industry), we would expect to see the ownership structure of firms characterized by relatively little outside equity (that is, 100 percent ownership of the equity by the manager) with almost all outside capital obtained through the use of debt.

The theory predicts the opposite would be true where the incentive effects of debt are large relative to the incentive effects of equity. Firms like conglomerates, in which it would be easy to shift outcome distributions adversely for bondholders (by changing the acquisition or divestiture policy), should be characterized by relatively lower utilization of debt. Conversely, in industries where the freedom of management to take riskier projects is severely constrained (for example, regulated industries such as public utilities), we should find more intensive use of debt financing.

The analysis suggests that in addition to the fairly well understood role of uncertainty in the determination of the quality of collateral, there is at least one other element of great importance—the ability of the owner of the collateral to change the distribution of outcomes by shifting either the mean outcome or the variance of the outcomes. A study of bank lending policies should reveal these to be important aspects of the contractual practices observed there.

6.6. *Application of the Analysis to the Large, Diffuse-Ownership Corporation*

While we believe the structure outlined in the preceding pages is applicable to a wide range of corporations, it is still in an incomplete state. One of the most serious limitations of the analysis is that, as it stands, we have not worked out in this paper its application to the very large, modern corporation whose managers own little or no equity. We believe our approach can be applied to this case, but space limitations preclude discussion of these issues here. They remain to be worked out in detail and will be included in a future paper.

6.7. *The Supply Side of the Incomplete Markets Question*

The analysis of this paper is also relevant to the incomplete market issue considered by Arrow (1964), Diamond (1967), Hakansson (1974a, b), Rubinstein (1974), Ross (1974), and others. The problems addressed in this literature derive from the fact that whenever the available set of financial claims on outcomes in a market fails to span the underlying state of space (see Arrow [1964] and Debreu [1959]), the resulting allocation is Pareto inefficient. A disturbing element in this literature surrounds the fact that the inefficiency conclusion is generally drawn without explicit attention in the analysis to the costs of creating new claims or of maintaining the expanded set of markets called for to bring about the welfare improvement.

The demonstration of a possible welfare improvement from the expansion of the set of claims by the introduction of new basic contingent claims or options can be thought of as an analysis of the demand conditions for new markets. Viewed from this perspective, what is missing in the literature on this problem is the formulation of a positive analysis of the supply of markets (or the supply of contingent claims). That is, what is it in the maximizing behavior of individuals in the economy that causes them to create and sell contingent claims of various sorts?

The analysis in this paper can be viewed as a small first step in the direction of formulating an analysis of the supply-of-markets issue which is founded in the self-interested maximizing behavior of individuals. We have shown why it is in the interest of a wealth-maximizing entrepreneur to create and sell claims such as debt and equity. Furthermore, as we have indicated above, it appears that extensions of these arguments will lead to a theory of the supply of warrants, convertible bonds, and convertible preferred stock. We are not suggesting that the specific analysis offered above is likely to be sufficient to lead to a theory of the supply of the wide range of contracts (both existing and merely potential) in the world at large. However, we do believe that framing the question of the completeness of markets in terms of the joining of both the demand and supply conditions will be very fruitful instead of implicitly assuming that new claims spring forth from some (costless) well-head of creativity unaided or unsupported by human effort.

7. Conclusions

The publicly held business corporation is an awesome social invention. Millions of individuals voluntarily entrust billions of dollars, francs, pesos, etc., of personal wealth to the care of managers on the basis of a complex set of contracting relationships which delineate the rights of the parties involved. The growth in the use of the corporate form as well as the growth in market value of established corporations suggests that at least, up to the present, creditors and investors have by and large not been disappointed with the results, despite the agency costs inherent in the corporate form.

Agency costs are as real as any other costs. The level of agency costs depends on, among other things, statutory and common law and human ingenuity in devising contracts. Both the law and the sophistication of contracts relevant to the modern corporation are the products of a historical process in which there were strong incentives for individuals to minimize agency costs. Moreover, there were alternative organizational forms available and opportunities to invent new ones. Whatever its shortcomings, the corporation has thus far survived the market test against potential alternatives.

References

Alchian, A. A., 1965. The basis of some recent advances in the theory of management of the firm, Journal of Industrial Economics, Nov., 30–44.

Alchian, A. A., 1968. Corporate and property rights, in: Economic policy and the regulation of securities (American Enterprise Institute, Washington, DC).

Alchian, A. A., 1974. Some implications of recognition of property right transactions costs, unpublished paper presented at the First Interlaken Conference on Analysis and Ideology, June.

Alchian, A. A., and W. R. Allen, 1969. Exchange and production: Theory in use (Wadsworth, Belmont, CA).

Alchian, A. A., and H. Demsetz, 1972. Production, information costs, and economic organization, American Economic Review LXII, no. 5, 777–95.

Alchian, A. A., and R. A. Kessel, 1962. Competition, monopoly and the pursuit of pecuniary gain, in: Aspects of labor economics (National Bureau of Economic Research, Princeton, NJ).

Arrow, K. J., 1963/4. Control in large organizations, Management Science 10, 397–408.

Arrow, K. J., 1964. The role of securities in the optimal allocation of risk bearing, Review of Economic Studies 31, no. 86, 91–96.

Atkinson, T. R., 1967. Trends in corporate bond quality, in: Studies in corporate bond finance 4 (National Bureau of Economic Research, New York).

Baumol, W. J., 1959. Business behavior, value and growth (Macmillan, New York).

Becker, G., 1957. The economics of discrimination (University of Chicago Press, Chicago, IL).

Becker, G. S., and G. J. Stigler, 1972. Law enforcement and compensation of enforcers, unpublished paper presented at the Conference on Capitalism and Freedom, Oct.

Benston, G., 1977. The impact of maturity regulation on high interest rate lenders and borrowers. Journal of Financial Economics 4, no. 1.

Berhold, M., 1971. A theory of linear profit sharing incentives, Quarterly Journal of Economics LXXXV, Aug., 460–82.

Berle, A. A., Jr., and G. C. Means, 1932. The modern corporation and private property (Macmillan, New York).

Black, F., and M. Scholes, 1973. The pricing of options and corporate liabilities, Journal of Political Economy 81, no. 3, 637–54.

Black, F., M. H. Miller, and R. A. Posner, 1974. An approach to the regulation of bank holding companies, unpublished manuscript (University of Chicago, Chicago, IL).

Branch, B., 1973. Corporate objectives and market performance, Financial Management, Summer, 24–29.

Coase, R. H., 1937. The nature of the firm, Economica, New Series, IV, 386–405. Reprinted in: Readings in price theory (Irwin, Homewood, IL) 331–51.

Coase, R. H., 1959. The Federal Communications Commission, Journal of Law and Economics II, Oct., 1–40.

Coase, R. H., 1960. The problem of social cost, Journal of Law and Economics III, Oct., 1–44.

Coase, R. H., 1964. Discussion, American Economics Review LIV, no. 3, 194–97.

Cyert, R. M., and C. L. Hedrick, 1972. Theory of the firm: Past, present and future: An interpretation, Journal of Economic Literature X, June, 398–412.

Cyert, R. M., and J. G. March, 1963. A behavioral theory of the firm (Prentice Hall, Englewood Cliffs, NJ).

De Alessi, L., 1973. Private property and dispersion of ownership in large corporations, Journal of Finance, Sept., 839–51.

Debreau, G., 1959. Theory of value (Wiley, New York).

Demsetz, H., 1967. Toward a theory of property rights, American Economic Review LVII, May, 347–59.

Demsetz, H., 1969. Information and efficiency: Another viewpoint, Journal of Law and Economics XII, April 1–22.

Diamond, P. A., 1967. The role of a stock market in a general equilibrium model with technological uncertainty, American Economic Review LVII, Sept., 759–76.

Evans, J. L., and S. H. Archer, 1968. Diversification and the reduction of dispersion: An empirical analysis, Journal of Finance, Dec.

Fama, E. F., 1970a. Efficient capital markets: A review of theory and empirical work, Journal of Finance XXV, no. 2.

Fama, E. F., 1970b. Multiperiod consumption-investment decisions, American Economic Review LX, March.

Fama, E. F., 1972. Ordinal and measurable utility, in: M. C. Jensen, ed., Studies in the theory of capital markets (Praeger, New York).

Fama, E. F., and M. Miller, 1972. The theory of finance (Holt, Rinehart and Winston, New York).

Friedman, M., 1970. The social responsibility of business is to increase its profits, New York Times Magazine, 13 Sept. 32ff.

Furubotn, E. G., and S. Pejovich, 1972. Property rights and economic theory: A survey of recent literature, Journal of Economic Literature X, Dec., 1137–62.

Galai, D., and R. W. Masulis, 1976. The option pricing model and the risk factor of stock, Journal of Financial Economics 3, no. 1/2, 53–82.

Hakansson, N. H., 1974a. The superfund: Efficient paths toward a complete financial market, unpublished manuscript.

Hakansson, N. H., 1974b. Ordering markets and the capital structures of firms with illustrations, Institute of Business and Economic Research Working Paper no. 24 (University of California, Berkeley, CA).

Heckerman, D. G., 1975. Motivating managers to make investment decisions, Journal of Financial Economics 2, no. 3, 273–92.

Hirshleifer, J., 1958. On the theory of optimal investment decisions, Journal of Political Economy, Aug., 329–52.

Hirshleifer, J., 1970. Investment, interest, and capital (Prentice-Hall, Englewood Cliffs, NJ).

Jensen, M. C., 1969. Risk, the pricing of capital assets, and the evaluation of investment portfolios, Journal of Business 42, no. 2, 167–247.

Jensen, M. C., 1974. Tests of capital market theory and implications of the evidence. Graduate School of Management Working Paper Series no. 7414 (University of Rochester, Rochester, NY).

Jensen, M. C., and J. B. Long, 1972. Corporate investment under uncertainty and Pareto optimality in the capital markets, Bell Journal of Economics, Spring, 151–74.

Jensen, M. C., and W. H. Meckling, 1976. Can the corporation survive? Center for Research in Government Policy and Business Working Paper no. PPS 76–4 (University of Rochester, Rochester, NY).

Klein, W. A., 1976. Legal and economic perspectives on the firm, unpublished manuscript (University of California, Los Angeles, CA).

Kraus, A., and R. Litzenberger, 1973. A state preference model of optimal financial leverage, Journal of Finance, Sept.

Larner, R. J., 1970. Management control and the large corporation (Dunellen, New York).

Lintner, J., 1965. Security prices, risk, and maximal gains from diversification, Journal of Finance XX, Dec., 587–616.

Lloyd-Davies, P., 1975. Risk and optimal leverage, unpublished manuscript (University of Rochester, Rochester, NY).

Long, J. B., 1972. Wealth, welfare, and the price of risk, Journal of Finance, May, 419–33.

Long, J. B., Jr., 1974. Discussion, Journal of Finance XXXIX, no. 12, 485–88.

Machlup, F., 1967. Theories of the firm: Marginalist, behavioral, managerial, American Economic Review, March, 1–33.

Manne, H. G., 1962. The "higher criticism" of the modern corporation, Columbia Law Review 62, March, 399–432.

Manne, H. G., 1965. Mergers and the market for corporate control, Journal of Political Economy, April, 110–20.

Manne, H. G., 1967. Our two corporate systems: Law and economics, Virginia Law Review 53, March, 259–84.

Manne, H. G., 1972. The social responsibility of regulated utilities, Wisconsin Law Review V, no. 4, 995–1009.

Marris, R., 1964. The economic theory of managerial capitalism (Free Press of Glencoe, Glencoe, IL).

Mason, E. S., 1959. The corporation in modern society (Harvard University Press, Cambridge, MA).

McManus, J. C., 1975. The costs of alternative economic organizations, Canadian Journal of Economics VIII, Aug., 334–50.

Meckling, W. H., 1976. Values and the choice of the model of the individual in the social sciences, Schweizerische Zeitschrift für Volkswirtschaft und Statistik, Dec.

Merton, R. C., 1973. The theory of rational option pricing, Bell Journal of Economics and Management Science 4, no. 1, 141–83.

Merton, R. C., 1974. On the pricing of corporate debt: The risk structure of interest rates, Journal of Finance XXIX, no. 2, 449–70.

Merton, R. C., and M. G. Subrahmanyam, 1974. The optimality of a competitive stock market, Bell Journal of Economics and Management Science, Spring, 145–70.

Miller, M. H., and F. Modigliani, 1966. Some estimates of the cost of capital to the electric utility industry, 1954–57, American Economic Review, June, 333–91.

Modigliani, F., and M. H. Miller, 1958. The costs of capital, corporation finance, and the theory of investment, American Economic Review 48, June, 261–97.

Modigliani, F., and M. H. Miller, 1963. Corporate income taxes and the cost of capital: A correction, American Economic Review, June, 433–43.

Monsen, R. J., and A. Downs, 1965. A theory of large managerial firms, Journal of Political Economy, June, 221–36.

Myers, S. C., 1975. A note on the determinants of corporate debt capacity, unpublished manuscript (London Graduate School of Business Studies, London).

Penrose, E., 1958. The theory of the growth of the firm (Wiley, New York).

Preston, L. E., 1975. Corporation and society: The search for a paradigm, Journal of Economic Literature XIII, June, 434–53.

Ross, S. A., 1973. The economic theory of agency: The principals problems, American Economic Review LXII, May, 134–39.

Ross, S. A., 1974a. The economic theory of agency and the principle of similarity, in: M. D. Balch et al., eds., Essays on economic behavior under uncertainty (North-Holland, Amsterdam).

Ross, S. A., 1974b. Options and efficiency, Rodney L. White Center for Financial Research Working Paper no. 3–74 (University of Pennsylvania, Philadelphia, PA).

Rubinstein, M., 1974. A discrete-time synthesis of financial theory, Parts I and II, Institute of Business and Economic Research Working Papers nos. 20 and 21 (University of California, Berkeley, CA).

Scitovsky, T., 1943. A note on profit maximisation and its implications. Review of Economic Studies XI, 57–60.

Sharpe, W. F., 1964. Capital asset prices: A theory of market equilibrium under conditions of risk, Journal of Finance XIX, Sept., 425–42.

Shubik, M., 1970. A curmudgeon's guide to microeconomics, Journal of Economic Literature VIII, June, 405–34.

Silver, M., and R. Auster, 1969. Entrepreneurship, profit and limits on firm size, Journal of Business 42, July, 277–81.

Simon, H. A., 1955. A behavioral model of rational choice, Quarterly Journal of Economics 69, 99–118.

Simon, H. A., 1959. Theories of decision making in economics and behavioral science, American Economic Review, June 253–83.

Smith, A., 1937. The wealth of nations, Cannan edition (Modern Library, New York).

Smith, C., 1976. Option pricing: A review, Journal of Financial Economics 3, nos. 1/2, 3–52.

Warner, J. B., 1975. Bankruptcy costs, absolute priority, and the pricing of risky debt claims, unpublished manuscript (University of Chicago, Chicago, IL).

Williamson, O. E., 1964. The economics of discretionary behavior: Managerial objectives in a theory of the firm (Prentice-Hall, Englewood Cliffs, NJ).

Williamson, O. E., 1970. Corporate control and business behavior (Prentice-Hall, Englewood Cliffs, NJ).

Williamson, O. E., 1975. Markets and hierarchies: Analysis and antitrust implications (The Free Press, New York).

Wilson, R., 1968. On the theory of syndicates, Econometrica 36, Jan., 119–32.

Wilson, R., 1969. La decision: Agregation et dynamique des orders de preference, Extrait (Editions du Centre National de la Recherche Scientifique, Paris), 288–307.

Discussion Questions

1. Define the agency relationship.

2. The authors listed three components of agency costs. What are those components? Distinguish between "inside" and "outside" equity.

3. Discuss the "agency problem"—that is, how can principals induce agents to act as if to maximize the principals' welfare?

4. What is meant by monitoring costs? Who bears these costs? Give some examples.

5. What is meant by bonding costs or bonding expenditures?

6. What are some examples of bankruptcy costs?

7. What are the agency costs of debt?

*Richard A. Lambert and David F. Larcker**

Executive Compensation, Corporate Decision Making, and Shareholder Wealth: A Review of the Evidence

For some time, one of the great debates has been how to ensure that executives of publicly traded firms make their decisions in the interests of shareholders and not themselves. One answer to this question lies in how corporate executives are compensated. This article is a thorough discussion of known ways to align the interests of executives and shareholders via executive compensation.

Introduction

In recent years the compensation of corporate management has become the focus of a major controversy. The level of executive pay and its relationship to corporate performance are now central issues in a generally heated debate among legislators, corporate directors, economists, financial journalists, and compensation professionals.

As a sampling of the rhetoric generated by this controversy, consider this pronouncement in Carol Loomis's widely cited *Fortune* article titled (provocatively, if not judiciously) "The Madness of Executive Compensation":

> In a totally rational world, top executives would get paid handsomely for first-class performance, and would lose out when they flopped. But to an extraordinary extent, those who flop still get paid handsomely.

*We would like to thank John Balkcom, Donald Chew, Alfred Rappaport, Lawrence Revsine, and Mark Ubelhart for helpful comments on earlier drafts.

Source: Reprinted with permission of *Midland Corporate Finance Journal* (Spring 1986), pp. 64–71. Richard A. Lambert is Professor of Accounting at Stanford University. David F. Larcker is the Ernst and Young Professor of Accounting at the Wharton School at the University of Pennsylvania.

Moreover, Loomis continues,

> It is widely believed that many compensation committees are rubber stamps, unwilling to be hard-nosed about the pay of top executives, particularly those chaps who are fellow members of the board.[1]

Or consider this more forceful expression of dissatisfaction with corporate compensation committees, which appeared in a recent *Wall Street Journal* editorial:

> Boards of directors, individual shareholders, and large institutions have got to clean up their own acts with respect to corporations that have poor performance and then make that performance even poorer by offering outrageous amounts of compensation to demonstrably incompetent executives.[2]

Finally, in another recent *Wall Street Journal* editorial, titled "Reform Executive Pay or Congress Will," Peter Drucker calls for executives to limit their compensation to a multiple of the compensation earned by the "rank and file."[3] And, perhaps taking its cue from Drucker's moralistic tone, the American Law Institute has added to the general furor by proposing amendments to the Business Judgment Rule that would change the composition of corporate boards of directors, further restrict the autonomy of corporate managements, and regulate executive compensation.[4]

Executive compensation consultants, while predictably far less hostile, have also been strongly critical of conventional compensation practices. But here the discussion has focused not on the appropriate *level* of executive pay, but rather on the proper criteria, the ideal "scoreboard" for evaluating managerial performance and awarding bonuses. The widespread use of short-term, accounting-oriented measures like EPS and EPS growth has come under attack, and a number of alternatives have been proposed to strengthen the unity of interest between management and stockholders. Some consultants have proposed real, or inflation-adjusted, returns on stockholders' equity (that is, the return on equity minus the cost of equity capital) as the ideal basis for incentive compensation.[5] Others have argued that discounted cash flow is the performance measure that corresponds most strongly to the process by which investors price corporate shares.[6]

Meanwhile, as the controversy rages on in political and business circles, academics have begun to explore some of the issues raised above. In contrast to the morass of baseless charge and countercharge in which the public debate has become enmired, researchers in the fields of economics, finance, and accounting have established the beginnings of a scientific inquiry into questions of managerial economics. The result to date has been a small, but rapidly growing body of empirical studies providing insights into matters like the following:

[1] *Fortune* (July 12, 1982).

[2] Graef Crystal, "Congress Thinks It Knows Best About Executive Compensation," *The Wall Street Journal* (July 30, 1984).

[3] "Reform Executive Pay or Congress Will," *The Wall Street Journal* (April 24, 1984).

[4] On other fronts, although generally only in isolated cases, shareholder activists have leveled charges of "excessive" compensation in attempts to oust incumbent directors in proxy fights. See, for example, the proxy fight discussions regarding Pantry Pride Inc. in *The Wall Street Journal,* Proxy Contest Announcement (November 21, 1984), p. 45.

[5] Louis J. Brindisi, "Creating Shareholder Value: A New Mission for Executive Compensation" (New York: Booz, Allen and Hamilton, Inc., 1984), and Jude Rich and Ennius Bergsma, "Pay Executives to Create Wealth," *Chief Executive* (1982).

[6] See, for example, Alfred Rappaport, "How to Design Value-Contributing Executive Incentives," *Journal of Business Strategy* 4 (1983).

- What are the consequences of the separation of ownership from control in the large public corporation? How effective are compensation contracts in overcoming conflicts of interest between management and stockholders?

- What are the pros and cons of various "scorecards" for evaluating managerial performance and awarding executive bonuses? What is the optimal "mix" of components—stock options, annual cash bonuses, long-term performance payments, etc.—in the total compensation package?

- Do compensation contracts "really matter" to executives? That is, do managers respond differently to different compensation plans?

- To what extent is annual executive compensation related (and, furthermore, to what extent *should* it be related) to year-to-year corporate performance and stockholder returns?

- How effective is the labor market for executives—that market which sets a manager's "opportunity wage"—in curbing management's natural tendency to pursue its self-interest at the expense of stockholders?

Our purpose in this article is to review the academic literature on executive compensation. We also discuss some of the more innovative incentive plans introduced by compensation professionals in recent years.

A Framework for Examining Executive Compensation

A recent development in the theory of corporate organization, known as "agency theory," has focused attention on the separation of ownership from control in large public corporations. In the context of this theory, management incentive compensation plans are viewed as one of several important means of reducing potential conflicts of interest between management and shareholders. (The others are the existence of a market for corporate control, which disciplines inefficient managers through the threat of takeover; and a market for executive labor, which in theory weighs an executive's past service to shareholders when determining his or her opportunities for alternative employment.) To the extent the separation of ownership from control is a serious problem in the large public corporation (and the recent proliferation of leveraged buyouts can be construed as evidence in support of this supposition), an effective compensation program can add value to the firm by improving the alignment of management incentives with stockholder interests.

There are three principal kinds of conflicts discussed in the agency literature. First, and most obviously, whereas shareholders' primary interest is in having a management team that maximizes their financial return, executives may derive "nonpecuniary" benefits ("perks," in the vernacular) from their control over corporate resources. They may authorize the purchase of superfluous corporate jets. Or, with far more serious consequences, they may seek to build a corporate empire through a series of large acquisitions at costly premiums that penalize their own shareholders.[7] (It is important to note that in this context *perk* means any expenditure that has a higher value to management

---

[7] For example, it is sometimes argued that founders of firms (e.g., Henry Ford) place such a high value on power and maintaining control over the operations of the firm that these actions decrease their personal wealth and the wealth of the shareholders. In this context, perquisite consumption can be very costly to shareholders. Similarly, the announcement of a "bad" corporate acquisition can decrease the total market value of the acquiring firm's stock by millions of dollars.

than to shareholders. Thus, "perks" have a potential value much larger than the sum of costs for club memberships, first-class air travel, etc.)

Second, management and shareholders can differ sharply in their attitudes toward the risk of potential investment strategies. Whereas shareholders can diversify their wealth by spreading it among different assets, a large portion of a manager's wealth (human capital, compensation earned, and stock in the firm) is tied to the fortunes of the company. Therefore, we would expect managers to be more risk averse than shareholders. Too great a difference in risk aversion might cause a manager to turn down a project that would benefit shareholders because the perceived personal risks are too high.

Third, there is a potential conflict between the decision-making time horizons of executives and shareholders. For example, an executive's investment decisions may be evaluated by the compensation committee over a shorter time period than shareholders use in assessing the eventual outcome of the same investment decisions. This pressure may in turn cause a manager to evaluate projects based on their immediate impact on profits, rather than according to the present value of cash flows over the life of the investment. A foreshortened decision-making horizon thus may motivate management to turn down profitable long-term investments.

From the perspective of agency theory, then, executive compensation contracts are *not* simply a tax-efficient vehicle for delivering pay to executives (although taxes offer at least a partial explanation for some features of compensation plans).[8] The primary function of incentive compensation plans is to control the kinds of conflicts of interest between management and shareholders described above. And, as we hope to show in the next section, the ability of the agency framework to identify the sources of conflicts between stockholders and executives is useful in determining the "optimal" design of a compensation plan.

Compensation "Scorecards" and Contract Design

How, then, are current compensation plans designed to control such conflicts of interest between management and stockholders? And, furthermore, how effective are they in accomplishing this end? In this section, we discuss the implications of the agency issues discussed above for choosing the appropriate performance measure, as well as the structure and components of the compensation package.

Before considering specific contract designs, it is useful to point out some of the difficulties that arise in evaluating managerial performance. For one thing, the separation between ownership and management prevents shareholders from directly observing much of management's activity. Also, because shareholders almost never possess management's familiarity with the operations of the firm, they may not be able to evaluate the consequences of those actions they can observe. As a result, they must often rely on reported *results* (on an accountant's periodic measure of net income,

---

[8] For some additional discussion of tax/incentive aspects of compensation contracts, see G. Hite and M. Long, "Taxes and Executive Stock Options," *Journal of Accounting and Economics* 4 (1982); M. Miller and M. Scholes, "Executive Compensation, Taxes and Incentives," in W. Sharpe and C. Cootner (eds.), *Financial Economics: Essays in Honor of Paul Cootner* (1982); C. Smith and R. Watts, "Incentive and Tax Effects of U.S. Executive Compensation Plans," *Australian Management Journal* (1983); R. Lambert and D. Larcker, "Stock Options and Managerial Incentives," working paper, Northwestern University (1984); and M. Scholes and M. Wolfson, "Employee Compensation and Taxes: Links with Incentives and with Investment and Financing Decisions," working paper, Stanford University (1984).

for example, or share price performance) as the basis for evaluating management's performance. Unfortunately, these results are likely to reflect the effects of a large number of factors that are not under management's control. This may make it difficult to determine whether poor results are due to "bad luck" or to poor decisions on the part of management.

Another problem is that the consequences of management's current decisions may extend over many years, and it is often difficult to foresee today their effects on the value of the firm in *future* periods. These difficulties suggest that compensation contracts (or any other disciplinary mechanism) can never be fully successful in resolving agency problems. But, given such limitations, let's see how the contracts are designed to deal with these management-shareholder conflicts.

Executive Expenditures and Risky Investments

One objective of a good compensation scheme is to motivate managers to make expenditure decisions that benefit shareholders. To approach this problem, consider the extreme (and improbable) case of an executive whose compensation is totally independent of his performance. An example would be a manager whose compensation consisted entirely of a *fixed* salary—one that, say, in real terms remained unchanged from year to year. Such a manager would have no incentive to increase shareholder wealth because he does not share in any of the resulting gains. He would be much more likely than other executives to avail himself of perquisites of all varieties, at the expense of his shareholders.

This incentive problem—one that all companies with outside stockholders face to at least some degree—can be reduced by making part of an executive's compensation depend upon the financial performance of the firm. By allowing managers to share in the company's gains, a compensation plan provides them with some incentive to develop strategies that will increase shareholder wealth. Also, since the executive now bears some of the costs of "perk" consumption, he will be less likely to evaluate corporate expenditures according to the personal satisfaction—and perhaps, in the case of some major investment decisions, the sense of power or prestige—they offer him.

Given this concern, it may seem that the optimal compensation scheme will bind executive compensation as tightly as possible to changes in the stock price of the firm. The problem with this solution, however, is that stock prices are often affected by factors beyond management's influence. This means that tying management's compensation very closely to the firm's stock price will greatly increase executives' individual exposure to risk. And imposing large personal risks on management can actually *reduce* shareholder wealth—in two ways. First, an increase in management's exposure to market risk will make the compensation scheme less attractive, all other things equal; and in return for bearing additional risk, executives collectively will require an increase in the general level of their compensation.[9] Second, increasing an executive's exposure to risk may cause him to become more conservative in his investment strategy. He may turn down risky projects that promise high expected returns to shareholders and accept only "safe" projects offering stable, but substandard returns.

---

[9] A recent study by Rick Antle and Abbie Smith has, in fact, shown that the average level of total compensation (salary plus bonus plus change in the value of stock holdings) is positively related to the riskiness of total compensation. See R. Antle and A. Smith, "Measuring Executive Compensation: Methods and an Application," working paper, University of Chicago (1984).

How can the compensation package be designed to give executives the incentive to increase profits and control expenditures, or "perks," while at the same time encouraging them to pursue risky, though profitable investment strategies? One possibility is to supplement stock price movements with other measures of firm performance, thereby providing compensation committees (and shareholders generally) with additional information that makes it easier to separate the effect of executives' actions from other factors that influence the firm's profits. In this way, an executive can be shielded from the "exogenous" or uncontrollable variables that affect the firm's profits, and his or her individual contribution can be more easily identified and evaluated.

To be effective, however, such measures must reflect the performance of management more clearly than do stock prices, or, at a minimum, they must provide information about managerial performance that stock prices do not. For example, if stock prices were always a fixed multiple of accounting earnings, there would be no benefit to basing executive compensation on both earnings and share price—because both measures would be providing the same information about management's performance. But because stock prices are not fixed multiples of EPS, this means that stock prices and accounting earnings provide somewhat different (although certainly not unrelated) indications of management's effectiveness. By combining several different measures of performance, some of the "noise" contained in each individual measure can be removed, offering a better assessment of managerial performance.[10]

An alternative is to weigh corporate performance against the performance of other comparable companies. In such *relative* performance schemes, executive compensation is set according to how well the company performs relative to a comparison or peer group.[11] The implicit assumption underlying this approach is that the construction of a peer group allows general market or macro-economic influences and industry-specific influences to be removed from the performance measure, thereby providing a better measure of an executive's distinctive contribution to the firm's profitability. The biggest difficulty in implementing such an approach is finding an appropriate peer group, especially for companies that have many different products. But for many firms operating in well-defined industries, such as banking, paper, and oil, relative performance measures are becoming commonplace features of the compensation plan.

Another way to encourage managers to take risks, while still controlling "perks," is to structure their compensation in such a manner as to offset their risk aversion. Consider a project that shareholders perceive to be a worthwhile risk (that is, the investment has a positive net present value after discounting at the required rate of return). As suggested, when a manager is more risk averse than shareholders, he may turn down a positive net-present-value project because he perceives the adverse consequences to *him* if the project performs poorly to dominate the favorable personal consequences if the project succeeds. The manager's risk aversion can be partially offset if his compensation contract is designed to make the adverse consequences associated with the "down-

---

[10] It is, of course, common to observe companies using multiple performance criteria in their compensation contracts. For example, Libbey-Owens-Ford Co. has a performance plan tied to increases in return on net assets and increases in sales. In a similar manner, Sears, Roebuck, and Co. bases its annual bonus payments on a combination of return on equity, growth in total revenues, net sales, gross profit, and growth in net premiums earned. The subset of performance criteria used by Sears for specific executives varies depending upon the business unit and executive level.

[11] For additional discussion of relative performance contracts, see Mark Ubelhart, "A New Look at Executive Compensation Plan," *Cash Flow* (1981); and R. Antle and A. Smith, "An Empirical Investigation into the Relative Performance Evaluation of Corporate Executives," working paper, University of Chicago (1984).

side" less severe, or to make the favorable consequences of the "upside" more attractive. Properly designed stock options, or accounting-based option contracts, may be the answer to neutralizing a manager's risk aversion. Options may be effective in encouraging management to invest in riskier projects because, while they carry no additional downside risk, their value generally increases as the volatility of the company's stock price rises, and they allow managers to share in the upside potential of the firm.

In general, then, agency theory implies that it is desirable to compensate executives on the basis of share price in order to give them incentives to control their expenditures and develop strategies that increase shareholder wealth. But the choice of how closely to tie management's compensation to share price must also consider the effect of exposing executives to greater market risk. The degree to which the executive's compensation should be tied to share price will therefore depend on the relative importance of these two incentive problems in the particular firm.

Decision-Making Horizon

The agency problem that results from differences in the decision-making time horizon of shareholders and executives can be partially resolved by changing either the "scorecard" or the payoff structure of compensation. The compensation "scorecard" can be changed from a measure with a "short-term" focus (such as yearly accounting earnings) to a measure that has an inherently "long-term" focus (for example, the market price of the common stock).[12]

Consider, for example, the situation where a manager is contemplating a capital investment with a positive expected net present value but an adverse impact on accounting earnings in the early years of the project. An executive compensated primarily on the basis of yearly accounting earnings may reject this project because of its effect on his "short-term" compensation. If the executive is instead compensated on the basis of share price (through, say, stock or stock options), he will be more likely to accept the project because he expects it to have a favorable impact on his compensation. The implicit assumption of this approach, of course, is that the executive believes that the "long-term" performance measure (that is, the stock price) will eventually, if not immediately, reward him by reflecting the "long-term" consequences of his investment decisions.[13]

An alternative, or perhaps complementary, way to lengthen the executive's decision-making horizon is to defer the payoff earned by the executive to some future point in time. Some corporations defer part of an executive's yearly bonus and require that the deferred compensation be paid in common stock. Since the executive's compensation is explicitly tied to the performance of the corporation in subsequent years, this type of bonus deferral will tend to lengthen his decision-making horizon.

In a similar manner, many corporations have also adopted compensation contracts known as "performance plans."[14] These contracts provide payoffs to executives if the growth in specified

---

[12] Throughout the analysis, we assume that the share price is the present value of the expected future cash flows that accrue to equity holders discounted at the appropriate risk-adjusted rate of return. Therefore, share price has an inherently "long-term" focus.

[13] For some evidence that the stock price impounds the consequences of unexpected changes in "long-term" investments, see J. McConnell and C. Muscarella, "Capitalized Value, Growth Opportunities, and Corporate Expenditure Announcements," working paper, Purdue University (1983).

[14] For example, 54 of the *Fortune* 100 have performance plans as of 1983. See Towers, Perrin, Forester, and Crosby, *1983 Executive Total Compensation Study,* New York: Towers, Perrin, Forester, and Crosby (1983).

accounting numbers (generally earnings per share or return on equity) over a three to five-year performance period exceeds some target. One important feature of performance plans is that the compensation earned from this contract is deferred until the end of this period. Nothing is earned if the executive leaves or is terminated during the term of the performance plan. And this stipulation, of course, could extend a manager's time horizon through at least the duration of the performance period.

Do Compensation Contracts Really Matter?

The next question we want to examine concerns whether executives really respond to the incentives provided by their compensation contracts. If the agency framework is useful in analyzing compensation questions, we should observe that executives compensated with different contracts will exhibit differences in their decision making. We now turn to a review of the empirical evidence on this question.

Academic research has recently begun to examine the incentive effects of compensation contracts. This research is typically conducted in one of two ways. First, researchers look for changes in executive decision making after a *new* compensation contract is adopted. For example, do managers compensated by a new "long-term" contract undertake more "long-term" investments? Second, studies attempt to ascertain whether the variation in existing compensation contracts across firms is associated with differences in executive decision making. For example, do managers receiving a substantial portion of their compensation from a bonus contract make different decisions than managers receiving only a modest bonus? The results of this set of studies provide some insights into agency problems related to executive expenditure decisions, risk aversion, and decision-making horizon.

Executive Expenditure Decisions

A typical funding formula for establishing the yearly bonus pool for executives is diagrammed in Figure 1. There is generally a threshold level of net income that must be surpassed before any bonus is paid (for example, net income must exceed five percent of total capital employed). Most proxy statement disclosures indicate that when net income exceeds this minimum standard, the bonus pool is computed as some percentage of net income above the threshold. The bonus pool also often has an explicit ceiling. For example, in some compensation plans, the bonus may not exceed total cash dividends paid or, perhaps, some target percentage of the total salaries of the executives participating in the bonus plan.

A recent study by Paul Healy has attempted to determine how executives actually respond to the incentives inherent in these kinds of net-income-based contracts.[15] Specifically, the question posed by Healy's study is this: Do executives adjust their expenditure decisions in order to increase the payoff from their yearly bonus contract?

The hypotheses of Healy's study can be illustrated by using Figure 1. Consider the case where an executive expects net income to be on the "flat" portion of the contract (denoted as *A* in -

---

[15] P. Healy, "Evidence on the Effect of Bonus Schemes on Accounting Procedure and Accrual Decisions," *Journal of Accounting and Economics* 7 (1985).

Figure 1   Typical Short-Term Bonus Contract

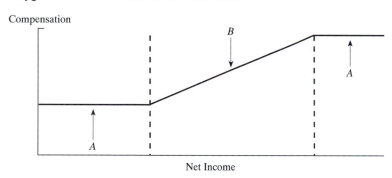

Figure 1). In this case, a manager would have an incentive to accelerate accounting recognition of expenses (say, maintenance) and defer recognition of revenues (for example, by delaying sale of goods until after the fiscal year is closed). Such accrual or deferral decisions would have no effect on the executive's bonus in the present year but would increase the probability of obtaining a bonus in subsequent periods. By contrast, an executive who expects net income to fall in the "sloped" portion of the contract (denoted as *B* in Figure 1) faces the opposite set of incentives. His or her bonus for the current period can be increased by accelerating the recognition of revenues and deferring the recognition of expenses.[16]

The results of Healy's study confirm our expectations. As predicted, managers who expect reported net income to fall below the bonus threshold appear to decrease revenues and increase expenses. The opposite pattern of behavior is observed when executives expect net income to fall between the bonus threshold and the ceiling.

A study conducted by Mark Wolfson examines the effects of bonus contracts on the behavior of executives in oil and gas partnerships.[17] Many of these partnerships are organized such that limited partners contribute capital to the enterprise and a drilling agent performs the exploration and development activity. The contracts specifying how the costs and revenues are shared are often designed to take advantage of tax code regulations. In one common sharing arrangement, the limited partners bear all of the drilling costs. After discovery of oil or gas, the drilling agent bears all of the costs necessary to complete the well. The limited partners and the drilling agent then share the revenues earned from the sale of oil or gas.

The arrangement ideally should be structured such that the drilling agent has an incentive to complete every well where the total revenues accruing to *both* parties are expected to exceed his costs to complete the well. An "agency" problem arises, however, because the drilling agent receives only part of the revenues associated with completion while bearing all of the costs. The

---

[16] The hypotheses of Healy's study are similar to those developed and empirically examined in D. Larcker and L. Revsine, "The Oil and Gas Accounting Controversy: An Analysis of Economic Consequences," *The Accounting Review* (1983).

[17] M. Wolfson, "Empirical Evidence of Incentive Problems and Their Mitigation in Oil and Gas Tax Shelter Programs," in J. Pratt and R. Zeckhauser, *Asymmetric Information, the Agency Problem, and Modern Business,* Harvard University Press.

drilling agent thus has an incentive to complete only those wells for which his share of the revenues exceeds the cost of completion. Thus, he is not likely to complete all of the wells that would benefit the limited partners.

If the limited partners view this agency problem to be serious, they will be less willing to invest funds in such partnerships. The drilling agent therefore has an incentive to devise a means of reducing this conflict of interest. One way to counteract this "noncompletion" incentive is to select only highly risky drilling programs, those whose expected outcome is highly variable. In this way, the wells are likely to be "so good" or "so bad" that the interests and objectives of the limited partners and the drilling agent are brought together. In such extreme cases, the fortunes of the drilling agent and limited partners are virtually identical: Either they both "win big," or they lose the initial investment by the limited partner.

Wolfson tested this hypothesis, and his results suggest that partnerships with contracts like those described engage in significantly more risky (exploratory) drilling than do partnerships that operate under different sharing arrangements.

A study by one of the present authors examines changes in the level of "perks" associated with the adoption of bonus contracts by major commercial banks.[18] In this study, "perks" are defined as occupancy, furniture, and salary expenditures, as well as the number of bank employees. (It is assumed that bank managers prefer to have more expensive working conditions and larger staffs than the level of expenditures desired by shareholders.)

This study determines specifically whether the ratio of management's expenditures on "perks" to operating revenue decreases following the adoption of an annual bonus contract. (This hypothesis follows, of course, from our earlier discussion: A manager compensated with a bonus contract bears part of the cost of expenditures on "perks," whereas a manager with only a fixed salary does not.) The results indicate that banks without bonus contracts had a significantly higher ratio of "perks" to operating revenue than did similar banks with bonus contracts. Moreover, there is some evidence that the ratio of nonpecuniary expenditures to revenue decreases following the adoption of the bonus plan. Thus, it appears that bonus contracts influence the expenditure decisions of bank managers.

Risk Aversion

Some evidence on the issue of whether executives behave as though they are more risk averse than shareholders has been provided by Yakov Amihud and Baruch Lev.[19] Their study examines executive motives in conglomerate mergers.

Finance theory maintains that mergers undertaken *solely* for corporate diversification do not benefit stockholders because they can costlessly duplicate such diversification by holding different securities. Executives, however, benefit from corporate diversification because they hold partially "undiversifiable" portfolios consisting of their compensation claims on the firm and their human capital. The authors hypothesize that because executives are more risk averse than shareholders,

[18] D. Larcker, "Short-Term Compensation Contracts, Executive Expenditure Decisions, and Corporate Performance: The Case of Commercial Banks," working paper, Northwestern University (1984).

[19] Y. Amihud and B. Lev, "Risk Reduction as a Managerial Motive for Conglomerate Mergers," *Bell Journal of Economics* 12 (1981).

executives undertake conglomerate mergers to decrease the variability of the value of the firm. By decreasing firm variability through conglomerate-type acquisitions, managers can effectively diversify—and thus increase the value of—their own "undiversifiable portfolios."

Amihud and Lev find, in fact, that companies with broadly diversified stock ownership—those in which there is no dominant shareholder to monitor corporate decisions—are more likely to engage in conglomerate or diversifying mergers than are firms with concentrated ownership interests.[20]

In a somewhat more direct analysis of the ability of compensation contracts to affect executive risk aversion, we examined changes in firm variability associated with the *initial* adoption of stock option plans.[21] We attempted to determine whether the adoption of a stock option contract motivates managers to increase the variability of equity returns.

Two possibilities are considered in this study. First, standard option pricing models suggest that the value of an option increases as the variability of stock prices increases. This suggests that the adoption of stock options will counteract executives' risk aversion and motivate them to increase firm variability. A second possibility is that standard option pricing models are not applicable to *executive* stock options. Executives cannot sell their options to other investors. Nor can they short their own stock, making it difficult to construct the riskless hedge required for option pricing models to work. In fact, under certain circumstances, stock options may actually *increase* the risk aversion of a manager, thereby motivating him to decrease firm variability.

An explanation of why the standard option pricing formulas may not be appropriate in valuing executive stock options is as follows: Consider the behavior of a risk-averse manager who cannot diversify or hedge the risk associated with the option's payoff. If he expects the options to finish far "in the money" (which is likely because options are usually granted with an exercise price equal to or below the stock price at the date of the grant), he may want to "bank" the value of that option by *decreasing* the variability of the firm's stock price, thus increasing the odds that the options will finish "in the money."

If, however, an executive's options are expected to finish "out of the money," then a manager may have an incentive to increase the variance of the firm's stock price in order to increase the probability that they will become valuable. This suggests that granting options that are initially "out of the money" may be the solution to overcoming managers' risk aversion.

The results of our study indicate that firms whose options are expected to finish "out of the money" tend to exhibit increasing stock price variability following the adoption of stock option plans. In contrast, companies whose options are expected to finish "in the money" tend to exhibit decreases in stock price variability.

Decision-Making Horizon

As discussed earlier, if the decision-making horizon of management is significantly shorter than that of shareholders, this can lead to "underinvestment" by the corporation. For example, if an executive

---

[20] For additional discussion of managerial incentives in acquisitions, see B. Lev, "Observations on the Merger Phenomenon and a Review of the Evidence," *Midland Corporate Finance Journal* 1 (1983); D. Larcker, "Managerial Incentives in Mergers and Their Impact on Shareholder Wealth," *Midland Corporate Finance Journal* 1 (1983); and R. Lambert and D. Larcker, "Golden Parachutes, Executive Decision-Making, and Shareholder Wealth," *Journal of Accounting and Economics* (forthcoming).

[21] R. Lambert and D. Larcker, "Stock Options and Managerial Incentives," working paper, Northwestern University (1984).

is being evaluated solely according to near-term accounting performance and a profitable investment project under consideration is expected to have an adverse impact in earnings in early years, he will have an incentive to reject that investment.

One possible way to mitigate this problem is to adopt a compensation contract designed to lengthen an executive's decision-making horizon. This presumes, of course, that compensation contracts can actually motivate a manager to lengthen his decision-making horizon. Although this issue cannot be examined directly, it is possible to determine whether the investment behavior of executives changes after a contractual change.

In a study published in 1983, one of the present authors examined whether the adoption of "long-term" compensation contracts was associated with increases in "long-term" investment.[22] The specific focus of this study was the adoption of "performance plans," those contracts that provide deferred compensation when certain "long-term" (generally ranging over a three- to six-year period) goals are met. The relative amount of capital investment of companies adopting performance plans was compared to the investment of similar firms without performance plans. The results of the study indicated that firms adopting performance plans had substantial increases in capital investment after the contractual change relative to similar firms without performance plans.

Stockholder Response to New Compensation Plans

The research on whether compensation contracts "really matter" suggests that the design of such contracts influences executive decision making. But how does this influence translate into shareholder wealth? Furthermore, how do investors respond to the adoption of new compensation plans?

Several studies have, in fact, documented that stock prices rise when companies announce the adoption of "long-term" compensation contracts.[23] These studies find that "long-term" contracts are associated with an approximately one to two percent increase in shareholder wealth. (Although these percentages might seem small in absolute terms, it is important to remember that the firms making these contractual changes are extremely large, and these percentages translate into millions of dollars of increases in shareholder value.) In short, compensation contracts do "appear to matter"—to investors as well as management.

The Relationship Between Pay and Performance

To this point, we have suggested that agency theory provides a framework for analyzing issues in executive compensation. We have also presented evidence that the theory is useful in predicting the "incentive effects" of different compensation contracts. In this section, we bring the theory to bear on the available evidence regarding the relationship between executive compensation and corporate performance.

---

[22] D. Larcker, "The Association Between Performance Plan Adoption and Corporate Capital Investment," *Journal of Accounting and Economics* 5 (1983).

[23] For an analysis of the security market response to the adoption of "long-term" compensation contracts, see D. Larcker, "The Association Between Performance Plan Adoption and Corporate Capital Investment," *Journal of Accounting and Economics* 5 (1983); and J. Brickley, S. Bhagat, and R. Lease, "The Impact of Long-Range Managerial Compensation Plans on Shareholder Wealth," *Journal of Accounting and Economics* 7 (1985). It is important to note that the market reaction to the disclosure of a new compensation plan will reflect not only the market's assessment of the desirability of the compensation scheme but also the market's assessment of any new strategy changes that are being introduced at the same time.

Much of the controversy surrounding executive compensation tends to focus on whether executive compensation is related to corporate performance. That is, are current compensation contracts really designed to "pay for performance"? Criticism of executive compensation in the financial press is based almost entirely upon intuition and personal observation—what financial economists call "anecdotal" evidence.[24] Although no formal statistical analysis is done, these articles generally conclude that there is little or no relationship between executive compensation and corporate performance or shareholder wealth. Corporate compensation practices are then pronounced "irrational," failing to distinguish between good and bad performance.

Two academic studies presented at the University of Rochester's recent Conference on Managerial Compensation and the Managerial Labor Market address this issue more systematically.[25] Both of these studies examine the correlation between changes in compensation and changes in *shareholder wealth* for large samples of major U.S. corporations, and both show a positive, statistically significant correlation between executive compensation and shareholder wealth. This empirical evidence is, of course, inconsistent with the charges often made in the financial press.

Such findings, however, should not be taken to imply that American corporations have attained the optimum in incentive compensation. In fact, the coefficients measuring the correlation between compensation and shareholder returns, although statistically significant, are rather small. Also, rather modest changes in compensation occur for large changes in shareholder wealth. For example, Kevin Murphy reports that a ten-percent change in the equity value of the firm is associated with only about a two-percent increase in total executive compensation. Therefore, although there is a statistical association between executive compensation and shareholder wealth, it is difficult to predict changes in executive compensation from changes in shareholder wealth. The correlation results, nevertheless, do suggest that executive compensation in American corporations is not total "madness."

One problem in interpreting these studies is that they typically exclude changes in the value of the executives' stock holdings and stock options from their measurement of compensation. Obviously, these components of executive wealth are tied *directly* to changes in shareholder wealth; executives with large holdings in their company's stock are clearly rewarded for good performance and penalized for bad performance through the change in value of their personal stock holdings. And, as other studies show, the stock holdings of top executives in their own companies often constitute a significant portion of their wealth. This suggests that financial press "studies" correlating only annual salary and bonus with accounting profitability measures may seriously understate the real relationship between corporate performance and total compensation.[26]

---

[24] One of the few attempts in the financial press to document its case more carefully is the *Fortune* article by Carol Loomis, which graphed executive compensation (defined as salary plus bonus) versus a single accounting measure of corporate performance. As discussed in more detail shortly, there are two problems with this study. First, instead of the change in shareholder wealth, return on equity is used as the measure of firm performance. Second, the analysis ignores the stock options and shares owned by the executive, the value of which are directly related to shareholder wealth.

[25] K. Murphy, "Corporate Performance and Managerial Remuneration," *Journal of Accounting and Economics* 7 (1985); and A. Coughlan and R. Schmidt, "Executive Compensation, Management Turnover, and Firm Performance: An Empirical Investigation," *Journal of Accounting and Economics* 7 (1985).

[26] For some additional evidence on the importance of equity holdings to managerial decision making, see G. Benston, "The Self-Serving Management Hypothesis: Some Evidence," *Journal of Accounting and Economics* 7 (1985); R. Walkling and M. Long, "Agency Theory, Managerial Welfare, and Takeover Bid Resistance," *Rand Journal of Economics* 15 (1984); and W. Lewellen, C. Loderer, and A. Rosenfeld, "Merger Decisions and Executive Stock Ownership," *Journal of Accounting and Economics* 7 (1985).

How Should Compensation Correlate with Shareholder Returns?

Given that a significant portion of the wealth of top executives is already directly tied to stock price performance, we are led to ask: In the best of all possible compensation plans, how *should* the non-stock components of compensation like salary, yearly bonus, and performance plans be related to annual stock price changes?

As suggested earlier, one implication of agency theory is that it may be desirable to base compensation on other measures of the firm's performance in order to "filter out" the effects of random events on stock prices. The "noise" in stock prices may impose too much risk on executives, exposing too much of their compensation to factors beyond their control. Such risks may in turn cause them to become excessively conservative in their investment policy. Therefore, in designing compensation plans, companies can find it necessary to use criteria other than stock price—accounting earnings, return on equity, cash flow, sales, comparisons with industry-average rates of return—to supplement the direct dependence of an executive's stock-related compensation on stock prices. In this sense, the absence of a strong relationship between firm performance and contemporaneous salary and bonus need not be an indication of the irrationality of corporate compensation practices.

To summarize, then, the positive statistical correlations detected in these studies suggest that executive compensation is not total "madness." However, without additional information about the seriousness of "agency" problems resulting from managerial risk aversion in specific firms, it is difficult to determine what the correlation would be between the "optional" compensation package and shareholder returns. Small positive correlations may represent an "optimal" contract for managers in highly cyclical industries, and thus expose them to some large risks they cannot control. Alternatively, in cases where risk aversion is not a serious concern, the same small positive correlations may imply that current compensation plans fail seriously in motivating management to act in the interest of its shareholders.

The Labor Market for Executives

The fact that changes in compensation are correlated with changes in shareholder wealth also tells us little about whether the *level* of executive compensation is correct. Large positive correlations between changes in compensation and shareholder wealth can exist at the same time that executives are being "overpaid" or, for that matter, seriously "underpaid." The level of executive compensation is determined, in theory at least, by the operation of a labor market for executive services. Moreover, to the extent that it effectively determines the relationship between executive performance and *future* levels of executive compensation, this labor market can provide an important means of motivating executives to serve their shareholders.

There are two important aspects of the labor market. First, the labor market sets the executive's opportunity wage, and this provides a lower bound on the amount of total compensation that must be paid to retain him. At the same time, the availability of other executives of comparable experience and ability at this opportunity wage provides some constraint on the level of compensation demanded by executives in their current jobs. This tells us, for example, that executives cannot simply pay themselves any compensation level they desire.

Second, the labor market has the potential to control agency problems.[27] When an executive makes decisions that harm stockholders, the labor market should lower the executive's current opportunity wage (as well as all future period levels of compensation). To the extent executives are penalized in this way for poor decisions, they have less incentive to behave in a manner that benefits themselves at the expense of their shareholders. (This disciplining effect of the labor market assumes, of course, that the labor market has good information about the shareholder consequences of an executive's decisions.)

There have been several empirical studies that have examined aspects of the labor market for corporate executives.

We recently completed a study examining the effects of large corporate acquisitions on subsequent executive pay in an attempt to determine whether the labor market seems to reflect the consequences of executive decisions on shareholder wealth.[28] Specifically, we analyzed the change in real executive compensation (relative to industry standards for firms of a similar size and industry) in the period surrounding the completion of a large acquisition.

Two possibilities were considered. First, there is a strong positive relationship between the level of executive compensation and firm size. This suggests that an executive can increase his compensation simply by increasing firm size, regardless of the impact of this size increase on shareholder wealth. Second, the labor market value of executives should reflect *both* the change in firm size and the effect on profitability caused by an acquisition. If the labor market takes into account changes in shareholder wealth in setting the executive's opportunity wage, we should observe increases in executive compensation only for those acquisitions producing increases in shareholder wealth.

The preliminary results of our study suggest that *real* (inflation-adjusted) executive compensation (relative to industry and size standards) increased following a substantial increase in firm size via acquisition. As predicted, however, virtually all of this increase went to executives making acquisitions that increased shareholder wealth. The managements of companies making acquisitions that reduced their share prices saw no increase in the relative level of their real compensation.

Another study presenting evidence of a rational labor market was performed by Anne Coughlan and Ron Schmidt. They attempted to determine whether changes in shareholder wealth are a good predictor of executive terminations.[29] (To be fired is, of course, to face the most extreme form of labor market discipline, especially when it makes it difficult to obtain another comparable job.) The study finds that terminations are more likely to occur after decreases in shareholder wealth.

A third study of the executive labor market focuses on changes in shareholder wealth at the time of an "unexpected" death of a chief executive officer (CEO).[30] The market's response to the announcement of the "unexpected" death of a CEO offers an ideal test of the value of a top executive to a firm. Assuming the search costs of obtaining a new CEO are small relative to the market value

---

[27] For additional discussion of this point, see Eugene Fama, "Agency Problems and the Theory of the Firm," *Journal of Political Economy* 88 (1980).

[28] R. Lambert and D. Larcker, "Executive Compensation Effects of Large Corporate Acquisitions," working paper, Northwestern University (1984).

[29] A. Coughlan and R. Schmidt, "Executive Compensation, Management Turnover, and Firm Performance: An Empirical Investigation," *Journal of Accounting and Economics* 7 (1985).

[30] W. Johnson, R. Magee, N. Nagarajan, and H. Newman, "An Analysis of the Stock Price Reaction to Sudden Executive Deaths: Implications for the Managerial Labor Market," *Journal of Accounting and Economics* (forthcoming).

of the firm, the effect of an "unexpected" CEO death on shareholder wealth will depend on the stock market's assessment of the value of the former CEO relative to the expected value of the new CEO. From the shareholder's perspective, the value of a CEO is the capitalized value of the CEO's expected future contributions to the value of the firm minus the capitalized value of the CEO's expected future compensation.

If CEOs, as is often alleged by the financial press, have the power to control boards of directors, one would expect the strength of a CEO's control to increase with his seniority. This implies, of course, that the former CEO would have more control over the board than the CEO expected to succeed him. And if such is the case, the former CEO should be paid more (relative to his contribution to the firm's value) than the expected payments to the new CEO. If the relatively "overpaid" CEO dies unexpectedly, the announcement of the death should be accompanied by a positive security market reaction.

The results of the study, however, show a pronounced *negative* security market reaction—at least to the deaths of those CEOs who were not the founders of their companies.[31] This result suggests that CEOs are not overpaid relative to their contribution to shareholder wealth (at least not when compared to alternative managers available in the labor market).[32]

Innovations in Compensation Design

The evidence on executive compensation and the market for managerial labor suggests that current executive compensation practices are not total "madness." This discussion should not be construed, however, to imply that there is no room for improvement in the design of compensation contracts. In fact, it is interesting to examine some of the recent innovations in compensation contract designs proposed (generally) by compensation consultants and, in some cases, adopted by corporations. Most of these innovative contracts seem designed primarily to deal with the kinds of "agency" problems we have been discussing throughout.

In 1983, for example, Johnson Controls, Inc. developed a unique seven-year performance plan for two of its most senior-level executives (both of whom were then about 60 years of age). In each of the seven years, the base amount of the plan (consisting of $300,000 and $100,000 for the two executives, respectively) was multiplied by a percentage that varied between 0 and 150 percent. The determination of each percentage was based upon the *ratio* of the average annual total shareholder return for Johnson Controls (over the ten-year period ending with the current year) to the average total shareholder return for a peer group of Fortune 500 companies over the same period.[33] Each of

---

[31] However, the study does find a significant positive reaction to the announcement of the unexpected death of an executive who was the corporate founder. This is consistent with the hypothesis that corporate founders, who often own a substantial portion of the firm's stock, are able to exercise control over the board of directors that enables them to be paid more relative to their contribution to firm value than their successors.

[32] It is important to realize that the security market reaction to a CEO death is more complex than simply the difference in capitalized value of the compensation paid to the new CEO relative to the old CEO. The magnitude of the change in shareholder wealth depends upon the new CEO's contribution to firm value minus compensation paid (in technical terms, the CEO's marginal product) relative to the old CEO's contribution to the firm value minus compensation.

[33] Notice that this contract is similar to the market-indexed option suggested by Mark Ubelhart in *Midland Corporate Finance Journal* (Winter 1985). See "Business Strategy, Performance Measurement, and Compensation" and also an earlier article, "A New Look at Executive Compensation Plans," *Cash Flow* (1981). Relative shareholder value compensation contracts have also been adopted by Clevepak Corp. and U.S. West.

the yearly awards was then invested in a hypothetical portfolio consisting of the stock of Johnson Controls. The payment of the total value of this hypothetical portfolio was deferred until the end of the seven-year performance period.

There are several interesting aspects of this performance plan. First, the term of the contract extends approximately three years *beyond* the retirement of the two executives. This feature appears to be an attempt to lengthen the decision-making horizon of executives—especially in the case of those near retirement age. This contract explicitly motivates the executives to consider the impact of their decisions on the company after they leave the corporation.

Second, the "scorecard" for the annual changes in the value of the performance plan is formally tied to changes in shareholder wealth over the prior ten years. This is unusual because performance plans are typically based upon earnings per share or return on equity growth rates. One explanation for the choice of changes in shareholder wealth is that the board of directors was attempting to lengthen the executives' decision-making horizon by selecting a scorecard that has a longer performance evaluation horizon than yearly accounting numbers.

Finally, the performance plan is based on *relative* changes in shareholder wealth. This appears to be an attempt to isolate that portion of changes in shareholder wealth that is under management's control from economy- and industry-wide effects. The choice of a ten-year period for assessing the performance of the company may be an attempt to "wash out" other random elements that affect performance in a single year.

Another example of an innovative compensation scheme is the performance unit plan adopted by TRW in 1983 for 28 of its key executives. Under this plan, the value of each performance unit varies according to how TRW ranks relative to 98 peer companies. More interesting, performance is measured using the ratio of the market value of the firm (equity plus debt) to the *inflation-adjusted* value of net assets (typically referred to as the "q ratio"). The key feature of the TRW contract is that the impact of inflation on accounting measures is explicitly considered. This is important because inflation can severely distort historical accounting measures of corporate performance. For example, corporations (or divisions within corporations) with "old" assets will produce a higher return on assets than otherwise similar corporations (or divisions) with "newer" assets. Since asset age and changes in price level are explicitly considered in the TRW approach, this should produce a more reasonable accounting-based comparison between TRW and peer companies and among the divisions of TRW as well.

A more general, conceptual innovation in compensation design has been proposed by Booz, Allen, and Hamilton, Inc. The consulting firm's compensation specialists have developed what they call a "Strategic Reward Map" (see Figure 2). The Strategic Reward Map has two dimensions. The first is called "risk posture." It is measured by the ratio of contingent compensation (i.e., the sum of yearly bonus, stock options, SARs, performance plans, restricted stock, and phantom stock) to yearly salary. This dimension attempts to capture the degree to which an executive's compensation is "at risk." The second dimension is called "time focus." It is measured by the ratio of long-term compensation (i.e., the sum of stock options, SARs, performance plans, restricted stock, and phantom stock) to the annual bonus. This dimension attempts to capture the degree to which an executive's compensation is obtained from long-term (multiyear) performance measures versus short-term (single-year) performance measures. In terms of the agency theory framework, the risk posture and time focus variables are measures of the (1) potentially non-diversifiable risk imposed upon the executive and (2) the executive's decision-making horizon.

Figure 2   Strategic Reward Map (Booz, Allen, and Hamilton)

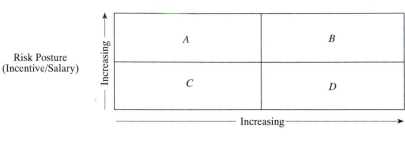

Time Focus
(Long-Term Incentives/Short-Term Incentives)

The Strategic Reward Map has several potential applications. First, it provides a simple way to synthesize the critical elements and compare compensation practices within a sample of firms. Second, it provides a convenient way to track changes in the "mix" of compensation components over time. Also, it may be possible to develop recommendations regarding contractual design in various portions of the map. For example, consider a firm that has a large market share in a profitable industry with substantial barriers to entry, but where product or service innovation is unlikely to be profitable. For this type of company, it may be desirable to motivate managers to be conservative in their decision making and to be most concerned with the short-term impact of their actions (that is, make few changes and simply manage the existing customer relationships). The executive compensation contracts would accordingly produce a risk posture and time focus in the quadrant labeled *C* in Figure 2. By contrast, if the profitability of the firm depends upon executives undertaking risky investments with long-term payoffs, then the compensation plan should be structured so that it falls in quadrant *B*.[34]

Another approach deserving mention—one that has been widely popularized by executive compensation and management consulting firms—is to measure corporate performance by the "spread" between return on equity (ROE) and the equity cost of capital.[35] One can justify the use of ROE "spread," just as one can justify the use of many financial surrogates, by arguing that this measure provides additional information about managerial actions not contained in stock price changes. But this measure is typically cited as the appropriate scorecard for compensation purposes because of its strong positive correlation with the ratio of the market value of equity to historical book value. This empirical correlation is then used to justify the statement that the most direct way to create shareholder value is to increase the spread between ROE and the equity cost of capital.

There are a number of serious flaws with this argument for using ROE "spread," at least as the sole basis for evaluating managerial performance. For one thing, ROE is an *accounting* measure,

[34] One must be careful, however, not to impose so much risk on the manager that he becomes too conservative in his decision-making.

[35] See Louis Brindisi. "Creating Shareholder Value: A New Mission for Executive Compensation" (New York: Booz, Allen, and Hamilton, Inc.) (1984); and J. Rich and J. Larson, "Why Some Long-Term Incentives Fail," *Compensation Review* (1984) for a discussion of "spread" in a compensation context. One case of adoption of this approach is First Tennessee Corp.'s executive compensation plan.

one that has all of the inherent problems associated with the historical cost accounting system (for example, inflation distortions and arbitrary cost allocations). The equity cost of capital, however, is a *market-determined* required rate of return for investing capital in risky projects, and it is at best unclear how the cost of capital relates to the ROE. Moreover, all of the empirical analysis supporting "spread" uses the ratio of market to book as the primary measure of management's success in creating shareholder value. But it is not obvious that shareholders' primary interest is served by managements intent on maximizing their company's price-to-book ratio. The most direct measure of interest to shareholders is the rate of return on their shares. And we are aware of no evidence that indicates that "spread" is directly associated with total shareholder return (or, better yet, with the rate of shareholder return in excess of the normal rate of return given the company's risk).

In fact, it is easy to illustrate that managers compensated on the basis of ROE "spread" may be motivated to decrease shareholder wealth. For example, assume that a manager is considering the adoption of two investment projects, both of which are expected to have a return that exceeds the firm's cost of capital. Assume the ROE "spread" for project A exceeds the "spread" for project B. If the manager is compensated on the basis of ROE "spread" *alone,* he can maximize the "spread" and his compensation by selecting only project A. In this example, the use of "spread" (or any rate of return measure) can have the unfortunate effect of motivating the manager to reject projects that would increase shareholder wealth.[36]

Given this potential problem of "underinvestment" (as well as the potential for manipulating accounting-based measures in general), we recommend caution in using the ROE "spread" as the principal measure of corporate success and as the "scorecard" for computing management incentive awards.

Summary

Our review of the academic research has provided an analysis of a variety of issues concerning executive compensation. We began by using agency theory as an economic framework to identify potential conflicts of interest between management and shareholders. Viewed in this context, the primary function of a corporate compensation plan is to reduce such conflicts by providing management with the strongest possible incentives to maximize shareholder value.

The framework enables us to offer some specific suggestions for reducing management-stockholder conflicts through the design of compensation contracts. Empirical tests in the agency literature show that executives respond predictably to the incentives built into compensation contracts. Furthermore, *changes* in compensation plans affect executive decision making in ways consistent with our theory of corporate managers as self-interested economic agents.

The available evidence on the relationship between executive pay and corporate performance documents a positive relationship between senior executives' annual incomes and annual shareholder returns. This correlation becomes especially clear when changes in the value of executive holdings in their own company's stock and stock options (which are often quite substantial) are included in the calculation of income.

---

[36] One solution to this problem is to change the compensation contract from one based upon rate of return to one based upon residual income. See C. Horngren, *Cost Accounting: A Management Emphasis,* Prentice-Hall (1982), Chapter 20 for some additional discussion of this point.

The labor market for executives also plays a critical role in curbing management's tendency to pursue its self-interest at the expense of its stockholders. Research bearing on the executive labor market suggests that an executive's opportunity wage—and, in fact, the ability to retain his job—is related to the effect of his decisions on his shareholders. Also, research showing negative market responses to unexpected deaths of CEOs suggests that most executives are not able to exercise enough control over boards of directors to pay themselves more (relative to their contribution to the firm's profits) than the compensation required by alternative managers.

In general, the emerging body of research on the economic consequences of executive compensation suggests, contrary to most discussions in the popular press, that executive compensation is not total "madness." This, of course, does not imply that the conflicts are totally resolved or that all companies are equally proficient at controlling these conflicts.[37]

The recent trend of corporate reorganizations (spin-offs, leveraged buyouts, and so forth) may also reflect attempts by executives and shareholders to control management incentive problems.[38] One of the more plausible arguments why management groups and investors are paying substantial premiums over market to take firms private is the radical improvement in management incentives. Taking the firm private greatly reduces and, in some cases, eliminates the separation of ownership and control that characterizes most large public corporations. Corporate spin-offs also promise improvements in management incentives. By separating operating units that were previously combined, spin-offs allow the performance of the individual operating units to be evaluated more accurately, thereby improving the ability of the parent company to reward and thus motivate divisional operating managers.

References

Amihud, Y., and B. Lev. "Risk Reduction as a Managerial Motive for Conglomerate Mergers," *Bell Journal of Economics* 12 (1981).

Antle, R., and A. Smith. "An Empirical Investigation into the Relative Performance Evaluation of Corporate Executives," working paper, University of Chicago (1984).

Antle, R., and A. Smith. "Measuring Executive Compensation: Methods and an Application," working paper, University of Chicago (1984).

Benston, G. "The Self-Serving Management Hypothesis: Some Evidence," *Journal of Accounting and Economics* 7 (1985).

Brickley, J., S. Bhagat, and R. Lease. "The Impact of Long-Range Managerial Compensation Plans on Shareholder Wealth," *Journal of Accounting and Economics* 7 (1985).

Coughlan, A., and R. Schmidt. "Executive Compensation, Management Turnover, and Firm Performance: An Empirical Investigation," *Journal of Accounting and Economics* 7 (1985).

DeAngelo, H., DeAngelo L., and E. Rice. "Going Private: The Effects of a Change in Corporate Ownership Structure," *Midland Corporate Finance Journal* 2 (1984).

---

[37] It is important to note that our focus has been primarily directed to the use of compensation contracts and external labor markets to motivate managers to work in shareholders' interests. We have not discussed the disciplining effects of competition within the internal labor market and the market for corporate control. Obviously, the role that compensation contracts play in motivating managers is influenced by the ability of these other mechanisms to discipline managers into selecting actions that increase shareholder wealth.

[38] For additional discussion of these issues, see G. Hite and J. Owers, "The Restructuring of Corporate America: An Overview," *Midland Corporate Finance Journal* 2 (1984); K. Schipper and A. Smith, "The Corporate Spin-Off Phenomenon," *Midland Corporate Finance Journal* 2 (1984); and H. DeAngelo, L. DeAngelo, and E. Rice, "Going Private: The Effects of Change in Corporate Ownership Structure," *Midland Corporate Finance Journal* 2 (1984).

Fama, E. "Agency Problems and the Theory of the Firm," *Journal of Political Economy* 88 (1980).

Healy, P. "Evidence on the Effect of Bonus Schemes on Accounting Procedure and Accrual Decisions," *Journal of Accounting and Economics* 7 (1985).

Hite, G., and M. Long. "Taxes and Executive Stock Options," *Journal of Accounting and Economics* 4 (1982).

Hite, G., and J. Owers. "The Restructuring of Corporate America: An Overview," *Midland Corporate Finance Journal* 2 (1984).

Horngren, C. *Cost Accounting: A Managerial Emphasis,* Prentice-Hall, (1982).

Johnson, W. B., R. Magee, N. Nagarajan, and H. Newman. "An Analysis of the Stock Price Reaction to Sudden Executive Deaths: Implications for the Managerial Labor Market," *Journal of Accounting and Economics* 7 (1985).

Lambert, R., and D. Larcker. "Golden Parachutes, Executive Decision-Making, and Shareholder Wealth," *Journal of Accounting and Economics* 7 (1985).

Lambert, R., and D. Larcker. "Executive Compensation Effects of Large Corporate Acquisitions," working paper, Northwestern University (1984).

Larcker, D. "Managerial Incentives in Mergers and Their Impact on Shareholder Wealth," *Midland Corporate Finance Journal* 1 (1983).

Larcker, D. "The Association Between Performance Plan Adoption and Corporate Capital Investment," *Journal of Accounting and Economics* 5 (1983).

Larcker, D. "Short-Term Compensation Contracts, Executive Expenditure Decisions, and Corporate Performance: The Case of Commercial Banks," working paper, Northwestern University (1984).

Larcker, D., and L. Revsine. "The Oil and Gas Accounting Controversy: An Analysis of Economic Consequences," *The Accounting Review* (1983).

Lev, B. "Observations on the Merger Phenomenon and a Review of the Evidence," *Midland Corporate Finance Journal* 1 (1983).

Lewellen, W., C. Loderer, and A. Rosenfeld. "Merger Decisions and Executive Stock Ownership," *Journal of Accounting and Economics* 7 (1985).

McConnell, J., and C. Muscarella. "Capitalized Value, Growth Opportunities, and Corporate Expenditure Announcements," working paper, Purdue University (1983).

Miller, M., and M. Scholes. "Executive Compensation, Taxes, and Incentives," in W. Sharpe and C. Cootner (eds.), *Financial Economics: Essays in Honor of Paul Cootner* (1982).

Murphy, K. "Corporate Performance and Managerial Remuneration," *Journal of Accounting and Economics* 7 (1985).

Rappaport, A. "How to Design Value-Contributing Executive Incentives," *Journal of Business Strategy* 4 (1983).

Rich, J., and E. Bergsma. "Pay Executives to Create Wealth," *Chief Executive* (1982).

Rich, J., and J. Larson, "Why Some Long-Term Incentives Fail," *Compensation Review* (1984).

Schipper, K., and A. Smith. "The Corporate Spin-Off Phenomenon," *Midland Corporate Finance Journal* 2 (1984).

Scholes, M., and M. Wolfson. "Employee Compensation and Taxes: Links with Incentives and with Investment and Financing Decisions," working paper, Stanford University (1984).

Smith, C., and R. Watts. "Incentive and Tax Effects of U.S. Executive Compensation Plans," *Australian Management Journal* (1983).

Towers, Perrin, Forester, and Crosby. *1983 Executive Total Compensation Study.* New York: Towers, Perrin, Forester, and Crosby (1983).

Ubelhart, M. "A New Look at Executive Compensation Plans," *Cash Flow* (1981).

Walkling, R., and M. Long. "Agency Theory, Managerial Welfare, and Takeover Did Resistance," *Rand Journal of Economics* 15 (1984).

Wolfson M. "Empirical Evidence of Incentive Problems and Their Mitigation in Oil and Gas Tax Shelter Programs." In J. Pratt and R. Zeckhauser, *Principles and Agents: The Structure of Business,* Harvard Business School Press, 1985.

Discussion Questions

1. Do you think that executive compensation should be related to the performance of the corporation? Explain.

2. If executive compensation is tied to corporate performance, what are some *bad* ways it can be accomplished, and what are some *good* ways? Why?

3. What conflicts tend to exist between the interests of the managers and those of the shareholders of a large, publicly traded firm?

*J. Fred Weston**

A (Relatively) Brief History of Finance Ideas

Professor Weston presents an overview of the central ideas in finance. Instead of presenting these as matters of fact, however, he categorizes the concepts and presents them within a 60-year historical context.

Most curricula in departments of economics include the history of economic thought. The rationale is that we understand current ideas better with perspectives on their evolution. The same benefits are likely to emerge from efforts to trace how the main concepts of financial management and financial economics have evolved. Historical perspectives are particularly useful in comprehending the new concepts and ideas that have emerged in rapid succession in recent years.

Review and analysis of financial history suggest five generalizations. One, the new developments of each historical period and the creators of these developments were responding to the pressing economic, financial, and sociopolitical problems of the period. Two, financial thought has also responded to the maturation of financial markets, internationalization, and increased competition. Three, the development and/or uses of new tools, new mathematical models, and new methodologies have facilitated the creation of theories to explain financial behavior. Four, practice has reflected the new learning with varying time lags but has also stimulated the development of theory to understand, explain, and predict financial behavior. Five, new ideas have built on the ideas provided by previous knowledge.

These propositions will be supported by the materials developed in the following eight sections:

I. An overview of the central ideas of finance

II. Historical review of the impact of economic developments on the content of the finance field

III. The emergence of selected areas of finance

*This effort grew out of an invited presentation to the FMA Senior Statespersons' Breakfast in San Francisco on October 24, 1992. I am grateful to Richard S. Bower for the topic and to Jerry L. Stevens, the Editor, for his counsel. I appreciate the help from Paul Alapat, Yehning Chen, Susan Chiu, David Hirshleifer, Chi-Cheng Hsia, Marilyn McElroy, Eduardo Schwartz, and especially Harry DeAngelo, Jonathan Howe, and Clement Krouse. I also benefited from the comments of two anonymous reviewers and Dorothy Silvers, Line Editor.

Source: Reprinted with permission of *Financial Practice and Education* (Spring/Summer 1994), pp. 7–26. J. Fred Weston is Cordner Professor Emeritus of Managerial Economics and Finance at The Anderson Graduate School of Management at UCLA.

IV. The working capital management area in historical perspective

V. Financial strategy and growth

VI. International finance

VII. The proliferation (explosion) of the literature of finance

VIII. Coping with the knowledge explosion

I. Overview of the Central Ideas of Finance

Finance ideas can be divided into eleven central areas:

1. Investment Decisions (Capital Budgeting)

2. The Efficient Markets Hypothesis (EMH)

3. Portfolio Decisions (Gains to Diversification)

4. Risk and Return (Factor Models)

5. Pricing Derivative Securities (Option Pricing Theory)

6. Capital Structure, Dividend Decisions, Optimal Contractual Choice

7. Valuation and Growth Opportunities

8. International Finance

9. Agency, Auctions, Games, Information, Recontracting

10. Takeovers, Governance, and Control

11. The Timing of Cash Inflows and Outflows (Short-Term Financial Management)

The central propositions related to these areas will be briefly stated as a basis for subsequent discussions.

1. Investment Decisions (Capital Budgeting).   Fisher separation is the idea that investment decisions can be separated from considerations about individual preferences. If capital markets are perfect, managers maximize owners' wealth by investing until the rate of return is equal to the opportunity cost of capital. Individuals can delegate investment decisions to the managers of firms, and the appropriate decision rule is the same, independent of shareholders' time preferences for consumption. The investment rule is to undertake projects until the marginal rate of return equals the market-determined discount rate (the opportunity cost of capital). Given a perfectly competitive capital market, the important Fisher separation concept applies as well to the full set of traditional capital structure and related decisions (DeAngelo [23]).

2. The Efficient Markets Hypothesis (EMH).   EMH holds that current prices reflect all available information. The no-arbitrage profit condition is also implied. Any two securities or portfolios with the same state-contingent payoff vectors must be priced identically. This is the single-price law of markets. If short selling is allowed, a second necessary condition for market equilibrium is the absence of any riskless arbitrage opportunity. Noise traders or uninformed investors are contrasted with informed investors, who trade on information. Noise trading makes it possible for informed investors to earn a normal return on the investment in information gathering (Kyle [66]). A second approximation to EMH adjusts for noise traders and the limited ability of arbitrage by rational investors to fully offset their activity.

3. Portfolio Decisions (Gains to Diversification).   Diversification eliminates nonsystematic risk. Only systematic risk is priced. On a mean-variance-efficient frontier, each investor picks a point for a particular degree of risk aversion; such portfolios will combine two assets: the risk-free asset and the common risky portfolio, the market (M). Two-fund separation still holds in the absence of a risk-free asset by combining M with a zero beta portfolio.

4. Risk and Return (Factor Models).   The tradeoff between risk and return has been emphasized in recent generations of finance textbooks. This central proposition of financial economics is based on the concept that risk-averse investors must be promised a higher nominal return to bear a higher risk. For broad classes of securities, solid evidence is consistent with this proposition; that is, historical returns on equities are higher than for straight bonds.

However, for more narrowly defined securities and portfolios, less agreement is found on the identification of risk factors and other variables that appear to influence security returns. At the theoretical level, the law of one price, the arbitrage condition, and the equilibrium condition all utilize linear pricing relationships. Security and portfolio expected returns are related to their sensitivities to pervasive factors, as formulated in factor models such as CAPM and APT. In empirical tests, a wide range of variables have been used to explain returns.

5. Pricing Derivative Securities (Option Pricing Theory).   Derivative securities are assets whose values are based on the values of other assets. Pricing derivatives is based on the principle that close substitutes have the same price. Calls, puts, swaps, futures, and forward contracts are examples of derivative securities whose payoffs are contingent on the values of other assets. Derivative securities can be formed by the use of options such as calls and puts or by combining short and long positions in options, in futures or forward contracts, or in combinations of other assets with differing degrees of perceived risk. Derivative securities provide opportunities for risk management (hedging) and spanning with new securities (financial engineering).

6. Capital Structure, Dividend Decisions, Optimal Contractual Choice.   The key aspects of corporate finance involve financial structure and dividend policy, for which Modigliani and Miller (M&M) developed irrelevance propositions. Departures from the M&M conditions give rise to many challenging corporate finance policy decision issues, including optimal contractual choice.

7. Valuation and Growth Opportunities.   Assets are valued by their appropriately discounted expected future cash flow distributions. If actions or decisions do not affect the probability distributions of the future cash flows, the capital structure and dividend irrelevance propositions follow. The related value additivity principle states that the value of the firm is equal to the sum of the values of its projects. When the idealized assumptions of pure and perfect markets are relaxed, capital structure and dividend policies can change the cost of capital and, therefore, the value of the firm. The relation between profitability rates and the cost of capital defines growth opportunities and is central in models for estimating the intrinsic value of firms. Some have suggested that capital structure issues should be

financing episodes were of great significance. In Dewing's view, dividend policy also had an impact on the liquidity and subsequent strength of the corporation. Dewing's subsequent textbooks in corporate finance set the pattern for what is now referred to as the traditional corporate finance approach. Because the early consolidations involved large aggregates, the nature and terms of the financial contracts were matters of critical significance. As a result, traditional business finance included a heavy emphasis on institutional detail and description of financial instruments and contracts.

B. The 1920s

In the 1920s, major industries began to develop or mature. Some of the most significant were the radio, chemical, automobile, and steel industries. Large-scale national advertising emerged. Marketing and distribution methods reflected the advances in communications and transportation. Mergers were employed to round out marketing lines. Profit margins were high, but the inventory recession and sharp price declines of 1920–1921 again emphasized the importance of financial structure. Inventory price fluctuations and periodic financial stringency stimulated attention to liquidity considerations.

C. The 1930s

The recession that began in 1929 was unprecedented in its duration and severity. In the business field, it caused a wave of financial reorganizations and bankruptcies. A scramble for liquidity took place. The public began to claim their deposits from the commercial banks. The banks in turn reduced their lines of credit. Forced inventory liquidations ensued. Prices declined, and the inventory liquidations did not provide sufficient funds to meet obligations. Bank runs and bankruptcies cascaded. The need for safe leverage and liquidity was again dramatized.

With the reduced rate of business activity, losses resulted. Fixed financial charges were especially burdensome. In the public utility holding company systems, financial leverage had been magnified through the pyramiding of layers of intermediate entities. When operating revenue declined, the systems could not support the heavy burdens of financial charges, and a devastating collapse of the far-flung systems followed. Most railroads were able to cover current operating expenses, but debilitating deficits resulted from the overhang of heavy, fixed financial charges resulting from high debt ratios. As a consequence, virtually the entire railroad industry went through reorganization. Again, leverage decisions had an important role.

These events of the 1930s seemed to underline the importance of traditional business finance. The errors of unsound financial structure, particularly the consequences of heavy debt charges, were again demonstrated. The emphasis of traditional business finance on the analysis of financial structure and liquidity was again supported.

The financial distress of the 1930s resulted in major legislative enactments that increased federal regulation of the securities markets. The issuing and trading of securities became subject to monitoring by the Securities and Exchange Commission (SEC). Significant changes were made in the "rules of the game" to which financial managers and financial intermediaries were required to conform.

D. The 1940s

The 1940s were, of course, dominated by World War II and its immediate aftermath. All activity was subordinated and directed to the war effort. Many industries shifted to production for the defense effort. The conduct of the war required specialized products without peacetime uses. The specialized investments required to produce these goods required large outlays. The use of these facilities was of uncertain duration, with little or no application in the peacetime economy. It was, therefore, necessary to finance such programs primarily from government resources. Financial officers of firms were involved in arranging the financing programs with government help.

Expanded operations in wartime programs required additional plant and equipment, mainly financed by the government, but working capital requirements remained a challenge to financial managers. In the period immediately after World War II, financing the expansion of capacity and of working capital required for the growth of sales of peacetime products assumed crucial proportions for private financial policy.

E. Early 1950s

The early 1950s were years of rapid economic expansion but were clouded with the threat of a major postwar recession. Rising labor costs led to the substitution of capital equipment for labor. The rapid growth of firms coupled with a depressed equity market in the early 1950s and a tightening money market caused managers to place great emphasis on the conservation of cash. Cash-flow management became critical to profitability and value maximization. The orientation of financial management as the "outsider looking in" and the emphasis on financial ratio analysis as the tool of the outside analyst were shifted. The uses and applications of internal financial management procedures and controls received increased attention. Cash budget forecasting developed. Internal managerial controls, such as aging receivables, analysis of purchases, and the application of inventory controls, were stressed. The activities of financial managers began to broaden the scope.

F. Late 1950s and the 1960s

By the late 1950s, profit opportunities in mature industries began to narrow. The limited profit opportunities in traditional industrial activity fostered development of the theory of capital budgeting. With relatively tight money and a limited range of opportunities, management began to place increasing importance on careful assessment of resource allocation. The narrowing of the margin between prospective profitability and the cost of funds stimulated cost-of-capital analysis to determine appropriate investment hurdle rates. The higher market valuations placed on differential cash flow growth encouraged the creation of new techniques of planning and control.

G. Late 1970s and the 1980s

The foregoing provides illustrations of the generalization that financial practice in each historical period was responding to the pressing problems of the day. A review of the decade of the 1980s underscores how financial thought has responded to the maturation of financial markets, to internationalization, and to increased competition.

The developments and their impacts summarized in Exhibit 2 reflect the changing environments evolving since the late 1970s. These developments can be summarized into the following categories.
1. The Rise of International Competition.   The revolutions in transportation and communications have produced increasingly competitive world markets for many products. The completion of the transnational railroads in the U.S. in the 1880s resulted in a large common market that stimulated

Exhibit 2   Changes in Late 1970s through the 1980s

Economic Developments	Impact on the Finance Field
• Increased international competition	• Increased importance of agency problems
• Changing technologies—pace of innovation increased	• Increased pace of takeovers, acquisitions, and mergers
• Changing manufacturing methods—flexible manufacturing systems	• Rise of new forms of financing for small- and medium-sized firms, including highly leveraged transactions (HLTs) and high-yield securities (junk bonds)
• Changed management of human resources—hierarchy to participative management	• Innovations in option pricing theory and the creation of many forms of financial derivatives
• Fluctuating exchange rates—changing prices of buying and selling goods and companies	• Increased use of the futures, forward, and swap markets
• Deregulation in financial services	• Increased use of spreadsheet and computer-assisted analysis
• Persistent U.S. government deficits, large balance of payments deficits—continuing uncertainty and fear of inflation and/or high interest rates	• New financial products and innovations in financial services—the explosion of the financial engineering industry
• Frequent changes in tax laws	• Development of short-term financial models and integration into general finance theory as well as more sophisticated computer-assisted short-term financial management analysis
• Increased power of relatively low-cost personal computers	
• Weaknesses in governance and control systems exposed	

horizontal mergers and national firms. The emergence of world markets in the 1980s has created new competitive pressures as well as opportunities. Transnational mergers have increased the size and number of large multinational enterprises. Europe's 1992 integration initiatives have stimulated another wave of mergers.

2. Changing Technologies.   The pace of technological change has continued to accelerate, increasing competition between products and between their producers. Threats of losing markets and customers in an increasingly dynamic world have grown.

3. Management Adjustments.   External environments have changed in many dimensions and increased in turbulence. As a consequence, firms have had to readjust their management systems, their selection of product markets, their research and manufacturing methods, their methods of marketing, and their management of human resources. The challenge to finance has been to develop information flows that enable firms to anticipate changes and to have quick reaction responses to threats and opportunities. Strategy and strategic planning have developed to help firms more effectively realign to changing environments and the increased pace of competition from product changes and new management methods.

4. Deregulation.   Deregulation has taken place in airlines, banking, the savings and loan industry, in other financial services, broadcasting, cable, communications, transportation, and oil and gas. The readjustments in these industries included M&As, which accounted for 37 percent of merger activity by value between 1981 and 1986.

5. Fluctuating Exchange Rates.   Fluctuating exchange rates affect the prices of raw materials, the prices of goods sold, and the prices of buying and selling foreign companies. Fluctuating exchange rates require continuous readjustments in the selection of types and locations of production methods, marketing activities, and growth strategies including alliances, licensing, and takeovers.

6. Innovations in Finance.   The increased use of computers and formal models plus "rocket scientist" applications of finance theory produced many models directly applied in financial practice. These innovations were reinforced by competitive pressures. Deregulation in the financial intermediation industries permitted greater freedom and flexibility in lending and investing activities, which encouraged an inflow of capital, resulting in excess capacity in financial services. Excess capacity placed pressure on profit margins and stimulated new types of activities in which the financial intermediaries possessed limited managerial experience or capabilities. Some new practices were highly speculative—in part because of perverse incentives created by government policies such as deposit insurance.

7. Increased Use of Debt.   The long period of economic expansion during most of the 1980s encouraged financial managers to increase (book) debt ratios and to decrease interest coverage ratios. Jensen [55, 56] provided a conceptual justification for the use of debt in his free cash-flow theory. In addition, one of the innovations in the financing of takeovers and mergers was the increased use of below-investment-grade debt obligations ("junk bonds"). Their fluctuations in value created investor distress as well as opportunities.

8. Changes in Tax Policy.   Four major revisions in the tax laws were enacted during the 1980s, shifting the relative advantages of the use of debt and equity. The changes also stimulated new tax-planning strategies.

With the foregoing background, we can now turn to depicting some patterns in the flow of the history of financial thought.

III. The Emergence of Selected Areas of Finance

A panorama is presented in Exhibit 3 that provides a time line of the introduction of new concepts and ideas in finance during the last 60 years.

The topics covered in the present section are:

A. Investment Decisions and Valuation

B. Capital Structure Theory

C. Factor Models—CAPM and APT

D. Derivative Securities

E. Games and Information

F. Takeovers and Corporate Control

G. Financial Distress

Full sections are then developed on Short-Term Financial Management, Financial Strategy and Growth, and International Finance before the paper concludes with discussions of The Literature of Finance and Coping with the Knowledge Explosion.

Exhibit 3   Emergence of Major Ideas in Finance by Initial Year of Decade

1930	1940	1950	1960	1970	1980	1990
Interest Rates and Investment Decisions: Fisher 1930	*Financial Markets and Business Finance:* Jacoby & Saulnier 1947	*Capital Budgeting:* Dean 1951	*Dividend Policy:* Miller & Modigliani 1961	*Efficient Capital Markets:* Fama 1970, 1991	*Corporate Control and Restructuring:* Jensen & Ruback 1983; Weston & Chung 1983; Chung & Weston 1982	*Risk Management:* Smith, Smithson, & Wilford 1990
Valuation Theory: Williams 1938		*Working Capital Management:* Baumol 1952; Stone 1972; Smith 1973; Kim & Atkins 1978; Sartoris & Hill 1983; Gentry 1988; Kim & Srinivasan 1988, 1991; Hill & Sartoris 1988, 1993	*CAPM:* Sharpe 1964; Lintner 1965; Mayers 1972; Merton 1973b	*Conglomerate Performance:* Weston & Mansinghka 1971; Weston, Smith, & Shrieves 1972	*Financial Strategy:* Myers 1984a	
		Merger Analysis: Weston 1953	*Financial Distress:* Altman 1968; Warner 1977	*Critique of CAPM:* Merton 1972; Roll 1977	*Synthetic Securities:* Cox & Rubinstein 1985	
		Dividend Growth Model: Gordon & Shapiro 1956	*Event Analysis:* Fama, Fisher, Jensen, & Roll 1969; Brown & Warner 1980	*Option Pricing:* Black & Scholes 1973; Merton 1973a; Rubinstein 1976	*Portfolio Insurance:* Rubinstein & Leland 1981	
		Auctions, Games, Information: Luce & Raiffa 1957; Vickrey 1961		*International Finance:* Solnik 1974; Adler & Dumas 1982; Levi 1983; Solnik 1991	*Financial Engineering:* Finnerty 1988; Smith & Smithson 1990	
		Capital Structure: Durand 1952; Modigliani & Miller 1958; Miller 1977; Myers 1977, 1984b; Myers & Majluf 1984; Titman 1984		*Contingent Claims Analysis:* Brennan & Schwartz 1978		
				BOP: Sharpe 1978; Cox, Ross & Rubinstein 1979; Rendleman & Bartter 1979		
				APT: Ross 1976; Roll & Ross 1980; Bower, Bower & Logue 1984; Chen, Roll & Ross 1986		
				Financial Contracting: Smith & Warner 1979; Emery & Finnerty 1992		

A. Investment Decisions and Valuation

The origins of some fundamental concepts of finance are found in the writings of Irving Fisher, particularly *The Theory of Interest* [34]. As J. Hirshleifer observed in his *Investment, Interest, and Capital* [49], the logical structure of Fisher's work was explaining individual investment decisions as intertemporal choices among consumption opportunities (under certainty) and viewing interest rates as equilibrium prices clearing markets for consumption claims. Hirshleifer extended Fisher's work, particularly in dealing with the treatment of intertemporal decisions under uncertainty. Similarly, fundamental concepts of valuation theory emanated from the John B. Williams book [138].

Significant new empirical studies were begun in the late 1930s under the auspices of the National Bureau of Research (NBER). Neil H. Jacoby, Raymond J. Saulnier, and their associates produced a series of monographs on new developments in financial forms and institutions related to the changing economic and financial environments. They produced monographs on subjects such as financing uses and sources, equipment financing, receivables financing, direct placement, etc. Some of the studies were purely descriptive in setting forth cross-sectional patterns in asset structures and their financing sources. But, in general, the aim of these NBER studies was to relate innovations in financial practices to developments in the economy and financial markets (Jacoby and Saulnier [52]).

In the early 1950s, Joel Dean published his *Managerial Economics* [21] and his companion book, *Capital Budgeting* [22]. These two books stimulated a stream of studies stemming from top management's concerns with investment decisions on plant, equipment, and product development. Current textbook chapters on capital budgeting still owe a considerable debt to the pioneering work of Joel Dean and his associates. Stimulated by an attempt to deal with one of the analytical aspects of equipment decisions was the paper by Gordon and Shapiro [41], which studied the required rate of profit in capital equipment analysis. The article included a formulation that came to be known as the Gordon-Shapiro dividend growth valuation model.

In 1950, a conference sponsored by the NBER was held on the theory of business finance. At this conference David Durand, of MIT, presented a paper contrasting what came to be called the NOI versus NI approach to the cost of capital and the value of the firm (Durand [27]). In the NOI approach, net operating income represents the flow that is capitalized; partitioning the flow between returns to debt and returns to equity could not affect a firm's cost of capital or its value. In the NI approach, a change in leverage could affect both the value of the firm and its cost of capital. Durand [27] and the later empirical work of Myron J. Gordon [40] appeared to support the NI theory. This was a period in the United States during which relatively mature large corporations did most of their financing from cash retentions.

B. Capital Structure Theory

Modigliani and Miller (M&M) [81] opted for the NOI approach. Based on a framework similar to the fundamental methodology of microeconomics, which starts with idealized assumptions of pure and perfect competition in factor and product markets, M&M formulated the propositions of capital structure and dividend irrelevance. Ultimately, the M&M propositions had a great impact because they specified that, under assumptions similar to those for perfect competition in microeconomics, the cost of capital (and, therefore, firm value) could not be affected by leverage or dividend changes. Subsequent developments (to which both Miller and Modigliani contributed) analyzed how the relaxation of individual M&M conditions influenced the cost of capital and valuation. These studies (see Weston [131] for references) demonstrated how other variables such as taxes (corporate, personal, capital gains), bankruptcy risks and costs, asymmetric information, signaling, and product durability (Titman [126]) could influence leverage and dividend decisions.

Another important conceptual development was agency theory and its applications, formulated by Jensen and Meckling [59]. The implications of agency problems were developed for many areas of finance, thereby adding important new dimensions to their analysis. For example, the understanding of capital structure was advanced by Smith and Warner [109] in their paper on financial contracting, which analyzed the implications of debt covenants. The considerable subsequent literature in this area has been reviewed by Emery and Finnerty [28], who pointed out the importance of the interactions of various financial contracting considerations in determining the characteristics of debt instruments.

C. Risk and Return (Factor Models)

Markowitz [71, 72] had demonstrated how efficient portfolios could be constructed by the use of mean-variance analysis. Drawing on these insights and their implications, the Sharpe-Lintner capital asset pricing model (CAPM) emerged in 1964 (Lintner [69], Sharpe [104]). Only systematic risk is priced in the equation for measuring the required return on an asset. The risk component of the required return to an individual security is measured by the covariance of its returns with the returns on the market portfolio. This was another powerful development in financial economics, leading to the award in 1990 of a share of the Nobel Prize to Bill Sharpe (as well as to Harry Markowitz and Merton Miller).

The early CAPM models employed a risk-free asset. If no risk-free asset exists, Black [6] showed how the use of a zero beta portfolio preserves the major results of the CAPM. Mayers [73] demonstrated that the CAPM can be extended to include non-marketable assets such as human capital. The appropriate measure of risk is still the covariance, but with two portfolios, one composed of marketable assets and another of nonmarketable assets. Merton [76] formulated an intertemporal capital asset pricing model in continuous time. If the risk-free rate is stochastic, a third fund is necessary to hedge against unanticipated changes in the future risk-free rate, so that the resulting model exhibits three-fund separation.

Early empirical work provided some confirmation for CAPM. The empirical security market line appeared to have a somewhat higher intercept and a somewhat smaller slope than the theoretical CAPM, resulting in higher than predicted empirical returns for low beta companies and lower than predicted empirical returns for high beta companies. But in the late 1970s, when the prime rate rose above 20 percent, some uses of CAPM in cost of capital calculations in regulatory proceedings as well as in internal financial decision making were (to put it kindly) incautious at best.

In addition, subsequent work challenged CAPM on both theoretical and empirical grounds. Roll [92] emphasized the sensitivity of the position and shape of the efficient frontier to the selection of the index for measuring the "market." The recent work by Fama and French [31] found that traditional betas had no explanatory power in studies of returns over long time periods, whereas firm size and book-to-market ratios did. In response, Roll and Ross wrote: " . . . the recent paper by Fama and French [31] forcefully resurrects an old finding that there is virtually no detectable cross-sectional beta/return relation. . . . Earlier papers reported the same result" ([94] p. 2). After listing many such papers, they performed some analytics that brought them to a number of conclusions, such as the following:

As we have seen, though, the empirical findings are not by themselves sufficient to cause rejection of the theory. The cross-sectional relation is very sensitive to the choice of an index and indices can be quite close to each other and to the mean/variance frontier and yet still produce significantly different cross-sectional slopes, positive, negative or zero. The finding that a market index proxy does not explain cross-sectional returns is consistent with even a very close, but unobserved true market index being efficient.

Furthermore, since all of the estimates are subject to serious sampling error, the proxy itself may actually produce a positive cross-sectional expected return/true beta relation which cannot be detected in the sample mean return/estimated beta relation. ([94], p. 12)

Meanwhile, CAPM has been attacked from another direction. The multifactor approach to asset returns in Merton [74], Roll and Ross [93], and Ross [95], and the later empirical work (see, for example, Chen, Roll, and Ross [15]), explained asset returns better than CAPM, took care of the size effect, etc. In the arbitrage pricing theory (APT) formulation, returns are related to unexpected changes in industrial production, inflation, the shape of the maturity yield curve, and the shape of the risk yield curve. Another potential factor, given the great impact of the OPEC cartel policies of 1973 and 1979, is the price of oil. Fama [30] observed,

On the other hand . . . the results . . . are sensitive to the assets used in the tests and the way the βs of economic factors are estimated is disturbing . . . the multifactor models are licenses to search the data for variables that, *ex post,* describe the cross-section of average returns. It is perhaps no surprise, then, that these variables do well in competitions on the data used to identify them.

Burton Malkiel, in a chapter titled "Risk and Return: A New Look" in a NBER book edited by Benjamin M. Friedman [36], suggested that the factors to consider from an economic standpoint were market risks (beta), economy risk (national income or gross domestic product or an index of industrial production), inflation risk (interest rate risk), and the dispersion of analysts' forecasts on grounds that "this risk variable may serve as a good proxy for a variety of systematic risks" [p. 40]. Without settling all of the issues raised by APT, it has been demonstrated that one can get some useful information and insights by reasonable and straightforward applications of APT (D. H. Bower, R. S. Bower, and D. E. Logue [8]).

It is generally true that a well-constructed multivariate model will "explain" more than a univariate model. A central problem in finance is that the theories call for the use of expectations. But historical data are used in empirical tests. In addition, the empirical parameters are unstable over time. Nevertheless, single-factor and multifactor models agree on some broad patterns. Equities should yield more than straight bonds. Junior bonds should yield more than senior bonds. The bonds of highly leveraged firms should yield more, other things being equal, than the bonds of less leveraged firms. Convertible securities with equity-like characteristics should yield more than straight bonds. Indeed, the empirical tests of CAPM based on comparisons among different types of securities without exception find a positive intercept and a significant positive relationship between beta risks of securities classes and their returns.

It is remarkable that many of the new intellectual developments in finance portrayed in Exhibit 1 have received immediate acceptance and use by practitioners. Many of these advances were stimulated by financial practice as well. Even where controversy remains, we obtain many useful insights from the theoretical models. They have enriched our understanding and have improved the way we handle practical problems. They inform our judgments and enable us to avoid conceptual errors. Even where the controversies between alternative models continue, the sparks of these clashes can illuminate and guide the practitioner.

D. Derivative Securities

A whole new way of looking at finance followed from the development of the option pricing model associated with Black and Scholes [7]; Cox, Ross, and Rubinstein [19]; and Merton [75]. Their work, in turn, led to more complex studies of contingent claims analysis such as the use of stochastic calculus in option pricing constructs by Brennan and Schwartz [11]. Sharpe [105] originated binomial option pricing (BOP) models to simplify his classroom exposition of the closed form solutions provided by the option pricing models of Black and Scholes. The BOP has been a versatile tool for analyzing uncertain streams and the role of derivative securities. Cox and Rubinstein [18] provided a comprehensive, definitive treatise on options and option markets. Among their notable contributions is the demonstration that synthetic securities and derivatives could be developed from combined long and short positions in a variety of instruments.

Applications of the analytic frameworks stimulated by BOP have led to work on synthetic and derivative securities—financial engineering that has created a wide range of new types of securities and transactions. Portfolio insurance is a concept directly derived from thinking in the BOP framework (Rubinstein and Leland [99]). Derivative securities combined with innovations in the use of forward and futures markets, along with their expression in the form of swaps and related transactions and institutions, have led to a risk management literature (Smith, Smithson, and Wilford [108]). The use of options in areas such as capital budgeting has enriched the analysis by considering options to defer investments, to shut down the use of durable goods temporarily, and to abandon operations before the end of their physical life (Brennan and Schwartz [12]). Options concepts have provided insights and contributed to the development of the literature and practice in the three important areas of financial strategy, financial engineering, and risk management.

Economic, financial, and competitive changes have increased the need to manage and reallocate risk and to relate risks to alternative patterns of future states and alternative scenarios. Dynamism in the economic, financial, political, and cultural environments has highlighted the tensions in control mechanisms at every level—world, nation, and organization (business units)—emphasizing the need to deal with governance, control, and agency issues and their costs. The resulting effects on volatility and the market micro-structure have been analyzed by Damodaran and Subrahmanyam [20]. Another review considers the role of general equilibrium analysis in the field of contingent claims and examines the nature of the stochastic processes for underlying security market assets (Hodges, Selby, Clewlow, Strickland, and Xu [50]).

E. Games and Information

The seminal studies of Luce and Raiffa [70] and Vickrey [127] introduced a literature on auctions, games, and information. A readable introduction with numerous examples is provided by Rasmusen [89]. Game theory models have increasingly found their way into the mainstream of finance literature (Rasmusen [90], Thakor [125]). They provide language and analytical concepts increasingly used throughout finance. The richness of the materials is conveyed by a sample of the materials covered in Thakor's review paper. Game theory is defined as the analysis of decisions and actions of agents involved in particular interactions (or games). When more than one decision maker is involved, their actions and decisions affect each other. The game may be played cooperatively (collusion) or noncooperatively. A strategy combination is a Nash equilibrium if no player has incentives to deviate from this strategy, given that the other players do not deviate. Other concepts of equilibrium are also introduced, and criteria for evaluating them are formulated. Applications to financial decisions are presented by Rasmusen, Thakor, and others.

F. Takeovers and Corporate Control

The areas of M&A, corporate control, and restructuring, which gathered momentum in the 1970s, exploded in the 1980s. Exhibit 4 provides an overview of the many forms of restructuring and their event returns to shareholders. Most produced event-related, positive, "abnormal" returns.

The returns from takeover and restructuring activities have been analyzed by the use of one, or a combination of, the theories summarized in Exhibit 5.

A large and growing literature has sought to test and analyze the reasons and results of the many forms of takeovers and restructuring. (See the many publications by Jarrell, Brickley, and Netter [53] and by Jensen, his students, and associates [56–61].) Textbook summaries and numerous references are found in Gaughan [37] and in Weston, Chung, and Hoag [134].

Effective summaries of the theoretical materials are found in Hirshleifer [45, 46]. Theoretical models start with the Grossman and Hart [43] free-rider problem, which can be summarized by a simple numerical example. The stock of the target (T) firm is selling for $40. A bidder (B) offers $60 in a takeover (tender offer). An atomistic shareholder in T feels that since B has offered $60, the company must be worth more than that to B. So the small shareholder in T does not tender since his "vote" will not influence the result. If the tender offer succeeds, the small shareholder in T expects to hold a share of stock that will rise in value above $60. If this particular tender offer does not succeed, the small shareholder in T believes that the increased value discovered by the bidder and the competitive market for corporate control will cause the price of the stock to rise above $60.

Grossman and Hart solve the free-rider problem by post-acquisition dilution, that is, selling off assets of the acquired company to another company controlled by the successful bidders. Other methods of solving the free-rider problem have been proposed. Shleifer and Vishny [106] solve the problem by having a large shareholder (or equivalently a bidder with a relatively large foothold) who pays the full value of his expected improvement and profits on his initial stake. With different assumptions about the process, Hirshleifer and Titman [48] solve the free-rider problem and deal with other issues through a model in which the individual (atomistic) shareholder is indifferent between tendering and not tendering. Other models posit methods by which shareholders of the bidder firm may become pivotal (Holmstrom and Nalebuff [51]). Analysis of multiple bidders moves to the realm of a game-theoretic framework. Seminal papers in this area include Fishman [35] and Hirshleifer and Png [47].

Alternative methods of payment used by the bidder and the role of taxes in the transaction are additional topics that cut across the several issues outlined above. Also important are the issues of takeover defenses, managerial voting power and compensation, corporate governance, and corporate control.

A widely accepted view of the history and theory of takeover activities has been articulated by Jensen [54–61]. According to Jensen, agency problems were aggravated by "the regulatory banishment of active investors in the 1930s" ([58], p. 659). Prevented by government antitrust policy from takeovers in their core lines of business activity, American corporations embarked on diversification programs during the conglomerate merger movement of the 1960s. Beginning in the mid-70s, it was recognized that diversification was unsound, and the premiums of 30–50 percent received by targets

---

Exhibit 4 Forms of Restructuring and Their Financial Results

Form of Restructuring	Event Returns (%)
Takeovers	
Merger Studies	
Acquired firms	20
Acquiring firms	2 to 3
Tender Offer Studies	
Acquired firms	30 to 35
Acquiring firms	−1 to +4
Sell-offs	
Spin-offs	2 to 4
Divestitures	
Sellers	0.5 to 1
Buyers	0.34
Equity Carve-outs	2
Changes in Ownership Structure	
Exchange Offers	
Debt for equity	14
Preferred for equity	8
Share Repurchases	16
Going Private	20
Leveraged Buyouts (Early Ones)	40 to 50
Leveraged Cash-outs	20 to 30
ESOPs	−4 to +4
Joint Ventures	
Participant firms	2.5
Scaled by investment	23
Corporate Control	
Unequal Voting Rights	
Value of control	5 to 6
Dual-class recapitalizations	−1
Proxy Contests	10
Premium Buy-backs	
Greenmail	−2
Standstill agreements	−4
Merger Defenses	−4 to +4

---

reflected the value of reversing unsound conglomeration. The activity of the 1980s provides lessons for improving management practice: "decentralization, downsizing, increased pay for performance and equity holdings by managers and employees, increased cooperation with active investors and the use of leverage at divisional levels to increase the incentives for efficiency. . ." ([58], p. 665). Jensen concluded that new legislation at the end of the 1980s interfered with the self-correcting adjustment processes already under way.

Exhibit 5   Theories of Mergers and Takeovers

   I. Efficiency Theories—Potential for social benefits

    A. *Differential efficiency*—acquirer's superior management improves efficiency in target

    B. *Inefficient management*—target management is inefficient

   II. Operating Synergy—Economies of scale and scope; complementarities of organizational capabilities

   III. Financial Synergy—Lower cost of capital from joining of imperfectly correlated cash-flow streams

   IV. Underutilized Debt Capacity—Potential justification for increased leverage

   V. Strategic—Realignment to changing environments

   VI. Market Below Replacement Cost—When the "q-ratio" is below one, buy the securities of a firm to acquire capacity

   VII. Undervaluation

    A. *Short-term myopia*—market participants undervalue corporations with long-term investment programs

    B. *Information*—announcement reveals "sitting on a gold mine" or prospective "kick in pants"

    C. *Asymmetric information*—target management knows more than the bidder or public

   VIII. Signaling—Tender offer may signal that future cash flows will rise

   IX. Incentives Alignment—Creation of executive compensation packages to better align managerial incentives with those of shareholders

   X. Agency Problems and Managerialism—Agency costs due to separation of ownership and control

   XI. Winner's Curse

    A. Winning bid based on most optimistic estimates

    B. *Hubris hypothesis*—errors of overoptimism in evaluating takeovers

   XII. Market Position—Larger firms possess market power

   XIII. Redistribution—Shareholders gain at the expense of other stakeholders

   XIV. Tax Influences—Possible better utilization of tax credits, etc.

My assessment of the relevant theory and evidence has a somewhat different emphasis. The conglomerate merger activity of the 1960s was not accounted for by "American corporations, dominant in their product markets, flush with cash . . ." (Jensen [58], p. 659). Almost 50 percent of the firms regarded as most active in conglomerate acquisitions were seeking to adjust to the uncertainties of the defense market or were in exhausting-resource areas such as petroleum and forest products. Other conglomerates, such as ITT, were seeking to diminish undue dependence on foreign markets and unstable governments, to develop their domestic business, and to reduce their dependence on the telephone equipment market as well. Firms that had had high market shares in individual product market lines had less pressure to engage in diversification during the 1960s.

The following major causative factors that changed the takeover market reflected fundamental changes in the external environments to which firms must relate:

(1) The internationalization of competition eroded the competitive advantage of U.S. producers in important markets.

(2) Changing production and managerial technologies altered the scope and boundaries of markets, resulting in new forms of domestic competition as well (autos, steel, computers).

(3) The rise of discretionary consumer incomes resulted in inter-product competition (recreation competes with expenditures on clothing).

(4) Financial innovation made all firms subject to takeover, including hostile tender offers.

Diversification activities of large firms such as General Electric have increased during the 1980s, and the scope of activity of the largest firms broadened rather than narrowed during the last decade.

The activities of the 1980s highlighted issues of corporate governance. The securities legislation of the 1930s provided investors with additional information and restricted the activities of commercial banks and investment bankers. Nonbank financial institutions such as insurance companies, pension funds, and mutual funds became holders of about half of corporate equity by the 1990s. But despite their increasing share of corporate ownership, institutional investors did not seek to influence corporate managements directly. They voted by purchasing the shares of companies with good performance and selling the shares of poor performers. The leveraged buyout firms were at least in part a response to weaknesses in corporate control mechanisms. Leveraged buyouts enabled managers to achieve substantial ownership positions, providing them with incentives to behave like owners. This object lesson in the values of responsible corporate governance stimulated institutional investors by 1993 to become activists in influencing the selection of the chief executives at major companies such as IBM, General Motors, and American Express. In substantial measure, the takeovers and buyouts of the 1980s signaled major changes in corporate control and governance mechanisms in the United States.

G. *Financial Distress*

Related areas of analysis include financial distress, reorganization, bankruptcy, high-yield securities, junk bonds, and highly leveraged transactions (HLTs). Although the prevailing U.S. bankruptcy law was enacted in 1978, its impact was not recognized until after the 1980s. The key provision is that the debtor management (which guided the firm into financial distress) remains in possession of the company and has a dominant role in formulating reorganization proposals. Some have argued that the ease of using the bankruptcy laws was an important factor in the "overleveraging" of the 1980s. Between 1980 and 1990, the number of annual bankruptcy filings tripled, and the assets of public companies filing for bankruptcies surpassed $80 billion per year in both 1990 and 1991, exceeding by at least 50 times the levels of the early eighties. The size of the distressed security market in 1990 has been estimated at a book value of over $350 billion (Altman [3]).

Many important issues have been raised by the rise of bankruptcies, junk bonds, and distressed securities. The nature of the subject is conveyed by Exhibit 6.

Exhibit 6   Topics Related to Financial Distress

I. The Nature of Financial Distress

II. Causes of Financial Distress
    A. Economic and other environmental factors
    B. Managerial policies and other internal problems

III. Prediction of Financial Distress
    A. Accounting data
    B. Financial market data

IV. Alternative Remedies for Financial Distress
    A. Recontracting, extension, composition
    B. Voluntary
    C. Court-supervised

V. Voluntary Procedures
    A. Financial restructuring
    B. Reorganizing policies and operations
    C. Asset divestitures and sales
    D. Capital infusion
    E. The turn-around entrepreneurs
    F. Potential impediments to private restructuring
        1. Free-rider problem
        2. Asymmetric information
        3. Conflicts of interest

VI. Operation of the 1978 Bankruptcy Act in the United States
    A. Strong position of debtor
    B. Fairness
    C. Feasibility
    D. Absolute priority
    E. Writedowns
    F. Valuation and value trends

VII. Issues Related to Financial Distress
    A. Theory of the firm
    B. Costs of financial distress
    C. Costs of bankruptcy
    D. Effects on the underinvestment problem
    E. Effects on risk premiums on debt and equity
    F. Returns to shareholders and other stakeholders
    G. Effects on executives—turnover and compensation
    H. Effects on capital structure policies
    I. Effects on dividend policies

Important questions are posed by the topics in Exhibit 6. What are the effects of financial distress and financial reorganization rules on lenders and the availability of financing for enterprise? Are the direct and indirect costs of bankruptcy large enough to impact models of the firm? Are resources dissipated or enhanced by the reorganization processes? Should the bankruptcy statutes and other legal rules be changed? These and related issues were explored in a two-volume collection of papers edited by Jensen and Ruback [61]. Other book-length treatments include those by Altman [3] and Branch and Ray [9]. Progress will be further advanced by the emergence of formal models of financial distress (Gertner and Sharfstein [39], John and John [62], and Wruck [139]).

The widespread activity and burgeoning literature have given rise to the development of courses on financial distress in the finance curriculum. In addition, sessions on this topic have been appearing regularly during the annual meetings of the Financial Management Association. It is clear that these expanding areas of academic research and teaching have represented responses to substantial changes in the economic environment.

IV. Short-Term Financial Management (STFM)

Because of its importance in financial practice, the working capital management area continues to be significant. In recent years this area has come to be called short-run financial management (Gentry [38]) or short-term financial management (Hill and Sartoris [44]). In reporting the results of a survey on the activities of financial managers, Weston [130] found that:

(1) working capital management represented a major activity in the day-to-day responsibilities of finance officers;

(2) the decisions were important to the success of the firm and required a high level of competence;

(3) these activities had to be related to the longer-term policies and decisions involved in the investment and financing activities of the firm, as well as to the other management activities in the firm.

In an early state-of-the-art paper, K. V. Smith [111] summarized eight approaches to working capital management:

> The first three, aggregate guidelines, constraint set, and cost balancing, are partial models; the next two approaches, probability models and portfolio theory, stress future uncertainty and interdependencies; while the last three approaches, mathematical programming, multiple goals, and financial simulation, have a broader, systematic focus.

Models of the management of corporate cash balances had been developed by Baumol [5] and by Miller and Orr [80]. Many other important facets of cash management were further developed by Bernell K. Stone [117–122].

A subsequent state-of-the-art paper by James Gentry [38] articulated effectively the many important dimensions and contributions of the literature on short-run or short-term financial management. In a discussion both comprehensive and analytical, Gentry demonstrated the important role of STFM for the development of ideas in finance. He recognized the contributions of analyzing STFM in a CAPM valuation framework. Another important advance was initiated by Kim and Atkins [63] in 1978, who first used the net-present-value approach to judge accounts receivables investments. Their model was further developed by Sartoris and Hill [101] and other writers.

Gentry also set forth the reasons why the cash management literature began to blossom in the 1970s. The economic environment of high inflation and high interest rates increased the importance of effective cash management. More-accessible computer technology made it economical to analyze cash receipts and disbursements on a daily basis.

Important contributions to the analysis of receivables were made by Carpenter and Miller [14] and by Stone [120]. Contributions to the theory of accounts receivable and the role of factors were made by Mian and Smith [77] and by Janet Smith [110]. In discussing future directions, Gentry called attention to the framework developed by Srinivasan and Kim [115, 116] in grouping cash management decisions as operational and infrastructural. Gentry also explained how the development of electronic and computer technologies has created a revolution in the management and control of current assets and current liabilities. He also noted the future potential of artificial intelligence and expert systems. The present brief overview inadequately captures the full content of Gentry's wide-ranging panoramic vistas and the writers whose contributions he described. Kim and Srinivasan have continued the momentum of WCM research with their two-volume book, *Advances in Working Capital Management* [64, 65].

V. Financial Strategy and Growth

Another area of growing importance is the relationship between strategy and finance. Gentry [38] commented on the potential of the strategy literature (Porter [86, 87]) and the shareholder value literature (Donaldson [26], Rappaport [88]). These writings demonstrated a crucial link between financial strategy and corporate strategy. They call attention to the critical parameters ("value drivers") relating the free cash flows of a firm to its cumulative performance in the financial markets.

The options–contingent claims literature also suggests links between finance and strategy. These ideas have been developed in the paper by Brennan and Schwartz [12] on evaluating natural resource investments. A number of asset options provide opportunities for strategic decision making. A taxonomy of asset options would include the abandonment option, the option to defer development, the option to expand or grow, the option to shrink, and the option to switch projects.

Growth in investment opportunities and sales represents a powerful force for value creation. Surprisingly, the concept of growth has received a somewhat disjointed treatment in the financial literature. Capital structure papers generally make a zero-growth assumption. In the Miller and Modigliani 1961 dividend paper [79], sources of *alternative* patterns of growth and growth opportunities are analyzed.

Growth is generally most meaningfully measured with reference to free cash flows. In the basic models of Gordon-Shapiro and those of Miller-Modigliani, all of the key variables grow at the same rate. The same assumption is made in models used by financial consultants (see, for example Rappaport [88]). These include sales and (since they are usually specified as a fixed ratio to sales) assets, working capital, fixed assets, and cash flows as well.

Most of the finance literature on capital structure and in central models such as the CAPM, OPM, and APT is in the spirit of the static classic models of Marshallian economics. This is true in empirical tests as well. For example, the Fama and French [31] study does not consider growth as a variable. Yet the two variables they identify as important influences on historically measured returns are the market-to-book ratio and the price-earnings ratio. It is well established in the finance textbook literature that both measures are greatly influenced by growth in the firm's cash flows as well as reflecting risk factors.

VI. International Finance

In their paper, "International Portfolio Choice and Corporation Finance: A Synthesis," Adler and Dumas [1] provided an overview of the central theories and related empirical studies of the major issues in international finance. Their findings are supported by later analytical treatments (see, for example, Levi [67]; Solnik [114]).

Adler and Dumas observed that the basic structure of the theory of international finance mirrors that of domestic financial theory. We start from a micro-theory of individual portfolio choice to obtain (via aggregation and market clearing) equilibrium pricing relationships and risk-return tradeoffs. We thereby get objectives for value-maximizing firms from which decision rules can be formulated. The logical sequence is the same whether there is one capital market or more. Nations or capital markets are defined by subsets of investors who use the same price index in deflating their anticipated nominal monetary returns.

A. Purchasing Power Parity (PPP)

The purchasing power parity theorem states that in competitive markets the exchange-adjusted prices of identical tradable goods and financial assets must be equal worldwide (taking account of information and transaction costs). PPP deals with the rates at which domestic goods are exchanged for foreign goods. Thus if X dollars buy a bushel of wheat in the United States, the X dollars should also buy a bushel of wheat in the United Kingdom. Expressed equivalently, the purchasing power parity doctrine states that people will value currencies for what they will buy. If an American dollar buys the same basket of goods and services as five units of a foreign currency, we should have an exchange rate of five foreign currency units to the dollar, or each foreign currency unit should be worth $0.20.

PPP is distinguished from commodity price parity (CPP)—the law of one price. CPP is an arbitrage condition that holds between the prices of identical traded goods in two locations in the absence of trade barriers. It may also hold for nontraded goods that are close substitutes for traded goods. PPP is a relationship between baskets of goods or weighed average price levels. CPP is a sufficient condition for PPP.

In practice, price levels are measured by indices calculated relative to some base period yielding *relative* PPP. For PPP to hold, the price indexes must be a valid representation of consumption possibilities and preferences. PPP could hold despite differences in tastes and nontraded goods with sufficient substitutability between goods to produce high correlations between the price movements of individual commodities.

The empirical evidence reveals deviations from PPP that are large and persist for long but variable periods. Sources of deviations from PPP include differences in factor costs and production functions. While improvements in technology and communications along with changes in regulations have greatly enhanced the mobility of capital—both financial and intellectual—other factors of production remain relatively immobile. Differences in consumption baskets reflecting differences in national tastes also contribute to PPP deviations. Other explanations include taxes, tariffs, transactions costs, asymmetric information, imperfect competition, and measurement error.

B. *International Returns and Portfolio Choice*

International returns are stable but fat-tailed distributions. Adler and Dumas suggested that for various reasons the distributions may be regarded as approximately normal, but the correlations of returns across nations are small. Hence a potential for international diversification to reduce risk is "unquestionable" (Adler and Dumas [1], p. 938). The construction of optimal international portfolios and evaluation of their benefits involve complex issues.

Adler and Dumas first considered optimal portfolio choice in a unified world capital market with no transactions costs or taxes, but with nationally heterogeneous consumption preferences. All investors have access to the same menu of financial assets plus one default-free, short-term bond per country. All bonds are risky in real terms. Currency translation raises difficulties, and the estimation problems are especially severe in testing an international asset pricing model (IAPM). The nonstationarity of the parameters coupled with the use of historical data where expected values are required causes a serious wedge between models and tests. Merton [76] has suggested a solution at the theoretical level using state variables to estimate the parameters, but the technique has not been implemented in practice.

International asset pricing models are fully valid only when investors use the same price index in deflating returns. Nevertheless, Adler and Dumas indicate that it is possible to derive an expression for the forward exchange rate as a function of the distribution of the future spot rate corresponding to the maturity of the forward contract. But the forward rate differs from the expected value of the stock rate by two premiums. One stems from the risk aversion of investor speculators. The other premium would exist under risk neutrality arising from random inflation. Thus there is nominal risk as well as real risk.

In their final section, Adler and Dumas analyzed hedging policy. The observed that in a complete, perfect, and unified international capital market, corporate hedging would be unnecessary. In the real world with the imperfections they have discussed, measuring exposure and methods of hedging exposures involve a large number of variables. Among the factors that make measuring exposure and dealing with exposure through hedging difficult are (1) the impact of PPP deviations on sales prices and unit costs; (2) the indirect impact of fluctuating exchange rates and the impact via sales prices on quantities sold, and consequently on production schedules; (3) the impact of fluctuating exchange rates on replacement costs and purchase prices of physical assets used in the production process; (4) their impact on short-term nominal net assets with maturities equal to the planning horizon date; (5) the impact of exchange rates on longer-term nominal net assets whose maturities fall beyond the planning horizon end date; and (6) an additional variable: when a firm tenders or bids for a project or a sales contract abroad, it is uncertain whether it will succeed; nevertheless, in anticipation of undertaking the project, it may be prudent to enter into hedging actions, not necessarily in forward markets, but possibly by taking positions in currency options markets, puts, calls, and swaps.

The survey by Adler and Dumas and subsequent literature demonstrate that the key issues for international portfolio choice and corporate finance have been identified but are far from resolved. Even at the practical level, methods of measuring exchange risk exposures and dealing with them have not been worked out. Nor is there agreement on issues such as whether Japanese firms have lower financing costs and therefore a financially derived competitive advantage (FDCA). A widely held view is that this is so. An alternative view is that FDCA is confused with the more rapid rate of improvement in business practices and productivity, which resulted in both favorable trade and favorable exchange rate movements for Japan. (Cf. J. F. Weston [132].)

VII. A Flowering of Finance Journals

Related to the explosion of information and concepts has been a parallel expansion in the number of financial and finance-related journals. This is presented in the form of a time line in Exhibit 7. Of the 36 journals covered in J. L. Heck's 1992 *Finance/Accounting Literature Database for the Personal Computer,* we see the numbers of new finance journals increasing, particularly during the 1980s. If the 1980s was the decade of the deal, it was also a period that spawned new financial journals.

The Brealey and Edwards [10] bibliography of finance covers 120 periodicals organized by 328 key words and 529 topics. It contains over 12 thousand entries, 56 percent of which appeared in 1980–1989, and 30 percent in 1970–1979, or 86 percent since 1970 and 99.2 percent since 1950. So those who obtained their Ph.D. training before 1970 covered 14 percent of the literature in B&E; those with doctorates before 1950 covered less than 1 percent of the B&E references. Moral: Your Ph.D. enables you to keep up with the literature and to contribute to its further development.

A confident prediction can be set forth based on the data and patterns described above. Recent years have seen the multiplication of new concepts, new propositions, and new ways of looking at financial data and decisions. The analysis, research, and writing stimulated by this intellectual growth have resulted in a proliferation of journals to record the theory, evidence, and practice produced by the burgeoning research activity. The history of thought and ideas teaches us that invention nurtures more invention. Innovation feeds on itself, so we can expect the two horns of plenty depicted in Exhibits 3 and 7 to further extend and widen their boundaries. Thus, it is becoming more difficult to be conversant with all areas of finance and to keep up with even that sample of journals covered in the reference volumes on finance literature.

VIII. Coping with the Knowledge Explosion

From the above review, two related questions naturally arise. One, what will be important in the future? Two, how do we cope with such an explosion of concepts and literature? We can best answer the two questions together. Clearly, some core ideas and methodologies will have become and will continue to be essential in the toolbox of the financial economist and financial manager. These include the following:

- Utility and behavioral theory—how individuals make decisions and choices and react to risk

- Elements of game theory—for understanding decisions and choices; competitive behavior

- Basic concepts of microeconomics—demand-supply elasticity equilibrium; behavior and reactions of rivals

- Basic concepts of macroeconomics—the nature of the unstable environment in which financial decisions are made

- Option pricing models—the key to understanding synthetic securities and risk management

- Event analysis techniques—to analyze the market's initial assessment of the value impacts of change

- Performance measurement—to measure longer-run effects of decisions and actions

- The microstructure of security prices—to understand price formation and security price dynamics

- Factor models—both single and multiple, to analyze broad influences on asset returns

Exhibit 7   The Flowering of Finance Journals

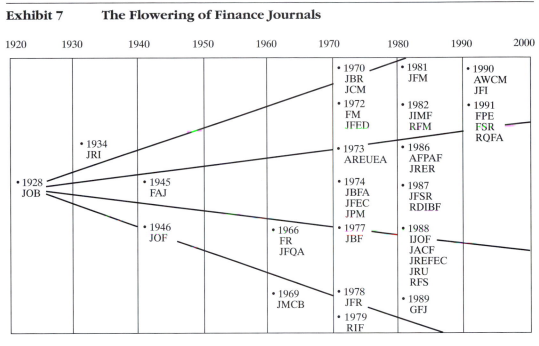

| 1920 | 1930 | 1940 | 1950 | 1960 | 1970 | 1980 | 1990 | 2000 |

- 1970
  JBR
  JCM
- 1972
  FM
  JFED
- 1973
  AREUEA
- 1974
  JBFA
  JFEC
  JPM
- 1977
  JBF
- 1978
  JFR
- 1979
  RIF

- 1981
  JFM
- 1982
  JIMF
  RFM
- 1986
  AFPAF
  JRER
- 1987
  JFSR
  RDIBF
- 1988
  IJOF
  JACF
  JREFEC
  JRU
  RFS
- 1989
  GFJ

- 1990
  AWCM
  JFI
- 1991
  FPE
  FSR
  RQFA

- 1934
  JRI
- 1928
  JOB
- 1945
  FAJ
- 1946
  JOF
- 1966
  FR
  JFQA
- 1969
  JMCB

Explanation of Abbreviations

AFPAF—Advances in Financial Planning and Forecasting
AWCM—Advances in Working Capital Management
FAJ—Financial Analysts Journal
FM—Financial Management
FPE—Financial Practice and Education
FR—Financial Review
FSR—Financial Services Review
GFJ—Global Finance Journal
IJOF—International Journal of Finance
AREUEA—Journal of the American Real Estate & Urban
         Economics Association
JACF—Journal of Applied Corporate Finance
JBR—Journal of Bank Research
JBF—Journal of Banking and Finance
JOB—Journal of Business
JBFA—Journal of Business Finance and Accounting
JCM—Journal of Cash Management
JOF—Journal of Finance
JFQA—Journal of Financial and Quantitative Analysis

JFEC—Journal of Financial Economics
JFED—Journal of Financial Education
JFI—Journal of Financial Intermediation
JFR—Journal of Financial Research
JFSR—Journal of Financial Services Research
JFM—Journal of Futures Markets
JIMF—Journal of International Money and Finance
JMCB—Journal of Money, Credit and Banking
JPM—Journal of Portfolio Management
JREFEC—Journal of Real Estate Finance and Economics
JRER—Journal of Real Estate Research
JRI—Journal of Risk and Insurance
JRU—Journal of Risk and Uncertainty
RDIBF—Recent Developments in International Banking
         and Finance
RIF—Research in Finance
RFS—Review of Financial Studies
RFM—Review of Futures Markets
RQFA—Review of Quantitative Finance and Accounting

- International parity conditions—global markets require an understanding of the international dimensions of asset pricing and returns

These are core conceptual areas. They are applicable to a wide range of issues and problems. They are also effectively employed on a narrow range of issues as well. But most important, they are not to be used in isolation. They must be integrated with the planning and operating activities of the firm as a whole. They are not ends in themselves but contributors to the growth and performance of the firm as a whole. They must interact effectively with the other decision processes in the firm.

The quantitative techniques to understand and employ the core ideas can vary. In this day, calculus is a minimum. Matrix algebra and facility with the calculus of variations including stochastic calculus provide access to important literature.

Knowledge of econometrics is another essential tool. We must not only learn it, but also use it to understand its powers and limitations. This is true for MBAs and practicing managers, as well as their mentors.

The most important managerial attributes are energy, drive, interpersonal skills, experience, and, above all, good judgment. The foregoing presentation has been slanted toward the values of formal analysis, but, while quantitative techniques perform an essential function, not everyone can be or need be a quantitative whiz. The art of case studies is increasingly converging to rigorous testing of propositions, in addition to illuminating the results of more formal quantitative methodologies (see, for example, Baker [4]; Ruback [96, 97]).

Since innovation builds on the reservoir of concepts and tools, we can expect the explosion of literature and knowledge to continue. Although competence in key techniques and methodologies can be applied to a wide array of issues and problems, we are likely to see selectivity and specialization of research, teaching, and practicing scope. We get good at what we spend most of our time doing. So in addressing the challenges of the future, we can be what we want to be by relating our studies and activities to our interests, aptitudes, and aspirations.

References

1. Michael Adler and Bernard Dumas. "International Portfolio Choice and Corporation Finance: A Synthesis." *Journal of Finance* 38 (June 1983), pp. 925–984.
2. Edward I. Altman. "Financial Ratios, Discriminant Analysis and the Prediction of Corporate Bankruptcy." *Journal of Finance* 23 (September 1968), pp. 589–609.
3. ____. *Corporate Financial Distress and Bankruptcy: A Complete Guide to Predicting & Avoiding Distress and Profiting from Bankruptcy.* New York, John Wiley, 1993.
4. George P. Baker. "Beatrice: A Study in the Creation and Destruction of Value." *Journal of Finance* 47 (July 1992), pp. 1081–1119.
5. William J. Baumol. "The Transactions Demand for Cash: An Inventory Theoretic Approach." *Quarterly Journal of Economics* 66 (November 1952), pp. 545–556.
6. Fischer Black. "Capital Market Equilibrium with Restricted Borrowing." *Journal of Business* (July 1972), pp. 444–455.
7. ____ and Myron Scholes. "The Pricing of Options and Corporate Liabilities." *Journal of Political Economy* 81 (May-June 1973), pp. 637–659.
8. Dorothy H. Bower, Richard S. Bower, and Dennis E. Logue. "Arbitrage Pricing Theory and Utility Stock Returns." *Journal of Finance* 39 (September 1984), pp. 1041–1054.
9. Ben Branch and Hugh Ray. *Bankruptcy Investing: How to Profit from Distressed Companies.* Dearborn, IL, Financial Publishing, 1992.
10. Richard Brealey and Helen Edwards. *A Bibliography of Finance.* Cambridge, MA, MIT Press, 1991.
11. Michael J. Brennan and Eduardo S. Schwartz. "Finite Difference Methods and Jump Processes Arising in the Pricing of Contingent Claims: A Synthesis." *Journal of Financial and Quantitative Analysis* 13 (September 1978), pp. 461–474.
12. ____. "Evaluating Natural Resource Investments." *Journal of Business* (April 1985), pp. 135–157.

13. S. Brown and J. Warner. "Measuring Security Price Performance." *Journal of Financial Economics* 8 (1980), pp. 205–258.

14. M. D. Carpenter and J. E. Miller. "A Reliable Framework for Monitoring Accounts Receivable." *Financial Management* (Winter 1979), pp. 37–40.

15. Nai-fu Chen, Richard Roll, and Stephen A. Ross. "Economic Forces and the Stock Market." *Journal of Business* 56 (1986), pp. 383–403.

16. K. S. Chung and J. Fred Weston. "Diversification and Mergers in a Strategic Long-Range-Planning Framework." Chapter 13 in *Mergers and Acquisitions,* M. Keenan and L. J. White, eds. Lexington, MA, D. C. Heath, 1982, pp. 315–347.

17. Thomas E. Copeland and J. Fred Weston. *Financial Theory and Corporate Policy,* 3rd ed. Reading, MA, Addison-Wesley, 1988.

18. John C. Cox and Mark Rubinstein. *Options Markets.* Englewood Cliffs, NJ, Prentice-Hall, 1985.

19. John C. Cox, Stephen A. Ross, and Mark Rubinstein. "Option Pricing: A Simplified Approach." *Journal of Financial Economics* 7 (September 1979), pp. 229–263.

20. Aswath Damodaran and Marti G. Subrahmanyam. "The Effects of Derivative Securities on the Markets for the Underlying Assets in the United States: A Survey." In New York University Salomon Center, *Financial Markets, Institutions & Instruments* 1, 1992, pp. 1–22.

21. J. Dean. *Managerial Economics.* Englewood Cliffs, NJ, Prentice-Hall, 1951.

22. ____. *Capital Budgeting: Top-Management Policy on Plant, Equipment, and Product Development.* New York, Columbia University Press, 1951.

23. H. C. DeAngelo. "Competition and Unanimity." *American Economic Review* (March 1981), pp. 18–28.

24. Arthur S. Dewing. *Corporate Promotions and Reorganizations.* Cambridge, MA, Harvard University Press, 1914.

25. ____. *The Financial Policy of Corporations,* New York, Ronald Press, 1920.

26. Gordon Donaldson. *Managing Corporate Wealth: The Operation of a Comprehensive Financial Goals System.* Praeger Special Studies, 1984.

27. David Durand. *Conference on Research and Business Finance.* New York, National Bureau of Economic Research, 1952.

28. Douglas R. Emery and John D. Finnerty. "A Review of Recent Research Concerning Corporate Debt Provisions." In New York University Salomon Center, *Financial Markets, Institutions & Instruments* 1 (1992), pp. 23–39.

29. Eugene F. Fama. "Efficient Capital Markets: A Review of Theory and Empirical Work." *Journal of Finance* 25 (1970), pp. 383–417.

30. "Efficient Capital Markets: II." *Journal of Finance* 46 (December 1991), pp. 1575–1617.

31. ____ and Kenneth R. French. "The Cross-Section of Expected Stock Returns." *Journal of Finance* 47 (June 1992), pp. 427–465.

32. Eugene F. Fama, Lawrence Fisher, Michael C. Jensen, and Richard Roll. "The Adjustment of Stock Prices to New Information." *International Economic Review* 10 (1969), pp. 1–21.

33. John D. Finnerty. "Financial Engineering in Corporate Finance: An Overview." *Financial Management* (Winter 1988), pp. 14–33.

34. Irving Fisher. *The Theory of Interest.* New York, Macmillan, 1930.

35. M. J. Fishman. "A Theory of Preemptive Takeover Bidding." *RAND Journal of Economics* 19 (Spring 1988), pp. 88–101.

36. Benjamin M. Friedman, ed. *The Changing Roles of Debt and Equity in Financing U.S. Capital Formation.* Chicago, University of Chicago Press, 1982.

37. Patrick A. Gaughan. *Mergers & Acquisitions.* New York, HarperCollins, 1991.

38. James A. Gentry. "State of the Art of Short-Run Financial Management." *Financial Management* 17 (Summer 1990), pp. 41–57.

39. Robert Gertner and David Scharfstein. "A Theory of Workouts and the Effects of Reorganization Law." *Journal of Finance* 46 (September 1991), pp. 1189–1222.

40. Myron J. Gordon. *The Investment, Financing and Valuation of the Corporation.* Homewood, IL, Irwin, 1962.

41. _____ and E. Shapiro. "Capital Equipment Analysis: The Required Rate of Profit." *Management Science* 3 (October 1956), pp. 102–110.

42. Benjamin Graham and David L. Dodd. *Security Analysis.* New York, McGraw-Hill, 1934.

43. S. J. Grossman and O. D. Hart. "Takeover Bids, the Free-Rider Problem, and the Theory of the Corporation." *The Bell Journal of Economics* 11 (Spring 1980), pp. 42–64.

44. Ned C. Hill and William L. Sartoris. *Short-Term Financial Management.* New York, Macmillan, 1988, 1993.

45. David Hirshleifer. "Takeovers." In *The New Palgrave Dictionary of Money & Finance,* Peter Newman, Murray Milgate, and John Eatwell, eds. New York, Stockton Press, 1992a, pp. 638–645.

46. _____. "Mergers and Acquisitions: Strategic and Informational Issues." ms., September 4, 1992b, forthcoming in the *North-Holland Finance Handbook.*

47. _____ and I. P. Png. "Facilitation of Competing Bids and the Price of a Takeover Target." *The Review of Financial Studies* 2 (1989), pp. 587–606.

48. _____ and S. Titman. "Share Tendering Strategies and the Success of Hostile Takeover Bids." *Journal of Political Economy* 98 (1990), pp. 295–324.

49. J. Hirshleifer. *Investment, Interest, and Capital.* Englewood Cliffs, NJ, Prentice-Hall, 1970.

50. Stewart D. Hodges, Michael J. P. Selby, Les J. Clewlow, Chris R. Strickland, and Xinzhong G. Xu. "Recent Developments in Derivative Securities: 20 Years on from Black and Scholes." In New York University Salomon Center, *Financial Markets, Institutions & Instruments* 1, 1992, pp. 41–61.

51. B. Holmstrom and B. Nalebuff. "To the Raider Goes the Surplus?: A Reexamination of the Free-Raider Problem." *Journal of Economics & Management Strategy* 1 (Spring 1992), pp. 37–62.

52. Neil H. Jacoby and Raymond J. Saulnier. *Business Finance and Banking.* New York, National Bureau of Economic Research, 1947.

53. G. A. Jarrell, J. A. Brickley, and J. M. Netter. "The Market for Corporate Control: The Empirical Evidence Since 1980." *Journal of Economic Perspectives* 2 (Winter 1988), pp. 49–68.

54. M. C. Jensen, ed. "Symposium on the Market for Corporate Control: The Scientific Evidence." *Journal of Financial Economics* 11 (April 1983).

55. _____. "Agency Costs of Free Cash Flow, Corporate Finance and Takeovers." *American Economic Review* (May 1986), pp. 323–329.

56. _____. "The Takeover Controversy: Analysis and Evidence." Chapter 20 in *Knights, Raiders, and Targets,* J. C. Coffee, Jr., L. Lowenstein, and S. Rose-Ackerman, eds. New York, Oxford University Press, 1988a.

57. _____. "Takeovers: Their Cause and Consequences." *Journal of Economic Perspectives* 2 (Winter 1988b), pp. 21–48.

58. _____. "Market for Corporate Control." In *The New Palgrave Dictionary of Money & Finance,* Peter Newman, Murray Milgate, and John Eatwell, eds. New York, Stockton Press, 1992, pp. 657–666.

59. _____ and W. Meckling. "Theory of the Firm: Managerial Behavior, Agency Costs and Ownership Structure." *Journal of Financial Economics* (October 1976), pp. 305–360.

60. _____ and R. S. Ruback. "The Market for Corporate Control: The Scientific Evidence." *Journal of Financial Economics* 11 (April 1983), pp. 5–50.

61. _____, eds. "Symposium on the Structure and Governance of Enterprise," *Journal of Financial Economics* 27, Part I (September 1990); Part II (October 1990).

62. Kose John and Teresa A. John. "Coping with Financial Distress: A Survey of Recent Literature in Corporate Finance." In New York University Salomon Center, *Financial Markets, Institutions & Instruments* 1, 1992, pp. 63–78.

63. Y. H. Kim and J. C. Atkins. "Evaluating Investments in Accounts Receivable: A Wealth Maximization Framework," *Journal of Finance* (May 1978), pp. 403–412.

64. Yong H. Kim and Venkat Srinivasan, eds. *Advances in Working Capital Management.* Greenwich, CT, JAI Press, Vol. 1, 1988.

65. _____, eds. *Advances in Working Capital Management.* Greenwich, CT, JAI Press, Vol. 2, 1991.

66. A. S. Kyle. "Continuous Auctions and Insider Trading." *Econometrica* 53 (November 1985), pp. 1315–1336.

67. Maurice Levi. *International Finance: Financial Management and the International Economy.* New York, McGraw-Hill, 1983.

68. John Lintner. "Distribution of Incomes of Corporations Among Dividends, Retained Earnings, and Taxes." *American Economic Review* 46 (May 1956), pp. 97–113.

69. _____. "The Valuation of Risk Assets and the Selection of Risky Investments in Stock Portfolios and Capital Budgets." *Review of Economics and Statistics* 47 (1965), pp. 13–37.

70. R. Duncan Luce and Howard Raiffa. *Games and Decisions.* New York, Dover, 1957.

71. H. M. Markowitz. "Portfolio Selection." *Journal of Finance* 7 (March 1952), pp. 77–91.

72. _____. *Portfolio Selection: Efficient Diversification of Investments.* New York, Wiley, 1959.

73. D. Mayers. "Non-Marketable Assets and the Capital Market Equilibrium Under Uncertainty." In Jensen, ed., *Studies in the Theory of Capital Markets.* New York, Praeger, 1972, pp. 223–248.

74. Robert C. Merton. "An Analytic Derivation of the Efficient Portfolio Frontier." *Journal of Financial and Quantitative Analysis* (September 1972), pp. 1851–1872.

75. _____. "Theory of Rational Option Pricing." *Bell Journal of Economics and Management Science* 4 (Spring 1973a), pp. 141–183.

76. _____. "An Intertemporal Capital Asset Pricing Model." *Econometrica* (September 1973b), pp. 867–888.

77. Shehzad L. Mian and Clifford W. Smith, Jr. "Accounts Receivable Management Policy: Theory and Evidence." *Journal of Finance* 47 (March 1992), pp. 169–200.

78. Merton H. Miller. "Debt and Taxes." *Journal of Finance* 32 (May 1977), pp. 261–275.

79. _____ and F. Modigliani. "Dividend Policy, Growth, and the Valuation of Shares." *Journal of Business* (October 1961), pp. 411–433.

80. Merton H. Miller and Daniel Orr. "A Model of the Demand for Money by Firms." *Quarterly Journal of Economics* 80 (August 1966), pp. 413–435.

81. F. Modigliani and M. Miller. "The Cost of Capital, Corporation Finance and the Theory of Investment." *American Economic Review* (June 1958), pp. 261–297.

82. Stewart C. Myers. "Determinants of Corporate Borrowing." *Journal of Financial Economics* 5 (November 1977), pp. 147–175.

83. _____. "Finance Theory and Financial Strategy." *Interfaces* 14 (January-February 1984a), pp. 126–137.

84. _____. "The Capital Structure Puzzle." *Journal of Finance* 39 (July 1984b), pp. 575–592.

85. _____ and Nicholas S. Majluf. "Corporate Financing and Investment Decisions When Firms Have Information That Investors Do Not Have." *Journal of Financial Economics* 13 (1984), pp. 187–221.

86. Michael Porter. *Competitive Strategy.* New York, Free Press, 1980.

87. _____. *Competitive Advantage.* New York, Free Press, 1985.

88. A. Rappaport. *Creating Shareholder Value.* New York, Free Press, 1986.

89. Eric Rasmusen. *Games and Information: An Introduction to Game Theory.* Oxford, UK, Basil Blackwell, 1989.

90. _____. "Game Theory and Finance." In Peter Newman, Murray Milgate, and John Eatwell, eds. *The New Palgrave Dictionary of Money & Finance.* New York, Stockton Press, 1992, pp. 217–219.

91. Richard J. Rendleman, Jr., and Brit J. Bartter. "Two-State Options Pricing." *Journal of Finance* 34 (December 1979), pp. 1093–1110.

92. Richard Roll. "A Critique of the Asset Pricing Theory's Tests Part I: On Past and Potential Testability of the Theory." *Journal of Financial Economics* 4 (1977), pp. 129–176.

93. ____ and Stephen A. Ross. "An Empirical Investigation of the Arbitrage Pricing Theory." *Journal of Finance* 35 (1980), pp. 1073–1103.

94. ____. "On the Cross-Sectional Relation Between Expected Returns and Betas." Unpublished manuscript (July 8, 1992).

95. Stephen A. Ross. "The Arbitrage Theory of Capital Asset Pricing." *Journal of Economic Theory* 13 (1976), pp. 341–360.

96. Richard S. Ruback. "The Conoco Takeover and Stockholder Returns." *Sloan Management Review* 23 (Winter 1982), pp. 13–33.

97. ____. "The Cities Service Takeover: A Case Study." *Journal of Finance* 38 (May 1983), pp. 319–330.

98. Mark Rubinstein. "The Valuation of Uncertain Income Streams and the Pricing of Options." *Bell Journal of Economics* 7 (Autumn 1976), pp. 407–425.

99. ____ and Hayne E. Leland. "Replicating Options with Positions in Stock and Cash." *Financial Analysts Journal* 37 (July-August 1981), pp. 63–72.

100. W. L. Sartoris and N. C. Hill. "Evaluating Credit Policy Alternatives: A Present Value Framework." *Journal of Financial Research* (Spring 1981), pp. 81–89.

101. ____. "A Generalized Cash Flow Approach to Short-Term Financial Decisions," *Journal of Finance* 38 (1983), pp. 349–360.

102. Jay Shanken. "The Arbitrage Pricing Theory: Is It Testable." *Journal of Finance* 37 (1982), pp. 1129–1140.

103. ____ and M. I. Weinstein. "Macroeconomics Variables and Asset Pricing: Estimation and Tests." Unpublished manuscript (1990).

104. William F. Sharpe. "Capital Asset Prices: A Theory of Market Equilibrium Under Conditions of Risk." *Journal of Finance* 19 (1964), pp. 425–442.

105. ____. *Investments.* Englewood Cliffs, NJ, Prentice-Hall, 1978.

106. A. Scleifer, and R. W. Vishny. "Large Shareholders and Corporate Control." *Journal of Political Economy* 94 (1986), pp. 461–488.

107. Clifford W. Smith, Jr., and Charles W. Smithson. *The Handbook of Financial Engineering: New Financial Product Innovations, Applications, and Analyses.* New York, Harper Business, 1990.

108. ____ and D. Sykes Wilford. *Managing Financial Risk.* New York, Harper, 1990.

109. Clifford W. Smith Jr., and J. B. Warner. "On Financial Contracting: An Analysis of Bond Covenants." *Journal of Financial Economics* 7 (1979), pp. 117–161.

110. J. K. Smith. "Trade Credit and Informational Asymmetry." *Journal of Finance* (September 1987), pp. 863–872.

111. K. V. Smith. "State of the Art of Working Capital Management." *Financial Management* (Autumn 1973), pp. 50–55.

112. ____. "On Working Capital as an Investment by the Firm." In *Readings on the Management of Working Capital,* K. V. Smith, ed. St. Paul, MN, West Publishing Company, 1980, pp. 609–624.

113. B. H. Solnik. "An Equilibrium Model of the International Capital Market." *Journal of Economic Theory* 8 (August 1974), pp. 500–524.

114. ____. *International Investments.* 2nd ed., Reading, MA, Addison-Wesley, 1991.

115. V. Srinivasan and Y. H. Kim. "Deterministic Cash Flow Management: State of the Art and Research Direction." *Omega* (1986a), pp. 145–166.

116. ____. "Decision Support for Integrated Cash Management." *Decision Support Systems* (December 1986b), pp. 347–363.

117. B. K. Stone. "The Use of Forecasts and Smoothing in Control Limit Models for Cash Management." *Financial Management* (Spring 1972), pp. 72–84.

118. ____. "Cash Planning and Credit Line Determination with a Financial Statement Simulator: A Cash Report on Short-Term Financial Planning." *Journal of Financial and Quantitative Analysis* (December 1973), pp. 711–729.

119. ____. "Allocating Credit Lines, Planned Borrowing and Tangible Services Over a Company's Banking System." *Financial Management* (Summer 1974), pp. 65–78.

120. ____. "The Payments–Pattern Approach of the Forecasting and Control of Accounts Receivable." *Financial Management* (Autumn 1976), pp. 65–82.

121. ____. "Design of a Receivable Collection System." *Management Science* (August 1981), pp. 876–880.

122. ____. "The Design of a Company's Banking System." *Journal of Finance* (May 1983), pp. 373–385.

123. ____ and N. C. Hill. "Cash Transfer Scheduling for Efficient Cash Concentration." *Financial Management* (Autumn 1980), pp. 35–43.

124. ____ and T. Miller. "Daily Cash Forecasting: A Structuring Framework." *Journal of Cash Management* (October 1981), pp. 35–50.

125. Anjan V. Thakor. "Game Theory in Finance." *Financial Management* 20 (Spring 1991), pp. 71–94.

126. S. Titman. "The Effect of Capital Structure on a Firm's Liquidation Decision." *Journal of Financial Economics* (March 1984), pp. 137–151.

127. William Vickrey. "Counterspeculation, Auctions, and Competitive Sealed Tenders." *Journal of Finance* 16 (March 1961), pp. 8–37.

128. J. B. Warner. "Bankruptcy Costs: Some Evidence." *Journal of Finance* 32 (May 1977), pp. 337–347.

129. J. Fred Weston, *The Role of Mergers in the Growth of Large Firms.* Berkeley, CA, University of California Press, 1953.

130. ____. "Finance Function." *Journal of Finance* 9 (September 1954), pp. 265–282.

131. ____. "What MM Have Wrought." *Financial Management* (Summer 1989), pp. 29–38.

132. ____. "Some Financial Perspectives on Comparative Costs of Capital." *Business Economics* 26 (April 1991), pp. 33–37.

133. ____ and K. S. Chung. "Some Aspects of Merger Theory." *Midwest Finance Journal* 12 (1983), 1–38.

134. ____ and Susan E. Hoag. *Mergers, Restructuring, and Corporate Control.* Englewood Cliffs, NJ, Prentice Hall, 1990.

135. ____ and Thomas E. Copeland. *Managerial Finance,* 9th ed., Ft. Worth, TX, Dryden, 1992.

136. ____ and Surendra K. Mansinghka. "Tests of the Efficiency of Conglomerate Firms." *Journal of Finance* 26 (September 1971), pp. 919–936.

137. J. Fred Weston, Keith V. Smith, and Ronald E. Shrieves. "Conglomerate Performance Using the Capital Asset Pricing Model." *Review of Economics and Statistics* 54 (November 1972), pp. 357–363.

138. J. B. Williams. *The Theory of Investment Value.* Harvard University Press, 1938.

139. Karen Hopper Wruck. "Financial Distress, Reorganization, and Organizational Efficiency." *Journal of Financial Economics* 27 (1990), pp. 419–444.

Discussion Questions

1. Describe the "Fisher separation" as it applies to capital budgeting.

2. What are the implications of the efficient markets hypothesis?

3. Explain why portfolio diversification can be expected to eliminate nonsystematic risk.

4. Discuss the premise that investors will always receive higher expected returns the higher the risk.

5. What is a derivative security?

6. For what are Modigliani and Miller (M&M) most famous in the financial management literature?

hypothesis about, investment behavior. We illustrate geometrically relations between beliefs and choice of portfolio according to the "expected returns—variance of returns" rule.

One type of rule concerning choice of portfolio is that the investor does (or should) maximize the discounted (or capitalized) value of future returns.[1] Since the future is not known with certainty, it must be "expected" or "anticipated" returns that we discount. Variations of this type of rule can be suggested. Following Hicks, we could let "anticipated" returns include an allowance for risk.[2] Or we could let the rate at which we capitalize the returns from particular securities vary with risk.

The hypothesis (or maxim) that the investor does (or should) maximize discounted return must be rejected. If we ignore market imperfections, the foregoing rule never implies that there is a diversified portfolio that is preferable to all nondiversified portfolios. Diversification is both observed and sensible; a rule of behavior that does not imply the superiority of diversification must be rejected both as a hypothesis and as a maxim.

The foregoing rule fails to imply diversification no matter how the anticipated returns are formed, whether the same or different discount rates are used for different securities, no matter how these discount rates are decided upon or how they vary over time.[3] The hypothesis implies that the investor places all his funds in the security with the greatest discounted value. If two or more securities have the same value, then any of these or any combination of these is as good as any other.

We can see this analytically: Suppose there are N securities; let r_{it} be the anticipated return (however decided upon) at time t per dollar invested in security i; let d_{it} be the rate at which the return on the ith security at time t is discounted back to the present; let X_i be the relative amount invested in security i. We exclude short sales; thus $X_i \geq 0$ for all i. Then the discounted anticipated return of the portfolio is

$$R = \sum_{t=1}^{\infty} \sum_{i=1}^{N} d_{it} r_{it} X_i$$

$$= \sum_{i=1}^{N} X_i \left(\sum_{t=1}^{\infty} d_{it} r_{it} \right)$$

$R_i = \sum_{t=1}^{\infty} d_{it} r_{it}$ is the discounted return of the ith security; therefore,

$R = \Sigma X_i R_i$ where R_i is independent of X_i. Since $X_i \geq 0$ for all i and $\Sigma X_i = 1$, R is a weighted average of R_i with the X_i as non-negative weights. To maximize R, we let $X_i = 1$ for i with maximum R_i. If several Ra_a, $a = 1, \ldots, K$ are maximum, then any allocation with

$$\sum_{a=1}^{K} Xa_a = 1$$

maximizes R. In no case is a diversified portfolio preferred to all nondiversified portfolios.[4]

[1] See, for example, J. B. Williams, *The Theory of Investment Value* (Cambridge, Mass.: Harvard University Press, 1938), pp. 55–75.

[2] J. R. Hicks, *Value and Capital* (New York: Oxford University Press, 1939), p. 126. Hicks applies the rule to a firm rather than to a portfolio.

[3] The results depend on the assumption that the anticipated returns and discount rates are independent of the particular investor's portfolio.

[4] If short sales were allowed, an infinite amount of money would be placed in the security with highest r.

It will be convenient at this point to consider a static model. Instead of speaking of the time series of returns from the ith security ($r_{i1}, r_{i2}, \ldots, r_{it}, \ldots$), we will speak of "the flow of returns" (r_i) from the ith security. The flow of returns from the portfolio as a whole is $R = \Sigma X_i r_i$. As in the dynamic case, if the investor wished to maximize "anticipated" return from the portfolio, he would place all his funds in that security with maximum anticipated returns.

There is a rule which implies both that the investor should diversify and that he should maximize expected return. The rule states that the investor does (or should) diversify his funds among all those securities which give maximum expected return. The law of large numbers will ensure that the actual yield of the portfolio will be almost the same as the expected yield.[5] This rule is a special case of the expected returns-variance of returns rule (to be presented below). It assumes that there is a portfolio that gives both maximum expected return and minimum variance, and it commends this portfolio to the investor.

This presumption, that the law of large numbers applies to a portfolio of securities, cannot be accepted. The returns from securities are too intercorrelated. Diversification cannot eliminate all variance.

The portfolio with the maximum expected return is not necessarily the one with minimum variance. There is a rate at which the investor can gain expected return by taking on variance, or reduce variance by giving up expected return.

We saw that the expected returns or anticipated returns rule is inadequate. Let us now consider the expected returns-variance of returns (E-V) rule. It will be necessary to first present a few elementary concepts and results of mathematical statistics. We will then show some implications of the E-V rule. After this we will discuss its plausibility.

In our presentation we try to avoid complicated mathematical statements and proofs. As a consequence, a price is paid in terms of rigor and generality. The chief limitations from this source are (1) we do not derive our results analytically for the n-security case; instead, we present them geometrically for the 3 and 4 security cases; (2) we assume *static* probability beliefs. In a general presentation we must recognize that the probability distribution of yields of the various securities is a function of time. The writer intends to present, in the future, the general, mathematical treatment that removes these limitations.

We will need the following elementary concepts and results of mathematical statistics:

Let Y be a random variable, i.e., a variable whose value is decided by chance. Suppose, for simplicity of exposition, that Y can take on a finite number of values $y_1, y_2, \ldots, y_N$. Let the probability that $Y = y_1$ be p_1; that $Y = y_2$ be p_2, etc. The expected value (or mean) of Y is defined to be

$$E = p_1 y_1 + p_2 y_2 + \ldots p_N y_N.$$

The variance of Y is defined to be

$$V = p_1(y_1 - E)^2 + p_2(y_2 - E)^2 + \ldots p_N(y_N - E)^2.$$

V is the average squared deviation of Y from its expected value. V is a commonly used measure of dispersion. Other measures of dispersion, closely related to V, are the standard deviation, $\sigma = \sqrt{V}$ and the coefficient of variation, σ/E.

Suppose we have a number of random variables: $R_1, \ldots, R_n$. If R is a weighted sum (linear combination) of the R_i

[5] Williams, *op. cit.*, pp. 68, 69.

$$R = a_1R_1 + a_2R_2 + \ldots + a_nR_n,$$

then R is also a random variable. (For example, R_1 may be the number which turns up on one die, R_2 that of another die, and R the sum of these numbers. In this case $n = 2$, $a_1 = a_2 = 1$.)

It will be important for us to know how the expected value and variance of the weighted sum (R) are related to the probability distribution of the $R_1, \ldots, R_n$. We state these relations below; we refer the reader to any standard text for proof.[6]

The expected value of a weighted sum is the weighted sum of the expected values—i.e., $E(R) = a_1E(R_1) + a_2E(R_2) + \ldots + a_nE(R_n)$. The variance of a weighted sum is not as simple. To express it we must define *covariance*. The covariance of R_1 and R_2 is

$$\sigma_{12} = E \{ [R_1 - E(R_1)] [R_2 - E(R_2)] \},$$

i.e., the expected value of [(the deviation of R_1 from its mean) times (the deviation of the R_2 from its mean)]. In general we define the covariance between R_i and R_j as

$$\sigma_{ij} = E \{ [R_i - E(R_i)] [R_j - E(R_j)] \}.$$

σ_{ij} may be expressed in terms of the familiar correlation coefficient (ρ_{ij}). The covariance between R_i and R_j is equal to [(their correlation) times (the standard deviation of R_i) times (the standard deviation of R_j)]:

$$\sigma_{ij} = \rho_{ij}\sigma_i\sigma_j.$$

The variance of a weighted sum is

$$V(R) = \sum_{i=1}^{N_i} a^2_i V(X_i) + 2 \sum_{i=1}^{N_i} \sum_{t>1}^{N_i} a_i a_j \sigma_{ij}.$$

If we use the fact that the variance of R_i is σ_{ij}, then

$$V(R) = \sum_{i=1}^{N} \sum_{j=1}^{N} a_i a_j \sigma_{ij}.$$

Let R_i be the return on the ith security. Let μ_i be the expected value of R_i, and let σ_{ij} be the covariance between R_i and R_j (thus σ_{ii} is the variance of R_i). Let X_i be the percentage of the investor's assets that are allocated to the ith security. The yield (R) on the portfolio as a whole is

$$R = \sum_i R_i X_i.$$

The R_i (and consequently R) are considered to be random variables.[7] The X_i are not random variables, but are fixed by the investor. Since the X_i are percentages, we have $\sum X_i = 1$. In our analysis we will exclude negative values of the X_i (i.e., short sales); therefore, $X_i \geq 0$ for all i.

The return (R) on the portfolio as a whole is a weighted sum of random variables (where the investor can choose the weights). From our discussion of such weighted sums we see that the expected return E from the portfolio as a whole is

---

[6] For example, J.V. Uspensky, *Introduction to Mathematical Probability* (New York: McGraw-Hill, 1937), chapter 9, pp. 161–81.

[7] That is, we assume that the investor does (and should) act as if he had probability beliefs concerning these variables. In general, we would expect that the investor could tell us, for any two events (A and B), whether he personally considered A more

(*continued on p. 117*)

Figure 1

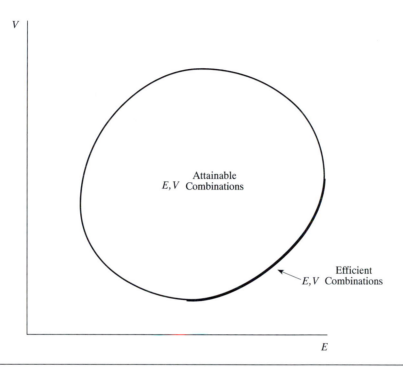

$$E = \sum_{i=1}^{N} X_i \mu_i$$

and the variance is

$$V = \sum_{i=1}^{N} \sum_{j=1}^{N} \sigma_{ij} X_i X_j.$$

For fixed probability beliefs (μ_i, σ_{ij}) the investor has a choice of various combinations of E and V depending on his choice of portfolio $X_1, \ldots, X_N$. Suppose that the set of all obtainable (E,V) combinations were as in Figure 1. The E-V rule states that the investor would (or should) want to select one of those portfolios that give rise to the (E,V) combinations indicated as efficient in the figure—i.e., those with minimum V for given E or more and maximum E for given V or less.

There are techniques by which we can compute the set of efficient portfolios and efficient (E,V) combinations associated with given μ_i and σ_{ij}. We will not present these techniques here. We will,

<hr/>

[7](*continued from p. 116*)

likely than B, B more likely than A, or both equally likely. If the investor were consistent in his opinions on such matters, he would possess a system of probability beliefs. We cannot expect the investor to be consistent in every detail. We can, however, expect his probability beliefs to be roughly consistent on important matters that have been carefully considered. We should also expect that he will base his actions upon these probability beliefs—even though they be in part subjective.

This paper does not consider the difficult question of how investors do (or should) form their probability beliefs.

however, illustrate geometrically the nature of the efficient surfaces for cases in which N (the number of available securities) is small.

The calculation of efficient surfaces might possibly be of practical use. Perhaps there are ways, by combining statistical techniques and the judgment of experts, to form reasonable probability beliefs (μ_i, σ_{ij}). We could use these beliefs to compute the attainable efficient combinations of (E, V). The investor, being informed of what (E, V) combinations were attainable, could state which he desired. We could then find the portfolio that gives this desired combination.

Two conditions—at least—must be satisfied before it would be practical to use efficient surfaces in the manner described above. First, the investor must desire to act according to the E-V maxim. Second, we must be able to arrive at reasonable μ_i and σ_{ij}. We will return to these matters later.

Let us consider the case of three securities. In the three security case our model reduces to

1) $E = \sum_{i=1}^{3} X_i \mu_i$

2) $V = \sum_{i=1}^{3} \sum_{j=1}^{3} X_i X_j \sigma_{ij}$

3) $\sum_{i=1}^{3} X_i = 1$

4) $X_i \geq 0$ for $i = 1, 2, 3$.

From (3) we get

3') $X_3 = 1 - X_1 - X_2$.

If we substitute (3') in equation (1) and (2), we get E and V as functions of X_1 and X_2. For example, we find

1') $E = \mu_3 + X_1(\mu_1 - \mu_3) + X_2(\mu_2 - \mu_3)$.

The exact formulas are not too important here (that of V is given below).[8] We can simply write

a) $E = E(X_1, X_2)$

b) $V = V(X_1, X_2)$

c) $X_1 \geq 0, X_2 \geq 0, 1 - X_1 - X_2 \geq 0$

By using relations (a), (b), (c), we can work with two-dimensional geometry.

The attainable set of portfolios consists of all portfolios that satisfy constraints (c) and (3') (or equivalently [3] and [4]). The attainable combinations of X_1, X_2 are represented by the triangle abc in Figure 2. Any point to the left of the X_2 axis is not attainable because it violates the condition that $X_1 \geq 0$. Any point below the X_1 axis is not attainable because it violates the condition that $X_2 \geq 0$. Any point above the line $(1 - X_1 - X_2 = 0)$ is not attainable because it violates the condition that $X_3 = 1 - X_1 - X_2 \geq 0$.

We define an *isomean* curve to be the set of all points (portfolios) with a given expected return. Similarly, an *isovariance* line is defined to be the set of all points (portfolios) with a given variance of return.

---

[8] $V = X_1^2(\sigma_{11} - 2\sigma_{13} + \sigma_{33}) + X_2^2(\sigma_{22} - 2\sigma_{23} + \sigma_{33}) + 2X_1 X_2(\sigma_{12} - \sigma_{13} - \sigma_{23} + \sigma_{33}) + 2X_1(\sigma_{13} - \sigma_{33}) + 2X_2(\sigma_{22} - \sigma_{33}) + \sigma_{22}$

Figure 2

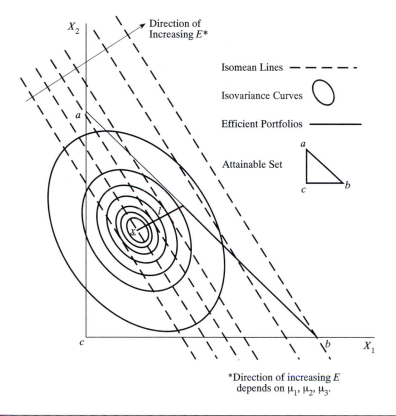

*Direction of increasing E
depends on μ_1, μ_2, μ_3.

An examination of the formulae for E and V tells us the shapes of the isomean and isovariance curves. Specifically, they tell us that typically[9] the isomean curves are a system of parallel straight lines; the isovariance curves are a system of concentric ellipses (see Figure 2). For example if $\mu_2 \neq \mu_3$, equation 1' can be written in the familiar form $X_2 = a + bX_1$; specifically (1)

$$X_2 = \frac{E - \mu_3}{\mu_2 - \mu_3} - \frac{\mu_1 - \mu_3}{\mu_2 - \mu_3} X_1.$$

Thus the slope of the isomean line associated with $E = E_0$ is $-(\mu_1 - \mu_3)/(\mu_2 - \mu_3)$; its intercept is $(E_0 - \mu_3)/(\mu_2 - \mu_3)$. If we change E, we change the intercept but not the slope of the isomean line. This confirms the contention that the isomean lines form a system of parallel lines.

Similarly, by a somewhat less simple application of analytic geometry, we can confirm the contention that the isovariance lines form a family of concentric ellipses. The "center" of the system is

[9] The isomean "curves" are as described above except when $\mu_1 = \mu_2 = \mu_3$. In the latter case all portfolios have the same expected return and the investor chooses the one with minimum variance. As to the assumptions implicit in our description of the isovariance curves, see footnote 12.

Figure 3

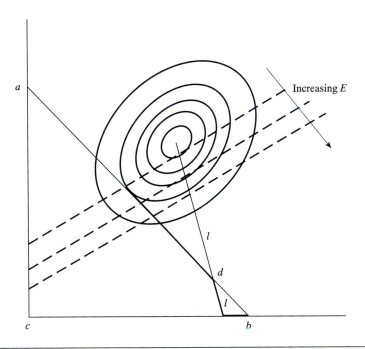

the point that minimizes V. We will label this point X. Its expected return and variance we will label E and V. Variance increases as you move away from X. More precisely, if one isovariance curve, C_1, lies closer to X than another, C_2, then C_1 is associated with a smaller variance than C_2.

With the aid of the foregoing geometric apparatus let us seek the efficient sets. X, the center of the system of isovariance ellipses, may fall either inside or outside the attainable set. Figure 4 illustrates a case in which X falls inside the attainable set. In this case X is efficient. For no other portfolio has a V as low as X; therefore, no portfolio can have either smaller V (with the same or greater E) or greater E with the same or smaller V. No point (portfolio) with expected return E less than E is efficient. For we have $E > E$ and $V < V$.

Consider all points with a given expected return E—i.e., all points on the isomean line associated with E. The point of the isomean line at which V takes on its least value is the point at which the isomean line is tangent to an isovariance curve. We call this point $\hat{X}(E)$. If we let E vary, $\hat{X}(E)$ traces out a curve.

Algebraic considerations (which we omit here) show us that this curve is a straight line. We will call it the critical line l. The critical line passes through X for this point minimizing V for all points with $E(X_1, X_2) = E$. As we go along l in either direction from X, V increases. The segment of the critical line from X to the point where the critical line crosses the boundary of the attainable set is part of the efficient set. The rest of the efficient set is (in the case illustrated) the segment of the ab line from d to b. b is the point of maximum attainable E. In Figure 3, X lies outside the admissible area but the critical line cuts the admissible area. The efficient line begins at the attainable point with minimum variance (in this case on the ab line). It moves toward b until it intersects the critical

Figure 4

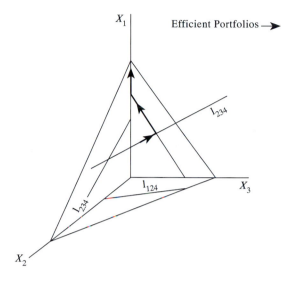

line, moves along the critical line until it intersects a boundary, and finally moves along the boundary to b. The reader may wish to construct and examine the following other cases: (1) X lies outside the attainable set, and the critical line does not cut the attainable set. In this case there is a security that does not enter into any efficient portfolio. (2) Two securities have the same μ_i. In this case the isomean lines are parallel to a boundary line. It may happen that the efficient portfolio with maximum E is a diversified portfolio. (3) A case wherein only one portfolio is efficient.

The efficient set in the 4 security case is, as in the 3 security and also the N security case, a series of connected line segments. At one end of the efficient set is the point of minimum variance; at the other end is a point of maximum expected return[10] (see Figure 4).

Now that we have seen the nature of the set of efficient portfolios, it is not difficult to see the nature of the set of efficient (E,V) combinations. In the 3 security case $E = a_0 + a_1 X_1 + a_2 X_2$ is a plane;

---

[10] Just as we used the equation $\sum_{i=1}^{4} X_i = 1$ to reduce the dimensionality in the 3 security case, we can use it to represent the 4 security case in three-dimensional space. Eliminating X_4, we get $E = E(X_1, X_2, X_3)$, $V = V(X_1, X_2, X_3)$. The attainable set is represented, in three-space, by the tetrahedron with vertices $(0,0,0)$, $(0,0,1)$, $(0,1,0)$, $(1,0,0)$, representing portfolios with, respectively, $X_4 = 1$, $X_3 = 1$, $X_2 = 1$, $X_1 = 1$.

Let s_{123} be the subspace consisting of all points with $X_4 = 0$. Similarly, we can define $s_{a1}, \ldots, a$ to be the subspace consisting of all points with $X_i = 0$, $i \neq a_1, \ldots, a$. For each subspace $s_{a1}, \ldots, a$ we can define a *critical line* $la_1, \ldots, a$. This line is the locus of points P where P minimizes V for all points in $s_{a1}, \ldots, a$ with the same E as P. If a point is in $s_{a1}, \ldots, a$ and is efficient it must be on $la_1, \ldots, a$. The efficient set may be traced out by starting at the point of minimum available variance, moving continuously along various $la_1, \ldots, a$ according to definite rules, and ending in a point that gives maximum E. As in the two-dimensional case, the point with minimum available variance may be in the interior of the available set or on one of its boundaries. Typically, we proceed along a given critical line until either this line intersects one of a larger subspace or meets a boundary (and simultaneously the critical line of a lower-dimensional subspace). In either of these cases the efficient line turns and continues along the new line. The efficient line terminates when a point with maximum E is reached.

Figure 5

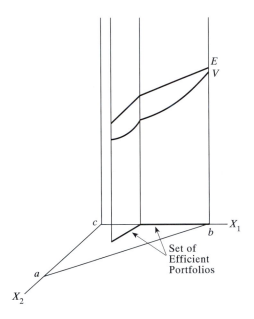

$V = b_0 + b_1X_1 + b_2X_2 + b_{12}X_1X_2 + b_{11}X^2_1 + b_{22}X^2_2$ is a paraboloid.[11] As shown in Figure 5, the section of the E-plane over the efficient portfolio set is a series of connected line segments. The section of the V-paraboloid over the efficient portfolio set is a series of connected parabola segments. If we plotted V against E for efficient portfolios, we would again get a series of connected parabola segments (see Figure 6). This result obtains for any number of securities.

Various reasons recommend the use of the expected return-variance of return rule, both as a hypothesis to explain well-established investment behavior and as a maxim to guide one's own action. The rule serves better, we will see, as an explanation of, and guide to, "investment" as distinguished from "speculative" behavior.

Earlier we rejected the expected returns rule on the grounds that it never implied the superiority of diversification. The expected return-variance of return rule, on the other hand, implies diversification for a wide range of μ_i, σ_{ij}. This does not mean that the E-V rule never implies the superiority of an undiversified portfolio. It is conceivable that one security might have an extremely higher yield and lower variance than all other securities, so much so that one particular undiversified portfolio would give maximum E and minimum V. But for a large, presumably representative range of μ_i, σ_{ij} the E-V rule leads to efficient portfolios, almost all of which are diversified.

Not only does the E-V hypothesis imply diversification, it implies the "right kind" of diversification for the "right reason." The adequacy of diversification is not thought by investors to depend solely on the number of different securities held. A portfolio with sixty different railway securities,

---

[11] See footnote 8.

Figure 6

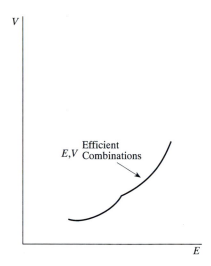

for example, would not be as well diversified as the same size portfolio with some railroad, some public utility, mining, various sort of manufacturing, etc. The reason is that it is generally more likely for firms within the same industry to do poorly at the same time than for firms in dissimilar industries.

Similarly, when trying to make variance small, it is not enough to invest in many securities. It is necessary to avoid investing in securities with high covariances among themselves. We should diversify across industries because firms in different industries, especially industries with different economic characteristics, have lower covariances than firms within an industry.

The concepts "yield" and "risk" appear frequently in financial writings. Usually if the term "yield" were replaced by "expected yield" or "expected return," and "risk" by "variance of return," little change of apparent meaning would result.

Variance is a well-known measure of dispersion about the expected. If instead of variance the investor was concerned with standard error, $\sigma = \sqrt{V}$, or with the coefficient of dispersion, σ/E, his choice would still lie in the set of efficient portfolios.

Suppose an investor diversifies between two portfolios—i.e., if he puts some of his money in one portfolio, the rest of his money in the other. An example of diversifying among portfolios is the buying of the shares of two different investment companies. If the two original portfolios have *equal* variance, then typically[12] the variance of the resulting (compound) portfolio will be less than the variance of either original portfolio. This is illustrated by Figure 7. To interpret Figure 7, we note that a portfolio (P) that is built out of two portfolios $P' = (X'_1, X'_2)$ and $P'' = (X''_1, X''_2)$ is of the form $P = \lambda P' + (1 - \lambda)P'' = (\lambda X' + (1 - \lambda)X''_1, \lambda X'_2 + (1 - \lambda)X''_2)$. P is on the straight line connecting P' and P''.

---

[12] In no case will variance be increased. The only case in which variance will not be decreased is if the returns from both portfolios are perfectly correlated. To draw the isovariance curves as ellipses it is both necessary and sufficient to assume that no two distinct portfolios have perfectly correlated returns.

Figure 7

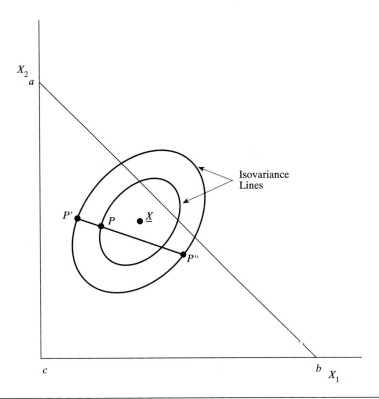

The *E-V* principle is more plausible as a rule for investment behavior as distinguished from speculative behavior. The third moment[13] M_3 of the probability distribution of returns from the portfolio may be connected with a propensity to gamble. For example, if the investor maximizes utility (*U*) which depends on *E* and *V*($U = U(E, V)$, $\partial U/\partial E > 0$, $\partial U/\partial E < 0$), he will never accept an actuarially fair[14] bet. But if $U = U(E, V, M_3)$ and if $\partial U/\partial M_3 \neq 0$, then there are some fair bets that would be accepted.

Perhaps—for a great variety of investing institutions that consider yield to be a good thing; risk, a bid thing; and gambling to be avoided—*E, V* efficiency is reasonable as a working hypothesis and a working maxim.

Two uses of the *E-V* principle suggest themselves. We might use it in theoretical analyses or we might use it in the actual selection of portfolios.

---

[13] If *R* is a random variable that takes on a finite number of values $r_1, \ldots, r_n$ with probabilities $p_1, \ldots, p_n$ respectively, and expected value *E*, then $M_3 = \sum_{i=1}^{n} p_i(r_i - E)^3$.

[14] One in which the amount gained by winning the bet times the probability of winning is equal to the amount lost by losing the bet times the probability of losing.

In theoretical analyses we might inquire, for example, about the various effects of a change in the beliefs generally held about a firm, or a general change in preference as to expected return versus variance of return, or a change in the supply of a security. In our analyses the X_i might represent individual securities, or they might represent aggregates such as bonds, stocks and real estate.[15]

To use the E-V rule in the selection of securities, we must have procedures for finding reasonable μ_i and σ_{ij}. These procedures, I believe, should combine statistical techniques and the judgment of practical men. My feeling is that the statistical computations should be used to arrive at a tentative set of μ_i and σ_{ij}. Judgment should then be used in increasing or decreasing some of these μ_i and σ_{ij} on the basis of factors and nuances not taken into account by the formal computations. Using this revised set of μ_i and σ_{ij}, the set of efficient E, V combinations could be computed, the investor could select the combination he preferred, and the portfolio that gave rise to this E, V combination could be found.

One suggestion as to tentative μ_i, σ_{ij} is to use the observed μ_i, σ_{ij} for some period of the past. I believe that better methods, which take into account more information, can be found. I believe that what is needed is essentially a "probabilistic" reformulation of security analysis. I will not pursue this subject here, for this is "another story." It is a story of which I have read only the first page of the first chapter.

In this paper we have considered the second stage in the process of selecting a portfolio. This stage starts with the relevant beliefs about the securities involved and ends with the selection of a portfolio. We have not considered the first stage: the formation of the relevant beliefs on the basis of observation.

Discussion Questions

1. Explain why Markowitz chose to analyze portfolios instead of single securities.

2. Contrast the calculation for mean returns for the portfolio with the calculation for portfolio variance in returns.

3. Of all the attainable combinations of portfolio expected returns and expected variance in returns, which are the ones you would prefer? Explain.

4. What is the "right kind" of diversification?

5. Comment on the use of variance to measure risk in portfolio return.

6. You have just read an article by Harry Markowitz, whose work ultimately revolutionized portfolio theory. What are the key concepts of this theory?

---

[15] Care must be used in using and interpreting relations among aggregates. We cannot deal here with the problems and pitfalls of aggregation.

*William F. Sharpe**

Capital Asset Prices: A Theory of Market Equilibrium under Conditions of Risk

*The Markowitz model was a huge contribution to theoretical considerations in portfolio manage-
ment, but the input data requirements and the computational complexities limited its use on Wall
Street. Following some contributions by several researchers including James Tobin, Professor
William Sharpe produced his now famous Capital Asset Pricing Model (CAPM) and its also-famous
Beta. Part of Professor Sharpe's contribution was to avoid computational problems of computing
portfolio variances from covariance in returns between each security. He used returns on the market portfolio (the entire stock market) as his sole benchmark, and his Beta coefficient measured how
returns of a given security covaried with market returns. For a portfolio of ten securities, the Sharpe
model would require calculation of 10 Betas as opposed to 100 covariance calculations necessary
for the Markowitz approach. Further, portfolio beta (risk) is the linear-weighted average of betas of
individual stocks, instead of the complex computation required for portfolio variance using covariances of individual stocks. The resulting model developed by Sharpe and others has been called the
Capital Asset Pricing Model (CAPM), and it has had a profound impact on theory and practice in
financial management.*

I. Introduction

One of the problems that has plagued those attempting to predict the behavior of capital markets is
the absence of a body of positive microeconomic theory dealing with conditions of risk. Although
many useful insights can be obtained from the traditional models of investment under conditions of

*A great many people provided comments on early versions of this paper that led to major improvements in the exposition.
In addition to the referees, who were most helpful, the author wishes to express his appreciation to Dr. Harry Markowitz of
the Rand Corporation, Professor Jack Hirshleifer of the University of California at Los Angeles, and to Professors Yoram
Barzel, George Brabb, Bruce Johnson, Walter Oi, and R. Haney Scott of the University of Washington.

Source: Reprinted with permission from *The Journal of Finance* (September 1964), pp. 425–442. William F. Sharpe is a Professor of Finance.

certainty, the pervasive influence of risk in financial transactions has forced those working in this area to adopt models of price behavior that are little more than assertions. A typical classroom explanation of the determination of capital asset prices, for example, usually begins with a careful and relatively rigorous description of the process through which individual preferences and physical relationships interact to determine an equilibrium pure interest rate. This is generally followed by the assertion that somehow a market risk-premium is also determined, with the prices of assets adjusting accordingly to account for differences in their risk.

A useful representation of the view of the capital market implied in such discussions is illustrated in Figure 1. In equilibrium, capital asset prices have adjusted so that the investor, if he follows rational procedures (primarily diversification), is able to attain any desired point along a *capital market line*.[1] He may obtain a higher expected rate of return on his holdings only by incurring additional risk. In effect, the market presents him with two prices: the *price of time,* or the pure interest rate (shown by the intersection of the line with the horizontal axis) and the *price of risk,* the additional expected return per unit of risk borne (the reciprocal of the slope of the line).

At present there is no theory describing the manner in which the price of risk results from the basic influences of investor preferences, the physical attributes of capital assets, etc. Moreover, lacking such a theory, it is difficult to give any real meaning to the relationship between the price of a single asset and its risk. Through diversification, some of the risk inherent in an asset can be avoided so that its total risk is obviously not the relevant influence on its price; unfortunately, little has been said concerning the particular risk component that is relevant.

In the last ten years a number of economists have developed *normative* models dealing with asset choice under conditions of risk. Markowitz,[2] following Von Neumann and Morgenstern, developed an analysis based on the expected utility maxim and proposed a general solution for the portfolio selection problem. Tobin[3] showed that under certain conditions Markowitz's model implies that the process of investment choice can be broken down into two phases: first, the choice of a unique optimum combination of risky assets; and second, a separate choice concerning the allocation of funds between such a combination and a single riskless asset. Recently, Hicks[4] has used a model similar to that proposed by Tobin to derive corresponding conclusions about individual investor behavior, dealing somewhat more explicitly with the nature of the conditions under which the process of investment choice can be dichotomized. An even more detailed discussion of this process, including a rigorous proof in the context of a choice among lotteries, has been presented by Gordon and Gangolli.[5]

---

[1] Although some discussions are also consistent with a nonlinear (but monotonic) curve.

[2] Harry M. Markowitz, *Portfolio Selection, Efficient Diversification of Investments* (New York: John Wiley and Sons, 1959). The major elements of the theory first appeared in his article "Portfolio Selection," *The Journal of Finance,* XII (March 1952), 77–91.

[3] James Tobin, "Liquidity Preference as Behavior Towards Risk," *The Review of Economic Studies,* XXV (February 1958), 65–86.

[4] John R. Hicks. "Liquidity," *The Economic Journal,* LXXII (December 1962), 787–802.

[5] M. J. Gordon and Ramesh Gangolli, "Choice Among and Scale of Play on Lottery Type Alternatives," College of Business Administration, University of Rochester, 1962. For another discussion of this relationship, see W. F. Sharpe, "A Simplified Model for Portfolio Analysis,"*Management Science,* Vol. 9, No. 2 (January 1963), 277–293. A related discussion can be found in F. Modigliani and M. H. Miller, "The Cost of Capital, Corporation Finance, and the Theory of Investment," *The American Economic Review,* XLVIII (June 1958), 261–297.

Figure 1

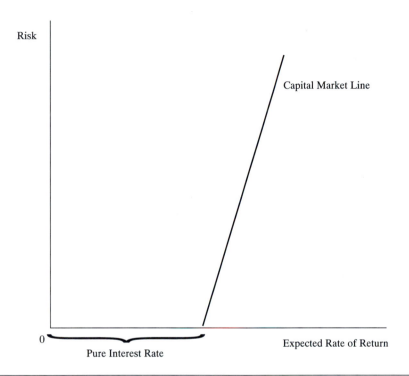

Although all the authors cited use virtually the same model of investor behavior,[6] none has yet attempted to extend it to construct a *market* equilibrium theory of asset prices under conditions of risk.[7] We will show that such an extension provides a theory with implications consistent with the assertions of traditional financial theory described above. Moreover, it sheds considerable light on the relationship between the price of an asset and the various components of its overall risk. For these reasons it warrants consideration as a model of the determination of capital asset prices.

Part II provides the model of individual investor behavior under conditions of risk. In Part III the equilibrium conditions for the capital market are considered and the capital market line derived. The implications for the relationship between the prices of individual capital assets and the various components of risk are described in Part IV.

---

[6] Recently, Hirshleifer has suggested that the mean-variance approach used in the articles cited is best regarded as a special case of a more general formulation due to Arrow. See Hirshleifer's "Investment Decision Under Uncertainty," *Papers and Proceedings of the Seventy-Sixth Annual Meeting of the American Economic Association,* Dec. 1963, or Arrow's "Le Role des Valeurs Boursieres pour la Repartition la Meilleure des Risques," *International Colloquium on Econometrics,* 1952.

[7] After preparing this paper the author learned that Mr. Jack L. Treynor, of Arthur D. Little, Inc., had independently developed a model similar in many respects to the one described here. Unfortunately, Mr. Treynor's excellent work on this subject is, at present, unpublished.

II. Optimal Investment Policy for the Individual

The Investor's Preference Function

Assume that an individual views the outcome of any investment in probabilistic terms; that is, he thinks of the possible results in terms of some probability distribution. In assessing the desirability of a particular investment, however, he is willing to act on the basis of only two parameters of this distribution—its expected value and standard deviation.[8] This can be represented by a total utility function of the form

$$U = f(E_w, \sigma_w),$$

where E_w indicates expected future wealth and σ_w the predicted standard deviation of the possible divergence of actual future wealth from E_w.

Investors are assumed to prefer a higher expected future wealth to a lower value, ceteris paribus ($dU/dE_w > 0$). Moreover, they exhibit risk aversion, choosing an investment offering a lower value of σ_w to one with a greater level, given the level of E_w ($dU/d\sigma_w < 0$). These assumptions imply that indifference curves relating E_w and σ_w will be upward sloping.[9]

To simplify the analysis, we assume that an investor has decided to commit a given amount (W_i) of his present wealth to investment. Letting W_t be his terminal wealth and R the rate of return on his investment:

$$R \equiv \frac{W_t - W_i}{W_i},$$

we have

$$W_t = R W_i + W_i.$$

This relationship makes it possible to express the investor's utility in terms of R, since terminal wealth is directly related to the rate of return:

$$U = g(E_R, \sigma_R).$$

Figure 2 summarizes the model of investor preferences in a family of indifference curves; successive curves indicate higher levels of utility as one moves down and/or to the right.[10]

---

[8] Under certain conditions the mean-variance approach can be shown to lead to unsatisfactory predictions of behavior. Markowitz suggests that a model based on the semi-variance (the average of the squared deviations below the mean) would be preferable; in light of the formidable computational problems, however, he bases his analysis on the variance and standard deviation.

[9] While only these characteristics are required for the analysis, it is generally assumed that the curves have the property of diminishing marginal rates of substitution between E_w and σ_w, as do those in our diagrams.

[10] Such indifference curves can also be derived by assuming that the investor wishes to maximize expected utility and that his total utility can be represented by a quadratic function of R with decreasing marginal utility. Both Markowitz and Tobin present such a derivation. A similar approach is used by Donald E. Farrar in *The Investment Decision Under Uncertainty* (Prentice-Hall, 1962). Unfortunately Farrar makes an error in his derivation; he appeals to the Von-Neumann-Morgenstern cardinal utility axioms to transform a function of the form

$$E(U) = a + bE_R - cE_R2 - c\sigma_R2$$

into one of the form

$$E(U) = k_1E_R - k_2\sigma_R2.$$

(*continued on p. 131*)

Figure 2

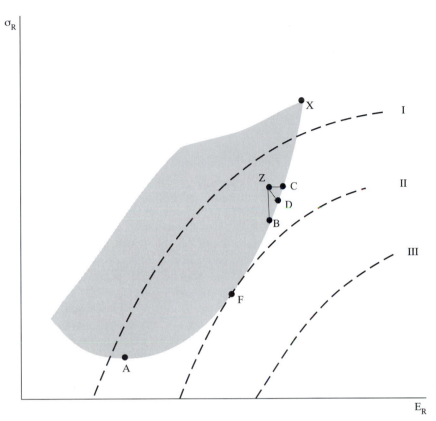

The Investment Opportunity Curve

The model of investor behavior considers the investor as choosing from a set of investment opportunities, one that maximizes his utility. Every investment plan available to him may be represented by a point in the E_R, σ_R plane. If all such plans involve some risk, the area composed of such points will have an appearance similar to that shown in Figure 2. The investor will choose from among all possible plans the one placing him on the indifference curve representing the highest level of utility (point F). The decision can be made in two stages: first, find the set of efficient investment plans; and, second, choose one from among this set. A plan is said to be efficient if (and only if) there is no

---

[10] (*continued from p. 130*)

That such a transformation is not consistent with the axioms can readily be seen in this form, since the first equation implies nonlinear indifference curves in the E_R, σ_R^2 plane while the second implies a linear relationship. Obviously, no three (different) points can lie on both a line and a nonlinear curve (with a monotonic derivative). Thus, the two functions must imply different orderings among alternative choices in at least some instance.

alternative with either (1) the same E_R and a lower σ_R, (2) the same σ_R and a higher E_R, or (3) a higher E_R and a lower σ_R. Thus investment Z is inefficient since investments B, C, and D (among others) dominate it. The only plans that would be chosen must lie along the lower right-hand boundary (AFBDCX)—the *investment opportunity curve.*

To understand the nature of this curve, consider two investment plans—A and B, each including one or more assets. Their predicted expected values and standard deviations of rate of return are shown in Figure 3. If the proportion α of the individual's wealth is placed in plan A and the remainder $(1 - \alpha)$ in B, the expected rate of return of the combination will lie between the expected returns of the two plans:

$$E_{Rc} = \alpha E_{Ra} + (1 - \alpha)\, E_{Rb}.$$

The predicted standard deviation of return of the combination is

$$\sigma_{RC} = \sqrt{\alpha^2 \sigma_{Ra}^2 + (1 - \alpha)^2\, \sigma_{Rb}^2 + 2 r_{ab}\, \alpha(1 - \alpha)\, \sigma_{Ra}\, \sigma_{Rb}}.$$

Note that this relationship includes r_{ab}, the correlation coefficient between the predicted rates of return of the two investment plans. A value of +1 would indicate an investor's belief that there is a precise positive relationship between the outcomes of the two investments. A zero value would indicate a belief that the outcomes of the two investments are completely independent and −1 that the investor feels that there is a precise inverse relationship between them. In the usual case, r_{ab} will have a value between 0 and +1.

Figure 3 shows the possible values of E_{Rc} and σ_{Rc} obtainable with different combinations of A and B under two different assumptions about the value of r_{ab}. If the two investments are perfectly correlated, the combinations will lie along a straight line between the two points, since in this case both E_{Rc} and σ_{Rc} will be linearly related to the proportions invested in the two plans.[11] If they are less than perfectly positively correlated, the standard deviation of any combination must be less than that obtained with perfect correlation (since r_{ab} will be less); thus, the combinations must lie along a curve below the line AB.[12] AZB shows such a curve for the case of complete independence ($r_{ab} = 0$); with negative correlation, the locus is *even more U-shaped.*[13]

The manner in which the investment opportunity curve is formed is relatively simple conceptually, although exact solutions are usually quite difficult.[14] One first traces curves indicating E_R, σ_R

---

[11]

$$E_{Rc} = \alpha E_{Ra} + (1 - \alpha)\, E_{Rb} = E_{Rb} + (E_{Ra} - E_{Rb})\alpha$$

$$\sigma_{RC} = \sqrt{\alpha^2 \sigma_{Ra}^2 + (1 - \alpha)^2\, \sigma_{Rb}^2 + 2 r_{ab}\, \alpha(1 - \alpha)\sigma_{Ra}\, \sigma_{Rb}}$$

but $r_{ab} = 1$; therefore, the expression under the square root sign can be factored:

$$\sigma_{RC} = \sqrt{[\alpha \sigma_{Ra} + (1 - \alpha)\, \sigma_{Rb}]^2}$$

$$= \alpha \sigma_{Ra} + (1 - \alpha)\sigma_{Rb}$$

$$= \sigma_{Ra} + (\sigma_{Ra} - \sigma_{Rb})\alpha$$

[12] This curvature is, in essence, the rationale for diversification.

[13] When $r_{ab} = 0$, the slope of the curve at point A is $-\dfrac{\sigma_{Ra}}{E_{Rb} - E_{Ra}}$; at point B it is $\dfrac{\sigma_{Rb}}{E_{Rb} - E_{Ra}}$. When $r_{ab} = -1$, the curve degenerates to two straight lines to a point on the horizontal axis.

[14] Markowitz has shown that this is a problem in parametric quadratic programming. An efficient solution technique is described in his article, "The Optimization of a Quadratic Function Subject to Linear Constraints," *Naval Research Logistics Quarterly,* Vol. 3 (March and June, 1956), 111–133. A solution method for a special case is given in the author's "A Simplified Model for Portfolio Analysis," *op. cit.*

Figure 3

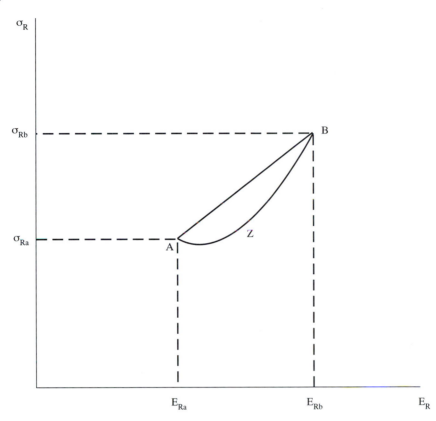

values available with simple combinations of individual assets, then considers combinations of combinations of assets. The lower right-hand boundary must be either linear or increasing at an increasing rate ($d^2\sigma_R/dE^2_R > 0$). As suggested earlier, the complexity of the relationship between the characteristics of individual assets and the location of the investment opportunity curve makes it difficult to provide a simple rule for assessing the desirability of individual assets, since the effect of an asset on an investor's overall investment opportunity curve depends not only on its expected rate of return (E_{Ri}) and risk (σ_{Ri}), but also on its correlations with the other available opportunities ($r_{i1}, r_{i2}, \ldots, r_{in}$). However, such a rule is implied by the equilibrium conditions for the model, as we will show in Part IV.

The Pure Rate of Interest

We have not yet dealt with riskless assets. Let P be such an asset; its risk is zero ($\sigma_{Rp} = 0$) and its expected rate of return, E_{Rp}, is equal (by definition) to the pure interest rate. If an investor places α of his wealth in P and the remainder in some risky asset A, he would obtain an expected rate of return:

$$E_{Rc} = \alpha E_{Rp} + (1 - \alpha) E_{Ra}.$$

The standard deviation of such a combination would be

$$\sigma_{Rc} = \sqrt{\alpha^2 \sigma^2_{Rp} + (1 - \alpha)^2 \sigma_{Ra}^2 + 2r_{pa} \alpha (1 - \alpha) \sigma_{Rp} \sigma_{Ra}},$$

but since $\sigma_{Rp} = 0$, this reduces to

$$\sigma_{Rc} = (1 - \alpha) \sigma_{Ra}.$$

This implies that all combinations involving any risky asset or combination of assets plus the riskless asset must have values of E_{Rc} and σ_{Rc} that lie along a straight line between the points representing the two components. Thus in Figure 4 all combinations of E_R and σ_R lying along the line PA are attainable if some money is loaned at the pure rate and some placed in A. Similarly, by lending at the pure rate and investing in B, combinations along PB can be attained. Of all such possibilities, however, one will dominate: that investment plan lying at the point of the original investment opportunity curve where a ray from point P is tangent to the curve. In Figure 4 all investments lying along the original curve from X to ϕ are dominated by some combination of investment in ϕ and lending at the pure interest rate.

Consider next the possibility of borrowing. If the investor can borrow at the pure rate of interest, this is equivalent to disinvesting in P. The effect of borrowing to purchase more of any given investment than is possible with the given amount of wealth can be found simply by letting α take on negative values in the equations derived for the case of lending. This will obviously give points lying along the extension of line PA if borrowing is used to purchase more of A, points lying along the extension of PB if the funds are used to purchase B, etc.

As in the case of lending, however, one investment plan will dominate all others when borrowing is possible. When the rate at which funds can be borrowed equals the lending rate, this plan will be the same one that is dominant if lending is to take place. Under these conditions, the investment opportunity curve becomes a line (PϕZ in Figure 4). Moreover, if the original investment opportunity curve is not linear at point ϕ, the process of investment choice can be dichotomized as follows: first, select the (unique) optimum combination of risky assets (point ϕ) ; and, second, borrow or lend to obtain the particular point on PZ at which an indifference curve is tangent to the line.[15]

Before proceeding with the analysis, it may be useful to consider alternative assumptions under which only a combination of assets lying at the point of tangency between the original investment opportunity curve and a ray from P can be efficient. Even if borrowing is impossible, the investor will choose ϕ (and lending) if his risk-aversion leads him to a point below ϕ on the line Pϕ. Since a large number of investors choose to place some of their funds in relatively risk-free investments, this is not an unlikely possibility. Alternatively, if borrowing is possible but only up to some limit, the choice of ϕ would be made by all but those investors willing to undertake considerable risk. These alternative paths lead to the main conclusion, thus making the assumption of borrowing or lending at the pure interest rate less onerous than it might initially appear to be.

[15] This proof was first presented by Tobin for the case in which the pure rate of interest is zero (cash). Hicks considers the lending situation under comparable conditions but does not allow borrowing. Both authors present their analysis using maximization subject to constraints expressed as equalities. Hicks' analysis assumes independence and thus ensures that the solution will include no negative holdings of risky assets; Tobin's covers the general case, thus his solution would generally include negative holdings of some assets. The discussion in this paper is based on Markowitz's formulation, which includes non-negativity constraints on the holdings of all assets.

Figure 4

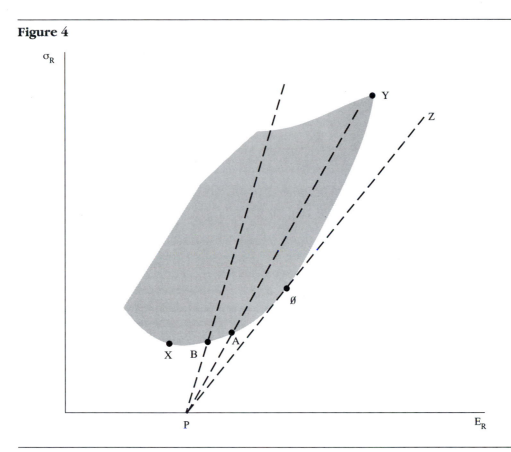

III. Equilibrium in the Capital Market

In order to derive conditions for equilibrium in the capital market, we invoke two assumptions. First, we assume a common pure rate of interest, with all investors able to borrow or lend funds on equal terms. Second, we assume homogeneity of investor expectations:[16] Investors are assumed to agree on the prospects of various investments—the expected values, standard deviations, and correlation coefficients described in Part II. Needless to say, these are highly restrictive and undoubtedly unrealistic assumptions. However, since the proper test of a theory is not the realism of its assumptions but the acceptability of its implications, and since these assumptions imply equilibrium conditions that form a major part of classical financial doctrine, it is far from clear that this formulation should be rejected—especially in view of the dearth of alternative models leading to similar results.

Under these assumptions, given some set of capital asset prices, each investor will view his alternatives in the same manner. For one set of prices the alternatives might appear as shown in

[16] A term suggested by one of the referees.

Figure 5

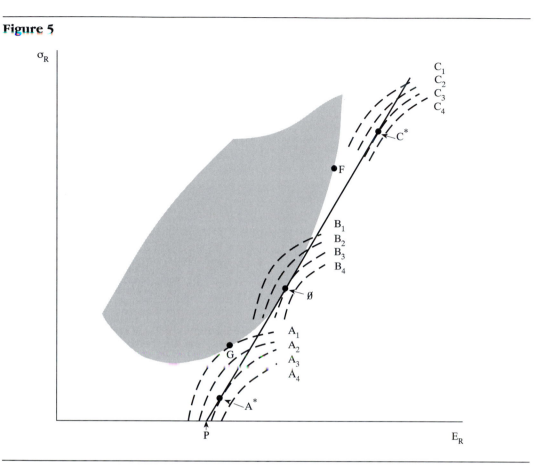

Figure 5. In this situation, an investor with the preferences indicated by indifference curves A_1 through A_4 would try to lend some of his funds at the pure interest rate and to invest the remainder in the combination of assets shown by point ϕ, since this would give him the preferred overall position A^*. An investor with the preferences indicated by curves B_1 through B_4 would try to invest all his funds in combination ϕ, while an investor with indifference curves C_1 through C_4 would invest all his funds plus additional (borrowed) funds in combination ϕ in order to reach his preferred position (C^*). In any event, all would attempt to purchase only those risky assets that enter combination ϕ.

The attempts by investors to purchase the assets in combination ϕ and their lack of interest in holding assets not in combination ϕ would, of course, lead to a revision of prices. The prices of assets in ϕ will rise, and, since an asset's expected return relates future income to present price, their expected returns will fall. This will reduce the attractiveness of combinations that include such assets; thus, point ϕ (among others) will move to the left of its initial position.[17] On the other hand, the

---

[17] If investors consider the variability of future dollar returns unrelated to present price, both E_R and σ_R will fall; under these conditions, the point representing an asset would move along a ray through the origin as its price changes.

prices of assets not in ϕ will fall, causing an increase in their expected returns and a rightward movement of points representing combinations that include them. Such price changes will lead to a revision of investors' actions; some new combination or combinations will become attractive, leading to different demands and thus to further revisions in prices. As the process continues, the investment opportunity curve will tend to become more linear, with points such as ϕ moving to the left and formerly inefficient points (such as F and G) moving to the right.

Capital asset prices must, of course, continue to change until a set of prices is attained for which every asset enters at least one combination lying on the capital market line. Figure 6 illustrates such an equilibrium condition.[18] All possibilities in the shaded area can be attained with combinations of risky assets, while points lying along the line PZ can be attained by borrowing or lending at the pure rate plus an investment in some combination of risky assets. Certain possibilities (those lying along PZ from point A to point B) can be obtained in either manner. For example, the E_R, σ_R values shown by point A can be obtained solely by some combination of risky assets; alternatively, the point can be reached by a combination of lending and investing in combination C of risky assets.

It is important to recognize that in the situation shown in Figure 6 many alternative combinations of risky assets are efficient (i.e., lie along line PZ), and thus the theory does not imply that all investors will hold the same combination.[19] On the other hand, all such combinations must be perfectly (positively) correlated, since they lie along a linear border of the E_R, σ_R region.[20] This provides a key to the relationship between prices of capital assets and different types of risk.

IV. The Prices of Capital Assets

We have argued that in equilibrium there will be a simple linear relationship between the expected return and standard deviation of return for efficient combinations of risky assets. Thus far, nothing has been said about such a relationship for individual assets. Typically, the E_R, σ_R values associated with single assets will lie above the capital market line, reflecting the inefficiency of undiversified holdings. Moreover, such points may be scattered throughout the feasible region, with no consistent relationship between their expected return and total risk (σ_R). However, there will be a consistent relationship between their expected returns and what might best be called *systematic risk*, as we will now show.

Figure 7 illustrates the typical relationship between a single capital asset (point i) and an efficient combination of assets (point g) of which it is a part. The curve igg' indicates all E_R, σ_R values that can be obtained with feasible combinations of asset i and combination g. As before, we denote such

[18] The area in Figure 6 representing E_R, σ_R values attained with only risky assets has been drawn at some distance from the horizontal axis for emphasis. It is likely that a more accurate representation would place it very close to the axis.

[19] This statement contradicts Tobin's conclusion that there will be a unique optimal combination of risky assets. Tobin's proof of a unique optimum can be shown to be incorrect for the case of perfect correlation of efficient risky investment plans if the line connecting their E_R, σ_R points would pass through point P. In the graph on page 83 of the article (*op. cit.*), the constant-risk locus would, in this case, degenerate from a family of ellipses into one of straight lines parallel to the constant-return loci, thus giving multiple optima.

[20] E_R, σ_R values given by combinations of any two combinations must lie within the region and cannot plot above a straight line joining the points. In this case they cannot plot below such a straight line. But since only in the case of perfect correlation will they plot along a straight line, the two combinations must be perfectly correlated. As shown in Part IV, this does not necessarily imply that the individual securities they contain are perfectly correlated.

Figure 6

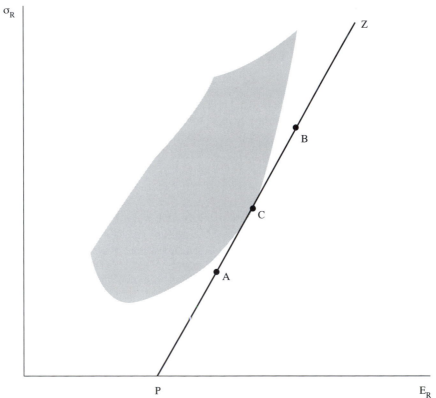

a combination in terms of a proportion α of asset i and $(1 - \alpha)$ of combination g. A value of $\alpha = 1$ would indicate pure investment in asset i while $\alpha = 0$ would imply investment in combination g. Note, however, that $\alpha = .5$ implies a total investment of more than half the funds in asset i, since half would be invested in i itself and the other half used to purchase combination g, which also includes some of asset i. This means that a combination in which asset i does not appear at all must be represented by some negative value of α. Point g' indicates such a combination.

In Figure 7 the curve igg' has been drawn tangent to the capital market line (PZ) at point g. This is no accident. All such curves must be tangent to the capital market line in equilibrium, since (1) they must touch it at the point representing the efficient combination and (2) they are continuous at that point.[21] Under these conditions a lack of tangency would imply that the curve intersects PZ. But then some feasible combination of assets would lie to the right of the capital

---

[21] Only if $r_{ig} = -1$ will the curve be discontinuous over the range in question.

Figure 7

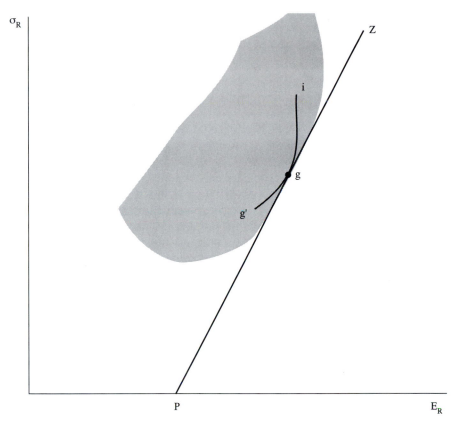

market line, an obvious impossibility since the capital market line represents the efficient bound-ary of feasible values of E_R and σ_R.

The requirement that curves such as igg' be tangent to the capital market line can be shown to lead to a relatively simple formula that relates the expected rate of return to various elements of risk for all assets that are included in combination g.[22] Its economic meaning can best be seen if

---

[22] The standard deviation of a combination of g and i will be:

$$\sigma = \sqrt{\alpha^2 \sigma_{Ri}^2 + (1-\alpha)^2 \sigma_{Rg}^2 + 2r_{ig}\,\alpha(1-\alpha)\,\sigma_{Ri}\,\sigma_{Rg}}$$

at $\alpha = 0$:

$$\frac{d\sigma}{d\alpha} = -\frac{1}{\sigma}\,[\sigma_{Rg}^2 - r_{ig}\sigma_{Ri}\,\sigma_{Rg}]$$

but $\sigma = \sigma_{Rg}$ at $\alpha = 0$. Thus,

$$\frac{d\sigma}{d\alpha} = -[\sigma_{Rg} - r_{ig}\sigma_{Ri}].$$

The expected return of a combination will be:

$$E = \alpha E_{Ri} + (1-\alpha)\,E_{Rg}.$$

(*continued on p. 140*)

the relationship between the return of asset i and that of combination g is viewed in a manner similar to that used in regression analysis.[22] Imagine that we were given a number of (ex post) observations of the return of the two investments. The points might plot as shown in Figure 8. The scatter of the R_i observations around their mean (which will approximate E_{Ri}) is, of course, evidence of the total risk of the asset—σ_{Ri}. But part of the scatter is due to an underlying relationship with the return on combination g, shown by B_{ig}, the slope of the regression line. The response of R_i to changes in R_g (and variations in R_g itself) account for much of the variation in R_i. It is this component of the asset's total risk that we term the *systematic* risk. The remainder,[24] being uncorrelated with R_g, is the unsystematic component. This formulation of the relationship between R_i and R_g can be employed *ex ante* as a predictive model. B_{ig} becomes the *predicted* response of R_i to changes in R_g. Then, given σ_{Rg} (the predicted risk of R_g), the systematic portion of the predicted risk of each asset can be determined.

This interpretation allows us to state the relationship derived from the tangency of curves such as igg' with the capital market line in the form shown in Figure 9. All assets entering efficient combination g must have (predicted) B_{ig} and E_{Ri} values lying on the line PQ.[25] Prices will adjust so that assets which are more responsive to changes in R_g will have higher expected returns than those which are less responsive. This accords with common sense. Obviously, the part of an asset's risk that is due to its correlation with the return on a combination cannot be diversified away when the asset is added to the combination. Since B_{ig} indicates the magnitude of this type of risk, it should be directly related to expected return.

The relationship illustrated in Figure 9 provides a partial answer to the question posed earlier concerning the relationship between an asset's risk and its expected return. But thus far we have argued only that the relationship holds for the assets which enter some particular efficient combina-

[22](*continued from p. 139*)

Thus, at all values of α:

$$\frac{dE}{d\alpha} = -[E_{Rg} - E_{Ri}]$$

and, at $\alpha = 0$:

$$\frac{d\sigma}{dE} = \frac{\sigma_{Rg} - r_{ig}\sigma_{Ri}}{E_{Rg} - E_{Ri}}.$$

Let the equation of the capital market line be

$$\sigma_R = s(E_R - P),$$

where P is the pure interest rate. Since igg' is tangent to the line when $\alpha = 0$, and since (E_{Rg}, σ_{Rg}) lies on the line,

$$\frac{\sigma_{Rg} - r_{ig}\sigma_{Ri}}{E_{Rg} - E_{Ri}} = \frac{\sigma_{Rg}}{E_{Rg} - P}$$

or

$$\frac{r_{ig}\sigma_{Ri}}{\sigma_{Rg}} = -\left[\frac{P}{E_{Rg} - P}\right] + \left[\frac{1}{E_{Rg} - P}\right]E_{Ri},$$

[23] This model has been called the diagonal model since its portfolio analysis solution can be facilitated by rearranging the data so that the variance-covariance matrix becomes diagonal. The method is described in the author's article cited earlier.

[24] Ex post, the standard error.

[25]

$$r_{ig} = \sqrt{\frac{B_{ig}^2\sigma_{Rg}^2}{\sigma_{Ri}^2}} = \frac{B_{ig}\sigma_{Rg}}{\sigma_{Ri}}$$

and

$$B_{ig} = \frac{r_{ig}\sigma_{Ri}}{\sigma_{Rg}}.$$

(*continued on p. 141*)

Figure 8

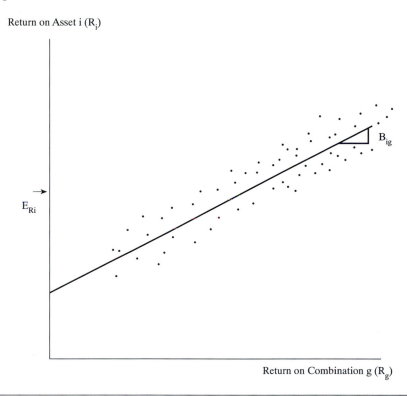

tion (g). Had another combination been selected, a different linear relationship would have been derived. Fortunately, this limitation is easily overcome. As shown in the footnote,[26] we may arbitrarily select *any* one of the efficient combinations, then measure the predicted responsiveness of *every*

---

[25](*continued from p. 140*)

The expression on the right is the expression on the left side of the last equation in footnote 22. Thus,

$$B_{ig} = -\left[\frac{P}{E_{Rg} - P}\right] + \left[\frac{1}{E_{Rg} - P}\right] E_{Ri}.$$

[26] Consider the two assets i and i*, the former included in efficient combination g and the latter in combination g*. As shown above,

$$B_{ig} = -\left[\frac{P}{E_{Rg} - P}\right] + \left[\frac{1}{E_{Rg} - P}\right] E_{Ri}$$

and

$$B_{i^*g^*} = -\left[\frac{P}{E_{Rg^*} - P}\right] + \left[\frac{1}{E_{Rg^*} - P}\right] E_{Ri^*}$$

Since R_g and R_{g^*} are perfectly correlated,

$$r_{i^*g^*} = r_{i^*g}.$$

(*continued on p. 142*)

Figure 9

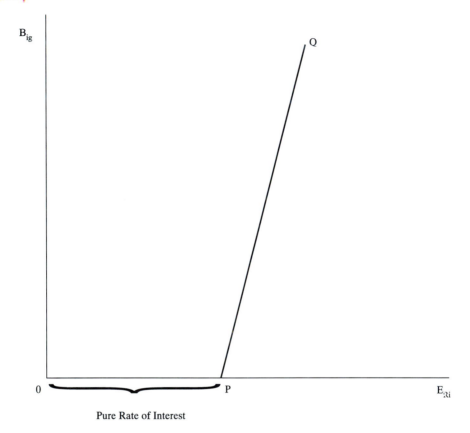

Pure Rate of Interest

---

asset's rate of return to that of the combination selected; these coefficients will be related to the expected rates of return of the assets in exactly the manner pictured in Figure 9.

The fact that rates of return from all efficient combinations will be perfectly correlated provides the justification for arbitrarily selecting any one of them. Alternatively, we may choose instead any variable perfectly correlated with the rate of return of such combinations. The vertical

[26](*continued from p. 141*)

Thus,

$$\frac{B_{i^*g^*}\sigma_{Rg^*}}{\sigma_{Ri^*}} = \frac{B_{i^*g}\sigma_{Rg}}{\sigma_{Ri^*}}$$

and

$$B_{i^*g^*} = B_{i^*g}\left[\frac{\sigma_{Rg}}{\sigma_{Rg^*}}\right].$$

Since both g and g* lie on a line that intercepts the E-axis at P,

$$\frac{\sigma_{Rg}}{\sigma_{Rg^*}} = \frac{E_{Rg} - P}{E_{Rg^*} - P}$$

(*continued on p. 143*)

axis in Figure 9 would then indicate alternative levels of a coefficient measuring the sensitivity of the rate of return of a capital asset to changes in the variable chosen.

This possibility suggests both a plausible explanation for the implication that all efficient combinations will be perfectly correlated and a useful interpretation of the relationship between an individual asset's expected return and its risk. Although the theory itself implies only that rates of return from efficient combinations will be perfectly correlated, we might expect that this would be due to their common dependence on the overall level of economic activity. If so, diversification enables the investor to escape all but the risk resulting from swings in economic activity—this type of risk remains even in efficient combinations. And, since all other types can be avoided by diversification, only the responsiveness of an asset's rate of return to the level of economic activity is relevant in assessing its risk. Prices will adjust until there is a linear relationship between the magnitude of such responsiveness and expected return. Assets that are unaffected by changes in economic activity will return the pure interest rate; those which move with economic activity will promise appropriately higher expected rates of return.

This discussion provides an answer to the second of the two questions posed in this paper. In Part III it was shown that with respect to equilibrium conditions in the capital market as a whole, the theory leads to results consistent with classical doctrine (i.e., the capital market line). We have now shown that with regard to capital assets considered individually, it also yields implications consistent with traditional concepts: It is common practice for investment counselors to accept a lower expected return from defensive securities (those which respond little to changes in the economy) than they require from aggressive securities (which exhibit significant response). As suggested earlier, the familiarity of the implications need not be considered a drawback. The provision of a logical framework for producing some of the major elements of traditional financial theory should be a useful contribution in its own right.

Discussion Questions

1. Note that in Figure 1 Professor Sharpe plots risk on the vertical axis and expected rate of return on the horizontal axis. It has become traditional to plot expected returns on the vertical axis and risk on the horizontal. Draw the capital market line of Figure 1 with the axes reversed.

2. Draw Figure 2 with the E_R vertical and the σ_R horizontal. Explain the elements of the figure.

3. Explain why $P\phi Z$ is the investment opportunity curve in Figure 4.

4. Explain what is meant by systematic risk and unsystematic risk.

---

[26](*continued from p. 142*)

and

$$B_{i^*g^*} = B_{i^*g}\left[\frac{E_{Rg} - P}{E_{Rg^*} - P}\right].$$

Thus,

$$-\left[\frac{P}{E_{Rg^*} - P}\right] + \left[\frac{1}{E_{Rg^*} - P}\right]E_{Ri^*} = B_{i^*g}\left[\frac{E_{Rg} - P}{E_{Rg^*} - P}\right],$$

from which we have the desired relationship between R_{i^*} and g:

$$B_{i^*g} = -\left[\frac{P}{E_{Rg} - P}\right] + \left[\frac{1}{E_{Rg} - P}\right]E_{Ri^*}.$$

B_{i^*g} must therefore plot on the same line as does B_{ig}.

5. Figure 8 shows a plot of return for security i plotted against returns on "combination," or market returns. What is the slope of the line called?

6. Plot Figure 9 with E_{Ri} and B_{ig} horizontal.

7. How does the use of B_{ig} (Beta) to measure portfolio risk eliminate the need to compute portfolio variance from the covariances of returns of securities in the portfolio?

Franco Modigliani and Gerald A. Pogue

An Introduction to Risk and Return: Concepts and Evidence, Part I

Relationships of risk and return are the cornerstone of thought in financial management. This article is an excellent introduction to these relationships and establishes the basis for the next article, which develops the capital asset pricing model.

---

1. Introduction

Portfolio theory deals with the selection of optimal portfolios by rational risk-averse investors—that is, by investors who attempt to maximize their expected portfolio returns consistent with individually acceptable levels of portfolio risk. Capital markets theory deals with the implications for security prices of the decisions made by these investors—that is, what relationship should exist between security returns and risk if investors behave in this optimal fashion. Together, portfolio and capital markets theories provide a framework for the specification and measurement of investment risk, for developing relationships between expected security return and risk, and for measuring the performance of managed portfolios such as mutual funds and pension funds.

The purpose of this article is to present a nontechnical introduction to portfolio and capital markets theories. Our hope is to provide a wide class of readers with an understanding of the foundation upon which the modern risk and performance measures are based, by presenting the main elements of the theory along with the results of some of the more important empirical tests. We are attempting to present not an exhaustive survey of the theoretical and empirical literature, but rather the main thread of the subject, leading the reader from the most basic concepts to the more sophisticated but practically useful results of the theory.

Source: Reprinted, with permission, from *Financial Analysts Journal,* March/April 1974. Copyright 1974, The Financial Analysts Federation, Charlottesville, Va. All rights reserved. Franco Modigliani is Institute Professor Emeritus, M.I.T. Gerald A. Pogue is former Professor of Finance at City University of New York.

2. Investment Return

Measuring historical rates of return is a relatively straightforward matter. We will begin by showing how investment return during a single interval can be measured and then present three commonly used measures of average return over a series of such intervals.

The return on an investor's portfolio during a given interval is equal to the change in value of the portfolio plus any distributions received from the portfolio expressed as a fraction of the initial portfolio value. It is important that any capital or income distributions made to the investor be included, or else the measure of return will be deficient. Equivalently, the return can be thought of as the amount (expressed as a fraction of the initial portfolio value) that can be withdrawn at the end of the interval while maintaining the principal intact. The return on the investor's portfolio, designated R_P, is given by

$$R_P = \frac{V_1 - V_0 + D_1}{V_0},$$ (1a)

where V_1 = the portfolio market value at the end of the interval,
  V_0 = the portfolio market value at the beginning of the interval,
  D_1 = cash distributions to the investor during the interval.

The calculation assumes that any interest or dividend income received on the portfolio securities and not distributed to the investor is reinvested in the portfolio (and thus reflected in V_1). Furthermore, the calculation assumes that any distributions occur at the end of the interval or are held in the form of cash until the end of the interval. If the distributions were reinvested prior to the end of the interval, the calculation would have to be modified to consider the gains or losses on the amount reinvested. The formula also assumes no capital inflows during the interval. Otherwise, the calculation would have to be modified to reflect the increased investment base. Capital inflows at the end of the interval, however, can be treated as just the reverse of distributions in the return calculation.

Thus, given the beginning and ending portfolio values, plus any contributions from or distributions to the investor (assumed to occur at the end of the interval), we can compute the investor's return using Equation (1a). For example, if the XYZ pension fund had a market value of $100,000 at the end of June, capital contributions of $10,000, benefit payments of $5,000 (both at the end of July), and an end-of-July market value of $95,000, the return for the month is a loss of 10 percent.

The arithmetic average return is an unweighted average of the returns achieved during a series of such measurement intervals. For example, if the portfolio returns (as measured by Equation [1a]) were −10 percent, 20 percent, and 5 percent in July, August, and September respectively, the average monthly return is 5 percent. The general formula is

$$R_A = \frac{R_{P1} + R_{P2} + \ldots + R_{PN}}{N},$$ (1b)

where R_A = the arithmetic average return,
  R_{PK} = the portfolio return during the interval k, $k = 1, \ldots, N$,
  N = the number of intervals in the performance-evaluation period.

The arithmetic average can thought of as the mean value of the withdrawals (expressed as a fraction of the initial portfolio value) that can be made at the end of each interval while maintaining the principal intact. In the above example, the investor must add 10 percent of the principal at the end of the first interval and can withdraw 20 percent and 5 percent at the end of the second and third, for a mean withdrawal of 5 percent of the initial value per period.

The time-weighted return measures the compound rate of growth of the initial portfolio during the performance-evaluation period, assuming that all cash distributions are reinvested in the portfolio. It is also commonly referred to as the "geometric" rate of return. It is computed by taking the geometric average of the portfolio returns computed from Equation (1a). For example, let us assume the portfolio returns were –10 percent, 20 percent, and 5 percent in July, August, and September, as in the example above. The time-weighted rate of return is 4.3 percent per month. Thus one dollar invested in the portfolio at the end of June would have grown at a rate of 4.3 percent per month during the three-month period. The general formula is

$$R_T = [(1 + R_{P1})(1 + R_{P2}) \ldots (1 + R_{PN})]^{1/N} - 1, \tag{1c}$$

where R_T = the time-weighted rate of return,

R_{PK} = the portfolio return during the interval k, $k = 1, \ldots, N$,

N = the number of intervals in the performance-evaluation period.

In general, the arithmetic and time-weighed average returns do not coincide. This is because, in computing the arithmetic average, the amount invested is assumed to be maintained (through additions or withdrawals) at its initial value. The time-weighted return, on the other hand, is the return on a portfolio that varies in size because of the assumption that all proceeds are reinvested. The failure of the two averages to coincide is illustrated in the following example: Consider a portfolio with a $100 market value at the end of 1972, a $200 value at the end of 1973, and a $100 market value at the end of 1974. The annual returns are 100 percent and – 50 percent. The arithmetic and time-weighted average returns are 25 percent and zero percent respectively. The arithmetic average return consists of the average of $100 withdrawn at the end of Period 1 and $50 replaced at the end of Period 2. The compound rate of return is clearly zero, the 100 percent return in the first period being exactly offset by the 50 percent loss in the second period on the larger asset base. In this example the arithmetic average exceeded the time-weighted average return. This always proves to be true, except in the special situation where the returns in each interval are the same, in which case the averages are identical.

The dollar-weighted return measures the average rate of growth of all funds invested in the portfolio during the performance-evaluation period—that is, the initial value plus any contributions less any distributions. As such, the rate is influenced by the timing and magnitude of the contributions and distributions to and from the portfolio. The measure is also commonly referred to as the "internal rate of return." It is important to corporations, for example, for comparison with the actuarial rates of portfolio growth assumed when funding their employee pension plans.

The dollar-weighted return is computed in exactly the same way that the yield to maturity on a bond is determined. For example, consider a portfolio with market value of $100,000 at the end of 1973 (V_0), capital withdrawals of $5,000 at the end of 1974, 1975, and 1976 (C_1, C_2, and C_3), and a market value of $110,000 at the end of 1976 (V_3). Using compound interest tables, the dollar-weighted rate of return is found by trial and error to be 8.1 percent per year during the three-year period. Thus each dollar in the fund grew at an average rate of 8.1 percent per year. The formula used is

$$V_0 = \frac{C_1}{(1+R_D)} + \frac{C_2}{(1+R_D)^2} + \frac{C_3}{(1+R_D)^3} + \frac{V_3}{(1+R_D)^3},$$ (1d)

where $R_D =$ the dollar-weighted rate of return.

What is the relationship between the dollar-weighted return (internal rate of return) and the previously defined time-weighted rate of return? It is easy to show that under certain special conditions both rates of return are the same. Consider, for example, a portfolio with initial total value of V_0. No further additions or withdrawals occur, and all dividends are reinvested. Under these special circumstances all of the C's in Equation (1d) are zero so that

$$V_0 = \frac{V_0(1+R_{P1})(1+R_{P2})(1+R_{P3})}{(1+R_D)^3},$$

where R_P's are the single-period returns. The numerator of the expression on the right is just the value of the initial investment at the end of the three periods (V_3). Solving for R_D we find

$$R = [(1+R_{P1})(1+R_{P2})(1+R_{P3})]^{1/3} - 1,$$

which is the same as the time-weighted rate of return R_T given by Equation (1c). However, when contributions or withdrawals to the portfolio occur, the two rates of return are not the same. Because the dollar-weighted return (unlike the time-weighted return) is affected by the magnitude and timing of portfolio contributions and distributions (which are typically beyond the portfolio manager's control), it is not useful for measuring the investment performance of the manager. For example, consider two identical portfolios (designated A and B) with year-end 1973 market values of $100,000. During 1974 each portfolio has a 20 percent return. At the end of 1974, portfolio A has a capital contribution of $50,000 and portfolio B a withdrawal of $50,000. During 1975, both portfolios suffer a 10-percent loss, resulting in year-end market values of $153,000 and $63,000 respectively. Now, both portfolio managers performed equally well, earning 20 percent in 1974 and −10 percent in 1975, for a time-weighted average return of 3.9 percent per year. The dollar-weighted returns are not the same, however, due to the different asset bases for 1975, equaling 1.2 percent and 8.2 percent for portfolios A and B respectively. The owners of portfolio B, unlike those of A, made a fortuitous decision to reduce their investment prior to the 1975 decline.

In the remainder of this article, when we mention rate of return, we will generally be referring to the single interval measure given by Equation (1a). However, from time to time we will refer to the arithmetic and geometric averages of these returns.

3. Portfolio Risk

The definition of investment risk leads us into much less well-explored territory. Not everyone agrees on how to define risk, let alone how to measure it. Nevertheless, there are some attributes of risk that are reasonably well accepted.

If an investor holds a portfolio of treasury bonds, he faces no uncertainty about monetary outcome. The value of the portfolio at maturity of the notes will be identical with the predicted value. In this case, the investor bears no monetary risk. However, if he has a portfolio composed of common stocks, it will be impossible to exactly predict the value of the portfolio as of any future date. The best he can do is make a best guess or most-likely estimate, qualified by statements about the range and likelihood of other values. In this case, the investor does bear risk.

One measure of risk is the extent to which the *future* portfolio values are likely to diverge from the expected or predicted value. More specifically, risk for most investors is related to the chance that future portfolio values will be less than expected. Thus, if the investor's portfolio has a current value of $100,000 and an expected value of $110,000 at the end of the next year, he will be concerned about the probability of achieving values less than $110,000.

Before proceeding to the quantification of risk, it is convenient to shift our attention from the terminal value of the portfolio to the portfolio rate of return, R_p, since the increase in portfolio value is directly related to R_p.[1]

A particularly useful way to quantify the uncertainty about the portfolio return is to specify the probability associated with each of the possible future returns. Assume, for example, that an investor has identified five possible outcomes for his portfolio return during the next year. Associated with each return is a subjectively determined probability, or relative chance of occurrence. The five possible outcomes are as follows:

Possible Return	Subjective Probability
50%	0.1
30	0.2
10	0.4
−10	0.2
− 30	0.1
	1.00

Note that the probabilities sum to 1.00 so that the actual portfolio return is confined to take one of the five possible values. Given this probability distribution, we can measure the expected return and risk for the portfolio.

The expected return is simply the weighted average of possible outcomes, where the weights are the relative chances of occurrence. The expected return on the portfolio is 10 percent, given by

$$E(R_p) = \sum_{j=1}^{5} P_j R_j \tag{2}$$
$$= 0.01(50.0) + 0.2(30.0) + 0.4(10.0) + 0.2(-10.0) + 0.2(-30.0)$$
$$= 10\%,$$

where the R_j's are the possible returns and the P_j's the associated probabilities.

If risk is defined as the chance of achieving returns less than expected, it would seem to be logical to measure risk by the dispersion of the possible returns below the expected value. However, risk measures based on below-the-mean variability are difficult to work with and are actually unnecessary as long as the distribution of future return is reasonably symmetric about the expected

---

[1] The transformation changes nothing of substance since

$$\overline{M}_T = (1 + \overline{R}_p)M_o$$
$$= M_o + M_o\overline{R}_p,$$

where $\overline{M}_T$ = terminal portfolio value,
   $\overline{R}_p$ = portfolio return.

Since M_T is a linear function of R_p, any risk measures developed for the portfolio return will apply equally to the terminal market value.

Exhibit 1   Possible Shapes for Probability Distributions

Symmetric Probability Distribution

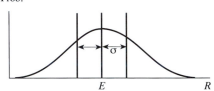

Probability Distribution Skewed to Left

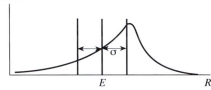

Probability Distribution Skewed to Right

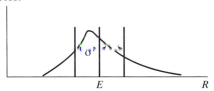

value.[2] Exhibit 1 shows three probability distributions: the first symmetric, the second skewed to the left, and the third skewed to the right. For a symmetric distribution, the dispersion of returns on one side of the expected return is the same as the dispersion on the other side.

Empirical studies of realized rates of return on diversified portfolios show that skewness is not a significant problem.[3] If future distributions are shaped like historical distributions, then it makes little difference whether we measure variability of returns on one or both sides of the expected return. If the probability distribution is symmetric, measures of the total variability of return will be twice as large as measures of the portfolio's variability below the expected return. Thus, if total variability is used as a risk surrogate, the risk rankings for a group of portfolios will be the same as when variability below the expected return is used. It is for this reason that total variability of returns has been so widely used as a surrogate for risk.

It now remains to choose a specific measure of total variability of returns. The measures most commonly used are the variance and standard deviation of returns.

---

[2] Risk measures based on below-the-average variation are analytically difficult to deal with. H. Markowitz, in Chapter 9 of [18], develops a semivariance statistic that measures variability below the mean and compares it with the more commonly used variance calculation.

[3] See, for example, M. E. Blume [2].

The variance of return is a weighted sum of the squared deviations from the expected return. Squaring the deviations ensures that deviations above and below the expected value contribute equally to the measure of variability, regardless of sign. The variance, designated σ_p^2 for the portfolio in the previous example, is given by

$$\sigma_p^2 = \sum_{j=1}^{5} P_j(R_j) - E(R_p)^2 \tag{3}$$
$$= 0.1(50.0 - 10.0)^2 + 0.2(30.0 - 10.0)^2 + 0.4(10.0 - 10.0)^2 +$$
$$0.2(-10.0 - 10.0)^2 + 0.1(-30.0 - 10.0)^2$$
$$= 480 \text{ percent squared.}$$

The standard deviation (σ_p) is defined as the square root of the variance. It is equal to 22 percent. The larger the variance or standard deviation, the greater the possible dispersion of future realized values around the expected value and the larger the investor's uncertainty. As a rule of thumb for symmetric distributions, it is often suggested that roughly two-thirds of the possible returns will lie within one standard deviation either side of the expected value and that 95 percent will be within two standard deviations.

Exhibit 2 shows the historical return distributions for a diversified portfolio. The portfolio is composed of approximately 100 securities, with each security having equal weight. The month-by-month returns cover the period from January 1945 to June 1970. Note that the distribution is approximately, but not perfectly, symmetric. The arithmetic average return for the 306-month period is 0.91 percent per month. The standard deviation about this average is 4.45 percent per month.

Exhibit 3 gives the same data for a single security, National Department Stores. Note that the distribution is highly skewed. The arithmetic average return is 0.81 percent per month over the 306-month period. The most interesting aspect, however, is the standard deviation of month-by-month returns—9.02 percent per month, more than double that for the diversified portfolio. This result will be discussed further in the next section.

Thus far our discussion of portfolio risk has been confined to a single-period investment horizon such as the next year; that is, the portfolio is held unchanged and evaluated at the end of the year. An obvious question relates to the effect of holding the portfolio for several periods—say for the next 20 years: Will the one-year risks tend to cancel out over time? Given the random-walk nature of security prices, the answer to this question is no. If the risk level (standard deviation) is maintained during each year, the portfolio risk for longer horizons will increase with the horizon length. The standard deviation of possible terminal portfolio values after N years is equal to $\sqrt{N}$ times the standard deviation after one year.[4] Thus the investor cannot rely on the "long run" to reduce his risk of loss.

---

[4] This result can be illustrated as follows. The portfolio market value after N years, $\overline{M}_N$, is equal to

$$\overline{M}_N = M_o[(1 + \overline{R}_{P1})(1 + \overline{R}_{P2}) \ldots (1 + \overline{R}_{PN})],$$

where $\overline{M}_o$ is the initial value and $\overline{R}_{pt}$ (t = 1, . . . , N) is the return during year t (as given by Equation [1a]). For reasonably small values of the annual returns, the above expression can be approximated by

$$\overline{M}_N = M_o[1 + \overline{R}_{P1} + \overline{R}_{P2} + \ldots + \overline{R}_{PN}].$$

Now, if the annual returns, $\overline{R}_{pt}$ are independently and identically distributed with variance σ^2, the variance of $\overline{M}_N$ will equal $(M_o)^2 N \sigma^2$, or N times the variance after one year. Therefore, the standard deviation of the terminal value will equal $\sqrt{N}$ times the standard deviation after one year. The key assumption of independence of portfolio returns over time is realistic, since security returns appear to follow a random walk through time.

A similar result could be obtained without the restriction of the size of the $\overline{R}_{pt}$ if we had dealt with continuously, as opposed to annually, compounded rates of return. However, the analysis would be more complicated.

Exhibit 2 Rate of Return Distribution for a Portfolio of 100 Securities (Equally Weighted)

January 1945–June 1970

	Range		Frequency	1 ||| 5 |||| 10 |||| 15 |||| 20 |||| 25 |||| 30 ||||35 |||| 40 |||| 45 |||| 50 |
1	−13.6210	−12.2685	1	*
2	−12.2685	−10.9160	2	**
3	−10.9160	−9.5635	2	**
4	−9.5635	−8.2110	3	8**
5	−8.2110	−6.8585	8	8*******
6	−6.8585	−5.5060	9	*********
7	−5.5060	−4.1535	17	8****************
8	−4.1535	−2.8010	18	******************
9	−2.8010	−1.4485	27	***************************
10	−1.4485	−0.0960	28	8***************************
11	−0.0960	1.2565	30	******************************
12	1.2565	2.6090	50	**
13	2.6090	3.9615	35	***********************************
14	3.9615	5.3140	33	*********************************
15	5.3140	6.6665	18	8*****************
16	6.6665	8.0190	14	**************
17	8.0190	9.3715	4	****
18	9.3715	10.7240	2	**
19	10.7240	12.0765	2	8*
20	12.0765	13.4290	3	***

Scaling factor = 1

Average return = 0.91 percent per month

Standard deviation = 4.45 percent per month

Number of observations = 306

Exhibit 3   Rate of Return Distribution for National Department Stores

January 1945–June 1970

	Range		Frequency	1		5		10		15		20		25		30		35		40		45		50
1	−32.3670	−29.4168	1	8																			
2	−29.4168	−26.4666	0																				
3	−26.4666	−23.5163	0																				
4	−23.5163	−20.5661	1	8																			
5	−20.5661	−17.6159	1	8																			
6	−17.6159	−14.6657	3	8**																			
7	−14.6657	−11.7155	13	8***********																			
8	−11.7155	−8.7653	11	8*********																			
9	−8.7653	−5.8151	39	8*************************************																			
10	−5.8151	−2.8649	47	8***																			
11	−2.8649	0.0853	45	8***																			
12	0.0853	3.0355	34	8********************************																			
13	3.0355	5.9857	28	8**************************																			
14	5.9857	8.9359	25	8***********************																			
15	8.9359	11.8861	17	8***************																			
16	11.8861	14.8363	17	8***************																			
17	14.8363	17.7865	9	8*******																			
18	17.7865	20.7366	8	8******																			
19	20.7366	23.6868	5	8****																			
20	23.6868	26.6370	2	8*																			

Scaling factor = 1
Average return = 0.81 percent per month
Standard deviation = 9.02 percent per month
Number of observations = 306

A final remark should be made before leaving portfolio risk measures. We have implicitly assumed that investors are risk averse, i.e., that they seek to minimize risk for a given level of return. This assumption appears to be valid for most investors in most situations. The entire theory of portfolio selection and capital asset pricing is based on the belief that investors *on the average* are risk averse.

4. Diversification

A comparison of the distribution of historical returns for the 100-stock portfolio (Exhibit 2) with the distribution for National Department Stores (Exhibit 3) reveals a curious relationship. While the standard deviation of returns for the security is double that of the portfolio, its average return is less. Is the market so imperfect that over a long period of time (25 years) it rewarded substantially higher risk with the lower average return?

No so. As we shall now show, not all of the security's risk is relevant. Much of the total risk (standard deviation of return) of National Department Stores was diversifiable. That is, if it had been combined with other securities, a portion of the variation in its returns could have been smoothed out or canceled by complementary variation in the other securities. The same portfolio diversification effect accounts for the low standard deviation of return for the 100-stock portfolio. In fact, the portfolio standard deviation was less than that of the typical security in the portfolio. Much of the total risk of the component securities had been eliminated by diversification. Since much of the total risk could be eliminated simply by holding a stock in a portfolio, there was no economic requirement for the return earned to be in line with total risk. Instead, we should expect realized returns to be related to that portion of security risk that cannot be eliminated by portfolio combination.

Diversification results from combining securities having less than perfect correlation (dependence) among their returns in order to reduce portfolio risk. The portfolio return, being simply a weighted average of the individual security returns, is not diminished by diversification. In general, the lower the correlation among security returns, the greater the impact of diversification. This is true regardless of how risky the securities of the portfolio are when considered in isolation.

Ideally, if we could find sufficient securities with uncorrelated returns, we could completely eliminate portfolio risk. This situation is unfortunately not typical in real securities markets, where returns are positively correlated to a considerable degree. Thus, while portfolio risk can be substantially reduced by diversification, it cannot be entirely eliminated. This can be demonstrated very clearly by measuring the standard deviations of randomly selected portfolios containing various numbers of securities.

In a study of the impact of portfolio diversification on risk, Wagner and Lau [27] divided a sample of 200 NYSE stocks into six subgroups based on the Standard and Poor's Stock Quality Ratings as of June 1960. The highest quality ratings (A+) formed the first group, the second highest ratings (A) the next group, and so on. Randomly selected portfolios were formed from each of the subgroups and contained from 1 to 20 securities. The month-by-month portfolio returns for the 10-year period through May 1970 were then computed for each portfolio (portfolio composition remaining unchanged). The exercise was repeated ten times to reduce the dependence on single samples, and the values for the ten trials were then averaged.

Table 1 shows the average return and standard deviation for portfolios from the first subgroup (A+ quality stocks). The average return is unrelated to the number of issues in the portfolio. On the other hand, the standard deviation of return declines as the number of holdings increases. On the av-

Table 1   Risk versus Diversification for Randomly Selected Portfolios of A+ Quality Securities

June 1960–May 1970

Number of Securities in Portfolio	Average Return (%/Month)	Std. Deviation of Return (%/Month)	Correlation with Market	
			R	R^2
1	0.88	7.0	0.54	0.29
2	0.69	5.0	0.63	0.40
3	0.74	4.8	0.75	0.56
4	0.65	4.6	0.77	0.59
5	0.71	4.6	0.79	0.62
10	0.68	4.2	0.85	0.72
15	0.69	4.0	0.88	0.77
20	0.67	3.9	0.89	0.80

Source: Wagner and Lau [27], Table C, p. 53.

erage, approximately 40 percent of the single security risk is eliminated by forming randomly selected portfolios of 20 stocks. However, it is also evident that additional diversification yields rapidly diminishing reduction in risk. The improvement is slight when the number of securities held is increased beyond, say, ten. Exhibit 4 shows the results for all six quality groups. The figure shows the rapid decline in total portfolio risk as the portfolios are expanded from 1 to 10 securities.

Returning to Table 1, we note from the next-to-last column in the table that the return on a diversified portfolio follows the market very closely. The degree of association is measured by the correlation coefficient (R) of each portfolio with an unweighted index of all NYSE stocks (perfect positive correlation results in a correlation coefficient of 1.0).[5] The 20-security portfolio has a correlation of 0.89 with the market. The implication is that the risk remaining in the 20-stock portfolio is predominantly a reflection of uncertainty about the performance of the stock market in general. Exhibit 5 shows the results for the six quality groups.

Correlation in Exhibit 5 is represented by the correlation coefficient squared, R^2 (possible values range from 0 to 1.0). The R^2 coefficient has a useful interpretation: It measures the proportion of variability in portfolio return that is attributable to variability in market returns. The remaining variability is risk, which is unique to the portfolio and, as Exhibit 4 shows, can be eliminated by proper diversification of the portfolio. Thus, R^2 measures the degree of portfolio diversification. A poorly diversified portfolio will have a small R^2 (0.30–0.40). A well diversified portfolio will have a much higher R^2 (0.85–0.95). A perfectly diversified portfolio will have an R^2 of 1.0; that is, all the risk in such a portfolio is a reflection of market risk. Exhibit 5 shows the rapid gain in diversification as the portfolio is expanded from one to two securities and up to ten securities. Beyond ten securities the gains tend to be smaller. Note that increasing the number of issues tends to be less efficient at achieving diversification

[5] Two securities with perfectly correlated return patterns will have a correlation coefficient of 1.0. Conversely, if the return patterns are perfectly negative correlated, the correlation coefficient will equal −1. Two securities with uncorrelated (i.e., statistically unrelated) returns will have a correlation coefficient of zero. The average correlation coefficient between returns for NYSE securities and the S&P 500 Stock Index during the 1945–1970 period was approximately 0.5.

Exhibit 4   Standard Deviation versus Number of Issues in Portfolio

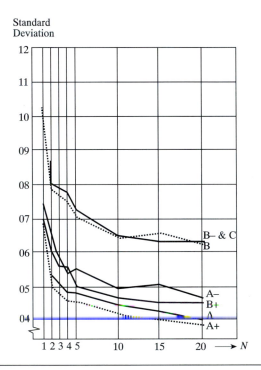

Source: Wagner and Lau (27), Exhibit 1, p. 50.

---

for the highest quality A+ issues. Apparently the companies of this group are more homogeneous than the companies grouped under the other quality codes.

The results show that while some risks can be eliminated via diversification, others cannot. Thus we are led to distinguish between a security's "unsystematic" risk, which can be washed away by mixing the security with other securities in a diversified portfolio, and its "systematic" risk, which cannot be eliminated by diversification. This proposition is illustrated in Exhibit 6. It shows total portfolio risk declining as the number of holdings increases. Increasing diversification gradually tends to eliminate the unsystematic risk, leaving only systematic, i.e., market-related, risk. The remaining variability results from the fact that the return on nearly every security depends to some degree on the overall performance of the market. Consequently, the return on a well diversified portfolio is highly correlated with the market, and its variability or uncertainty is basically the uncertainty of the market as a whole. Investors are exposed to market uncertainty, no matter how many stocks they hold.

5. The Risk of Individual Securities

In the previous section we concluded that the systematic risk of an individual security is that portion of its total risk (standard deviation of return) that cannot be eliminated by combining it with other

Exhibit 5   Correlation versus Number of Issues in Portfolio

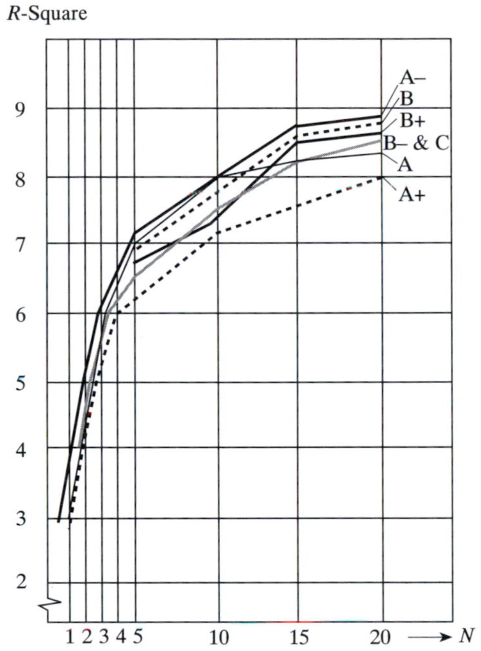

R-Square

Source: Wagner and Lau (27), Exhibit 2, p. 50.

securities in a well diversified portfolio. We now need a way of quantifying the systematic risk of a security and relating the systematic risk of a portfolio to that of its component securities. This can be accomplished by dividing security return into two parts: one dependent (i.e., perfectly correlated), and a second independent (i.e., uncorrelated) of market return. The first component of return is usually referred to as "systematic" and the second as "unsystematic." Thus we have

Security Return = Systematic Return + Unsystematic Return. (4)

Since the systematic return is perfectly correlated with the market return, it can be expressed as a factor, designated beta (β), times the market return, R_m. The beta factor is a market sensitivity index, indicating how sensitive the security return is to changes in the market level. The unsystematic return, which is independent of market returns, is usually represented by a factor epsilon (ϵ'). Thus the security return, R, may be expressed as

$$R = \beta R_m + \epsilon'. \qquad (5)$$

For example, if a security had a β factor of 2.0 (e.g., an airline stock), then a 10 percent market return would generate a systematic return for the stock of 20 percent. The security return for the period would be the 20 percent plus the unsystematic component. The unsystematic component depends on factors unique to the company, such as labor difficulties or higher than expected sales.

The security returns model given by Equation (5) is usually written in a way such that the average value of the residual term ϵ' is zero. This is accomplished by adding a factor, alpha (α), to

Exhibit 6   Systematic and Unsystematic Risk

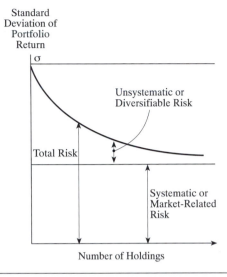

the model to represent the average value of the unsystematic returns over time. That is, we set $\epsilon' = \alpha + \epsilon$ so that

$$R = \alpha + \beta R_m + \epsilon, \tag{6}$$

where the average ϵ over time is equal to zero.

The model for security returns given by Equation (6) is usually referred to as the "market model." Graphically, the model can be depicted as a line fitted to a plot of security returns against rates of return on the market index. This is shown in Exhibit 7 for a hypothetical security.

The beta factor can be thought of as the slope of the line. It gives the expected increase in security return for a 1 percent increase in market return. In Exhibit 7, the security has a beta of 1.0. Thus, a 10 percent market return will result, on the average, in a 10 percent security return. The market-weighted average beta for all stocks is 1.0 by definition.

The alpha factor is represented by the intercept of the line on the vertical security return axis. It is equal to the average value over time of the unsystematic returns (ϵ') on the stock. For most stocks, the alpha factor tends to be small and unstable. (We shall return to alpha later.)

Using the definition of security return given by the market model, the specification of systematic and unsystematic risk is straightforward—they are simply the standard deviations of the two return components.[6]

---

[6] The relationship between the risk components is given by

$$\sigma^2 = \beta^2 \sigma^2_m + \sigma^2_\epsilon.$$

This follows directly from Equation (5) and the assumption of statistical independence of R_m and ϵ'. The R^2 term previously discussed is the ratio of systematic to total risk (both measured in terms of variance):

$$R^2 = \frac{\beta^2 \sigma^2_m}{\sigma^2}.$$

Note also that the R^2 is the square of the correlation coefficient between security and market returns.

Exhibit 7   The Market Model for Security Returns

Beta (β), the market sensitivity index, is the slope of the line. Alpha (α), the average of the residual returns, is the intercept of the line on the security axis. Epsilon (ϵ), the residual returns, is the perpendicular distances of the points from the line.

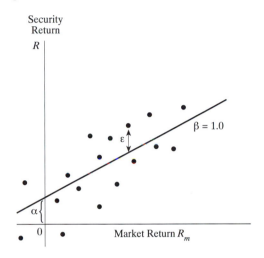

The systematic risk of a security is equal to β times the standard deviation of the market return:

$$\text{Systematic Risk} = \beta\sigma_m. \tag{7}$$

The unsystematic risk equals the standard deviation of the residual return factor ϵ:

$$\text{Unsystematic Risk} = \sigma_\epsilon. \tag{8}$$

Given measures of individual security systematic risk, we can now compute the systematic risk of portfolio. It is equal to the beta factor for the portfolio, β_p, times the risk of the market index, σ_m:

$$\text{Portfolio Systematic Risk} = \beta_p\sigma_m. \tag{9}$$

The portfolio beta factor can be shown to be simply an average of the individual security betas weighted by the proportion of each security in the portfolio, or

$$\beta_p = \sum_{j=1}^{N} X_j\beta_j, \tag{10}$$

where X_j = the proportion of portfolio market value represented by security j,

N = the number of securities.

Thus the systematic risk of the portfolio is simply a weighted average of the systematic risk of the individual securities. If the portfolio is composed of an equal dollar investment average in each stock (as was the case for the 100-security portfolio of Exhibit 2), the β_p is simply an unweighted average of the component security betas.

Table 2   Standard Deviations of 20-Stock Portfolios and Predicted Lower Limits

June 1960–May 1970

(1) Stock Quality Group	(2) Standard Deviation of 20-Stock Portfolios ($\sigma \cdot$%/Month)	(3) Average Beta Value for Quality Group β	(4) Lower Limit[a] $\beta \cdot \sigma_m$ (%/Month)
A+	3.94	0.74	3.51
A	4.17	0.80	3.80
A−	4.52	0.89	4.22
B+	4.45	0.87	4.13
B	6.27	1.24	5.89
B− & C	6.32	1.23	5.84

[a]σ_m = 4.75 percent per month.
Source: Wagner and Lau [27], p. 52, and Table C, p. 53.

The unsystematic risk of the portfolio is also a function of the unsystematic security risks, but the form is more complex.[7] The important point is that with increasing diversification this risk can be reduced toward zero.

With these results for portfolio risk, it is useful to return to Exhibit 4. The figure shows the decline in portfolio risk with increasing diversification for each of the six quality groups. However, the portfolio standard deviations for each of the six groups are decreasing toward different limits because the average risks (β) of the groups differ.

Table 2 shows a comparison of the standard deviations for the 20-stock portfolios with the predicted lower limits based on average security systematic risks. The lower limit is equal to the average beta for the quality group ($\overline{\beta}$) times the standard deviation of the market return (σ_m). The standard deviations in all cases are close to the predicted values. These results support the contention that portfolio systematic risk equals the average systematic risks of the component securities.

The main results of this section can be summarized as follows: First, as seen from Exhibit 4, roughly 40 to 50 percent of total security risk can be eliminated by diversification. Second, the remaining systematic risk is equal to the security β times market risk. Third, portfolio systematic risk is a weighted average of security systematic risks.

The implications of these results are substantial. First, we would expect realized rates of return over substantial periods of time to be related to the systematic as opposed to total risk of securities.

---

[7] Assuming the unsystematic returns (ϵ'_j) of securities to be uncorrelated (reasonably true in practice), the unsystematic portfolio risk is given by

$$\sigma^2(\epsilon'_p) = \sum_{j=1}^{N} X_j^2 \sigma^2(\epsilon'_j),$$

where $\sigma^2(\epsilon'j)$ is the unsystematic risk for stock j. Assume the portfolio is made up of equal investment in each security and $\overline{\sigma}^2(\epsilon')$ is the average value of the $\sigma^2(\epsilon'_j)$. Then, $X_j = 1/N$ and

$$\sigma^2(\epsilon'_p) = \frac{1}{N}\overline{\sigma}^2(\epsilon'),$$

which (assuming $\overline{\sigma}^2[\epsilon']$ is finite) obviously approaches zero as the number of issues in the portfolio increases.

Since the unsystematic risk is relatively easily eliminated, we should not expect the market to offer a risk premium for bearing it. Second, since security systematic risk is equal to the security beta times σ_m (which is common to all securities), beta is useful as a *relative* risk measure. The β gives the systematic risk of a security (or portfolio) relative to the risk of the market index. Thus it is often convenient to speak of systematic risk in relative terms (i.e., in terms of beta rather than beta times σ_m).

References

1. Fischer Black, Michael C. Jensen, and Myron S. Scholes. "The Capital Asset Pricing Model: Some Empirical Tests." Published in *Studies in the Theory of Capital Markets,* edited by Michael Jensen. New York, Praeger, 1972, pp. 79–121.

2. Marshall E. Blume. "Portfolio Theory: A Step Toward Its Practical Application." *Journal of Business,* Vol. 43 (April 1970), pp. 152–173.

3. Marshall E. Blume and Irwin Friend. "A New Look at the Capital Asset Pricing Model." *The Journal of Finance,* Vol. XXVIII (March 1973), pp. 19–33.

4. Richard A. Brealey. *An Introduction to Risk and Return from Common Stocks.* Cambridge, MA, MIT Press, 1969.

5. Eugene F. Fama. "Components of Investment Performance." *The Journal of Finance,* Vol. XXVII (June 1972), pp. 551–567.

6. Eugene F. Fama and James D. MacBeth. "Risk, Return and Equilibrium: Empirical Tests." Unpublished Working Paper No. 7237, University of Chicago, Graduate School of Business, August 1972.

7. Jack C. Francis. *Investment Analysis and Management.* New York, McGraw-Hill, 1972.

8. Irwin Friend and Marshall E. Blume. "Risk and the Long Run Rate of Return on NYSE Common Stocks." Working Paper No. 18–72, Wharton School of Commerce and Finance, Rodney L. White Center for Financial Research.

9. Nancy Jacob. "The Measurement of Systematic Risk for Securities and Portfolios: Some Empirical Results." *Journal of Financial and Quantitative Analysis,* Vol. VI (March 1971), pp. 815–834.

10. Michael C. Jensen. "The Performance of Mutual Funds in the Period 1945–1964." *The Journal of Finance,* Vol. XXIII (May 1968), pp. 389–416.

11. Michael C. Jensen. "Risk, the Pricing of Capital Assets, and the Evaluation of Investment Portfolios." *Journal of Business,* Vol. 42 (April 1969), pp. 167–247.

12. Michael C. Jensen. "Capital Markets: Theory and Evidence." *The Bell Journal of Economics and Management Science,* Vol. 3 (Autumn 1972), pp. 357–398.

13. Robert A. Levy. "On the Short Term Stationarity of Beta Coefficients." *Financial Analysts Journal,* Vol. 27 (November-December 1971), pp. 55–62.

14. John Lintner. "The Valuation of Risk Assets and the Selection of Risky Investments in Stock Portfolios and Capital Budgets." *Review of Economics and Statistics,* Vol. XLVII (February 1965), pp. 13–37.

15. John Lintner. "Security Prices, Risk, and Maximal Gains from Diversification." *The Journal of Finance,* Vol. XX (December 1965), pp. 587–616.

16. Norman E. Mains. "Are Mutual Fund Beta Coefficients Stationary?" Unpublished Working Paper, Investment Company Institute, Washington, DC, October 1972.

17. Harry M. Markowitz. "Portfolio Selection." *The Journal of Finance,* Vol. VII (March 1952), pp. 77–91.

18. Harry M. Markowitz. *Portfolio Selection: Efficient Diversification of Investments.* New York, John Wiley, 1959.

19. Merton H. Miller and Myron S. Scholes. "Rates of Returns in Relation to Risk: A Reexamination of Recent Findings." Published in *Studies in the Theory of Capital Markets,* edited by Michael Jensen, New York, Praeger, 1972, pp. 47–78.

beyond the return predicted by the CAPM on the basis of the asset's beta value. (More on the interpretation of alpha appears in Section 9.)

Beta for a security is calculated by regressing the observed security risk premiums, r, on the observed risk premiums on the market, r_m. By this procedure we are, in effect, estimating the parameters of the market model of Equation (16a). The equation of the fitted line is

$$r = \hat{\alpha} + \hat{\beta} r_m + \hat{\epsilon}, \tag{16b}$$

where $\hat{\alpha}$ is the intercept of the fitted line and $\hat{\beta}$ represents the stock's systematic risk. The $\hat{\epsilon}$ term represents variation about the line resulting from the unsystematic component of return. We have put hats (^) over the α, β, and ϵ terms to indicate that these are estimated values. It is important to remember that these estimated values may differ substantially from the true values because of statistical measurement difficulties. However, the extent of possible error can be measured, and we can indicate a range within which the true value is almost certain to lie.

Exhibit 8 shows a risk-premium plot and fitted line for National Department Stores. The market is represented by a weighted index of all NYSE securities. The plot is based on monthly data during the period from January 1945 to June 1970.

The estimated beta is 1.26, indicating above average systematic risk. The estimated alpha is –0.05 percent per month, indicating that the excess return on the security averaged –0.60 percent per year over the 25-year period. The correlation coefficient is 0.52; thus 27 percent of the variance of security returns resulted from market movements. The remainder was due to factors unique to the company.

Our interpretation of the estimated alpha and beta values must be conditioned by the degree of possible measurement error. The measurement error is estimated by "standard error" coefficients associated with alpha and beta.

For example, the standard error of beta is 0.12. Thus, the probability is about 66 percent that the true beta will lie between 1.26 ± 0.12 and about 95 percent that it will lie between 1.26 ± 0.24 (i.e., plus or minus two times the standard error). Thus we can say with high confidence that National Department Stores has above average risk (i.e., true beta greater than 1.0).

The standard error for alpha is 0.45, which is large compared with the estimated value of –0.05. Thus we cannot conclude that the true alpha is different from zero, since zero lies well within the range of estimated alpha plus or minus one standard error (i.e., -0.05 ± 0.45).

Table 3 presents the same type of regression results for a random collection of 30 NYSE stocks.[3] The table contains the following items: Column (1) gives the number of monthly observations, columns (2) and (3) the estimated alpha ($\hat{\alpha}$) and its standard error, columns (4) and (5) the estimated beta ($\hat{\beta}$) and its standard error, column (6) the unsystematic risk $\hat{\sigma}_\epsilon$, column (7) the R^2 in percentage terms, columns (8) and (9) the arithmetic average of monthly risk premiums and the standard deviation, and column (10) the geometric mean risk premium. The results are ranked in terms of descending values of estimated beta. The table includes summary results for the NYSE market index and the prime commercial paper risk-free rate.[4] The last two rows of the table give

---

[3] The sample was picked to give the broadest possible range of security beta values. This was accomplished by ranking all NYSE securities with complete data from 1945 to 1970 by their estimated beta values during this period. We then selected every twenty-fifth stock from the ordered list. The data was obtained from the University of Chicago CRSP (Center for Research in Security Prices) tape.

[4] The commercial paper results in Table 3 are rates of return, not risk premiums. The risk premiums would equal zero by definition.

Exhibit 8   Returns on National Department Stores versus NYSE Index (Percent per Month), January 1945–June 1970

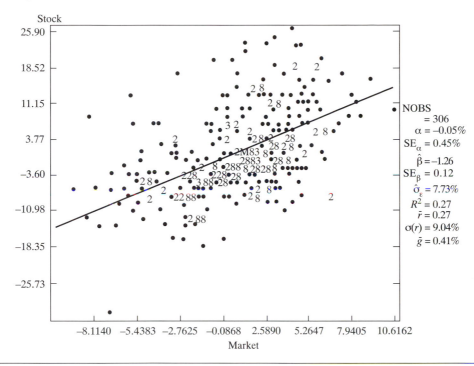

average values and standard deviations for the sample. The average beta, for example, is 1.05, slightly higher than the average of all NYSE stocks.

The beta value for a portfolio can be estimated in two ways. One method is to compute the beta of all portfolio holdings and weight the results by portfolio representation. However, this method has the disadvantage of requiring beta calculations for each individual portfolio asset. The second method is to use the same computation procedures used for stocks, but to apply them to the portfolio returns. In this way we can obtain estimates of portfolio betas without explicit consideration of the portfolio securities. We have used this approach to compute portfolio and mutual fund beta values.

Exhibit 9 shows the plot of the monthly risk premiums on the 100-stock portfolio against the NYSE index for the same 1945–1970 period. As in the case of National Department Stores, the best-fit line has been put through the points using regression analysis. The slope of the line ($\hat{\beta}$) is equal to 1.10, with a standard error of 0.03. Note the substantial reduction in the standard error term compared to the security examples. The estimated alpha is 0.14, with a standard error of 0.10. Again, we cannot conclude that the true alpha is different from zero. Note that the points group much closer to the line than in the National Department Store plot. This results, of course, from the fact that much of the unsystematic risk causing the points to be scattered around the regression line in Exhibit 8 has been eliminated. The reduction is evidenced by the R^2 measure of 0.87 (versus 0.27

returns, R_j, for a series of stocks ($j = 1, \ldots, N$) on the stocks' estimated beta values, $\hat{\beta}_j$, during the period studied. The equation of the fitted line is given by

$$\overline{R}_j = \gamma_0 + \gamma_1\beta_j + \mu_j, \tag{18a}$$

where γ_0 and γ_1 are the intercept and slope of the line and μ_j is the deviation of stock j from the line. By comparing Equations (17b) and (18a), we infer that if the CAPM hypothesis is valid, μ_j should equal $\overline{\epsilon}_j$ and hence should be small. Furthermore, it should be uncorrelated with β, and hence we can also infer that γ_0 and γ_1 should equal $\overline{R}_F$ and $\overline{R}_M - \overline{R}_F$ respectively.

The hypothesis is illustrated in Exhibit 11. Each plotted point represents one stock's realized return versus the stock's beta. The vertical distances of the points from the CAPM theoretical line (also called the "market line") represent the mean residual returns, $\overline{\epsilon}_j$. Assuming the CAPM to be correct, the $\overline{\epsilon}_j$ should be uncorrelated with the $\hat{\beta}_j$, and thus the regression equation fitted to these points should be (1) linear, (2) upward sloping with slope equal to $\overline{R}_M - \overline{R}_F$, and (3) should pass through the vertical axis at the risk-free rate.

Expressed in risk-premium form, the equation of the fitted line is

$$r_j = \gamma_0 + \gamma_1\beta_j + \mu_j, \tag{18b}$$

where $\overline{r}_j$ is the average realized risk premium for stock j. Comparing Equation (18b) to the CAPM in risk-premium form (Equation [15]), the predicted values for γ_0 and γ_1, are 0 and $\overline{r}_m$ the mean market risk premium ($\overline{R}_M - \overline{R}_F$). Thus shifting to risk premiums changes the predicted value only for γ_0, but not for γ_1.

Other Measures of Risk

The hypothesis just described is only true if beta is a complete measure of a stock's risk. Various alternative risk measures have been proposed, however. The most common alternative hypothesis states that expected return is related to the standard deviation of return—that is, to a stock's total risk, which includes both systematic and unsystematic components.

Which is more important in explaining average observed returns on securities, systematic or unsystematic risk? The way to find out is to fit an expanded equation to the data:

$$R_j = \gamma_0 + \gamma_1\hat{\beta}_j + \gamma_2(\hat{SE}_j) + \mu_j. \tag{19}$$

Here, $\hat{\beta}_j$ is a measure of systematic risk and $\hat{SE}_j$ a measure of unsystematic risk.[8] Of course, if the CAPM is exactly true, then γ_2 will be zero—that is, $\hat{SE}_j$ will contribute nothing to the explanation of observed security returns.

Tests of the Capital Asset Pricing Model

If the CAPM is right, empirical tests would show the following:

1. On the average, and over long periods of time, the securities with high systematic risk should have high rates of return.

---

[8] $\hat{SE}_j$ is an estimate of the standard error of the residual term in Equation (17a). Thus it is the estimated value for $\sigma(\epsilon_j)$, the unsystematic risk term defined in Equation (8). See column (6) of Tables 3 and 4 for typical values for securities and mutual funds.

Exhibit 11   Relationship between Average Return (R_j) and Security Risk (β_j).

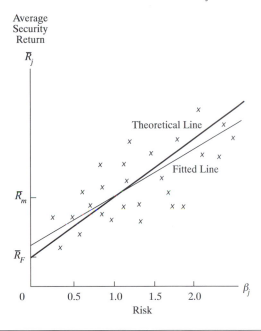

2. On the average, there should be a linear relationship between systematic risk and return.

3. The slope of the relationship (γ_1) should be equal to the mean market risk premium $(\overline{R}_M - \overline{R}_F)$ during the period used.

4. The constant term (γ_0) should be equal to the mean risk-free rate (R_F).

5. Unsystematic risk, as measured by $\hat{SE}_j$, should play no significant role in explaining differences in security returns.

These predictions have been tested in several recent statistical studies. We will review some of the more important ones. Readers wishing to skip the details may proceed to the summary at the end of this section. We will begin by summarizing results from studies based on individual securities, and then we will turn to portfolio results.

Results of Tests Based on Securities

The Jacob Study.   The Jacob study [9] deals with the 593 New York Stock Exchange stocks for which there is complete data from 1946 to 1965. Regression analyses were performed for the 1946–55 and 1956–65 periods, using both monthly and annual security returns. The relationship of mean security returns and beta values is shown in Table 6. The last two columns of the table give the theoretical values for the coefficients, as predicted by the CAPM.

Table 6   Results of the Jacob Study

$$\bar{r}_j = \gamma_0 + \gamma_1\beta_j + \mu_j$$

Tests Based on 593 Securities

Period	Return Interval	Regression Results[a]			Theoretical Values	
		γ_0	γ_1	$\bar{R}^2$	$\gamma_0 = 0$	$\gamma_1 = \bar{R}_M - \bar{R}_F$
46–55	Monthly	0.80	0.30 (0.07)b	0.02	0	1.10
	Yearly	8.90	5.10 (0.53)	0.14	0	14.40
56–65	Monthly	0.70	0.30 (0.06)	0.03	0	0.80
	Yearly	6.70	6.70 (0.53)	0.21	0	10.80

[a]Coefficient units are monthly data, percent per month; annual data, percent per year.
[b]Standard error.
Source: Jacob [9], Table 3, pp. 827–828.

The results show a significant positive relationship between realized return and risk during each of the ten-year periods. For example, in 1956–65 there was a 6.7 percent per year increase in average return for a one-unit increase in beta. Although the relationships shown in Table 6 are all positive, they are weaker than those predicted by the CAPM. In each period γ_1 is less and γ_0 is greater than the theoretical values.

The Miller-Scholes Study.   The Miller-Scholes research [19] deals with annual returns for 631 stocks during the 1954–63 period. The results of three of their tests are reported in Table 7. The tests are (1) mean return versus beta; (2) mean return versus unsystematic risk, $(\hat{SE}_j)^2$; and (3) mean return versus both beta and unsystematic risk.

The results for the first test show a significant positive relationship between mean return and beta. A one-unit increase in beta is associated with 7.1 percent increase in mean return.

The results for the second test do not agree with the CAPM's predictions. That is, high unsystematic risk is apparently associated with higher realized returns. However, Miller and Scholes show that this correlation may be largely spurious (i.e., it may be due to statistical sampling problems). For example, a substantial positive correlation exists between beta and $(\hat{SE}_j)^2$. Thus unsystematic risk will appear to be significant in tests from which beta has been omitted, even though it may be unimportant to the pricing of securities. This sort of statistical correlation need not imply a causal link between the variables.

Test number (3) includes both beta and $(\hat{SE}_j)^2$ in the regression equation. Both are found to be significantly positively related to mean return. The inclusion of $(\hat{SE}_j)^2$ has somewhat weakened the relationship of return and beta, however. A one-unit increase in beta is now associated with only a 4.2 percent increase in mean return.

Table 7   Results of the Miller-Scholes Study

$$\overline{R}_m = \gamma_0 + \gamma_1 \hat{\beta}_j + \gamma_2 (\hat{SE}_j)^2 + \mu_j$$
Annual Rates of Return 1954–1963
Tests Based in 631 Securities

Regression Results[a]				Theoretical Values		
$\hat{\gamma}_0$	$\hat{\gamma}_1$	$\hat{\gamma}_2$	R^2	γ_0	γ_1	γ_2
12.2	7.1		0.19	2.8	8.5	0
(0.7)[b]	(0.6)					
16.3		39.3	0.28	2.8	8.5	0
(0.4)		(2.5)				
12.7	4.2	31.0	0.33	2.8	8.5	0
(0.6)	(0.6)	(2.6)				

[a]Units of coefficients: percent per year.
[b]Standard error.
Source: Miller and Scholes [19], Table 1B, p. 53.

The interpretation of these results is again complicated by the strong positive correlation between beta and $(\hat{SE}_j)^2$ and by other sampling problems.[9] A significant portion of the correlation between mean return and $(SE_j)^2$ may well be a spurious result. In any case, the results do show that stocks with high systematic risk tend to have higher rates of return.

Results for Tests Based on Portfolio Returns

Tests based directly on securities clearly show the significant positive correlation between return and systematic risk. Such tests, however, are not the most efficient method of obtaining estimates of the magnitude of the risk-return trade-off. The tests are inefficient for two reasons.

The first problem is well-known to economists. It is called "errors in variables bias" and results from the fact that beta, the independent variable in the test, is typically measured with some error. These errors are random in their effect—that is, some stocks' betas are overestimated and some are underestimated. Nevertheless, when these estimated beta values are used in the test, the measurement errors tend to attenuate the relationship between mean return and risk.

By carefully grouping the securities into portfolios, much of this measurement error problem can be eliminated. The errors in individual stocks' betas cancel out so that the portfolio beta can be measured with much greater precision. This, in turn, means that tests based in portfolio returns will be more efficient than tests based on security returns.

The second problem relates to the obscuring effect of residual variation. Realized security returns have a large random component, which typically accounts for about 70 percent of the variation of

---

[9] For example, skewness in the distributions of stock returns can lead to spurious correlations between mean return and SE_j.
   See Miller and Scholes [19], pp. 66–71.

Table 8   Results of the Friend-Blume Study

**Returns from a Yearly Revision Policy for
Stocks Classified by Beta for Various Periods**

Holding Period

Portfolio No.	1929–1969		1948–1969		1956–1969	
	Beta	Mean Return	Beta	Mean Return	Beta	Mean Return
1	0.19	0.79%	0.45	0.99%	0.28	0.95%
2	0.49	1.00	0.64	1.01	0.51	0.98
3	0.67	1.10	0.76	1.25	0.66	1.12
4	0.81	1.28	0.85	1.30	0.80	1.18
5	0.92	1.26	0.94	1.35	0.91	1.17
6	1.02	1.34	1.03	1.37	1.03	1.14
7	1.15	1.42	1.12	1.32	1.16	1.10
8	1.29	1.53	1.23	1.33	1.30	1.18
9	1.49	1.55	1.36	1.39	1.48	1.15
10	2.02	1.59	1.67	1.36	1.92	1.10

Monthly arithmetic mean returns.
Source: Friend and Blume [8], Table 4, p. 10.

return. (This is the diversifiable or unsystematic risk of the stock.) By grouping securities into portfolios, we can eliminate much of this "noise" and thereby get a much clearer view of the relationship between return and systematic risk.

It should be noted that grouping does not distort the underlying risk-return relationship. The relationship that exists for individual securities is exactly the same for portfolios of securities.

The Friend-Blume Studies.   Professors Friend and Blume [3, 8] have conducted two interrelated risk-return studies. The first examines the relationship between long-run rates of return and various risk measures. The second is a direct test of the CAPM.

In the first study [8], Friend and Blume constructed portfolios of NYSE common stocks at the beginning of three different holding periods. The periods began at the ends of 1929, 1948, and 1956. All stocks for which monthly rate-of-return data could be obtained for at least four years preceding the test period were divided into ten portfolios. The securities were assigned on the basis of their betas during the preceding four years—the 10 percent of securities with the lowest betas to the first portfolio, the group with the next lowest betas to the second portfolio, and so on.

After the start of the test periods, the securities were reassigned annually. That is, each stock's estimated beta was recomputed at the end of each successive year, the stocks were ranked again on the basis of their betas, and new portfolios were formed. This procedure kept the portfolio betas reasonably stable over time.

The performance of these portfolios is summarized in Table 8. The table gives the arithmetic mean monthly returns and average beta values for each of the ten portfolios and for each test period.

For the 1929–69 period, the results indicate a strong positive association between return and beta. For the 1948–69 period, while higher beta portfolios had higher returns than portfolios with lower betas, there was little difference in return among portfolios with betas greater than 1.0. The 1956–69 period results do not show a clear relationship between beta and return. On the basis of these and other tests, the authors conclude that NYSE stocks with above-average risk have higher returns than those with below-average risk, but that there is little payoff assuming additional risk within the group of stocks with above-average betas.

In their second study [3], Blume and Friend used monthly portfolio returns during the 1955–68 period to test the CAPM. Their tests involved fitting the coefficients of Equation (18a) for three sequential periods: 1955–59, 1960–64, and 1965–68. The authors also added a factor to the regression equation to test for the linearity of the risk-return relationship.[10]

The values obtained for γ_0 and γ_1 are not in line with the Capital Asset Pricing Model's predictions, however. In the first two periods, γ_0 is substantially larger than the theoretical value. In the third period, the reverse situation exists, with γ_0 substantially less than predicted. These results imply that γ_1, the slope of the fitted line, is less than predicted in the first two periods and greater in the third.[11] Friend and Blume conclude that "the comparisons as a whole suggest that a linear model is a tenable approximation of the empirical relationship between return and risk for NYSE stocks over the three periods covered."[12]

Black, Jenson, and Scholes.   This study [1] is a careful attempt to reduce measurement errors that would bias the regression results. For each year from 1931 to 1965, the authors grouped all NYSE stocks into ten portfolios. The number of securities in each portfolio increased over the 35-year period from a low of 58 securities per portfolio in 1931 to a high of 110 in 1965.

Month-by-month returns for the portfolios were computed from January 1931 to December 1965. Average portfolio returns and portfolio betas were computed for the 35-year period and for a variety of sub-periods. The results for the complete period are shown in Table 9. The average monthly portfolio returns and beta values for the ten portfolios are plotted in Exhibit 12. The results indicate that over the complete 35-year period, average return increased by approximately 1.08 percent per month (13 percent per year) for a one-unit increase in beta. This is about three-quarters of the amount predicted by the CAPM. As Exhibit 12 shows, there appears to be little reason to question the linearity of the relationship over the 35-year period.

Black, Jenson, and Scholes also estimated the risk-return tradeoff for a number of sub-periods.[13] The slopes of the regression lines tend in most periods to understate the theoretical values, but are generally of the correct sign. Also, the sub-period relationships appear to be linear.

This paper provides substantial support for the hypothesis that realized returns are a linear function of systematic risk values. Moreover, it shows that the relationship is significantly positive over long periods of time.

---

[10] Their expanded test equation is

$$\overline{R}_j = \gamma_0 + \gamma_1\hat{\beta}_j + \gamma_2(\hat{\beta}_j)^2,$$

where, according to the CAPM, the expected value of γ_2 is zero.

[11] Table 1, p. 25, of Blume and Friend [3] presents period-by-period regression results.

[12] Blume and Friend [3], p. 26.

[13] Figure 6 of Black, Jensen, and Scholes [1], pp. 101–103, shows average monthly returns versus systematic risk for 17 nonoverlapping 2-year periods from 1932 to 1965.

Table 9   Results of the Black-Jensen-Scholes Study

$$R_p = \gamma_0 + \gamma_1 \beta_p + \mu_p$$
1931–1965
Tests Based on Ten Portfolios
(Averaging 75 Stocks per Portfolio)

Regression Results[a]			Theoretical Values	
γ_0	γ_1	R^2	$\gamma_0 = \overline{R}_F$	$\gamma_1 = \overline{R}_M - \overline{R}_F$
0.519	1.08	0.90	0.16	1.42
(0.05)[b]	(0.05)			

[a]Units of Coefficients: percent per month.
[b]Standard error.
Source: Black, Jensen, and Scholes [1], Table 4, p. 98, and Figure 7, p. 104.

Fama and MacBeth.   Fama and MacBeth [6] have extended the Black-Jensen-Scholes tests to include two additional factors. The first is an average of the β_j^2 for all individual securities in portfolio p, designated β_p^2. The second is a similar average of the residual standard deviations $(\hat{SE}_j)$ for all stocks in portfolio p, designated $\hat{SE}_p$. The first term tests for nonlinearities in the risk-return relationship, the second for the impact of residual variation.

The equation of the fitted line for the Fama-MacBeth study is given by

$$\overline{R}_p = \gamma_0 + \gamma_1 \hat{\beta}_p + \gamma_2 \hat{\beta}_p^2 + \gamma_3 \hat{SE}_p + \mu_p, \tag{20}$$

where, according to the CAPM, we should expect γ_2 and γ_3 to have zero values.

The results of the Fama-MacBeth tests show that while estimated values of γ_2 and γ_3 are not equal to zero for each interval examined, their average values tend to be insignificantly different from zero. Fama and MacBeth also confirm the Black-Jensen-Scholes result that the realized values of γ_0 are not equal to $\overline{R}_j$, as predicted by the CAPM.

Summary of Test Results

We will briefly summarize the major results of the empirical tests:

1. The evidence shows a significant positive relationship between realized returns and systematic risk. However, the slope of the relationship (γ_1) is usually less than predicted by the CAPM.

2. The relationship between risk and return appears to be linear. The studies give no evidence of significant curvature in the risk-return relationship.

3. Tests that attempt to discriminate between the effects of systematic and unsystematic risk do not yield definitive results. Both kinds of risk appear to be positively related to security returns. However, there is substantial support for the proposition that the relationship between return and unsystematic risk is at least partly spurious—that is, it partly reflects statistical problems rather than the true nature of capital markets.

Exhibit 12   Results of the Black-Jensen-Scholes Study, 1931–1965

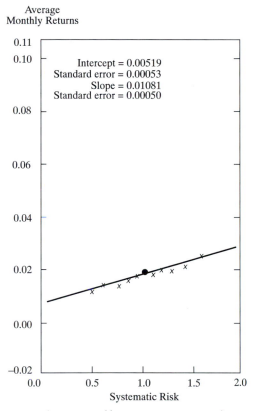

Average monthly returns versus systematic
risk for the 35-year period 1931–1965 for
ten portfolios and the market portfolio

Source: Black, Jensen, and Scholes [1], Fig. 7, p. 104.

Obviously, we cannot claim that the CAPM is absolutely right. On the other hand, the empirical tests do support the view that beta is a useful risk measure and that high-beta stocks tend to be priced in order to yield correspondingly high rates of return.

9. Measurement of Investment Performance

The basic concept underlying investment performance measurement follows directly from the risk-return theory. The return on managed portfolios, such as mutual funds, can be judged relative to the returns on unmanaged portfolios at the same degree of investment risk. If the return exceeds the standard, the portfolio manager has performed in a superior way, and vice versa. Given this, it remains to select a set of "benchmark" portfolios against which the performance of managed portfolios can be evaluated.

Performance Measures Developed from the Capital Asset Pricing Model

The CAPM provides a convenient and familiar standard for performance measurement; the benchmark portfolios are simply combinations of the riskless asset and the market index. The return standard for a mutual fund, for example, with beta equal to β_p, is equal to the risk-free rate $(\overline{R}_F)$ plus β_p times the average realized risk premium on the market $(\overline{R}_M - \overline{R}_F)$. Thus the return on the performance standard $(\overline{R}_S)$ is given by

$$\overline{R}_S = \overline{R}_F + \beta_P(\overline{R}_M - \overline{R}_F), \tag{21}$$

where $\overline{R}_M$ and $\overline{R}_F$ are the arithmetic average returns on the market index and riskless asset during the evaluation period. The performance measure, designated α_p, is equal to the difference in average returns between the fund and its standard; that is,

$$\alpha_p = \overline{R}_P - \overline{R}_S, \tag{22}$$

where $\overline{R}_P$ is the arithmetic average return on the fund. Under the CAPM assumption, the expected values of $\overline{R}_P$ and $\overline{R}_S$ are the same; therefore, the expected value for the performance measure $\hat{\alpha}_p$ is zero. Managed portfolios with positive estimated values for α_p have thus outperformed the standard, and vice versa. Estimated values of alpha $(\hat{\alpha}_p)$ are determined by regressing the portfolio risk premiums on the corresponding market risk premiums.

The interpretation of the estimated alpha must take into consideration possible statistical measurement errors. As we discussed in Section 7, the standard error of alpha (SE_α) is an indication of the extent of the possible measurement error. The larger the standard error, the less certain we can be that measured alpha is a close approximation of the true value.[14]

A measure of the degree of statistical significance of the estimated alpha value is given by the ratio of the estimated alpha to its standard error. The ratio, designated as t_α, is given by

$$t_\alpha = \hat{\alpha}_p/SE_\alpha. \tag{23}$$

The statistic t_α gives a measure of the extent to which the true value of alpha can be considered to be different from zero. If the absolute value of t_α is large, then we have more confidence that the true value of alpha is different from zero. Absolute values of t_α in excess of 2.0 indicate a probability of less than about 2.5 percent that the true value of alpha is zero.

These methods of performance measurement were originally devised by Michael Jensen [10, 11] and have been widely used in many studies of investment performance, including that of the recent SEC Institutional Investor Study [22].

A performance measure closely related to the Jensen alpha measure was developed by Jack L. Treynor [25]. The Treynor performance measure (designated TI)[15] is given by

$$TI = \alpha/\beta. \tag{24}$$

---

[14] See columns 2 and 3 of Table 4 for typical mutual fund α and SE_α values.

[15] Treynor's work preceded that of Jensen. In a discussion of Jensen's performance measure [26], Treynor showed that his measure (as originally presented in [25]) was equivalent to

$$TI = R_F - \alpha/\beta.$$

Since R_F is a constant, the TI index for ranking purposes is equivalent to that given in Equation (24).

Exhibit 13   Relationship between the Jensen and Treynor Measures of Investment Performance

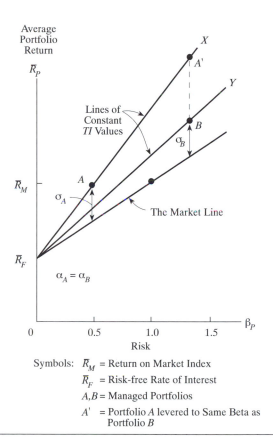

Symbols: $\bar{R}_M$ = Return on Market Index

$\bar{R}_F$ = Risk-free Rate of Interest

A,B = Managed Portfolios

A' = Portfolio A levered to Same Beta as Portfolio B

The difference between the α and *TI* performance measures is simply that the fund alpha value has been divided by its estimated beta. The effect, however, is significant, eliminating a so-called "leverage bias" from the Jensen alpha measures. This is illustrated in Exhibit 13.

Funds *A* and *B* in Exhibit 13 have the same alpha values. (The alphas are equal to the vertical distance on the diagram between the funds and the market line.) By combining portfolio *B* with the riskless rate (that is, by borrowing or lending at R_F), any return-risk combination along line *Y* can be obtained. But such points are clearly dominated by combinations along line *X*—attainable by borrowing or lending combined with fund *A*. As Exhibit 13 shows, the alpha for fund *A*, when levered to the same beta as fund *B* (Point *A'*), dominates the latter's alpha value.

The Treynor measure eliminates this leverage effect. All funds that lie along a line (such as *X* or *Y*) have the same *TI* value; therefore, borrowing or lending combined with any fund outcome will not increase (or decrease) its performance measure. The Treynor measure thus permits direct performance comparisons among funds with differing beta values.

Problems with the Market Line Standard

The tests of the CAPM summarized in Section 8 indicate that the average returns over time on securities and portfolios tend to deviate from the predictions of the model. Although the observed risk-return relationships seem to be linear, they are generally flatter than predicted by the CAPM, implying that the trade-off of risk for return is less than predicted.

This evidence raises some question as to whether the CAPM market line provides the best benchmark for performance measurement and suggests instead that other benchmark portfolios may be more appropriate. For example, under certain conditions, the "empirical" risk-return lines developed by Black, Jensen, and Scholes [1] and others would seem to be a reasonable alternative to the CAPM market line standard. This might be the case if the portfolio for which performance is being measured were restricted to exactly the same set of investment options used to create the empirical standard, that is, if the portfolio were fully invested in common stock and could not use leverage to increase its beta value. For such a portfolio, it would seem appropriate to measure performance relative to the empirical line, as opposed to the market line.

A comparison of these standards is illustrated in Exhibit 14. The market line performance measure (designated as α_1 in Exhibit 14) is equal to the vertical distance from the portfolio to the market line. The empirical line measure (designated α_2) is the vertical distance from the portfolio to the empirical line. Since, ideally, all the stocks used to develop the empirical line are contained in the market index, the empirical line, like the market line, would be expected to have a return equal to market return, $\overline{R}_M$, for beta equal to 1.0. The intercepts on the return axis, however, are typically different for the two lines. The market line intercept, by definition, is equal to the average risk-free rate. The empirical line intersects the return axis at a point different from $\overline{R}_F$, and typically above it. This intercept equals the average return on a portfolio with "zero beta," designated $\overline{R}_Z$. The existence of a long-run average return on the zero beta portfolio that differs from the riskless rate is a clear violation of the predictions of the CAPM. As of this time, there is no clear theoretical understanding of the reason for this difference.

To summarize, empirically based performance standards could, under certain conditions, provide alternatives to those of the CAPM market line standard. However, the design of appropriate empirical standards requires further research. In the interim, the familiar market line benchmarks can provide useful information regarding performance, although the information should not be regarded as being very precise.[16]

References

1. Fischer Black, Michael C. Jensen, and Myron S. Scholes. "The Capital Asset Pricing Model: Some Empirical Tests." Published in *Studies in the Theory of Capital Markets,* edited by Michael Jensen. New York, Praeger, 1972, pp. 79–121.

2. Marshall E. Blume. "Portfolio Theory: A Step Toward Its Practical Application." *Journal of Business,* Vol. 43 (April 1970), pp. 152–173.

3. Marshall E. Blume and Irwin Friend. "A New Look at the Capital Asset Pricing Model." *The Journal of Finance,* Vol. XXVIII (March 1973), pp. 19–33.

[16] There are a number of excellent references for further study of portfolio theory. Among these we would recommend books by Richard A. Brealey [4], Jack Clark Francis [7], and William F. Sharpe [24]. For a more technical survey of the theoretical and empirical literature, see Jensen [12].

Exhibit 14   Measurement of Investment Performance: Market Line versus Empirical Standard

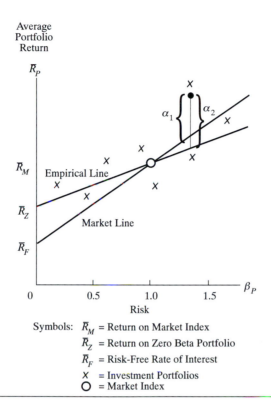

Symbols: $\bar{R}_M$ = Return on Market Index
$\bar{R}_Z$ = Return on Zero Beta Portfolio
$\bar{R}_F$ = Risk-Free Rate of Interest
X = Investment Portfolios
O = Market Index

4. Richard A. Brealey. *An Introduction to Risk and Return from Common Stocks.* Cambridge, Mass., MIT Press, 1969.

5. Eugene F. Fama. "Components of Investment Performance." *The Journal of Finance,* Vol. XXVII (June 1972), pp. 551–567.

6. Eugene F. Fama and James D. MacBeth. "Risk, Return and Equilibrium: Empirical Tests." Unpublished Working Paper No. 7237, University of Chicago, Graduate School of Business, August 1972.

7. Jack C. Francis. *Investment Analysis and Management.* New York, McGraw-Hill, 1972.

8. Irwin Friend and Marshall E. Blume. "Risk and the Long Run Rate of Return on NYSE Common Stocks." Working Paper No. 18–72. Wharton School of Commerce and Finance, Rodney L. White Center for Financial Research.

9. Nancy Jacob. "The Measurement of Systematic Risk for Securities and Portfolios: Some Empirical Results."*Journal of Financial and Quantitative Analysis,* Vol. Vl (March 1971), pp. 815–834.

10. Michael C. Jensen. "The Performance of Mutual Funds in the Period 1945–1964." *The Journal of Finance,* Vol. XXIII (May 1968), pp. 389–416.

11. Michael C. Jensen. "Risk, the Pricing of Capital Assets, and the Evaluation of Investment Portfolios." *Journal of Business,* Vol. 42 (April 1969), pp. 167–247.

12. Michael C. Jensen. "Capital Markets: Theory and Evidence." *The Bell Journal of Economics and Management Science,* Vol. 3 (Autumn 1972), pp. 357–398.

13. Robert A. Levy. "On the Short Term Stationarity of Beta Coefficients." *Financial Analysts Journal,* Vol 27 (November–December 1971), pp. 55–62.

14. John Lintner. "The Valuation of Risk Assets and the Selection of Risky Investments in Stock Portfolios and Capital Budgets." *Review of Economics and Statistics,* Vol. XLVII (February 1965), pp. 13–37.

15. John Lintner. "Security Prices, Risk, and Maximal Gains from Diversification." *The Journal of Finance,* Vol. XX (December 1965), pp. 587–616.

16. Norman E. Mains. "Are Mutual Fund Beta Coefficients Stationary?" Unpublished Working Paper, Investment Company Institute, Washington, DC, October 1972.

17. Harry M. Markowitz. "Portfolio Selection." *The Journal of Finance,* Vol. VII (March 1952), pp. 77–91.

18. Harry M. Markowitz. *Portfolio Selection: Efficient Diversification of Investments.* New York, John Wiley, 1959.

19. Merton H. Miller and Myron S. Scholes. "Rates of Returns in Relation to Risk: A Reexamination of Recent Findings." Published in *Studies in the Theory of Capital Markets,* edited by Michael Jensen. New York: Praeger, 1972, pp. 47–78.

20. Franco Modigliani and Gerald A. Pogue. A *Study of Investment Performance Fees.* Lexington, MA, Heath-Lexington Books, 1974.

21. Gerald A. Pogue and Walter Conway. "On the Stability of Mutual Fund Beta Values." Unpublished Working Paper, MIT, Sloan School of Management, June 1972.

22. Securities and Exchange Commission. *Institutional Investor Study Report of the Securities and Exchange Commission.* Chapter 4, "Investment Advisory Complexes," pp. 325–347. Washington, DC: U.S. Government Printing Office, 1971.

23. William F. Sharpe. "Capital Asset Prices: A Theory of Market Equilibrium under Conditions of Risk." *The Journal of Finance,* Vol. XIX (September 1964), pp. 425–442.

24. William F. Sharpe. *Portfolio Theory and Capital Markets.* New York, McGraw-Hill, 1970.

25. Jack L. Treynor. "How to Rate the Management of Investment Funds." *Harvard Business Review,* Vol. XLIII (January–February 1965), pp. 63–75.

26. Jack L. Treynor. "The Performance of Mutual Funds in the Period 1945–1964: Discussion." *The Journal of Finance,* Vol. XXIII (May 1968), pp. 418–419.

27. Wayne H. Wagner, and Sheila Lau. "The Effect of Diversification on Risk." *Financial Analysts Journal,* Vol. 26 (November–December 1971), pp. 48–53.

Discussion Questions

1. Summarize the assumptions that allow the theoretical derivation of the CAPM.

2. In the event that empirical testing shows the CAPM to explain relationships among risk, return, and value, is it of any importance whether the assumptions made for deriving the CAPM are indeed realistic? Discuss.

3. If the CAPM is to be useful, why is it necessary that beta values for a firm or mutual fund be predictable (have stationarity)?

4. Comment on the findings of the Levy study: that the stationarity of betas was related to the number of securities in the portfolio.

5. Discuss each of the five predictions listed for testing whether the CAPM is appropriate.

6. Summarize the results of the two studies described (the Jacob and the Miller-Scholes studies) that performed tests on individual securities.

7. Explain the two reasons given why CAPM tests on individual securities are less efficient than tests on portfolios.

8. Comment on the general results of the empirical tests on the CAPM.

Problems

1. Assume that the CAPM is valid and that the betas have stationarity. Use the relationship

$$E(R_p) = R_F + \beta_p(E(R_m) - R_F)$$

to compute $E(R_p)$ for portfolios of one security each. For each calculation, therefore, the $E(R_p)$ is an estimate of the cost of equity for that firm. Perform this calculation for the following firms: Homestake Mining Company, First National Store, American Ship Building, Phillip Jones Corporation, and City Investing Company.

Suggestions:

a. For your estimate of R_F, look up the current rate on thirty-day treasury bills.

b. Use the mean security value (times 12) in Table 3, column 10 for your estimate of the risk premium.

c. Use beta values from Table 3 for each firm indicated.

2. Critically evaluate the potential of this method for estimating the cost of equity for the firm. In your analysis, include a discussion of what rate is appropriate for the risk-free rate.

Barr Rosenberg and Andrew Rudd

The Corporate Uses of Beta

This article, published in 1983, was an important introduction of portfolio theory concepts for the benefit of corporate users in financial management. Some of the examples may seem unrealistic to you because the interest rates are so high. However, keep in mind that interest rates in the early 1980s were very high, and a risk-free rate of 13 percent on July 1, 1982, was certainly realistic.

Introduction

Of the many analytical methods collectively referred to as Modern Portfolio Theory, the Capital Asset Pricing Model (CAPM) is the most familiar to today's generation of MBA's. The popularity of the CAPM arises from its success in expressing a powerful theoretical insight in a simple, usable form. The primary use of the CAPM is to determine minimum required rates of return from investments in risky assets. The key variable in the CAPM is called "beta," a statistical measure of risk that has become as familiar as—and, indeed, interchangeable with—the CAPM itself. Over the past decade, beta has become the most widely recognized and applied measure of risk in the investment community.

In our view the recognition accorded beta and the CAPM is well deserved. The model captures the essential treatment of risk in capital markets, reflecting the crucial function of those markets in diversifying risk across the society. Although the original methodology and perspective of the CAPM have been refined in the last two decades, we believe the basic concepts underlying the model have stood the test of time.

Beta is an important tool for almost all institutional investors. Indeed, it is hard to find a major investment advisor or pension plan sponsor in the United States who does not use some aspect of Modern Portfolio Theory. By comparison, corporate financial managers have lagged behind in applying the modern analytical tools that have evolved from the CAPM. Finance theory maintains that the same CAPM-derived expected rates of return that have provided the benchmarks for evaluating the

Source: Reprinted with permission from *Issues in Corporate Finance* (New York: Stern, Steward, Putnam, and Macklis, 1983), pp. 42–52. Barr Rosenberg is Managing General Partner, Rosenberg Institutional Equity Management, Orinda, CA. Andrew Rudd is Chairman and CEO of BARRA, Inc., International Financial Consulting, Berkeley, CA.

performance of investment managers should also be used by corporate managers as the "hurdle rates" (or discount rates, in discounted cash flow applications) for evaluating corporate investments. These expected rates of return also furnish the standards by which corporate performance should be judged.

Probably the most formidable obstacle to applying the CAPM in corporate investment decisions has been the difficulty of making reasonable judgments about the betas or projects or internal divisions. The prices or values of such "non-trading" assets are not readily observable, and thus the standard statistical estimates of beta cannot be calculated using market data alone. Without such beta predictions, the CAPM is difficult to apply.

This article is concerned with advances in the area of risk prediction that have made it possible to project the relative risks associated with non-trading investments—whether SBU's, subsidiaries, or individual projects. With these advances, the CAPM can be used to obtain required rates of return that can be used in a wide variety of corporate financial decisions: capital budgeting, acquisition and divestiture pricing, performance comparison among divisions, and structuring management compensation contracts.

Before discussing these topics, we will begin by reviewing the role of the CAPM in determining the appropriate reward for risk.

The Reward for Risk Bearing

Financial managers have long realized that some projects were riskier than others and that these projects required a higher rate of return. A risky investment is, of course, one whose return is uncertain in advance; and in such a case, it is only the *expected* or average rate of return that can be projected.

For example, a project that requires an initial investment of $100 and returns $113 at the end of a year with certainty is a *riskless* project offering an investment rate of return of 13 percent. Compare this to another project that also requires a $100 investment, but with an uncertain outcome. Suppose the risky project has a 50 percent probability of success, in which case the investment would be worth $226 (providing an investment return of 226 percent), and a 50 percent probability of disaster, in which case the initial investment would be entirely lost (with a rate of return on investment of −100 percent). The expected value of this project is one-half of $226, and so again equals $113. If a company were to invest all of its funds in one or the other of these projects, what manager would not choose the one promising a certain 13 percent?

To justify undertaking the risky project, a higher payout in the event of success is required. Suppose instead that the success payout were $238. Then, the expected value would be one-half of $238, or $119. The excess of this $119 expectation over the $113 obtained from the riskless project would amount to a $6 expected premium on an investment of $100, or a 6 percent excess rate of return for the project. Faced with the choice between this risky investment and the riskless alternative above, the manager's decision would be more difficult. The important question would then become "Is this expected excess return of 6 percent enough to justify taking on the added investment risk?" It is questions like these that the CAPM was designed to answer.

The Portfolio Perspective

The concept of decision making in the presence of risk is a relatively old one, and it was first studied as a formal question in the 1920s. Probably the single most important development in investment theory was Harry Markowitz's insight that because investors are concerned with the return on their entire portfolio of assets, the risk of any individual project is relevant only insofar as it contributes to the risk of that portfolio.[1]

In other words, we cannot evaluate the risk of a project in isolation, but instead must consider each project within the context of all other assets that are held. For a corporation with many divisions, this suggests that the risk of each division should be considered within the context of all divisions. Consider again the case of the risky project above, with its 50 percent chance of returning $226 and 50 percent chance of returning nothing. Suppose further that the corporation considering the project is engaged in other risky businesses, such that if this project fails, the other businesses will pay off; and, conversely, if the other businesses fail, this project will succeed. In this case, the project provides a hedge against the risks of the other businesses, and actually *reduces* the risk of the corporation as a whole! Using this corporate-wide framework, such a risk-reducing investment would be chosen instead of the riskless alternative.

The portfolio perspective, in which the risk of each division is evaluated in the context of the whole, is an important advance on the naive "one-at-a-time approach" in which each division is evaluated in isolation. Even the corporate-wide perspective, however, is not broad enough for most corporate applications.[2] For the majority of corporate uses, the relevant context for measuring risk is *not* the individual corporation's portfolio of assets, but rather the cumulative portfolio of the corporation's stockholders—both actual and potential. In this broader perspective, the appropriate criterion for evaluating risk shifts from the corporate portfolio to the portfolio held by all investors, the "market portfolio" of the society.

The Simple Capital Asset Pricing Model

Corporate stockholders typically hold the shares of many companies in their portfolios. The portfolios of institutional investors (mutual fund managers, pension sponsors, investment advisor trust departments, insurance companies, and the like) include anywhere from a minimum of 30 to 40 to a maximum of several thousand common stocks. From their point of view, the success or failure of a given company is only one of many outcomes that influence the performance of their portfolio.

For such well-diversified investors, then, it is not the isolated equity risk of the individual corporation that counts, but rather its contribution to the risk of a diversified equity portfolio. The risk of almost all managed equity portfolios looks very much like the risk of the market portfolio of all equities; that is, their risk is very highly correlated with the risk of a market index.[3]

As a result, the individual corporation's contribution to the risk of investors' equity portfolios can be closely approximated by calculating its contribution to the risk of the portfolio of all outstanding equities, or the market portfolio. It is this risk contribution that is measured by a company's beta. The higher the beta, the greater the contribution to the risk of investors' portfolios. And the greater the risk, the higher the return expected by these investors for holding the security.

---

[1] Harry M. Markowitz: *Portfolio Selection: Efficient Diversification of Investment.* John Wiley, New York, 1959.

[2] Those uses for the corporate-wide perspective are analyzed in a related article now in preparation.

[3] For example, the equity portfolio held by large pension funds typically has correlations of .98 (where 1.0 represents perfect correlation) or higher with broad-based market indexes.

The simple Capital Asset Pricing Model captures this perspective.[4] According to the simple CAPM, an investment's required rate of return increases in direct proportion to its beta. The CAPM also implies that investors, in pricing common stocks, are concerned exclusively with *systematic* risk. A security's systematic risk, as measured by beta, is the sensitivity (or co-variance) of its returns to movements in the economy as a whole. Assets with high betas exaggerate general market developments, performing exceptionally well when the market goes up and exceptionally poorly when the market goes down.

All common stocks, of course, have additional risk. Such risk is called "residual" because it is the risk that remains after the systematic component has been removed. Residual risk is also sometimes called "diversifiable" because a properly structured portfolio can escape this risk entirely by diversifying it away. The reasoning underlying the CAPM is that, because residual risk can be eliminated cheaply through diversification, capital markets will not reward investors for bearing such risks. Consequently, stocks are priced as if investors' expected (and, on average and over long periods of time, their actual) returns are related only to the systematic risks of their portfolios.

Beta, then, is a measure of exposure to systematic risk only. It is also a measure of *relative* risk expressing systematic risk exposure in relation to all other securities and thus to the market as a whole. The market portfolio, by definition, has a beta of 1.0. A beta greater than 1 indicates above average systematic risk; a beta less than 1, below-average systematic risk. The betas of U.S. common stocks range from about 0.5 to somewhere above 2.0.[5]

At a beta of 1.0, the average level of risk, investors expect an average return. What is an average return? Intuitively, it should be the return on the average investor's portfolio. The average portfolio includes, at least in theory, all assets in the economy in proportion to their value. However, because the returns on this hypothetically all-inclusive "market portfolio" cannot be observed, we are forced to rely on broad stock market indices (often the S&P 500) as a proxy for "the market."[6]

With this as background, the simple CAPM states the following:

$$E(R) = R_F + B(E(R_M) - R_F)$$

where:
E(R) is the required or expected rate of return on the asset,
R_F is the risk-free return,
B is the beta of the asset,
$E(R_M)$ is the expected return on the market portfolio.

The required rate of return is equal to the sum of two terms: the risk-free return and an increment that compensates the investor for accepting the asset's risk. The compensation for risk is expressed

---

[4] We call it "simple" to contrast it from the extended models that have since been developed. This model had its origin in the work pursued independently by Professors William Sharpe, John Lintner, and Jan Mossin, aimed at understanding how capital asset prices are determined by the give and take of the competitive capital market.

[5] A negative beta would identify a common stock as a hedge against the systematic risk of the economy. Because of the extent to which the price of gold moves against the dollar, gold stocks come closest to having negative betas. Indeed, there may have been a few years in the early 1970s when the betas of gold stocks were actually zero or slightly negative. Since that time, however, they have risen.

[6] The market portfolio has holdings in every asset in proportion to the shares outstanding of that asset. Just as the shareholdings in the market portfolio are proportional to shares outstanding, the values of holdings in the market portfolio are in direct proportion to the value of outstanding shares in the market—that is, to the fraction of outstanding common stock value in each company.

as the asset's beta multiplied by the expected excess return of the market, $E(R_M) - R_F$. This expected excess return is sometimes referred to as the "risk premium."

Determining Required Rates of Return

To use the CAPM, three rates of return are needed: the short-term rate (or the rate on whatever maturity corresponds most closely to the term of the investment in question) on government securities, the market rate of return, and the after-tax cost of debt. The first and third of these are determined by market rates of interest and the tax law. Arriving at a figure for the expected excess rate of return on the equity market portfolio (i.e., $E(R) - R_F$) is more difficult.

One approach is to use average historical returns (including dividends plus market appreciation) as a substitute. This typically arrives at a number like 6 percent.[7]

In addition, surveys of investor opinion have been used to arrive at a consensus of expectations about the market's future performance. The collective response is then used to derive implied rates of return in the market.

An increasing number of services also provide realistic estimates of the required rate of return for equity investment.[8] In recent years, systematic long-term forecasting procedures have been used to project corporate earnings, dividends, and stock prices. The use of these projections (in discounted dividend valuation models) has in turn yielded realistic estimates of expected rates of return.

These alternative methods come up with prospective excess rates of return for the equity market that are, again, in the range of 6 percent, but often slightly lower.[9]

Extensions of the CAPM

Before illustrating some of the corporate applications of the CAPM, we want to comment briefly on the solidity of its theoretical foundations.

Because the "market portfolio of all assets" is only a theoretical construct whose risks and returns are not practically calculated, most applications of CAPM use some index of common stocks as a surrogate. As some academics have argued, the errors caused by the failure to use the right benchmark portfolio may be significant. Bonds, real estate, and human capital are all examples of investments whose returns and risks are not reflected in the performance of the S&P 500. And to the extent that certain corporate projects have characteristics more closely resembling such assets, the use of betas measured against the S&P 500 may not be appropriate.

A similar problem arises from the extension of common stock holdings across national boundaries. The existence of international investment means that the market portfolio of assets held by

---

[7] The most frequently cited study is R. G. Ibbotson and R. A. Sinquefield, *Stocks, Bonds, Bills and Inflation: The Past (1926–1976) and the Future (1977–2000)* (Charlottesville, VA: Financial Analysts Research Foundation, 1977).

[8] The goal is to describe the expectations in the minds of investors since it is these expectations that determine the investor's actions in valuing stocks. A service produces "reasonable" results if investors judge the results to be reasonable. In the 1960s, Value Line pioneered in providing a broad cross-section of long-term earnings and payout forecasts. This was indeed a pioneering effort, but the required rates of return inferred from valuation models applied to these earnings forecasts fluctuated enormously from year to year. In the recent past, however, a number of services have provided forecasts that are sufficiently representative of the consensus to produce expected rates of return that are accepted as plausible by the investor community.

[9] For the origins of the Dividend Discount Model, see John Burr Williams, *The Theory of Investment Value* (Cambridge, MA: Harvard University Press, 1938).

U.S. investors is not identical to the index of U.S. common stocks. It is our judgment that such problems are not likely to be serious for most corporate uses. In all but a few cases, the application of the CAPM using betas calculated against a broad stock market index should provide a good working approximation of the risks of corporate investments.

Second, problems arise from the unrealistic assumptions of the simple CAPM. Extensions of this model, taking into account a number of subtleties in the investment environment, come up with slightly different formulas for capital asset pricing. These questions will be the subject of academic research for years to come. On balance, though, we favor extensions of the CAPM in which beta remains the dominant determinant of valuation.[10]

Finally, there is the question of which particular definition of the market portfolio of common stocks will be used to define beta. Will it be the Standard & Poor's 500 stock index, a broader-based New York Stock Exchange index, or even the portfolio of all the common stocks in the United States that are publicly traded and meet the SEC requirement to file 10K reports? It seems that the wider the index, the better; and we thus prefer a broader index. But for most applications, the S&P 500 is broad enough.[11]

In sum, the simple CAPM relationship, using either the S&P 500 or a broader-based market weighted index as the basis for calculating beta, should serve well in most corporate applications. Only in the case of rate regulation, where a company's revenues are set by a regulatory agency in line with the CAPM, are refinements of the CAPM likely to have a significant effect.[12]

Capital Budgeting and the Cost of Capital

Perhaps the most common corporate financial decision is the valuation of a capital investment opportunity. In its most general form, we can isolate four steps in the analysis:

1. Estimation of the investment's after-tax cash flow.

2. Prediction of the investment's risk.

3. Estimation of the cost of capital (the expected rate of return demanded by investors for equivalent risk assets).

4. Calculation of the net present value of the investment by discounting the cash flows using the cost of capital.

Risk assessment and the calculation of expected returns are thus integral steps in the capital budgeting process. They produce the cost of capital that is used to discount expected cash flows back to their present value.

---

[10] See Barr Rosenberg, "The Capital Asset Pricing Model and the Market Model," *Journal of Portfolio Management* (Winter 1981), pp. 5–16, for a more complete discussion of this question.

[11] A definite conclusion can be reached on this subject. As we have complete data on the 10K filing companies, we can evaluate the potential error from more restrictive indexes. Statistical research at BARRA has confirmed that the error implied in the use of the S&P 500 as a market portfolio is tolerable for the definition of beta. See Andrew Rudd and Barr Rosenberg, "The 'Market Model' in Investment Management," *Journal of Finance* (May 1980), pp. 597–607.

[12] For readings on this subject, see, for example, the articles in the Autumn 1978 issue of *Financial Management* and the subsequent correspondence.

According to the CAPM, then, the relevant measure of risk is beta; and the relationship between risk and required return is the familiar CAPM itself, as specified in the equation above.

How does the computation proceed? Let us consider the example of XYZ Corporation, whose beta as of July 1, 1982, was 0.75.[13] Further, assume the long-run market risk premium is 6 percent and the risk-free rate is 13 percent. Putting these numbers into the CAPM equation gives the required rate of return (cost of equity):

$$13\% + 0.75(6\%) = 17.5\%$$

The CAPM implies that investors who expect the common stock of XYZ to provide an annual rate of return equal to (greater or less than) 17.5 percent will classify XYZ as fairly (under- or over-) valued.

Notice that this 17.5 percent figure is the company's cost of *equity* capital only. And while it does represent a minimal standard for the corporate-wide return on equity, it should not be used as a hurdle rate for capital budgeting decisions within XYZ. To obtain the cost of capital for discounting purposes, we have to adjust for the financial leverage of XYZ.

To illustrate, let's assume that XYZ's target capital structure is composed of 65 percent equity and 35 percent debt. Further, the after-tax cost of debt is estimated to be approximately 7.6 percent. Given these assumptions, XYZ Corporation's overall cost of debt and equity capital (also called the "weighted average cost of capital") is:

$$\frac{\text{equity}}{\text{proportion}} \cdot \frac{\text{cost of}}{\text{equity}} + \frac{\text{debt}}{\text{proportion}} \cdot \frac{\text{cost of}}{\text{debt}} =$$
$$(0.65)(17.5\%) + (0.35)(7.6\%) = 14.0\%$$

What does this 14.0 percent mean? It is the after-tax return that managers should require from any project that is a "clone" of XYZ. This figure is clearly important in investor relations as well, for it expresses investors' expectations about the company's return on its total capital investment. If, however, the investment under consideration differs significantly from the company norm, management should evaluate the investment according to its own beta, rather than the beta for the company as a whole.

To illustrate this point, let's look at one of XYZ's divisions, a producer of specialized electronic components that we will call "ABC." The most common procedure for applying the CAPM to non-trading assets is known as the "method of similars." This approach estimates the risk of a division or project using the average beta of a sample of companies engaged solely, or largely, in the same line of business.

In the case of ABC, the first step was to identify the division's most direct competitors. ABC was able to identify five direct competitors, but of these only two were publicly traded. The (value-weighted) average beta for the two competitors was 1.43, suggesting that this branch of the electronics business is substantially riskier than XYZ's other operations. But, because there are only two companies in the sample, this estimate of ABC's beta could be very inaccurate.

Consequently, the search for similars was extended to the more general SIC (Standard Industrial Classification) code, adding 15 companies to the sample. The average beta for these 15 companies

---

[13] XYZ is a diversified electronics company whose name has been deleted to preserve confidentiality. The figures mentioned in the text were derived by a Financial Strategy task force at XYZ.

Exhibit 2   Fundamental Beta Prediction for BCD

Average beta...1.00
Industry adjustment..−0.15
Financial leverage adjustment......................................0.00
Growth orientation adjustment ....−0.15
Earnings variation adjustment ....−0.05
Predicted fundamental beta.......................................0.65

The great advantage of the method of similars is its simplicity. All that is required is a group of publicly traded companies whose business risks, on average, are comparable to that of the investment in question. The disadvantage of the method of similars, besides the possibly arbitrary nature of the selection process, is its likelihood of inaccuracy. The list of similar companies is usually very small, and none of them is likely to be comparable, in all aspects, to the particular project. As a result, the range of uncertainty in the implied prediction can be quite wide.

In contrast to the simplicity of the method of similars, the mathematics supporting the application of the fundamental prediction method is quite complex. The fundamental method attempts to detect and estimate the strength of a systematic relationship between beta and fundamental characteristics by using a variant of linear regression. The estimation method is applied to a very large data base: typically ten or more years of data on over 1,000 companies. The effect of using such a large body of data is to eliminate or minimize estimation errors through the process of averaging. Because of the large data base and the sophistication of statistical methods, the results are relatively precise.

Once the fundamental prediction rule has been formulated, the additional data requirements for any single application are quite small: Descriptors for important fundamental characteristics must be calculated using various ratios that can be derived from standard accounting statements, and these descriptors collectively yield a prediction of beta. The descriptors, such as payout ratio and variance of earnings, can be calculated from historical data or from projections. If neither of these are available, they can be estimated using the published descriptors of similar companies.

These descriptors can be used to identify the unique characteristics of an investment, while the method of similars makes no such attempt to distinguish which characteristics of companies or investments contribute to their total risk profile. The calculation of these descriptors thus results not only in a prediction of beta, but also in a useful description of the investment's distinctive risk characteristics as they might be perceived by institutional investors.

Conclusions

The CAPM is a powerful tool for corporate capital budgeting and performance measurement. Its full potential, however, has not yet been realized, largely for the following reason. To be applied effectively the user must have credible estimates of the risk-free interest rate, the market risk premium, and the individual asset's (project's, division's) beta. The first factor, interest rates, can be observed regularly and therefore does not present a problem. The market risk premium can be estimated from historical data, or projected using a sophisticated statistical technique. Beta estimation, however, has been a major stumbling block in applying the CAPM.

In recent years, betas have been generated by measuring the relationship between a company's stock price movements and movements in a broad-based market index of common stocks. These estimates are more or less satisfactory, depending on the magnitude of the estimation error. But, in any case, this does not solve the problem of beta estimation for (non-traded) projects or divisions.

The CAPM has traditionally been applied in estimating required rates of return for non-trading divisions by using the "method of similars." While theoretically valid, this method has the drawback that the selection of comparable companies is often arbitrary, and this potential problem, combined with the fact that the number of similar companies is often very small, restricts the number of cases where the method can be used with confidence.

Over the past decade our research has focused on *predicting* beta by analyzing the fundamental characteristics of a company or project. The data required for this procedure can be derived from traditional accounting numbers such as those furnished by historical (or projected) balance sheets and income statements. The method can, therefore, be used to estimate the beta of divisions or even projects. And, even in the case of publicly traded companies, additional research has confirmed that fundamental analysis outperforms the traditional method of predicting beta. Joint predictions, using both stock market and fundamental data, are best.

In its application to divisions, fundamental prediction is also much less subject to criticism for vagueness or bias than the method of similars. Further, in linking the risk of a division to its tangible operating characteristics, the analysis becomes more intuitively understandable (and, perhaps, easier to apply) for the division manager.

In short, for corporate analysis involving investments in non-trading assets, fundamental risk prediction is likely to provide the following advantages: (a) improved accuracy, (2) the use of explicit formulas, and (3) the direct connection of beta to the operating characteristics of the company, division, or project in question.

References

Ibbotson, R. G., and R. A. Sinquefield. *Stocks, Bonds, Bills and Inflation: The Past (1925–1976) and the Future (1977–2000)*. Charlottesville, VA: Financial Analyst Research Foundation, 1977.

Lanstein and Sharpe. "Duration and Security Risk." *Journal of Financial and Quantitative Analysis,* November 1978, pp. 653–668.

Levy, Haim. "Tests of Capital Asset Pricing Hypotheses." *Research in Finance* (Volume 1, pp. 115–223, 1979).

Lintner, John. "The Valuation of Risky Assets and the Selection of Risky Investments in Stock Portfolios and Capital Budgets." *Review of Economics and Statistics* (February 1965), pp. 13–37.

Markowitz, Harry M. *Portfolio Selection: Efficient Diversification of Investment,* John Wiley, New York, 1959.

Mossin, Jan. "Equilibrium in Capital Asset Markets." *Econometrica* (October 1966), pp. 768–783.

Rosenberg, Barr. "The Capital Asset Pricing Model and the Market Model." *Journal of Portfolio Management* (Winter 1981), pp. 5–16.

Rosenberg, Barr, and James Guy. "Prediction of a Beta from Investment Fundamentals." *Financial Analysts Journal,* Part I (May/June 1976, pp. 3–15).

Rosenberg, Barr, and Vinay Marathe. "The Prediction of Investment Risk: Systematic and Residual." *Proceedings of the Seminar on the Analysis of Security Prices,* University of Chicago, November 1975, pp. 82–225.

Rudd, Andrew, and Henry Clasing. *Modern Portfolio Theory: The Principles of Investment Management* (Dow Jones-Irwin, 1982).

Figure 3   Actual Returns: Stock B versus Portfolio P

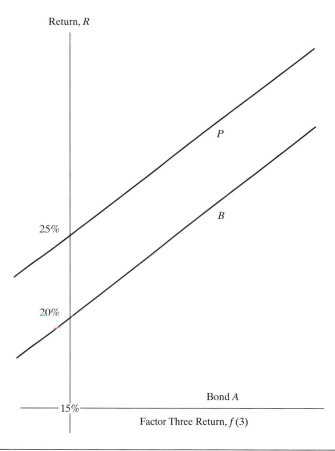

exchange traders exploit when the dollar/mark price differs from what a dollar could buy if it were first exchanged for marks. In well-functioning capital markets, such opportunities exist only momentarily, until they are closed by traders whose reward comes from eliminating such gaps.

When this arbitrage takes place, with investors reducing their holdings of stock B and covering themselves by purchasing the portfolio, the price of stock B falls and that of stock C rises. At the lower price, stock B becomes more attractive relative to stock C. This process terminates only when the portfolio and stock B offer the same expected return. In fact, as in the foreign exchange market or in the bond market, the process works sufficiently rapidly that a gap would probably be too fleeting for an outside investor even to notice. Arbitrage opportunities will no longer exist only when all three assets in Figure 2 lie on the same line; in any other case, there will always be another portfolio that beats (or is beaten by) one of the assets, no matter what unanticipated developments come to pass.

Figure 4 plots the line on which all three assets must fall. As we have drawn it, there is a direct positive relation between the expected return, E, on any portfolio or individual asset and its risk sensitivity, $b(3)$. The slope of this line measures the market price of this type of risk.

Figure 4   Equilibrium Expected Returns

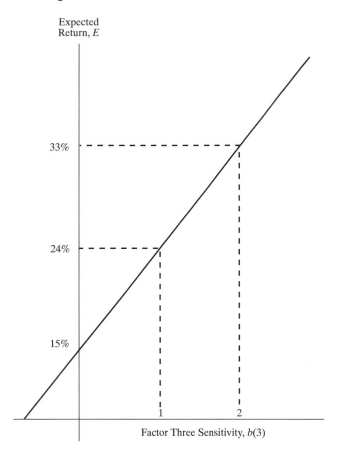

In Figure 4, the price of risk for factor three is displayed as the difference between the expected return at a sensitivity of one and the riskless return. As the riskless rate is 15 percent and assets with a factor three sensitivity of one have a 24 percent return, the market price of risk is 9 percent (24%−15%). This means that any asset with a $b(3)$ of one—i.e., any asset whose return rises or falls by 1 percent whenever the third factor rises or falls by 1 percent—will have an expected return 9 percent above the riskless return of 15 percent. An asset that is more sensitive will have a higher expected return; for example, the return for an asset with a b of two is 33 percent ($15\% + 2 \times 9\%$). In other words, the price of risk for factor three of 9 percent is the rate at which the investor is rewarded for assuming a unit of sensitivity to movements in this factor.

In summary, the expected return on any asset is directly related to that asset's sensitivity to unanticipated movements in major economic factors. If we let $E3$ stand for the return on a portfolio with a sensitivity of one to factor three ($E3$ equals 24 percent in the example of Figure 4), then the total expected return (E) on the portfolio may be computed as

$$E = r + (E1 - r)\,(b1) + (E2 - r)\,(b2) + (E3 - r)\,(b3) + (E4 - r)\,(b4). \tag{3}$$

This equation simply states the relationship we have proved: The expected return on any asset, E, exceeds the riskless return, r, by an amount equal to the sum of the products of the market prices of risk, $Ef - r$, and the sensitivities of the asset to each of the respective factors.

Examining the Factors

We have defined sensitivities as the responses of asset return to unanticipated movements in economic factors. But what are these factors? If we knew them, we could measure directly the sensitivities of individual stocks to each. We could, for example, attribute a particular fraction of the observed price movements in a given stock to movements in the economic factor.

Unfortunately, this is much more difficult than it sounds. To begin with, any one stock is so influenced by idiosyncratic forces that it is very difficult to determine the precise relation between its return and a given factor. At a more practical level, we have so much more data available on individual stock returns than we have on broad economic factors that this approach would be very inefficient. It would be a bit like attempting to see what happens to the yield on a Phoenix Power and Light bond when the money supply changes. A much better approach would be first to determine the impact of an index of municipal bond yields on the Phoenix bond; this can be done with considerable accuracy. We can then see how sensitive bond yields as a whole are to money supply changes. The sensitivity of the Phoenix bond to the money supply can then be determined as the product of these two sensitivities, each of which can be measured with some precision.

The biggest problem in the measurement of sensitivities, however, is separating unanticipated from anticipated factor movements. The bs measure the sensitivity of returns to *unanticipated* movements in the factors. By just looking at how a given asset relates to movements in the money supply, we would be including the influence of both anticipated and unanticipated changes, when only the latter are relevant. Anticipated changes are expected and have already been incorporated into expected returns. The unanticipated returns are what determine the bs, and their measurement is one of the more important components of the APT approach.

What economic factors relate to unanticipated returns on large portfolios? As noted above, empirical research indicates that the following four economic factors are relevant:[3]

1. Unanticipated changes in inflation,

2. Unanticipated changes in industrial production,

3. Unanticipated changes in risk premiums (as measured by the spread between low grade and high grade bonds), and

4. Unanticipated changes in the slope of the term structure of interest rates.

It is possible, of course, to think of many other potential systematic factors, but our research has found that many of them influence returns only through their impact on the above four factors. The money supply, for example, is an important variable, but it is not as good a yardstick against which to measure sensitivities because most of the influence of unpredicted money supply changes is captured by the other variables. For instance, the change in interest rates on a Friday (from before the money supply announcement to after) is an adequate measure of the surprise in the announcement.

It's hardly surprising that the variables listed above were found to be important determinants of market returns. They appear in the traditional discounted cash flow (DCF) valuation formula. Two of them—changes in industrial production and unanticipated inflation—are related to the numerator in the DCF formula, i.e., to the expected cash flows themselves. Expected industrial production is a proxy for the real value of future cash flows. Inflation enters because assets are not neutral; their nominal cash flow growth rates do not always match expected inflation rates.

The other two variables would seem intuitively to be more related to the denominator in the DCF formula—i.e., to the risk-adjusted discount rate. The risk premium measure is an amalgam of investor attitudes toward risk-bearing and perceptions about the general level of uncertainty. The term structure of interest rates enters because most assets have multiple-year cash flows and, for reasons relating to risk and time preferences, the discount rate that applies to distant flows is not the same as the rate that applies to flows in the near future.

These variables make intuitive sense, and it also makes sense that they are indeed "systematic." *Every* asset's value changes when one of these variables changes in an unanticipated way. Thus investors who hold portfolios that are more exposed to such changes—i.e., that contain assets whose bs are higher on average—will find that their portfolios' market values fluctuate with greater amplitude over time. They will be compensated by a higher total return in the long run, but they will have to bear up under more severe reactions to bear markets.

Strategic Portfolio Planning

No "off-the-shelf" approach to strategic planning is appropriate for all investment funds any more than one size of suit fits all customers. Below, we outline some general considerations that figure into the determination of investment goals.

The Structuring Decision

Traditionally, portfolio strategy is perceived as the choice of the proper mix of stocks and bonds (with real estate and other assets occasionally included). Every portfolio has its own pattern of sensitivities to the systematic economic factors. Stocks as a group and bonds as another group have different sensitivities to systematic risks; hence, the traditional approach may offer a rough solution to the choice of the optimal pattern of risk exposure. But the results can be improved significantly by examining the sensitivity of *each asset* to systematic risks.[4]

The first problem facing the architect of the fund's investment strategy is that of determining the most desirable exposure to systematic economic risks. Altering the mix of stocks and bonds in the portfolio will certainly affect the amount and type of risk exposure, but so will nearly every other purchase and sale decision. The strategist must first choose the desired level of exposure; then appropriate transactions can move the fund toward that desired position.

For example, assume that two of the empirically relevant exposures—to the general level of risk tolerance and to the term structure of interest rates—are held constant and that we are interested in the choice of exposure to inflation risk and to industrial production risk. In Figure 5, the horizontal axis depicts the sensitivity, or "exposure," of a portfolio to inflation risk. The vertical axis plots the same portfolio's exposure to production risk. We will refer to these sensitivities as the inflation and productivity "betas," respectively.

Figure 5   Sensitivities to Productivity and Inflation Risks

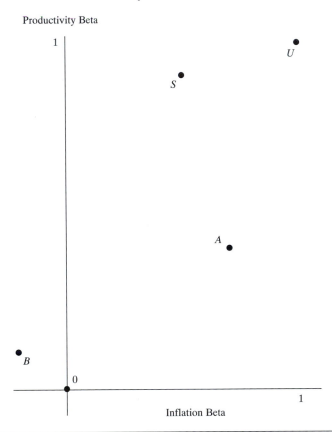

The betas measure the average response of a portfolio or an asset to unanticipated changes in the respective economic factors. For example, a portfolio with an inflation beta of 1 will tend to move up and down by 1 percent in response to a 1 percent unanticipated rate of inflation. A beta greater than 1, say an inflation beta of 1.5, means that the portfolio's returns are magnified by inflation, with a 1 percent unanticipated inflation leading to a 1.5 percent additional return on the portfolio. Similarly, if beta is less than 1, unanticipated inflation has a less than proportional impact on the portfolio's returns. A portfolio with a beta of 0.5 will show a 0.5 percent increase in return for every 1 percent unexpected inflation. And a portfolio with a beta of zero will, on average, be unaffected by unanticipated inflation. Of course, many assets actually have negative betas and tend to do worse than expected when inflation is greater than expected. A utility stock with an inflation beta of −0.3 loses 0.3 percent of return for each 1 percent unanticipated inflation.

In Figure 5, point *A* depicts a large investment fund with an inflation sensitivity of about 0.7 and a production sensitivity of 0.4. Is this a usual or an unusual pattern of sensitivities? There is no way to answer this question without referring to some landmarks.

One obvious landmark is the origin, O—the point at which both betas are zero. A portfolio at this point would be affected by neither unanticipated inflation nor by changes in expected industrial production. This may seem to be desirable, but it is not necessarily so. For one thing, such a portfolio offers no insurance against unexpected inflation risk; when inflation is greater than anticipated, this portfolio will, on average, not respond. Perhaps more importantly, there is a tradeoff between return and risk exposure. Moving a portfolio to O, where it will not respond to changes in inflation or to productivity, will have an impact on average return.

Point U represents unit sensitivity to both economic factors. A portfolio located at U will increase in value by 1 percent with either a 1 percent unexpected inflation or a 1 percent increase in expected industrial production. The expenditures of an investment portfolio such as a pension fund are probably exposed to the risk of inflation in an adverse way; unanticipated increases in inflation will, on average, increase expenditures. The inflation sensitivity of a portfolio at U will help to offset this. Industrial production, however, could tell a different story. Declines in industrial production will generally be associated with increases in unemployment, which in turn will place greater economic burdens on individuals and corporations. In addition, productivity changes will be associated with changes in the relative prices of the goods and services purchased by the plan sponsors and its beneficiaries, and these may also be adverse. But rather than helping the fund to insure against these risks, a portfolio with a productivity beta of 1 actually magnifies them. When industrial production turns down, so too does the return on the portfolio. Whether or not point U is attractive depends upon the particular situation of the fund.

Point B represents the typical pattern of sensitivities for a portfolio of long-term government bonds. Notice that it has a negative beta with inflation and a slightly positive beta with productivity. Investments in bonds are subject to significant adverse inflation effects and are also somewhat sensitive to productivity (although to a far lesser extent than equities). Productivity sensitivity is larger for corporate bonds than for governments, for obvious reasons.

Point S is the location of a broad-based market index of large, listed stocks. Although this is a useful reference point, it would be wrong to ascribe too much importance to it. The right choice of a pattern of sensitivities for a given fund depends upon a variety of considerations unique to that fund and to the markets in which its beneficiary is a buyer, and these will not generally result in choosing the market index of stocks. The market index should not be ignored, but neither should it be worshipped. It is simply a useful landmark on the horizon, a signpost that is a guide in unfamiliar territory.

APT and the CAPM

We now have the necessary apparatus to relate the well-known Capital Asset Pricing Model (CAPM) to APT. The CAPM asserts that only a single number—the CAPM "beta" against a market index—is required to measure risk. As Figure 6 illustrates, the CAPM beta measures the distance along a ray from the origin through S, where a broad-based market index is located. We assume that portfolio S is the market index used in computing CAPM betas; it could be any of the commonly used indexes, such as the S & P 500.

Portfolio S has a CAPM beta of 1.0 (by construction). Another portfolio, such as Qa, which is located halfway along the ray between O and S, has a CAPM beta of .5. Similarly, Qb has a CAPM beta of 2, because it is twice as far from the origin as S itself. Note that the CAPM beta of any

Figure 6 CAPM and APT Betas

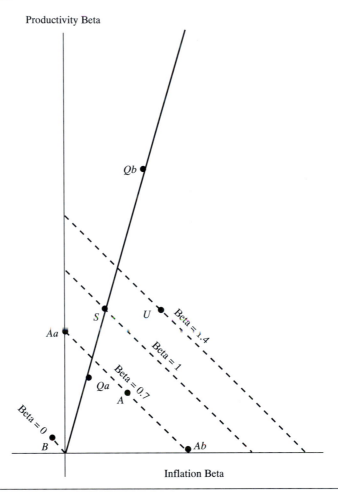

portfolio can be measured by its distance along the ray *relative* to the market index *S*. The CAPM beta is a relative risk measure.

But there are many portfolios that are not on the ray *OS*. For instance, portfolios such as *B, A,* and *U*, all of which have certain desirable properties, are located in the productivity-inflation space *off* the CAPM ray. What are their CAPM betas? It turns out that there are entire families of portfolios with a particular value of the CAPM beta whose members are not on the ray. The dashed lines in Figure 6 show some of these families. For example, portfolio *A* is in the family whose CAPM beta is 0.7, but so are all the portfolios along the dashed line that passes through *A*. There are portfolios in this family that have no inflation risk (such as *Aa*), and there are portfolios with no productivity risk (such as *Ab*). All of them have CAPM betas of 0.7. We doubt very much, however, that most investment managers and clients would regard them as equally desirable.

If S happens to be a mean-variance efficient portfolio, a so-called "optimized" portfolio, then all portfolios whose CAPM betas are the same will have equal returns on average over time. In this sense, the CAPM beta measures the overall desirability of an asset as perceived by the average investor in the marketplace. Even in this case, however, it is not necessarily true that a particular individual or client will consider all portfolios with the same expected return equally desirable. For example, portfolios Aa and Ab in Figure 6 might have the same long-term expected return, but they are exposed to far different types of risk, and neither is preferable for all funds.

Finally, there is usually no reason to think that a particular portfolio such as S, even though it is a broad index such as the S & P 500, is itself optimized. If it is not optimized, then portfolios A, Aa, and Ab will not have equal expected returns, even though they do have equal CAPM betas. Recent empirical evidence has shown unequivocally that most of the commonly used market indexes are not optimized portfolios. Under this condition, the CAPM beta is not even a reliable indicator of expected return and, as we have already seen, it is virtually worthless as a measure of the type of risk to which the portfolio is exposed.

Now consider fund A, located on the exposure terrain with an inflation sensitivity of 0.7 and a productivity sensitivity of 0.4. What should be the strategy for fund A? How should it go about making its strategic investment decision? To put the question another way, where should the fund go to in Figure 5? Should it move closer to S, the stock market index? Should it be somewhere between B and S, divided between bonds and stocks? Just "choosing between bonds and stocks" limits the fund to a position along a line between B and S. The strategic decision is clearly much broader than this.

The appropriate choice of risk exposure depends upon the uses to which the income generated by the fund is to be put. Just as different individuals choose to live in different places, different investment funds will choose different patterns of risk exposure.

Analyzing Portfolio Strategy

To choose the optimal pattern of risk sensitivities and move to the best position in Figure 5, we must examine the economic situation of the sponsors and the beneficiaries of the fund. To argue that there is one best strategy for everyone—such as "buying the market"—is simply wrong. In the case of pension systems, we might assume that the principal goal is to serve the interests of the beneficiaries by meeting the promised pension benefits with a minimum of additional taxes (if the plan is public) or of corporate contributions (if it is private), but this goal structure may not be appropriate in all cases (for example, for a nonprofit institution, such as a university).

The economic situations confronting the sponsor and the beneficiaries are determined by the markets within which they operate and by the uses to which they put funds. The sensitivity of prices in these markets to overall inflation, for example, is an important determinant of the proper investment policy. The location of the organization is important as well. A company that employs blue-collar workers in the Los Angeles area has a different pattern of expenditures than a white-collar service firm located in New York.

Although organizations do not constitute a homogeneous group, they all share broad economic concerns. The key questions involve (a) their patterns of expenditures, (b) their other sources of income, and (c) the economic conditions they will face. These questions can be answered by detailed economic study. In the case of a company, for example, central questions would be "what are its products, its costs and its prospects? How sensitive is it to the business cycle?" In the case of a museum, the study might begin with an examination of the markets for antiquities. How have these markets behaved, and what plans does the museum have for new acquisitions? Also of great importance is the need to meet current and forecast expenditures of a more prosaic sort, such as those related to maintenance and security. Such a study must be continually updated if the fund is to respond to changes in the economic environment and to changes in the goals and operations of the organization. But even before the initial study is concluded, it will have important implications for strategic portfolio decisions.

Given an economic profile of the organization, one can begin to structure the overall risk exposure of the portfolio. Expenditures on major commodity groups—on salaries and materials, say—should be compared with the general expenditure pattern in the country as a whole. For example, suppose that the organization spent less on food and relatively more on travel than the average investor. The higher expenditure on travel would render it more vulnerable to energy costs than the typical investor, whereas the lower expenditures on foodstuffs would make it less exposed to food prices.

At the strategic level, these considerations will influence the optimal pattern of risk exposure. To the extent that food prices coincide with general inflation, for example, the optimal portfolio could be less hedged against inflation—i.e., could have a lower inflation beta than a broad-based market average has. Similarly, to the extent that food prices tend to be somewhat independent of productivity risk, the organization could accept a higher sensitivity to productivity risk than a broad-based average has. By bearing more risk in this dimension, the portfolio could expect a higher return.

The influence of these kinds of considerations on the idiosyncratic risk of specific industry groupings has tactical implications. If the organization is unconcerned about inflation in agricultural prices, it would also wish to skew its portfolio out of this sector. Similarly, a sensitivity to energy costs might lead it to skew its portfolio holdings in the direction of the energy sector. An organization will wish to hold a pattern of investments tailored to its own needs. Its optimal portfolio will therefore have a pattern of investments that is modestly skewed from the broad-based market index owned by the average investor.

It should be emphasized that tactical portfolio adjustments can be accomplished without reducing the average return on the portfolio. The strategic decisions determining the level of exposure to systematic economic factors influence the average return, but the tactical decisions can be made without any sacrifice of portfolio return, because they deal merely with idiosyncratic risk.

Implementing the Strategy

To implement the chosen strategy, the fund may direct the investments itself, or it may select investment managers who will follow established investment policy guidelines. The adoption of the APT approach to strategy has implications for the choice and the evaluation of investment managers. If the strategy dictates that investments should be made in particular sectors, then it would be natural to look for managers who specialize in these sectors.

More generally, managers implicitly tend to choose portfolios that have particular patterns of sensitivities to the economic factors. One manager might, for example, focus on high price-earnings-ratio companies so that his portfolio has a characteristic pattern of sensitivities. Another might be heavily invested in utilities, and this would result in a different pattern of sensitivities. The investment strategy for the portfolio as a whole may be implemented by choosing a portfolio of managers in such a way that pooling them together results in the desired pattern of sensitivities. If, for example, manager A's portfolio typically has an inflation beta of 2 and manager B's portfolio has an inflation beta of 1, then a desired inflation of beta 1.4 for the overall strategy could be achieved by placing $0.40 with manager A for every $0.60 given to manager B.

Of course, the complete manager evaluation issue is more complicated than this. Given that a manager has a certain pattern of risk exposures, we also want to know whether he or she accomplishes this in the least costly fashion and with the least amount of idiosyncratic risk. This is the subject of performance evaluation, which is well-developed in the APT framework but is beyond the scope of this article.

Finally, a fund's choice of investments will generally be constrained by legal and other considerations. Typical of such constraints is the requirement that all investments be of a certain grade or from an approved list, or that the investments include bonds or equities from a particular issuer. The APT approach to strategy is particularly well-suited to these situations; because of its flexibility, it can be adapted to special situations when many traditional approaches cannot.

For example, suppose that the portfolio is constrained to hold a significant portion of its investments in the equities of the bonds of a particular company or government agency. For two related reasons it will generally be the case that this constraint is binding, in the sense that the fund would rather reduce its holdings of this security. First, the large holding subjects the fund to a substantial amount of idiosyncratic risk; second, the fund may already be implicitly subject to much of the risk associated with the issuer.

The total risk of this security, however, can be substantially mitigated if the remainder of the portfolio is explicitly selected to offset its influence. If the security in question has a lower than desired sensitivity to inflation risk—e.g., a beta of 0.6 when the desired beta is 0.9—then the influence of the holding on the inflation exposure of the portfolio may be countered by choosing alternative investments with inflation betas in excess of 0.9. As a result, however, the fund may be subjected to idiosyncratic risk, which would not be a problem if the constraints were absent.[5]

Summary

The APT approach to the portfolio strategy decision involves choosing the desirable degree of exposure to the fundamental economic risks that influence both asset returns and organizations. This focus differs from that of traditional investment analysis and is ideally suited to the management of large pools of funds.

Choosing the optimal degree of risk exposure requires an understanding of the level of risk exposure of the organization. Optimally, the pattern of risk exposure in the fund will balance the organization's current level of risk exposure. The fund should be positioned to hedge the organization against the economic uncertainties it faces.

Implementing this strategy may involve either choosing managers according to their typical pattern of exposure to economic risks and their ability to offer excess returns with low idiosyncratic risk or by choosing assets directly according to estimates of their exposure characteristics and relying upon diversification to remove idiosyncratic risk. The former approach is "active APT," whereas the latter approach may be quasipassive, inasmuch as systematic exposure is planned and implemented but there is no attempt at selection based on anticipated abnormal returns.

Notes

1. Arbitrage Pricing Theory was originated by Stephen A. Ross in "The Arbitrage Theory of Capital Asset Pricing," *Journal of Economic Theory*, December 1976, pp. 341–360. Theoretical refinements have been made by the following: Gregory Connor, "A Factor Pricing Theory for Capital Assets" (Working paper, Northwestern University, 1981); Gur Huberman, "A Simple Approach to Arbitrage Pricing Theory," *Journal of Economic Theory*, October 1982, pp. 183–191; Nai-fu Chen and Jonathan E. Ingersoll, Jr., "Exact Pricing in Linear Factor Models with Finitely Many Assets: A Note," *Journal of Finance*, June 1983, pp. 985–988; Philip H. Dybvig, "An Explicit Bound on Deviations from APT Pricing in a Finite Economy," *Journal of Financial Economics*, December 1983, pp. 483–496; Mark Grinblatt and Sheridan Titman, "Factor Pricing in a Finite Economy," *Journal of Financial Economics*, December 1983, pp. 497–507; Robert Stambaugh, "Arbitrage Pricing with Information," *Journal of Financial Economics*, November 1983, pp. 357–369; Gary Chamberlain and Michael Rothschild, "Arbitrage and Mean/Variance Analysis on Large Markets," *Econometrica*, forthcoming; and Jonathan Ingersoll, Jr., "Some Results in the Theory of Arbitrage Pricing," *Journal of Finance*, forthcoming.

2. Empirical testing with equities is described in the following: Richard Roll and Stephen A. Ross, "An Empirical Investigation of the Arbitrage Pricing Theory," *Journal of Finance*, December 1980, pp. 1073–1104; Nai-fu Chen, "Arbitrage Asset Pricing: Theory and Evidence" (Dissertation, Graduate School of Management, University of California at Los Angeles, 1981); Mark R. Reinganum, "The Arbitrage Pricing Theory: Some Empirical Results," *Journal of Finance*, May 1981, pp. 313–321; Patricia Hughes, "A Test of the Arbitrage Pricing Theory" (Working paper, University of British Columbia, August 1981); Lawrence Kryzanowski and Minh Chan To, "General Factor Models and the Structure of Security Returns," *Journal of Financial and Quantitative Analysis*, March 1983, pp. 31–52; and Stephen J. Brown and Mark I. Weinstein, "A New Approach to Testing Asset Pricing Models: The Bilinear Paradigm," *Journal of Finance*, June 1983, pp. 711–743. Tests with Treasury bills are presented in George Oldfield, Jr., and Richard J. Rogalski, "Treasury Bill Factors and Common Stock Returns," *Journal of Finance*, May 1981, pp. 337–350. Issues of testability are discussed by Jay Shanken, "The Arbitrage Pricing Theory: Is it Testable?" *Journal of Finance*, December 1982, pp. 1129–1140; Philip H. Dybvig and Stephen A. Ross, "Yes, the APT Is Testable" (Working paper, Yale University, June 1983); and Gunter Franke, "On Tests of the Arbitrage Pricing Theory" (Working paper, Universitat Giessen, 1983).

3. See Nai-fu Chen, Richard Roll, and Stephen A. Ross, "Economic Forces and the Stock Market" (Working paper, University of California at Los Angeles, 1983).

4. The systematic—and idiosyncratic—risks at the heart of the APT approach to investment strategy have been identified in technical econometric work. For assets on which data are available, the pattern of exposure of each asset is known.

5. In some countries other than the United States, constraints on investment are so stiff as to preclude achievement of the desired overall pattern of systematic risk exposure.

Discussion Questions

1. List the four factors presented in this article that contribute to unanticipated returns on large portfolios.

2. Why does each factor contain the word *unanticipated*?

3. If changes in the factors are unanticipated, how can the portfolio manager use this strategy to choose appropriate portfolios?

part **III**

Capital Budgeting

The presumption regarding articles appearing in Part III is that students are up to speed in the mathematics of finance and understand the NPV rule. The article by Alan Shapiro goes beyond the mechanical aspects of the NPV rule in introducing strategy into the matrix.

Analysis of risk in capital budgeting by firms is often done by varying the discount rate or by using the scenario analysis (pessimistic, most likely, and optimistic expectations). The Hertz article is a classic in the area of incorporating risk in the analysis; he describes Monte Carlo simulation to enable analysts to incorporate the full range of knowledge imperfections into the inputs for NPV calculations.

The final three articles present insightful perspectives from business executives regarding budgeting procedures.

Alan C. Shapiro

Corporate Strategy and the Capital Budgeting Decision

In its capital budgeting program the firm needs to establish strategic options in order to gain competitive advantage. It can either seek lower costs than its competitors, or it can differentiate its product in any number of ways. Among other things, this means the firm should identify its competitive edge and relentlessly attempt to enhance it.

The decade 1974 through 1983 was a dismal one for American business in general. It began with the deepest economic decline since the Depression and ended with national recoveries from back-to-back recessions in the early 1980s. Yet throughout these dark years, 13 companies on the Fortune 500 list of the largest U.S. industrial companies were money-making stars, earning consistently high returns. These firms averaged at least a 20-percent return on shareholders' equity (ROE) over this ten-year span. (To gain some perspective, a dollar invested in 1974 at a compound annual rate of 20 percent would have grown to $6.19 by the end of 1983, a healthy return even after allowing for the effects of inflation.) Moreover, none of these firms' ROE ever dipped below 15 percent during this difficult period.

The 13 were led by a profit superstar, American Home Products, whose ROE not only averaged 29.5 percent during the 1974–83 decade, but also has held above 20 percent for 30 straight years. To appreciate the significance of such a feat, one dollar invested at 20 percent compounded annually would be worth over $237 at the end of 30 years.

What type of firm can achieve such a remarkable record? Far from being the prototypical high-tech firm or a lucky oil company, American Home Products is the low-profile producer of Anacin, Chef Boy-Ar-Dee pasta products, Brach's candy, and Gulden's mustard, in addition to prescription drugs and nondrug products such as cardiovascular drugs, oral contraceptives, and infant formula.

In general, high-technology firms were not well represented among the 13, which included just IBM and two pharmaceutical companies, SmithKline Beckman and Merck. IBM, moreover, with an average ROE of 20.5 percent, ranked only 11th out of the 13, far behind such low-tech firms as

Source: Reprinted with permission from *Midland Corporate Finance Journal* (Spring 1985), pp. 22–36. Alan C. Shapiro is the Johnson Professor of Banking and Finance at USC.

Dow Jones (26.3 percent), Kellogg (24.8 percent), Deluxe Check Printers (24.1 percent), and Maytag (25.1 percent). It was even less profitable than a steel company (Worthington Industries—23.9 percent) and a chemical firm (Nalco Chemical—21.5 percent).

Although the 13 have earned extraordinary return on shareholders' equity capital, Exhibit 1 shows that returns to the shareholders themselves have been less than earthshaking. This is consistent with the efficient market hypothesis, the idea that prices of traded securities rapidly reflect all currently available information. Since the high return on equity capital earned by the 13 is not news to investors—these firms have consistently been outstanding performers—investors back in 1974 had already incorporated these expectations in their estimations of firm values. This means that a firm's expected high ROE is already "priced out" or capitalized by the market at a rate that reflects the anticipated riskiness of investing in the company's stock. As a result, investors will earn exceptional returns only if the firm turns out to do even better than expected, something that by definition is not possible to predict in advance. The fact that the 13's median annual total return to investors (stock price appreciation plus reinvested dividends) of 13.4 percent is almost identical to the Fortune 500's median return of 13.6 percent indicates that investor expectations about the relative performances of both groups of firms were substantially borne out.

This illustrates the key distinction between operating in an efficient financial market and operating in product and factor markets that are less than perfectly competitive. One can expect to consistently earn excess returns only in the latter markets; competition will ensure that excess returns in an efficient market are short-lived. However, it is evident from the generally dismal performance of the Fortune 500 that it is no mean trick to take advantage of those product and factor market imperfections that do exist.

The demonstrated ability of a firm such as Deluxe Check Printers—a firm on the trailing edge of technology, described as a "buggy whip company threatened with extinction by the 'checkless society'"—consistently to earn such extraordinary returns on invested capital must be due to something more than luck or proficiency at applying sophisticated techniques of investment analysis. That something is the knack for creating positive net present value (NPV) projects, projects with rates of return in excess of the required return. The scarcity of this skill is attested by the fact that aggregate profits of $68.8 billion for the Fortune 500 in 1983 were, in real terms, 22 percent below the $43.6 billion earned in 1974, a recession year. Keep in mind also that the Fortune 500 have been disciplined savers, re-investing over $300 billion of retained earnings in their businesses over the ten-year period. This massive reinvestment alone should have produced considerably higher real earnings than 1974's.

This evidence notwithstanding, it is usually taken for granted that positive NPV projects do exist and can be identified using fairly straightforward techniques. Consequently, the emphasis in most capital budgeting analyses is on estimating and discounting future project cash flows. Projects with positive net present values are accepted; those that fail this test are rejected.

It is important to recognize, however, that selecting positive NPV projects in this way is equivalent to picking under-valued securities on the basis of fundamental analysis. The latter can be done with confidence only if there are financial market imperfections that do not allow asset prices to reflect their equilibrium values. Similarly, the existence of economic rents—excess returns that lead to positive net present values—is the result of monopolistic control over product or factor supplies (i.e., "real market imperfections").

It is the thesis of this article that generating projects likely to yield positive excess returns is at least as important as the conventional quantitative investment analysis. This is the essence of

Exhibit 1   13 Stars of The Decade 1974–1983

Company	Average ROE 1974–1983	Total Return to Investors 1974–1983[a]
American Home Products	29.5%	6.6%
Dow Jones	26.3	29.8
Mitchell Energy	26.0	26.4
SmithKline Beckman	25.4	19.7
Kellogg	24.8	13.3
Deluxe Check Printers	24.1	13.4
Worthington Industries	23.9	41.7
Maytag	23.1	14.5
Merck	21.9	3.8
Nalco Chemical	21.5	11.4
IBM	20.5	11.3
Dover	20.3	26.6
Coca-Cola	20.3	2.9
Median total return to investors for the 13	13.4%	
Medial total return to investors for the Fortune 500	13.6%	

[a]Total return to investors as calculated by *Fortune,* April 30, 1984. It includes both price appreciation and dividend yield to an investor and assumes that any proceeds from cash dividends, the sale or rights and warrant offerings, and stock received in spinoffs were reinvested at the end of the year in which they were received. The return reported is the average annual return compounded over the ten-year period.

corporate strategy: creating and then taking advantage of imperfections in product and factor markets. Thus, an understanding of the strategies followed by successful firms in exploiting and defending those barriers to entry created by product and factor market imperfections is crucial to any systematic evaluation of investment opportunities. For one thing, it provides a qualitative means of identifying, or ranking, ex ante those projects most likely to have positive net present values. This ranking is useful because constraints of time and money limit the number and range of investment opportunities a given firm is likely to consider.

More important, a good understanding of corporate strategy should help uncover new and potential profitable projects. Only in theory is a firm fortunate enough to be presented, at no effort or expense on its part, with every available investment opportunity. Perhaps the best way to gain this understanding is to study a medley of firms, spanning a number of industries and nations, that have managed to develop and implement a variety of value-creating investment strategies. This is the basic approach taken here.

The first section discusses what happens to economic rents over time, and thus to opportunities for positive NPV projects, in a competitive industry. The second section considers in more detail the nature of market imperfections that give rise to economic rents and how one can design investments to exploit those imperfections. The third section presents the available evidence on the relationship between various competitive advantages and rates of return on invested capital. The fourth introduces a normative approach to strategic planning and investment analysis. The fifth and final section deals with the rationale and means for domestic firms to evolve into multinational corporations.

Competitive Markets and Excess Returns

A perfectly competitive industry is one characterized by costless entry and exit, undifferentiated products, and increasing marginal costs of production. These undifferentiated products, also known as commodities, are sold exclusively on the basis of price. In such an industry, as every student of microeconomics knows, each firm produces at the point at which price equals marginal cost. Long-run equilibrium exists when price also equals average cost. At this point, total revenue equals total cost for each firm taken individually and for the industry as a whole. This cost includes the required return on the capital used by each firm. Thus, in the long run, the actual return on capital in a competitive industry must equal the required return.

Any excess return quickly attracts new entrants to the market. Their additional capacity and attempts to gain market share lead to a reduction in the industry price and a lowering of returns to all market participants. In the early 1980s, for example, the high returns available in the video-game market, combined with the ease of entry into the business, attracted a host of competitors. This led to a red-ink bath for the industry in 1983, followed by the exit of a number of firms from the industry. Conversely, should the actual return for the industry be below the required return, the opposite happens. The weakest competitors exit the industry, resulting in an increase in the industry price and a boost in the overall return on capital for the remaining firms. This process, which is now taking place in the oil refining business, continues until the actual return once again equals the required return.

The message from this analysis is clear: The run-of-the-mill firm operating in a highly competitive, commodity-type industry is doomed from the start in its search for positive net present value projects. Only firms that can bring to bear on new projects competitive advantages that are difficult to replicate have any assurance of earning excess returns in the long run. These advantages take the form of either being the low-cost producer in the industry or being able to add value to the product—value for which customers are willing to pay a high (relative to cost) price. The latter type of advantage involves the ability to convert a commodity business into one characterized by products differentiated on the basis of service and/or quality. By creating such advantages, a firm can impose barriers to entry by potential competitors, resulting in a less-than-perfectly competitive market and the possibility of positive NPV projects.

Barriers to Entry and Positive Net Present Value Projects

As we have just seen, the ability to discourage new entrants to the market by erecting barriers to entry is the key to earning rates of return that consistently exceed capital costs. If these barriers did not exist, new competitors would enter the market and drive down the rate of return to the required return. High barriers to entry and the threat of a strong reaction from entrenched competitors will reduce the risk of entry and so prolong the opportunity to earn excess returns.

This analysis suggests that successful investments (those with positive NPVs) share a common characteristic: They are investments that involve creating, preserving, and even enhancing competitive advantages that serve as barriers to entry. In line with this conclusion, the successful companies described by Thomas Peters and Robert Waterman in their bestseller, *In Search of Excellence*, were able to define their strengths—marketing, customer contact, new product innovation, low-cost manufacturing, etc.—and then build on them. They have resisted the temptation to move into new businesses that look attractive but require corporate skills they do not have.

A clearer understanding of the potential barriers to competitive entry can help to identify potential value-creating investment opportunities. This section now takes a closer look at the five major sources of barriers to entry—economies of scale, product differentiation, cost disadvantages, access to distribution channels, and government policy—and suggests some lessons for successful investing.[1]

Economies of Scale

Economies of scale exist whenever a given increase in the scale of production, marketing, or distribution results in a less-than-proportional increase in cost. The existence of scale economies means that there are *inherent cost advantages in being large.* The more significant these scale economies, therefore, the greater the cost disadvantage faced by a new entrant to the market. Scale economies in marketing, service, research, and production are probably the principal barriers to entry in the mainframe computer industry, as GE, RCA, and Xerox discovered to their sorrow. It is estimated, for example, that IBM spent over $5 billion to develop its innovative System 360, which it brought out in 1963. In natural resource industries, firms such as Alcan, the Canadian aluminum company, and Exxon were able to fend off new market entrants by exploiting economies of scale in production and transportation.

High capital requirements go hand-in-hand with economies of scale. In order to take advantage of scale economies in production, marketing, or new product development, firms must often make enormous up-front investments in plant and equipment, research and development, and advertising. These capital requirements themselves serve as a barrier to entry; the more capital required, the higher the barrier to entry. This is particularly true in industries such as petroleum refining, mineral extraction, and mainframe computers.

A potential entrant to a market characterized by scale economies in production will be reluctant to enter unless the market has grown sufficiently to permit the construction and profitable utilization of an economically sized plant. Otherwise, the new entrant will have to cut price to gain market share, destroying in the process the possibility of abnormal profits. By expanding in line with growth in the market, therefore, entrenched competitors can preempt profitable market entry by new competitors.

Consider, for example, the economies of the cement industry. The low value-to-weight ratio of cement makes the cement business a very regional one; beyond a radius of about 150 to 200 miles from the cement plant, the costs of transport become prohibitive unless cheap water or rail transportation is available. At the same time, the significant economies of scale available in cement production limit the number of plants a given region can support. For instance, suppose that demand in a land-locked region is sufficient to support only one or two modern cement plants. By expanding production and adding substantial new capacity to that already available, a firm can significantly raise the price of market entry by new firms and make plant expansion or replacement by existing competitors look much less attractive. This type of move obviously requires a longer time frame and the willingness to incur potential losses until the market grows larger.

---

[1] See, for example, Michael E. Porter, "How Competitive Forces Shape Strategy," *Harvard Business Review,* March-April 1979, pp. 137–145, for a good summary and discussion of these barriers to entry and their implications for corporate strategy.

Scale economies are all-important in the grocery retailing business, on the level of the individual store as well as the city-wide market. Whether a store has $100,000 or $10,000,000 in annual sales, it still needs a manager. In addition, the cost of constructing and outfitting a supermarket doesn't increase in proportion to the number of square feet of selling space. Thus, the ratio of expenses to sales exhibits a significant decline as the volume of sales rises.

Similarly, whether it has 10 percent or 25 percent of a given market, a supermarket chain has to advertise and supply its stores from a warehouse. The higher the share of market, the lower the advertising cost per customer, the faster the warehouse will turn over its inventory, and the more likely its delivery trucks will be used to capacity. These cost efficiencies translate directly into a higher return on capital.

The relationship between the market dominance of a supermarket chain in a given market and its profitability is evident in the relative returns for firms following contrasting expansion strategies. Chains such as Kroger and Winn-Dixie, which have opted for deep market penetration in a limited geographic area (ranking number one or two in almost all their major markets), have realized returns on equity that far exceeded their equity costs. On the other hand, chains such as A&P and National Tea, which expanded nationally by gaining toe-hold positions in numerous, though scattered, markets, have consistently earned less than their required returns.

Computer store chains, to take another example, also enjoy significant economies of scale. These show up in the form of lower average costs for advertising, distribution, and training. Even more important, they receive larger discounts on their products from the manufacturers.

Lesson #1: Investments that are structured to fully exploit economies of scale are more likely to be successful than those that are not.

Product Differentiation

Some companies, such as Coca-Cola and Procter & Gamble, take advantage of *enormous advertising expenditures and highly developed marketing skills* to differentiate their products and keep out potential competitors wary of the high marketing costs and risks of new product introduction. Others sell expertise and high-quality products and service. For example, Nalco Chemical, a specialty chemical firm, is a problem solver and counselor to its customers while Worthington Industries, which turns semifinished steel into finished steel, has a reputation for quality workmanship that allows it to charge premium prices. As indicated in the introduction to this article, both have been handsomely rewarded for their efforts, with average equity returns exceeding 20 percent annually from 1974 to 1983.

Pharmaceutical companies have traditionally earned high returns by developing unique products that are protected from competition by patents, trademarks, and brand names. Three outstanding examples are SmithKline Beckman's Tagamet, for treating stomach ulcers, and Hoffman-La Roche's tranquilizers, Librium and Valium. American Home Products also owes a great deal of its profitability to several patented drugs.

Similarly, the development of technologically innovative products has led to high profits for firms such as Xerox and Philips (Netherlands). A fat R&D budget, however, is only part of the activity leading to commercially successful innovations. To a great extent, the risks in R&D are commercial, not technical. Firms that make technology pay off are those that closely link their R&D activities with market realities. They always ask what the customer needs. Even if they have strong technology, they do their marketing homework. This requires close contact with customers, as well as careful monitoring of the competition. Studies also indicate that top management involvement is extremely important in those firms that rely heavily and effectively on technology as a competitive weapon. This requires close coordination and communication between technical and business managers.

Failure to heed that message has led to Xerox's inability to replicate its earlier success in the photocopy business. In addition to its revolutionary copier technology, Xerox developed some of the computer industry's most important breakthroughs, including the first personal computer and the first network connecting office machines. But, through a lack of market support, it has consistently failed to convert its research prowess into successful high-tech products.

Service is clearly the key to extraordinary profitability for many firms. The ability to differentiate its computers from others through exceptional service has enabled IBM to dominate the worldwide mainframe computer business with a market share of over 75 percent. Similarly, Caterpillar Tractor has combined dedication to quality with outstanding distribution and after-market support to differentiate its line of construction equipment and so gain a commanding 35 percent share of the world market for earth-moving machinery. American firms, such as the auto companies, that have been somewhat lax in the area of product quality have fallen prey to those Japanese firms for which quality has become a religion.

What may not be obvious from these examples is that it is possible to differentiate anything, even commodity businesses such as fast food, potato chips, theme parks, candy bars, and printing. The answer seems to be quality and service as companies like McDonald's, Disney, Frito-Lay, Mars, and Deluxe Check Printers have demonstrated. Cleanliness and consistency of service are the hallmarks of Disney and McDonald's, with both rating at the top of almost everyone's list as the best mass service providers in the world. Similarly, it is said that Mars plants are kept so clean one can "eat off the factory floor."

High-quality work and dependability have helped Deluxe Check Printers flourish in a world supposedly on the verge of doing without checks. It fills better than 95 percent of orders in two days, and ships 99 percent error free.

Frito-Lay's special edge is a highly motivated 10,000 person sales force dedicated to selling its chips. They guarantee urban supermarkets and rural mom and pop stores alike a 99.5 percent chance of a daily call. Although they get only a small weekly salary, the sales people receive a 10 percent commission on all the Lay's, Doritos, and Tostitos they sell. So they hustle, setting up displays, helping the manager in any way possible, all the while angling for that extra foot of shelf space or preferred position that can mean additional sales income. There are also tremendous side benefits to close contact with the market. Frito can get a market test rolling in ten days and respond to a new competitive intrusion in 48 hours.

A similar level of service is provided by Sysco, a $2 billion firm in the business of wholesaling food to restaurants and other institutional business. It is a very mundane, low-margin business—one where low cost is seemingly all that matters. Yet, behind its slogan, "Don't sell food, sell peace of mind," Sysco earns margins and a return on capital that are the envy of the industry. Even in that business, a large number of customers will pay a little more for personalized service. And in a low-margin business, a little more goes a long way.

Sysco's secret was to put together a force of over 2,000 "marketing associates" who assure customers that "98 percent of items will be delivered on time." They also provide much more, going to extraordinary lengths to produce a needed item for a restauranteur at a moment's notice. Chairman John Baugh summed it up as follows:

> The typical food service company picks a case of frozen french fries out of the warehouse and drops it on the restaurant's back porch. Where is the skill in that? Where is the creativity? Service isn't a free lunch. The price tag (and cost) is higher; but even at the lower end of the market, most customers (not all, to be sure) will pay some additional freight for useful service.[2]

Other firms have made their owners wealthy by understanding that they too are *selling solutions to their customers' problems,* not hardware or consumables. John Patterson, the founder of National Cash Register, used to tell salesmen: "Don't talk machines, talk the prospect's business." Thomas Watson, the founder of IBM, patterned his sales strategy on that admonition. Thus, while other companies were talking technical specifications, his salesmen were marketing solutions to understood problems, such as making sure the payroll checks came out on time.

These days, Rolm Corp., a leader in the crowded market for office communications systems, is taking a page out of IBM's book. It has built up a service force of over 3,400 employees whose main job is to reassure customers mystified by the complexities of modern technology, while selling them more equipment. The common strategic vision and approaches of the two firms may help explain why IBM, when it decided to enter the telecommunications business, did so by acquiring Rolm (in 1984) rather than another firm.

The contrast between the approaches followed by IBM and DEC is particularly revealing. DEC has developed excellent narrow-purpose minicomputers, trusting that application solutions can be developed by others to justify advanced technology. That simple strategy—selling machines on their merits to scientists and engineers—worked spectacularly for two decades, turning DEC into the world's second-largest computer company. One consequence of that strategy, however, is that DEC never needed to and never did develop the kind of marketing orientation IBM is noted for.

The advent of the personal computer, which can perform many of the functions of a minicomputer at a fraction of the cost, has underscored the shortcomings inherent in DEC's product- rather than market-oriented strategy. As its traditional business has stagnated, DEC has attempted to reposition itself to compete in the nimble new world of personal computers. But it has failed thus far to adapt marketing and sales strategies to the new, less technically sophisticated customers it has tried to attract.

The results are painfully obvious. On October 18, 1983, DEC's stock nosedived 21 points after it announced that quarterly earnings would be 75 percent lower than the year before. Thus far at least, IBM, and its strategy of utilizing proven technology to market solutions to known problems, has prevailed in the marketplace.

Lesson #2: Investments designed to create a position at the high end of anything, including the high end of the low end, differentiated by a quality or service edge, will generally be profitable.

Cost Advantages

Entrenched companies often have cost advantages that are unavailable to potential entrants, independent of economies of scale. Sony and Texas Instruments, for example, take advantage of the *learning*

---

[2] Quoted in *Forbes,* October 11, 1982, p. 58.

curve to reduce costs and drive out actual and potential competitors. This concept is based on the old adage that you improve with practice. With greater production experience, costs can be expected to decrease because of more efficient use of labor and capital, improved plant layout and production methods, product redesign and standardization, and the substitution of less expensive materials and practices. This cost decline creates a barrier to entry because new competitors, lacking experience, face higher unit costs than established companies. By achieving market leadership, usually by price cutting, and thereby accumulating experience faster, this entry barrier can be most effectively exploited.

Proprietary technology, protected by legally enforceable patents, provides another cost advantage to established companies. This is the avenue taken by many of the premier companies in the world, including 3M, West Germany's Siemens, Japan's Hitachi, and Sweden's L. M. Ericsson.

Monopoly control of low-cost raw materials is another cost advantage open to entrenched firms. This was the advantage held for so many years by Aramco (Arabian-American Oil Company), the consortium of oil companies that until the early 1980s had exclusive access to low-cost Saudi Arabian oil.

McDonald's has developed yet another advantage vis-a-vis potential competitors: It has already acquired, at a relatively low cost, many of the best fast-food restaurant locations. Favorable locations are also important to supermarkets and department stores.

A major cost advantage enjoyed by IBM's personal computer is the fact that software programs are produced first for it since it has a commanding share of the market. Only later—if at all—are these programs, which now number in the thousands, rewritten for other brands. Companies that don't develop IBM look-alikes must either write their own software, pay to have existing software modified for their machines, or wait until the software houses get around to rewriting their programs.

Sometimes, however, new entrants enjoy a cost advantage over existing competitors. This is especially true in industries undergoing deregulation, such as the airlines and trucking. In both of these industries regulation long insulated firms from the rigors of competition and fare wars. Protected as they were, carriers had little incentive to clamp down on costs. And still they were quite profitable. The excess returns provided by the regulatory barrier to entry were divided in effect between the firm's stockholders and their unionized employees.

Deregulation has exposed these firms to new competitors not saddled with outmoded work rules and high-cost employees. For example, new low-cost competitors in the airline industry, such as People's Express and Southwest Airlines, have much lower wages (about half of what big airlines pay) and more flexible work rules (which, for example, permit pilots to load baggage and flight attendants to man reservations phones).

One firm that managed to stay ahead of the game is Northwest Airlines. For years, Northwest has been run as if competition were fierce, while still making the most of the protections of regulations. It gained a reputation for fighting labor-union demands and hammered away to increase productivity. As a result, Northwest's overhead costs are only about 2 percent of total costs, compared with about 5 percent for major competitors. Similarly, its labor costs are about two-thirds the industry average. Consequently, it is the most efficient of the major airlines, which has greatly enhanced its competitive position.

Lesson #3: Investments aimed at achieving the lowest delivered cost position in the industry, coupled with a pricing policy to expand market share, are likely to succeed, especially if the cost reductions are proprietary.

Access to Distribution Channels

Gaining distribution and shelf space for their products is a major hurdle that newcomers to an industry must overcome. Most retailers of personal computers, for example, limit their inventory to around five lines. Currently, over 200 manufacturers are competing for this very limited amount of shelf space. Moreover, the concentration of retail outlets among chains means that new computer makers have even fewer avenues to the consumer. This presents new manufacturers with a Catch-22: You don't get shelf space until you are a proven winner, but you can't sell until you get shelf space.

Conversely, well-developed, better yet unique, distribution channels are a major source of competitive advantage for firms such as Avon, Tupperware, Procter & Gamble, and IBM. Avon, for example, markets its products directly to the consumer on a house-to-house basis through an international network of 900,000 independent sales representatives. Using direct sales has enabled Avon to reduce both its advertising expenditures and the amount of money it has tied up in the business. Potential competitors face the daunting task of organizing, financing, and motivating an equivalent sales force. Thus, its independent representatives are the entry barrier that allows Avon consistently to earn exceptional profit margins in a highly competitive industry. Similarly, the sales forces of Frito-Lay, Sysco, and IBM help those firms distribute their products and raise the entry barrier in three very diverse businesses.

Conversely, the lack of a significant marketing presence in the U.S. is perhaps the greatest hindrance to Japanese drug makers attempting to expand their presence in the U.S. Marketing drugs in the U.S. requires considerable political skill in maneuvering through the U.S. regulatory process, as well as rapport with American researchers and doctors. This latter requirement means that pharmaceutical firms must develop extensive sales forces to maintain close contact with their customers. There are economies of scale here: the cost of developing such a sales force is the same, whether it sells one product or one hundred. Thus, only firms with extensive product lines can afford a large sales force, raising a major entry barrier to Japanese drug firms trying to go it alone in the U.S.

One way the Japanese drug firms have found to get around this entry barrier is to form joint ventures with American drug firms, in which the Japanese supply the patents and the American firms provide the distribution network. Such licensing arrangements are a common means of entering markets requiring strong distribution capabilities. Union Carbide, for example, follows a strategy of using high R&D expenditures to generate a diversified and innovative line of new products. Since each new product line requires a different marketing strategy and distribution network, firms like Union Carbide are more willing to trade their technology for royalty payments and equity in a joint venture with companies already in the industry.

Lesson #4: Investments devoted to gaining better product distribution often lead to higher profitability.

Government Policy

We have already seen in the case of the airline, trucking, and pharmaceutical industries that government regulations can limit, or even foreclose, entry to potential competitors. Other government policies that raise partial or absolute barriers to entry include import restrictions, environmental controls, and licensing requirements. For example, American quotas on Japanese cars have limited the ability of companies such as Mitsubishi and Mazda to expand their sales in the U.S., leading to a higher return on investment for American car companies. Similarly, environmental regulations that restrict the development of new quarries have greatly benefited those firms, such as Vulcan Materials, that already had operating quarries. The effects of licensing restrictions on the taxi business in New York City are reflected in the high price of a medallion (giving one the right to operate a cab there), which in turn reflects the higher fares that the absence of competition has resulted in.

A change in government regulations can greatly affect the value of current and prospective investments in an industry. For example, the Motor Carrier Act of 1935 set up a large barrier to entry into the business as it allowed the Interstate Commerce Commission to reject applicants to the industry. The Act also allowed the truckers themselves to determine their rates collectively, typically on the basis of average operating efficiency. Thus carriers with below-average operating costs were able to sustain above-average levels of profitability. It is scarcely surprising, then, that the major trucking companies pulled out all the stops in lobbying against deregulation. As expected, the onset of trucking deregulation, which greatly reduced the entry barrier, has led to lower profits for trucking companies and a significant drop in their stock prices.

Lesson #5: Investments in projects protected from competition by government regulation can lead to extraordinary profitability. However, what the government gives, the government can take away.

Investment Strategies and Financial Returns: Some Evidence

Ultimately, the viability of a value-creating strategy can only be assessed by examining the empirical evidence. Theory and intuition tell us that companies which follow strategies geared towards creating and preserving competitive advantages should earn higher returns on their investments than those which do not. And so they do.

William K. Hall studied eight major domestic U.S. industries and the diverse strategies followed by member firms.[3] The period selected for this study was 1975–1979, a time of slow economic growth and high inflation. These were especially hard times for the eight basic industries in Hall's study. They all faced significant cost increases that they were unable to offset fully through price increases. In addition, companies in each of these industries were forced by regulatory agencies to make major investments to comply with a variety of health, environmental, safety, and product performance standards. To compound their problems, competition from abroad grew stronger during this period. Foreign competition achieved high market shares in three of the industries (steel, tire and rubber, and automotive); moderate shares in two others (heavy-duty trucks and construction and materials handling equipment); and entry positions in the other three (major home appliances, beer, and cigarettes).

The net result of these adverse trends is that profitability in the eight basic industries has generally fallen to or below the average for manufacturers in the United States. According to Table 1, the average return on equity for these eight industries was 12.9 percent, substantially below the 15.1 percent median return for the Fortune 1000. A number of firms in these industries have gone bankrupt, are in financial distress, or have exited their industry.

---

[3] William K. Hall, "Survival Strategies in a Hostile Environment," *Harvard Business Review,* September-October 1980, pp. 75–85.

Table 1 Return on Equity in Eight Basic Industries: 1975–1979[a]

Industry	Return on Equity	Leading Firm	Return on Equity
Steel	7.1%	Inland Steel	10.9%
Tire and rubber	7.4	Goodyear	9.2
Heavy-duty trucks	15.4	Paccar	22.8
Construction and materials handling equipment	15.4	Caterpillar	23.5
Automotive	15.4	General Motors	19.8
Major home appliances	10.1	Maytag	27.2
Beer	14.1	G. Heilman Brewing	25.8
Cigarettes	18.2	Philip Morris	22.7
Average—eight industries	12.9	Average—leading companies	20.2
Median—Fortune 1000	15.1		

[a]From William K. Hall, "Survival Strategies in a Hostile Environment."

Yet this tells only part of the story. As Table 1 also shows, some companies survived, indeed prospered, in this same hostile environment. They did this by developing business strategies geared towards achieving one or both of the following competitive positions within their respective industries and then single-mindedly tailoring their investments to attain these positions:

1. Become the lowest total delivered cost producer in the industry, while maintaining an acceptable service/quality combination relative to competition.

2. Develop the highest product/service/quality differentiated position within the industry, while maintaining an acceptable delivered cost structure.

Table 2 provides a rough categorization of the strategies employed by the two top-performing companies in each of the eight industries studied. In most cases, the industry profit leaders chose to occupy only one of the two competitive positions. Perhaps this is because the resources and skills necessary to achieve a low-cost position are incompatible with those needed to attain a strongly differentiated position.

At least three of the 16 leaders, however, combined elements of both strategies with spectacular success. Caterpillar has combined lowest-cost manufacturing with outstanding distribution and after-sales service to move well ahead of its domestic and foreign competitors in profitability. Similarly, the U.S. cigarette division of Philip Morris has become the industry profit leader by combining the lowest-cost manufacturing facilities in the world with high-visibility brands, supported by high-cost promotion. Finally, Daimler Benz employs elements of both strategies, but in different business segments. It has the lowest cost position in heavy-duty trucks in Western Europe, along with its exceptionally high-quality, feature-differentiated line of Mercedes Benz cars.

Other examples of the benefits of attaining the low-cost position in an industry or picking and exploiting specialized niches in the market abound. For example, the low-cost route to creating positive NPV investments has been successfully pursued in, of all places, the American steel industry. The strategy has involved building up-to-date mini-mills employing non-union workers who earn

Table 2   Competitive Strategies Employed by Leaders in Eight Basic Industries[a]

Industry	Low Cost Leader	Meaningful Differentiation	Both Employed Simultaneously
Steel	Inland Steel	National	—
Tire and rubber	Goodyear	Michelin (French)	—
Heavy-duty trucks	Ford, Daimler Benz (German)	—	—
Construction and materials handling equipment	—	John Deere	Caterpillar
Automotive	General Motors	Daimler Benz	—
Major home appliances	Whirlpool	Maytag	—
Beer	Miller	G. Heilman Brewing	—
Cigarettes	R. J. Reynolds	—	Philip Morris

[a]From William K. Hall, "Survival Strategies in a Hostile Environment."

substantially less than members of the United Steelworkers Union. Mini-mills melt scrap, which is cheaper in the U.S. than anywhere else, and their modern plant and equipment and simplified work practices greatly reduce their need for labor. Chapparal Steel of Midlothian, Texas, a big—and profitable—mini-mill, has pared its labor costs to a mere $29 on a ton of structural steel. This compares with average labor costs of $75 a ton at big integrated U.S. plants.

The chief disadvantage is that their steelmaking capabilities are limited. They can't, for example, make the industry's bread-and-butter item: flat-rolled steel. But in the product areas where mini-mills do compete—rod, bar, and small beams and shapes—big producers have all but surrendered. So, too, have foreign mills. In just two years, Nucor Corp's mini-mill in Plymouth, Utah, cut the Japanese share of California's rod and bar market from 50 to 10 percent.

Taking a different tack, Armstrong Rubber Co. has specialized in grabbing small market segments overlooked by its rivals. Today, Armstrong ranks second in industrial tires and second or third in both the replacement market for all-season radials and in tires for farm equipment and off-road recreational vehicles. Its niche-picking strategy relies heavily on the design and production innovations arising from its large investments in research and development.

A number of chemical firms, including Hercules, Monsanto, Dow, and Belgium's Solvay, have attempted to lessen their dependence on the production of commodity chemicals and plastics by investing heavily in highly profitable specialty products for such industries as electronics and defense. These specialty chemicals are typically sold in smaller quantities but at higher prices than traditional bulk commodity chemicals. Perhaps the most successful chemical "niche picker" is Denmark's Novo Industri—one of the world's largest producers of enzymes and insulin, and a pioneer in genetic engineering techniques. Novo's continued success is largely due to its ability to find and exploit small but profitable market niches. For instance, industry analysts credit Novo's success at selling enzymes in Japan to the company's ability to outdo even Japanese purity standards and to concentrate on small specialty markets that Japan's chemical giants can't be bothered with. In fact, most of Novo's markets appear too small for giant chemical firms such as Germany's Hoechst or Du Pont to pursue.

James River Corp. has combined cost cutting with product differentiation to achieve spectacular growth and profits in the paper-goods industry, an industry where many companies are struggling to hold their own. Typically, James River buys other companies' cast-off paper mills and remakes them in its own image. It abandons all or most of the commodity-grade paper operations. It refurbishes old equipment and supplements it with new machinery to produce specialty products (automobile and coffee filters, airline ticket paper, peel-off strips for Band-Aids, and cereal-box liners) that are aimed at specific markets and provide higher profits with less competition. At the same time, James River cuts costs by extracting wage concessions from workers and dismissing most executives. It also raises the productivity of those employees who stay by allowing many of them to join the company's lucrative *profit-sharing* programs. James River's success in following this two-pronged strategy is reflected in its 1983 net income of $55.1 million, 332 times larger than its 1970 earnings of $166,000.

Designing an Investment Strategy

Although a strong competitive edge in technology or marketing skills may enable a firm to earn excess returns, these barriers to entry will eventually erode, leaving the firm susceptible to increased competition. Existing firms are entering new industries, and there are growing numbers of firms from a greater variety of countries, leading to new, well-financed competitors able to meet the high marketing costs and enormous capital outlays necessary for entry. Caterpillar Tractor, for example, faces a continuing threat from low-cost foreign competitors, especially Japan's Komatsu, which is second in worldwide sales. To stay on top, therefore, a firm's strategy must be constantly evolving, seeking out new opportunities and fending off new competitors.

Xerox clearly illustrates the problems associated with losing a competitive edge. For many years, Xerox was the king of the copier market, protected by its patents on xerography, with sales and earnings growing over 20 percent annually. The loss of its patent protection has brought forth numerous well-heeled competitors, including IBM, 3M, Kodak, and the Japanese, resulting in eroding profits and diminishing growth prospects. Xerox has tried to transfer its original competitive advantage in technology to new products designed for the so-called office of the future. However, its difficulties in closely coordinating its R&D and marketing efforts have led to a series of serious, self-confessed blunders in acquisitions, market planning, and product development. For example, as mentioned earlier, the basic technology for the personal computer was developed by Xerox's Palo Alto Research Center in the early 1970s, but it remained for Apple Computer and IBM to capitalize on this revolutionary product.

More recently, Xerox's 1982 acquisition of Crum & Forster, a property and casualty insurance company, has called into question the company's strategy. It is unclear how Xerox, for whom high technology has been the chief competitive advantage, can earn excess returns in a business in which it has no experience. As we have already seen, firms that stick to their knitting are more likely to succeed than those that don't.

Common sense tells us that, in order to achieve excess returns over time, the distinctive competitive advantage held by the firm must be difficult or costly to replicate. If it is easily replicated, it will not take long for actual or potential competitors to apply the same concept, process, or organizational structure to their operations. The competitive advantage of experience, for example, will evaporate unless a firm can keep the tangible benefits of its experience proprietary and force its competitors to go through the same learning process. Once a firm loses its competitive advantage, its profits will erode to a point where it can no longer earn excess returns. For this reason, the firm's competitive advantage has to be constantly monitored and maintained so as to ensure the existence of an effective barrier to entry into the market. Should these barriers to entry break down, the firm must react quickly either to reconstruct them or build new ones.

Caterpillar has reacted to Komatsu's challenge by attempting to slash its costs, closing plants, shifting production overseas, forcing union and nonunion workers alike to take pay cuts, eliminating many positions, and pressuring its suppliers to cut prices and speed deliveries. To get lower prices, the company is shopping around for hungrier suppliers, including foreign companies. This is reflected in its philosophy of worldwide sourcing, as described by its director of purchasing: "We're trying to become international in buying as well as selling. We expect our plants, regardless of where they're located, to look on a world-wide basis for sources of supply."[4] For example, German and Japanese companies now supply crankshafts once made exclusively in the U.S.

One important source of extra profit is the quickness of management to recognize and use information about new, lower-cost production opportunities. The excess profits, however, are temporary, lasting only until competitors discover these opportunities for themselves. For example, purchasing the latest equipment will provide a temporary cost advantage, but this advantage will disappear as soon as competitors buy the equipment for their own plants. Only if the equipment is proprietary will the firm be able to maintain its cost advantage. Along the same line, many American electronics and textile firms shifted production facilities to Taiwan, Hong Kong, and other Asian locations to take advantage of lower labor costs there. However, as more firms took advantage of this cost reduction opportunity, competition in the consumer electronics and textiles markets in the U.S. intensified, causing domestic prices to drop and excess profits to dissipate. In fact, firms in competitive industries must continually seize new nonproprietary cost reduction opportunities, not to earn excess returns but simply to make normal profits, or just survive.

Similarly, marketing-oriented firms can earn excess returns by being among the first to recognize and exploit new marketing opportunities. For example, Crown Cork & Seal, the Philadelphia-based bottle-top maker and can maker, reacted to slowing growth in its U.S. business by expanding overseas. It set up subsidiaries in such countries as Thailand, Malaysia, Ethiopia, Zambia, Peru, Ecuador, Brazil, and Argentina. In so doing, as it turns out, they guessed correctly that in those developing, urbanizing societies, people would eventually switch from home-grown produce to food in cans and drinks in bottles.

Profitable markets, however, have a habit of eventually attracting competition. Thus, to be assured of having a continued supply of value-creating investments on hand, the firm must institutionalize its strategy of cost reduction and/or product differentiation. Successful companies seem to do this by creating a corporate culture—a set of shared values, norms, and beliefs—that has as one of its elements an obsession with some facet of their performance in the marketplace. McDonald's has an obsessive concern for quality control, IBM for customer service, and 3M for innovation. Forrest Mars set the tone for his company by going into a rage if he found an improperly wrapped candy bar leaving the plant. In order to maintain its low-cost position in the structural steel market, Chapparal Steel has teams of workers and foremen scour the world in search of the latest production machinery and methods.

---

[4] As quoted in *The Wall Street Journal* (August 10, 1971), p. 1.

Conversely, AT&T's manufacturing orientation, which focused on producing durable products with few options, was well-suited to the regulated environment in which it operated throughout most of its existence. But such an inward-looking orientation is likely to be a significant barrier to the company's ability to compete against the likes of IBM and other market-oriented, high-tech companies that react quickly to consumer demand. Prior to the breakup of AT&T, the manufacturers at Western Electric, AT&T's manufacturing arm, freely decided which products to make and when. They controlled the factories, supplying telephones to a captive market of Bell companies. AT&T was essentially an order taker, no more needing a sales force than any other utility does. There were no competitors forcing quicker market reaction nor any marketers challenging manufacturers' decisions.

Although AT&T claims that it is now "market-driven," evidence abounds that the company's older entrenched manufacturing mentality is still dominant. Unless AT&T can change its corporate culture—a difficult and demanding task for any company, much less for a giant set in its ways—and marry manufacturing and marketing, it will have a difficult time competing with firms such as IBM in the office automation and computer business it has set its sights on.

The basic insight here is that sustained success in investing is not so much a matter of building new plants as of seeking out lower-cost production processes embodied in these plants, coming up with the right products for these plants to produce, and adding the service and quality features that differentiate these products in the marketplace. In other words, it comes down to people and how they are organized and motivated. The cost and difficulty of creating a corporate culture that adds value to capital investment is the ultimate barrier to entry; unlike the latest equipment, money alone can't buy it.

In the words of Maurice R. (Hank) Greenberg, president of American Insurance Group (A.I.G.), a worldwide network of insurance companies that has enjoyed spectacular success by pioneering in territory relatively unpopulated by competitors, "You can't imitate our global operation. It's just incapable of being reproduced. Domestically, we have some imitators for pieces of our business, but not the entire business. And in any event, you can only imitate what we've done. You can't imitate what we're thinking. You can't copy what we're going to do tomorrow."[5]

Corporate Strategy and Foreign Investment

Most of the firms we have discussed are multinational corporations (MNCs) with worldwide operations. For many of these MNCs, becoming multinational was the end result of an apparently haphazard process of overseas expansion. But, as international operations become a more important source of profit and as domestic and foreign competitors become more aggressive, it is apparent that domestic survival for many firms is increasingly dependent on their success overseas. To ensure this success, multinationals must develop global strategies that will enable them to maintain their competitive edge both at home and abroad.

Overseas Expansion and Survival

It is evident that if one's competitors gain access to lower-cost sources of production abroad, following them overseas may be a prerequisite for domestic survival. One strategy often followed by

---

[5] Wyndham Robertson, "Nobody Tops A.I.G. in Intricacy—or Daring," *Fortune,* May 22, 1978, p. 99.

firms for whom cost is the key consideration, such as Chapparal Steel, is to develop a global scanning capability to seek out lower-cost production sites or production technologies worldwide.

Economies of Scale.   A somewhat less obvious factor motivating foreign investment is the effect of economies of scale. We have already seen that in a competitive market, prices will be forced close to marginal costs of production. Hence, firms in industries characterized by high fixed costs relative to variable costs must engage in volume selling just to break even.

A new term has arisen to describe the size necessary in certain industries to compete effectively in the global marketplace: *world scale.* These large volumes may be forthcoming only if firms expand overseas. For example, companies manufacturing products such as mainframe computers that require huge R&D expenditures often need a larger customer base than that provided by even a market as large as the United States in order to recapture their investment in knowledge. Similarly, firms in capital-intensive industries with significant economies of scale in production may also be forced to sell overseas in order to spread their overhead over a higher volume of sales.

To take an extreme case, L. M. Ericsson, the highly successful Swedish manufacturer of telecommunications equipment, is forced to think internationally when designing new products since its domestic market is too small to absorb the enormous R&D expenditures involved and to reap the full benefit of production scale economies. Thus, when Ericsson developed its revolutionary AXE digital switching system, it geared its design to achieve global market penetration.

Many firms have found that a local market presence is necessary in order to continue selling overseas. For example, a local presence has helped Data General adapt the design of its U.S. computers and software to the Japanese market, giving the company a competitive edge over other U.S. companies selling computers in Japan. Data General has also adopted some Japanese manufacturing techniques and quality-control procedures that will improve its competitive position worldwide.

More firms are preparing for global competition. For example, although Black & Decker has a 50 percent market share worldwide in power tools, new competitors like the Japanese are forcing the company to change its manufacturing and marketing operations. Black & Decker's new strategy is based on a marketing concept known as "globalization," which holds that the world is becoming more homogenized and that distinctions between markets are disappearing. By selling standardized products worldwide, a firm can take advantage of economies of scale, thereby lowering costs and taking business from MNCs that customize products for individual markets. Until recently, the latter strategy of customization was the one that Black & Decker followed; the Italian subsidiary made tools for Italians, the British subsidiary tools for Britons.

By contrast, Japanese power-tool makers such as Makita Electric Works don't care that Germans prefer high-powered, heavy-duty drills and that Americans want everything lighter. Instead, Makita's strategy, which has been quite successful, is based on the notion that if you make a good drill at a low price, it will sell from Brooklyn to Baden-Baden. In response, Black & Decker recently unveiled 50 new power tools, each standardized for world production. It plans to standardize future products as well, making only minimal concessions, which require only minor modifications, to cultural differences.

Knowledge Seeking.   Some firms enter foreign markets for the purpose of gaining information and experience that is expected to prove useful elsewhere. For instance, Beecham, an English firm, deliberately set out to learn from its U.S. operations how to be more competitive, first in the area of consumer products and later in pharmaceuticals. This knowledge proved highly valuable in competing with American and other firms in its European markets. Unilever, the Anglo-Dutch corporation, learned to adapt to world markets, with impressive results, the marketing skills it acquired in the U.S. through its American affiliate Lever Bros.

In industries characterized by rapid product innovation and technical breakthroughs by foreign competitors, it pays constantly to track overseas developments. The Japanese excel in this. Japanese firms systematically and effectively collect information on foreign innovation and disseminate it within their own research and development, marketing, and production groups. The analysis of new foreign products as soon as they reach the market is an especially long-lived Japanese technique. One of the jobs of Japanese researchers is to tear down a new foreign computer and analyze how it works as a base on which to develop a product of their own that will outperform the original. In a bit of a switch, as pointed out above, Data General's Japanese operation is giving the company a close look at Japanese technology, enabling it quickly to pick up and transfer back to the United States new information on Japanese innovations in the areas of computer design and manufacturing. Similarly, Ford Motor Co. has used its European operations as an important source of design and engineering ideas and management talent.

Designing a Global Expansion Strategy

The ability to pursue systematically policies and investments congruent with worldwide survival and growth depends on four interrelated elements:

1. The first, and the key to the development of a successful global strategy, is to understand and then capitalize on those factors that have led to success in the past. In order for domestic firms to become global competitors, therefore, the sources of their domestic advantage must be transferable abroad. A competitive advantage predicated on government regulation, such as import restrictions, clearly doesn't fit in this category.

2. Second, this global approach to investment planning necessitates a systematic evaluation of individual entry strategies in foreign markets, a comparison of the alternatives, and selection of the optimal mode of entry.

3. The third important element is a continual audit of the effectiveness of current entry modes. As knowledge about a foreign market increases, for example, or sales potential grows, the optimal market penetration strategy will likely change.

4. Fourth, top management must be committed to becoming and/or staying a multinational corporation. Westinghouse demonstrated its commitment to international business by creating the new position of President-international and endowing its occupant with a seat on the company's powerful management committee. A truly globally oriented firm—one that asks, "Where in the *world* should we develop, produce, and sell our products and services?"—also requires an intelligence system capable of systematically scanning the world and understanding it along with people who are experienced in international business and know how to use the information generated by the system.

Summary and Conclusions

We have seen that rates of return in competitive industries are driven down to their required returns. Excess profits quickly attract new entrants to the market, lowering returns until actual and required returns are again equal. Thus, the run-of-the-mill firm operating in a highly competitive market will be unable consistently to find positive net present value investments—ones which earn excess returns relative to their required returns. The key to generating a continual flow of positive NPV projects, therefore, is to erect and maintain barriers to entry against competitors. This involves either building defenses against potential competitors or finding positions in the industry where competition is the weakest.

The firm basically has two strategic options in its quest for competitive advantage: It can seek lower costs than its competitors, or it can differentiate its product in a number of ways, including high advertising expenditures, product innovation, high product quality, and first-rate service.

Each of these options involves a number of specific investment decisions: construction of efficient-scale facilities and vigorous pursuit of cost reduction through accumulated experience, in the case of cost leadership; if product differentiation is the main goal, the focus is on advertising, R&D, quality control, customer-service facilities, distribution networks, and the like. The more an investment widens a firm's competitive advantage and reduces the chances of successful replication by competitors, the greater the likelihood that investments will be successful.

Despite our understanding of the subject matter, it is difficult to give a set of rules to follow in developing profitable investment strategies. If it were possible to do so, competitors would follow them and dissipate any excess returns. One must be creative and quick to recognize new opportunities. Nevertheless, without dictating what should be done in every specific circumstance, there are some basic lessons we have learned from economic theory and the experiences of successful firms. The basic lessons are these:

1. Invest in projects that take advantage of your competitive edge. The corollary is, stick to doing one or two things and doing them well; don't get involved in businesses you are unfamiliar with.

2. Invest in developing, maintaining, and enhancing your competitive advantages.

3. Develop a global scanning capability. Don't be blindsided by new competitors or lower-cost production techniques or locations.

4. Pick market niches where there is little competition. Be prepared to abandon markets where competitors are catching up and apply your competitive advantages to new products or markets.

Assuming that a firm does have the necessary resources to be successful internationally, it must carefully plan for the transfer of these resources overseas. For example, it must consider how it can best utilize its marketing expertise, innovative technology, or production skills to penetrate a specific foreign market. Where a particular strategy calls for resources the firm lacks, such as an overseas distribution network, corporate management must first decide how and at what cost these resources can be acquired. It must then decide whether (and how) to acquire the resources or change its strategy.

Discussion Questions

1. How do you suggest the firm should go about securing investment proposals that are consistent with strategies identified here?

2. Describe the five lessons discussed in this article and give one example of each.

3. Contrast this article's concept of establishing strategic options for investing with a more random selection process designed, for example, to maximize diversification.

David B. Hertz

Risk Analysis in Capital Investment

This article was the first to describe the Monte Carlo simulation method for capital investment analysis under risk or uncertainty. Although articles have since appeared on various details of the method, none has provided the comprehensive and definitive treatment given here.

The simulation method has several advantages First, simulation enables the analyst to handle very complicated problems. Second, compared with the single-valued estimate approach, simulation allows the experts providing input data to indicate the probable accuracy of their estimates as well as expected values. Third, the method enables the analyst to make a sensitivity analysis of any stochastic variable merely by holding all other variables constant (presumably at their expected values). Finally, since the output is a probability distribution of NPV or IRR, decision makers have substantial information about the reward-risk profile of the project. For example, output data could include the worst, best, most likely, and expected outcomes, and the probabilities would be estimated for IRR > cost of capital, IRR > 0, IRR > riskless rate, IRR > "sensational," NPV > "ruinous" outcome, or NPV > 0. Software is now readily available for Monte Carlo simulation.

The problematic aspects of the method are securing appropriate input data, incorporating interdependence among the variables, correct modeling of the project variables, and correct specification of independence or correlation of cash flows over time.

Of all the decisions that business executives must make, none is more challenging—and none has received more attention—than choosing among alternative capital investment opportunities. What makes this kind of decision so demanding, of course, is not the problem of projecting return on investment under any given set of assumptions. The difficulty is in the assumptions and in their impact. Each assumption involves its own degree—often a high degree—of uncertainty; and, taken together, these combined uncertainties can multiply into a total uncertainty of critical proportions. This is where the element of risk enters, and it is in the evaluation of risk that the executive has been able to get little help from currently available tools and techniques.

Source: Reprinted by permission of *Harvard Business Review.* "Risk Analysis in Capital Investments" by David B. Hertz, January–February 1963, pp. 95–106.

There is a way to help the executive sharpen his key capital investment decisions by providing him with a realistic measurement of the risks involved. Armed with this measurement, which evaluates for him the risk at each possible level of return, he is then in a position to measure more knowledgeably alternative courses of action against corporate objectives.

Need for New Concept

The evaluation of a capital investment project starts with the principle that the productivity of capital is measured by the rate of return we expect to receive over some future period. A dollar received next year is worth less to us than a dollar in hand today. Expenditures three years hence are less costly than expenditures of equal magnitude two years from now. For this reason we cannot calculate the rate of return realistically unless we take into account (a) when the sums involved in the investment are spent and (b) when the returns are received.

Comparing alternative investments is thus complicated by the fact that they usually differ not only in size but also in the length of time over which expenditures will have to be made and benefits returned.

It is these facts of investment life that long ago made apparent the shortcomings of approaches that simply averaged expenditures and benefits, or lumped them, as in the number-of-years-to-payout method. These shortcomings stimulated students of decision making to explore more precise methods for determining whether one investment would leave a company better off in the long run than would another course of action.

It is not surprising, then, that much effort has been applied to the development of ways to improve our ability to discriminate among investment alternatives. The focus of all of these investigations has been to sharpen the definition of the value of capital investments to the company. The controversy and furor that once came out in the business press over the most appropriate way of calculating these values has largely been resolved in favor of the discounted cash flow method as a reasonable means of measuring the rate of return that can be expected in the future from an investment made today.

Thus we have methods which, in general, are more or less elaborate mathematical formulas for comparing the outcomes of various investments and the combinations of the variables that will affect the investments.[1] As these techniques have progressed, the mathematics involved has become more and more precise, so that we can now calculate discounted returns to a fraction of a percent.

But the sophisticated businessman knows that behind these precise calculations are data which are not that precise. At best, the rate-of-return information he is provided with is based on an average of different opinions with varying reliabilities and different ranges of probability. When the expected returns on two investments are close, he is likely to be influenced by "intangibles"—a precarious pursuit at best. Even when the figures for two investments are quite far apart, and the choice seems clear, there lurks in the back of the businessman's mind memories of the Edsel and other ill-fated ventures.

In short, the decision maker realizes that there is something more he ought to know, something in addition to the expected rate of return. He suspects that what is missing has to do with the nature

---

[1] See, for example, Joel Dean, *Capital Budgeting* (New York, Columbia University Press, 1951); "Return on Capital as a Guide to Managerial Decisions," *National Association of Accounts Research Report No. 35,* December 1, 1959; and Bruce F. Young, "Overcoming Obstacles to Use of Discounted Cash Flow for Investment Shares," *NAA Bulletin,* March 1963, p. 15.

of the data on which the expected rate of return is calculated, and with the way those data are processed. It has something to do with uncertainty, with possibilities and probabilities extending across a wide range of rewards and risks.

The Achilles Heel

The fatal weakness of past approaches thus has nothing to do with the mathematics of rate-of-return calculation. We have pushed along this path so far that the precision of our calculation is, if anything, somewhat illusory. The fact is that, no matter what mathematics are used, each of the variables entering into the calculation of rate of return is subject to a high level of uncertainty. For example:

The useful life of a new piece of capital equipment is rarely known in advance with any degree of certainty. It may be affected by variations in obsolescence or deterioration, and relatively small changes in use life can lead to large changes in return. Yet an expected value for the life of the equipment—based on a great deal of data from which a single best possible forecast has been developed—is entered into the rate-of-return calculation. The same is done for the other factors that have a significant bearing on the decision at hand.

Let us look at how this works out in a simple case—one in which the odds appear to be all in favor of a particular decision:

The executives of a food company must decide whether to launch a new packaged cereal. They have come to the conclusion that five factors are the determining variables: advertising and promotion expense, total cereal market, share of market for this product, operating costs, *and* new capital investment. *On the basis of the "most likely" estimate for each of these variables the picture looks very bright—a healthy 30 percent return. This future, however, depends on each of the "most likely" estimates coming true in the actual case. If each of these "educated guesses" has, for example, a 60 percent chance of being correct, there is only an 8 percent chance that all five will be correct (.60 × .60 × .60 × .60 × .60). So the "expected" return is actually dependent on a rather unlikely coincidence. The decision maker needs to know a great deal more about the other values used to make each of the five estimates and about what he stands to gain or lose from various combinations of these values.*

This simple example illustrates that the rate of return actually depends on a specific combination of values of a great many different variables. But only the expected levels of ranges (e.g., worst, average, best; or pessimistic, most likely, optimistic) of these variables are used in formal mathematical ways to provide the figures given to management. Thus, predicting a single most likely rate of return gives precise numbers that do not tell the whole story.

The "expected" rate of return represents only a few points on a continuous curve of possible combinations of future happenings. It is a bit like trying to predict the outcome in a dice game by saying that the most likely outcome is a "7." The description is incomplete because it does not tell us about all the other things that could happen. In Exhibit 1, for instance, we see the odds on throws of only two dice having six sides. Now suppose that each die has 100 sides and there are eight of them! This is a situation more comparable to business investment, where the company's market share might become any one of 100 different sizes and where there are eight different factors (pricing, promotions, and so on) that can affect the outcome.

Nor is this the only trouble. Our willingness to bet on a roll of the dice depends not only on the odds but also on the stakes. Since the probability of rolling a "7" is 1 in 6, we might be quite willing

Exhibit 1   Describing Uncertainty—A Throw of the Dice

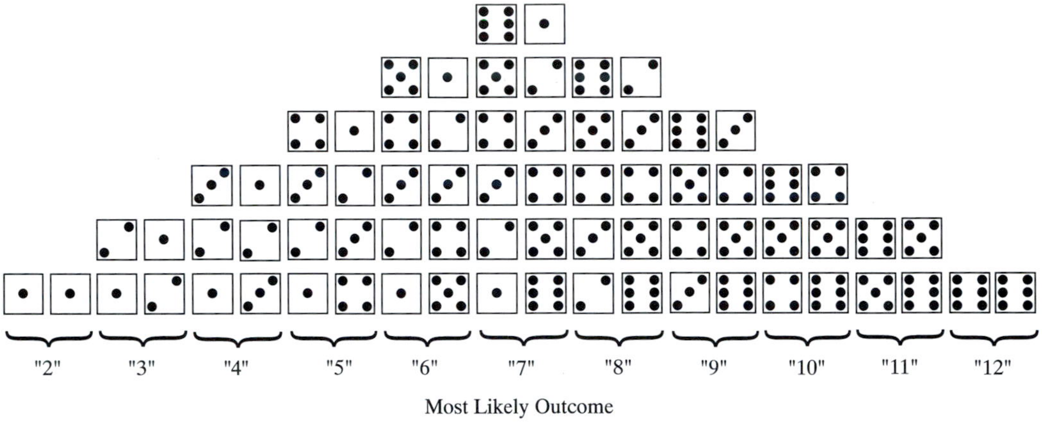

"2"   "3"   "4"   "5"   "6"   "7"   "8"   "9"   "10"   "11"   "12"

Most Likely Outcome

to risk a few dollars on that outcome at suitable odds. But would we be equally willing to wager $10,000 or $100,000 at those same odds, or even at better odds? In short. risk is influenced both by the odds on various events occurring and by the magnitude of the rewards or penalties which are involved when they do occur, To illustrate again:

Suppose that a company is considering an investment of $1 million. The "best estimate" of the probable return is $200,000 a year. It could well be that this estimate is the average of three possible returns—a 1-in-3 chance of getting no return at all, a 1-in-3 chance of getting $200,000 per year, a 1-in-3 chance of getting $400,000 per year. Suppose that getting no return at all would put the company out of business. Then, by accepting this proposal, management is taking a 1-in-3 chance of going bankrupt.

If only the "best estimate" analysis is used, management might go ahead, however, unaware that it is taking a big chance. If all the available information were examined, management might prefer an alternative proposal with a smaller, but more certain (i.e., less variable), expectation.

Such considerations have led almost all advocates of the use of modern capital-investment-index calculations to plead for a recognition of the elements of uncertainty. Perhaps Ross G. Walker sums up current thinking when he speaks of "the almost impenetrable mists of any forecast."[2]

How can the executive penetrate the mists of uncertainty that surround the choices among alternatives?

Limited Improvements

A number of efforts to cope with uncertainty have been successful up to a point, but all seem to fall short of the mark in one way or another:

---

[2] "The Judgment Factor in Investment Decisions," *HBR*, March-April 1961, p. 99.

1. *More accurate forecasts.* Reducing the error in estimates is a worthy objective. But no matter how many estimates of the future go into a capital investment decision, when all is said and done, the future is still the future. Therefore, however well we forecast, we are still left with the certain knowledge that we cannot eliminate all uncertainty.

2. *Empirical adjustments.* Adjusting the factors influencing the outcome of a decision is subject to serious difficulties. We would like to adjust them so as to cut down the likelihood that we will make a "bad" investment, but how can we do that without at the same time spoiling our chances to make a "good" one? And in any case, what is the basis for adjustment? We adjust, not for uncertainty, but for bias.

   For example, construction estimates are often exceeded. If a company's history of construction costs is that 90 percent of its estimates have been exceeded by 15 percent, then in a capital estimate there is every justification for increasing the value of this factor by 15 percent. This is a matter of improving the accuracy of the estimate.

   But suppose that new-product sales estimates have been exceeded by more than 75 percent in one-fourth of all historical cases, and have not reached 50 percent of the estimate in one-sixth of all such cases? Penalties for overestimating are very tangible, and so management is apt to reduce the sales estimate to "cover" the one case in six—thereby reducing the calculated rate of return. In doing so, it is possibly missing some of its best opportunities.

3. *Revising cutoff rates.* Selecting higher cutoff rates for protecting against uncertainty is attempting much the same thing. Management would like to have a possibility of return in proportion to the risk it takes. Where there is much uncertainty involved in the various estimate of sales, costs, prices, and so on, a high calculated return from the investment provides some incentive for taking the risk. That is, in fact, a perfectly sound position. The trouble is that the decision maker still needs to know explicitly what risks he is taking—and what the odds are on achieving the expected return.

4. *Three-level estimates.* A start at spelling out risks is sometimes made by taking the high, medium, and low values of the estimated factors and calculating rates of return based on various combinations of the pessimistic, average, and optimistic estimates. These calculations give a picture of the range of possible results, but do not tell the executive whether the pessimistic result is more likely than the optimistic one—or, in fact, whether the average result is much more likely to occur than either of the extremes. So, although this is a step in the right direction, it still does not give a clear enough picture for comparing alternatives.

5. *Selected probabilities.* Various methods have been used to include the probabilities of specific factors in the return calculation. L. C. Grant discusses a program for forecasting discounted cash flow rates of return where the service life is subject to obsolescence and deterioration. He calculates the odds that the investment will terminate at any time after it is made depending on the probability distribution of the service-life factor. After calculating these factors for each year through maximum service life, he then determines an overall expected rate of return.[3]

Edward G. Bennion suggests the use of game theory to take into account alternative market growth rates as they would determine rate of return for various alternatives. He uses the estimated probabilities that specific growth rates will occur to develop optimum strategies. Bennion points out:

---

[3] "Monitoring Capital Investments," *Financial Executive,* April 1963, p. 19.

"Forecasting can result in a negative contribution to capital budget decisions unless it goes further than merely providing a single most probable prediction. . . . [With] an estimated probability coefficient for the forecast, plus knowledge of the payoffs for the company's alternative investments and calculation of indifference probabilities . . . the margin of error may be substantially reduced, and the businessman can tell just how far off his forecast may be before it leads him to a wrong decision."[4]

Note that both of these methods yield an expected return, each based on only one uncertain input factor—service life in the first case, market growth in the second. Both are helpful, and both tend to improve the clarity with which the executive can view investment alternatives. But neither sharpens up the range of "risk taken" or "return hoped for" sufficiently to help very much in the complex decisions of capital planning.

Sharpening the Picture

Since every one of the many factors that enter into the evaluation of a specific decision is subject to some uncertainty, the executive needs a helpful portrayal of the effects that the uncertainty surrounding each of the significant factors has on the returns he is likely to achieve. Therefore, the method we have developed at McKinsey & Company, Inc., combines the variabilities inherent in all the relevant factors. Our objective is to give a clear picture of the relative risk and the probable odds of coming out ahead or behind in the light of uncertain foreknowledge.

A simulation of the way these factors may combine as the future unfolds is the key to extracting the maximum information from the available forecasts. In fact, the approach is very simple, using a computer to do the necessary arithmetic. (Recently, a computer program to do this was suggested by S. W. Hess and H. A. Quigley for chemical process investments.[5])

To carry out the analysis, a company must follow three steps:

1. Estimate the range of values for each of the factors (e.g., range of selling price, sales growth rate, and so on) and within that range the likelihood of occurrence of each value.

2. Select at random from the distribution of values for each factor one particular value. Then combine the values for all of the factors and compute the rate of return (or present value) from that combination. For instance, the lowest in the range of prices might be combined with the highest in the range of growth rate and other factors. (The fact that the factors are independent should be taken into account, as we shall see later.)

3. Do this over and over again to define and evaluate the odds of the occurrence of each possible rate of return. Since there are literally millions of possible combinations of values, we need to test the likelihood that various specific returns on the investment will occur. This is like finding out by recording the results of a great many throws what percent of 7's or other combinations we may expect in tossing dice. The result will be a listing of the rates of return we might achieve, ranging from a loss (if the factors go against us) to whatever maximum gain is possible with the estimates that have been made.

   For each of these rates the chances that it may occur are determined. (Note that a specific return can usually be achieved through more than one combination of events. The more combinations

[4] "Capital Budgeting and Game Theory," *HBR,* November-December 1956, p. 123.

[5] "Analysis of Risk in Investments Using Monte Carlo Techniques," *Chemical Engineering Symposium Series 42: Statistics and Numerical Methods in Chemical Engineering* (New York, American Institute of Chemical Engineering, 1963), p. 55.

for a given rate, the higher the chances of achieving it—as with 7's in tossing dice.) The average expectation is the average of the values of all outcomes weighted by the chances of each occurring.

The variability of outcome values from the average is also determined. This is important since, all other factors being equal, management would presumably prefer lower variability for the same return if given the choice. This concept has already been applied to investment portfolios.[6]

When the expected return and variability of each of a series of investments have been determined, the same techniques may be used to examine the effectiveness of various combinations of them in meeting management objectives.

Practical Test

To see how this new approach works in practice, let us take the experience of a management that has already analyzed a specific investment proposal by conventional techniques. Taking the same investment schedule and the same expected values actually used, we can find what results the new method would produce and compare them with the results obtained when conventional methods were applied. As we shall see, the new picture of risks and returns is different from the old one. Yet the differences are attributable in no way to changes in the basic data—*only to the increased sensitivity of the method to management's uncertainties about the key factors.*

Investment Proposal

In this case a medium-size industrial chemical producer is considering a $10 million extension to its processing plant. The estimated service life of the facility is 10 years; the engineers expect to be able to utilize 250,000 tons of processed material worth $510 per ton at an average processing cost of $435 per ton. Is this investment a good bet? In fact, what is the return that the company may expect? What are the risks? We need to make the best and fullest use we can of all the market research and financial analyses that have been developed, so as to give management a clear picture of this project in an uncertain world.

The key input factors management has decided to use are

1. Market size
2. Selling prices
3. Market growth rate
4. Share of market (which results in physical sales volume)
5. Investment required
6. Residual value of investment
7. Operating costs
8. Fixed costs
9. Useful life of facilities.

[6]See Harry Markowitz, *Portfolio Selection, Efficient Diversification of Investments* (New York, John Wiley and Sons, 1959); Donald E. Fararr, *The Investment Decision Under Uncertainty* (Englewood Cliffs, New Jersey, Prentice-Hall, Inc., 1962); William F. Sharpe, "A Simplified Model for Portfolio Analysis," *Management Science,* January 1963, p. 277.

These factors are typical of those in many company projects that must be analyzed and combined to obtain a measure of the attractiveness of a proposed capital facilities investment.

Obtaining Estimates

How do we make the recommended type of analysis of this proposal?

Our aim is to develop for each of the nine factors listed a frequency distribution or probability curve. The information we need includes the possible range of values for each factor, the average, and some ideas as to the likelihood that the various possible values will be reached. It has been our experience that for major capital proposals managements usually make a significant investment in time and funds to pinpoint information about each of the relevant factors. An objective analysis of the values to be assigned to each can, with little additional effort, yield a subjective probability distribution.

Specifically, it is necessary to probe and question each of the experts involved—to find out, for example, whether the estimated cost of production really can be said to be exactly a certain value or whether, as is more likely, it should be estimated to lie within a certain range of values. It is that range which is ignored in the analysis management usually makes. The range is relatively easy to determine; if a guess has to be made—as it often does—it is easier to guess with some accuracy a range rather than a specific single value. We have found from past experience at McKinsey & Company, Inc., that a series of meetings with management personnel to discuss such distributions is most helpful in getting at realistic answers to the *a priori* questions. (The term *realistic answers* implies all the information management does *not* have as well as all that it does have.)

The ranges are directly related to the degree of confidence that the estimator has in his estimate. Thus, certain estimates may be known to be quite accurate. They would be represented by probability distributions stating, for instance, that there is only 1 chance in 10 that the actual value will be different from the best estimate by more than 10 percent. Others may have as much as 100 percent ranges above and below the best estimate.

Thus, we treat the factor of selling price for the finished product by asking executives who are responsible for the original estimates these questions:

1. Given that $510 is the expected sales price, what is the probability that the price will exceed $550?
2. Is there any chance that the price will exceed $650?
3. How likely is it that the price will drop below $475?

Managements must ask similar questions for each of the other factors, until they can construct a curve for each. Experience shows that this is not as difficult as it might sound. Often information on the degree of variation in factors is readily available. For instance, historical information on variations in the price of a commodity is readily available. Similarly, management can estimate the variability of sales from industry sales records. Even for factors that have no history, such as operating costs for a new project, the person who makes the "average" estimate must have some idea of the degree of confidence he has in his prediction, and therefore he is usually only too glad to express his feelings. Likewise, the less confidence he has in his estimate, the greater will be the range of possible values that the variable will assume.

This last point is likely to trouble businessmen. Does it really make sense to seek estimates of variations? It cannot be emphasized too strongly that the less certainty there is in an "average" estimate, *the more important it is to consider the possible variation in that estimate.*

Further, an estimate of the variation possible in a factor, no matter how judgmental it may be, is always better than a simple "average" estimate, since it includes more information about what is known and what is not known. It is, in fact, this very *lack* of knowledge which may distinguish one investment possibility from another, so that for rational decision making it *must* be taken into account.

This lack of knowledge is in itself important information about the proposed investment. To throw any information away simply because it is highly uncertain is a serious error in analysis which the new approach is designed to correct.

Computer Runs

The next step in the proposed approach is to determine the returns that will result from random combinations of the factors involved. This requires realistic restrictions, such as not allowing the total market to vary more than some reasonable amount from year to year. Of course, any method of rating the return which is suitable to the company may be used at this point; in the actual case management preferred discounted cash flow for the reasons cited earlier, so that method is followed here.

A computer can be used to carry out the trials for the simulation method in very little time and at very little expense. Thus, for one trial actually made in this case, 3,600 discounted cash flow calculations, each based on a selection of the nine input factors, were run in two minutes at a cost of $15 for computer time. The resulting rate-of-return probabilities were read out immediately and graphed. The process is shown schematically in Exhibit 2.

Data Comparisons

The nine input factors described earlier fall into three categories:

1. *Market analyses.* Included are market size, market growth rate, the firm's share of the market, and selling prices. For a given combination of these factors, sales revenues may be determined.
2. *Investment cost analyses.* Being tied to the kinds of service-life and operating-cost characteristics expected, these are subject to various kinds of error and uncertainty; for instance, automation progress makes service life uncertain.
3. *Operating and fixed costs.* These also are subject to uncertainty, but are perhaps the easiest to estimate.

These categories are not independent, and for realistic results our approach allows the various factors to be tied together. Thus, if price determines the total market, we first select from a probability distribution the price for the specific computer run and then use for the total market a probability distribution that is logically related to the price selected.

We are now ready to compare the values obtained under the new approach with the values obtained under the old. This comparison is shown in Exhibit 3.

Valuable Results

How do the results under the new and old approaches compare?

In this case, management had been informed, on the basis of the "one best estimate" approach, that the expected return was 25.2 percent before taxes. When we ran the new set of data through the

Exhibit 2   Simulation for Investment Planning

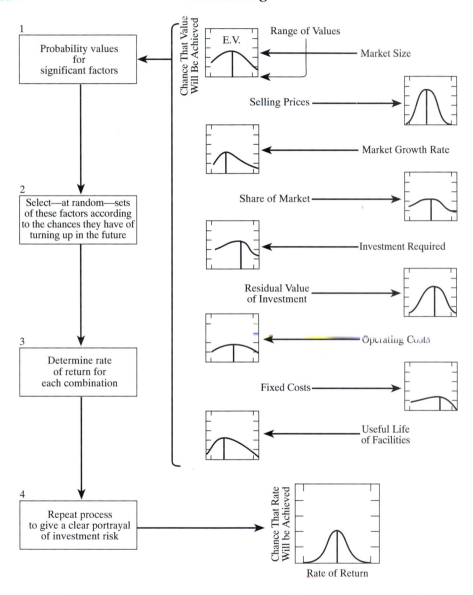

computer program, however, we got an expected return of only 14.6 percent before taxes. This surprising difference not only is due to the fact that under the new approach we use a range of values; it also reflects the fact that we have weighted each value in the range by the chances of its occurrence.

Exhibit 3   Comparison of Expected Values under Old and New Approaches

	Conventional "Best Estimate" Approach	New Approach
Market Analysis		
1. *Market size*		
Expected value (in tons)	250,000	250,000
Range	—	100,000–340,000
2. *Selling prices*		
Expected value (in dollars/ton)	$510	$510
Range	—	$385–$575
3. *Market growth rate*		
Expected value	3%	3%
Range	—	0–6%
4. *Eventual share of market*		
Expected value	12%	12%
Range	—	3%–17%
Investment Cost Analyses		
5. *Total investment required*		
Expected value (in millions)	$9.5	$9.5
Range	—	$7.0–$10.5
6. *Useful life of facilities*		
Expected value (in years)	10	10
Range	—	5–15
7. *Residual value (at 10 years)*		
Expected value (in millions)	$4.5	$4.5
Range	—	$3.5–$5.0
Other Costs		
8. *Operating costs*		
Expected value (in dollars/ton)	$435	$435
Range	—	$370–$545
9. *Fixed costs*		
Expected value (in thousands)	$300	$300
Range	—	$250–$375

Note: Range figures in right-hand column represent approximately 1 percent to 99 percent probabilities. That is, there is only a 1 in 100 chance that the value actually achieved will be respectively greater or less than the range.

Our new analysis thus may help management avoid an unwise investment. In fact, the general result of carefully weighing the information and lack of information in the manner I have suggested is to indicate the true nature of otherwise seemingly satisfactory investment proposals. If this practice were followed by managements, much regretted overcapacity might be avoided.

The computer program developed to carry out the simulation allows for easy insertion of new variables. In fact, some programs have previously been suggested that take variability into account.[7] But most programs do not allow for dependence relationships between the various input factors. Further, the program used here permits the choice of a value for price from one distribution, which value determines a particular distribution (from among several) that will be used to determine the value for sales volume. To show how this important technique works:

Suppose we have a wheel, as in roulette, with the numbers from 0 to 15 representing one price for the product or material, the numbers 16 to 30 representing a second price, the numbers 31 to 45 a third price, and so on. For each of these segments we would have a different range of expected market volumes; e.g., $150,000–$200,000 for the first, $100,000–$150,000 for the second, $75,000–$100,000 for the third, and so forth. Now suppose that we spin the wheel and the ball falls in 37. This would mean that we pick a sales volume in the $75,000–$100,000 range. If the ball goes in 11, we have a different price and we turn to the $150,000–$200,000 range for a sales volume.

Most significant, perhaps, is the fact that the program allows management to ascertain the sensitivity of the results to each or all of the input factors. Simply by running the program with changes in the distribution of an input factor, it is possible to determine the effect of added or changed information (or the lack of information). It may turn out that fairly large changes in some factors do not significantly affect the outcomes. In this case, as a matter of fact, the management was particularly concerned about the difficulty in estimating market growth. Running the program with variations in this factor quickly demonstrated to us that for average annual growths from 3 percent and 5 percent there was no significant difference in the expected outcome.

In addition, let us see what the implications are of the detailed knowledge the simulation method gives us. Under the method using single expected values, management arrives only at a hoped-for expectation of 25.2 percent after taxes (which, as we have seen, is wrong unless there is no variability in the various input factors—a highly unlikely event). On the other hand, with the method we propose, the uncertainties are clearly portrayed:

Percent Return	Probability of Achieving at Least the Return Shown
0%	96.5%
5	80.6
10	75.2
15	53.8
20	43.0
25	12.6
30	0

This profile is shown in Exhibit 4. Note the contrast with the profile obtained under the conventional approach. This concept has been used also for evaluation of new product introductions, acquisitions of new businesses, and plant modernization.

---

[7] See Frederick S. Hillier, "The Derivation of Probabilistic Information for the Evaluation of Risky Investments," *Management Science,* April 1963, p. 443.

Exhibit 4   Anticipated Rates of Return under Old and New Approaches

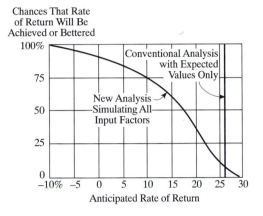

Comparing Opportunities

From a decision-making point of view, one of the most significant advantages of the new method of determining rate of return is that it allows management to discriminate among measures of (1) expected return based on weighted probabilities of all possible returns, (2) variability of return, and (3) risks.

To visualize this advantage, let us take an example which is based on another actual case but simplified for purposes of explanation. The example involves two investments under consideration, A and B.

Selected Statistics

	Investment A	Investment B
Amount of investment	$10,000,000	$10,000,000
Life of investment (in years)	10	10
Expected annual net cash inflow	$1,300,000	$1,400,000
Variability of cash inflow		
One chance in 50 of being *greater* than	$1,700,000	$3,400,000
One chance in 50 of being *less*[a] than	$900,000	($600,000)
Expected return on investment	5.0%	6.8%
Variability of return on investment		
One chance in 50 of being *greater* than	7.0%	15.5%
One chance in 50 of being *less*[a] than	3.0%	(4.0%)
Risk of investment		
Chances of loss	Negligible	1 in 10
Expected size of loss		$200,000

[a]In the case of negative figures (indicated by parentheses), "less than" means "worse than."

When the investments are analyzed, the data tabulated and plotted in Exhibit 5 are obtained. We see that

Investment B has a higher expected return than Investment A.

Investment B also has substantially more variability than Investment A. There is a good chance that Investment B will earn a return which is quite different from the expected return of 6.8 percent, possibly as high as 15 percent or as low as a loss of 5 percent. Investment A is not likely to vary greatly from the expected 5 percent return.

Investment B involves far more risk than does Investment A. There is virtually no chance of incurring a loss on Investment A. However, there is 1 chance in 10 of losing money on Investment B. If such a loss occurs, its expected size is approximately $200,000.

Clearly, the new method of evaluating investments provides management with far more information on which to base a decision. Investment decisions made only on the basis of maximum expected return are not unequivocally the best decisions.

Conclusion

The question management faces in selecting capital investments is, first and foremost, what information is needed to clarify the key differences among various alternatives? There is agreement as to the basic factors that should be considered—markets, prices, costs, and so on. And the way the future return on the investment should be calculated, if not agreed on, is at least limited to a few methods, any of which can be consistently used in a given company. If the input variables turn out as estimated, any of the methods customarily used to rate investments should provide satisfactory (if not necessarily maximum) returns.

In actual practice, however, the conventional methods do *not* work as satisfactorily. Why? The reason, as we have seen earlier in this article, and as every executive and economist knows, is that the estimates used in making the advance calculations are just that—estimates. More accurate estimates would be helpful, but at best the residual uncertainty can easily make a mockery of corporate hopes. Nevertheless, there is a solution. To collect realistic estimates for the key factors means to find out a great deal about them. Hence the kind of uncertainty that is involved in each estimate can be evaluated ahead of time. Using this knowledge of uncertainty, executives can maximize the value of the information for decision making.

The value of the computer programs in developing clear portrayals of the uncertainty and risk surrounding alternative investments has been proved. Such programs can produce valuable information about the sensitivity of the possible outcomes to the variability of input factors and to the likelihood of achieving various possible rates of return. This information can be extremely important as a backup to management judgment. To have calculations of the odds on all possible outcomes lends some assurance to the decision makers that the available information has been used with maximum efficiency.

This simulation approach has the inherent advantage of simplicity. It requires only an extension of the input estimates (to the best of our ability) in terms of probabilities. No projection should be pinpointed unless we are *certain* of it.

The discipline of thinking through the uncertainties of the problem will in itself help to ensure improvement in making investment choices. For to understand uncertainty and risk is to understand the key business problem—and the key business opportunity. Since the new approach can be

Exhibit 5   Comparison of Two Investment Opportunities

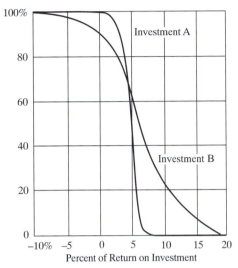

applied on a continuing basis to each capital alternative as it comes up for consideration and progresses toward fruition, gradual progress may be expected in improving the estimation of the probabilities of variation.

Last, the courage to act boldly in the face of apparent uncertainty can be greatly bolstered by the clarity of portrayal of the risks and possible rewards. To achieve these lasting results requires only a slight effort beyond what most companies already exert in studying capital investments.

Discussion Questions

1. What is a "stochastic" variable?

2. Draw a picture of a probability distribution for NPV. Label on it the type of information obtainable from this probability distribution, if it were known.

3. Draw NPV probability distributions for projects A and B, each with the same mean and variance but such that you would obviously prefer A to B.

4. Describe the Monte Carlo simulation method of capital budgeting as proposed by Hertz. In your description, explain how the input information is secured, how the simulation is accomplished, and how the results might be interpreted. Highlight the strengths and weaknesses of this simulation technique.

5. List the five efforts to cope with uncertainty indicated by Hertz; point out what improvement they offered and where they fell short.

Problems

1. You are given the following probability distribution for the outlay (O) on a project:

P(O = $100,000) = 0.2
P(O = $110,000) = 0.3
P(O = $120,000) = 0.4
P(O = $130,000) = 0.1

As an exercise in what it means to take random samples, take 100 random samples from the above probability distribution and record the results on a histogram. Summarize the results.

Hint:

a. To accomplish the random sampling, let the digits

0, 1   represent $100,000

2, 3, 4   represent   110,000

5, 6, 7, 8 represent   120,000 and

9   represent   130,000

b. If you do not have a random digit table, use arbitrarily selected columns of digits from present value tables. Use the digits which are the furthest to the right of the decimal point.

2. You have the following information for a project:

Outlay = $100,000
Cost of capital = 10 percent
Salvage value = $0.0
Cash flow: P(CF = 10,000) = 0.3
                  P(CF = 15,000) = 0.5
                  P(CF = 20,000) = 0.2
Life of project: P(L = 8 years) = 0.2
                  P(L = 10 years) = 0.4
                  P(L = 12 years) = 0.3
                  P(L = 14 years) = 0.1

Ignore tax and depreciation; make ten trials for NPV and plot a histogram of the results. (Assume that cash flows are perfectly correlated through time; i.e., whatever the outcome of a random sample of the CF distribution, that is the CF for each year over the life of the project.)

Marc Ross*

Capital Budgeting Practices of Twelve Large Manufacturers

This paper contains descriptions of the capital budgeting procedures of twelve large firms. An important conclusion of the study is that a common practice in capital budgeting procedures results in capital rationing for small projects. The challenge involves devising a procedure that avoids systematically denying capital to small, potentially high-return prospects.

I. Introduction

Surveys of capital budgeting practices among large firms have indicated a widespread use of discounted cash flow (DCF) methods, especially internal rate of return.[1] At the same time, many firms state that they also continue to use simple payback or related methods [8]. The study reported here sheds light on the differences between theory and practice in the implementation of DCF analysis.

Surveys have shown that many firms use either a weighted average cost of capital or the cost of a specific source of funds in determining a hurdle rate. Most firms, however, employ some form of capital rationing—that is, they restrict capital expenditures even though it generally means neglecting profitable projects.[2] Under rationing, projects compete against each other, not against a profitability standard. The study reported here uses empirically determined hurdle rates and other data to examine these capital allocation practices.

*I would like to express my pleasure in working with the project group at the Alliance to Save Energy: Robin Miller, Bob Rauch, Mike Reid, and Jim Wolf. The help of Carliss Baldwin of the School of Business Administration, Harvard University for extensive comments on an early draft is also appreciated. I also thank the editor and the anonymous reviewers of *Financial Management* for their extensive and useful suggestions.

Source: Reprinted with permission of *Financial Management* (Winter 1986), pp. 15–22. Marc Ross is a Professor of Physics at University of Michigan, Ann Arbor.

[1] Two recent surveys of the literature are those by Scott and Petty [9] and Gurnani [5].

[2] See the surveys by Gitman and Forrester [4] and Petty, Scott, and Bird [6]. A survey of capital budgeting practices is presented by Fremge [3].

A. *The Alliance Study*

The study, by the Alliance to Save Energy [1], was undertaken to evaluate tax incentives for industrial energy conservation. It was supported by the John D. and Catherine T. MacArthur Foundation. Data were gathered, primarily in 1981–82, from 15 large firms, with three each from the steel, paper, aluminum, and petroleum refining industries. Since the author did not participate in the petroleum refining interviews, petroleum refining is omitted here. The firms studied accounts for about one-third of the combined sales of the four industries. Much of the information collected is proprietary, and the firms cannot be identified.

Information was gathered from two sources at each firm: one to three days of interviews, and records of the analysis of energy-related investment projects. The interviews focused on examples of projects at the margin of acceptability and on the financial analysis of these projects.

Although the study was designed to address tax incentives, its field-study approach and its focus on energy conservation projects lent themselves to learning about the investment decision-making process in general. The field-study approach enabled examination of actual operating procedures, and since energy conservation is not usually an area of proprietary concern, discussions were often open and information generously provided. Moreover, respondents stated that the capital budgeting process for energy conservation is essentially the same as for other discretionary projects of the same size.

B. *The Sample Data*

The firms typically categorize capital investments as either mandatory (regulations and contracts, capitalized maintenance, replacement of antiquated equipment, product quality) or discretionary (expanded markets, new businesses, cost cutting). Decision making is different for mandatory and discretionary projects. We culled the project data to omit (the few) projects that appeared to be mandatory. We also omitted many projects for which the financial information was inadequate for our analysis. The final sample contained some 400 projects: roughly 100 completed projects, almost all in 1980–1981, and 300 projects either underway or prospective, primarily intended for the period 1982–1985.

Interviews at the firms showed that most firms' decision-making processes are different for different project sizes. Typical levels of approval authority are shown in Exhibit 1. Using the size categories from Exhibit 1, we found the data to contain roughly 300 small and very small projects, 100 medium-sized projects, and 12 large projects. Unlike the samples of small and medium projects, that of large projects was probably not representative of those under consideration across these industries, because some firms did not provide data on large projects (due to proprietary concerns). In this study most of the information thus concerns discretionary projects of $10 million or less.

The data were complete (except for very small projects) for four of the twelve firms under consideration; i.e., they spanned all energy conservation projects under consideration regardless of project size. Complete records for projects based at one or more plants were obtained for five more firms. For the remaining firms, only samples of the projects under consideration were obtained.

II. Example of a Project Proposal

Decision making on smaller projects can be succinctly described by a hypothetical example. Typical features that we observed are incorporated; the specifics would, of course, vary.

Exhibit 1   Project Size and Decision-Making Authority

Project Size	Typical Boundaries	Primary Site for Investment Decision
Very small	Up to $100,000	Plant
Small	$100,000 to $1 million	Division
Medium	$1 million to $10 million	Corporate investment committee
Large	Over $10 million	CEO and board

Bill Johnson is part of an energy-conservation team (created in 1979) at a large plant of a basic-materials manufacturer. On the initiative of a vendor, he has identified an approach to cutting energy costs at a heater: advanced combustion controls, which could reduce excess air in the combustion zone.[3]

Bill looks into other approaches, such as total replacement of the heater or added heat exchangers (to capture heat from the stack gases to preheat the product). However, the projects overlap; he can advocate at most one.

Opinions on technical issues are sought out by Bill, especially from an operating engineer at the facility where the heater is located and from his supervisor. He obtains rough quotes from vendors and estimates annual benefits for several schemes. A critical test for the combustion-control option is passed in a discussion with the manager of the facility in question. These managers are typically like kings in their realms. Their tastes and the production problems they face may lead them to veto any modification out of hand. The facility manager is primarily concerned with technological risks, such as a long breaking-in period and possible operational problems. Use of automatic controls would involve operating the heater close to conditions that are analogous to being at the edge of a cliff; a small mistake could be very damaging. Bill selected a project for this particular heater in part because he knows that this facility manager is open to new technology. He is able to tell the manager that one of the control options has been applied in a similar situation and has operated without trouble.

Bill gets the go-ahead for detailed design work on the control option. One consideration is that, since the likely project cost is over $100,000 (but less than a million), the final investment decision would be made at division headquarters. Bill knows that the plant manager has many things to ask for at the division and would prefer that the decision on this project be kept at the plant level. He cannot bring the cost below $100,000, however. He also knows that other alternatives would create a project in the $1 million to $10 million range, putting the final decision with the Corporate Investment Committee (CIC). Paradoxically, while he knows that the CIC is more generous in approving projects than the division, he wants to avoid going to the CIC because a very extensive case would have to be prepared, and enthusiastic support would be needed from the division, plant, and facility managers. That would be hard to get for a project that cuts costs but has no other production benefits. He has observed that higher-level managers give higher priority to new markets than to cost cutting and that lower-level managers give higher priority to maintaining and improving the manufacturing process

---

[3] His idea could also have come from an energy-conservation audit of the plant, corporate energy conservation staff, professional literature, or contacts with peers.

(with respect to product quality, flexibility and reliability of production, production capacity, etc.) than to cost cutting.

The control system is designed by Bill with the help of a vendor and representatives of plant service organizations, and in collaboration with the operating engineer. He obtains good capital cost quotes and calculates initial-year operating costs and benefits. He calculates the ratio of capital cost to first year net benefits (without considering taxes) and calls this the payback.

Bill notes with concern that the cost is higher than his preliminary estimate, so that the payback is 1.7 years, near the cut-off on projects approved by the division in the past two years. Bill's plant is relatively modern, and the businesses with which the heater is associated are sound; if the project were at a less-favored location, the division would certainly not approve it. A substantial risk that the plant or production line will be shut down creates an expectation of substantially reduced profitability, even where management does not expect the shutdown to occur soon.

Using a microcomputer, Bill calculates several after-tax DCF measures of investment worth. He has instructions for certain aspects of the evaluation: He must assign a ten-year life to all projects, although he suspects the life of this project will be shorter because the technology will probably become obsolete. He must use 6 percent per year escalation of all prices over the project life, in spite of the different expectations he has for natural gas and other factors.[4] He assumes that the heater is operated at design levels and that the energy saved per year is constant over the ten-year period. No risk assessment is included in the analysis. In any case, although the DCF evaluations are carried out, the project is discussed at the plant in terms of its 1.7 year payback.

The request for funds includes a two-page financial analysis prepared by computer, a brief technical description of the project and very brief comments on its possible impacts on production and on pollution. The request is sent to the plant manager. He has an overview of the requests that will go from the plant to the division. Although he is not especially impressed by a cost-cutting project with this payback, he wants to get experience with advanced control systems and is satisfied the project will not interfere with production, so he approves the request. It is then forwarded to Corporate Engineering for technical evaluation. The plant manager or Corporate Engineering often returns a request at this stage, putting it on hold or asking for substantial changes. This time it goes through.

The request is sent to division headquarters as part of a group of requests. On the basis of an earlier planning process, the plant manager knows that the total requested is in line with the capital the division expects to allocate to his plant.

Decision makers at the division include a vice president who has responsibility for the products made at the facility in question. He has a good relationship with the facility manager and knows about the request from personal conversation. He notes the project's internal rate of return of 44 percent, but pays no attention to the NPV or profitability index, which are also shown in the financial analysis. He is accustomed to the fact that standard project life and escalation rates have been used in the evaluation, and believes this to be an effective procedure for preventing some plant managers from exaggerating the benefits of their projects. The vice president believes the engineering estimate of capital costs and initial benefits to be unbiased. He has his own ideas about rates of inflation, which lead him to feel that the calculated IRR may be a few points high. As an expert in the

---

[4] Although many interviewees in our study discussed the uncertainty of future energy prices, the recent steep drop in oil and gas prices was not expected or even hinted at by anyone in our interviews. In the following, no consideration of this price drop is made.

prospects of the business in question, he believes this facility will operate at a full schedule for the next few years, and so he is satisfied with this aspect of the analysis.

The division has a fixed amount of capital to allocate, similar to that of the previous year.[5] At the critical meeting on the project in question, it is learned that the requests for mandatory projects are larger than usual.[6] Considering the funds remaining, if all discretionary projects were ranked by their IRR, this particular project would not make it. On the other hand, division management likes to approve requests from this plant manager because he is cautious in his proposals and is very effective in other respects. The project is approved but it is noted that implementation may be delayed.

III. Financial Analysis of Projects

As the example suggests, many of the firms studied severely simplify the DCF evaluation of projects and, in any case, rely primarily on simple payback. (It should be kept in mind that projects of the kind under study have, as suggested in the hypothetical example, very simple benefit streams.) Exhibit 2 summarizes the observations at the twelve firms.

Not surprisingly, perhaps, sensitivity analysis for various potential risks is typically avoided. For example, reduced production because of weak sales or changes in the production process could affect the benefit stream from an energy-saving project. However, only a few of the firms studied have considered such contingencies. Two chemical firms retroactively studied the performance of energy-conservation projects associated with organic chemicals and found that, while engineering analyses proved fairly accurate in a narrow sense, benefits and economic lives tended to be less than predicted because of unanticipated changes in production rates and technology. These insights were not formally incorporated into the financial analyses.

The practice at most firms is thus to keep both the financial analysis of smaller projects, and the process of communicating this analysis to decision makers, extremely simple [7]. Decisions are then based on the primary quantitative measure from the analysis supplemented by informal adjustments made in the minds of decision makers. The analysis of large projects was more detailed in the few cases we saw. For example, detailed DCF analyses were carried out, often including sensitivity analyses with respect to parameters like rates of price escalation.

IV. Rates of Return for Project Approval

Many firms have internally published, or de jure, hurdle rates for project approval. These rates may or may not correspond to the apparent, or de facto, rates that empirically characterize projects actually approved. At some firms the de jure rates were described as being out of date or intended only for a first cut, to help decide if preparation of a project proposal merits more effort.

At some firms, however, the de jure and de facto rates are essentially the same. These firms have a decentralized capital budgeting process: Project decisions are made locally, with heavy

---

[5] If division management wanted to, they could increase this capital allocation by making a good case for it. But this would require a major effort and would use up some of the division's "credit" with corporate headquarters. Division management feels it has more pressing problems to address.

[6] Requests for mandatory projects are not accompanied by financial analyses. They are generally approved after consideration of the project's nature and its cost, the priorities developed at the plant level, and the reputation of the plant and its management.

Exhibit 2   Distribution of Twelve Firms by Measure of Investment Worth Used for Smaller Projects

Measures Calculated	Number of Firms	Measure Primarily Relied Upon	Number of Firms
IRR[a]	5	IRR, with both variable project life and price escalation	5
Simplified IRR and simple payback[b]	5	IRR, with fixed life and/or escalation	3
Simple payback only[c]	2	Simple payback	4

[a]NPV and other DCF measures were also calculated but not referred to in discussion or in other documents.
[b]Of the five, one approximated the DCF calculation so it could be easily hand calculated, and all required use of a single economic life for all projects and/or a single uniform price escalation rate.
[c]Or a return on investment directly based on simple payback.

reliance on a uniform rate of return criterion. Capital requirements are forwarded to higher management, and although there may be restraints at a given time or for a given business, the capital is typically provided. We call these flexible-budgeting firms.

A different approach to capital budgeting is followed at many firms. At these firms, project approval is not based on an announced or assumed hurdle rate. While people are typically aware, as suggested in the hypothetical example, of hurdle rates characterizing past decisions, the critical approval decision is based on competition among projects for an essentially fixed sum. We call firms employing this procedure capital-rationing firms.

The de facto rates reported here are all based on a uniform calculation of (nominal-dollar) internal rate of return (IRR).[7] For this purpose, we examined projects at flagship plants associated with relatively solid product lines with stable process technology and with well established lives. For almost all the firms, there were data on such projects. These projects roughly share the financial risks of the firm as a whole.

De facto hurdle rates for project approval were determined in part from the data on proposed and approved projects. Almost all projects in the sample were completed, approved, or expected to be approved. In other words, very few projects were being considered (and were included in the sample) which were not expected to be approved. The IRR distribution of these projects is very broad, but it has a few projects with IRRs that are close to the lowest IRR for an approved project. Hence, this lowest IRR is taken as the apparent hurdle rate. In addition, apparent hurdle rates were determined from information on projects specifically identified at the firm as barely acceptable. Hurdle rate results from these two sources of information were consistent (within roughly ± 5 percentage points in the rate of return).[8]

[7] For comparative purposes it is important to choose project parameters that reflect the expectations at the firm, rather than mimicking the overly simple financial analyses sometimes made there. For example, in the cases of organic chemical products mentioned in the previous section, the adjustments suggested by the firms' studies were incorporated.

[8] Another issue in hurdle rate determination is possible time dependence. Were they rising because of the 1982 recession? Were they falling because the best energy-conservation projects had already been selected? Data from four firms that extended several years into the past and/or were planned several years into the future showed no significant change in hurdle

(*continued on p. 269*)

V. Hurdle Rate Results

Our information is consistent with the expectation that all twelve firms had de facto hurdle rates for large projects close to the corporate average cost of capital (about 15 percent).[9] Only four firms gave this treatment to the smaller projects, however. For the other eight firms, hurdle rates for small and/or medium projects were high. Among the eight, all six providing information on small projects show very high hurdle rates (35 percent to 60 percent), and all six providing information on medium projects show moderately high hurdle rates (25 percent to 40 percent). These data are summarized in Exhibit 3.

The firms studied thus fall into two classes:

(i) firms with uniform de facto hurdle rates near the corporate average cost of capital for all discretionary projects, i.e., flexible-budgeting firms, and

(ii) firms with de facto hurdle rates that are high for small projects, moderately high for medium projects, and fairly near the cost of capital for large projects.

We found through interviews that most of the second group of firms explicitly employ capital rationing at lower levels of decision making. That is, fixed sums are allocated to those groups, below the level of CEO and Board, that make decisions about capital projects, with the result that much less discretionary investment is undertaken in smaller projects than would be justified by conventional analysis. The rest of the firms in this group deny that they impose capital rationing, but at the plant/division level perceptions and behavior conform to capital rationing. The sample data suggest that the rationing of capital is most severe at plant and division levels but, surprisingly, is often severe even at the level of the corporate investment committee (which typically makes the effective decision on medium-sized projects).

The results from our sample of firms are consistent with survey results that half or more of large firms impose capital rationing on all projects ([4], [7]). Our new finding is that capital rationing, as practiced, has an especially severe impact on smaller projects.

Not surprisingly, financial analysis of smaller projects at flexible-budgeting firms tends to be more sophisticated than at capital-rationing firms. All of the former employ DCF analysis, and essential attention is given to details in the calculation. At only one of the eight capital-rationing firms is a DCF analysis with essential details carried out.

Although the firms cannot be named, general observations can be made. The flexible-budgeting firms are all relatively strong financially. From comments made at a few capital-rationing firms, it seemed that interest coverage might be negatively correlated with the effective hurdle rate. It is, roughly. A linear regression (using data from nine firms) of hurdle rates, HR, for small projects (in percent) against interest coverage (four-year average), IC, yielded HR = 60 − 5 × IC, with $r^2 \approx 0.5$. (The hurdle rates also correlate rather well with other financial characteristics of the firms.) The reason for such a correlation is probably related to inhibitions on capital spending resulting from the difficulties that firms with poorer ratings face in raising capital, as discussed subsequently.

---

[8] (*continued from p. 268*)

rates. Interviews confirmed that there was no major change in project opportunities and that the firms' financial practices were not changing rapidly, except for delays in capital spending associated with the 1982 recession. These delays were not reflected in the information we collected.

[9] Two of these firms showed us their methods of calculating cost of capital; they correspond closely to textbook procedures. See, for example, Van Horne [10].

Exhibit 3   Investment Hurdle Rates by Project Size: Flexible-Budgeting and Capital-Rationing Firms

	Hurdle Rate Range[a] (Percent)		Number in Sample (Firms, Projects)	
	Flexible Budgeting Firms	Capital Rationing Firms	Flexible Budgeting Firms	Capital Rationing Firms
Size of Project[b]				
Small	14–17	35–60	(4, 197)	(6, 96)
Medium	14–17	25–40	(4, 19)	(6, 73)
Large	—	15–25[c]	—	(3, 12)

[a]Internal rate of return, discounting nominal dollar flows.
[b]See Exhibit 1 for definitions.
[c]Based on a very small project sample; return on least profitable project is shown.

VI. Possible Rationales for Severe Capital Rationing for Smaller Projects

The high hurdle rates for smaller projects do not primarily reflect greater uncertainty about return on investment for smaller projects at capital-rationing firms. Such concerns have, to a large degree, been taken into account:

(i) Engineering data on the projects (i.e., within their design context) are relatively accurate. This has been confirmed by retrospective studies of projects at several of the firms.

(ii) The disadvantages of projects associated with less favored plants and product lines, with rapidly changing products and processes, and with short-lived types of equipment were compensated for in the hurdle-rate determinations. The sample of low-risk projects at flagship plants defines the hurdle rates for almost all the firms. Without doubt, incomplete financial analysis of smaller projects at most capital-rationing firms leads to some discounting by management of even the least risky projects. This does not appear, however, to be a major consideration.

There was no suggestion from our interviewees at capital-rationing firms that smaller projects at better plants and product lines suffer from a degree of uncertainty that would justify subjecting them to higher hurdle rates. Instead, as discussed at several interviews, *all* cost-cutting projects in the firm's major businesses suffer from the same downside uncertainty as the firm as a whole: the risk of low capacity utilization, especially during recessions. The evidence indicates, then, that limitations in capital budgeting procedures, rather than unusual risk levels, are the direct cause of high hurdle rates for smaller projects. What, then, is the cause of these capital budgeting procedures?

Two explanations were suggested at interviews at capital-rationing firms, both of which have merit:

(i) The shadow cost of capital is much higher than the average cost of capital to the firm. Under this explanation, capital rationing is imposed on firms by outside suppliers of capital.

(ii) Top corporate management is preoccupied with many other responsibilities and assigns low priority to cost cutting. Also, top management feels unable to decentralize or delegate open-ended responsibility for investment in smaller projects, especially since information and decision costs for smaller projects are relatively high.

With respect to the first explanation, mature businesses typically provide for plant and equipment expenditures from their stream of earnings. For most of the capital-rationing firms, the earnings would not be sufficient to allow expeditious implementation of all profitable cost-cutting projects. Our interviews showed that many perceived it would be potentially damaging for their firm to attempt to raise additional equity funds and that lenders would resist the raising of debt money beyond some debt-equity or interest-coverage ratios (independent of the profitability of the investments). For example, rating services might draw negative conclusions about an attempt to raise additional capital, with the result that the firm could no longer borrow in certain markets and its bonds could not be purchased by certain institutional investors. The sense that an equity offering would, in particular, reduce stock prices is confirmed by a general analysis of public offerings of industrial stocks by Asquith and Mullins [2].

Interviewees perceived the effect to be strongly differentiated, however, depending on the general purpose of the investment: Debt *can* be raised by the capital-rationing firms without unacceptably weakening their financial rating for certain major acquisitions. In the recent past, many of the firms in the study have made major acquisitions. For added investment to modernize existing plants, however, the cost of capital is perceived to be very high.

Let us turn to the second explanation. For firms in a poor financial position, a perception that characterized a majority of the capital-rationing firms, arrangements for any financing from outside sources would be extraordinarily time consuming for top management. Given their priorities, top management often copes with productivity improvement by allocating relatively small fixed sums to divisions and plants. That leaves them the time to carefully analyze the large projects and the modes of financing them.

A related perspective was offered at some interviews. Many energy-conservation projects' lack of impact on production capacity, product quality, and product flexibility is perceived as a reason for giving them a low priority. Cost-cutting projects can be postponed, it is thought, without losing much of the opportunity, whereas market opportunities associated with new or improved products or increased production may be altogether fleeting.

How important are the smaller projects being postponed, or neglected altogether, at capital-rationing firms? There was enough information from six of the firms to roughly answer this question. Smaller energy-conservation projects (i.e., those decided below the CEO-Board level) accounted for 2 percent to 15 percent of total capital spending by these six firms. The highest fractions in this range were associated with flexible-budgeting firms or firms in very high energy-to-value-added businesses, and the lowest fractions were associated with capital-rationing firms with somewhat lower energy costs. The average difference in these energy-conservation expenditures between flexible-budgeting and capital-rationing firms was roughly 10 percent of total plant and equipment expenditures.[10] In

---

[10] Of the six firms, four practice capital rationing, with two each in the high and lower energy to value-added categories. One flexible-budgeting firm is in each of the two energy to value-added categories.

addition, the estimated returns for these smaller projects were substantially higher than for the average project.[11] One can infer that the profits being postponed by capital-rationing firms could be substantial.

The author concludes that capital rationing is not, as some might suspect, a rational scheme for focusing effort on the most profitable investment opportunities. The evidence on the high returns of smaller projects shows that the average large project is less profitable than the smaller projects being neglected by capital-rationing firms. Capital rationing is a bureaucratic process that was not responsive at the time of our study to the substantial opportunities for profits offered by small and medium-sized energy-related projects.

VII. Suggestions for Improved Capital Budgeting

We will focus on suggestions for efficient involvement of top management in decisions on smaller projects.

(i) Information on Individual Projects: Communication is difficult at large firms, and people at all levels are busy, so the financial analysis of a smaller project and the reporting of it must be kept simple and intuitively clear. It should include easily digested information on the project's definition and input parameters, as well as internal evidence that the analysis has been done correctly and consistently with that of other projects.

(ii) Analysis of Groups of Projects: The second suggestion is less familiar. For those firms that feel unable to decentralize investment decision making with uniform hurdle rates, we suggest that top management solicit from their staff, for selected plants and product lines, ambitious modernization proposals consisting of coherent combinations of smaller projects. The idea is to elicit a proposal for a program of smaller projects whose total cost is large enough to command the careful attention of top management on a par with large projects costing perhaps $100 million or more. Not only would such an approach make it possible for top management to evaluate the potential of smaller projects, but also it would free the people who define projects, like Bill Johnson of our hypothetical example, to consider competing projects of different size on their merits (without being biased by considering where the decision would be made) and to define a coherent program of projects rather than using a piecemeal approach.

It is essential that such modernization programs be solicited by top management and that the means of analyzing and presenting the programs be well developed.[12] Ad hoc efforts from below are not likely to succeed.

VIII. Summary

Results have been presented from an in-depth study of capital budgeting for discretionary projects at twelve firms in the process industries. They indicate that, while discounted cash flow techniques

---

[11] There are three principal reasons why there were so many highly profitable energy conservation projects: (i) rapidly increased prices for energy, (ii) dramatic improvements in available energy-related technology such as control systems, and (iii) qualitative changes in the management of energy projects (e.g., assignment of responsibilities, improved engineering capabilities, metering, and new cost accounting procedures). Given fixed energy prices, this opportunity might be largely, but not completely, used up in five years at a flexible-budgeting firm. Other categories of small projects also offer high profitability for some of the same reasons, e.g., automation based on new microprocessors.

[12] Helpful software (ENVEST) has been developed by M. W. Reid at the Alliance to Save Energy.

are nominally used at most firms, it is important to ask whether the calculations are carried out incorporating essential details and whether it is a DCF criterion or simple payback that is actually relied on. For their smaller projects, most firms in the sample severely simplify their DCF analysis and/or rely primarily on simple payback.

Results (in eight of the twelve firms studied) also indicate that project approval at many firms follows different criteria depending on the locus of the decision. The effect of this is that smaller projects are subject to high de facto hurdle rates. At these firms only large projects are observed to face a hurdle rate near the cost of capital. Only four of the twelve firms studied impose uniform hurdle rates regardless of the locus of decision making (or the size of project). Not surprisingly, firms with thorough financial analysis of smaller projects tend to be the same firms that do not discriminate against smaller projects.

These results suggest the importance of asking how capital budgeting practices differ at the plant, division, investment committee, and CEO and Board levels. A large firm's capital budgeting practices for smaller projects can be indicative of the firm's effectiveness in using information and skills from its lower levels.

References

1. Alliance to Save Energy. *Industrial Investment in Energy Efficiency: Opportunities, Management Practices, and Tax Incentives.* Washington, DC (July 1983).
2. P. Asquith and D. W. Mullins, Jr. "Equity Issues and Offering Dilution." *Journal of Financial Economics* (Jan./Feb. 1986), pp. 61–89.
3. J. M. Fremge. "Capital Budgeting Practices: A Survey." *Management Accounting,* U.S. (May 1973), pp. 19–25.
4. L. J. Gitman and J. R. Forrester, Jr. "A Survey of Capital Budgeting Techniques Used by Major U.S. Firms." *Financial Management* (Fall 1977), pp. 66–71.
5. C. Gurnani. "Capital Budgeting: Theory and Practice." *Engineering Economist,* 30 (Fall 1984), pp. 19–46.
6. J. W. Petty, D. F. Scott, and M. M. Bird. "The Capital Expenditure Decision-Making Process of Large Corporations." *Engineering Economist,* 20 (Spring 1975), pp. 159–172.
7. E. M. Rudden. "The Misuse of a Sound Investment Tool." *The Wall Street Journal* (Nov. 1, 1982). p. 30.
8. L. D. Schall, G. L. Sundem, and W. R. Geijsbeek, Jr. "Survey and Analysis of Capital Budgeting Methods." *Journal of Finance* (March 1978), pp. 281–87.
9. D. F. Scott, Jr., and J. W. Petty. "Capital Budgeting Practices in Large American Firms: A Retrospective Analysis and Synthesis." *The Financial Review,* 19 (May 1984), pp. 111–23.
10. J. C. Van Horne. *Financial Management and Policy,* 5th ed. Englewood Cliffs, NJ, Prentice-Hall, 1980.

Discussion Questions

1. What are the implications of a division having a fixed amount of capital available for investment each period?
2. Explain what is meant by capital rationing.
3. Why did the author argue that capital rationing did not result in the firm's focusing on the most profitable projects?
4. How can the firm design a capital budgeting procedure that would avoid the capital rationing described in this study?

Samuel C. Weaver, Hershey Foods Corporation, Moderator; Donald Peters, E.G.&G.; Roger Cason, E.I. DuPont, DeNemours and Co.; and Joe Daleiden, Ameritech; Panelists.

Capital Budgeting

Procedures and strategies for capital decision making by three large firms are described in this article. The presenters are knowledgeable and well trained in finance methodology, and they describe candidly the approaches their firms take, including the problems they face in implementing these procedures.

This article and the one following are taken from panel discussions presented at the 1988 Annual Meetings of the Financial Management Association.

Samuel C. Weaver: Welcome to the special session on capital budgeting practices. Our panelists are representatives from companies of varying sizes, but on a relative scale they would all be considered very large companies. We are going to begin with Roger, and then Don, Joe, and I will follow. We have some unique presentations, and I hope we can have a productive exchange with the audience.

Roger Cason: Good afternoon. I am Roger Cason, and I am in one of the industrial departments of the DuPont Company. I'm going to give a presentation that has very few numbers and absolutely no statistics of any kind. I am going to briefly describe our department and some of our practices so you will know more of my background. Then I want to look at what I view from my position in DuPont as trends, and finally close with a list of what I feel are problems—what I feel we don't do very well and I suspect trouble other companies as well.

I guess DuPont needs no introduction. We are in ninth place in the Fortune 500. I am in the Chemicals and Pigments Department, which makes a variety of chemicals, mostly titanium dioxide. We also make freon and a wide variety of other industrial chemicals, most of which are commodities in nature.

Source: Reprinted with permission of *Financial Management* (Spring 1989), pp. 10–17. Samuel C. Weaver is Director of Corporate Financial Planning and Analysis at Hershey Foods Corporation; Donald Peters is VP of Planning at E.G. & G., Inc. (scientific instruments); Roger Cason is retired and formerly of E.I. DuPont, DeNemours and Co., and now a business and financial consultant; Joe Daleiden is retired and formerly of Ameritech.

Sam sent the three of us a questionnaire to use as a think piece to help us get a grasp on what we should cover in our discussions. From this, I've listed the company perspective on some of our procedures. Like most other companies of any size, some are fairly formal. The minutia guidance is provided by the Finance Department, while the broad guidance is provided by an organization called Corporate Planning, a staff arm of our Executive Committee. Our principle methodology at the moment is Internal Rate of Return. Most of the numbers that get ground out and published are IRR numbers, and our projected cash flows, hurdle rates, and cost of capital all include inflation; in other words, we don't work with so-called real returns.

Our cost of capital is estimated periodically by a variety of methods, all of which lead to about the same answer. We currently have a published rate of 12 percent internally. In real life, that figure is little used. It is a good first screen for sifting out a lot of really bad ideas, but beyond that our actual capital budgeting process is very much capital-ration driven, and so the typical hurdle rate is unfortunately never published. But we all understand that if a project is not well above 12 percent, it won't even be considered. The typical hurdle rates are frequently a good bit higher, depending upon where the cut occurs on any one year's budget.

Finally, just to mention the one thing several of us were asked to cover at least in passing, when we do a capital lease analysis we do use the long-term cost of debt, which is one of the occasional controversies.

Now, here are what I view as trends within our company. Not too many years ago, appropriation requests tended to be thought of almost in isolation. Someone would bring in an idea, and the approving body, normally the Executive Committee, would focus only on that idea and either approve it or not. Now there is a tendency to view the capital budgeting process. Approving a project is just one piece of the overall planning process, which works not decision-by-decision but business-by-business. So business plans will be drawn up to look ahead one, two, five, and ten years into the future for each major business segment, and this plan may or may not involve major capital investment. If it does, the capital investment will be studied, and preliminary numbers will be drawn up of the type learned about in a beginning finance class, and then the process will move forward.

The net result is that the business plan has to make sense, and the individual appropriations within the business plan also have to make sense. Obviously, this leads to a process where there is a certain amount of moving back and forth between the business plan and the specific appropriation requests. There is a final authorization step in each project, but this tends to be almost ceremonial. By the time each project is turned in for approval, the decision has already been made, unless some dreadful change has occurred in the environment.

There is a greater emphasis on examining business plans in general rather than individual projects. Money should be concentrated in good businesses (meaning good for us), so even attractive projects in unattractive businesses may not get funded.

Also, we now include capital leases as part of our capital budgeting system along with regular appropriation requests. Unfortunately, operating leases are still a way to beat the capital budgeting system under some circumstances, and we haven't quite found a way to reach out and capture them in a way that is administratively practical.

The last trend I'd like to mention is that we are finally putting more and more emphasis on the fundamentals and less on minutia. We used to have a world-class assortment of minutia on projects that we had to work through. We've gotten rid of all that and now look more at the basics.

What I call my personal list of problems probably looks like that of a lot of others in this room. We really don't do a very good job of dealing with uncertainty when evaluating business plans. The high hurdle rates are one approach, but are not very satisfying intellectually.

Meaningful post audits are a problem for us. We have a post audit system that covers the larger projects—those $2 million or over that were submitted to make money. The results aren't sound for a variety of reasons. One is that superficial answers are accepted. Somebody may say, "This project just barely broke even because the selling price never met our expectations." Selling price is just a surrogate for competitive conditions, market conditions, and so forth, and we haven't really dug in when things go bad to find out what really happened, where our thinking went wrong.

I also think we are still struggling with how to evaluate operating lease situations, and different people in the company have different views on how to do it. I have my way of doing it, and of course I think I'm right, but some of my compatriots have a rather different view, and they also think they are right.

We are still learning how to effectively evaluate foreign projects. In the past, we didn't take adequate account of blocked currency and all sorts of other problems that were run into overseas. We used a simplifying set of assumptions. Needless to say, they did not measure up in real life, and we're doing our best now to incorporate real life into our overseas evaluations.

There is also the problem of occasionally letting the desire for functional excellence, which is a buzz word in DuPont at the moment, degenerate into the search for functional perfection, causing an emphasis on minutia and other details that is not very effective.

The last item is not really a capital budgeting problem but is generated by capital budgeting. After a great deal of educating our managers, we finally made them aware of the fact that conceptually there is something called cost of capital, and that this is a cost just like electricity, or labor, or ingredients, or anything else. That cost must be covered. When the managers look over an appropriation request, we'll have this type of discussion with them. They immediately pull out their monthly operating statements, their monthly P&L. They want to know if they're meeting their cost of capital or not. I think that's a valid question, and we really don't know how to answer it. We have all these figures, the IRRs and NPVs, which work for a specific decision. Unfortunately, we run businesses year-by-year, and it would be really nice to know if we're meeting our cost of capital in the long range. If any of you are struggling for a research idea, I guess that would be my number one choice. I would like now to turn the meeting over to Don Peters.

Donald Peters: Thank you, Roger. This is a return to the Financial Management Association for me. I was first involved with the FMA in the early years, when Vic Andrews was the editor of the journal. I attended one or two FMA meetings, and for a half-dozen years or so was an associate editor of the journal. I think I was probably the only practitioner among the associate editors for a long time, and it's delightful to see practitioner activity again in the FMA. That was one of the original objectives that attracted me to it. Sam, I congratulate you for the time and effort you have spent in getting practitioners here. I encourage everyone to recognize that although it's a little tough for the incentives to be right for the practitioners, the goal of bridging the gap between practice and academia is a worthy one. I would urge you to bend over backwards to facilitate and support it.

Now, I would like to talk a little about E.G.&G. We publicly indicate our goals are to grow at 15 percent per year and to contribute a 20 percent return on equity. If you look at our history from about 1970–1985, we basically achieved those goals throughout that entire period of time. In 1986 we took a 20 percent EPS drop, recovered 20 percent in 1987, and we're well on our way to meeting the 15 percent goal in 1988.

Last week I had a study done, and there are only two companies in the Fortune 500 that have achieved 15 percent growth and 20 percent return on equity each year for the last five years. Those two are Abbott Labs and the Deluxe Corporation (whom you may recognize as the Deluxe check printers). So how can we achieve these goals? By providing an orientation to technology, through diversification, and by offering products and services to meet the needs of carefully selected, well-defined government and industry markets worldwide. (Careful selection is part of what E.G.&G. is all about. We are approaching $1.5 billion in sales and are number 277 on the Fortune 500.)

To manage ourselves, we use a strategic planning system that keeps track of entities called business elements: well-defined businesses that have a strategy. We understand customers and competition within each of these business elements. There are 160 elements and approximately 40 divisions.

These elements cover a variety of businesses. You might appropriately ask how all this fits together. We are, in fact, held together by a system of outlook and commitment to strategic planning. We have a highly articulate system, a set of beliefs within the company that are widely accepted. Within that, one of the stronger statements we could make is that a strategically advantaged position effectively implemented leads to above-average financial performance. In other words, if you can understand what business you are in, if you have decided to make it a good business and can determine an appropriate strategy and effectively implement it, then you're going to be successful. To relate this to the notion of capital budgeting, we would say a strategically advantaged business—in other words, one whose strategy we are comfortable with—ought to invest or ought to be able to invest as necessary in order to implement its chosen strategy. That statement in some sense is biased towards the capital investments needed by a business that has an appropriate strategy. Finally, as a kind of definitional statement, let me say that good businesses would have the characteristic of having strategic advantage. They would grow, and they would have a high return on investment.

We manage the company through a planning and control process that consists essentially of developing a strategic plan in the spring. Each of the above divisions prepares a strategic plan within which they define the business elements, their competitors, the competitive advantages and disadvantages, any emerging new technology that might impact the business, etc. In short, they establish a strategy. They may be resubmitting from the previous year; they may not be changing any of their definitions. But every division goes through this.

We have review teams of two senior operating managers, a planning executive and a financial executive, who review all of these operations in this process. There are frequent communications about what is taking place within each one of these businesses. This process provides us with much information, insight, and sharing about what is going on. In fact, there is even sharing from one business element in one part of the company to another business element totally remote from it.

In addition to the spring planning process, in the fall we develop a plan that looks ahead into the next calender year. We specify our primary interests in the one-year plan. Our first step is to confirm that the strategy has not changed, the second is to review how we are implementing the strategy that we stated in the spring, and the third is an identification of what the commitment to financial performance is in the coming year. Finally, we have a process of monthly reporting and reviewing where the departments make their results known, using the one-year plan as the reference base.

Capital expenditures within this process are not singularly emphasized; they are part of the whole picture. Typically, a major capital expenditure first appears in the strategic plan. However, there are exceptions. We have had circumstances when an appropriate kind of project is identified outside the strategic plan. But typically, most of the kind of thinking that relates to a capital investment will appear in a strategic plan.

Major projects are specifically listed in the one-year plan. The one-year plan has the usual kind of statement as to what the capital additions, depreciation, etc., are going to be. It is essentially the profit and loss statement of the business element and division.

Decisions to actually proceed with a capital investment are documented and approved with a capital expenditure request. Approval authority is delegated very low in the organization for projects of $0.5 million or less. There is a corporate office review for projects greater than $0.5 million. There is a lease-buy analysis in all cases where leases are involved which aggregate $100,000 or more, and anything that involves real estate and information systems is studied by those functions that exist within the corporate office.

I come to the area of capital budgeting with the somewhat radical view that deciding whether a business is a good business or a bad business is a very subjective experience. It is not something that is done mechanically, but by real people in real organizations. Given that, the whole purpose of capital budgeting procedures has to be oriented to facilitate and support subjective decisions. Within an organization, I would argue that decision criteria and performance criteria should be identical, or as nearly identical as practical. Related to that, if using incentives, those incentives ought to be related to the variables on which the decisions are being made.

Secondly, we should understand decision criteria and performance criteria. Frequently, fairly complicated and sophisticated mathematics are used when we think about economics and finance. Management decisions, as I said before, are not rational optimizations—they are subjective judgments made with limited and biased information and much uncertainty about the future. Measures should be selected and even designed in the context of the above observation, not merely transferred from theories or models that rely on normative optimization, which I think is frequently what happens.

My information base is going to go back a few years. I am going to call on Bierman and Schmidt, whom I quoted in my 1972 coupon rate paper. Bierman and Schmidt understand the problem. They describe exactly how people make decisions and then say, "Even withstanding all of that, it is probably safe to say net present value is the appropriate way to go." I disagree. You have to start with a subjective environment and think about what kind of decision is needed, and then design your performance measure to do what you want it to in that particular environment. Measures should be selected to encourage superior financial performance and reinforce the strategic evaluation of business. That means you are trying to think about what your measure does, what your measure makes people think about, and what it makes them talk about. Hopefully, you are emphasizing what is really important in making the business better. Measures and criteria should be robust, not particularly sensitive to modest changes and assumptions that cannot be objectively verified.

The two assumptions that are most troubling in my experience are the cost of capital and the end value of a project. I am thinking of capital budgeting as it relates to providing capital in the way of equipment or up-front investments in a facility for an ongoing business. We do not look at acquisitions in exactly this way. In acquisitions or in establishing a new business, there is an additional issue that has to be considered, namely, the price of the acquisition. Thus, I am thinking of capital budgeting in the context of supporting an ongoing business.

To do so, we emphasize what are essentially accounting returns—the first of which is a return on net investment or operating profit over average net investment, where net investment is defined to be what the manager controls. It excludes cash, which is controlled at the corporate level. The return essentially focuses on what we call operating capital, close to what you would think of as working capital minus cash plus the net fixed assets.

The dilemma then comes as to what to do about the fact that an accounting rate of return drops when an additional investment is made in a project. Here again, try to think of a manager who is making a subjective decision about making an investment and who is trying to bring into that thinking present value concepts, which would seem to be clearly the most valuable part of what finance has to offer.

We created the notion that essentially there ought to be a way to create a long-range measure of the return on net investments that is consistent with present value. This notion that we created or focused on was an equivalent project in which equivalence was defined in terms of net present value, and the equivalent project is essentially identical to what is actually being proposed in net present value terms. If you do that kind of thinking and proceed with the mathematics, you end up with the statement of what we call the equivalent return on net investments. We use the cost of capital as the discount rate and typically a five-year horizon. The Treasurer's Department provides us with a calculation of the cost of capital, the cost of debt prevailing over the long-term after-tax rate, cost of equity, long-term government bonds adjusted for risk using capital asset pricing model, and debt and equity rated in proportion to the current market values.

To establish hurdle rates, we thought in terms of a Gordon model. We assumed that essentially we wanted to be self-financing at a selected level of growth. That was a very heroic goal when it was first established in 1972. It required nearly a tripling of the return on net investment of the commercial operations within E.G.&G. from what those businesses operated at in 1970–1971. We established five-year goals for the growth of groups and divisions.

We are now tracking people in terms of their ability to provide strategies, to grow businesses, and to meet return on investment goals over five-year periods and then go back to the planning and control process. What we do in the spring with the strategic plans allows us to understand and think about how these plans and strategies relate to earnings in each of the businesses. The fall provides an opportunity to think about the one-year plan and the implication of that in terms of achieving what was predicated and predicted in the spring. Finally, the monthly reporting provides the opportunity to review the actual against the planned. So in this way the whole corporation is tied together, and measurement and decision making are tightly linked with one another.

I indicated that the initial goal was 170 percent over the level of achievement when established in 1972. By 1983–1984, we had already over-achieved our goal. Then, in 1986, there was a 20 percent drop. Hopefully, we are on our way back up from that position. What is going to affect return on equity is the performance in the Department of Energy of non-commercial operations whose equipment levels are government owned and operated. The second factor that is going to impact return on equity is the capital structure. In 1984 there was a 10 percent repurchase of E.G.&G.'s stock. So with that, I'll end my presentation. Joe, would you like to take it from here?

Joe Daleiden: Thank you. The Ameritech family of companies is a regional holding company for the Midwest. As assets, we have the five Bell companies and a service company, a communication company, which is a sister provider company, and a company to provide the information systems to the Bell companies. In the enterprise group we have Ameritech Credit, Cellular Mobile, and a publishing company. Our result in revenues is almost $10 billion.

The interesting aspect of our company is capital expenditures. We spend $2 billion. Now, that would not be a big problem if we could spend it in one lump sum. We could do that if we were like some electric companies who have only one or two major decisions, and thus can really study them. Our problem is that we have maybe one or two decisions a year that might involve an acquisition of $100 or $200 million. When working on those, we have the benefit of all sorts of people studying and researching. However, most of our decisions are much, much smaller. In fact, we probably have another group of decisions in the $10 million range. There might be ten or twenty of those in a year. We also have hundreds of decisions that are $1 million and thousands of decisions that are $0.5 million or less.

That is what becomes a problem. How does one devise a set of techniques that cannot be centrally administered in the sense that every decision cannot benefit from an expert study (i.e., the people in the field have to do the studies)? A theoretical model so elegant that no one understands it can't be used. We had to come up with something usable, something maybe not so obvious intuitively, but simple enough that it can be utilized to the best advantage.

We also have to use a strategy that can measure people in the aggregate to make sure they are following the general rules. When dealing with thousands of investments, we still have to rely on the person in the field to make the right decisions.

We have come up with a system that gives the right tools to the people in the field, and they utilize these tools to sift their projects through a group of screens to determine whether or not the project should be approved. The screens are similar to those of any other company—project risk, cost of capital, all the elements that go into a project. One of the difficulties is looking at risk, which again was not something we had to concern ourselves with in the past, but now we do. I will show you how we are trying that.

First, let me just explain why we even want to look at project risk, because there are a lot of people that would not bother. Project risk is inherent in a project's cost of capital. Although one project might be riskier than another, on the average it is reflected in the beta and your CAPM model. The problem with this type of thinking is that in the past, most of our projects were engineering-type projects in which we developed a new money-saving technology. We could estimate that very, very finitely because we knew we were going to use say eight installers or ten operators to implement this. When there wasn't a lot of risk in taking on a project, we could be very certain.

Now more and more of our projects have to do with revenue generation. So trying to look at revenues and trying to estimate the possible variance in revenues become an integral part of the process. When we first attempted this, it was generally decided that we would accept only those projects that have 20 or 25 percent return, which should sift out riskier projects. The trouble with this simplistic notion is that there could be a case where, if an arbitrary hurdle rate such as 20 percent is used, and the cash flow is divided by that, the resulting present value could be negative and a project with very little risk could be washed out. Again, if it was an expense-saving project that could be estimated very, very carefully, and we only came out to 18 percent return, would we want the project dropped because of this blanket 20 percent hurdle rate? No. What could happen, though, is we would drop those surer 18 percent projects and take on projects that might promise a 30 or 40 percent return, and over time we would push the company into a higher-risk organization without ever consciously making that decision.

I don't like the idea of using hurdle rates, merely because they disguise what is really going on. We began looking around to see what other methods we could adopt, and we reviewed what other companies were doing. We decided to ask the people in the field to risk-adjust the cash flows. We told them not to play with the discount rate, not to use a hurdle rate, and not to raise the discount rate arbitrarily. We asked them to just take the cash flows and come up with three estimates—the best case, the worst case, and the most likely. The expected cash flows probably should be broken down between a revenue and an expense. The revenues could be made by marketing and the expense by the engineers. Giving us a best case and worse case will pick up any skewness that is in a particular project. Sometimes the people in the field might say they felt very uncomfortable with this. But we all make these kind of decisions every day. Of course, we are only going to use this for certain types of projects. Obviously, there are some projects that we have to undertake because of the service we have to provide through the telephone company.

Theories that are being developed today are farther and farther away from the practical applications of actually using them. As a practical matter, I think what is most important in improving the estimates and the overall capital budgeting process is tracking. One of our companies institutionalized tracking. Now we can confront the person in marketing who put his name on the revenue estimates if he said A was going to happen and it didn't. And we can go back to the engineer who said she was going to cut 50 people out in the work force by doing B and ask her what happened to those 50 people.

When the company announced that it was going to begin tracking, that year's budgets had already been submitted. But the company told every division to take back their submissions and think about the fact that everyone who worked on the project was going to be tracked, and then resubmit the estimates. Seven hundred projects never came back—they just disappeared. Many of the others had much lower estimates.

There are traditional measures that are used in the process of project selection. I'm sure you all know the problems with IRR, and I am not going to discuss them here. But these problems are a concern to us, and so we came up with something that we call the project rate of return. Basically, the only difference is that cash flows are reinvested at the corporate cost of capital as opposed to the project rate. We are using this to avoid the higher rate of return that occurs when one reinvests the project return. The problem is that it doesn't correctly rank projects having different study lengths. What is implicit in this is that there is going to be a lower rate of return, but it will occur over a much longer period of time. We won't want to take on that project unless we have some reason to believe that we could make it into a very high winner. In reality, we don't know if we're going to be able to do that, so we would probably want to take the one with the highest NPV. Then why don't we take all the projects with the positive NPV?

It's simply unrealistic to think that a company can take on every single project with a positive NPV and provide them with the amount of funding their developers desire. We use a ranking system that enables us to draw the line and say, "Here is the amount of money you get to spend on this project." When ranking by NPV, you have to make sure that you don't pick one project with a return of, say, $150 over two projects that have a return of, say, $100 each. You have to maximize shareowner wealth.

I just showed you why project rate of return does not always work and why NPV doesn't always work. Nothing always works. What we came up with is what we call the project selection index (PSI). We deliberately use the term "selection index," even though the results are returns, because this type of return isn't comparable to the return the bank gives on a bond, and we didn't want to confuse the two. But, basically, it is looking at NPV and dividing it by the present value of the outflows.

There are two interesting differences between this and some of my fellow panelists' ideas. First of all, instead of looking at the investment only, we consider all outflows as coming from the share-owner. Any negative flows are potential money that is taken out of the shareowners' pocket. Whether that's called investment or expense seems irrelevant. The fact is, from the shareowners' perspective we're taking money they have or could have. Naturally, the shareholders want to know what they are getting in return. That is the rationale for evaluating all negative cash flows instead of just investments.

The second difference is that we use a common denominator. If two different denominators are used, then there is the problem of using one measure with project Y and coming up with 50 over 100 or 50 percent, and using another measure with project Z and getting 1000 over 2000, which is also 50 percent. If both projects are 50 percent, which do I select? The two 50 percents are not equal. Since we have determined that the denominator would be equal in the sense that the total investment would be equal, we don't have to worry about choosing one package of projects over another. They both have the same denominator, so one package would yield a higher total aggregate return.

That is the formulation for our index. We add the risk factors to the risk-adjusted PSI, which allows us to rank our projects, although it does not cover the problem of multiyear projects in an optimized portfolio of investments. It shows it does make a difference which method you pick in terms of a rank ordering of projects. The PSI is the one we are putting our money on for the time being. Thank you very much.

Sam Weaver: First of all, let me express my gratitude to the three other panelists for their insightful presentations. I would also like to briefly go over what's been discussed up to this point. Roger gave us an excellent overview of a lot of the specific difficulties he encounters at DuPont. Don talked about, among other things, a message that comes through loud and clear when working with corporate America. We all want to deal with internal rates of return, or project rates of return, or an adjustment factor, or a net present value, but the simple truth of the matter is that bonuses are based on accounting rates of return. There are very few incentive plans that will bring the economics into play. So what you heard Don talking about is a typical real-world problem and people in other companies have already studied how to link the accounting rates of return that bonuses are based on with investment or economics rates of return. That is what Don was looking to do. Joe gave an excellent presentation. You will see that what Joe was calling project rate of return, I am going to call terminal rate of return. In the literature, it is actually referred to as modified internal rate of return—that is, if you can find literature that discusses it. This is a subject that is very thinly written about.

I'm intending to cover several topics. I'd like to begin with a financial overview to familiarize you with Hershey's capital program background, and then from there how we budget for capital projects, how we evaluate capital projects, how we monitor and control them as they are being undertaken, and then how we perform post-completion audits. At Hershey, we really don't do a good job in that area.

To put Hershey into perspective size-wise for you, sales were a little over $2.4 billion in 1987. We're not sure what 1988 is going to look like, because we sold our restaurant business and bought

Cadbury-USA this summer. We generate about $320 million of operating income and about $150 million of net income. Capital expenditures fluctuate around $100 million.

The financial considerations which I want to discuss are as applicable to capital budgeting as to acquisition or divestiture analysis. Our capital program is a four-phase, four-prong approach. I wanted to highlight to you the approval levels so you know that we are really only involved with projects over $0.5 million. Projects below this level down to $10,000 are the responsibility of each operating division.

We used to use a category system for classifying projects. Projects were classified as profit adding, which generated incremental profit, and profit maintaining. To be honest, after ten years at Hershey I have yet to decipher the distinction between these two projects. Profit maintaining is simply making sure your profits remain constant. Because it is that type of project, you never had to go through an economic rate of return. Likewise, other administrative (such as personal computers, mainframes, new desks, etc.), environmental, and RND projects were always thought of as necessary.

Now we are looking at a revised system. The three major categories would be conventional capital, new products, and research and development. Essentially, what we are attempting is a move into an era where we can start evaluating all major capital projects over $50,000. Also, we are looking at much lower, realistic hurdle rates that compensate for the risk underlying projects.

When we do annual budgets, we have a menu of projects. We plan to spend $100 million in capital, but only about half of the projects will actually be undertaken due to priority adjustments. We can't plan for a number of years because we just don't have solid ideas about what our priorities are going to be next year, let alone five years from now.

Approval at annual budget time is not authorization to go ahead with the project. Each project is individually reviewed. We look at payback period. We also look at net present value, internal rates of return, and something analogous to Joe's project rate of return which I call terminal rate of return or modified internal rate of return. The terminal rate of return or modified internal rate of return, depending on the hurdle rate, reflects the net present value.

There is a tendency in major Fortune 500 firms to not use NPV. Senior management prefers to use rates of return. I can tell you whether a 10 percent rate of return is good. I know what interest rates are. I know what the cost of capital is. But as we all know, internal rates of return can give you a very erroneous answer. The terminal rate of return will always give an answer consistent with net present value, as long as the reinvestment rate is identical to the discount rate that would have been used for net present value. From a technical point of view, this gives the right answer and in such a way that management can understand it as a rate of return. So it satisfies both constituencies. That is why we began using terminal rate of return.

We have an enormous amount of capital capacity. Unfortunately, we don't have enough projects on the drawing board to utilize all of our capacity. So all I need to do is be consistent with net present value. I am assuming that we do have sources of capital if we really need it. We're not going to take on anything monumental, but we do have the necessary capital for our normal projects. And that concludes our presentations.

Discussion Questions

1. Describe capital rationing as explained by Mr. Cason of DuPont.
2. In the case of E.G.&G., discuss how capital budgeting fits into the larger process of strategic planning.

3. Comment on the scope of the annual capital budget for Ameritech.

4. Describe how Ameritech incorporates risk into its capital budgeting procedure.

5. What was the impact of the plan to "track" investments on the number submitted by Ameritech employees? Explain why this occurred.

6. Comment on the project selection index used by Ameritech. Was this method presented in your textbook?

7. Mr. Weaver of Hershey indicated that bonuses are tied to accounting returns. What impact might this have on capital budgeting methodology?

8. All three presenters seemed to indicate that not all projects with positive NPVs are adopted, due to budget limitations. Discuss what this means in terms of the overall capital budgeting procedure.

Samuel C. Weaver, Hershey Foods Corporation, Moderator; Peter J. Clemmens III, Vulcan Materials Company; Jack A. Gunn, Southwestern Bell Corporation; and Bruce D. Dannenburg, Digital Equipment

Divisional Hurdle Rates and the Cost of Capital

The panelists present a discussion of the conceptual need for divisional hurdle rates for multi-divisional firms; they also discuss their procedures for estimating divisional hurdle rates. While all agreed on the conceptual need to estimate divisional hurdle rates, they also agreed that measurement problems are substantial.

Samuel C. Weaver: For about the past six years I have been involved as a practitioner with the questions of how to set divisional hurdle rates and project hurdle rates. Today we are going to talk about just that. Jack will present first, then Pete, Bruce, and I will follow. Jack, will you begin?

Jack A. Gunn: Good morning. Southwestern Bell is one of the largest holding companies, with many subsidiaries. Southwestern Bell Telecom is our subsidiary that sells equipment in the residential and business areas. When we purchased Metromedia Paging, the paging and cellular operations were split. The cellular operation went to Mobile Systems, and we retained the paging division. We own Gulf Printing Company. We have a new subsidiary technology resource, which is where all the engineers and those people interested in applications for telephone services are employed. We have a capital corporation that takes care of issuing bonds and stocks as required. We have an asset management organization, and we have Southwestern Bell Corporation, which is primarily the legal and lobbying operation in Washington, DC.

Source: Reprinted with permission of *Financial Management* (Spring 1989), pp. 18–25. Samuel C. Weaver is Director of Corporate Financial Planning and Analysis at Hershey Food Corporation; Peter J. Clemmens III is Senior VP-West for Vulcan Materials Company (construction materials group); Jack A. Gunn is Associate Director of Financial Planning for Southwestern Bell Corporation; and Bruce D. Dannenburg is of Digital Equipment Corporation.

In 1987 we made a little over $8 billion in gross revenue and netted $1.047 billion. Telecom is the largest part of the company right now, and as the cellular division continues to grow, we can expect some revenue growth. We have $21.5 billion in assets. The telephone company is responsible for about $18.5 billion of those assets, and so is by far the largest subsidiary. We have a debt ratio in the low 40s with long-term debt and equity about $8 billion.

The telephone company operates in Arkansas, Kansas, Missouri, Oklahoma, and Texas. The other subsidiaries operate all over the world, from Australia to the United Kingdom.

The notion of divisional cost of capital can be applied in various places within the company. One potential application in corporate treasury is in establishing a required return for each of the subsidiaries. Furthermore, a required return can also be established for particular projects. Most of my background is in the phone company, so I will talk primarily about this area. We looked at divisional cost of capital in the context of how it could be employed when studying new products and services. Divisional cost of capital is also used when the engineers study capital deployment decisions in particular locations and on specific pieces of equipment.

In the strategic planning department, they use the concept of divisional cost of capital in evaluating international opportunities. We use the discount rate as a weighted average cost of capital, based on capital structure, market-based cost of debt and market-based cost of equity. In establishing the returns for subsidiaries, the treasury department uses a modified multistage dividend discount model.

There is no doubt that the use of discounted cash flow techniques is increasing in our company. Principally it began on the network side, but it is becoming more and more prevalent on the product side as well. That would confirm the general trends as noted in some survey articles. I can also confirm the surveys that say the hardest part of these studies is identifying relevant cash flows. It gets particularly difficult in the phone company because there are tremendous joint common costs on an incremental basis. Typically, projects tend to be either huge winners or huge losers.

In 1984, it dawned on us that there really was no good processing place to evaluate new products and services in the phone company. As part of the pitch to put the process together, it was proposed that we should think about cash flow, risk adjusted discount rates, and probability simulation. The basis for this reasoning was to use advanced finance concepts to help deal with uncertainty, to help understand the potential outcomes of a decision, and to help make decisions faster.

We had a situation in our particular work group in which we didn't have many resources to use in a project. We elected to go with the CAPM type of approach because the beta is readily available. Basically, we were just trying to decide if this was an issue worth pursuing. We asked ourselves, do we want to try to take the treasury-determined equity cost, the return cost, and decide whether or not we should factor it up and down in the context of what we were doing in the phone company?

We began with the study called the EDA or the analysis of operating results, a cost accounting study that starts at the top and allocates everything to some service category. We thought we would try those service categories because they were generally accepted within the company and within the industry. We were going to use leverage-adjusted betas to take capital structure out as an issue. We wanted to try to isolate business risk. So the formula we basically used was as follows: K_L (or K for a particular business line) equals a risk-free rate plus some beta determined for the business line, over the corporate beta, and then we calculate a quasi-telephone company risk premium.

The preliminary analysis indicated that there could be some small differences in risk. The toughest part was identifying comparable firms and single product firms who competed with the products we offered. It was virtually impossible to find any. We started off with eight broad lines of business. We could only find enough data for three of them, which ruled out some of the areas where growth had occurred. For example, publishing got ruled out. Some of the billing services were ruled out because the competitors were large companies (like Sears), and we couldn't isolate the billing operation.

At that point, we decided the next stage would be to test the results to see if we would get the same relative differences in risk for the categories on the assumption that there are some predictive problems with beta. So we designed a series of tests to do just that. About that time, interest shifted elsewhere, and we've never had time to do the tests. As a result, we have not incorporated detailed divisional cost of capital into the cash flow analysis on new products at the phone company.

Our researchers are also working on the probability simulation side of the process. In designing the models that we use, they are trying to make it easy for financially unsophisticated analysts to apply the techniques of probability simulation. They are trying to identify a series of questions or some sort of a program that can be used as a system to help if this particular distribution characterized uncertainty on this input variable better than a normal distribution. Then the next step in the program would be to input data appropriate to subjectively describe the distribution. So, as time goes on and the process progresses, that could well be implemented into the procedures.

Another area in decision making that is new for our company is the question of what should be the appropriate return for international projects. During my brief stint in corporate planning, I had an opportunity to work on an international project in South America. The country we were studying had inflation of 20 percent per month, and their capital expatriation laws were quite severe, so we had a problem with determining an appropriate return. Right now, our corporate involvement in looking at specific projects like that is very small.

But the fact of the matter is, there are more and more opportunities presenting themselves that need to be evaluated. The return requirement currently is judgmental. As we get more involved in this area, we are going to need to do more work.

No doubt about it, we at Southwestern Bell find the idea and the notion of divisional cost of capital conceptually appealing. We will apply it where we can identify comparable firms and where we can solve the analytical techniques. Obviously, Treasury's burden of proof in a regulatory proceeding is far higher than the burden of proof on me in a new product process. Once again, I think as the industry continues to deregulate and the subsidiaries expand, the real growth for the corporation will not be in the telephone company. As the growth occurs in those other subsidiaries, it is going to be even more important to incorporate this concept. This is a new area for us, and we are still in the learning process, but we find it interesting and will apply it. Thank you.

Peter J. Clemmens III: Good morning. I am Pete Clemmens, Chief Financial Officer of Vulcan Materials Company. We are an industrial company based in Birmingham, Alabama. If you were to ask me to define our company in a few words, I would say that Vulcan Materials Company is an international producer of industrial materials and commodity products that are essential to the standard of living in advanced industrial societies. We hold substantial positions in two basic industries, construction aggregates and industrial chemicals.

We are the world's largest producer of crushed stone, shipping 111 million tons last year. We have three chemical plants, making us the second largest producer of chlorinated solvents in this country, just behind Dow. We produce five of the six chlorinated solvents. Our capacity is 24 percent of the U.S. production capacity for chloral solvents.

Sales from continuing operations have more than doubled over the last ten years, due primarily to the increased shipments in construction materials. In 1987 sales were $923 million. Although our sales have never reached $1 billion, they probably will this year.

In 1987, our net earnings were $114 million. We will exceed that this year by 20 percent. Over the past five years our earnings have grown at a compounded annual average rate of over 16 percent. Given the fact that we are in two cyclical businesses, this is a fairly stable record. This is due to the fact that the chemical business and the construction materials business have complementary cycles; when the construction materials business decreases, the chemicals business increases.

One of the strengths of our company is the funding provided from operations. The annual compound rate of growth over the last ten years is about 10 percent. For the most recent five-year period, it is 13 percent. In 17 of the last 19 years, our cash flow has increased. The only two years that it decreased, it was down 5 percent one year and 1 percent another. That is one of the reasons why we are such a strong company financially.

Our debt ratio has declined from 27 percent ten years ago to less than 10 percent today. In fact, we actually have more than enough cash to offset debt. Our stock prices also did very well. We are one of the few companies that have a stock price higher now than before last year's crash.

During the last four years we have ranked around 300 in sales in the Fortune 500. However, in 1987 we were in the top 15 percent in total return to investors. We don't have much leverage, so in return on assets we were even higher. In 1987, I think we were ranked 43.

Everything that I have shown up to this point can be calculated from public information. But our hurdle rates are confidential, so everything that I'm going to tell you from now on is a lie. But I am using the lies to illustrate how we operate. I make one caveat before we start talking about this, and that is that hurdle rates are important. We review our hurdle rates periodically. This presentation today is the same one that I just made to our Board several weeks ago. The last time we reviewed our hurdle rates was in 1985, and before that the last time was in 1982, so it's roughly a three-year cycle. We don't sit down every three years to review the hurdle rates, but as often as we think we need to. In between those periods, we will make minor adjustments if we see a reason to do so. But the caveat I make is that we spend time talking about hurdle rates quite extensively, and then they are essentially forgotten.

When we evaluate investments, the assumptions and projections made by the operating people overwhelm the hurdle rate. So hurdle rates are important, but not as important as looking at each project, understanding each strategy, and challenging the assumptions.

We follow a few general concepts. We use internal rate of return as the investment measure. I understand the reason for using net present value; we just like to talk in terms of rates of return. Before we used internal rate of return, we used an accounting measure of return. Many of the operating people know how to run a quarry or produce chemicals and sell those products, but they don't have a lot of understanding of all the financial concepts behind hurdle rates. We didn't want to change the way we look at things in terms of moving to a net present value. We felt that staying with an internal rate of return was much easier for many financial people to understand.

When we evaluate a project, our project cash flows are solely project related. There are no financing cash flows in a project. If there is subsidized financing, we then calculate the present value of the subsidy and use that as a negative initial investment. But, except for subsidized interest rates or subsidized financing, we would not consider financing at all in the cash flows of a project.

We make all of our projections in constant dollars. This is much easier for our operating people. They don't have to project inflation. They input their numbers in the computer in constant dollars and let the computer generate the nominal dollars and then deflate back into constant dollar returns.

The hurdle rates we develop are average hurdle rates for a project of average risk. If there is a project of higher or lower risk, we expect the divisions to identify the reasons for that, and we try to mentally adjust for those factors.

All of the corporate and group expenses are included in the project cash flows, even on an allocated basis, the reason being that we think that is the best estimate of the incremental or cash flows associated with the project, even though corporate expenses can't be directly related to a project. We also assume in the projections that all our projects are equity only—no debt. Eventually, we adjust the hurdle rate to reflect a risk-adjusted, leveraged beta. But I'm getting ahead of myself.

Let me start at the beginning, when our divisional hurdle rates are based upon our real pre-tax cost of capital. Real pre-tax cost of capital is the corporation's cost of capital before taking into account specifically the tax deductible shield set up by the cost of debt and expected inflation. The corporation's cost of capital is the same for all divisions. In addition, a minimum excess return is also added across all divisions. In our case, the minimum excess is about a percentage point and is assessed to cover our aspirations of elevating ourselves beyond our required return. From this basis, we begin to look at each of our divisions, both the construction aggregates and industrial chemicals divisions. The adjustments that we apply are as follows.

First of all, we attempt to adjust the betas underlying our cost of capital and the capital that we pass on to our divisions, using the capital asset pricing model. By doing this we take a look at our competitors. We look for pure plays and calculate an average industry beta. We convert the stock beta to an asset beta that takes into account our targeted leverage, and from that we develop either an increment or decrement to our cost of capital.

The final adjustment that we generate leading to divisional cost of capital is an item that we call "shortfall." We have an excellent program of post-completion audits. We are able to look back over time as far as 16 years ago and examine what each of the divisions had submitted as major projects versus the realities experienced by the projects. Did what they say back in 1972 come to pass throughout the 15-year projection period?

We are able to yearly monitor more current projects for the changes that are affecting underlying assumptions of each capital project. From this, we assess management's capability of projecting the future and their eventual rates of return. Not too surprising, we tend to find that our divisional management tends to be a shade optimistic on their project submissions. As a result of that, to cover the optimism that is present within capital project proposals, we include (calculated by divisions) a shortfall. That is to say, an average deficit that in the past has been experienced by a division falling short of the actual implementation returns versus the projected rates of return. This shortfall is the final piece of our divisional hurdle rates. Thank you very much.

Bruce D. Dannenburg: Digital Equipment Corporation's business consists of the design, manufacture, sales, and service of networked computer systems, associated peripheral equipment, and related network communication and software products. In 1988 we enjoyed net income of over $1.3 billion on revenues of $11.5 billion. Capital spending doubled in 1988 to $1.5 billion.

Most financially sophisticated companies use some form of discounted cash flow (DCF) analysis when evaluating the expected return on investment of product development efforts. An integral step in performing this analysis is the determination of the appropriate hurdle rate (discount rate) to be used in discounting the forecasted cash flow generated by the project. This hurdle rate should reflect the systematic risk of the project's cash flow stream.

Their determination of the appropriate risk-adjusted hurdle rate presents a predicament to corporate management: Does the financial evaluation of different product development projects within the firm require the use of multiple hurdle rates? If so, how can the required risk adjustments be determined?

These concerns prompted another look at the way product development project hurdle rates were determined by Digital. This study has resulted in the technique outlines in this presentation, which has since been adopted as corporate policy at Digital.

Research and development is an area of uncertainty and risk regarding the future payoffs of an R&D program. The amount of risk decreases across the spectrum of R&D activities as one moves from basic research to product development activities. Risk also decreases as one moves from R&D projects focused on non-traditional product lines (or products for which market acceptance is particularly uncertain) to projects focused on more traditional product lines.

Extending the "pure play" technique to the development project level is one way of determining the risk-adjusted hurdle rate for the project. The need for a quantitative, financially oriented project selection technique is clear: to promote unbiased, risk-adjusted financial resource allocation within the product development division of a firm. If the product development, project selection decision is treated as a capital investment decision, the proper hurdle rate to use for "normal" risk projects is a firm's weighted average cost of debt and equity funds, the firm's weighted average cost of capital (WACC).

Since R&D is a speculative activity by nature, it makes sense that the average WACC of firms in an R&D-intensive industry would be higher than those of other industries, such as consumer products or electric utilities, where future payoffs are more certain. There is a positive linear relationship between rates of return in the financial market and the uncertainty (risk) of the future payoffs.

"Business risk" is the component of primary interest for determining a risk-adjusted hurdle rate for evaluating a development project. The market, the product, and the technology utilized (the MPT mix) are the key factors in determining the level of business risk.

At Digital, we use a matrix concept wherein the X-axis represents risk associated with development categories ranging from product development (low risk) to advanced development (moderate risk) and basic research (high risk). The Y-axis represents the risk associated with product lines—traditional (low risk) and non-traditional (high risk).

Normal R&D programs are focused on the development of new products along a traditional product line and based on an established technology. This places the project's normal MPT mix in the lower left portion of the risk matrix. Any new product development effort along traditional product lines for this firm should be evaluated at the company's weighted average cost of capital, with no additional risk adjustment. As a project moves from "normal" risk to areas of less traditional products or markets, or toward the more speculative (basic research) end of the R&D spectrum, the systematic risk of the potential project differs from the systematic risk of the company as a whole. In these cases, we try to quantitatively differentiate between different levels of project risk by adjusting the hurdle rate to correspond to the level of systematic risk of the project.

Since a project beta is unobservable in the financial marketplace, the pure play technique is used to estimate the systematic risk of a non-normal risk project to the firm. We attempt to derive a proxy beta from a publicly traded, single product line firm which competes in the targeted marketplace and uses equivalent risk technology. Once the pure play firm is identified, its beta is adjusted to the evaluating firm's level of financial leverage and used as an estimate of the unobservable project beta. The CAPM and WACC formulas are then used to determine the risk-adjusted project hurdle rate.

The same financial metrics are used to determine the risk-adjusted project hurdle rate as are used to determine the firm's WACC, except that the leverage-adjusted pure play beta is substituted for the evaluating firm's beta.

Since true pure play firms are often difficult to identify, or may not even exist, this technique can be made more practical by designing a risk class schedule for the firm to use in evaluating its product development programs. A number of companies can be identified that develop or compete in businesses having similar technological risks. A leverage-adjusted beta would be calculated for each of these firms.

The firms would then be grouped by product type and ranked according to risk level, using clusters of similar value leverage-adjusted betas. An average leverage-adjusted beta per product line type would be calculated, and several risk-adjusted hurdle rate classes determined, depending on how speculative the product line. All of the betas shown are leverage adjusted to reflect the evaluating firm's capital structure.

In conclusion, when a single hurdle rate is used for the DCF evaluation of all of a firm's product development projects, it may lead to inaccurate analysis because the required rate of return and the systematic risk of the cash flows may not be equal for all projects. The CAPM and WACC models, together with the pure play technique, can be used to determine the appropriate risk-adjusted hurdle rate to evaluate each product development project. Combining these theories and applying them to the practice of financial management helps improve project selection decisions, promote an appropriate risk-adjusted resource allocation of a firm's development budget, and provide a more accurate assessment of the financial "goodness" of the development project. Thank you.

Sam Weaver: Before I begin my presentation, I would like to highlight a common thread that seems to run throughout all of our presentations. You can clearly see that there is a drastic need in the real world for divisional hurdle rates. In fact, as you heard all three presenters say (and Bruce in a bit more detail), there is a need not only for divisional hurdle rates but for project specific hurdle rates as well. Quite frankly, the state of the art is not that well refined to help the practitioner develop answers. We try to develop project or divisional hurdle rates by adjusting the cost of capital while always testing ourselves on the reasonableness of the final result.

I'd like to give you a brief overview of Hershey Foods. You obviously know our candy bars. We are also a pasta company, and in 1987 we had approximately $2.4 billion in sales. We had an operating income of $320 million and enjoyed a net income of $148 million. A lot has happened since December 31, 1987. We sold our restaurant operation, Friendly Ice Cream, and we also purchased the operating assets of Cadbury-USA. Today Hershey is very different from what the numbers of 1987 would reveal.

My presentation will give you a feel for how we look at divisional hurdle rates. In order to do that, you need to get an understanding of how we determine the cost of capital. Furthermore, we are in an evolutionary state wherein we have a current hurdle rate methodology that can be improved upon. I'll try to give you a glimpse of where we are currently and where we want to be, and then give a few final parting comments.

To begin with, we calculate our cost of capital based upon weighted average cost of debt and equity, using a targeted three-year-plan capital structure. We do calculate the cost of capital based on current book weights as well as market values. We calculate our cost of debt based upon our historical cost of debt after taxes. Our cost of equity is calculated using two methodologies, the dividend growth model and the capital asset pricing model. Both give fairly similar results, but we rely upon the dividend growth model. In that respect, after a survey of a number of our competitors we found that we're unique in the food industry in that we do use (and admit to using) the dividend growth model to calculate our cost of equity. It makes sense for us. We do pay a dividend, and it has a steady, stable growth rate. We can tell you what our growth is expected to be from now until 1995 through our strategic planning process. The dividend growth model makes sense in our case.

On the other hand, the capital asset pricing model often provides less than adequate statistical qualities. When you plot Hershey's excess return versus the market's excess returns, our betas are not necessarily statistically significantly different than zero and the correlation factors are anywhere from 0.2 to 0.3. On one occasion I had an opportunity to calculate our beta and found that I had to go the third decimal place on the R-squared before I got a non-zero value. It was the most random series I ever saw. I'm not willing to bet my career on that type of correlation. So again, we use the dividend growth model and calculate an approximate cost of equity.

Based upon our targeted capital structure, our cost of capital is 12 percent. It's not 12.00 percent; it's 12 percent. In fact, given all the assumptions and the softness in the numbers going into the cost of capital, it's impossible to measure the cost of capital to the nearest tenth of a percent, let alone hundredth of a percent. Consequently, when we use market weights, targeted capital structure weights, or current book value weights, it really doesn't change the answer. Our cost of capital is still 12 percent.

Our current hurdle rate methodology is basically a divisional hurdle rate procedure that is based upon a modified, let me call it "Gup-Norwood," approach that further adjusts each divisional cost of capital much as Peter described. Our current technique is based upon Benton Gup's article of a few years ago wherein he described a systematic approach that attempts to quantify the divisional risk premium based on past divisional performance and management's views. In coming up with this divisional risk premium, we first evaluate objective risk. How has the division performed against its plans? We also evaluate subjective risk by using a questionnaire that addresses eighteen different identified areas, and we ask our senior management to rank each division's risk accordingly. Of course, we average the objective and subjective risk components to develop a divisional risk premium.

Currently, we have a second adjustment to the cost of capital called a surcharge, or an increment for support projects. By support projects, I mean administrative projects such as my PC, the mainframe computer, an office building, etc. We also include as support projects environmental control or R&D projects. This surcharge is assessed against our normal capital expenditure projects, based upon each division's mix of support projects, and presents an area where I can see a tremendous opportunity for improvement. As you'll see in our proposed methodology, we do try to eliminate this surcharge. Currently, the divisional hurdle rate begins with the cost of capital, adds a premium for divisional risk as calculated by a modified Gup-Norwood approach, and adds an increment for support projects.

Corporations tend to be evolving creatures. Major evolutionary steps occurred about a year ago. At that time, organizational changes resulted in corporate finance assuming responsibility for the capital expenditure program instead of corporate engineering. The financial people at Hershey Foods have long recognized the need to develop a hurdle rate methodology that not only looks at divisional risk but also highlights the distinction between project categories. That is to say, a divisional hurdle rate does not recognize the business risk difference between a new product and the replacement of a Hershey Kiss line. Obviously, different risk profiles underlie those investment decisions.

In January 1988, a task team was formed to review hurdle rates. The charter was to review not only divisional hurdle rates but division and project hurdle rates, very much as Bruce was explaining they do with R&D type of projects at DEC. What developed from this task team is a new procedure that we're extremely hopeful will be implemented at Hershey Foods. Underlying this procedure, we have identified a number of categories of projects, each with a slightly different risk profile. Given that risk profile, what we did as a task team was to challenge ourselves and consider various hurdle rates that we would attach to each category by division. Nothing objective about this except that it started with the cost of capital, 12 percent, and adjusted it slightly for optimistic estimation errors which would underlie a project. This rate was attached to our least-risky projects. On the upside we made observations about senior management's desires for new products and new markets. The guidance from observing what they wanted as a rate of return in the past formed the standard going forward. The other categories had hurdle rates attached, based upon this continua.

In fact, as a parting comment and again supported by my fellow panel members, I would like to suggest that perhaps as researchers we've been looking at the wrong area as far as divisional hurdle rates are concerned. Think in terms of the portfolio investor. For years we have been looking at defining the capital market line or security market line, but in the ultimate decision of where should the investor be on that capital market or on that security market line, we've always had to rely on a combination with utility analysis. I truly believe that the comments you have heard here today strongly support an attempt at merging the description of the corporation's investment line along with the preferences (utility functions) of the corporation. As a result of that, an important issue is trying to understand the subjective preferences of a corporation. That is, what rate of return does management feel comfortable with in taking on a particular project at a given risk level? Perhaps this is an area for further research and further discussion. My thanks to my fellow panel members as well as to you, the audience.

Discussion Questions

1. Should the firm compute a cost of capital for each division, or should there be one cost of capital for the entire firm? Explain.

2. What is meant by a "leverage-adjusted beta"?

3. What problem was Mr. Gunn referring to when he mentioned the difficulty of finding comparable firms and single product firms?

4. According to Mr. Clemmens, "assumptions and projections made by the operating people overwhelm the hurdle rate." What did he mean?

5. Mr. Clemmens indicated that financing costs are not included in the project cash flows. Comment.

6. Mr. Clemmens and Mr. Dannenburg referred to "pure play" a few times. Explain what this is.

7. Mr. Weaver referred to using a dividend growth model in the estimation of the cost of equity at Hershey. Why did he feel this model was appropriate for Hershey?

part IV

Capital Structure and Dividend Policy

Miller and Modigliani (M&M) turned the academic finance world upside down with their 1958 article which shows that, if corporate income taxes are ignored and if capital markets are perfect, the value of the firm is invariant with its capital structure. They followed that in 1963 with the article included here that admits the existence of corporate income taxes and shows that the use of leverage could increase the value of the firm. To this day, the debate on capital structure and a great deal of research regarding it continue. The article by Stewart Myers is a comprehensive review of "the capital structure puzzle," and the article by Pinegar and Wilbricht allows managers to tell us what they think about the capital structure issue.

Miller and Modigliani also created a new controversy with their 1961 article, included here, which makes the perfect capital markets assumption and shows that the dividend policy of a corporation doesn't matter. This issue has also been hotly debated and researched. The article by Lease and Loewenstein summarizes the research and presents the status of that debate.

Merton H. Miller and Franco Modigliani

Corporate Income Taxes and the Cost of Capital: A Correction

This is the second of the famous M&M articles on capital structure. The first article by Miller and Modigliani, published in the American Economic Review *in 1958, contains the argument that a corporation cannot increase the value of the firm by using debt as part of its permanent capital structure. Their argument was based on the premise that investors could assume personal debt to help finance the purchase of unlevered shares, if the value of the levered shares is greater than that of unlevered ones. Their famous arbitrage argument shows that there is no reason for leverage to increase value. Importantly, M&M set a new standard for the conceptual exploration of financial issues.*

In their 1958 article, M&M assumed perfect capital markets and an absence of corporate income taxes. The article reproduced here was published in the American Economic Review *in 1963 to show the impact of corporate income taxes on the leverage issue. Because the tax shelter effect of debt grows with increases in debt, the conclusion appears to be that more debt is better than less debt for the combined stockholders and debt holders. However, M&M (and others) have pointed out that there are practical limits to the use of debt. In the years following M&M's work on capital structure, various investigators have shown that the present value of expected bankruptcy costs increases with leverage, leading to the likelihood that an optimal capital structure exists.*

The purpose of this communication is to correct an error in our paper "The Cost of Capital, Corporation Finance and the Theory of Investment" (this *Review,* June 1958). In our discussion of the effects of the present method of taxing corporations on the valuation of firms, we said (p. 272):

> The deduction of interest in computing taxable corporate profits will prevent the arbitrage process from making the value of all firms in a given class proportional to the expected returns generated by their physical assets. Instead, it can be shown (by the same type of proof used for the original version of Proposition I) that *the market values of firms in each class must be proportional in equilibrium to their expected returns net of taxes* (*that is, to the sum of the interest paid and expected net stockholder income*). (Italics added.)

Source: Reprinted with permission of the *American Economic Review.* Merton H. Miller is the Robert R. McCormick Distinguished Service Professor of Finance at the Graduate School of Business at the University of Chicago. Franco Modigliani is Institute Professor Emeritus, M.I.T.

The statement in italics, unfortunately, is wrong. For even though one firm may have an *expected* return after taxes (our $\overline{X}^\tau$) twice that of another firm in the same risk-equivalent class, it will not be the case that the *actual* return after taxes (our X^τ) of the first firm will always be twice that of the second, if the two firms have different degrees of leverage.[1] And since the distribution of returns after taxes of the two firms will not be proportional, there can be no "arbitrage" process which forces their values to be proportional to their expected after-tax returns.[2] In fact, it can be shown—and this time it really will be shown—that "arbitrage" will make values within any class a function not only of expected after-tax returns, but of the tax rate and the degree of leverage. This means, among other things, that the tax advantages of debt financing are somewhat greater than we originally suggested and, to this extent, the quantitative difference between the valuations implied by our position and by the traditional view is narrowed. It still remains true, however, that under our analysis the tax advantages of debt are the *only* permanent advantages so that the gulf between the two views in matters of interpretation and policy is as wide as ever.

I. Taxes, Leverage, and the Probability Distribution of After-Tax Returns

To see how the distribution of after-tax earnings is affected by leverage, let us again denote by the random variable X the (long-run average) earnings before interest and taxes generated by the currently owned assets of a given firm in some stated risk class, k.[3] From our definition of a risk class it follows that X can be expressed in the form $\overline{X}Z$, where $\overline{X}$ is the expected value of X, and the random variable $Z = X/\overline{X}$, having the same value for all firms in class k, is a drawing from a distribution, say $f_k(Z)$. Hence the random variable X^τ, measuring the after-tax return, can be expressed as:

$$X^\tau = (1 - \tau)(X - R) + R = (1 - \tau)X + \tau R = (1 - \tau)\overline{X}Z + \tau R \tag{1}$$

where τ is the marginal corporate income tax rate (assumed equal to the average), and R is the interest bill. Since $E(X^\tau) \equiv \overline{X}^\tau = (1 - \tau)\overline{X} + \tau R$ we can substitute $\overline{X}^\tau - \tau R$ for $(1 - \tau)\overline{X}$ in (1) to obtain:

$$X^\tau = (\overline{X}^\tau - \tau R)Z + \tau R = \overline{X}^\tau\left(1 - \frac{\tau R}{\overline{X}^\tau}\right)Z + \tau R. \tag{2}$$

Thus, if the tax rate is other than zero, the shape of the distribution of X^τ will depend not only on the "scale" of the stream $\overline{X}^\tau$ and on the distribution of Z, but also on the tax rate and the degree of leverage (one measure of which is $R/\overline{X}^\tau$). For example, if Var $(Z) = \sigma^2$, we have:

---

[1] With some exceptions, which will be noted when they occur, we shall preserve here both the notation and the terminology of the original paper. A working knowledge of both on the part of the reader will be presumed.

[2] Barring, of course, the trivial case of universal linear utility functions. Note that in deference to Professor Durand (see his Comment on our paper and our reply, this *Review*, Sept. 1959, 49, 639–69) we here and throughout use quotation marks when referring to arbitrage.

[3] Thus our X corresponds essentially to the familiar EBIT concept of the finance literature. The use of EBIT and related "income" concepts as the basis of valuation is strictly valid only when the underlying real assets are assumed to have perpetual lives. In such a case, of course, EBIT and "cash flow" are one and the same. This was, in effect, the interpretation of X we used in the original paper and we shall retain it here both to preserve continuity and for the considerable simplification it permits in the exposition. We should point out, however, that the perpetuity interpretation is much less restrictive than might appear at first glance. Before-tax cash flow and EBIT can also safely be equated even where assets have finite lives as soon as these assets attain a steady state age distribution in whch annual replacements equal annual depreciation. The subject of finite lives of assets will be further discussed in connection with the problem of the cut-off rate for investment decisions.

$$\text{Var }(X^\tau) = \sigma^2(\overline{X^\tau})^2 \left(1 - \tau \frac{R}{\overline{X^\tau}}\right)^2$$

implying that for given $\overline{X^\tau}$ the variance of after-tax returns is smaller, the higher τ and the degree of leverage.[4]

II. The Valuation of After-Tax Returns

Note from equation (1) that, from the investor's point of view, the long-run average stream of after-tax returns appears as a sum of two components: (1) an uncertain stream $(1 - \tau)\overline{X}Z$; and (2) a sure stream τR.[5] This suggests that the equilibrium market value of the combined stream can be found by capitalizing each component separately. More precisely, let ρ^τ be the rate at which the market capitalizes the expected returns net of tax of an unlevered company of size $\overline{X}$ in class k, i.e.,

$$\rho^\tau = \frac{(1 - \tau)\overline{X}}{V_U} \quad \text{or} \quad V_U = \frac{(1 - \tau)\overline{X}}{\rho^\tau},^6$$

and let r be the rate at which the market capitalizes the sure streams generated by debts. For simplicity, assume this rate of interest is a constant independent of the size of the debt so that

$$\tau = \frac{R}{D} \quad \text{or} \quad D = \frac{R}{\tau}.^7$$

Then we would expect the value of a levered firm of size $\overline{X}$, with a permanent level of debt D_L in its capital structure, to be given by:

$$V_L = \frac{(1 - \tau)\overline{X}}{\rho\tau} + \frac{\tau R}{r} = V_U + \tau D_L.^8 \tag{3}$$

In our original paper we asserted instead that, within a risk class, market value would be proportional to expected after-tax return $\overline{X^\tau}$ (cf. our original equation [11]) which would imply:

---

[4] It may seem paradoxical at first to say that leverage *reduces* the variability of outcomes, but remember we are here discussing the variability of total returns, interest plus net profits. The variability of stockholder net profits will, of course, be greater in the presence than in the absence of leverage, though relatively less so than in an otherwise comparable world of no taxes. The reasons for this will become clearer after the discussion in the next section.

[5] The statement that τR—the tax saving per period on the interest payments—is a sure stream is subject to two qualifications. First, it must be the case that firms can always obtain the tax benefit of their interest deductions either by offsetting them directly against other taxable income in the year incurred; or, in the event no such income is available in any given year, by carrying them backward or forward against past or future taxable earnings; or, in the extreme case, by merger of the firm with (or its sale to) another firm that can utilize the deduction. Second, it must be assumed that the tax rate will remain the same. To the extent that neither of these conditions holds exactly then some uncertainty attaches even to the tax savings, though, of course, it is of a different kind and order from that attaching to the stream generated by the assets. For simplicity, we shall here ignore these possible elements of delay or of uncertainty in the tax saving; but it should be kept in mind that this neglect means that the subsequent valuation formulas overstate, if anything, the value of the tax saving for any given permanent level of debt.

[6] Note that here, as in our original paper, we neglect dividend policy and "growth" in the sense of opportunities to invest at a rate of return greater than the market rate of return. These subjects are treated extensively in our paper, "Dividend Policy, Growth and the Valuation of Shares," *Jour. Bus.*, Univ. Chicago, Oct. 1961, 411–33.

[7] Here and throughout, the corresponding formulas when the rate of interest rises with leverage can be obtained merely by substituting $r(L)$ for r, where L is some suitable measure of leverage.

[8] The assumption that the debt is permanent is not necessary for the analysis. It is employed here both to maintain continuity with the original model and because it gives an upper bound on the value of the tax saving. See in this connection footnote 5 and footnote 9.

$$V_L = \frac{\overline{X}^\tau}{\rho^\tau} = \frac{(1-\tau)\overline{X}}{\rho^\tau} + \frac{\tau R}{\rho^\tau} = V_U + \frac{r}{\rho^\tau}\, \tau D_L. \tag{4}$$

We will now show that if (3) does not hold, investors can secure a more efficient portfolio by switching from relatively overvalued to relatively undervalued firms. Suppose first that unlevered firms are overvalued or that

$$V_L - \tau D_L < V_U.$$

An investor holding m dollars of stock in the unlevered company has a right to the fraction m/V_U of the eventual outcome, i.e., has the uncertain income

$$Y_U = \left(\frac{m}{V_U}\right)(1-\tau)\overline{X}Z.$$

Consider now an alternative portfolio obtained by investing m dollars as follows: (1) the portion,

$$m\left(\frac{S_L}{S_L + (1-\tau)D_L}\right),$$

is invested in the stock of the levered firm, S_L; and (2) the remaining portion,

$$m\left(\frac{(1-\tau)D_L}{S_L + (1-\tau)D_L}\right),$$

is invested in its bonds. The stock component entitles the holder to a fraction,

$$\frac{m}{S_L + (1-\tau)D_L},$$

of the net profits of the levered company or

$$\left(\frac{m}{S_L + (1-\tau)D_L}\right)[(1-\tau)(\overline{X}Z - R_L)].$$

The holding of bonds yields

$$\left(\frac{m}{S_L + (1-\tau)D_L}\right)[(1-\tau)R_L].$$

Hence the total outcome is

$$Y_I = \left(\frac{m}{S_L + (1-\tau)D_L}\right)[(1-\tau)\overline{X}Z]$$

and this will dominate the uncertain income Y_U if (and only if)

$$S_L + (1-\tau)D_L \equiv S_L + D_L - \tau D_L \equiv V_L - \tau D_L < V_U.$$

Thus, in equilibrium, V_U cannot exceed $V_L - \tau D_L$, for if it did investors would have an incentive to sell shares in the unlevered company and purchase the shares (and bonds) of the levered company.

Suppose now that $V_L - \tau D_L > V_U$. An investment of m dollars in the stock of the levered firm entitles the holder to the outcome

$$Y_L = (m/S_L)[(1-\tau)(\bar{X}Z - R_L)]$$
$$= (m/S_L)(1-\tau)\bar{X}Z - (m/S_L)(1-\tau)R_L.$$

Consider the following alternative portfolio: (1) borrow an amount $(m/S_L)(1-\tau)D_L$ for which the interest cost will be $(m/S_L)(1-\tau)R_L$ (assuming, of course, that individuals and corporations can borrow at the same rate, r); and (2) invest m plus the amount borrowed, i.e.,

$$M + \frac{m(1-\tau)D_L}{S_L} = m\frac{S_L + (1-\tau)D_L}{S_L} = (m/S_L)[V_L - \tau D_L]$$

in the stock of the unlevered firm. The outcome so secured will be

$$(m/S_L)\left(\frac{V_L - \tau D_L}{V_U}\right)(1-\tau)\bar{X}Z.$$

Subtracting the interest charges on the borrowed funds leaves an income of

$$Y_U = (m/S_L)\left(\frac{V_L - \tau D_L}{V_U}\right)(1-\tau)\bar{X}Z - (m/S_L)(1-\tau)R_L$$

which will dominate Y_L if (and only if) $V_L - \tau D_L > V_U$. Thus, in equilibrium, both $V_L - \tau D_L > V_U$ and $V_L - \tau D_L < V_U$ are ruled out and (3) must hold.

III. Some Implications of Formula (3)

To see what is involved in replacing (4) with (3) as the rule of valuation, note first that both expressions make the value of the firm a function of leverage and the tax rate. The difference between them is a matter of the size and source of the tax advantages of debt financing. Under our original formulation, values within a class were strictly proportional to expected earnings after taxes. Hence the tax advantage of debt was due solely to the fact that the deductibility of interest payments implied a higher level of after-tax income for any given level of before-tax earnings (i.e., higher by the amount τR since $\bar{X}^\tau = (1-\tau)\bar{X} + \tau R$). Under the corrected rule (3), however, there is an additional gain due to the fact that the extra after-tax earnings, τR, represent a sure income in contrast to the uncertain outcome $(1-\tau)\bar{X}$. Hence τR is capitalized at the more favorable certainty rate, $1/r$, rather than at the rate for uncertain streams, $1/\rho^\tau$.[9]

Since the difference between (3) and (4) is solely a matter of the rate at which the tax savings on interest payments are capitalized, the required changes in all formulas and expressions derived from (4) are reasonably straightforward. Consider, first, the before-tax earnings yield, i.e., the ratio of expected earnings before interest and taxes to the value of the firm.[10] Dividing both sides of (3) by V and by $(1-\tau)$ and simplifying we obtain:

[9] Remember, however, that in one sense formula (3) gives only an upper bound on the value of the firm since $\tau R/r = \tau D$ is an exact measure of the value of the tax saving only where both the tax rate and the level of debt are assumed to be fixed forever (and where the firm is certain to be able to use its interest deduction to reduce taxable income either directly or via transfer of the loss to another firm). Alternative versions of (3) can readily be developed for cases in which the debt is not assumed to be permanent, but rather to be outstanding only for some specified finite length of time. For reasons of space, we shall not pursue this line of inquiry here beyond observing that the shorter the debt period considered, the closer does the valuation formula approach our original (4). Hence, the latter is perhaps still of some interest if only as a lower bound.

[10] Following usage common in the field of finance we referred to this yield as the "average cost of capital." We feel now, however, that the term "before-tax earnings yield" would be preferable both because it is more immediately descriptive and because it releases the term "cost of capital" for use in discussions of optimal investment policy (in accord with standard usage in the capital budgeting literature).

$$\frac{\overline{X}}{V} = \frac{\rho^\tau}{1 - \tau} \left[1 - \tau \frac{D}{V} \right] \tag{31.c}$$

which replaces our original equation (31) [see Merton H. Miller and Franco Modigliani, "Cost of Capital, Corporation Finance and the Theory of Investment," *American Economic Review* (June 1958), p. 294]. The new relation differs from the old in that the coefficient of D/V in the original (31) was smaller by a factor of τ/ρ^τ.

Consider next the after-tax earnings yield, i.e., the ratio of interest payments plus profits after taxes to total market value.[11] This concept was discussed extensively in our paper because it helps to bring out more clearly the differences between our position and the traditional view, and because it facilitates the construction of empirical tests of the two hypotheses about the valuation process. To see what the new equation (3) implies for this yield we need merely substitute $\overline{X}^\tau - \tau R$ for $(1 - \tau)\overline{X}$ in (3) obtaining:

$$V = \frac{\overline{X}^\tau - \tau R}{\rho^\tau} + \tau D = \frac{\overline{X}^\tau}{\rho^\tau} + \tau \frac{\rho^\tau - r}{\rho^\tau} \ D, \tag{5}$$

from which it follows that the after-tax earnings yield must be:

$$\frac{\overline{X}^\tau}{V} = \rho^\tau - \tau(\rho^\tau - r)D/V. \tag{11.c}$$

This replaces our original equation (11) [Miller and Modigliani, "Cost of Capital," p. 272] in which we had simply $\overline{X}^\tau/V = \rho^\tau$. Thus, in contrast to our earlier result, the corrected version (11.c) implies that even the after-tax yield is affected by leverage. The predicted rate of decrease of $\overline{X}^\tau/V$ with D/V, however, is still considerably smaller than under the naive traditional view, which, as we showed, implied essentially $\overline{X}^\tau/V = \rho^\tau - (\rho^\tau - r)D/V$. See our equation (17) and the discussion immediately preceding it (p. 277).[12] And, of course, (11.c) implies that the effect of leverage on $\overline{X}^\tau/V$ is *solely* a matter of the deductibility of interest payments whereas, under the traditional view, going into debt would lower the cost of capital regardless of the method of taxing corporate earnings.

Finally, we have the matter of the after-tax yield on *equity* capital, i.e., the ratio of net profits after taxes to the value of the shares.[13] By subtracting D from both sides of (5) and breaking $\overline{X}^\tau$ into its two components—expected net profits after taxes, $\overline{\pi}^\tau$, and interest payments, $R = rD$—we obtain after simplifying:

$$S = V - D = \frac{\overline{\pi}^\tau}{\rho^\tau} - (1 - \tau) \left(\frac{\rho^\tau - r}{\rho^\tau} \right) D. \tag{6}$$

From (6) it follows that the after-tax yield on equity capital must be:

$$\frac{\overline{\pi}^\tau}{S} = \rho^\tau + (1 - \tau) [\rho^\tau - r]D/S \tag{12.c}$$

---

[11] We referred to this yield as the "after-tax cost of capital." Cf. the previous footnote.

[12] The i_k^* of (17) is the same as ρ^τ in the present context, each measuring the ratio of net profits to the value of the shares (and hence of the whole firm) in an unlevered company of the class.

[13] We referred to this yield as the "after-tax cost of equity capital." Cf. footnote 9.

which replaces our original equation (12), $\bar{\pi}^\tau/S = \rho^\tau + (\rho^\tau - r)D/S$. The new (12.c) implies an increase in the after-tax yield on equity capital as leverage increases which is smaller than that of our original (12) by a factor of $(1 - \tau)$. But again, the linear increasing relation of the corrected (12.c) is still fundamentally different from the naive traditional view which asserts the cost of equity capital to be completely independent of leverage (at least as long as leverage remains within "conventional" industry limits).

IV. Taxes and the Cost of Capital

From these corrected valuation formulas we can readily derive corrected measures of the cost of capital in the capital budgeting sense of the minimum prospective yield an investment project must offer to be just worth undertaking from the standpoint of the present stockholders. If we interpret earnings as perpetuities, as we did in the original paper, then we actually have two equally good ways of defining this minimum yield: either by the required increase in before-tax earnings, $d\underline{X}$, or by the required increase in earnings net of taxes, $d\overline{X}(1 - \tau)$.[14] To conserve space, however, as well as to maintain continuity with the original paper, we shall concentrate here on the before-tax case with only brief footnote references to the net-of-tax concept.

Analytically, the derivation of the cost of capital in the above sense amounts to finding the minimum value of $d\overline{X}/dI$ for which $dV = dI$, where I denotes the level of new investment.[15] By differentiating (3) we see that:

$$\frac{dV}{dI} = \frac{1 - \tau}{\rho^\tau}\frac{d\overline{X}}{dI} + \tau\frac{dD}{dI} \geq 1 \quad \text{if}\frac{d\overline{X}}{dI} \geq \frac{1 - \tau\dfrac{dD}{d}I}{1 - \tau} \quad \rho^\tau. \tag{7}$$

Hence the before tax required rate of return cannot be defined without reference to financial policy. In particular, for an investment considered as being financed entirely by new equity capital $dD/dI = 0$ and the required rate of return or marginal cost of equity financing (neglecting flotation costs) would be:

$$\rho^S = \frac{\rho^\tau}{1 - \tau}.$$

This result is the same as that in the original paper (see equation [32], p. 294) and is applicable to any other sources of financing where the remuneration to the suppliers of capital is not deductible for tax purposes. It applies, therefore, to preferred stock (except for certain partially deductible issues of public utilities) and would apply also to retained earnings were it not for the favorable tax treatment of capital gains under the personal income tax.

For investments considered as being financed entirely by new debt capital $dI = dD$ we find from (7) that:

---

[14] Note that we use the term "earnings net of taxes" rather than "earnings after taxes." We feel that to avoid confusion the latter term should be reserved to describe what will actually appear in the firm's accounting statements, namely the net cash flow including the tax savings on the interest (our $\overline{X}^\tau$). Since financing sources cannot in general be allocated to particular investments (see below), the after-tax or accounting concept is not useful for capital budgeting purposes, although it can be extremely useful for valuation equations as we saw in the previous section.

[15] Remember that when we speak of the minimum required yield on an investment we are referring in principle only to investments which increase the *scale* of the firm. That is, the new assets must be in the same "class" as the old. See in this connection, J. Hirshleifer, "Risk, the Discount Rate and Investment Decisions," *Am. Econ. Rev.,* May 1961, *51,* 112–20 (especially pp. 119–20). See also footnote 16.

$$\rho^D = \rho^\tau \qquad\qquad (33.c)$$

which replaces our original equation (33) in which we had:

$$\rho^D = \rho^S - \frac{\tau}{1-\tau}\, r. \qquad\qquad (33)$$

Thus for borrowed funds (or any other tax-deductible source of capital) the marginal cost or before-tax required rate of return is simply the market rate of capitalization for net of tax unlevered streams and is thus independent of both the tax rate and the interest rate. This required rate is lower than that implied by our original (33), but still considerably higher than that implied by the traditional view (see exp. pp. 276–277 of our paper) under which the before-tax cost of borrowed funds is simply the interest rate, r.

Having derived the above expressions for the marginal costs of debt and equity financing it may be well to warn readers at this point that these expressions represent at best only the hypothetical extremes insofar as costs are concerned and that neither is directly usable as a cut-off criterion for investment planning. In particular, care must be taken to avoid falling into the famous "Liquigas" fallacy of concluding that if a firm intends to float a bond issue in some given year then its cut-off rate should be set that year at ρ^D; while, if the next issue is to be an equity one, the cut-off is ρ^S. The point is, of course, that no investment can meaningfully be regarded as 100 percent equity financed if the firm makes any use of debt capital—and most firms do, not only for the tax savings, but for many other reasons having nothing to do with "cost" in the present static sense (cf. our original paper, pp. 292–293). And no investment can meaningfully be regarded as 100 percent debt financed when lenders impose strict limitations on the maximum amount a firm can borrow relative to its equity (and when most firms actually plan on normally borrowing less than this external maximum so as to leave themselves with an emergency reserve of unused borrowing power). Since the firm's long-run capital structure will thus contain both debt and equity capital, investment planning must recognize that, over the long pull, *all* of the firm's assets are really financed by a mixture of debt and equity capital even though only one kind of capital may be raised in any particular year. More precisely, if L^* denotes the firm's long-run "target" debt ratio (around which its actual debt ratio will fluctuate as it "alternately" floats debt issues and retires them with internal or external equity) then the firm can assume, to a first approximation at least, that for any particular investment $dD/dI = L^*$. Hence, the relevant marginal cost of capital for investment planning, which we shall here denote by ρ^*, is:

$$\rho^* = \frac{1-\tau_L^*}{1-\tau}\, \rho^\tau = \rho^S - \frac{\tau}{1-\tau}\, \rho^D L^* = \rho^S(1-L^*) + \rho^D L^*.$$

That is, the appropriate cost of capital for (repetitive) investment decisions over time is, to a first approximation, a weighted average of the costs of debt and equity financing, the weights being the proportions of each in the "target" capital structure.[16]

---

[16] From the formulas in the text one can readily derive corresponding expressions for the required net-of-tax yield, or net-of-tax cost of capital for any given financing policy. Specifically, let $\tilde{\rho}(L)$ denote the required net-of-tax yield for investment financed with a proportion of debt $L = dD/dI$. (More generally L denotes the proportion financed with tax deductible sources of capital.) Then from (7) we find: (*continued on p. 307*)

V. Some Concluding Observations

Such, then, are the major corrections that must be made to the various formulas and valuation expressions in our earlier paper. In general, we can say that the force of these corrections has been to increase somewhat the estimate of the tax advantages of debt financing under our model and consequently to reduce somewhat the quantitative difference between the estimates of the effects of leverage under our model and under the naive traditional view. It may be useful to remind readers once again that the existence of a tax advantage for debt financing—even the larger advantage of the corrected version—does not necessarily mean that corporations should at all times seek to use the maximum possible amount of debt in their capital structures. For one thing, other forms of financing, notable retained earnings, may in some circumstances be cheaper still when the tax status of investors under the personal income tax is taken into account. More important, there are, as we pointed out, limitations imposed by lenders [see Miller and Modigliani, "Cost of Capital," pp. 292–293], as well as many other dimensions (and kinds of costs) in real-world problems of financial strategy which are not fully comprehended within the framework of static equilibrium models, either our own or those of the traditional variety. These additional considerations, which are typically grouped under the rubric of "the need for preserving flexibility," will normally imply the maintenance by the corporation of a substantial reserve of untapped borrowing power. The tax advantage of debt may well tend to lower the optimal size of that reserve, but it is hard to believe that advantages of the size contemplated under our model could justify any substantial reduction, let alone their complete elimination. Nor do the data indicate that there has in fact been a substantial increase in the use of debt (except relative to preferred stock) by the corporate sector during the recent high tax years.[17]

As to the differences between our modified model and the traditional one, we feel that they are still large in quantitative terms and still very much worth trying to detect. It is not only a matter of the two views having different implications for corporate financial policy (or even for national tax

---

[16] (*continued from p. 306*)

$$\tilde{\rho}(L) = (1 - \tau) \frac{d\overline{X}}{dI} = (1 - L\tau)\rho^{\tau} \qquad (8)$$

and the various costs can be found by substituting the appropriate value for L. In particular, if we substitute in this formula the "target" leverage ratio, L^*, we obtain:

$$\tilde{\rho}^* \equiv \tilde{\rho}(L^*) = (1 - \tau L^*)\rho^{\tau}$$

and $\tilde{\rho}^*$ measures the average net-of-tax cost of capital in the sense described above.

Although the before-tax and the net-of-tax approaches to the cost of capital provide equally good criteria for investment decisions when assets are assumed to generate perpetual (i.e., non-depreciating) streams, such is not the case when assets are assumed to have finite lives (even when it is also assumed that the firm's assets are in a steady state age distribution so that our X or EBIT is approximately the same as the net cash flow before taxes). See footnote 3 above. In the latter event, the correct method for determining the desirability of an investment would be, in principle, to discount the net-of-tax stream at the net-of-tax cost of capital. Only under this net-of-tax approach would it be possible to take into account the deductibility of depreciation (and also to choose the most advantageous depreciation policy for tax purposes). Note that we say that the net-of-tax approach is correct "in principle" because, strictly speaking, nothing in our analysis (or anyone else's, for that matter) has yet established that it is indeed legitimate to "discount" an uncertain stream. One can hope that subsequent research will show the analogy to discounting under the certainty case is a valid one; but, at the moment, this is still only a hope.

[17] See, e.g., Merton H. Miller, "The Corporate Income Tax and Corporate Financial Policies," in *Staff Reports to the Commission on Money and Credit* (forthcoming).

policy). But since the two positions rest on fundamentally different views about investor behavior and the functioning of the capital markets, the results of tests between them may have an important bearing on issues ranging far beyond the immediate one of the effects of leverage on the cost of capital.

Discussion Questions

1. Refer to formula (3). Explain how this formula was rationalized and what it shows.

2. If the total value of the firm can be increased by using leverage, does this mean that debt should be utilized as permanent financing for the corporation?

3. If the total value of the firm can be increased by using leverage, does this mean that the use of debt should always increase? If the use of debt should always increase, what are the logical limits on how high the proportion of debt could or should become?

Stewart C. Myers

The Capital Structure Puzzle

This article is a thoughtful treatise on what we know about the capital structure of the firm. On the one hand we have theory and evidence that there is an optimal capital structure. On the other hand, however, there exists just as much theory and evidence that there is no such thing as an optimal structure of long-term debt and equity.

This paper's title is intended to remind you of Fischer Black's well-known note on "The Dividend Puzzle," which he closed by saying, "What should the corporation do about dividend policy? We don't know." [6, p. 8] I will start by asking, "How do firms choose their capital structures?" Again, the answer is, "We don't know."

The capital structure puzzle is tougher than the dividend one. We know quite a bit about dividend policy. John Lintner's model of how firms set dividends [20] dates back to 1956, and it still seems to work. We know stock prices respond to unanticipated dividend changes, so it is clear that dividends have information content—this observation dates back at least to Miller and Modigliani (MM) in 1961 [28]. We do not know whether high dividend yield increases the expected rate of return demanded by investors, as adding taxes to the MM proof of dividend irrelevance suggests, but financial economists are at least hammering away at this issue.

By contrast, we know very little about capital structure. We do not know how firms choose the debt, equity, or hybrid securities they issue. We have only recently discovered that capital structure changes convey information to investors. There has been little if any research testing whether the relationship between financial leverage and investors' required return is as the pure MM theory predicts. In general, we have inadequate understanding of corporate financing behavior and of how that behavior affects security returns.

I do not want to sound too pessimistic or discouraged. We have accumulated many helpful insights into capital structure choice, starting with the most important one, MM's No Magic in Leverage Theorem (Proposition I) [31]. We have thought long and hard about what these insights imply for optimal capital structure. Many of us have translated these theories, or stories, of optimal capital

Source: Reprinted with permission from *The Journal of Finance* (July 1984), pp. 515–592. Stewart C. Myers is the Gordon Y Billard Professor of Finance at M.I.T.

structure into more or less definite advice to managers. But our theories don't seem to explain actual financing behavior, and it seems presumptuous to advise firms on optimal capital structure when we are so far from explaining actual decisions. I have done more than my share of writing on optimal capital structure, so I take this opportunity to make amends and to try to push research in some new directions.

I will contrast two ways of thinking about capital structure:

1. *A static tradeoff* framework, in which the firm is viewed as setting a target debt-to-value ratio and gradually moving towards it, in much the same way that a firm adjusts dividends to move towards a target payout ratio.

2. An old-fashioned *pecking order* framework, in which the firm prefers internal to external financing, and debt to equity if it issues securities. In the pure pecking order theory, the firm has no well-defined target debt-to-value ratio.

Recent theoretical work has breathed new life into the pecking order framework. I will argue that this theory performs at least as well as the static trade-off theory in explaining what we know about actual financing choices and their average impacts on stock prices.

Managerial and Neutral Mutation Hypotheses

I have arbitrarily, and probably unfairly, excluded "managerial" theories which might explain firm's capital structure choices.[1] I have chosen not to consider models which cut the umbilical cord that ties managers' acts to stockholders' interests.

I am also sidestepping Miller's Idea of "neutral mutation."[2] He suggests that firms fall into some financing patterns or habits which have no material effect on firm value. The habits may make managers feel better, and since they do no harm, no one cares to stop or change them. Thus someone who identifies these habits and uses them to predict financing behavior would not be explaining anything important.

The neutral mutations idea is important as a warning. Given time and imagination, economists can usually invent some model that assigns apparent economic rationality to any random event. But taking neutral mutation as a strict null hypothesis makes the game of research too tough to play. If an economist identifies costs of various financing strategies, obtains independent evidence that the costs are really there, and then builds a model based on these costs which explains firms' financing behavior, then some progress has been made, even if it proves difficult to demonstrate that, say, a type *A* financing strategy gives higher firm value than a type *B*. (In fact, we would never see type *B* if all firms follow value-maximizing strategies.)

There is another reason for not immediately embracing neutral mutations: We know investors are interested in the firm's financing choices, because stock prices change when the choices are

---

[1] The finance and economics literature has at least three "managerial" strands: (1) descriptions of managerial capitalism, in which the separation of ownership and control is taken as a central fact of life, for example Berle and Means [5]; (2) agency theory, pioneered for finance by Jensen and Meckling [18]; and (3) the detailed analysis of the personal risks and rewards facing managers and how their responses affect firms' financing or investment choices. For examples of Strand (3), see Ross's articles on financial signalling [36, 37].

[2] Put forward in "Debts and Taxes" [27], esp. pp. 272–73. Note that Miller did not claim that all of firms' financing habits are neutral mutations, only that some of them may be. I doubt that Miller intended this idea as a strict null hypothesis (see below).

announced. The change might be explained as an "information effect" having nothing to do with financing per se—but, again, it is a bit too easy to wait until the results of an event study are in, and then to think of an information story to explain them. On the other hand, if one starts by assuming that managers have special information, builds a model of how that information changes financing choices, and predicts which choices will be interpreted by investors as good or bad news, then some progress has been made.

So this paper is designed as a one-on-one competition of the static tradeoff and pecking-order stories. If neither story explains actual behavior, the neutral mutations story will be there faithfully waiting.

The Static Tradeoff Hypothesis

A firm's optimal debt ratio is usually viewed as determined by a tradeoff of the costs and benefits of borrowing, holding the firm's assets and investment plans constant. The firm is portrayed as balancing the value of interest tax shields against various costs of bankruptcy or financial embarrassment. Of course, there is controversy about how valuable the tax shields are, and which, if any, of the costs of financial embarrassment are material, but these disagreements give only variations on a theme. The firm is supposed to substitute debt for equity, or equity for debt, until the value of the firm is maximized. Thus the debt-equity tradeoff is as illustrated in Figure 1.

Costs of Adjustment

If there are no costs of adjustment and the static tradeoff theory is correct, then each firm's observed debt-to-value ratio should be its optimal ratio. However, there must be costs, and therefore lags, in adjusting to the optimum. Firms can not immediately offset the random events that bump them away from the optimum, so there should be some cross-sectional dispersion of actual debt ratios across a sample of firms having the same target ratio.

Large adjustment costs could possibly explain the observed wide variation in actual debt ratios, since firms would be forced into long excursions away from their optimal ratios. But there is nothing in the usual static tradeoff stories suggesting that adjustment costs are a first-order concern—in fact, they are rarely mentioned. Invoking them without modelling them is a cop-out.

Any cross-sectional test of financing behavior should specify whether firms' debt ratios differ because they have different optimal ratios or because their actual ratios diverge from optimal ones. It is easy to get the two cases mixed up. For example, think of the early cross-sectional studies which attempted to test MM's Proposition I. These studies tried to find out whether differences in leverage affected the market value of the firm (or the market capitalization rate for its operating income). With hindsight, we can quickly see the problem: If adjustment costs are small, and each firm in the sample is at, or close to, its optimum, then the in-sample dispersion of debt ratios must reflect differences in risk or in other variables affecting optimal capital structure. But then MM's Proposition I cannot be tested unless the effects of risk and other variables on firm value can be adjusted for. By now we have learned from experience how hard it is to hold "other things constant" in cross-sectional regressions.

Of course, one way to make sense of these tests is to assume that adjustment costs are small, but managers don't know, or don't care, what the optimal debt ratio is, and thus do not stay close to it. The researcher then assumes some (usually unspecified) "managerial" theory of capital structure

Figure 1 The Static-Tradeoff Theory of Capital Structure

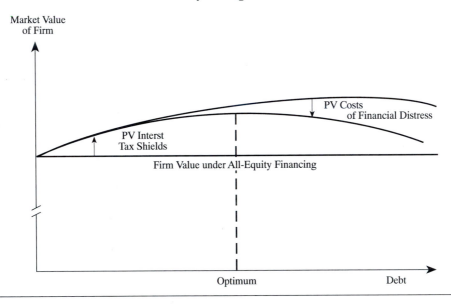

choice. This may be a convenient assumption for a cross sectional test of MM's Proposition I, but not very helpful if the object is to understand financing behavior.[3]

But suppose we don't take this "managerial" fork. Then if adjustment costs are small and firms stay near their target debt ratios, I find it hard to understand the observed diversity of capital structures across firms that seem similar in a static tradeoff framework. If adjustment costs are large, so that some firms take extended excursions away from their targets, then we ought to give less attention to refining our static tradeoff stories and relatively more to understanding what the adjustment costs are, why they are so important, and how rational managers would respond to them.

But I am getting ahead of my story. On to debt and taxes.

---

[3] The only early cross-sectional study I know of which sidesteps these issues is MM's 1966 paper on the cost of capital for the electric utility industry [28]. Their "corrected" theory says that firm value is independent of capital structure except for the value added by the present value of interest tax shields. Thus tax-paying firms would be expected to substitute debt for equity, at least up to the point where the probability of financial distress starts to be important. However, the regulated firms MM examined had little tax incentive to use debt, because their interest tax shields were passed through to consumers. If a regulated firm pays an extra one dollar of interest, and this saves T_c in corporate income taxes, regulators are supposed to reduce the firm's pre-tax operating income by $T_c/(1 - T)$, the grossed-up value of the tax saving, This roughly cancels out any tax advantage of borrowing. Thus regulated firms should have little incentive to borrow enough to flirt with financial distress, and their debt ratios could be dispersed across a conservative range.

Moreover, MM's test could pick up the present value of interest tax shields *provided* they adjusted for differences in operating income. Remember, interest tax shields are not eliminated by regulation, just offset by reductions in allowed operating income.

Thus regulated firms are relatively good subjects for cross-sectional tests of static tradeoff theories. MM's theory seemed to work fairly well for three years in the mid-1950s. Unfortunately, MM's equations didn't give sensible coefficients when fitted on later data (see, for example, Robicheck, McDonald, and Higgins [35]). There has been little further work attempting to extend or adapt MM's 1966 model. In the meantime, theory has moved on.

Debt and Taxes

Miller's famous "Debt and Taxes" paper [27] cuts us loose from the extreme implications of the original MM theory, which made interest tax shields so valuable that we could not explain why all firms were not awash in debt. Miller described an equilibrium of *aggregate* supply and demand for corporate debt, in which personal income taxes paid by the marginal investor in corporate debt just offset the corporate tax saving. However, since the equilibrium determines only aggregates, debt policy should not matter for any single tax-paying firm. Thus Miller's model allows us to explain the dispersion of actual debt policies without having to introduce non-value-maximizing managers.[4]

Trouble is, this explanation works only if we assume that all firms face approximately the same marginal tax rate, and *that* is an assumption we can immediately reject. The extensive trading of depreciation tax shields and investment tax credits, through financial leases and other devices, proves that plenty of firms face low marginal rates.[5]

Given significant differences in effective marginal tax rates, and given that the static tradeoff theory works, we would expect to find a strong tax effect in any cross-sectional test, regardless of whose theory of debt and taxes you believe.

Figure 2 plots the net tax gain from corporate borrowing against the expected realizable tax shield from a future deduction of one dollar of interest paid. For some firms this number is 46 cents, or close to it. At the other extreme, there are firms with large unused loss carryforwards which pay no immediate taxes. An extra dollar of interest paid by these firms would create only a potential future deduction, usable when and if the firm earns enough to work off prior carryforwards. The expected realizable tax shield is positive but small. Also, there are firms paying taxes today which cannot be sure they will do so in the future. Such a firm values expected future interest tax shields at somewhere between zero and the full statutory rate.

In the "corrected" MM theory [28] any tax-paying corporation gains by borrowing; the greater the marginal tax rate, the greater the gain. This gives the top line in the figure. In Miller's theory, the personal income taxes on interest payments would exactly offset the corporate interest tax shield, provided that the firm pays the full statutory tax rate. However, any firm paying a lower rate would see a net loss to corporate borrowing and a net gain to lending. This gives the bottom line.

There are also compromise theories, advanced by DeAngelo and Masulis [12], Modigliani [30], and others, indicated by the middle dashed line in the figure. The compromise theories are appealing because they seem less extreme than either the MM or Miller theories. But regardless of which theory holds, the *slope* of the line is always positive. The *difference* between (1) the tax advantage of borrowing to firms facing the full statutory rate, and (2) the tax advantage of lending (or at least *not* borrowing) to firms with large tax loss carryforwards is exactly the same as in the "extreme" theories. Thus, although the theories tell different stories about aggregate supply and demand of corporate debt, they make essentially the same predictions about which firms borrow more or less than average.

So the tax side of the static tradeoff theory predicts that IBM should borrow more than Bethlehem Steel, other things equal, and that General Motors' debt-to-value ratio should be more than Chrysler's.

---

[4] Although Miller's "Debt and Taxes" model [27] was a major conceptual step forward, I do not consider it an adequate description of how taxes affect optimum capital structure or expected rates of return on debt and equity securities. See Gordon and Malkiel [16] for a recent review of the evidence.

[5] Cordes and Scheffrin [8] present evidence on the cross-sectional dispersion of effective corporate tax rates.

Figure 2   The Net Tax Gain to Corporate Borrowing

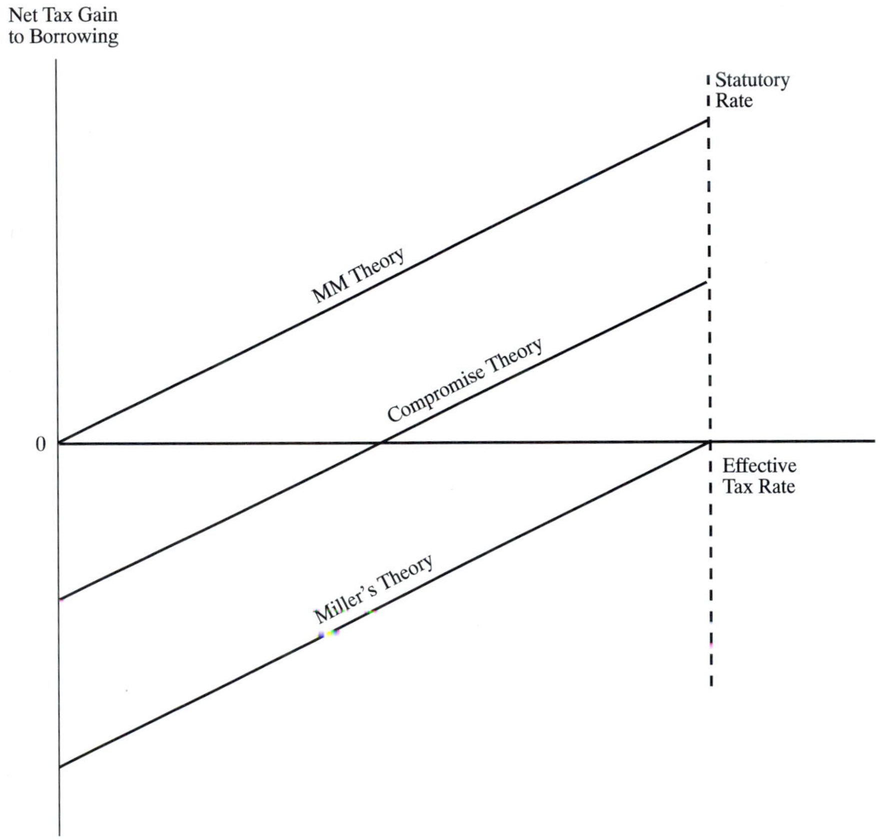

Net Tax Gain
to Borrowing

Costs of Financial Distress

Costs of financial distress include the legal and administrative costs of bankruptcy, as well as the subtler agency, moral hazard, monitoring, and contracting costs which can erode firm value even if formal default is avoided. We know these costs exist, although we may debate their magnitude. For example, there is no satisfactory explanation of debt covenants unless agency costs and moral hazard problems are recognized.

The literature on costs of financial distress supports two qualitative statements about financial behavior.[6]

1. Risky firms ought to borrow less, other things equal. Here "risk" would be defined as the variance rate of the market value of the firm's assets. The higher the variance rate, the greater the

---

[6] I have discussed these two points in more detail in [32 and 33].

probability of default on any given package of debt claims. Since costs of financial distress are caused by threatened or actual default, safe firms ought to be able to borrow more before expected costs of financial distress offset the tax advantages of borrowing.

2. Firms holding tangible assets-in-place having active second-hand markets will borrow less than firms holding specialized, intangible assets or valuable growth opportunities. The expected cost of financial distress depends not just on the probability of trouble, but the value lost if trouble comes. Specialized, intangible assets or growth opportunities are more likely to lose value in financial distress.

The Pecking Order Theory

Contrast the static tradeoff theory with a competing popular story based on a financial pecking order:

1. Firms prefer internal finance.

2. They adapt their target dividend payout ratios to their investment opportunities, although dividends are sticky and target payout ratios are only gradually adjusted to shifts in the extent of valuable investment opportunities.

3. Sticky dividend policies, plus unpredictable fluctuations in profitability and investment opportunities, mean that internally generated cash flow may be more or less than investment outlays. If it is less, the firm first draws down its cash balance or marketable securities portfolio.[7]

4. If external finance is required, firms issue the safest security first. That is, they start with debt, then possibly hybrid securities such as convertible bonds, then perhaps equity as a last resort. In this story, there is no well-defined target debt-equity mix, because there are two kinds of equity, internal and external, one at the top of the pecking order and one at the bottom. Each firm's observed debt ratio reflects its cumulative requirements for external finance.

The Pecking Order Literature

The pecking order hypothesis is hardly new.[8] For example, it comes through loud and clear in Donaldson's 1961 study of the financing practices of a sample of large corporations. He observed [13, p. 67] that "Management strongly favored internal generation as a source of new funds even to the exclusion of external funds except for occasional unavoidable 'bulges' in the need for funds." These bulges were not generally met by cutting dividends: Reducing the "customary cash dividend payment . . . was unthinkable to most managements except as a defensive measure in a period of extreme financial distress" (p. 70). Given that external finance was needed, managers rarely thought of issuing stock:

> *Though few companies would go so far as to rule out a sale of common under any circumstances, the large majority had not had such a sale in the past 20 years and did not anticipate one in the foreseeable future. This was particularly remarkable in view of the very high Price-Earnings ratios of recent*

---

[7] If it is more, the firm first pays off debt or invests in cash or marketable securities. If the surplus persists, it may gradually increase its target payout ratio.

[8] Although I have not seen the term "pecking order" used before.

years. Several financial officers showed that they were well aware that this had been a good time to sell common, but the reluctance still persisted. (pp. 57–58).

Of course, the pecking order hypothesis can be quickly rejected if we require it to explain everything. There are plenty of examples of firms issuing stock when they could issue investment-grade debt. But when one looks at aggregates, the heavy reliance on internal finance and debt is clear. For all non-financial corporations over the decade 1973–1982, internally generated cash covered, on average, 62 percent of capital expenditures, including investment in inventory and other current assets. The bulk of required external financing came from borrowing. Net new stock issues were never more than 6 percent of external financing.[9] Anyone innocent of modern finance who looked at these statistics would find the pecking order idea entirely plausible, at least as a description of typical behavior.

Writers on "managerial capitalism" have interpreted firms' reliance on internal finance as a byproduct of the separation of ownership and control: Professional managers avoid relying on external finance because it would subject them to the discipline of the capital market.[10] Donaldson's 1969 book was not primarily about managerial capitalism, but he nevertheless observed that the financing decisions of the firms he studied were *not* directed towards maximizing shareholder wealth, and that scholars attempting to explain those decisions would have to start by recognizing the "managerial view" of corporate finance [14, Ch. 2].

This conclusion is natural given the state of finance theory in the 1960s. Today, it is not so obvious that financing by pecking order goes against shareholders' interests.

External Financing with Asymmetric Information

I used to ignore the pecking order story because I could think of no theoretical foundation for it that would fit in with the theory of modern finance. An argument could be made for internal financing to avoid issue costs, and if external finance is needed, for debt to avoid the still higher costs of equity. But issue costs in themselves do not seem large enough to override the costs and benefits of leverage emphasized in the static tradeoff story. However, recent work based on asymmetric information gives predictions roughly in line with the pecking order theory. The following brief exposition is based on a forthcoming joint paper by me and Nicholas Majluf [34], although I will here boil down that paper's argument to absolute essentials.

Suppose the firm has to raise N dollars in order to undertake some potentially valuable investment opportunity. Let y be this opportunity's net present value (NPV) and x be what the firm will be worth if the opportunity is passed by. The firm's manager knows what x and y are, but investors in capital markets do not: They see only a joint distribution of possible values $(\tilde{x}, \tilde{y})$. The information asymmetry is taken as given. Aside from the information asymmetry, capital markets are perfect and semi-strong form efficient. MM's Proposition I holds in the sense that the stock of debt relative to real assets is irrelevant if information available to investors is held constant.

The *benefit* to raising N dollars by a security issue is y, the NPV of the firm's investment opportunity. There is also a possible cost: The firm may have to sell the securities for less than they are really worth. Suppose the firm issues *stock* with an aggregate market value, when issued, of N. (I

---

[9] These figures were computed from Brealey and Myers [7], Table 14–3, p. 291.

[10] For example, see Berle [4] or Berle and Means [5].

will consider debt issues in a moment.) However, the manager knows the shares are really worth N_1. That is, N_1 is what the new shares will be worth, other things equal, when investors acquire the manager's special knowledge.

Majluf and I discuss several possible objectives managers might pursue in this situation. The one we think makes the most sense is maximizing the "true" or "intrinsic" value of the firm's *existing* shares. That is, the manager worries about the value of the "old" shareholders' stake in the firm. Moreover, investors know the manager will do this. In particular, the "new" investors who purchase any stock issue will assume that the manager is *not* on their side, and will rationally adjust the price they are willing to pay.

Define ΔN as the amount by which the shares are over- or undervalued: $\Delta N \equiv N_1 - N$. Then the manager will issue and invest when

$$y \geq \Delta N. \tag{1}$$

If the manager's inside information is unfavorable, ΔN is negative and the firm will always issue, even if the only good use for the funds raised is to put them in the bank—a zero-NPV investment.[11] If the inside information is favorable, however, the firm may pass up a positive-NPV investment opportunity rather than issue undervalued shares.

But if management acts this way, its decision to issue will signal bad news to both old and new shareholders. Let V be the market value of firm (price per share times number of shares) it does *not* issue, and V' be market value if it does issue; V' includes the value of the newly issued shares. Thus, if everyone knows that managers will act according to Inequality (1), the conditions for a rational expectations equilibrium are[12]

$$V = E(\tilde{x} \mid \text{no issue}) = E(\tilde{x} \mid y < \Delta N) \tag{2a}$$

$$V' = E(\tilde{x} + \tilde{y} + N \mid \text{issue}) = E(\tilde{x} + \tilde{y} + N \mid y \geq \Delta N). \tag{2b}$$

The total dollar amount raised is fixed by assumption, but the number of new shares needed to raise that amount is not. Thus ΔN is endogenous: It depends on V'. For example, if the firm issues, the fraction of all shares held by "new" stockholders is N/V'. The manager sees the true value of their claim as:

$$N_1 = N\backslash V' (x + y + N) \tag{3}$$

Thus, given N, x, and y, and given that stock is issued, the greater the price *per share*, the less value is given up to new stockholders, and the less ΔN is.

---

[11] If the firm always has a zero-NPV opportunity available to it, the distribution of $\tilde{y}$ is truncated at $y = 0$. I also assume that $\tilde{x}$ is non-negative.

[12] The simple model embodied in (1) and (2) is a direct descendent of Akerlof's work [1]. He investigated how markets can fail when buyers cannot verify the quality of what they are offered. Faced with the risk of buying a lemon, the buyer will demand a discount, which in turn discourages the potential sellers who do *not* have lemons. However, in Majluf's and my model, the seller is offering not a single good, but a partial claim on two, the investment project (worth y) and the firm without the project (worth x). The information asymmetry applies to both goods—for example, the manager may receive inside information that amounts to good news about x and bad news about y, or vice versa, or good or bad news about both.

Moreover, the firm may suffer by not selling stock, because the investment opportunity is lost. Management will sometimes issue even when stock is undervalued by investors. Consequently, investors on the other side of the transaction do not automatically interpret every stock issue as an attempted ripoff—if they did, stock would never be issued in a rational expectations equilibrium.

Majluf and I have discussed the assumptions and implications of this model in considerable detail. But here are the two key points.

1. *The cost of relying on external financing.* We usually think of the cost of external finance as administrative and underwriting costs, and in some cases underpricing of the new securities. Asymmetric information creates the possibility of a different sort of cost: the possibility that the firm will choose *not* to issue, and will therefore pass up a positive-NPV investment. This cost is avoided if the firm can retain enough internally generated cash to cover its positive-NPV opportunities.

2. *The advantages of debt over equity issues.* If the firm does seek external funds, it is better off issuing debt than equity securities. The general rule is "Issue safe securities before risky ones."

This second point is worth explaining further. Remember that the firm issues and invests if y, the NPV of its investment opportunity, is greater than or equal to ΔN, the amount by which the new shares are undervalued (if $\Delta N > 0$) or overvalued (if $\Delta N < 0$). For example, suppose the investment requires $N = \$10$ million, but in order to raise the amount the firm must issue shares that are really worth $12 million. It will go ahead only if project NPV is at least $2 million. If it is worth only $1.5 million, the firm refuses to raise the money for it; the intrinsic overall value of the firm is reduced by $1.5 million, but the old shareholders are $0.5 million better off.

The manager could have avoided this problem by building up the firm's cash reserves—but that is hindsight. The only thing he can do now is to redesign the security issue to reduce ΔN. For example, if ΔN could be cut to $0.5 million, the investment project could be financed without diluting the true value of existing shares. The way to reduce ΔN is to issue the safest possible securities—strictly speaking, securities whose future value changes least when the manager's inside information is revealed to the market.

Of course, ΔN is endogenous, so it is loose talk to speak of the manager controlling it. However, there are reasonable cases in which the absolute value of ΔN is always less for debt than for equity. For example, if the firm can issue default-risk free debt, ΔN is zero, and the firm never passes up a valuable investment opportunity. Thus, the ability to issue default-risk free debt is as good as cash in the bank. Even if default risk is introduced, the absolute value of ΔN will be less for debt than for equity if we make the customary assumptions of option pricing models.[13] Thus, if the manager has favorable information ($\Delta N > 0$), it is better to issue debt than equity.

This example assumes that new shares or risky debt would be underpriced. What if the manager's inside information is *unfavorable,* so that any risky security issue would be *overpriced?* In this case, wouldn't the firm want to make ΔN as *large* as possible, to take maximum advantage of new investors? If so, stock would seem better than debt (and warrants better still). The decision rule seems to be "Issue debt when investors undervalue the firm, and equity, or some other risky security, when they overvalue it."

The trouble with this strategy is obvious once you put yourself in investors' shoes. If you know the firm will issue equity only when it is overpriced, and debt otherwise, you will refuse to buy

---

[13] This amounts to assuming that changes in firm value are lognormally distributed, that managers and investors agree on the variance rate, and that managers know the current value of $\tilde{x} + \tilde{y}$ but investors do not. If there is asymmetric information about the variance rate, but not about firm value at the time of issue, the pecking order could be reversed. See Giammarino and Neave [15].

equity unless the firm has already exhausted its "debt capacity"—that is, unless the firm has issued so much debt already that it would face substantial additional costs in issuing more. Thus investors would effectively force the firm to follow a pecking order.

Now this is clearly too extreme. The model just presented would need lots of fleshing out before it could fully capture actual behavior. I have presented it just to show how models based on asymmetric information can predict the two central ideas of the pecking order story: first, the preference for internal finance, and, second, the preference for debt over equity if external financing is sought.

What We Know about Corporate Financing Behavior

I will now list what we know about financing behavior and try to make sense of this knowledge in terms of the two hypotheses sketched above. I begin with five facts about financing behavior and then offer a few generalizations from weaker statistical evidence or personal observation. Of course, even "facts" based on apparently good statistics have been known to melt away under further examination, so read with caution.

Internal versus External Equity

Aggregate investment outlays are predominantly financed by debt issues and internally generated funds. New stock issues play a relatively small part. Moreover, as Donaldson has observed, this is what many managers say they are trying to do.

This fact is what suggested the pecking order hypothesis in the first place. However, it might also be explained in a static tradeoff theory by adding significant transaction costs of equity issues and noting the favorable tax treatment of capital gains relative to dividends. This would make external equity relatively expensive. It would explain why companies keep target dividend payouts low enough to avoid having to make regular stock issues.[14] It would also explain why a firm whose debt ratio soars above target does not immediately issue stock, buy back debt, and re-establish a more moderate debt-to-value ratio. Thus firms might take extended excursions *above* their debt targets. (Note, however, that the static tradeoff hypothesis as usually presented rarely mentions this kind of adjustment cost.)

But the out-of-pocket costs of *repurchasing* shares seems fairly small. It is thus hard to explain extended excursions *below* a firm's debt target by an augmented static tradeoff theory—the firm could quickly issue debt and buy back shares. Moreover, if personal income taxes are important in explaining firms' apparent preferences for internal equity, then it's difficult to explain why *external* equity is not strongly *negative*—that is, why most firms haven't gradually moved to materially lower target payout ratios and used the released cash to repurchase shares.

Timing of Security Issues

Firms apparently try to "time" stock issues when security prices are "high." *Given that they seek external finance,* they are more likely to issue stock (rather than debt) after stock prices have risen

---

[14] Regulated firms, particularly electric utilities, typically pay dividends generous enough to force regular trips to the equity market. They have a special reason for this policy: It improves their bargaining position vs. consumers and regulators. It turns the opportunity cost of capital into cash requirements.

than after they have fallen. For example, past stock price movements were one of the best-performing variables in Marsh's study [22] of British firms' choices between new debt and new equity issues. Taggart [39] and others[15] have found similar behavior in the United States.

This fact is embarrassing to static tradeoff advocates. If firm value rises, the debt-to-value ratio falls, and firms ought to issue *debt,* not equity, to rebalance their capital structures.

The fact is equally embarrassing to the pecking order hypothesis. There is no reason to believe that the manager's inside information is systematically more favorable when stock prices are "high." Even if there were such a tendency, investors would have learned it by now, and would interpret the firm's issue decision accordingly. There is no way firms can *systematically* take advantage of purchasers of new equity in a rational expectations equilibrium.

Borrowing against Intangibles and Growth Opportunities

Firms holding valuable intangible assets or growth opportunities tend to borrow less than firms holding mostly tangible assets. For example, Long and Malitz [21] found a significant negative relationship between rates of investment in advertising and research and development (R&D) and the level of borrowing. They also found a significant *positive* relationship between the rate of capital expenditure (in fixed plant and equipment) and the level of borrowing.

Williamson [41] reached the same conclusion by a different route. His proxy for a firm's intangibles and growth opportunities was the difference between the market value of its debt and equity securities and the replacement cost of its tangible assets. The higher this proxy, he found, the less the firm's debt-to-value ratio.

There is plenty of indirect evidence indicating that the level of borrowing is determined not just by the value and risk of the firm's assets, but also by the type of assets it holds. For example, without this distinction, the static tradeoff theory would specify all target debt ratios in terms of market, not book values. Since many firms have market values far in excess of book values (even if those book values are restated in current dollars), we ought to see at least a few such firms operating comfortably at *very* high book debt ratios—and, of course, we do not. This fact begins to make sense, however, as soon as we realize that book values reflect assets-in-place (tangible assets and working capital). Market values reflect intangibles and growth opportunities as well as assets-in-place. Thus, firms do not set target book debt ratios because accountants certify the books. Book asset values are proxies for the values of assets in place.[16]

Exchange Offers

Masulis [23, 24] has shown that stock prices rise, on average, when a firm offers to exchange debt for equity, and fall when they offer to exchange equity for debt. This fact could be explained in various ways. For example, it might be a tax effect. If most firms' debt ratios are below their optimal ratios (i.e., to the left of the optimum in Figure 1), and if corporate interest tax shields have significant positive value, the debt-for-equity exchanges would tend to move firms closer to optimum capital structure. Equity-for-debt swaps would tend to move them farther away.

---

[15] Jalilvand and Harris [17], for example.

[16] The problem is not that intangibles and growth opportunities are risky. The *securities* of growth firms may be excellent collateral. But the firm which borrows against intangibles or growth opportunities may end up reducing their value.

The evidence on exchanges hardly builds confidence in the static tradeoff theory as a description of financing behavior. If the theory were right, firms would be sometimes above, and sometimes below, their optimum ratios. Those above would offer to exchange equity for debt. Those below would offer debt for equity. In both cases, the firm would move closer to the optimum. Why should an exchange offer be good news if in one direction and bad news if in the other?

As Masulis points out, the firm's willingness to exchange debt for equity might signal that the firm's debt capacity had, in management's opinion, increased. That is, it would signal an increase in firm value or a reduction in firm risk. Thus, a debt-for-equity exchange would be good news, and the opposite exchange bad news.

This "information effect" explanation for exchange offers is surely right in one sense. Anytime an announcement affects stock price, we can infer that the announcement conveyed information. That is not much help except to prove that managers have some information investors do not.

The idea that an exchange offer reveals a change in the firm's target debt ratio, and thereby signals changes in firm value or risk, sounds plausible. But an equally plausible story can be told without saying anything about a target debt ratio. If the manager with superior information acts to maximize the intrinsic value of existing shares, then the announcement of a stock issue should be bad news, other things equal, because stock issues will be more likely when the *manager* receives bad news.[17] On the other hand, stock retirements should be good news. The news in both cases has no evident necessary connection with shifts in target debt ratios.

It may be possible to build a model combining asymmetric information with the costs and benefits of borrowing emphasized in static tradeoff stories. My guess, however, is that it will prove difficult to do this without also introducing some elements of the pecking order study.

Issue or Repurchase of Shares

The fifth fact is no surprise, given the fourth. On average, stock price falls when firms announce a stock issue. Stock prices rise, on average, when a stock repurchase is announced. This fact has been confirmed in several studies, including those by Korwar [19], Asquith and Mullins [2], Dann and Mikkleson [10], and Vermaelen [40], and DeAngelo, DeAngelo, and Rice [11].

This fact is again hard to explain by a static tradeoff model, except as an information effect in which stock issues or retirements signal changes in the firm's target debt ratio. I've already commented on that.

The simple asymmetric information model I used to motivate the pecking order hypothesis does predict that the announcement of a stock issue will cause stock price to fall. It also predicts that stock price should *not* fall, other things equal, if default-risk debt is issued. Of course, no private company can issue debt that is absolutely protected from default, but it seems reasonable to predict that the average stock price impact of high-grade debt issues will be small relative to the average impact of stock issues. This is what Dann and Mikkleson [10] find.

These results may make one a bit more comfortable with asymmetric information models of the kind sketched above, and thus a bit more comfortable with the pecking order story.

That's the five facts. Here now are three items that do not qualify for that list—just call them "observations."

---

[17] This follows from the simple model presented above. See Myers and Majluf [34] for a formal proof.

Existence of Target Ratios

Marsh [22] and Taggart [39] have found some evidence that firms adjust towards a target debt-to-value ratio. However, a model based solely on this partial adjustment process would have a very low R^2. Apparently the static tradeoff model captures only a small part of actual behavior.[18]

Risk

Risky firms tend to borrow less, other things equal. For example, both Long and Malitz [21] and Williamson [41] found significant negative relationships between unlevered betas and the level of borrowing. However, the evidence on risk and debt policy is not extensive enough to be totally convincing.

Taxes

I know of no study clearly demonstrating that a firm's tax status has predictable, material effects on its debt policy.[19] I think the wait for such a study will be protracted.

Admittedly it's hard to classify firms by tax status without implicitly classifying them on other dimensions as well. For example, firms with large tax loss carryforwards may also be firms in financial distress, which have high debt ratios almost by definition. Firms with high operating profitability, and therefore plenty of unshielded income, may also have valuable intangible assets and growth opportunities. Do they end up with a higher or lower than average debt-to-value ratio? Hard to say.

Conclusion

People feel comfortable with the static tradeoff story because it sounds plausible and yields an interior optimum debt ratio. It rationalizes "moderate" borrowing.

Well, the story may be moderate and plausible, but that does not make it right. We have to ask whether it explains firms' financing behavior. If it does, fine. If it does not, then we need a better theory before offering advice to managers.

The static tradeoff story works to some extent, but it seems to have an unacceptably low R^2. Actual debt ratios vary widely across apparently similar firms. Either firms take extended excursions from their targets or the targets themselves depend on factors not yet recognized or understood.

At this point we face a tactical choice between two research strategies. First, we could try to expand the static tradeoff story by introducing adjustment costs, possibly including those stemming from asymmetric information and agency problems. Second, we could *start* with a story based on asymmetric information and expand it by adding only those elements of the static tradeoff which have clear empirical support. I think we will progress farther faster by the latter route.

Here is what I think is really going on. I warn you that the following "modified pecking order" story is grossly oversimplified and underqualified. But I think it is generally consistent with the empirical evidence.

---

[18] Of course, we could give each firm its own target and leave that target free to wander over time. But then we would explain everything and know nothing. We want a theory which predicts how debt ratios vary across firms and time.

[19] For example, both Williamson [41] and Long and Malitz [21] introduced proxies for firms' tax status, but failed to find any significant, independent effect on debt ratios.

1. Firms have good reasons to avoid having to finance real investment by issuing common stock or other risky securities. They do not want to run the risk of falling into the dilemma of either passing by positive-NPV projects or issuing stock at a price they think is too low.

2. They set target dividend payout ratios so that normal rates of equity investment can be met by internally generated funds.

3. The firm may also plan to cover part of normal investment outlays with new borrowing, but it tries to restrain itself enough to keep the debt safe—that is, reasonably close to default-risk free. It restrains itself for two reasons: first, to avoid any material costs of financial distress; and second, to maintain financial slack in the form of reserve borrowing power. "Reserve borrowing power" means that it can issue safe debt if it needs to.

4. Since target dividend payout ratios are sticky, and investment opportunities fluctuate relative to internal cash flow, the firm will from time to time exhaust its ability to issue safe debt. When this happens, the firm turns to less risky securities first—for example, risky debt or convertibles before common stock.

The crucial difference between this and the static tradeoff story is that, in the modified pecking order story, observed debt ratios will reflect the cumulative requirement for external financing—a requirement cumulated over an extended period.[20] For example, think of an unusually profitable firm in an industry generating relatively slow growth. That firm will end up with an unusually low debt ratio compared to its industry's average, *and it won't do much of anything about it.* It won't go out of its way to issue debt and retire equity to achieve a more normal debt ratio.

An unprofitable firm in the same industry will end up with a relatively high debt ratio. If it is high enough to create significant costs of financial distress, the firm *may* rebalance its capital structure by issuing equity. On the other hand, it may not. The same asymmetric information problems which sometimes prevent a firm from issuing stock to finance real investment will sometimes also block issuing stock to retire debt.[21]

If this story is right, average debt ratios will vary from industry to industry because asset risk, asset type, and requirements for external funds also vary by industry. But a long-run industry average will not be a meaningful target for individual firms in that industry.

Let me wrap this up by noting the two clear gaps in my description of "what is really going on." First, the modified pecking order story depends on sticky dividends, but does not explain why they are sticky. Second, it leaves us with at best a fuzzy understanding of when and why firms issue common equity. Unfortunately, I have nothing to say on the first weakness, and only the following brief comments on the second.

The modified pecking order story recognizes both asymmetric information and costs of financial distress. Thus the firm faces two increasing costs as it climbs up the pecking order: It faces higher odds of incurring costs of financial distress, and also higher odds that future positive-NPV projects will be passed by because the firm will be unwilling to finance them by issuing common stock or other risky securities. The firm may choose to reduce these costs by issuing stock now even

---

[20] The length of that period reflects the time required to make a significant shift in a target dividend payout ratio.

[21] The factors that make financial distress costly also make it difficult to escape. The gain in firm value from rebalancing is highest when the firm has gotten into deep trouble and lenders have absorbed a significant capital loss. In that case, rebalancing gives lenders a windfall gain. That is why firms in financial distress often do not rebalance their capital structures.

if new equity is not needed immediately to finance real investment, just to move the firm *down* the pecking order. In other words, financial slack (liquid assets or reserve borrowing power) is valuable, and the firm may rationally issue stock to acquire it. (I say "may" because the firm which issues equity to buy financial slack faces the same asymmetric information problems as a firm issuing equity to finance real investment.) The optimal *dynamic* issue strategy for the firm under asymmetric information is, as far as I know, totally unexplored territory.[22]

References

1. Akerlof, G. A. "The Market for 'Lemons': Quality and the Market Mechanism." *Quarterly Journal of Economics,* 84 (August 1970), 488–500.

2. Asquith, P., and D. W. Mullins. "Equity Issues and Stock Price Dilution." Working Paper, Harvard Business School, May 1983.

3. Barges, A. *The Effect of Capital Structure on the Cost of Capital.* Prentice-Hall, Englewood Cliffs, NJ, 1963.

4. Berle, A. *The 20th Century Capitalist Revolution.* Harcourt, Brace and World, 1954.

5. Berle, A., and G. Means. *The Modern Corporation and Private Property.* MacMillan, New York, 1932.

6. Black, F. "The Dividend Puzzle." *Journal of Portfolio Management,* 2 (Winter 1976), 5–8.

7. Brealey, R. A., and S. C. Myers. *Principles of Corporate Finance,* 2nd Ed. McGraw-Hill, New York, 1984.

8. Cordes, J. J., and S. M. Sheffrin. "Estimating the Tax Advantage of Corporate Debt." *The Journal of Finance,* 38 (March 1983), 95–105.

9. Dann, L. Y. "Common Stock Repurchases: An Analysis of Returns to Bondholders and Stockholders." *Journal of Financial Economics,* 9 (June 1981), 113–38.

10. Dann, L. Y., and W. H. Mikkleson. "Convertible Debt Issuance, Capital Structure Change and Financing-Related Information: Some New Evidence." Working Paper, Amos Tuck School of Business Administration, 1983.

11. DeAngelo, H., L. DeAngelo, and E. M. Rice. "Minority Freezeouts and Stockholder Wealth." Working Paper, Graduate School of Business Administration, University of Washington, 1982.

12. DeAngelo, H., and R. Masulis. "Optimal Capital Structure under Corporate and Personal Taxation." *Journal of Financial Economics,* 8 (March 1980), 3–29.

13. Donaldson, G. *Corporate Debt Capacity: A Study of Corporate Debt Policy and the Determination of Corporate Debt Capacity.* Boston, Division of Research, Harvard Graduate School of Business Administration, 1961.

14. Donaldson, G. *Strategy for Financial Mobility.* Boston, Division of Research, Harvard Graduate School of Business Administration, 1969.

15. Giammarino, R. M., and E. H. Neave. "The Failure of Financial Contracts and the Relevance of Financial Policy." Working Paper, Queens University, 1982.

16. Gordon, R. H., and G. B. Malkiel. "Corporation Finance." In H. J. Aaron and J. A. Pechman, *How Taxes Affect Economic Behavior.* Brookings Institution, Washington, DC, 1981.

17. Jalilvand, A., and R. S. Harris. "Corporate Behavior in Adjusting Capital Structure and Dividend Policy: An Econometric Study." *The Journal of Finance,* 39 (March 1984), 127–45.

---

[22] If the information asymmetry disappears from time to time, then the firm clearly should stock up with equity before it reappears. This observation is probably not much practical help, however, because we lack an objective proxy for changes in the degree of asymmetry.

18. Jensen, M. C., and W. Meckling. "Theory of the Firm: Managerial Behavior, Agency Costs and Capital Structure." *Journal of Financial Economics,* 3 (October 1976), 11–25.

19. Korwar, A. N. "The Effect of New Issues of Equity: An Empirical Examination." Working Paper, University of California, Los Angeles, 1981.

20. Lintner, J. "Distribution of Incomes of Corporations among Dividends, Retained Earnings and Taxes." *American Economic Review,* 46 (May 1956), 97–113.

21. Long, M. S., and E. B. Malitz. "Investment Patterns and Financial Leverage." Working Paper, National Bureau of Economic Research, 1983.

22. Marsh, P. R. "The Choice between Equity and Debt: An Empirical Study." *The Journal of Finance,* 37 (March 1982), 121–44.

23. Masulis, R. W. "The Effects of Capital Structure Change on Security Prices: A Study of Exchange Offers." *Journal of Financial Economics,* 8 (June 1980), 139–77.

24. Masulis, R. W. "The Impact of Capital Structure Change on Firm Value." *The Journal of Finance,* 38 (March 1983), 107–26.

25. Mikkelson, W. H. "Capital Structure Change and Decreases in Stockholders' Wealth: A Cross-Sectional Study of Convertible Security Calls." Forthcoming in B. Friedman, Ed., *Corporate Capital Structures in the United States* (National Bureau of Economic Research Conference Volume).

26. Mikkelson, W. H. "Convertible Calls and Security Returns." *Journal of Financial Economics,* 9 (June 1981), 113–38.

27. Miller, M. "Debt and Taxes." *The Journal of Finance,* 32 (May 1977), 261–75.

28. Miller, M., and F. Modigliani. "Dividend Policy, Growth and the Valuation of Shares." *Journal of Business,* 34 (October 1961), 411–33. "Some Estimates of the Cost of Capital to the Electric Utility Industry, 1954–1957." *American Economic Review,* 56 (June 1966), 333–91.

29. Miller, M. H., and K. Rock. "Dividend Policy under Information Asymmetry." Working Paper, Graduate School of Business, University of Chicago, November 1982.

30. Modigliani, F. "Debt, Dividend Policy, Taxes, Inflation and Market Valuation." *The Journal of Finance,* 37 (May 1982), 255–73.

31. Modigliani, F., and M. Miller. "The Cost of Capital, Corporation Finance and the Theory of Investment." *American Economic Review,* 53 (June 1958), 261–97.

32. Myers, S. "Determinants of Corporate Borrowing." *Journal of Financial Economics,* 5 (November 1977), 147–76.

33. Myers, S. "The Search for Optimal Capital Structure." *Midland Corporate Finance Journal,* 1 (Spring 1984), 6–16.

34. Myers, S., and N. Majluf. "Corporate Financing and Investment Decisions When Firms Have Information Investors Do Not Have." *Journal of Financial Economics,* forthcoming.

35. Robicheck, A. A., J. MacDonald, and R. Higgins. "Some Estimates of the Cost of Capital to the Electric Utility Industry, 1954–1957: Comment." *American Economic Review,* 57 (December 1967), 1278–88.

36. Ross, S. A. "Some Notes on Financial-Incentive Signalling Models, Activity Choice and Risk Preferences." *The Journal of Finance,* 33 (June 1978), 777–92.

37. Ross, S. A. "The Determination of Financial Structure: The Incentive-Signalling Approach." *Bell Journal of Economics,* 8 (Spring 1977), 23–40.

38. Smith, C., and Warner, J. "On Financial Contracting: An Analysis of Bond Covenants." *Journal of Financial Economics,* 7 (June 1979), 117–61.

39. Taggart, R. "A Model of Corporate Financing Decisions." *The Journal of Finance,* 32 (December 1977), 1467–84.

40. Vermaelen, T. "Common Stock Repurchases and Market Signalling: An Empirical Study." *Journal of Financial Economics,* 9 (June 1981), 139–83.

Exhibit 2 Relative Importance of Capital Structure Model Inputs and/or Assumptions in Governing Financing Decisions of Major U.S. Industrial Firms

Inputs/Assumptions by Order of Importance	Percentage of Responses within Each Rank[a]						
	Unimportant	2	3	4	Important	Not Ranked	Mean[b]
1. Projected cash flow from asset to be financed	1.7	1.1	9.7	29.5	58.0	0.0	4.41
2. Avoiding dilution of common shareholders' claims	2.8	6.3	18.2	39.8	33.0	0.0	3.94
3. Risk of asset to be financed	2.8	6.3	20.5	36.9	33.0	0.6	3.91
4. Restrictive covenants on senior securities	9.1	9.7	18.7	35.2	27.3	0.0	3.62
5. Avoiding mispricings of securities to be issued	3.4	10.8	27.3	39.8	18.7	0.0	3.60
6. Corporate tax rate	4.0	9.7	29.5	42.6	13.1	1.1	3.52
7. Voting control	17.6	10.8	21.0	31.2	19.3	0.0	3.24
8. Depreciation and other non-debt tax shields	8.5	17.6	40.9	24.4	7.4	1.1	3.05
9. Correcting mispricings of outstanding securities	14.8	27.8	36.4	14.2	5.1	1.7	2.66
10. Personal tax rates of debt and equity holders	31.2	34.1	25.6	8.0	1.1	0.0	2.14
11. Bankruptcy costs	69.3	13.1	6.8	4.0	4.5	2.3	1.58

[a]These estimates are based on 176 responses.

[b]Means are calculated by assigning scores of 1 through 5 for rankings from "unimportant" to "important," respectively, and by multiplying each score by the fraction of responses within each rank. A score of 0 is assigned when a source is not ranked.

almost half of the managers (47.2 percent) indicated their securities were correctly priced more than 80 percent of the time, another 40.3 percent indicated fair pricing between 50 and 80 percent of the time, and 11.9 percent said their securities were correctly priced less than 50 percent of the time. Thus, many managers disagree with the notion of efficient markets at least part of the time.

Despite these perceptions, however, managers may not deliberately attempt to signal their firms' true value. The low mean rank in Exhibit 2 on correcting mispricings of outstanding securities (2.66) is inconsistent with an overt signal. Therefore, the relation between the perceptions of market efficiency and managers' rankings of the factors in Exhibit 2 were cross-classified to determine whether financing choices are affected by managers' perceptions of fair market prices.

Market efficiency responses were grouped by whether managers believe their securities are correctly priced more than 80 percent of the time or 80 percent or less. Exhibit 2 responses were also categorized into "low" (ranks 1 and 2), "medium" (rank 3), and "high" (ranks 4 and 5) ranges. Then, two Pearson chi-square statistics were computed, based first on the high, medium, and low ranges and then on the high and the low.

The p-values for these statistics represent the probability of incorrectly inferring an association between managers' perceptions of market efficiency and the importance assigned to the factors in Exhibit 2. Ideally, such probabilities should be low. However, only two of the factors had p-values of 0.100 or lower.[9] Specifically, perceptions of market efficiency appear to influence the importance assigned to risk (p-values = 0.065 and 0.021) and to the restrictive covenants on senior securities (p-values = 0.194 and 0.071). Almost all of the managers (95 percent) who said the market is inefficient also said that asset risk is highly important. In comparison, 82 percent of the managers who believe the market is efficient categorize risk as highly important. The corresponding fractions for the restrictive covenants are 0.83 and 0.70.

Although the above fractions are statistically higher when managers believe the market is inefficient, they are not low even when managers perceive their securities to be correctly priced. Thus, perceptions of market efficiency appear to have little impact on financing decisions, and deliberate signals of firm value through the debt-equity choice seem unlikely.[10]

Tax-Cum-Bankruptcy Cost and Other Static Tradeoff Models.   Of the three capital structure categories discussed above, the static tradeoff models seem least well supported by the data in Exhibit 2. From these models, restrictive covenants on senior securities, the corporate tax rate, voting control, and depreciation and other non-debt tax shields are the most important inputs. Nevertheless, the respective mean ranks of 3.62, 3.52, 3.24, and 3.05 indicate only moderate concern for these factors. (Boquist and Moore [1] also find little support for the hypothesis that non-debt tax shields help determine the debt-equity choice at the individual firm level.) The mean ranks for the personal tax rates of debt and equity holders (2.14) and for bankruptcy costs (1.58) are even less supportive of the static tradeoff theories.

Although the low ranking of bankruptcy costs is not surprising given the size and success of the firms in our sample, the extensive treatment of tax arguments in the finance literature coupled with the recent major changes in the tax law suggest that taxes should be more important to managers in making financing decisions. Nevertheless, responses to a separate series of questions relating to the Tax Reform Act of 1986 indicate that the relative rankings above are accurate.

The first question of that series asked what effect the Tax Reform Act would have on after-tax cash flows. Half of the managers indicated their cash flows would increase, 26.7 percent indicated a decrease, and 22.7 percent indicated the Act would have no effect. Asked next how their capital structure was likely to change as a result of the Tax Reform Act, 82.4 percent of the managers indicated no revision in their capital structure would be made. Of the managers indicating no change, 83.4 percent said other factors are more important than tax laws in determining their financing mix. Additionally, 4.8 percent said that no change would be made because tax laws could change again soon; 0.7 percent indicated that changes had already been made in anticipation of the new tax law; 3.4 percent indicated that the precise implications of the tax law were not clear; and 7.6 percent listed a combination of the above reasons or did not respond to the question. Hence, tax factors do not appear to be the fundamental determinants of the debt-equity choice even for the large, successful firms in our sample.

---

[9] The probability of observing at least two significant factors at the 0.100 level by random chance alone is 0.910. Therefore, the association between the managers' perception of market efficiency and capital structure inputs is dubious.

[10] A chi-square statistic was also computed to determine whether managers' perceptions of market efficiency influence their preference for a target capital structure or a financing hierarchy. The p-value for that test (0.453) indicates that perceived mispricings are not critical determinants of that choice.

Exhibit 3   Relative Importance of Various Financial Planning Principles in Governing Financing Decisions of Major U.S. Industrial Firms

Planning Principle by Order of Importance	Percentage of Responses within Each Rank[a]						Mean[b]
	Unimportant	2	3	4	Important	Not Ranked	
1. Maintaining financial flexibility	0.6	0.0	4.5	33.0	61.4	0.6	4.55
2. Ensuring long-term survivability	4.0	1.7	6.8	10.8	76.7	0.0	4.55
3. Maintaining a predictable source of funds	1.7	2.8	20.5	39.2	35.8	0.0	4.05
4. Maximizing security prices	3.4	4.5	19.3	33.5	37.5	1.7	3.99
5. Maintaining financial independence	3.4	4.5	22.2	27.3	40.9	1.7	3.99
6. Maintaining a high debt rating	2.3	9.1	32.4	43.2	13.1	0.0	3.56
7. Maintaining comparability with other firms in the industry	15.9	36.9	33.0	10.8	2.8	0.6	2.47

[a]These estimates are based on 176 responses.

[b]Means are calculated by assigning scores of 1 through 5 for rankings from "unimportant" to "important," respectively, and by multiplying each score by the fraction of responses within each rank. A score of 0 is assigned when a source is not ranked.

Financial Planning Principles.   Managers' relative disinclination toward capital structure theory, in general, is further reflected in their rankings of seven financial planning principles summarized in Exhibit 3. Five of the seven principles there have mean ranks of 3.90 or higher. In contrast, only 3 of the 11 inputs in Exhibit 2 had mean ranks that high. Financial planning principles, therefore, dominate specific capital structure models in governing financing decisions for the firms in the sample. This finding is underscored by the observation from Exhibit 3 that maximizing security prices also has a lower mean rank (3.99) than three of the other financial planning principles. Given these findings and the absence of a strong relation between managers' perceptions of market efficiency and the importance attached to information factors in Exhibit 2, the evidence suggests that the projected cash flow, risk of the assets to be financed, and avoiding dilution of common shareholders' claims are more closely associated with financial planning principles than with information-related capital structure theories.

C. Factors Governing Preferences for Specific Financing Sources

Spearman rank correlations between the preferences listed in Exhibit 1 and the relative rankings listed in Exhibits 2 and 3 were calculated to determine which of the planning principles and/or capital structure inputs guide the selection of each funding source. Significant correlations are reported in Exhibit 4.[11] The funding source, the factor that is significant, and the direction of the relation are listed in the first through third columns, respectively.

[11] The significance level is 0.05. Obviously, more correlations are significant at the 0.10 level; however, interpreting those correlations is more difficult because higher significance levels induce more "noise."

Exhibit 4   Significant Correlations between Managerial Preferences for Funding Sources and the Perceived Importance of Capital Structure Model Inputs and/or Financial Planning Principles[a]

Funding Source	Capital Structure Input or Planning Principle	Direction of Relationship
Internal equity	None	NA
External common equity	Avoiding dilution	Negative
Straight debt	Maximizing security prices	Positive
Convertible debt	Cash flow Survivability	Negative
		Positive
Straight preferred	Comparability	Negative
Convertible preferred	None	NA

[a]The correlations are calculated with the nonparametric Spearman rank statistic, and the significance level is 0.05.

For internal equity and convertible preferred stock, no significant correlations exist. The lack of variation in the preferences reported in Exhibit 1 for these sources may explain this finding.[12] In contrast, the negative relation between managerial preferences for external equity and avoiding dilution of common shareholders' claims suggests that dilution deters new equity issues. Straight debt is used to maximize security prices; none of the theoretical factors, however, has a significant correlation. Preferences for convertible debt relate negatively to the importance attached to expected cash flows from new assets and positively to maintaining the long-term survivability of the firm. These relations suggest that managers concerned about "hanging" the convertible because of cash flow shortages in early stages of an asset's life nonetheless issue the debt if the investment is crucial to the firm's long-run survivability. Finally, the negative correlation between the preference for straight preferred stock and the importance assigned to maintaining comparability with other firms is consistent with the explanation (given in footnote 7) that preferred stock is used mainly for specialized needs.

Although the above explanations are plausible, they are also almost certainly oversimplified. By definition, the judgment required to make sound financing decisions implies that managers balance the need to avoid dilution against (for example) the need to grow and to maintain financial flexibility. Hence, multiple factors bear on the financing choice, and several financing alternatives may be considered simultaneously. Perhaps such complexities explain why managers are guided more by planning principles than by the implied precision of our theoretical models.[13]

---

[12] The same argument explains why maintaining financial flexibility in Exhibit 3 is uncorrelated with any of the financing sources in Exhibit 1. Over 94 percent of the respondents ranked maintaining financial flexibility as being very important (i.e., as a 4 or a 5). The lack of variability in the responses concerning internal equity and financial flexibility suggests something akin to an identity: Internal equity is the most preferred source because it provides the greatest flexibility.

[13] It is possible that planning principles frequently cause managers to finance their firms in ways predicted by capital structure models even though the principles—not the models—provide the motivation. For example, Kim and Sorenson [10] present evidence that supports Myers [15] and many of the tax-cum-bankruptcy cost models. However, the irresponsiveness of most managers in this sample to changes induced by the Tax Reform Act illustrates why knowing the motivation for financing decisions is important.

D. *Financing Decisions and Other Sources and Uses of Funds*

The importance of capital structure decisions (in general) relative to other decisions managers make can be assessed by examining responses relating to firms' sources and uses of funds. When presented with an attractive new growth opportunity that could not be undertaken without departing from the target capital structure or financing hierarchy, cutting the dividend, or selling off other assets, 82.4 percent of the managers indicated they would deviate from their target capital structure or financing hierarchy. In contrast, 1.7 percent said they would cut the dividend, and 3.4 percent said they would forgo the investment opportunity. The remainder said they would sell off other assets or pursue some combination of all the alternatives. Thus, the financing decision is the most flexible of all the sources and uses of funds constraints. That is, it is least binding. To the extent this is true and to the extent motivations for capital structure changes are complex and imprecise, interpreting common stock price responses to unanticipated capital structure changes will continue to pose difficult challenges to finance researchers.

IV. Conclusion

Corporate managers in this sample are more likely to follow a financing hierarchy than to maintain a target debt-equity ratio. Further, models based on corporate and/or personal taxes and bankruptcy and other leverage-related costs are not as useful in determining the financing mix as are models that suggest that new financing reveals aspects of the firm's marginal asset performance. However, the importance managers attach to specific capital structure theories is not related to managerial perceptions of market efficiency. Thus, most managers do not overtly signal firm value through capital structure adjustments. In general, financial planning principles are more important in governing the financing decisions of the firm than are specific capital structure theories. Moreover, the capital structure decision, per se, is less binding than either the investment or the dividend decision of the firm.

References

1. J. A. Boquist and W. T. Moore. "Interindustry Leverage Differences and the DeAngelo-Masulis Tax Shield Hypothesis." *Financial Management* (Spring 1984), pp. 5–9.
2. H. DeAngelo and R. W. Masulis. "Optimal Capital Structure Under Corporate and Personal Taxation." *Journal of Financial Economics* (June 1980), pp. 3–29.
3. A. Dewing. *Financial Policies of Corporations,* 5th ed., New York, Ronald Press, 1953.
4. G. Donaldson. *Corporate Debt Capacity: A Study of Corporate Debt Policy and the Determination of Corporate Debt Capacity.* Boston, Division of Research, Harvard School of Business, 1961.
5. E. Fama. "Agency Problems and the Theory of the Firm." *Journal of Political Economy* (April 1980), pp. 288–307.
6. R. A. Haugen and L. W. Senbet. "The Insignificance of Bankruptcy Costs to the Theory of Optimal Capital Structure." *Journal of Finance* (May 1978), pp. 383–93.
7. M. C. Jensen. "Agency Costs of Free Cash Flow, Corporate Finance, and Takeovers." *American Economic Review* (May 1986), pp. 323–29.
8. M. C. Jensen and W. H. Meckling. "Theory of the Firm: Managerial Behavior, Agency Costs and Ownership Structure." *Journal of Financial Economics* (October 1976), pp. 305–60.
9. E. H. Kim. "A Mean Variance Theory of Optimal Capital Structure and Corporate Debt Capacity." *Journal of Finance* (March 1978), pp. 45–64.

10. W. S. Kim and E. H. Sorensen. "Evidence on the Impact of the Agency Costs of Debt on Corporate Debt Policy." *Journal of Financial and Quantitative Analysis* (June 1986), pp. 131–44.

11. A. Kraus and R. H. Litzenberger. "A State Preference Model of Optimal Financial Leverage." *Journal of Finance* (September 1973), pp. 911–22.

12. M. H. Miller. "Debt and Taxes." *Journal of Finance* (May 1977), pp 261–76.

13. M. H. Miller and K. Rock. "Dividend Policy Under Asymmetric Information." *Journal of Finance* (September 1985), pp. 1031–51.

14. F. Modigliani and M. H. Miller. "The Cost of Capital, Corporation Finance, and the Theory of Investment." *American Economic Review* (June 1958), pp. 261–97.

15. S. C. Myers. "Determinants of Corporate Borrowing." *Journal of Financial Economics* (November 1977), pp. 147–76.

16. ———. "The Capital Structure Puzzle." *Journal of Finance* (July 1984), pp. 575–92.

17. S. C. Myers and N. S. Majluf. "Corporate Financing and Investment Decisions When Firms Have Information That Investors Do Not Have." *Journal of Financial Economics* (June 1984), pp. 187–221.

18. S. A. Ross., "The Determination of Financial Structure: The Incentive Signalling Approach." *Journal of Economics* (Spring 1977), pp. 23–40.

19. D. F. Scott, Jr. and D. J. Johnson. "Financing Policies and Practices in Large Corporations." *Financial Management* (Summer 1982), pp. 51–59.

20. J. H. Scott. "A Theory of Optimal Capital Structure." *Bell Journal of Economics* (Spring 1976), pp. 33–54.

21. C. W. Smith. "Investment Banking and the Capital Acquisition Process." *Journal of Financial Economics* (January/February 1986), pp. 3–25.

22. C. W. Smith and J. B. Warner. "On Financial Contracting: An Analysis of Bond Covenants." *Journal of Financial Economics* (June 1979), pp. 117–61.

23. E. Solomon. *The Theory of Financial Management.* New York, Columbia University Press, 1963.

24. R. A. Taggart, Jr. "Capital Budgeting and the Financing Decision: An Exposition." *Financial Management* (Summer 1977), pp. 59–64.

25. S. Titman. "The Effect of Capital Structure on a Firm's Liquidation Decision." *Journal of Financial Economics* (March 1984), pp. 137–51.

Appendix

The following is a reproduction of the survey sent to chief financial officers.

Instructions: Please answer the following questions as they relate to decisions you make in raising new long-term funds.

1. In raising new funds, your firm

    a. Seeks to maintain a target capital structure by using approximately constant proportions of several types of long-term capital simultaneously. (Answer questions 3 through 9.)

    b. Follows a hierarchy in which the most advantageous sources of funds are exhausted before other sources are used. (Answer questions 2 through 9.)

2. Rank the following sources of long-term funds in order of preference for financing new investments (1 = first choice, 6 = last choice).

Rank:

    a. ____ Internal equity (retained earnings)

    b. ____ External common equity

    c. ____ Straight debt

    d. ____ Convertible debt

    e. ____ Straight preferred stock

    f. ____ Convertible preferred stock

3. Please indicate the relative importance of the following considerations in governing your firm's financing decisions. (On a scale of 1 to 5, where 1 = Unimportant and 5 = Important.)

    a. ____ Maximizing prices of publicly traded securities

    b. ____ Maintaining financial flexibility

    c. ____ Ensuring long-term survivability of the firm

    d. ____ Maintaining financial independence

    e. ____ Maintaining comparability with firms in the industry

    f. ____ Maintaining a high debt rating

    g. ____ Maintaining a predictable source of funds

4. Approximately what percent of the time would you estimate that your firm's outstanding securities are priced fairly by the market?

    a. More than 80 percent of the time

    b. Between 50 and 80 percent of the time

    c. Less than 50 percent of the time

5. Given an attractive new growth opportunity that could not be taken without departing from your target capital structure or financing hierarchy, cutting the dividend, or selling off other assets, what action is your firm most likely to take?

    a. Forgo the growth opportunity.

    b. Deviate from the target capital structure or financing hierarchy.

    c. Cut the dividend.

    d. Sell off other assets.

6. Indicate the relative importance of the following factors in governing your firm's financing decisions. (On a scale of 1 to 5, where 1 = Unimportant and 5 = Important.)

    a. ____ The corporate tax rate

    b. ____ Personal tax rates of your debt and equity holders

    c. ____ The level of depreciation and other non-debt tax shields

    d. ____ Costs of bankruptcy

    e. ____ Voting control

    f. ____ Restrictive covenants of senior securities

    g. ____ Projected cash flow or earnings from the assets to be financed

    h. ____ Riskiness of the assets to be financed

    i. ____ Avoiding dilution of common shareholders' claims

    j. ____ Avoiding mispricings of securities to be issued

    k. ____ Correcting mispricings of outstanding securities

7. Other things held constant, the Tax Reform Act of 1986 will have the effect of

    a. Increasing your firm's after-tax cash flows.

    b. Decreasing your firm's after-tax cash flows.

    c. Leaving your firm's after-tax cash flows unchanged.

8. As a result of the Tax Reform Act of 1986, your firm is likely to

    a. Increase the proportion of debt used in the capital structure.

    b. Decrease the proportion of debt used in the capital structure.

    c. Leave the proportion of debt used in the capital structure unchanged.

9. If your firm does not plan to alter the proportion of debt currently used in its capital structure as a result of the Tax Reform Act of 1986, which of the following explanations most closely corresponds to your reasons?

    a. Tax laws could be changed again soon.

    b. Changes have already been made in the capital structure in anticipation of the Tax Reform Act of 1986.

    c. The precise implications of the Tax Reform Act of 1986 are not clear.

    d. Other factors are more important than tax laws in determining your capital structure.

Discussion Questions

1. Describe the pecking order theory of capital structure. What evidence supports this concept?

2. How should bankruptcy costs impact the capital structure decision?

3. What did managers indicate with respect to the tax-related aspects of capital structure?

4. Describe a situation in which a firm could not simultaneously make decisions reflecting its perceived optimal investment policy, optimal dividend policy, and optimal capital structure policy. According to the study, which so-called optimal area will have the most flexibility in the opinion of the firm's managers? Is this reasonable?

*Merton H. Miller and Franco Modigliani**

Dividend Policy, Growth, and the Valuation of Shares

The issue at hand was, and is, can a corporation adopt a dividend policy, such as high or low pay-out, or dividend stabilization, that will maximize the present value of the shares? It was generally assumed that such was the case until this article was published in 1961. Professors Miller and Modigliani eloquently argue that, while the value of the stock is the present value of future dividends, nevertheless, dividend policy *does not influence value.*

This article, along with their earlier one on capital structure, set a new standard for the investigation of financial management issues. Miller and Modigliani on the financial management side and Markowitz and Sharpe and others on the portfolio side, along with the arrival of general-use digital computers and financial data bases, initiated a revolution in academic finance in the 1960s and 1970s.

The effect of a firm's dividend policy on the current price of its shares is a matter of considerable importance, not only to the corporate officials who must set the policy, but to investors planning portfolios and to economists seeking to understand and appraise the functioning of the capital markets. Do companies with generous distribution policies consistently sell at a premium over those with niggardly payouts? Is the reverse ever true? If so, under what conditions? Is there an optimum payout ratio or range of ratios that maximizes the current worth of the shares?

Although these questions of fact have been the subject of many empirical studies in recent years, no consensus has yet been achieved. One reason appears to be the absence in the literature of a complete and reasonably rigorous statement of those parts of the economic theory of valuation bearing directly on the matter of dividend policy. Lacking such a statement, investigators have not yet been able to frame their tests with sufficient precision to distinguish adequately between the various contending hypotheses. Nor have they been able to give a convincing explanation of what their test results do imply about the underlying process of valuation.

Source: Reprinted with permission from Merton H. Miller, "Dividend Policy, Growth, and Valuation of Shares," *Journal of Business* (October 1961), pp. 411–433. Merton Miller is the Robert R. McCormick Distinguished Service Professor of Finance at the Graduate School of Business at the University of Chicago. Franco Modigliani is Institute Professor Emeritus, M.I.T.

In the hope that it may help to overcome these obstacles to effective empirical testing, this paper will attempt to fill the existing gap in the theoretical literature on valuation. We shall begin, in Section I, by examining the effects of differences in dividend policy on the current price of shares in an ideal economy characterized by perfect capital markets, rational behavior, and perfect certainty. Still within this convenient analytical framework we shall go on in Sections II and III to consider certain closely related issues that appear to have been responsible for considerable misunderstanding of the role of dividend policy. In particular, Section II will focus on the long-standing debate about what investors "really" capitalize when they buy shares, and Section III on the much mooted relations between price, the rate of growth of profits, and the rate of growth of dividends per share. Once these fundamentals have been established, we shall proceed in Section IV to drop the assumption of certainty and to see the extent to which the earlier conclusions about dividend policy must be modified. Finally, in Section V, we shall briefly examine the implications for the dividend policy problem of certain kinds of market imperfections.

I. Effect of Dividend Policy with Perfect Markets, Rational Behavior, and Perfect Certainty

The Meaning of the Basic Assumptions

Although the terms "perfect markets," "rational behavior," and "perfect certainty" are widely used throughout economic theory, it may be helpful to start by spelling out the precise meaning of these assumptions in the present context.

1. In "perfect capital markets," no buyer or seller (or issuer) of securities is large enough for his transactions to have an appreciable impact on the then ruling price. All traders have equal and costless access to information about the ruling price and about all other relevant characteristics of shares (to be detailed specifically later). No brokerage fees, transfer taxes, or other transaction costs are incurred when securities are bought, sold, or issued, and there are no tax differentials either between distributed and undistributed profits or between dividends and capital gains.

2. "Rational behavior" means that investors always prefer more wealth to less and are indifferent as to whether a given increment to their wealth takes the form of cash payments or an increase in the market value of their holdings of shares.

3. "Perfect certainty" implies complete assurance on the part of every investor as to the future investment program and the future profits of every corporation. Because of this assurance, there is, among other things, no need to distinguish between stocks and bonds as sources of funds at this stage of the analysis. We can, therefore, proceed as if there were only a single type of financial instrument which, for convenience, we shall refer to as shares of stock.

The Fundamental Principle of Valuation

Under these assumptions the valuation of all shares would be governed by the following fundamental principle: the price of each share must be such that the rate of return (dividends plus capital gains per dollar invested) on every share will be the same throughout the market over any given interval of time. That is, if we let

$$d_j(t) = \text{dividends per share paid by firm } j \text{ during period } t$$

$$p_j(t) = \text{the price (ex any dividend in } t-1 \text{) of a share in firm } j \text{ at the start of period } t,$$

we must have

$$\frac{d_j(t) + p_j(t+1) - p_j(t)}{p_j(t)} = \rho(t) \text{ independent of } j; \tag{1}$$

or, equivalently,

$$p_j(t) = \frac{1}{1 + \rho(t)} \left[d_j(t) + p_j(t+1) \right] \tag{2}$$

for each j and for all t. Otherwise, holders of low-return (high-priced) shares could increase their terminal wealth by selling these shares and investing the proceeds in shares offering a higher rate of return. This process would tend to drive down the prices of the low-return shares and drive up the prices of high-return shares until the differential in rates of return had been eliminated.

The Effect of Dividend Policy

The implications of this principle for our problem of dividend policy can be seen somewhat more easily if equation (2) is restated in terms of the value of the enterprise as a whole rather than in terms of the value of an individual share. Dropping the firm subscript j since this will lead to no ambiguity in the present context and letting

$$n(t) = \text{the number of shares of record at the start of } t$$

$$m(t+1) = \text{the number of new shares (if any) sold during } t \text{ at the ex dividend closing price } p(t+1), \text{ so that}$$

$$n(t+1) = n(t) + m(t+1)$$

$$V(t) = n(t)\, p(t) = \text{the total value of the enterprise and}$$

$$D(t) = n(t)\, d(t) = \text{the total dividends paid during } t \text{ to holders of record at the start of } t,$$

we can rewrite (2)

$$\begin{aligned} V(t) &= \frac{1}{1 + \rho(t)} \left[D(t) + n(t)\, p(t+1) \right] \\ &= \frac{1}{1 + \rho(t)} \left[D(t) + V(t+1) - m(t+1)\, p(t+1) \right]. \end{aligned} \tag{3}$$

The advantage of restating the fundamental rule in this form is that it brings into sharper focus the three possible routes by which current dividends might affect the current market value of the firm $V(t)$, or equivalently the price of its individual shares, $p(t)$. Current dividends will clearly affect $V(t)$ via the first term in the bracket, $D(t)$. In principle, current dividends might also affect $V(t)$

indirectly via the second term, $V(t + 1)$, the new ex dividend market value. Since $V(t + 1)$ must depend only on future and not on past events, such could be the case, however, only if both (a) $V(t + 1)$ were a function of future dividend policy and (b) the current distribution $D(t)$ served to convey some otherwise unavailable information as to what that future dividend policy would be. The first possibility being the relevant one from the standpoint of assessing the effects of dividend policy, it will clarify matters to assume, provisionally, that the future dividend policy of the firm is known and given for $t + 1$ and all subsequent periods and is independent of the actual dividend decision in t. Then $V(t + 1)$ will also be independent of the current dividend decision, though it may very well be affected by $D(t + 1)$ and all subsequent distributions. Finally, current dividends can influence $V(t)$ through the third term, $-m(t + 1)\, p(t + 1)$, the value of new shares sold to outsiders during the period. For the higher the dividend payout in any period, the more the new capital that must be raised from external sources to maintain any desired level of investment.

The fact that the dividend decision affects price not in one but in these two conflicting ways—directly via $D(t)$ and inversely via $-m(t)\, p(t + 1)$—is, of course, precisely why one speaks of there being a dividend policy *problem*. If the firm raises its dividend in t, given its investment decision, will the increase in the cash payments to the current holders be more or less than enough to offset their lower share of the terminal value? Which is the better strategy for the firm in financing the investment: to reduce dividends and rely on retained earnings or to raise dividends but float more new shares?

In our ideal world at least these and related questions can be simply and immediately answered: The two dividend effects must always exactly cancel out so that the payout policy to be followed in t will have *no* effect on the price at t.

We need only express $m(t + 1) \cdot p(t + 1)$ in terms of $D(t)$ to show that such must indeed be the case. Specifically, if $I(t)$ is the given level of the firm's investment or increase in its holding of physical assets in t and if $X(t)$ is the firm's total net profit for the period, we know that the amount of outside capital required will be

$$m(t + 1)\, p(t + 1) = I(t) - [X(t) - D(t)]. \tag{4}$$

Substituting expression (4) into (3), the $D(t)$ cancel and we obtain for the value of the firm as of the start of t

$$
\begin{aligned}
V(t) &\equiv n(t)\, p(t) \\
&= \frac{1}{1 + \rho(t)}\, [X(t) - I(t) + V(t + 1)].
\end{aligned}
\tag{5}
$$

Since $D(t)$ does not appear directly among the arguments and since $X(t)$, $I(t)$, $V(t + 1)$, and $\rho(t)$ are all independent of $D(t)$ (either by their nature or by assumption), it follows that the current value of the firm must be independent of the current dividend decision.

Having established that $V(t)$ is unaffected by the current dividend decision, it is easy to go on to show that $V(t)$ must also be unaffected by any future dividend decisions as well. Such future decisions can influence $V(t)$ only via their effect on $V(t + 1)$. But we can repeat the reasoning above and show that $V(t + 1)$—and hence $V(t)$—is unaffected by dividend policy in $t + 1$; that $V(t + 2)$—and hence $V(t + 1)$ and $V(t)$—is unaffected by dividend policy in $t + 2$; and so on for as far into the future as we care to look. Thus, we may conclude that given a firm's investment policy, the dividend payout policy it chooses to follow will affect neither the current price of its shares nor the total return to its shareholders.

Like many other propositions in economics, the irrelevance of dividend policy, given investment policy, is "obvious, once you think of it." It is, after all, merely one more instance of the general principle that there are no "financial illusions" in a rational and perfect economic environment. Values there are determined solely by "real" considerations—in this case the earning power of the firm's assets and its investment policy—and not by how the fruits of the earning power are "packaged" for distribution.

Obvious as the proposition may be, however, one finds few references to it in the extensive literature on the problem.[1] It is true that the literature abounds with statements that in some "theoretical" sense, dividend policy ought not to count; but either that sense is not clearly specified or, more frequently and especially among economists, it is (wrongly) identified with a situation in which the firm's internal rate of return is the same as the external or market rate of return.[2]

A major source of these and related misunderstandings of the role of the dividend policy has been the fruitless concern and controversy over what investors "really" capitalize when they buy shares. We say fruitless because as we shall now proceed to show, it is actually possible to derive from the basic principle of valuation (1) not merely one, but several valuation formulas, each starting from one of the "classical" views of what is being capitalized by investors. Though differing somewhat in outward appearance, the various formulas can be shown to be equivalent in all essential respects including, of course, their implication that dividend policy is irrelevant. While the controversy itself thus turns out to be an empty one, the different expressions do have some intrinsic interest since, by highlighting different combinations of variables, they provide additional insights into the process of valuation and they open alternative lines of attack on some of the problems of empirical testing.

II. What Does the Market "Really" Capitalize?

In the literature on valuation one can find at least the following four more or less distinct approaches to the valuation of shares: (1) the discounted cash flow approach; (2) the current earnings plus future investment opportunities approach; (3) the stream of dividends approach; and (4) the stream of earnings approach. To demonstrate that these approaches are, in fact, equivalent it will be helpful to begin by first going back to equation (5) and developing from it a valuation formula to serve as a point of reference and comparison. Specifically, if we assume, for simplicity, that the market rate of yield $\rho(t) = \rho$ for all t,[3] then, setting $t = 0$, we can rewrite (5) as

$$V(0) = \frac{1}{1 + \rho} [X(0) - I(0)] + \frac{1}{1 + \rho} V(1). \tag{6}$$

---

[1] Apart from the references to it in our earlier papers, especially [16], the closest approximation seems to be that in Bodenborn [1, p. 492], but even his treatment of the role of dividend policy is not completely explicit. (The numbers in brackets refer to references listed on p. 364.)

[2] See p. 354.

[3] More general formulas in which $\rho(t)$ is allowed to vary with time can always be derived from those presented here merely by substituting the cumbersome product

$$\prod_{\tau=0}^{t} [1 + \rho(\tau)] \text{ for } (1 + \rho)^{t+1}.$$

Since (5) holds for all t, setting $t = 1$ permits us to express $V(1)$ in terms of $V(2)$, which in turn can be expressed in terms of $V(3)$ and so on up to any arbitrary terminal period T. Carrying out these substitutions, we obtain

$$V(0) = \sum_{t=0}^{T-1} \frac{1}{(1 + \rho)^{t+1}} [X(t) - I(t)] + \frac{1}{(1 + \rho)^T} V(T). \tag{7}$$

In general, the remainder term $(1 + \rho)^{-T} \cdot V(T)$ can be expected to approach zero as T approaches infinity[4] so that (7) can be expressed as

$$V(0) = \lim_{T \to \infty} \sum_{t=0}^{T-1} \frac{1}{(1 + \rho)^{t+1}} \times [X(t) - I(t)], \tag{8}$$

which we shall further abbreviate to

$$V(0) = \sum_{t=0}^{\infty} \frac{1}{(1 + \rho)^{t+1}} [X(t) - I(t)]. \tag{9}$$

The Discounted Cash Flow Approach

Consider now the so-called discounted cash flow approach familiar in discussions of capital budgeting. There, in valuing any specific machine we discount at the market rate of interest the stream of cash receipts generated by the machine; plus any scrap or terminal value of the machine; and minus the stream of cash outlays for direct labor, materials, repairs, and capital additions. The same approach, of course, can also be applied to the firm as a whole, which may be thought of in this context as simply a large, composite machine.[5] This approach amounts to defining the value of the firm as

$$V(0) = \sum_{t=0}^{T-1} \frac{1}{(1 + \rho)^{t+1}} \times [\mathcal{R}(t) - \mathcal{O}(t)] + \frac{1}{(1 + \rho)^T} V(T), \tag{10}$$

where $\mathcal{R}(t)$ represents the stream of cash receipts and $\mathcal{O}(t)$ of cash outlays, or, abbreviating, as above, to

$$V(0) = \sum_{t=0}^{\infty} \frac{1}{(1 + \rho)^{t+1}} [\mathcal{R}(t) - \mathcal{O}(t)]. \tag{11}$$

But we also know, by definition, that $[X(t) - I(t)] = [\mathcal{R}(t) - \mathcal{O}(t)]$ since $X(t)$ differs from $\mathcal{R}(t)$ and $I(t)$ differs from $\mathcal{O}(t)$ merely by the "cost of goods sold" (and also by the depreciation expense if we wish to interpret $X(t)$ and $I(t)$ as net rather than gross profits and investment). Hence (11) is formally equivalent to (9), and the discounted cash flow approach is thus seen to be an implication of the valuation principle for perfect markets given by equation (1).

---

[4] The assumption that the remainder vanishes is introduced for the sake of simplicity of exposition only and is in no way essential to the argument. What is essential, of course, is that $V(0)$, i.e., the sum of the two terms in (7), be finite, but this can always be safely assumed in economic analysis. See below, n. 14.

[5] This is, in fact, the approach to valuation normally taken in economic theory when discussing the value of the *assets* of an enterprise, but much more rarely applied, unfortunately, to the value of the liability side. One of the few to apply the approach to the shares as well as the assets is Bodenhorn in [1], who uses it to derive a formula closely similar to (9) above.

The Investment Opportunities Approach

Consider next the approach to valuation which would seem most natural from the standpoint of an investor proposing to buy out and operate some already-going concern. In estimating how much it would be worthwhile to pay for the privilege of operating the firm, the amount of dividends to be paid is clearly not relevant, since the new owner can, within wide limits, make the future dividend stream whatever he pleases. For him the worth of the enterprise, as such, will depend only on: (*a*) the "normal" rate of return he can earn by investing his capital in securities (i.e., the market rate of return); (*b*) the earning power of the physical assets currently held by the firm; and (*c*) the opportunities, if any, that the firm offers for making additional investments in real assets that will yield more than the "normal" (market) rate of return. The latter opportunities, frequently termed the "good will" of the business, may arise, in practice, from any of a number of circumstances (ranging all the way from special locational advantages to patents or other monopolistic advantages).

To see how these opportunities affect the value of the business, assume that in some future period t the firm invests $I(t)$ dollars. Suppose, further, for simplicity, that starting in the period immediately following the investment of the funds, the projects produce net profits at a constant rate of $\rho^*(t)$ per cent of $I(t)$ in each period thereafter.[6] Then the present worth as of t of the (perpetual) stream of profits generated will be $I(t) \rho^*(t)/\rho$, and the "good will" of the projects (i.e., the difference between worth and cost) will be

$$I(t) \frac{\rho^*(t)}{\rho} - I(t) = I(t) \left[\frac{\rho^*(t) - \rho}{\rho} \right].$$

The present worth as of now of this future "good will" is

$$I(t) \left[\frac{\rho^*(t) - \rho}{\rho} \right] (1 + \rho)^{-(t + 1)},$$

and the present value of all such future opportunities is simply the sum

$$\sum_{t = 0}^{\infty} I(t) \frac{\rho^*(t) - \rho}{\rho} (1 + \rho)^{-(t + 1)}.$$

Adding in the present value of the (uniform perpetual) earnings, $X(0)$, on the assets currently held, we get as an expression for the value of the firm

$$V(0) = \frac{X(0)}{\rho} + \sum_{t = 0}^{\infty} I(t) \times \frac{\rho^*(t) - \rho}{\rho} (1 + \rho)^{-(t + 1)}. \tag{12}$$

To show that the same formula can be derived from (9), note first that our definition of $\rho^*(t)$ implies the following relation between the $X(t)$:

$$X(1) = X(0) + \rho^*(0) I(0),$$

---

[6] The assumption that $I(t)$ yields a uniform perpetuity is not restrictive in the present certainty context since it is always possible by means of simple, present-value calculations to find an equivalent uniform perpetuity for any project, whatever the time shape of its actual returns. Note also that $\rho^*(t)$ is the *average* rate of return. If the managers of the firm are behaving rationally, they will, of course, use ρ as their cut-off criterion. In this event we would have $\rho^*(t) \geq \rho$. The formulas remain valid, however, even where $\rho^*(t) < \rho$.

$$X(t) = X(t-1) + \rho^*(t-1)\,I(t-1)$$

and by successive substitution

$$X(t) = X(0) + \sum_{\tau=0}^{t-1} \rho^*(\tau)I(\tau),$$

$$t = 1, 2 \ldots \infty.$$

Substituting the last expression for $X(t)$ in (9) yields

$$V(0) = [X(0) - I(0)]\,(1+\rho)^{-1} + \sum_{t=1}^{\infty}\left[X(0) + \sum_{\tau=0}^{t-1}\rho^*(\tau)I(\tau) - I(t)\right](1+\rho)^{-(t+1)}$$

$$= X(0)\sum_{t=1}^{\infty}(1+\rho)^{-t} - I(0)\,(1+\rho)^{-1} + \sum_{t=1}^{\infty}\left[\sum_{\tau=0}^{t-1}\rho^*(\tau)I(\tau) - I(t)\right]\times(1+\rho)^{-(t+1)}$$

$$= X(0)\sum_{t=1}^{\infty}(1+\rho)^{-t} + \sum_{t=1}^{\infty}\left[\sum_{\tau=0}^{t-1}\rho^*(\tau)I(\tau) - I(t-1)\times(1+\rho)\right](1+\rho)^{-(t+1)}.$$

The first expression is, of course, simply a geometric progression summing to $X(0)/\rho$, which is the first term of (12). To simplify the second expression, note that it can be rewritten as

$$\sum_{t=0}^{\infty} I(t)\left[\rho^*(t)\sum_{\tau=t+2}^{\infty}(1+\rho)^{-\tau} - (1+\rho)^{-(t+1)}\right].$$

Evaluating the summation within the brackets gives

$$\sum_{t=0}^{\infty} I(t)\left[\rho^*(t)\frac{(1+\rho)^{-(t+1)}}{\rho} - (1+\rho)^{-(t+1)}\right] = \sum_{t=0}^{\infty} I(t)\left[\frac{\rho^*(t)-\rho}{\rho}\right](1+\rho)^{-(t+1)},$$

which is precisely the second term of (12).

Formula (12) has a number of revealing features and deserves to be more widely used in discussions of valuation.[7] For one thing, it throws considerable light on the meaning of those much abused terms "growth" and "growth stocks." As can readily be seen from (12), a corporation does not become a "growth stock" with a high price-earnings ratio merely because its assets and earnings are growing over time. To enter the glamor category, it is also necessary that $\rho^*(t) > \rho$. For if $\rho^*(t) = \rho$, then however large the growth in assets may be, the second term in (12) will be zero and the firm's price-earnings ratio would not rise above a humdrum $1/\rho$. The essence of "growth," in short, is not expansion, but the existence of opportunities to invest significant quantities of funds at higher than "normal" rates of return.

Notice also that if $\rho^*(t) < \rho$, investment in real assets by the firm will actually reduce the current price of the shares. This should help to make clear, among other things, why the "cost of capital" to the firm is the same regardless of how the investments are financed or how fast the firm is growing. The function of the cost of capital in capital budgeting is to provide the "cut-off rate" in the sense of the minimum yield that investment projects must promise to be worth undertaking from the point of view of the current owners. Clearly, no proposed project would be in the interest of the

---

[7] A valuation formula analogous to (12) though derived and interpreted in a slightly different way is found in Bodenhorn [1]. Variants of (12) for certain special cases are discussed in Walter [20].

current owners if its yield were expected to be less than ρ since investing in such projects would reduce the value of their shares. In the other direction, every project yielding more than ρ is just as clearly worth undertaking since it will necessarily enhance the value of the enterprise. Hence, the cost of capital or cut-off criterion for investment decisions is simply ρ.[8]

Finally, formula (12) serves to emphasize an important deficiency in many recent statistical studies of the effects of dividend policy (such as Walter [19] or Durand [4, 5]). These studies typically involve fitting regression equations in which price is expressed as some function of current earnings and dividends. A finding that the dividend coefficient is significant—as is usually the case—is then interpreted as a rejection of the hypothesis that dividend policy does not affect valuation.

Even without raising questions of bias in the coefficients,[9] it should be apparent that such a conclusion is unwarranted since formula (12) and the analysis underlying it imply only that dividends will not count given current earnings *and growth potential.* No general prediction is made (or can be made) by the theory about what will happen to the dividend coefficient if the crucial growth term is omitted.[10]

The Stream of Dividends Approach

From the earnings and earnings opportunities approach we turn next to the dividend approach, which has, for some reason, been by far the most popular one in the literature of valuation. This approach too, properly formulated, is an entirely valid one though, of course, not the only valid approach as its more enthusiastic proponents frequently suggest.[11] It does, however, have the disadvantage in contrast with previous approaches of obscuring the role of dividend policy. In particular, uncritical use of the dividend approach has often led to the unwarranted inference that, since the investor is buying dividends and since dividend policy affects the amount of dividends, then dividend policy must also affect the current price.

Properly formulated, the dividend approach defines the current worth of a share as the discounted value of the stream of dividends to be paid on the share in perpetuity. That is

$$p(t) = \sum_{\tau = 0}^{\infty} \frac{d(t + \tau)}{(1 + \rho)^{\tau + 1}} .$$ (13)

---

[8] The same conclusion could also have been reached, of course, by "costing" each particular source of capital funds. That is, since ρ is the going market rate of return on equity, any new shares floated to finance investment must be priced to yield ρ; and withholding funds from the stockholders to finance investment would deprive the holders of the chance to earn ρ on these funds by investing their dividends in other shares. The advantage of thinking in terms of the cost of capital as the cut-off criterion is that it minimizes the danger of confusing "costs" with mere "outlays."

[9] The serious bias problem in tests using current reported earnings as a measure of $X(0)$ was discussed briefly by us in [16].

[10] In suggesting that recent statistical studies have not controlled adequately for growth we do not mean to exempt Gordon in [8] or [9]. It is true that his tests contain an explicit "growth" variable, but it is essentially nothing more than the ratio of retained earnings to book value. This ratio would not in general provide an acceptable approximation to the "growth" variable of (12) in any sample in which firms resorted to external financing. Furthermore, even if by some chance a sample was found in which all firms relied entirely on retained earnings, his tests then could not settle the question of dividend policy. For if all firms financed investment internally (or used external financing only in strict proportion to internal financing as Gordon assumes in [8]), then there would be no way to distinguish between the effects of dividend policy and investment policy.

[11] See, e.g., the classic statement of the position in J. B. Williams [21]. The equivalence of the dividend approach to many of the other standard approaches is noted to our knowledge only in our [16] and, by implication, in Bodenhorn [1].

To see the equivalence between this approach and previous ones, let us first restate (13) in terms of total market value as

$$V(t) = \sum_{\tau=0}^{\infty} \frac{D_t(t+\tau)}{(1+\rho)^{\tau+1}}, \tag{14}$$

where $D_t(t+\tau)$ denotes that portion of the total dividends $D(t+\tau)$ paid during period $t+\tau$ that accrues to the shares of record as of the start of period t (indicated by the subscript). That equation (14) is equivalent to (9) and hence also to (12) is immediately apparent for the special case in which no outside financing is undertaken after period t, for in that case

$$D_t(t+\tau) = D(t+\tau) = X(t+\tau) - I(t+\tau).$$

To allow for outside financing, note that we can rewrite (14) as

$$V(t) = \frac{1}{1+\rho} \left[D_t(t) + \sum_{\tau=1}^{\infty} \frac{D_t(t+\tau)}{(1+\rho)^{\tau}} \right]$$

$$= \frac{1}{1+\rho} \left[D(t) + \sum_{\tau=0}^{\infty} \frac{D_t(t+\tau+1)}{(1+\rho)^{\tau+1}} \right]. \tag{15}$$

The summation term in the last expression can be written as the difference between the stream of dividends accruing to all the shares of record as of $t+1$ and that portion of the stream that will accrue to the shares newly issued in t, that is,

$$\sum_{\tau=0}^{\infty} \frac{D_t(t+\tau+1)}{(1+\rho)^{\tau+1}} = \left(1 - \frac{m(t+1)}{n(t+1)} \right) \times \sum_{\tau=0}^{\infty} \frac{D_{t+1}(t+\tau+1)}{(1+\rho)^{\tau+1}}. \tag{16}$$

But from (14) we know that the second summation in (16) is precisely $V(t+1)$ so that (15) can be reduced to

$$V(t) = \frac{1}{1+\rho} \left[D(t) + \left(1 - \frac{m(t+1)\,p(t+1)}{n(t+1)\,p(t+1)} \right) \times V(t+1) \right]$$

$$= \frac{1}{1+\rho} [D(t) + V(t+1) - m(t+1)\,p(t+1)], \tag{17}$$

which is (3) and which has already been shown to imply both (9) and (12).[12]

There are, of course, other ways in which the equivalence of the dividend approach to the other approaches might have been established, but the method presented has the advantage perhaps of providing some further insight into the reason for the irrelevance of dividend policy. An increase in current dividends, given the firm's investment policy, must necessarily reduce the terminal value of

---

[12] The statement that equations (9), (12), and (14) are equivalent must be qualified to allow for certain pathological extreme cases, fortunately of no real economic significance. An obvious example of such a case is the legendary company that is expected *never* to pay a dividend. If this were literally true, then the value of the firm by (14) would be zero; by (9) it would be zero (or possibly negative since zero dividends rule out $X(t) > I(t)$ but not $X(t) < I(t)$); while by (12) the value might still be positive. What is involved here, of course, is nothing more than a discontinuity at zero since the value under (14) and (9) would be positive and the equivalence of both with (12) would hold if that value were also positive as long as there was some period T, however far in the future, beyond which the firm would pay out $\varepsilon > 0$ percent of its earnings, however small the value of ε.

existing shares because the part of the future dividend stream that would otherwise have accrued to the existing shares must be diverted to attract the outside capital from which, in effect, the higher current dividends are paid. Under our basic assumptions, however, ρ must be the same for all investors, new as well as old. Consequently the market value of the dividends diverted to the outsiders, which is both the value of their contribution and the reduction in terminal value of the existing shares, must always be precisely the same as the increase in current dividends.

The Stream of Earnings Approach

Contrary to widely held views, it is also possible to develop a meaningful and consistent approach to valuation running in terms of the stream of earnings generated by the corporation rather than of the dividend distributions actually made to the shareholders. Unfortunately, it is also extremely easy to misstate or misinterpret the earnings approach as would be the case if the value of the firm were to be defined as simply the discounted sum of future total earnings.[13] The trouble with such a definition is not, as is often suggested, that it overlooks the fact that the corporation is a separate entity and that these profits cannot freely be withdrawn by the shareholders; but rather that it neglects the fact that additional capital must be acquired at some cost to maintain the future earnings stream at its specified level. The capital to be raised in any future period is, of course, $I(t)$ and its opportunity cost, no matter how financed, is ρ percent per period thereafter. Hence, the current value of the firm under the earnings approach must be stated as

$$V(0) = \sum_{t=0}^{\infty} \frac{1}{(1+\rho)^{t+1}} \times [X(t) - \sum_{\tau=0}^{t} \rho I(\tau)]. \tag{18}$$

That this version of the earnings approach is indeed consistent with our basic assumptions and equivalent to the previous approaches can be seen by regrouping terms and rewriting equation (18) as

$$V(0) = \sum_{t=0}^{\infty} \frac{1}{(1+\rho)^{t+1}} X(t) - \sum_{t=0}^{\infty} \left(\sum_{\tau=t}^{\infty} \frac{\rho I(t)}{(1+\rho)^{\tau+1}} \right)$$
$$= \sum_{t=0}^{\infty} \frac{1}{(1+\rho)^{\tau+1}} X(t) - \sum_{t=0}^{\infty} \frac{1}{(1+\rho)^{\tau+1}} \times \left(\sum_{\tau=0}^{\infty} \frac{\rho I(t)}{(1+\rho)^{\tau+1}} \right). \tag{19}$$

Since the last inclosed summation reduces simply to $I(t)$, the expression (19) in turn reduces to simply

$$V(0) = \sum_{t=0}^{\infty} \frac{1}{(1+\rho)^{\tau+1}} [X(t) - I(t)], \tag{20}$$

which is precisely our earlier equation (9).

Note that the version of the earnings approach presented here does not depend for its validity upon any special assumptions about the time shape of the stream of total profits or the stream of dividends per share. Clearly, however, the time paths of the two streams are closely related to each other (via financial policy) and to the stream of returns derived by holders of the shares. Since these relations are of some interest in their own right and since misunderstandings about them have

---

[13] In fairness, we should point out that there is no one, to our knowledge, who has seriously advanced this view. It is a view whose main function seems to be to serve as a "straw man" to be demolished by those supporting the dividend view. See, e.g., Gordon [9, esp. pp. 102–3]. Other writers take as the supposed earnings counter-view to the dividend approach not a relation running in terms of the *stream* of earnings but simply the proposition that price is proportional to current earnings, i.e., $V(0) = X(0)/\rho$. The probable origins of this widespread misconception about the earnings approach are discussed further on p. 355.

contributed to the confusion over the role of dividend policy, it may be worthwhile to examine them briefly before moving on to relax the basic assumptions.

III. Earnings, Dividends, and Growth Rates

The Convenient Case of Constant Growth Rates

The relation between the stream of earnings of the firm and the stream of dividends and of returns to the stockholders can be brought out most clearly by specializing (12) to the case in which investment opportunities are such as to generate a constant rate of growth of profits in perpetuity. Admittedly, this case has little empirical significance, but it is convenient for illustrative purposes and has received much attention in the literature.

Specifically, suppose that in each period t the firm has the opportunity to invest in real assets a sum $I(t)$ that is k percent as large as its total earnings for the period; and that this investment produces a perpetual yield of ρ^* beginning with the next period. Then, by definition

$$
\begin{aligned}
X(t) &= X(t-1) + \rho^* I(t-1) \\
&= X(t-1)\left[1 + k\rho^*\right] \\
&= X(0)\left[1 + k\rho^*\right]^t
\end{aligned}
\tag{21}
$$

and $k\rho^*$ is the (constant) rate of growth of total earnings. Substituting from (21) into (12) for $I(t)$ we obtain

$$
\begin{aligned}
V(0) &= \frac{X(0)}{\rho} + \sum_{t=0}^{\infty}\left(\frac{\rho^*-\rho}{\rho}\right)\times kX(0)\left[1+k\rho^*\right]^t\times(1+\rho)^{-(t+1)} \\
&= \frac{X(0)}{\rho}\left[1 + \frac{k(\rho^*-\rho)}{1+\rho}\times\sum_{t=0}^{\infty}\left(\frac{1+k\rho^*}{1+\rho}\right)^t\right].
\end{aligned}
\tag{22}
$$

Evaluating the infinite sum and simplifying, we finally obtain[14]

$$
V(0) = \frac{X(0)}{\rho}\left[1 + \frac{k(\rho^*-\rho)}{\rho-k\rho^*}\right] = \frac{X(0)(1-k)}{\rho-k\rho^*},
\tag{23}
$$

which expresses the value of the firm as a function of its current earnings, the rate of growth of earnings, the internal rate of return, and the market rate of return.[15] Note that (23) holds not just for period 0, but for every t. Hence if $X(t)$ is growing at the rate $k\rho^*$, it follows that the value of the enterprise, $V(t)$, also grows at that rate.

[14] One advantage of the specialization (23) is that it makes it easy to see what is really involved in the assumption here and throughout the paper that the $V(0)$ given by any of our summation formulas is necessarily finite (cf. above, n. 4). In terms of (23) the condition is clearly $k\rho^* < \rho$, i.e., that the rate of growth of the firm be less than market rate of discount. Although the case of (perpetual) growth rates greater than the discount factor is the much-discussed "growth stock praradox" (e.g. [6]), it has no real economic significance as we pointed out in [16, esp. n. 17, p. 664]. This will be apparent when one recalls that the discount rate ρ, though treated as a constant in partial equilibrium (relative price) analysis of the kind presented here, is actually a variable from the standpoint of the system as a whole. That is, if the assumption of finite value for all shares did not hold, because for some shares $k\rho^*$ was (perpetually) greater than ρ, then ρ would necessarily rise until an overall equilibrium in the capital markets had been restored.

[15] An interesting and more realistic variant of (22), which also has a number of convenient features from the standpoint of developing empirical tests, can be obtained by assuming that the special investment opportunities are available not in perpetuity but
(*continued on p. 353*)

The Growth of Dividends and the Growth of Total Profits

Given that total earnings (and the total value of the firm) are growing at the rate $k\rho^*$, what is the rate of growth of dividends per share and of the price per share? Clearly, the answer will vary depending on whether or not the firm is paying out a high percentage of its earnings and thus relying heavily on outside financing. We can show the nature of this dependence explicitly by making use of the fact that, whatever the rate of growth of dividends per share, the present value of the firm by the dividend approach must be the same as by the earnings approach. Thus let

g = the rate of growth of dividends per share or, what amounts to the same thing, the rate of growth of dividends accruing to the shares of the current holders (i.e., $D_0(t) = D_0(0)[1 + g]^t$;

k_τ = the fraction of total profits retained in each period (so that $D(t) = X(0)[1 - k_\tau]$);

$k_e = k - k_\tau$ = the amount of external capital raised per period, expressed as a fraction of profits in the period.

Then the present value of the stream of dividends to the original owners will be

$$D_0(0) \sum_{t=0}^{\infty} \frac{(1 + g)^t}{(1 + \rho)^{t+1}} = \frac{D(0)}{\rho - g}$$
$$= \frac{X(0)[1 - k_\tau]}{\rho - g}. \tag{24}$$

By virtue of the dividend approach we know that (24) must be equal to $V(0)$. If, therefore, we equate it to the right-hand side of (23), we obtain

$$\frac{X(0)[1 - k_\tau]}{\rho - g} = \frac{X(0)[1 - (k_\tau + k_e)]}{\rho - k\rho^*}$$

---

[15] *(continued from p. 352)*

only over some finite interval of T periods. To exhibit the value of the firm for this case, we need only replace the infinite summation in (22) with a summation running from $t = 0$ to $t = T - 1$. Evaluating the resulting expression, we obtain

$$V(0) = \frac{X(0)}{\rho} \left\{ 1 + \frac{k(\rho^* - \rho)}{\rho - k\rho^*} \times \left[1 - \left(\frac{1 + k\rho^*}{1 + \rho} \right)^T \right] \right\}. \tag{22a}$$

Note that (22a) holds even if $k\rho^* > \rho$, so that the so-called growth paradox disappears altogether. If, as we should generally expect, $(1 + k\rho^*)/(1 + \rho)$ is close to one, and if T is not too large, the right-hand side of (22a) admits a very convenient approximation. In this case, in fact, we can write

$$\left[\frac{1 + k\rho^*}{1 + \rho} \right]^T \cong 1 + T(k\rho^* - \rho)$$

the approximation holding, if, as we should expect, $(1 + k\rho^*)$ and $(1 + \rho)$ are both close to unity. Substituting this approximation into (22a), and simplifying, finally yields

$$V(0) \cong \frac{X(0)}{\rho} \left[1 + \frac{k(\rho^* - \rho)}{\rho - k\rho^*} \times T(\rho - k\rho^*) \right]$$
$$= \left[\frac{X(0)}{\rho} + kX(0) \times \left(\frac{\rho^* - \rho}{\rho} \right) T \right]. \tag{22b}$$

The common sense of (22b) is easy to see. The current value of a firm is given by the value of the earning power of the currently held assets plus the market value of the special earning opportunity multiplied by the number of years for which it is expected to last.

from which it follows that the rate of growth of dividends per share and the rate of growth of the price of a share must be[16]

$$g = k\rho^* \frac{1 - k_\tau}{1 - k} - k_e\rho \frac{1}{1 - k} . \tag{25}$$

Notice that in the extreme case in which all financing is internal ($k_e = 0$ and $k = k_\tau$), the second term drops out and the first becomes simply $k\rho^*$. Hence the growth rate of dividends in that special case is exactly the same as that of total profits and total value and is proportional to the rate of retention k_τ. In all other cases, g is necessarily less than $k\rho^*$ and may even be negative, despite a positive $k\rho^*$, if $\rho^* < \rho$ and if the firm pays out a large fraction of its income in dividends. In the other direction, we see from (25) that even if a firm is a "growth" corporation ($\rho^* > \rho$), then the stream of dividends and price per share must grow over time even though $k_\tau = 0$, that is, even though it pays off *all* its earnings in dividends.

The relation between the growth rate of the firm and the growth rate of dividends under various dividend policies is illustrated graphically in Figure 1, in which for maximum clarity the natural logarithm of profits and dividends have been plotted against time.[17]

Line A shows the total earnings of the firm growing through time at the constant rate $k\rho^*$, the slope of A. Line B shows the growth of (1) the stream of total earnings minus capital outlays and (2) the stream of dividends to the original owners (or dividends per share) in the special case in which all financing is internal. The slope of B is, of course, the same as that of A, and the (constant) difference between the curves is simply $\ln(1 - k)$, the ratio of dividends to profits. Line C shows the growth of dividends per share when the firm uses both internal and external financing. As compared with the pure retention case, the line starts higher but grows more slowly at the rate g given by (25). The higher the payout policy, the higher the starting position and the slower the growth up to the other limiting case of complete external financing, Line D, which starts at $\ln X(0)$ and grows at a rate of $(k/1 - k) \cdot (\rho^* - \rho)$.

The Special Case of Exclusively Internal Financing

As noted above, the growth rate of dividends per share is not the same as the growth rate of the firm except in the special case in which all financing is internal. This is merely one of a number of pecu-

---

[16] That g is the rate of price increase per share as well as the rate of growth of dividends per share follows from the fact that by (13) and the definition of g

$$
\begin{aligned}
p(t) &= \sum_{\tau=0}^{\infty} \frac{d(t + \tau)}{(1 + \rho)^{\tau+1}} \\
&= \sum_{\tau=0}^{\infty} \frac{d(0)[1 + g]^{t+\tau}}{(1 + \rho)^{\tau+1}} \\
&= (1 + g)^t \sum_{\tau=0}^{\infty} \frac{d(\tau)}{(1 + \rho)^{\tau+1}} \\
&= p(0)[1 + g]^t.
\end{aligned}
$$

[17] That is, we replace each discrete compounding expression such as $X(t) = X(0)[1 + k\rho^*]^t$ with its counterpart under continuous discounting $X(t) = X(0)_e^{k\rho^* t}$, which, of course, yields the convenient linear relation in $X(t) = \ln X(0) + k\rho^* t$.

Figure 1   Growth of Dividends per Share in Relation to Growth in Total Earnings

A. Total earnings: $\ln X(t) = \ln X(0) + k\rho^* t$;

B. Total earnings minus capital invested: $\ln [X(t) - I(t)] = \ln X(0)[1 - k] + k\rho^* t$;
   Dividends per share (all financing internal): $\ln D_o(t) = \ln D(0) + gt = \ln X(0)[1 - k] + k\rho^* t$;

C. Dividends per share (some financing external): $\ln D_o(t) = \ln D(0) + gt$;

D. Dividends per share (all financing external): $\ln D_o(t) = \ln X(0) + (k/1 - k)(\rho^* - \rho)]t$.

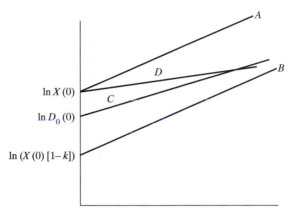

liarities of this special case on which, unfortunately, many writers have based their entire analysis. The reason for the preoccupation with this special case is far from clear to us. Certainly no one would suggest that it is the only empirically relevant case. Even if the case were in fact the most common, the theorist would still be under an obligation to consider alternative assumptions. We suspect that in the last analysis, the popularity of the internal financing model will be found to reflect little more than its ease of manipulation combined with the failure to push the analysis far enough to disclose how special and how treacherous a case it really is.

In particular, concentration on this special case appears to be largely responsible for the widely held view that, even under perfect capital markets, there is an optimum dividend policy for the firm that depends on the internal rate of return. Such a conclusion is almost inevitable if one works exclusively with the assumption, explicit or implicit, that funds for investment come *only* from retained earnings. For in that case *dividend policy* is indistinguishable from *investment policy;* and there *is* an optimal investment policy which does in general depend on the rate of return.

Notice also from (23) that if $\rho^* = \rho$ and $k = k_r$, the term $[1 - k_r]$ can be canceled from both the numerator and the denominator. The value of the firm becomes simply $X(0)/\rho$, the capitalized value of current earnings. Lacking a standard model for valuation more general than the retained earnings case, it has been all too easy for many to conclude that this dropping out of the payout ratio $[1 - k_r]$ when $\rho^* = \rho$ must be what is meant by the irrelevance of dividend policy and that $V(0) = X(0)/\rho$ must constitute the "earnings" approach.

Still another example of the pitfalls in basing arguments on this special case is provided by the recent and extensive work on valuation by M. Gordon.[18] Gordon argues, in essence, that because of increasing uncertainty the discount rate $\hat{\rho}(t)$ applied by an investor to a future dividend payment will rise with t, where t denotes not a specific date but rather the distance from the period in which the investor performs the discounting.[19] Hence, when we use a single uniform discount rate ρ as in (22) or (23), this rate should be thought of as really an average of the "true" rates $\hat{\rho}(t)$, each weighted by the size of the expected dividend payment at time t. If the dividend stream is growing exponentially, then such a weighted average ρ would, of course, be higher the greater the rate of growth of dividends g since the greater will then be the portion of the dividend stream arising in the distant as opposed to the near future. But if all financing is assumed to be internal, then $g = k_r\rho^*$ so that given ρ^*, the weighted average discount factor ρ will be an increasing function of the rate of retention k_r, which would run counter to our conclusion that dividend policy has no effect on the current value of the firm or its cost of capital.

For all its ingenuity, however, and its seeming foundation in uncertainty, the argument clearly suffers fundamentally from the typical confounding of dividend policy with investment policy that so frequently accompanies use of the internal financing model. Had Gordon not confined his attention to this special case (or its equivalent variants), he would have seen that while a change in dividend policy will necessarily affect the size of the expected dividend payment on the share in any future period, it need not, in the general case, affect either the size of the *total* return that the investor expects during that period or the degree of uncertainty attaching to that total return. As should be abundantly clear by now, a change in dividend policy, given investment policy, implies a change only in the distribution of the total return in any period as between dividends and capital gains. If investors behave rationally, such a change cannot affect market valuations. Indeed, if they valued shares according to the Gordon approach and thus paid a premium for higher payout ratios, then holders of the low payout shares would actually realize consistently higher returns on their investment over any stated interval of time.[20]

Corporate Earnings and Investor Returns

Knowing the relation of g to $k\rho^*$, we can answer a question of considerable interest to economic theorists, namely: What is the precise relation between the earnings of the corporation in any period $X(t)$ and the total return to the owners of the stock during that period?[21] If we let $G_t(t)$ be the capital gains to the owners during t, we know that

---

[18] See esp. [8]. Gordon's views represent the most explicit and sophisticated formulation of what might be called the "bird-in-the-hand" fallacy. For other, less elaborate, statements of essentially the same position see, among others, Graham and Dodd [11, p. 443] and Clendenin and Van Cleave [3].

[19] We use the notation $\hat{\rho}(t)$ to avoid any confusion between Gordon's purely subjective discount rate and the objective, market-given yields $\rho(t)$ in Section I. To attempt to derive valuation formulas under uncertainty from these purely subjective discount factors involves, of course, an error essentially analogous to that of attempting to develop the certainty formulas from "marginal rates of time preference" rather than objective market opportunities.

[20] This is not to deny that growth stocks (in our sense) may well be "riskier" than non-growth stocks. But to the extent that this is true, it will be due to the possibly greater uncertainty attaching to the size and duration of future growth opportunities and hence to the size of the future stream of total returns quite apart from any questions of dividend policy.

[21] Note also that the above analysis enables us to deal very easily with the familiar issue of whether a firm's cost of equity capital is measured by its earnings/price ratio or by its dividend/price ratio. Clearly, the answer is that it is measured by neither, except under very special circumstances. For from (23) we have for the earnings/price ratio

(*continued on p. 357*)

$$D_r(t) + G_r(t) = X(t) \times (1 - k_r) + gV(t) \tag{26}$$

since the rate of growth of price is the same as that of dividends per share. Using (25) and (26) to substitute for g and $V(t)$ and simplifying, we find that

$$D_r(t) + G_r(t) = X(t) \left[\frac{\rho(1 - k)}{\rho - k\rho^*} \right]. \tag{27}$$

The relation between the investors' return and the corporation's profits is thus seen to depend entirely on the relation between ρ^* and ρ. If $\rho^* = \rho$ (i.e., the firm has no special "growth" opportunities), then the expression in brackets becomes 1 and the investor returns are precisely the same as the corporate profits. If $\rho^* < \rho$, however, the investors' return will be less than the corporate earnings; and, in the case of growth corporations the investors' return will actually be greater than the flow of corporate profits over the interval.[22]

Some Implications for Constructing Empirical Tests

Finally, the fact that we have two different (though not independent) measures of growth in $k\rho^*$ and g and two corresponding families of valuation formulas means, among other things, that we can proceed by either of two routes in empirical studies of valuation. We can follow the standard practice of the security analyst and think in terms of price per share, dividends per share, and the rate of

---

[21] (*continued from p. 356*)

$$\frac{X(0)}{V(0)} = \frac{\rho - k\rho^*}{1 - k},$$

which is equal to the cost of capital ρ, only if the firm has no growth potential (i.e., $\rho^* = \rho$). And from (24) we have for the dividend/price ratio

$$\frac{D(0)}{V(0)} = \rho - g,$$

which is equal to ρ only when $g = 0$; i.e., from (25), either when $k = 0$; or, if $k > 0$, when $\rho^* < \rho$ and the amount of external financing is precisely

$$k_e = \frac{\rho^*}{\rho} k[1 - k_r],$$

so that the gain from the retention of earnings exactly offsets the loss that would otherwise be occasioned by the unprofitable investment.

[22] The above relation between earnings per share and dividends plus capital gains also means that there will be a systematic relation between retained earnings and capital gains. The "marginal" relation is easy to see and is always precisely one for one regardless of growth or financial policy. That is, taking a dollar away from dividends and adding it to retained earnings (all other things equal) means an increase in capital gains of one dollar (or a reduction in capital loss of one dollar). The "average" relation is somewhat more complex. From (26) and (27) we can see that

$$G_r(t) = k_r X(t) + kX(t) \frac{\rho^* - \rho}{\rho - k\rho^*}.$$

Hence, if $\rho^* = \rho$ the total capital gain received will be exactly the same as the total retained earnings per share. For growth corporations, however, the capital gain will always be greater than the retained earnings (and there will be a capital gain of

$$kX(t) \left[\frac{\rho^* - \rho}{\rho - k\rho^*} \right]$$

even when all earnings are paid out). For non-growth corporations the relation between gain and retentions is reversed. Note also that the absolute difference between the total capital gain and the total retained earnings is a constant (given ρ, k and ρ^*) unaffected by dividend policy. Hence the *ratio* of capital gain to retained earnings will vary directly with the payout ratio for growth corporations (and vice versa for non-growth corporations). This means, among other things, that it is dangerous to attempt to draw inferences about the relative growth potential or relative managerial efficiency of corporations solely on the basis of the ratio of capital gains to retained earnings (cf. Harkavy [12, esp. pp. 289–94]).

growth of dividends per share; or we can think in terms of the total value of the enterprise, total earnings, and the rate of growth of total earnings. Our own preference happens to be for the second approach primarily because certain additional variables of interest—such as dividend policy, leverage, and size of firm—can be incorporated more easily and meaningfully into test equations in which the growth terms is the growth of total earnings. But this can wait. For present purposes, the thing to be stressed is simply that two approaches, properly carried through, are in no sense *opposing* views of the valuation process, but rather equivalent views, with the choice between them largely a matter of taste and convenience.

IV. The Effects of Dividend Policy under Uncertainty

Uncertainty and the General Theory of Valuation

In turning now from the ideal world of certainty to one of uncertainty, our first step, alas, must be to jettison the fundamental valuation principle as given, say, in our equation (3)

$$V(t) = \frac{1}{1 + \rho(t)} [D(t) + n(t)p(t + 1)]$$

and from which the irrelevance proposition as well as all the subsequent valuation formulas in Sections II and III were derived. For the terms in the bracket can no longer be regarded as given numbers, but must be recognized as "random variables" from the point of view of the investor as of the start of period t. Nor is it at all clear what meaning can be attached to the discount factor $1/[1 + \rho(t)]$ since what is being discounted is not a given return, but at best only a probability distribution of possible returns. We can, of course, delude ourselves into thinking that we are preserving equation (3) by the simple and popular expedient of drawing a bar over each term and referring to it thereafter as the mathematical expectation of the random variable. But, except for the trivial case of universal linear utility functions, we know that $V(t)$ would also be affected, and materially so, by the higher order moments of the distribution of returns. Hence there is no reason to believe that the discount factor for expected values, $1/[1 + \rho(t)]$, would in fact be the same for any two firms chosen arbitrarily, not to mention that the expected values themselves may well be different for different investors.

All this is not to say, of course, that there are insuperable difficulties in the way of developing a testable theory of rational market valuation under uncertainty.[23] On the contrary, our investigations of the problem to date have convinced us that it is indeed possible to construct such a theory—though the construction, as can well be imagined, is a fairly complex and space-consuming task. Fortunately, however, this task need not be undertaken in this paper, which is concerned primarily with the effects of dividend policy on market valuation. For even without a full-fledged theory of what *does* determine market value under uncertainty we can show that dividend policy at least is *not* one of the determinants. To establish this particular generalization of the previous certainty results we need only invoke a corresponding generalization of the original postulate of rational behavior to allow for the fact that, under uncertainty, choices depend on expectations as well as tastes.

---

[23] Nor does it mean that all the previous certainty analysis has no relevance whatever in the presence of uncertainty. There are many issues, such as those discussed in Sections I and II, that really relate only to what has been called the pure "futurity" component in valuation. Here, the valuation formulas can still be extremely useful in maintaining the internal consistency of the reasoning and in suggesting (or criticizing) empirical tests of certain classes of hypotheses about valuation, even though the formulas themselves cannot be used to grind out precise numerical values for specific real-world shares.

"Imputed Rationality" and "Symmetric Market Rationality"

This generalization can be formulated in two steps as follows. First, we shall say that an individual trader "imputes rationality to the market" or satisfies the postulate of "imputed rationality" if, in forming expectations, he assumes that every other trader in the market is (*a*) rational in the previous sense of preferring more wealth to less regardless of the form an increment in wealth may take, and (*b*) imputes rationality to all other traders. Second, we shall say that a market as a whole satisfies the postulate of "symmetric market rationality" if every trader both behaves rationally and imputes rationality to the market.[24]

Notice that this postulate of symmetric market rationality differs from the usual postulate of rational behavior in several important respects. In the first place, the new postulate covers not only the choice behavior of individuals but also their expectations of the choice behavior of others. Second, the postulate is a statement about the market as a whole and not just about individual behavior. Finally, though by no means least, symmetric market rationality cannot be deduced from individual rational behavior in the usual sense since that sense does not imply imputing rationality to others. It may, in fact, imply a choice behavior inconsistent with imputed rationality unless the individual actually believes the market to be symmetrically rational. For if an ordinarily rational investor had good reason to believe that other investors would not behave rationally, then it might well be rational for him to adopt a strategy he would otherwise have rejected as irrational. Our postulate thus rules out, among other things, the possibility of speculative "bubbles" wherein an individually rational investor buys a security he knows to be overpriced (i.e., too expensive in relation to its expected *long-run* return to be attractive as a permanent addition to his portfolio) in the expectation that he can resell it at a still more inflated price before the bubble bursts.[25]

The Irrelevance of Dividend Policy Despite Uncertainty

In Section I we were able to show that, given a firm's investment policy, its dividend policy was irrelevant to its current market valuation. We shall now show that this fundamental conclusion need not be modified merely because of the presence of uncertainty about the future course of profits, investment, or dividends (assuming again, as we have throughout, that investment policy can be regarded as separable from dividend policy). To see that uncertainty about these elements changes nothing essential, consider a case in which current investors believe that the future streams of total earnings and total investment whatever actual values they may assume at different points in time

---

[24] We offer the term "symmetric market rationality" with considerable diffidence and only after having been assured by game theorists that there is no accepted term for this concept in the literature of that subject even though the postulate itself (or close parallels to it) does appear frequently. In the literature of economics a closely related, but not exact, counterpart is Muth's "hypothesis of rational expectations" [18]. Among the more euphonic, though we feel somewhat less revealing, alternatives that have been suggested to us are "putative rationality" (by T. J. Koopmans), "bi-rationality" (by G. L. Thompson), "empathetic rationality" (by Andrea Modigliani), and "pan-rationality" (by A. Ando).

[25] We recognize, of course, that such speculative bubbles have actually arisen in the past (and will probably continue to do so in the future), so that our postulate can certainly not be taken to be of universal applicability. We feel, however, that it is also not of universal inapplicability since from our observation speculative bubbles, though well publicized when they occur, do not seem to us to be a dominant, or even a fundamental, feature of actual market behavior under uncertainty. That is, we would be prepared to argue that, as a rule and on the average, markets do not behave in ways which do not obviously contradict the postulate so that the postulate may still be useful, at least as a first approximation, for the analysis of long-run tendencies in organized capital markets. Needless to say, whether our confidence in the postulate is justified is something that will have to be determined by empirical test of its implications (such as, of course, the irrelevance of dividend policy).

will be identical for two firms, 1 and 2.[26] Suppose further, provisionally, that the same is believed to be true of future total dividend payments from period one on so that the only way in which the two firms differ is possibly with respect to the prospective dividend in the current period, period 0. In terms of previous notation we are thus assuming that

$$\tilde{X}_1(t) = \tilde{X}_2(t) \qquad t = 0 \dots \infty$$

$$\tilde{I}_1(t) = \tilde{I}_2(t) \qquad t = 0 \dots \infty$$

$$\tilde{D}_1(t) = \tilde{D}_2(t) \qquad t = 1 \dots \infty,$$

the subscripts indicating the firms and the tildes being added to the variables to indicate that these are to be regarded from the standpoint of current period, not as known numbers but as numbers that will be drawn in the future from the appropriate probability distributions. We may now ask: "What will be the return, $\tilde{R}_1(0)$ to the current shareholders in firm 1 during the current period?" Clearly, it will be

$$\tilde{R}_1(0) = \tilde{D}_1(0) + \tilde{V}_1(1) - \tilde{m}_1(1)\,\tilde{p}_1(1). \tag{28}$$

But the relation between $\tilde{D}_1(0)$ and $\tilde{m}_1 \tilde{p}_1$ is necessarily still given by equation (4), which is merely an accounting identity so that we can write

$$\tilde{m}_1(1)\,\tilde{p}_1(1) = \tilde{I}_1(0) - [\tilde{X}_1(0) - \tilde{D}_1(0)], \tag{29}$$

and, on substituting in (28), we obtain

$$\tilde{R}_1(0) = \tilde{X}_1(0) - \tilde{I}_1(0) + \tilde{V}_1(1) \tag{30}$$

for firm 1. By an exactly parallel process we can obtain an equivalent expression for $\tilde{R}_2(0)$.

Let us now compare $\tilde{R}_1(0)$ with $\tilde{R}_2(0)$. Note first that, by assumption, $\tilde{X}_1(0) = \tilde{X}_2(0)$ and $\tilde{I}_1(0) = \tilde{I}_2(0)$. Furthermore, with symmetric market rationality, the terminal values $\tilde{V}_i(1)$ can depend only on prospective future earnings and investment and dividends from period 1 on and these too, by assumption, are identical for the two companies. Thus symmetric rationality implies that every investor must expect $\tilde{V}_1(1) = \tilde{V}_2(1)$ and hence finally $\tilde{R}_1(0) = \tilde{R}_2(0)$. But if the return to the investors is the same in the two cases, rationality requires that the two firms command the same current value so that $V_1(0)$ must equal $V_2(0)$ regardless of any difference in dividend payments during period 0. Suppose now that we allow dividends to differ not just in period 0 but in period 1 as well, but still retain the assumption of equal $\tilde{X}_i(t)$ and $\tilde{I}_i(t)$ in all periods and of equal $\tilde{D}_i(t)$ in period 2 and beyond. Clearly, the only way differences in dividends in period 1 can effect $\tilde{R}_i(0)$ and hence $V_i(0)$ is via $\tilde{V}_i(1)$. But, by the assumption of symmetric market rationality, current investors know that as of the start of period 1 the then investors will value the two firms rationally, and we have already shown that differences in the current dividend do not affect current value. Thus we must have $\tilde{V}_1(1) = \tilde{V}_2(1)$—and hence $V_1(0) = V_2(0)$—regardless of any possible difference in dividend payments during period 1. By an obvious extension of the reasoning to $\tilde{V}_i(2)$, $\tilde{V}_i(3)$, and so on, it must follow that the current valuation is unaffected by differences in dividend

---

[26] The assumption of two identical firms is introduced for convenience of exposition only, since it usually is easier to see the implications of rationality when there is an explicit arbitrage mechanism, in this case, switches between the shares of the two firms. The assumption, however, is not necessary and we can, if we like, think of the two firms as really corresponding to two states of the same firm for an investor performing a series of "mental experiments" on the subject of dividend policy.

payments in *any* future period and thus that dividend policy is irrelevant for the determination of market prices, given investment policy.[27]

Dividend Policy and Leverage

A study of the above line of proof will show it to be essentially analogous to the proof for the certainty world in which, as we know, firms can have, in effect, only two alternative sources of investment funds: retained earnings or stock issues. In an uncertain world, however, there is the additional financing possibility of debt issues. The question naturally arises, therefore, as to whether the conclusion about irrelevance remains valid even in the presence of debt financing, particularly since there may very well be interactions between debt policy and dividend policy. The answer is that it does, and while a complete demonstration would perhaps be too tedious and repetitious at this point, we can at least readily sketch out the main outlines of how the proof proceeds. We begin, as above, by establishing the conditions from period 1 on that lead to a situation in which $\tilde{V}_1(1)$ must be brought into equality with $\tilde{V}_2(1)$ where the V, following the approach in our earlier paper [17], is now to be interpreted as the total market value of the firm, debt plus equity, not merely equity alone. The return to the original investors taken as a whole—and remember that any individual always has the option of buying a proportional share of both the equity and the debt—must correspondingly be broadened to allow for the interest on the debt. There will also be a corresponding broadening of the accounting identity (4) to allow, on the one hand, for the interest return and, on the other, for any debt funds used to finance the investment in whole or in part. The net result is that both the dividend component and the interest component of total earnings will cancel out, making the relevant (total) return, as before, $[\tilde{X}_i(0) - \tilde{I}_i(0) + \tilde{V}_i(1)]$, which is clearly independent of the current dividend. It follows, then, that the value of the firm must also therefore be independent of dividend policy given investment policy.[28]

The Informational Content of Dividends

To conclude our discussion of dividend policy under uncertainty, we might take note briefly of a common confusion about the meaning of the irrelevance proposition occasioned by the fact that in the real world a change in the dividend rate is often followed by a change in the market price (sometimes spectacularly so). Such a phenomenon would not be incompatible with irrelevance to the extent that it was merely a reflection of what might be called the "informational content" of dividends, an attribute of particular dividend payments hitherto excluded by assumption from the discussion and proofs. That is, where a firm has adopted a policy of dividend stabilization with a long-established and generally appreciated "target payout ratio," investors are likely to (and have good reason to) interpret a change in the dividend rate as a change in management's views of future profit

---

[27] We might note that the assumption of symmetric market rationality is sufficient to derive this conclusion but not strictly necessary if we are willing to weaken the irrelevance proposition to one running in terms of long-run, average tendencies in the market. Individual rationality alone could conceivably bring about the latter, for over the long pull rational investors could enforce this result by buying and holding "undervalued" securities because this would ensure them higher long-run returns when eventually the prices became the same. They might, however, have a long, long wait.

[28] This same conclusion must also hold for the current market value of all the shares (and hence for the current price per share), which is equal to the total market value minus the given initially outstanding debt. Needless to say, however, the price per share and the value of the equity at *future* points in time will not be independent of dividend and debt policies in the interim.

prospects for the firm.[29] The dividend change, in other words, provides the occasion for the price change though not its cause, the price still being solely a reflection of future earnings and growth opportunities. In any particular instance, of course, the investors might well be mistaken in placing this interpretation on the dividend change, since the management might really only be changing its payout target or possibly even attempting to "manipulate" the price. But this would involve no particular conflict with the irrelevance proposition, unless, of course, the price changes in such cases were not reversed when the unfolding of events had made clear the true nature of the situation.[30]

V. Dividend Policy and Market Imperfections

To complete the analysis of dividend policy, the logical next step would presumably be to abandon the assumption of perfect capital markets. This is, however, a good deal easier to say than to do principally because there is no unique set of circumstances that constitutes "imperfection." We can describe not one but a multitude of possible departures from strict perfection, singly and in combinations. Clearly, to attempt to pursue the implications of each of these would only serve to add inordinately to an already overlong discussion. We shall instead, therefore, limit ourselves in this concluding section to a few brief and general observations about imperfect markets that we hope may prove helpful to those taking up the task of extending the theory of valuation in this direction.

First, it is important to keep in mind that from the standpoint of dividend policy, what counts is not imperfection per se but only imperfection that might lead an investor to have a systematic preference as between a dollar of current dividends and a dollar of current capital gains. Where no such systematic preference is produced, we can subsume the imperfection in the (random) error term always carried along when applying propositions derived from ideal models to real-world events.

Second, even where we do find imperfections that bias individual preferences—such as the existence of brokerage fees which tend to make young "accumulators" prefer low-payout shares and retired persons lean toward "income stocks"—such imperfections are at best only necessary but not sufficient conditions for certain payout policies to command a permanent premium in the market. If, for example, the frequency distribution of corporate payout ratios happened to correspond exactly with the distribution of investor preferences for payout ratios, then the existence of these preferences would clearly lead ultimately to a situation whose implications were different in no fundamental respect from the perfect market case. Each corporation would tend to attract to itself a "clientele" consisting of those preferring its particular payout ratio, but one clientele would be entirely as good as another in terms of the valuation it would imply for the firm. Nor, of course, is it necessary for the distributions to match exactly for this result to occur. Even if there were a "shortage" of some particular payout ratio, investors would still normally have the option of achieving their particular saving objectives without paying a premium for the stocks in short supply simply by buying appropriately weighted combinations of the more plentiful payout ratios. In fact, given the great range of corporate payout ratios known to be available, this process would fail to eliminate

---

[29] For evidence on the prevalence of dividend stabilization and target ratio, see Lintner [15].

[30] For a further discussion of the subject of the informational content of dividends, including its implications for empirical tests of the irrelevance proposition, see Modigliani and Miller [16, pp. 666–68].

permanent premiums and discounts only if the distribution of investor preferences were heavily concentrated at either of the extreme ends of the payout scale.[31]

Of all the many market imperfections that might be detailed, the only one that would seem to be even remotely capable of producing such a concentration is the substantial advantage accorded to capital gains as compared with dividends under the personal income tax. Strong as this tax push toward capital gains may be for high-income individuals, however, it should be remembered that a substantial (and growing) fraction of total shares outstanding is currently held by investors for whom there is either no tax differential (charitable and educational institutions, foundations, pension trusts, and low-income retired individuals) or where the tax advantage is, if anything, in favor of dividends (casualty insurance companies and taxable corporations generally). Hence, again, the "clientele effect" will be at work. Furthermore, except for taxable individuals in the very top brackets, the required difference in before-tax yields to produce equal after-tax yields is not particularly striking, at least for moderate variations in the composition of returns.[32] All this is not to say, of course, that differences in yields (market values) caused by differences in payout policies should be ignored by managements or investors merely because they may be relatively small. But it may help to keep investigators from being too surprised if it turns out to be hard to measure or even to detect any premium for low-payout shares on the basis of standard statistical techniques.

Finally, we may note that since the tax differential in favor of capital gains is undoubtedly the major *systematic* imperfection in the market, one clearly cannot invoke "imperfections" to account for the difference between our irrelevance proposition and the standard view as to the role of dividend policy found in the literature of finance. For the standard view is not that low-payout companies command a premium, but that, in general, they will sell at a discount![33] If such indeed were the case—and we, at least, are not prepared to concede that this has been established—then the analysis presented in this paper suggests there would be only one way to account for it; namely, as the result of systematic irrationality on the part of the investing public.[34]

To say that an observed positive premium on high payouts was due to irrationality would not, of course, make the phenomenon any less real. But it would at least suggest the need for a certain measure of caution by long-range policymakers. For investors, however naive they may be when they enter the market, do sometimes learn from experience and perhaps, occasionally, even from reading articles such as this.

---

[31] The above discussion should explain why, among other reasons, it would not be possible to draw any valid inference about the relative preponderance of "accumulators" as opposed to "income" buyers or the strength of their preferences merely from the weight attaching to dividends in a simple cross-sectional regression between value and payouts (as is attempted in Clendenin [2, p. 50] or Durand [5, p. 651]).

[32] For example, if a taxpayer is subject to a marginal rate of 40 percent on dividends and half that or 20 percent on long-term capital gains, then a before-tax yield of 6 percent consisting of 40 percent dividends and 60 percent capital gains produces an after-tax yield of 4.32 percent. To net the same after-tax yield on a stock with 60 percent of the return in dividends and only 40 percent in capital gains would require a before-tax yield of 6.37 percent. The difference would be somewhat smaller if we allowed for the present dividend credit, though it should also be kept in mind that the tax on capital gains may be avoided entirely under present arrangements if the gains are not realized during the holder's lifetime.

[33] See, among many, many others, Gordon [8, 9], Graham and Dodd [11, esp. chapters xxxiv and xxxvi], Durand [4, 5], Hunt, Williams, and Donaldson [13, pp. 647–49], Fisher [7], Gordon and Shapiro [10], Harkavy [12], Clendenin [2], Johnson, Shapiro, and O'Meara [14], and Walter [19].

[34] Or, less plausibly, that there is a systematic tendency for external funds to be used more productively than internal funds.

References

1. Bodenhorn, Diran. "On the Problem of Capital Budgeting." *Journal of Finance,* XIV (December 1959), 473–92.

2. Clendenin, John. "What Do Stockholders Like?" *California Management Review,* I (Fall 1958), 47–55.

3. Clendenin, John, and Van Cleave, M. "Growth and Common Stock Values." *Journal of Finance,* IX (September 1954), 365–76.

4. Durand, David. *Bank Stock Prices and the Bank Capital Problem.* ("Occasional Paper" No. 54.) New York: National Bureau of Economic Research, 1957.

5. ———. "The Cost of Capital and the Theory of Investment: Comment." *American Economic Review,* XLIX (September 1959), 639–54.

6. ———. "Growth Stocks and the Petersburg Paradox." *Journal of Finance,* XII (September 1957), 348–63.

7. Fisher, G. R. "Some Factors Influencing Share Prices." *Economic Journal,* LXXI, No. 281 (March 1961), 121–41.

8. Gordon, Myron. "Corporate Saving, Investment and Share Prices." *Review of Economics and Statistics.*

9. ———. "Dividends, Earnings and Stock Prices." *ibid.,* XLI, No. 2, Part I (May 1959), 99–105.

10. Gordon, Myron, and Shapiro, Eli. "Capital Equipment Analysis: The Required Rate of Profit." *Management Science,* III, 1956, 102–10.

11. Graham, Benjamin, and Dodd, David. *Security Analysis.* 3d ed. New York: McGraw-Hill, 1951.

12. Harkavy, Oscar. "The Relation between Retained Earnings and Common Stock Prices for Large Listed Corporations." *Journal of Finance,* VIII (September 1953), 283–97.

13. Hunt, Pearson, Williams, Charles, and Donaldson, Gordon. *Basic Business Finance.* Homewood, IL: Irwin, 1958.

14. Johnson, L. R., Shapiro, Eli, and O'Meara, J. "Valuation of Closely Held Stock for Federal Tax Purposes: Approach to an Objective Method." *University of Pennsylvania Law Review,* C, 166–95.

15. Lintner, John. "Distribution of Incomes of Corporations among Dividends, Retained Earnings and Taxes." *American Economic Review,* XLVI (May 1956), 97–113.

16. Modigliani, Franco, and Miller, Merton. "'The Cost of Capital, Corporation Finance and the Theory of Investment': Reply." *American Economic Review,* XLIX (September 1959), 655–69.

17. ———. "The Cost of Capital, Corporation Finance and the Theory of Investment," *ibid.,* XLVIII (1958), 261–97.

18. Muth, John F. "Rational Expectations and the Theory of Price Movements." *Econometrica.*

19. Walter, James E. "A Discriminant Function for Earnings-Price Ratios of Large Industrial Corporations." *Review of Economics and Statistics,* XLI (February 1959), 44–52.

20. ———. "Dividend Policies and Common Stock Prices." *Journal of Finance,* XI (March 1956), 29–41.

21. Williams, John B. *The Theory of Investment Value.* Cambridge, MA: Harvard University Press, 1938.

Discussion Questions

1. What is meant by "perfect capital markets," "rational behavior," and "perfect certainty"?

2. Explain the interaction among earnings, new investment in plant and equipment, and dividends.

3. John Burr Williams argues that the value of a common stock is the present value of future expected dividends. Does this article use the same basic assumption, or is it different?

4. How can the value of a stock be the present value of future dividends if dividend policy doesn't matter?

5. How can an investor construct her own stream of future dividends (dividend policy), given the basic earning power of the firm?

6. If personal tax rates on capital gains are different from the tax rate on dividend income, would the firm's dividend policy become relevant? Why?

*Ronald C. Lease and Uri Loewenstein**

Dividend Policy: Its Impact on Firm Value

Professors Lease and Loewenstein review the theory and evidence in the area of dividend policy. They provide guidelines for the financial manager in formulating a perspective regarding dividends and dividend policy for the firm.

Abstract

This paper provides a review and synthesis of the literature on dividend policy. Beginning with the seminal works in this area by Lintner (1956) and Miller and Modigliani (1961), the paper traces the evolution of the literature up through recent working papers. After demonstrating the irrelevance of dividend policy under perfect capital markets in both the certainty and uncertainty cases, market imperfections are systematically introduced with a discussion of how they might impact the irrelevance conclusion. This discussion concludes that, with the introduction of market imperfections, the importance of dividend policy becomes an empirical issue. The classic Lintner paper on how managers make the dividend decision is reviewed. Next, the empirical evidence related to dividend policy relevance is summarized. Given the prior discussion, a concluding section offers tentative advice on how practicing financial managers should go about making the dividend decision.

I. Introduction

A fundamental assumption in most of the finance literature is that managers work to maximize the wealth of the firm's *present* stockholders. Since share price is the critical variable in this wealth maximization framework, we must address the issue of how share price is determined in the marketplace. What economic process gives rise to the prices of securities that are reported daily in the

*We thank Avner Kalay and Jim Schallheim for useful comments and suggestions.

Source: Reprinted with permission from Ronald Lease and Uri Loewenstein. Ronald C. Lease and Uri Loewenstein are Professors of Finance at the University of Utah.

financial press? Of specific interest in this literature review is how, if at all, a firm's dividend policy affects the price of its common stock.[1]

The value of any asset, real or financial, is a function of the size, timing, and risk of the cash flows that accrue to the owner of the asset.[2] With respect to outside stockholders, firms distribute cash in two major ways: (1) cash dividends and (2) stock repurchases.[3] The most significant method for distributing cash, however, is via cash dividends.[4] In 1990 U.S. firms paid out over $105 billion in cash dividends.[5]

Given the above discussion, the following quote by Fisher Black may seem perplexing:

- Why do corporations pay dividends?
- Why do investors pay attention to dividends?

Perhaps the answers to these questions are obvious. Perhaps dividends represent the return to the investor who put his money at risk in the corporation. Perhaps corporations pay dividends to reward existing shareholders, and to encourage others to buy new issues of common stock at high prices. Perhaps investors pay attention to dividends because only through dividends or the prospect of dividends do they receive a return on their investment or the chance to sell their shares at a higher price in the future.

Or perhaps the answers are not so obvious. Perhaps a corporation that pays no dividends is demonstrating confidence that it has attractive investment opportunities that might be missed if it paid dividends. If it makes these investments, it may increase the value of the shares by more than the amount of the lost dividends. If that happens, its shareholders may be doubly better off. They end up with capital appreciation greater than the dividends they missed out on, and they find they are taxed at lower effective rates on capital appreciation than on dividends.

In fact, I claim that the answers to these questions are not obvious at all. The harder we look at the dividend picture, the more it seems like a puzzle, with pieces that just don't fit together.[6]

Although Professor Black's observations were made some time ago, financial economists still are wrestling with the "dividend puzzle." To fully appreciate the significance of this enigma, we must back up in time over three decades. It was in 1961 that Miller and Modigliani (M&M) approached the dividend policy question for the first time using the tools of the economist.[7] To avoid commingling

---

[1] By dividend policy, we mean the policy that management follows in making the dividend payout decision, i.e., the size and time series pattern of cash distributions to shareholders via dividend payments.

[2] Real assets, tangible and intangible, are listed on the left-hand side of the firm's balance sheet. Financial assets, such as bonds and stocks, are listed on the right-hand side of the balance sheet.

[3] Inside stockholders—e.g., managers and board members—may receive cash in other ways, such as a variety of compensation plans.

[4] Most firms pay dividends quarterly. The firm's board of directors states the size of the dividend on the "announcement date," which follows the board meeting. Further, the announcement states that the cash payment will be made to registered shareholders on a specific "record date." However, because of delays in the share transfer process, the stock goes "ex-dividend" four business days before the record date. After the stock goes ex-dividend, the shares trade *without* the rights to the *forthcoming* quarterly dividend. The dividend checks are mailed to shareholders of record on the "payment date," which is about two weeks after the record date.

[5] Aggregate dividend payments are reported in the *Federal Reserve Bulletin*. The average annual dividend yield on common stocks between 1926 and 1990 was 4.72 percent. This yield represents 39 percent of the *total* long-term return on the S&P 500 Index (see *Stocks, Bonds, Bills and Inflation: 1991 Yearbook,* Ibbotson Associates: Chicago). The remaining component of the total return is capital gains yield.

[6] F. Black, "The Dividend Puzzle," *Journal of Portfolio Management,* Winter 1976, p. 5.

[7] See M. Miller and F. Modigliani, "Dividend Policy, Growth, and the Valuation of Shares," *Journal of Business,* October 1961. This seminal publication, along with their other path-breaking research in financial economics, earned Professors Miller and Modigliani Nobel Prizes in economics (1990 and 1988, respectively).

too many complicating issues at one time, they framed their analysis in a perfect capital market context (PCM).[8] Their conclusion, which showed that the dividend policy decision is irrelevant—i.e., dividend policy has no impact on shareholder wealth—was contrary to the well-accepted conventional wisdom that dividends were vastly preferred, by some unspecified multiple, to retained earnings.[9] By this traditional position, the more generous the dividend policy, the higher the share price, all other things equal.

We begin our development in this paper by reviewing the economic arguments of M&M. Following M&M's impeccable logic, we demonstrate that under PCM dividend policy is irrelevant, both in the certainty case and in the uncertainty case.[10] We go on to relax the PCM assumptions, one by one, in an attempt to identify which imperfections, if any, might cause dividend policy to become a relevant decision variable. The results of this exercise are ambiguous; we find that some market imperfections suggest that dividend policy may be important while others suggest irrelevance. Next, we review how managers actually make their dividend decisions. Although managers behave as though dividend policy is a critical decision variable, their behavior does not imply that the market actually values that attention. Given the conflicting impacts of market imperfections, the relevance of dividend policy becomes an empirical question. Accordingly, we review the empirical evidence—i.e., what do "real world" stock price and other data suggest about how dividend policy affects equity valuation? We provide a summary of what we know and do not know about this issue. Finally, we offer tentative suggestions for practicing financial managers.

II. Stock Valuation

As mentioned above, cash flows expected to accrue to the owner of an asset—specifically, the size, timing, and risk of these cash flows determine the value of any real or financial asset.[11] For a share of common stock, the expected cash flows include dividends plus the selling price realized when the stock is sold.

If you are considering the purchase of a share of common stock, expect to hold it one year before selling it ex-dividend at price p_1, how much would you be willing to pay today, or p_0?[12] If you estimate the stock is in a risk class requiring k_e as an expected return, you would be willing to pay

$$p_0 = \frac{d_1}{(1 + k_e)^1} + \frac{p_1}{(1 + k_e)^1},$$ (1)

[8] Under perfect capital markets, the following conditions are assumed:

1. Information is costless and available to everyone on an equal basis. This assumption implies that *all* individuals are symmetrically informed.
2. No distorting taxes exist (e.g., as between capital gains and ordinary income).
3. Flotation and transactions costs are nonexistent.
4. No contracting or agency costs exist.
5. No investor or firm individually exerts enough power in the markets to influence the price of a security; i.e., investors are price takers.

[9] See B. Graham, D. Dodd, and S. Cottle, *Security Analysis* (Homewood, IL: Irwin, 1961).

[10] In the certainty case, future operating cash flows and investment opportunities are known without question. Under the uncertainty case, these future cash flows and investments are random variables drawn from market consensus probability distributions.

[11] Remember, the motivation for investment is to provide for future consumption.

[12] Selling ex-dividend means that you will receive the time = 1 dividend, d_1.

where d_1 and p_1 are the expected year-end dividend and share price respectively. But why would the individual who purchases your share be willing to pay p_1 at the end of year 1? Unless you believe in the "bigger fool" theory, that buyer must believe future cash flows justify the price p_1.[13] If the buyer also plans to hold the stock one year and receive d_2 before selling the share for p_2, his or her expectation must be such that

$$p_1 = \frac{d_2}{(1 + k_e)^1} + \frac{p_2}{(1 + k_e)^1}.$$

Substituting p_1 into Equation (1),

$$p_0 = \frac{d_1}{(1 + k_e)^1} + \frac{\dfrac{d_2}{(1 + k_e)^1} + \dfrac{P_2}{(1 + k_e)^1}}{(1 + k_e)^1}, \text{ or}$$

$$p_0 = \frac{d_1}{(1 + k_e)^1} + \frac{d_2}{(1 + k_e)^2} + \frac{P_2}{(1 + k_e)^2}. \tag{2}$$

Following the same rationale, ask how price p_2 is established and develop an expression similar to Equation (2) in terms of d_3 and p_3. Substituting the p_2 value into Equation (2),

$$p_0 = \frac{d_1}{(1 + k_e)^1} + \frac{d_2}{(1 + k_e)^2} + \frac{d_3}{(1 + k_e)^3} + \frac{P_3}{(1 + k_e)^3}.$$

Repetition of this process for $p_3, p_4, \ldots p_N$ will yield

$$p_0 = \frac{d_1}{(1 + k_e)^1} + \frac{d_2}{(1 + k_e)^2} + \ldots + \frac{d_N}{(1 + k_e)^N} + \frac{P_N}{(1 + k_e)^N}.$$

As $N \to \infty$, the final term approaches zero, and we can summarize the expression as

$$p_0 = \sum_{t=1}^{\infty} \frac{d_t}{(1 + k_e)^t}. \tag{3}$$

Equation (3) indicates that the price today, p_0, is a discounted cash stream of all future dividends. Thus, even though no specific owner has the intention of holding the stock until infinity, the share price is determined by discounting this infinite future cash flow stream at the required rate of return. On reflection, this valuation process makes economic sense. Asset values are based on cash flows, and expected cash dividends are the primary conduit for cash to flow from the corporation to the investor.[14] Notice that we have said nothing about the pattern or size of the d_t's. Elements in this vector may have any pattern, and, in fact, may be zero.[15]

---

[13] By "bigger fool," we mean that the buyer at $t = 1$ will be willing to buy the share without considering the economic fundamentals from the prior owner, who also ignored future cash flows.

[14] In perfect markets, corporate share repurchases are a perfect substitute for cash dividends. Further, corporate liquidation is considered another alternative, albeit unique, to cash dividends.

[15] This cash flow pattern is in sharp contrast to the promised cash payments for bonds, where the interest and principal payments contractually are determined in advance at the time the bonds are issued.

Given the share price valuation model we have just developed, consider whether the specific dividend policy (see footnote 1) a firm adopts can influence shareholder wealth. We will show that *given its investment decision,* the specific dividend policy adopted by a firm is *irrelevant* to shareholders, given perfect capital markets.[16]

III. Dividend Policy and Owner's Wealth

To illustrate the irrelevance of dividend policy, we will first assume *perfect certainty* with regard to our forecast of cash flows. In other words, *all* aspects of the firm's future, including investment opportunities, are known with complete certainty. Further, we assume perfect capital markets. These two simplifying assumptions will assist us in developing the economic intuition on the issue of dividend policy. Next, we will introduce uncertainty with respect to the firm's future cash flows. Finally, we will relax the perfect capital market assumptions to see if market imperfections impact the issue of dividend policy relevance.

Dividend Policy under Certainty

Imagine we establish a new firm that is entirely equity financed for our analytical convenience. This all-equity capital structure allows us to avoid evaluating the joint impact of dividend policy and financial leverage policy upon firm value.[17] To simplify the algebra, assume that dividends, operating cash flows, investment outlays, and new (equity) financing all occur at the *start* of each period.

Let:

S_0 = Pre-dividend market value of *all* common stock outstanding at $t = 0$

D_t = Total dividends paid at the start of time t to shares outstanding at $t = 0$

i = Market rate of interest on all securities in all periods[18]

F_t = New equity funds raised at the start of time t

X_t = Operating cash flows received by the firm at the start of time t. X_t depends only upon previous investments plus any cash flows upon firm liquidation.

I_t = Investment in all assets (including increases in the cash level) undertaken at time t.

The total market value of our all-equity firm at $t = 0$ as in Equation (3), or

$$S_0 = \sum_{t=0}^{T} \frac{D_t}{(1 + i)^t},$$ (3)

where T is some future period when the firm is liquidated. In any given period, the *total sources* of cash flows for the firm *must equal* the *total uses* of cash flows, or

---

[16] We assume firms accept all positive NPV projects. This guideline is called the NPV Rule.

[17] While we can make our dividend policy points using any capital structure, an all-equity capital structure simplifies the derivation.

[18] We easily could allow i to vary by time period. Note, in the certainty case, the rate of return on *all* financial assets in any given period is *equal.* This return equality is driven by the economic fact that yield differences are a product of variations in the risk or uncertainty of the underlying asset. Here we have assumed uncertainty away.

Sources $=$ Uses, or[19]

$$X_t + F_t = D_t + I_t + (1 + i)F_{t-1}. \tag{4}$$

By rearranging Equation (4), we can show that

$$D_t = X_t + F_t - I_t - (1 + i)F_{t-1}. \tag{5}$$

Substituting Equation (5) into Equation (3), we have

$$S_0 = X_0 + F_0 - I_0 - (1 + i)F_{-1} + \frac{X_1 + F_1 - I_1 - (1 + i)F_0}{(1 + i)^1} + \sum_{t=2}^{T} \ldots$$

Since we started up our hypothetical firm at $t = 0$, X_0 and F_{-1} are both zero. Thus, we have

$$S_0 = F_0 - I_0 + \frac{X_1 + F_1 - I_1 - (1 + i)F_0}{(1 + i)^1} + \sum_{t=2}^{T} \ldots$$

Note that F_0 and $-(1 + i)F_0/(1 + i)^1$ cancel out.

Similarly, $F_1/(1 + i)^1$ cancels with the third term, or $-(1 + i)F_1/(1 + i)^2$. We can continue and arrive at

$$S_0 = \sum_{t=0}^{T} \frac{(X_t - I_t)}{(1 + i)^t}. \tag{6}$$

Equation (6) expresses the current value of the all-equity firm as the discounted flow of $(X_t - I_t)$, which is the residual cash flow to shareholders, i.e., cash flow from operations less investments in all positive NPV projects identified for the period. This net cash flow is referred to as the *residual dividend*, i.e., the cash left for shareholders after the investment decision. If the quantity $(X_t - I_t)$ is negative, which means positive NPV project investment outlays exceed operating cash flows, the firm must make up the negative shortfall by raising funds in the external capital markets. Any other action would violate the NPV Rule.

Note that D_t does not appear in Equation (6). Since neither the X_t's or the I_t's are a function of dividend policy under the above assumptions (specifically perfect capital markets and the NPV Rule), dividend policy is irrelevant. By this statement we mean that paying out a dividend, D_t, that exceeds $(X_t - I_t)$ does not increase owners' wealth. This conclusion holds in spite of the fact that the value of the firm is solely a function of *residual dividends* and the market rate of interest.

If the residual amount $(X_t - I_t)$ is not paid out—i.e., is retained in the firm—the firm implicitly has increased I_t since sources must equal uses. However, I_t already includes *all* wealth-increasing projects, since the firm follows the NPV Rule. Therefore, retention of all or part of $(X_t - I_t)$ implies that the firm is investing in negative NPV projects. As we know, this action will decrease owners' wealth via a share price decline.

However, the above conclusion may seem paradoxical. Dividends count (see Equation (3)), but dividend policy does not count (see Equation (6))? What kind of financial alchemy can produce this result?

---

[19] For convenience, we assume the prior period's financing, F_{t-1}, is repaid at the end of $t - 1$, or at the start of period t. At the start of t, new financing, F_t, replaces the old financing. Incremental financing also may be obtained. Any refinancing assumption will serve us just as well.

A brief example may clarify the concept. The firm receives operating cash flows, X_t, in any period t. The firm makes the decision to invest in all positive NPV projects, I_t, in that period. If the firm makes a decision to pay out dividends in excess of $(X_t - I_t)$, the firm will have to raise an incremental amount ΔF_t in the market to fund the *incremental* dividend, ΔD_t, over and above the *residual* dividend available. This assertion can be verified by reexamining Equation (5), or

$$D_t = X_t + F_t - I_t - (1 + i)F_{t-1}.$$

If the firm decides to increase the residual dividend with external financing, what will be the repayment consequences of this incremental financing during the next period? The incremental repayment will equal $(1 + i)\Delta F_t$. Therefore, next period's dividend will be reduced by $(1 + i)\Delta F_t$. In our example, where we retire incremental financing at the end of each period, we have

$$\Delta D_t = \Delta F_t = \frac{(1 + i)\Delta F_t}{(1 + i)}.$$

The first term is the incremental dividend paid in t, the second term is the incremental financing raised in t to pay the extra dividend, and the third term is the present value of the incremental financing repaid one period away.[20] Thus, what the stockholders gain in extra dividends in period t, they give up in the next period, $t + 1$, plus interest. *You get it now, or you get it later!* In present-value terms, what is gained in extra ΔD_t today is offset exactly by future dividends lost, which, in turn, are worth ΔD_t today.

Given the linkage of market value to dividends, an extra dollar of dividends paid out today over and above the residual, $(X_t - I_t)$, will result in a loss of market value of exactly one dollar since this price decline is the present value of future dividends sacrificed. The trade-off implies a dollar's worth of market value today, or capital gain. With perfect markets and no differential taxes, this offsetting price decline implies irrelevance.

For instance, say management decides to increase the dividend by $1 today. The shareholder receives a check for an additional dollar. Simultaneously, the market recognizes the firm has raised an additional dollar of external financing that must be repaid next period plus interest at i. This decision decreases the firm's ability to pay dividends next period by $1(1 + i)$. What will happen to the stock price? Since stock price is the present value of future dividends and next period's dividend will drop by $1(1 + i)$, the present value of this reduction is

$$\frac{\$1(1 + i)}{(1 + i)},$$

or $1. Hence, the share price will drop $1. The extra dollar in dividend is exactly offset by a loss of $1 in market value.[21]

---

[20] If the firm refuses to cut the dividend next period by $(1 + i)\Delta F_t$, it will have to raise this additional amount in the market at $t + 1$. Then, in period $t + 2$ the firm will owe $-(1 + i)^2\Delta F_t$, and so on. Eventually, the "piper" will have to be paid, however. What is the present value of ultimate repayment postponed for n periods or $-(1 + i)^n\Delta F_t$? It will be $-(1 + i)^n\Delta F_t/(1 + i)^n$, which is also equal to the extra dividend in t.

[21] Even if the $1 of additional financing is never repaid, our conclusion does not change. The firm will still have to pay financing costs annually of $1(i)$. The present value of this as a perpetuity is $1(i)/(i)$, or $1.

Dividend Policy under Uncertainty

In the preceding analysis, we assumed complete certainty concerning all future cash flows. This setting implies the market has complete knowledge of the future capital investment outlays (I_t), operating cash flows (X_t), as well as dividends (D_t). Thus, in perfect capital markets with certainty, all stock in all firms is priced to yield an identical (risk-free) rate of return.

However, what happens to the conclusion of dividend policy irrelevance when we recognize that the investment, earnings, and dividend streams are uncertain? Probability distributions replace certain amounts for the cash flows. In this situation, will the value of the firm still be independent of its dividend policy?[22] The answer is yes! The irrelevance proposition still holds.

A frequently heard argument attacking the irrelevance proposition is that less uncertainty is attached to dividend payments received now versus dividend retention for reinvestment in projects whose future returns are uncertain (commonly called the "bird in the hand principle"). This discussion implies that the firm with the higher dividend payment (or the more stable dividend payment) will be valued more highly.[23]

This argument can be refuted rather quickly if we recall the assumptions and basic decision process. Remember, the investment decision is a given—i.e., take all positive NPV projects. While the future investment opportunities and project returns are uncertain, investors have formulated expectations about these future cash flows. Whether the firm retains funds to finance this investment program or whether it distributes the money in dividends and raises the necessary investment dollars in the capital market is irrelevant. The value of the firm remains unchanged since in either case the *uncertainty regarding the future* is unaffected. In one case, the current shareholders bear the project uncertainty; in the other case, the new equityholders share in it. No basis exists to argue that one group is willing to pay more for the claim on future earnings than the other; hence, dividend policy is irrelevant under uncertainty. We simply substitute the required rate of return on equity, k_e, for the risk-free rate, i, in the above equations.

Summary

Given the cash flows available from operations, X_t, the investment decision, I_t, and the need to refund past financing, the dividend policy decision can be simply a *residual decision.*[24] To pay dividends in excess of this residual amount (see Equation (5)) suggests that dividends are an active management decision variable. We have shown that this "managed" component of the dividend payment is irrelevant in the valuation process. Stock price will fall by the amount of the "excess" dividend paid.

This irrelevance conclusion, however, is not accepted by all academics or financial managers. Some strongly believe a "managed" dividend policy can have a positive impact on owners' wealth, or share price will not drop by the full amount of the incremental dividend paid. However, if dividend policy is important to shareholders, some of our assumptions must be in error. We have shown

---

[22] We can also view this question as whether the discount rate used in discounting the stream of dividends is affected by the choice of dividend policy.

[23] See M. Gordon, "Dividends, Earnings, and Stock Prices," *Review of Economics and Statistics,* May 1959.

[24] Again, this policy, which is no better or no worse than any other policy, implies paying what (if anything) is left over, or $(X_t - I_t)$.

the certainty assumption is not critical to our argument. Therefore, the perfect capital market assumptions must be at the root of our undoing *if* dividend policy counts.

Let us proceed to examine "real-world" phenomena. Will the departure from perfect capital markets cause us to alter our basic conclusions? We do not pretend that the perfect capital markets assumption is realistic. However, to destroy the irrelevance arguments, real-world imperfections and investor preferences will have to impact valuation *systematically* for dividend policy to become a relevant decision variable.

IV. Analysis of the Perfect Capital Market Assumptions

We will now relax, one by one, the perfect capital markets (PCM) assumptions we discussed earlier. Specifically,

PCM Assumption 1: Information is costless and available to everyone on an equal basis. This assumption implies that *all* individuals—outside and inside shareholders, managers and non-managers alike—are symmetrically informed.

We realize that the speed of information dissemination is important in security markets so that investors who receive information faster do not gain at the expense of investors who receive information slower. Further, this information should be available at zero or negligible cost.[25]

How can this information availability question be related to the issue of dividend policy? Many researchers contend that dividends do have significant information content, and thus an announced change in dividend policy can impact share price by providing "new" inside information previously known only to management. Given the way corporations establish and alter dividend policy, and the market's reaction to these changes, this argument has some merit.[26] The actual process that managers follow in making the dividend decision is discussed below.

Let us not lose perspective, however. Future operating cash flows and risk determine firm value. These future cash flows depend upon the firm's investment decision and its ability to manage its assets effectively. Dividends merely reflect this basic source of value. Management could use dividend changes to communicate its new perspective on future cash flows—its "insider information." However, dividend changes are just one of several ways to communicate inside information. Management could announce new expectations for residual cash available for dividends in the

---

[25] The theory of efficient markets suggest that all that is known or knowable about a stock is impounded in its present price, and stock price movements become strictly a function of the random arrival of new information. With the abundance of sources to convey information, such as satellite communications, around-the-clock global securities trading, the electronic and printed media, telephones, fax machines, and ticker tapes, and the literal army of "greedy" and smart analysts scurrying about for pieces of new information, the differential availability of *publicly available* information is not likely to exist. Further, *no* scientific empirical evidence exists that demonstrates that one class of investors (other than insiders, of course!) consistently outperforms another group of investors.

[26] See R. Pettit, "The Impact of Dividend and Earnings Announcements: A Reconciliation," *Journal of Business,* January 1976. In addition, see G. Charest, "Dividend Information, Stock Returns and Market Efficiency," *Journal of Financial Economics,* June-September 1978. These studies demonstrate a favorable (unfavorable) market reaction to a higher (lower) than expected dividend announcement. An alternative explanation for stock price reactions to dividend announcements is the "wealth transfer hypothesis." That is, stockholders are able to transfer wealth from bondholders by paying out larger than expected dividends. However, also see G. Handjinicolaou and A. Kalay, "Wealth Redistributions or Changes in Firm Value: An Analysis of Returns to Bondholders and Stockholders around Dividend Announcements," *Journal of Financial Economics,* March 1984. They show that the "information content hypothesis" dominates the "wealth transfer hypothesis" in explaining price reactions to dividend announcements.

future without altering the residual dividend today. Manipulating dividends to accomplish this communication is not an economic necessity.[27]

Nevertheless, proponents of the "information content hypothesis" argue that dividends are a perfect device to communicate inside information. Managers can use dividends to convey their assessment of future prospects for the firm without giving away the exact nature of the inside information and by "putting money where their mouth is."[28]

A related line of theoretical research involves using dividends as a "signal" of firm traits, i.e.; dividends are used to separate and distinguish firms in terms of their quality. However, for a "signalling equilibrium" to be effective, a cost must be associated with the signal.[29] Moreover, the cost of the signal must be higher for inferior firms so that they cannot "mimic" superior firms. Researchers who derive dividend signalling models use tax-related costs (see below), or costs associated with foregoing positive NPV investment to pay out dividends.[30]

PCM Assumption 2: No distorting taxes exist, e.g., as between capital gains and ordinary income.

In our tax environment, capital gains *historically* have been taxed at a substantially lower rate than dividends.[31] In addition, capital gains can be deferred until the stock actually is sold. Therefore, even if tax rates nominally are equal for dividends and capital gains, these rates effectively are lower for capital gains given the time value of money. Thus, retention versus cash dividends may have a positive impact on owners' wealth. The conclusion of this line of reasoning is that firms should tailor their dividend policy toward no or low payouts.[32]

However, others have suggested the possibility of effectively sheltering dividend income from taxes.[33] By borrowing additional sums of money to create tax-deductible interest expenses to offset

---

[27] If management attempted to manipulate the market with misleading announcements regarding their ability to sustain the dividend change, we would expect they could get away with this maneuver only once.

[28] By giving away inside information, we mean revealing the exact nature of proprietary information that would assist the firm's competitors.

[29] A signalling equilibrium is the state where each firm reveals its "quality" (e.g., a financially strong or weak firm) by a signalling mechanism (in this case, the amount of dividend paid). Market participants are able to correctly differentiate firm quality by observing the signal.

[30] See M. Miller and K. Rock, "Dividend Policy under Asymmetric Information," *Journal of Finance,* September 1985, who use dividends to signal unobserved current earnings, and K. John and J. Williams, "Dividends, Dilution and Taxes: A Signalling Equilibrium," *Journal of Finance,* September 1985, where dividends are utilized to signal future earnings. Also see P. Kumar, "Shareholder-Manager Conflict and the Information Content of Dividends," *Review of Financial Studies,* Summer 1988. Kumar attempts to show the existence of "coarse" signalling equilibria, where dividend changes reflect only broad changes in the firm's prospects. Therefore, dividends are "smoothed" relative to earnings (see corporate dividend decisions below).

[31] The Tax Reform Act of 1986 presumably eliminates the differential taxes between dividends and capital gains. However, if history repeats itself, you can count on Congress changing the tax rules again and again. In fact, several proposals to institute another reduced capital gains tax rate are being studied by Congress.

[32] See D. Farrar and L. Selwyn, "Taxes, Corporate Financial Policy and Return to Investors," *National Tax Journal,* December 1967. If $(X_t - I_t)$ is positive, share repurchase would be preferable to cash dividends. This procedure would minimize taxes paid.

[33] See M. Miller and M. Scholes, "Dividends and Taxes," *Journal of Financial Economics,* December 1978. However, D. Peterson, J. Peterson, and J. Ang find little evidence that investors engage in the strategies that Miller and Scholes suggest to avoid taxes on dividends. (See "Direct Evidence on the Marginal Rate of Taxation on Dividend Income," *Journal of Financial Economics,* June 1985.)

dividend income, and by adjusting risk through insurance policies, Keogh Plans, or IRAs, investors may avoid taxes on dividends entirely. If tax avoidance is possible, the differential tax argument may be irrelevant.

Further complicating the tax issue is the fact that some investors—e.g., pension funds—pay no taxes on either capital gains or dividends. Other investors—e.g., traders or short-term investors—have paid equal tax rates on dividends and capital gains under the U.S. tax code even before the Tax Reform Act of 1986.[34] Therefore, these investors should be indifferent to dividend policies from a tax standpoint. Finally, some investors pay less tax on dividends than on capital gains—e.g., corporations. Corporations do not have to pay income taxes on 70 percent of the dividends they receive from other corporations. Therefore, capital gains are taxed at a higher effective rate for corporate investors than dividends.[35]

PCM Assumption 3: Flotation and transactions costs are nonexistent.

Flotation costs can be substantial, particularly for new equity issues.[36] To the extent a firm pays out an extra dollar of dividends and, given a fixed investment policy, has to raise an extra dollar of new capital in the markets, flotation costs suggest that a residual dividend policy would be superior. In general, flotation costs would dictate going to the markets only when investment cash outlays and required capital retirements exceed operating cash inflows.

Transactions costs incurred by individual stockholders represent a potential imperfection which may result in a "managed" dividend policy having a positive impact on share price. A wide variety of investors, forming potential "dividend clientele" groups, may exist in the markets, each with a unique set of tax circumstances and consumption preferences. Some evidence suggests that investors tend to gravitate to firms with growth and payout characteristics that satisfy these tax and consumption circumstances.[37] High income individuals, *ceteris paribus,* may prefer high-growth firms with correspondingly low payouts. Low income or retired individuals may prefer a high and stable level of dividends for consumption purposes and, therefore, prefer mature, low-growth and high payout firms. Particularly with this latter set of investors, or dividend clientele, a firm that follows a strictly residual dividend policy will inject uncertainty regarding the amount of dividend to be paid each period.

Given the previously discussed trade-off between dividends and capital gains, these income-oriented investors could sell off part of their capital gains in lieu of receiving dividends, i.e., create "homemade" dividends. However, this procedure entails inconvenience and transactions costs. Hence, a stabilizing "managed" dividend policy *may* be received favorably and have a positive impact on share price.

---

[34] The above discussion of the deferral of capital gains does not apply to these investors since, by definition, they realize their gains (or losses) in the short run.

[35] Indeed, corporations might actually be involved in "dividend capture" activities to exploit the tax advantage of returns in the form of dividends. See J. Karpoff and R. Walkling, "Dividend Capture in NASDAQ Stocks," *Journal of Financial Economics,* December 1990.

[36] Empirical research suggests that equity issues by mature industrial firms are rare. See A. Kalay and A. Shimrat, "Firm Value and Seasoned Issues of Equity: Price Pressure, Wealth Redistribution or Negative Information," *Journal of Financial Economics,* September 1987.

[37] The evidence supporting tax-induced dividend clienteles is not strong, however. See W. Lewellen, K. Stanley, R. Lease, and G. Schlarbaum, "Some Direct Evidence on the Dividend Clientele Phenomenon," *Journal of Finance,* December 1978.

believes it can be sustained in the future. A dividend decrease is made only if adverse circumstances are not expected to pass quickly.

Managers believe that the market looks at the firm's earnings and has some notion of a "fair payout" ratio.[45] Hence, managers generally have an ideal or target dividend payout rate on earnings and make considerable effort to smooth changes to achieve the target. Smaller, step-wide adjustments are made rather than sudden movements toward the target level of payout.

Having compiled this survey information, Lintner developed a model to see if management's actual behavior followed this verbalized process, or

$$\Delta D_{it} = A_i + C_i(r_i E_{it} - D_{i(t-1)}) + U_{it},$$

where

ΔD_{it} = the change in dividends observed from period $t - 1$ to t for firm i,

A_i = the intercept term for firm i,

C_i = the speed of adjustment coefficient for firm i,

r_i = the target payout ratio for firm i,

E_{it} = the earnings after taxes in period t for firm i,

$D_{i(t-1)}$ = the dividend payout last period for firm i,

U_{it} = the error term for firm i in period t.

Lintner fit his regression model with actual corporate dividend data and found an r^2, or explained variance, of 85 percent. Further, the intercept term, A_i, was significant and positive. This finding indicates that managements consciously do avoid dividend cuts even when earnings decline.[46]

Thus, Lintner's results show us that management does try to do what they described verbally, or

1. Stabilize dividends with gradual, sustainable increases when possible.

2. Establish an appropriate target payout ratio.

3. Avoid dividend cuts if at all possible.

Given this observed pattern of management behavior, we see why the informational content argument for dividend is so often cited as suggesting that dividend policy is important. However, again the question can be asked: "Is the dividend announcement the only way to convey management's insider information?" Could the information be disseminated some other way?

The arguments on the relevance or irrelevance of dividend policy should leave the reader uncomfortable. While the finance literature has provided inordinate discussion on the strengths and weaknesses of the various arguments, the issue boils down to an empirical question: Does dividend policy matter?

---

[45] By payout ratio, we mean dividends per share dividend by earnings per share, or DPS/EPS.

[46] An updated study of the corporate dividend decision using several alternative models did not significantly improve upon Lintner's results. See G. Fama and H. Babiak, "Dividend Policy: An Empirical Analysis," *Journal of the American Statistical Association,* December 1968.

V. Empirical Evidence: Does Dividend Policy Count?

Just because managers behave as though dividend policy is a critical decision variable, it does not follow that the market values their efforts. As Merton Miller suggested with respect to the capital structure decision, the dividend policy decision might be a "neutral mutation"—a policy that causes no harm but creates no value.[47]

We have suggested that because of market imperfections—specifically taxes, flotation costs, transactions costs, asymmetric information, and agency costs—a firm's dividend policy might impact the value of its shares. Therefore, let's look at the empirical evidence regarding these imperfections.

Since the tax system historically has penalized dividends relative to capital gains, Brennan added a dividend yield variable to the Capital Asset Pricing Model.[48] He reasoned that stocks in firms with higher dividend yields should have higher pre-tax returns than equity in firms with lower payouts. This higher yield would compensate investors for higher taxes and, therefore, equate after-tax returns holding constant for systematic risk. Empirical tests of Brennan's model, however, have not yielded definitive results with respect to the significance of the dividend yield coefficient.[49] Due to econometric and data problems, the studies often present conflicting conclusions. However, on balance, the weight of the evidence leans *slightly* toward concluding the market requires extra return for higher dividend yields.[50]

Contrary results, however, are found in a unique study by John Long. He examined the prices of two classes of common stock in a firm (Citizens Utilities Company of Atlanta, Georgia) with two classes of common stock. One class pays a cash dividend while the other class provides an equivalent dollar value in extra shares via a stock split.[51] Tax models of dividend policy predict the stock split shares will sell at a premium relative to the cash dividend shares. Surprisingly, Long found the opposite. The cash dividend shares sold at a significant premium to the other class of shares. This result, although it represents only one firm, suggests that the market values cash dividends over capital gains.

If taxes play a large role in the composition of investors' portfolios, high-tax-bracket investors should hold low dividend yield stocks to escape taxes, while low-tax-bracket investors should be more indifferent to the dividend policies of firms. In other words, tax-induced dividend clienteles should exist. Lewellen, Stanley, Lease, and Schlarbaum examined the dividend yields on portfolios held by individual investors in a cross-section of tax brackets.[52] They found weak support, suggesting that high-tax-bracket investors chose stocks that paid lower dividend yields.

---

[47] See M. Miller, "Debt and Taxes," *Journal of Finance,* May 1977.

[48] See M. Brennan, "Taxes, Market Valuation, and Corporate Financial Policy," *National Tax Journal,* December 1970.

[49] See F. Black and M. Scholes, "The Effects of Dividend Yield and Dividend Policy on Common Stock Prices and Returns," *Journal of Financial Economics,* May 1974. Also see R. Litzenberger and R. Ramaswamy, "The Effect of Personal Taxes and Dividends on Capital Asset Prices: Theory and Empirical Evidence," *Journal of Financial Economics,* June 1979. In addition, see P. Hess, "Tests for Tax Effects in the Pricing of Financial Assets," *Journal of Business,* October 1983. Finally, see M. Miller and M. Scholes, "Dividends and Taxes: Some Empirical Evidence," *Journal of Financial Economics,* December 1982.

[50] However, in a recent working paper, A. Kalay and R. Michaely (1992) are unable to find cross-sectional differences in the returns associated with dividend yields. They argue that excess returns, on the week around the ex-dividend day, are a still unexplained phenomenon that is not consistent with the tax hypothesis.

[51] See J. Long, "The Market Valuation of Cash Dividends: A Case to Consider," *Journal of Financial Economics,* June 1978.

[52] See W. Lewellen, K. Stanley, R. Lease, and G. Schlarbaum, "Some Direct Evidence on the Dividend Clientele Phenomenon," *Journal of Finance,* December 1978.

Finally, a popular avenue of research of the "tax effect" and the "tax-induced clientele effect" has been the stock price behavior around the ex-dividend day. Stockholders owning the stock at the close of trading on the day *before* the ex-dividend day are entitled to the *next* dividend payment. Therefore, the stock price will drop at the opening of trading on the ex-date to reflect the loss of ownership of the forthcoming dividend. In an economy with preferential treatment of capital gains, the drop in price should be smaller than the forthcoming dividend. That is, a dollar of dividend paid out by the firm is worth less (after taxes) than a dollar of capital gains.

Elton and Gruber authored an influential academic study of stock price behavior around the ex-dividend day. They found less than a full-dividend price drop on the ex-dividend day during periods of differential taxation. Their study concludes that the ex-dividend price behavior of stocks is evidence of investor preference for capital gains over cash dividends.[53] In a more recent study, Mike Barclay studied the ex-dividend price behavior of stock in the United States prior to any income tax.[54] He found the price dropped by the full amount of the dividend during this pre-tax period. In contrast, other researchers found anomalous stock price behavior around ex-dividend days where taxes should not have played a role.[55]

Investigations of stock prices and returns in other countries with different tax codes—e.g., Britain and Canada—present similar, less than conclusive results. In general, the empirical studies that relate taxes, dividends, and firm value or realized returns show mixed results (with perhaps a *slight* tilt toward concluding that the market has a distaste for, or equivalently, requires a higher return for, stocks with higher dividend yields).

Empirical studies that cleanly model how dividend policy impacts firm value due to corporate flotations costs and investor transactions costs are, unfortunately, not available. Disentangling these potential effects from other imperfections on stock prices and returns is difficult. However, even if these effects could be modeled explicitly, the impacts are offsetting, as we pointed out above. Flotation costs seem to favor a residual policy, and transactions costs seem to suggest that a managed stable policy is preferred.

The agency theory models that suggest dividend policy can help reduce agency conflicts between bondholders and stockholders and managers and stockholders have, to date, not been tested.[56] Agency theory is a relatively recent development in financial economics. Further, these models currently do not specify an empirically testable functional relationship between dividend payout and agency costs. Finally, agency relationships may be too "firm-specific" to test by using the aggregated data that has been used to test the tax models.

[53] See E. Elton and M. Gruber, "Marginal Stockholder Tax Rates and the Clientele Effect," *Review of Economics and Statistics,* June 1970. They also report results that are consistent with the formation of clienteles. However, more recent research questions the ability to detect such clienteles with the available data. See A. Kalay, "The Ex-Dividend Day Behavior of Stock Prices: A Re-Examination of the Clientele Effect," *Journal of Finance,* September 1982.

[54] See M. Barclay, "Dividends, Taxes, and Common Stock Prices: The Ex-Dividend Day Behavior of Common Stock Prices before the Income Tax," *Journal of Financial Economics,* September 1987. The first modern income tax code in the U.S. went into effect in 1913. Barclay's sample period was between 1900 and 1910.

[55] See K. Eades, P. Hess, and H. Kim, "On Interpreting Security Returns during the Ex-Dividend Period," *Journal of Financial Economics,* March 1984. See also M. Grinblatt, R. Masulis, and S. Titman, "The Valuation Effects of Stock Splits and Stock Dividends," *Journal of Financial Economics,* December 1984.

[56] This discussion of agency theory, as well as dialogue contained in some other sections in this review, benefitted from the insights provided by J. Brickley and J. McConnell in "Dividend Policy," *The New Palgrave Dictionary of Money and Finance* (New York: MacMillan, 1990), eds. J. Eatwell and P. Newman.

With respect to whether managers use dividend policy to convey news about changes in firm value based on their "inside" or "asymmetric" information, empirical studies are more definitive.[57] Studies have shown that stock prices significantly rise when dividends are increased by more than the expected amount, and vice versa.[58] Moreover, research has shown that dividend announcements convey information over and above the information that is conveyed by earnings announcements.[59] Healy and Palepu find that investors interpret announcements of dividend initiations and omissions as managers' forecast of future earnings changes.[60]

Further, Brickley has shown that "specially designated dividends," which bear such labels as "special" or "extra" when announced by the board, convey less favorable information than do increases in regular dividends.[61] This finding suggests that the market regards the specially designated dividend as more temporary versus the permanent increase implied by an increase in the regular dividend.

However, share repurchase by the firm in lieu of cash dividends also is consistent with the signalling models as a way of reducing asymmetric information. As we noted earlier, share repurchase is an alternative to cash dividends. Managers may tend to repurchase their own shares when they think the firm's stock is undervalued. Accordingly, stock prices should increase at the announcement of share repurchase programs.

Empirical evidence shows that stock prices do respond positively when firms announce share repurchase programs.[62] However, the economic factors that lead managers to choose cash dividends versus stock repurchases are not well understood. To develop a theory that explains the choice between payout mechanisms, the differential costs and benefits between the alternatives must be specified.

In aggregate, managers historically have favored cash dividends relative to stock repurchase in spite of the fact that the tax code seems to favor stock repurchase. Therefore, in the view of management, cash dividends must possess substantial benefits relative to stock repurchase.

Based on asymmetric information arguments, two recent papers suggest that managers can use stock repurchases versus cash dividends to benefit themselves at the expense of outside

---

[57] S. Bhattacharya was the first to develop a theoretical model suggesting that managers could "signal" via dividend adjustments. See S. Bhattacharya, "Imperfect Information, Dividend Policy, and the 'Bird in Hand Fallacy,'" *Bell Journal of Economics,* Spring 1979. Also see a paper by the same author titled "Nondissipative Signalling Structures and Dividend Policy," *Quarterly Journal of Economics,* December 1980. In these models, managers are assumed to have asymmetric information not available to investors at large, mainly future earnings or cash flow projections.

[58] See R. Pettit, "Dividend Announcements, Security Performance, and Capital Market Efficiency," *Journal of Finance,* December 1972. Also see P. Asquith and D. Mullins, "The Impact of Initiating Dividend Payments on Shareholder Wealth," *Journal of Business,* January 1983. Interestingly, the timing of the dividend announcement also seems to convey information. Early announcements get a positive response from the market, while late announcements are regarded as bad news. See A. Kalay and U. Loewenstein, "The Informational Content of the Timing of Dividend Announcements," *Journal of Financial Economics,* July 1986.

[59] See J. Aharony and I. Swary, "Quarterly Dividend and Earnings Announcements and Stockholders' Returns: An Empirical Analysis," *Journal of Finance,* March 1980.

[60] See P. Healy and K. Palepu, "Earnings Information Conveyed by Dividend Initiations and Omissions," *Journal of Financial Economics,* September 1988.

[61] See J. Brickley, "Shareholder Wealth, Information Signaling, and the Specially Designated Dividend: An Empirical Study," *Journal of Financial Economics,* August 1983.

[62] See L. Dann, "Common Stock Repurchases: An Analysis of Returns to Bondholders and Stockholders," *Journal of Financial Economics,* June 1981; R. Masulis, "Stock Repurchase by Tender Offer: An Analysis of the Causes of Common Stock Price Changes," *Journal of Finance,* May 1980; and T. Vermaelen, "Common Stock Repurchases and Market Signalling: An Empirical Study," *Journal of Financial Economics,* June 1981.

shareholders.[63] If managers "time" their repurchases in periods when they think, based on outside information, that their stock is undervalued, selling shareholders lose while remaining shareholders, including non-selling managers, win. With regular cash dividends, however, "such gaming activity" cannot be conducted to the disadvantage of selling shareholders. Since the market is aware of managers' ability to exploit inside information, a higher market price will be attached to firms with a regular cash dividend policy versus a more sporadic share repurchase policy, *ceteris paribus*. This observation might explain the reason cash dividends are much more commonly used as a method of cash disbursement than is stock repurchase.

VI. Conclusion

In this paper we have reviewed the basic stock valuation model and have shown how share value is determined by the residual dividend in a world with perfect capital markets in both the certainty and uncertainty cases. In this environment, we concluded that dividend policy was irrelevant—a trivial detail that managers could well ignore.

However, when we relaxed our perfect capital market assumptions, we opened a "can of worms." Certain market imperfections seem to favor a managed dividend policy, others favor a residual dividend policy, while yet other imperfections are ambiguous as to their impact.

Next we examined how managers make the dividend decision in the "real world." Regardless of the valuation impact of dividend policy, managers behave as though dividend policy is an important decision variable.

Finally, we turned to the empirical evidence on whether dividend policy affects stock value or required returns. Unfortunately, we found the evidence is mixed and generally inconclusive. Given all the troublesome econometric problems involved with "holding all other factors constant" to isolate any dividend policy valuation effect, we basically concluded that no clear-cut evidence exists regarding the value of dividend policy. The accumulated evidence led Stewart Myers to suggest the following:

> There is scant evidence to date that investors pay a premium for stocks with either high or low dividend yields. Apparently dividend policy is irrelevant, or its effects are minimal compared with the effects of other variables.[64]

What is unknown dominates what is known about dividend policy. Little evidence suggests an appropriate dividend payout level. However, compelling evidence suggests that stock price changes accompany changes in cash dividends and stock repurchase announcements. This price reaction presumably reflects asymmetric information between managers and the market. However, the reason that managers choose dividend changes to communicate inside information relative to other communication channels is unknown. Nor do we have a theory about the nature of the information that is being provided via dividend changes or stock repurchases, or the linkage between this information and share price.

---

[63] See M. Barclay and C. Smith, "Corporate Payout Policy: Cash Dividends versus Share Repurchase," *Journal of Financial Economics,* October 1988. Also see A. Ofer and A. Thakor, "A Theory of Stock Price Response to Alternative Corporate Cash Disbursement Methods: Stock Repurchases and Dividends," *Journal of Finance,* June 1987.

[64] S. Myers, *Modern Developments in Financial Management* (New York: Praeger, 1976), p. 70.

However, we should take heart by noting that important strides have been made since the original M&M irrelevance hypothesis in 1961. The nature of the market imperfections that might cause dividend policy to matter were not understood then. While taxes, flotation costs, and transactions were identified quickly as having the potential to impact the argument, signalling theory and agency theory were developed later as potential explanations for relevance.

We anticipate that current and future research into the illusive dividend issue will yield more definitive conclusions. Once a model is developed and empirically supported, managers may have another tool that they can use to maximize firm value.

In the meantime, what is a financial manager to do? Consider these tentative suggestions:

1. No matter what dividend policy your firm adopts, *never* let dividend policy affect your investment decision. While the valuation impacts of dividend policy are unclear, we know that taking positive NPV projects increases shareholder wealth.

2. Never underpay dividends. Only retain funds within the firm that pass the NPV Rule. Do not forget that cash buildup, unless it is temporary, is an investment decision.

3. If residual cash flows are realized and the extra cash is expected to be temporary, consider a share repurchase versus a dividend increase. While we do not understand the signalling mechanism of dividend policy, we know that dividend cuts are met by share price declines. Therefore, avoid temporary dividend increases. Use share repurchases instead. Further, this procedure will avoid disrupting any dividend clientele that may exist.

4. Do not spend too much time worrying about the dividend decision. Management time has an opportunity cost. Remember Brealey and Myers' third law—"You can make a lot more money on the left-hand of the balance sheet than on the right."[65] Given the relative efficiency of the capital market compared to the productive goods market, their advice is well taken.[66]

References

Aharony, J., and I. Swary. "Quarterly Dividend and Earnings Announcements and Stockholders' Returns: An Empirical Analysis." *Journal of Finance,* March 1980.

Asquith, P., and D. Mullins. "The Impact of Initiating Dividend Payments on Shareholder Wealth." *Journal of Business,* January 1983.

Barclay, M. "Dividends, Taxes, and Common Stock Prices: The Ex-Dividend Day Behavior of Common Stock Prices Before the Income Tax." *Journal of Financial Economics,* September 1987.

Barclay, M., and C. Smith. "Corporate Payout Policy: Cash Dividends versus Share Repurchase." *Journal of Financial Economics,* October 1988.

---

[65] See R. Brealey and S. Myers, *Principles of Corporate Finance,* 4th ed. (New York: McGraw-Hill, 1991), p. 464. By this statement the authors mean that managers have much more potential for increasing shareholder wealth with good "productive" investment decisions on the left-hand side of the balance sheet than with capital structure and dividend decisions, which impact the right-hand side of the balance sheet.

[66] A word of caution! For the "purist," the suggestions provided above are a bit strong and might not always be followed literally because of other market imperfections, especially agency problems. For example, sometimes under conditions of financial distress the Net Present Value Rule is not in the best interest of the stockholders (suggestion 1). Occasionally, and again under conditions of financial distress, bond covenants may prevent the manager from paying out any dividends (suggestion 2). However, these cases are the exceptions to the general validity of the suggestions.

Bhattacharya, S. "Imperfect Information, Dividend Policy, and the 'Bird in the Hand Fallacy.'" *Bell Journal of Economics,* Spring 1979.

Bhattacharya, S. "Nondissipative Signalling Structures and Dividend Policy." *Quarterly Journal of Economics,* December 1980.

Black, F. "The Dividend Puzzle." *Journal of Portfolio Management,* Winter 1976.

Black, F., and M. Scholes. "The Effects of Dividend Yield and Dividend Policy on Common Stock Prices and Returns." *Journal of Financial Economics,* May 1974.

Brealey, R., and S. Myers. *Principles of Corporate Finance,* 4th ed. New York: McGraw-Hill, 1991.

Brennan, M. "Taxes, Market Valuation, and Corporate Financial Policy." *National Tax Journal,* December 1970.

Brickley, J. "Shareholder Wealth, Information Signaling, and the Specially Designated Dividend: An Empirical Study." *Journal of Financial Economics,* August 1983.

Brickley, J., and J. McConnell. "Dividend Policy." *The New Palgrave Dictionary of Money and Finance,* eds. J. Eatwell and P. Newman. New York: MacMillan, 1990.

Charest, G. "Dividend Information, Stock Returns and Market Efficiency." *Journal of Financial Economics,* June-September 1978.

Dann, L. "Common Stock Repurchases: An Analysis of Returns to Bondholders and Stockholders." *Journal of Financial Economics,* June 1981.

Eades, K., P. Hess, and H. Kim. "On Interpreting Security Returns during the Ex-Dividend Period." *Journal of Financial Economics,* March 1984.

Easterbrook, F. "Two Agency-Cost Explanations of Dividends." *American Economic Review,* September 1984.

Elton, E., and M. Gruber. "Marginal Stockholder Tax Rates and the Clientele Effect." *Review of Economics and Statistics,* June 1970.

Fama, G., and II. Babiak. "Dividend Policy; An Empirical Analysis." *Journal of the American Statistical Association,* December 1968.

Farrar, D., and L. Selwyn. "Taxes, Corporate Financial Policy and Return to Investors." *National Tax Journal,* December 1967.

Gordon, M. "Dividends, Earnings, and Stock Prices." *Review of Economics and Statistics,* May 1959.

Graham, B., D. Dodd, and S. Cottle. *Security Analysis.* Homewood, IL: Irwin, 1961.

Grinblatt, M., R. Masulis, and S. Titman. "The Valuation Effects of Stock Splits and Stock Dividends." *Journal of Financial Economics,* December 1984.

Handjinicolaou, G., and A. Kalay. "Wealth Redistributions or Changes in Firm Value: An Analysis of Returns to Bondholders and Stockholders around Dividend Announcements." *Journal of Financial Economics,* March 1984.

Healy, P., and K. Palepu. "Earnings Information Conveyed by Dividend Initiations and Omissions." *Journal of Financial Economics,* September 1988.

Hess, P. "Tests for Tax Effects in the Pricing of Financial Assets." *Journal of Business,* October 1983.

Jensen, M. "Agency Costs of Free Cash Flow, Corporate Finance, and Takeover." *American Economic Review,* May 1986.

Jensen, M., and W. Meckling. "The Theory of the Firm: Managerial Behavior, Agency Costs, and Ownership Structure." *Journal of Financial Economics,* October 1976.

John, K., and A. Kalay. "Costly Contracting and Optimal Payout Constraints." *Journal of Finance,* May 1982.

John, K., and J. Williams. "Dividends, Dilution and Taxes: A Signalling Equilibrium." *Journal of Finance,* September 1985.

Kalay, A. "Stockholder-Bondholder Conflicts and Dividend Constraints." *Journal of Financial Economics,* July 1982.

Kalay, A. "The Ex-Dividend Day Behavior of Stock Prices: A Re-Examination of the Clientele Effect." *Journal of Finance,* September 1982.

Kalay, A., and U. Loewenstein. "The Informational Content of the Timing of Dividend Announcements." *Journal of Financial Economics,* July 1986.

Kalay, A., and R. Michaely. "Dividends and Taxes: A Re-Examination." Working paper, University of Utah, April 1992.

Kalay, A., and A. Shimrat. "Firm Value and Seasoned Issues of Equity: Price Pressure, Wealth Redistribution or Negative Information." *Journal of Financial Economics,* September 1987.

Karpoff, J., and R. Walkling. "Dividend Capture in NASDAQ Stocks." *Journal of Financial Economics,* December 1990.

Kumar, P. "Shareholders-Manager Conflict and the Information Content of Dividends." *Review of Financial Studies,* Summer 1988.

Lewellen, W., K. Stanley, R. Lease, and G. Schlarbaum. "Some Direct Evidence on the Dividend Clientele Phenomenon." *Journal of Finance,* December 1978.

Lintner, J. "Distribution of Income of Corporations among Dividends, Retained Earnings, and Taxes." *American Economic Review,* May 1956.

Litzenberger, R., and K. Ramaswamy. "The Effect of Personal Taxes and Dividends on Capital Asset Prices: Theory and Empirical Evidence." *Journal of Financial Economics,* June 1979.

Long, J. "The Market Valuation of Cash Dividends: A Case to Consider." *Journal of Financial Economics,* June 1978.

Masulis, R. "Stock Repurchase by Tender Offer: An Analysis of the Causes of Common Stock Price Changes." *Journal of Finance,* May 1980.

Miller, M. "Debt and Taxes." *Journal of Finance,* May 1977.

Miller, M., and F. Modigliani. "Dividend Policy, Growth, and the Valuation of Shares," *Journal of Business,* October 1961.

Miller, M., and K. Rock. "Dividend Policy under Asymmetric Information." *Journal of Finance,* September 1985.

Miller, M., and M. Scholes. "Dividends and Taxes." *Journal of Financial Economics,* December 1978.

Miller, M., and M. Scholes. "Dividends and Taxes: Some Empirical Evidence." *Journal of Financial Economics,* December 1982.

Myers, S. *Modern Developments in Financial Management.* New York: Praeger, 1976.

Ofer, A., and A. Thakor. "A Theory of Stock Price Response to Alternative Corporate Cash Disbursement Methods: Stock Repurchases and Dividends." *Journal of Finance,* June 1987.

Peterson, D., P. Peterson, and J. Ang. "Direct Evidence on the Marginal Rate of Taxation on Dividend Income." *Journal of Financial Economics,* June 1985.

Pettit, R. "Dividend Announcements, Security Performance, and Capital Market Efficiency." *Journal of Finance,* December 1972.

Pettit, R. "The Impact of Dividend and Earnings Announcements: A Reconciliation." *The Journal of Business,* January 1976.

Rozeff, M. "Growth, Beta and Agency Costs as Determinants of Dividend Payout Ratios." *Journal of Financial Research,* Fall 1982.

Schleifer, A., and R. Vishny. "Large Stockholders and Corporate Control." *Journal of Political Economy,* June 1986.

Vermaelen, T. "Common Stock Repurchases and Market Signalling: An Empirical Study." *Journal of Financial Economics,* June 1981.

Discussion Questions

1. What conditions are assumed for a perfect capital market context?

2. Show why the value of a common stock is the present value of future dividends, even for investors who plan to get returns from a high future price rather than holding for the long term.

3. Explain the logic of the "residual" dividend policy.

4. How can dividend changes be used to communicate management's inside information?

5. Discuss some of the tax issues surrounding dividend policy.

6. How do transaction expenses interfere with the shareholder's ability to manufacture a customized dividend pattern?

7. Why might bondholders care if the dividends are on the high or the low side?

8. Summarize the results of the John Lintner study.

9. What is your conclusion regarding dividend policy, now that you have read the arguments and the evidence?

part V

Long-Term Financing

Firms issue debt and stock and retain earnings to finance growth in long-term assets. As the process of securing long-term capital is an infrequent event, financial managers tend not to be experts about the process, and there are many practical and legal pitfalls. For these reasons, investment banking firms are engaged to help issuers design, price, and issue securities.

The article by Clifford Smith contains a wealth of information about this process and its attendant costs; Rogowski and Sorensen present a discussion of the competitive developments in investment banking, particularly as they pertain to shelf registration.

A financing tool not generally well understood is leasing, probably because the cost of leasing is not easily computed. The article by Schallheim et al. presents a discussion of equipment leasing and the determinants of leasing costs.

In the 1980s, many innovations were developed to solve financing problems. The resulting new financial instruments and processes are generally referred to as *financial engineering*. The Finnerty article is a review of financial engineering—what it is and why it occurs.

Clifford W. Smith, Jr. *

Investment Banking and the Capital Acquisition Process

This paper reviews the theory and evidence on the process by which corporations raise debt and equity capital and the associated effects on security prices. Findings from related transactions are used to test hypotheses about the stock price patterns accompanying announcements of security offerings. Various contractual alternatives employed in security issues are examined—for example, rights or underwritten offers, negotiated or competitive bid, best efforts or firm commitment contracts, and shelf or traditional registration. Finally, incentives for underpricing new issues are analyzed.

1. Introduction

Corporations raise external capital by selling a range of different securities which they market in a variety of ways. The *Dealer's Digest* (1985) reports that $355.3 billion in public securities sales have been underwritten between 1980 and 1984. Of that total value, 24 percent is common stock, 5 percent is preferred stock, 2 percent is convertible preferred stock, 63 percent is debt, and 6 percent is convertible debt. Contracts negotiated between the issuing firm and underwriter constitute 95 percent of the offers, while in 5 percent the underwriter is selected through a competitive bid. Shelf registration accounts for 27 percent of the issues, while 73 percent are registered employing traditional procedures.

Capital markets play an important role in the theory of corporate financial economics; for example, capital market prices provide vital signals for corporate investment decisions. Yet we do not have a detailed understanding of the various contractual arrangements in the process of raising capital, or of the influence of this process on corporate financial and investment policy.

*I would like to thank Armen Alchian and the participants at the MERC Conference on Investment Banking and the Capital Acquisition Process, especially H. DeAngelo, M. Jensen, D. Mayers, R. Masulis, R. Schwert, R. Stulz, and J. Warner for their comments. This research was supported by the Managerial Economics Research Center, Graduate School of Management, University of Rochester.

Source: Reprinted with permission from the *Journal of Financial Economics* (January/February 1986), pp. 3–29 by Clifford W. Smith, Jr. Elsevier Science B.V., Amsterdam, The Netherlands. Clifford W. Smith, Jr. is the Clarey Professor of Finance and Economics at the William E. Simon Graduate School of Business Administration at the University of Rochester.

Section 2 examines the theory and evidence related to announcements of security offerings by public corporations. Average stock price reactions to public security issues are either negative or not significantly different from zero. Several hypotheses have been offered to explain these price reactions. The hypotheses also have implications for price reactions in related events, such as dividend changes and security repurchases. It is therefore possible to evaluate their relative merit by drawing on existing evidence about price reactions to these related announcements.

Section 3 examines the marketing of corporate securities. Securities can be sold through either a rights or an underwritten offering. Underwriters' services can be obtained through either a negotiated or a competitive bid contract. Finally, the securities can be registered with the Securities and Exchange Commission (SEC) through either the new shelf method or traditional registration procedures. Data on the costs, pricing, and frequency of use of these marketing methods for different securities provide a clearer understanding of the incentives important in choosing among them.

Section 4 examines the special case of initial public equity offerings. They are typically sold through either firm commitment or best effort contracts. Underwriters, on average, price initial public offerings significantly lower than their after-market price. The hypotheses which explain these choices are examined.

Section 5 presents brief concluding remarks, and suggests issues for further study.

2. On the Corporation's Choice of Security to Offer

A public corporation seeking external capital must first decide what type of claim to sell. In choosing the type of security to issue, it is important to understand the market reaction to the announcement. Table 1 summarizes two-day common stock price reactions adjusted for general market price changes (abnormal returns) to announcements of public issues of common stock, preferred stock, convertible preferred stock, straight debt, and convertible debt by industrial and utility firms. Four generalizations about relative magnitudes are suggested in Table 1: (1) the average abnormal returns are non-positive; (2) abnormal returns associated with announcements of common stock sales are negative and larger in absolute value than those observed with preferred stock or debt; (3) abnormal returns associated with announcements of convertible securities are negative and larger in absolute value than those for corresponding non-convertible securities; and (4) abnormal returns associated with sales of securities by industrials are negative and larger in absolute value than those for utilities.

There are several hypotheses for this pattern of relative stock price effects: (1) *Optimal Capital Structure*—firms have an optimal capital structure, and these price reactions reflect the change in the value of the firm associated with the adjustment of the firm's liability structure; (2) *Implied Cash Flow Change*—the stock price changes provide information about future expected net operating cash flows; (3) *Unanticipated Announcements*—stock price changes reflect only the unanticipated component of the announcement; hence the more predictable an event, the smaller the associated stock price change; (4) *Information Asymmetry*—corporate managers have more information than the marginal purchaser of securities; hence corporate managers are more likely to issue securities when they are overpriced in the market; (5) *Ownership Changes*—transactions that change the distribution of control rights in the firm affect the value of the firm's shares. These hypotheses are examined to identify the extent to which each helps explain the price effects in Table 1. The hypotheses are not mutually exclusive. However, each hypothesis also has implications for price

Table 1 Average Two-Day Abnormal Common Stock Returns and Average Sample Size (in Parentheses) from Studies of Announcements of Security Offerings

Returns are weighted averages by sample size of the returns reported by the respective studies. (Unless noted otherwise, returns are significantly different from zero.)

	Type of Issuer	
Type of Security Offering	**Industrial**	**Utility**
Common stock	−3.14[a]	−0.75[b]
	(155)	(403)
Preferred stock	−0.19[c*]	+0.08[d*]
	(28)	(249)
Convertible preferred stock	−1.44[d]	−1.38[d]
	(53)	(8)
Straight bonds	−0.26[e*]	−0.13[f*]
	(248)	(140)
Convertible bonds	−2.07[e]	n.a.[g]
	(73)	

[a]*Source:* Asquith and Mullins (1986), Kolodny and Suhler (1985), Masulis and Korwar (1986), Mikkelson and Partch (1986), Schipper and Smith (1986).
[b]*Source:* Asquith and Mullins (1986), Masulis and Korwar (1986), Pettway and Radcliffe (1985).
[c]*Source:* Linn and Pinegar (1985), Mikkelson and Partch (1986).
[d]*Source:* Linn and Pinegar (1985).
[e]*Source:* Dann and Mikkelson (1984), Eckbo (1986), Mikkelson and Partch (1986).
[f]*Source:* Eckbo (1986).
[g]Not available (virtually none are issued by utilities).
*Interpreted by the authors as not statistically significantly different from zero.

reactions to related announcements. Augmenting the observations in Table 1 with empirical evidence from the analysis of other events helps identify relative orders of importance.

2.1. Optimal Capital Structure and Relative Price Effects

With fixed investment policy and no contracting costs or taxes, the value of the firm is independent of the structure of its liabilities [Modigliani and Miller (1958)]. This capital structure irrelevance hypothesis implies that the function relating leverage and the value of the firm is a horizontal line. Alternatively, if taxes or contracting costs are important, or if investment policy and capital structure are interdependent, then the market value of the firm depends on the structure of its liabilities. In the case of the capital structure relevance hypothesis, the function relating firm value and leverage is concave.[1] But neither hypothesis by itself provides a satisfactory explanation of the estimates in Table 1. Maximizing behavior by firms implies that in voluntary transactions such as security sales, the firm should structure the transaction to yield the highest possible value of the firm. Thus,

[1] Various analyses emphasize different characteristics of claims such as corporate taxes [Modigliani and Miller (1962), Brennan and Schwartz (1978)], personal taxes [DeAngelo and Masulis (1980)], transactions costs of bankruptcy [Kraus and Litzenberger (1973)], and agency costs [Jensen and Meckling (1976), Myers (1977), Smith and Warner (1979)].

if a transaction moves a company along a given leverage-value function, the irrelevance hypothesis implies there should be no abnormal returns associated with announcements of security sales, while the capital structure relevance hypothesis implies the abnormal returns should be non-negative. Therefore, the negative returns in Table 1 are inconsistent with both predictions.

Reductions in firm value associated with apparently voluntary security sales present a puzzle. It is possible that security sales are optimal responses to an adverse change in the firm's prospects, and the negative price reaction is due to the revelation of the adverse change. Even if a security sale might itself increase the value of the firm, it could lead potential security holders to believe the firm has received bad news. Of course, if the announcement of the transaction is also associated with a shift in the leverage-value function, then the theory has no implication for the magnitudes observed in Table 1. Without a theory capable of differentiating between movement along a given leverage-value function and a shift in the function, it is difficult to test hypotheses about optimal capital structure by looking at the stock price reactions to announcements of security sales. Therefore, at the current stage of development, studies of financing decisions provide relatively weak tests of optimal capital structure theories.

2.2. Implied Changes in Expected Net Operating Cash Flow and Relative Price Effects

The firm's cash-flow identity states that sources must equal uses of funds. Therefore, an announcement of a new security sale must be matched either by an increase in new investment expenditure, a reduction in some liability (such as debt retirement or share repurchase), an increased dividend, or a reduction in expected net operating cash flow. In the Miller and Rock (1985) analysis of dividends, they hypothesize that investors draw inferences about implied changes in expected net operating cash flows from corporate dividend announcements. They suggest that larger-than-expected dividend payments are associated with larger-than-expected internally generated cash flows from operations, and thus the dividend increase represents good news for investors. The evidence in Table 1 is generally consistent with this hypothesis if the hypothesis is modified to consider security sales, so that unexpected security sales are associated with smaller-than-expected cash flows from operations, and thus security sales represent bad news for investors.

This argument can be generalized to consider other announcements which do not explicitly link sources and uses of funds. In general, to predict the implied change in cash flow, everything except net operating cash flow and the announcement policy variable is held fixed. Thus, announcements of security repurchases, increases in investment expenditures, or higher dividend payments are associated with implied increases in expected cash flow; and security offerings, reductions in investment expenditures, or lower dividend payments are associated with implied reductions in expected cash flow. If there is an implied increase in the corporation's expected net operating cash flow, the value of the firm should rise and there should be a corresponding increase in the value of the firm's equity.

Table 2 summarizes the evidence from studies of announcements of sales of new securities, stock repurchases, dividend changes, and changes in investment policy grouped by their effect on implied changes in expected cash flows. The evidence of generally positive abnormal returns in the upper panel of Table 2 associated with implied increases in cash flows, and generally negative abnormal return in the lower panel associated with implied decreases in cash flows, is consistent with the hypothesis that security market participants draw inferences about changes in operating cash flow from announcements that do not explicitly associate sources with uses of funds.

Table 2 Average Two-Day Common Stock Abnormal Returns and Average Sample Size from Studies of Changes in Financing, Dividend, and Investment Policy, Grouped by Implied Changes in Expected Corporate Cash Flows

Returns are weighted averages by sample size of the returns reported by the respective studies. (Unless otherwise noted, returns are significantly different from zero.)

Type of Announcement	Average Sample Size	Two-Day Announcement Period Return
Implied Increase in Expected Corporate Cash Flow		
Common stock repurchases		
intra-firm tender offer[a]	148	16.2%
open market repurchase[b]	182	3.6
targeted small holding[c]	15	1.6
Calls of non-convertible bonds[d]	133	−0.1*
Dividend increases		
dividend initiation[e]	160	3.7
dividend increase[f]	280	0.9
specially designated dividend[g]	164	2.1
Investment increases[b]	510	1.0
Implied Decrease in Expected Corporate Cash Flow		
Security sales		
common stock[i]	262	−1.6
preferred stock[j]	102	0.1*
convertible preferred[k]	30	−1.4
straight debt[l]	221	−0.2*
convertible debt[l]	80	−2.1
Dividend decreases[f]	48	−3.6
Investment decreases[h]	111	−1.1

[a]*Source:* Dann (1981), Masulis (1980), Vermaelen (1981), Rosenfeld (1982).
[b]*Source:* Dann (1980), Vermaelen (1981).
[c]*Source:* Bradley and Wakeman (1983).
[d]*Source:* Vu (1986).
[e]*Source:* Asquith and Mullins (1983).
[f]*Source:* Charest (1978), Aharony and Swary (1980).
[g]*Source:* Brickley (1983).
[h]*Source:* McConnell and Muscarella (1985).
[i]*Source:* Asquith and Mullins (1986), Masulis and Korwar (1986), Mikkelson and Partch (1986), Schipper and Smith (1986), Pettway and Radcliff (1985).
[j]*Source:* Linn and Pinegar (1985), Mikkelson and Partch (1986).
[k]*Source:* Linn and Pinegar (1985).
[l]*Source:* Dann and Mikkelson (1984), Eckbo (1986), Mikkelson and Partch (1986).
*Interpreted by the authors as not significantly different from zero.

The hypothesis that investors infer changes in net operating cash flows from investment, financing, and dividend policy announcements predicts nonpositive price reactions to announcements of security sales. However, this hypothesis does not predict differential reactions to debt versus equity sales, convertible versus non-convertible issues, or sales by industrial versus utility firms.

2.3. Unanticipated Announcements and Relative Price Effects

Because stock price changes reflect only the unanticipated component of the announcement, the magnitude of the stock price change at the announcement will vary inversely with the degree of predictability of the announcement if other effects are kept constant. The evidence in Tables 1 and 2 appears consistent with this hypothesis.

Predictability of Debt versus Equity Offers. Expected growth in assets or expected debt repayment (either from maturing issues or sinking-fund provisions) requires the firm to issue additional debt to maintain its capital structure.[2] Given a target capital structure and unchanged cash flows, debt repayment must be matched with new debt issuance. The more predictable are principal repayments, the more predictable are new debt issues. Similarly, the predictability of earnings (and thus internally generated equity) will determine the predictability of the new externally obtained equity funds. In general, a new debt issue is likely to be more predictable than a new equity issue because principal repayments are more predictable than earnings.

Another reason for the greater predictability of public debt offerings is related to the cost structures of public versus private debt. Flotation costs for publicly placed debt have a larger fixed component and more pronounced economies of scale than bank debt. Thus, a firm will tend to use bank lines of credit until an efficient public issue size is reached; then the firm will issue public debt and retire the bank debt. If potential security holders can observe the amount of bank borrowing and the pattern of public debt issuance, then predictable announcements of public bond issues should have smaller price reactions (see Marsh [1982] for evidence on the use of short-term debt to predict public debt issues).

Predictability of Industrial versus Utility Offers. Table 1 shows significant differences between the price reactions of industrials and utilities to new equity sales. Utilities appear to employ external capital markets more extensively than do industrials. If the higher frequency of use by utilities is associated with greater predictability of security issuance, then utilities should show a smaller observed stock price reaction to announcements of new security sales. But that raises the question of why the reliance on external capital markets differs between industrials and utilities.

A policy of paying larger dividends increases the frequency with which the corporation must go to capital markets to raise new equity (Rozeff [1982] and Easterbrook [1984]). If, when new funds are raised, the capital market provides effective monitoring of the firm's activities, then such a policy disciplines the firm more frequently and lowers agency costs. Firms with high investment rates and high demands for new capital frequently use capital markets anyway; for them the additional benefits of increased monitoring from higher dividends would be small. But utilities historically have both high demands for new capital and high dividend payout rates. I hypothesize that if the dividend rate is lowered and the frequency of selling new equity in capital markets is reduced, utility stockholders are likely to be damaged in the rate regulation process. By paying high dividends, the regulated firm subjects both its regulatory body as well as itself to capital market discipline more frequently. Stockholders are less likely to receive lower-than-normal levels of

---

[2] Note that the economics of scale documented in the schedule of flotation costs generally make it optimal to make discrete rather than continuous leverage adjustments. For simplicity, we ignore those flotation cost issues at present.

compensation due to lower allowed product prices when the regulatory authority is more frequently and effectively monitored by capital markets. Therefore, high dividends are a method of assuring a regulated firm's stockholders that they will receive a normal rate of return on the invested capital. This policy of high dividends also implies that the external security issuance by utilities is more predictable than for non-utilities. The smaller abnormal stock price changes for utilities than industrials is consistent with this hypothesis.[3]

Hypotheses about the predictability of announcements help explain the observed difference in announcement returns of common stock versus debt issues and industrials' versus utilities' offerings.[4] However, these hypotheses apparently do not explain differences in announcement returns between common and preferred stock or between convertible and nonconvertible issues.

2.4. Information Asymmetry and Relative Price Effects

Suppose that a potential purchaser of securities has less information than corporate managers, and corporate managers are more likely to issue securities when the market price of the firm's traded securities is higher than management's assessment of their value. This implies that the stock price effects of security issues will be greater the more the asymmetry in information between insiders and other security market participants (see Myers and Majluf [1984] and Myers [1984]). Since debt and preferred stock are more senior claims, their values are less sensitive to changes in firm value than is common stock, and thus the information asymmetry problem is less severe. Similarly, convertible debt and convertible preferred stock are more sensitive to changes in firm value than nonconvertible debt and preferred, but less so than common stock. Finally, in the rate regulation process, managers of utilities generally petition their respective regulatory authorities for permission for new security sales. This petitioning process could reduce the price reaction of utilities' announcements relative to industrials for any of three reasons: (1) it could reduce the differential information between manager and outsiders; (2) it could limit managers' discretion as to what security to sell; and (3) it could reduce managers' ability to time security offerings to take advantage of any differential information.

Thus, while the information asymmetry hypothesis does not predict the direction of announcement returns for debt or preferred issues, it offers a potential explanation of greater price changes associated with common stock than preferred or debt, for convertible than non-convertible issues, and for industrials than utilities.

While the evidence across classes of securities is consistent with the information asymmetry hypothesis, some data within security classes is apparently inconsistent. When Eckbo (1986) and Mikkelson and Partch (1986) disaggregate their bond data by rating class, neither study finds higher rated, less risky (and thus less sensitive to firm value) bonds to be associated with smaller abnormal returns. Eckbo also finds more negative abnormal returns to mortgage bonds than non-mortgage bonds.[5]

---

[3] Citizens Utilities is an apparent counterexample to this hypothesis. Because of its special tax status, it is allowed no new equity issues, and perhaps for that reason has a very low payout ratio. It also has an AAA rating and the highest rate of return to stockholders among all utilities, and it appears to have the best record in rate regulation proceedings. See also Long (1978).

[4] Also, the evidence in Table 2 of increases in dividends is consistent with this hypothesis. Dividend initiations are expected to have a larger unanticipated component than the ordinary dividend increases.

[5] As Stulz and Johnson (1985) argue, secured debt should be less sensitive to firm value than non-secured debt.

Table 3   Summary of Two-Day Announcement Effects Associated with Exchange Offers, Security Sales with Designated Uses of Funds, and Calls of Convertible Securities.

With sources and uses of funds associated, these transactions represent virtually pure financial structure changes.

Type of Transaction	Security Issued	Security Retired	Average Sample Size	Two-Day Announcement Period Return
Leverage-Increasing Transactions				
Stock repurchase[a]	Debt	Common	45	21.9%
Exchange offer[b]	Debt	Common	52	14.0
Exchange offer[b]	Preferred	Common	9	8.3
Exchange offer[b]	Debt	Preferred	24	2.2
Exchange offer[c]	Income bonds	Preferred	24	2.2
Transactions with No Change in Leverage				
Exchange offer[d]	Debt	Debt	36	0.6*
Security sale[f]	Debt	Debt	83	0.2*
Leverage-Reducing Transactions				
Conversion-forcing call[e]	Common	Convertible preferred	57	−0.4*
Conversion-forcing call[e]	Common	Convertible bond	113	−2.1
Security sale[f]	Convertible debt	Debt	15	−2.4
Exchange offer[b]	Common	Preferred	30	−2.6
Exchange offer[b]	Prefered	Debt	9	−7.7
Security sale[f]	Common	Debt	12	−4.2
Exchange offer[b]	Common	Debt	20	−9.9

[a]*Source*: Masulis (1980).
[b]*Source*: Masulis (1983). Note: These returns include announcement days of both the original offer and for about 40 percent of the sample, a second announcement of specific terms of the exchange.
[c]*Source*: McConnell and Schlarbaum (1981).
[d]*Source*: Dietrich (1984).
[e]*Source*: Mikkelson (1981).
[f]*Source*: Eckbo (1986), Mikkelson and Partch (1986).
*Not statistically different from zero.

The information asymmetry hypothesis can be distinguished from hypotheses about implied cash flow changes by examining evidence from events that explicitly associate sources and uses of funds. Just as the information asymmetry hypothesis implies no obvious predictions about dividend or investment announcements, the analysis of implied changes in net operating cash flows makes no prediction about the market reaction to announcements of exchange offers. The evidence in Table 3 from exchange offers, conversion-forcing calls of convertible securities, and security sales where the proceeds are used for debt retirement suggests that (1) the sign of the abnormal return and the sign of the leverage change are the same and (2) the larger the change in leverage, the greater is the absolute value of the abnormal price reaction. Thus, debt-for-common offers have larger stock price reactions than preferred-for-common offers, and common-for-debt offers have larger negative price reactions than common-for-preferred offers.

Combining the information symmetry hypothesis and the hypothesis on implied changes in net operating cash flows provides additional insight into the difference between reported announcement effects of debt and equity. For example, in the upper panel of Table 2, announcements of calls of nonconvertible debt are associated with implied increases in expected net operating cash flow but yield an insignificant negative return. However, this event is also on average associated with a reduction in leverage. When Vu (1986) disaggregates his sample of calls of bonds by change in leverage, he finds that for the 72 firms that decrease leverage, there are significant stock price announcement returns of −1.1 percent; for the 30 firms with no change in leverage, +0.3 percent; and for the 31 firms that increase leverage, +0.9 percent.

2.5. Changes in Ownership and Relative Price Effects

In some transactions, part of the observed price reaction reflects important changes in the ownership and control of the firm. Table 4 summarizes the results from studies of transactions with potentially important control implications. The upper panel summarizes results of transactions where the organization is restructured. The evidence suggests that organizational restructuring on average benefits stockholders. In the lower panel, value effects associated with a change in the distribution of ownership are examined. The evidence suggests that announcements of transactions that increase ownership concentration raise share prices, while those that reduce concentration lower share prices.

Organizational restructuring is sometimes accompanied by a security offering. For example, Schipper and Smith (1986) examine firms that sell common stock of a previously wholly owned subsidiary. In contrast to the negative returns from the sale of corporate common stock reported in Table 1, these "equity carve-outs" are associated with significant positive returns of 1.8 percent for the five days around the announcement.[6] There are important control implications of the public sale of a minority interest in a subsidiary. For example, management of the subsidiary can have a market-based compensation package that more accurately reflects subsidiary performance (see Smith and Watts [1982, 1984]). Schipper and Smith document that 94 percent of the carve-outs adopted incentive compensation plans based on the subsidiary's stock. The evidence from equity carve-outs is also consistent with the information asymmetry hypothesis. If management expects that the subsidiary is undervalued, then by segregating the subsidiary's cash flows and selling separate equity claims, the firm can more effectively capture that gain.

Some security sales involve potentially important ownership structure changes. For example, Masulis and Korwar (1986) isolate 56 offerings (not in Table 4) for which, in addition to the primary equity issue, there is also a registered secondary offering by the firm's management. The two-day announcement period return for the offers is −4.5 percent, compared to −3.1 percent for the average industrial equity offering.

---

[6] These positive returns are observed in spite of potentially large costs associated with these transactions. For example, the required information disclosures about the subsidiary are increased and the nature of the transactions that can take place between the parent and the subsidiary (to avoid potential conflict of interests between the parent's and subsidiary's outside stockholders) are restricted.

Table 4 Summary of Cumulative Abnormal Common Stock Returns and Average Sample Size from Studies of Announcements of Transactions That Change Corporate Control or Ownership Structure

Returns are weighted averages by sample size of the returns reported by the respective studies. (Unless otherwise noted, results are significantly different from zero.)

Type of Announcement	Average Sample Size	Cumulative Abnormal Returns
Organizational Restructuring		
Merger: Target[a]	113	20.0%
Bidder[a]	119	0.7*
Spin-off[b]	76	3.4
Sell-off: Seller[c]	279	0.7
Buyer[d]	118	0.7
Equity carve-out[e]	76	0.7*
Joint venture[f]	136	0.7
Going private[g]	81	30.0
Voluntary liquidation[b]	75	33.4
Life insurance company mutualization[i]	30	56.0
Savings & Loan Association charter conversion[j]	78	5.6
Proxy fight[k]	56	1.1
Ownership Restructuring		
Tender offer: Target[l]	183	30.0
Bidder[l]	183	0.8*
Large block acquisition[m]	165	2.6
Secondary distribution: Registered[n]	146	−2.9
Non-registered[n]	321	−0.8
Targeted share repurchase[o]	68	−4.8

[a] *Source:* Dodd (1980), Asquith (1983), Eckbo (1983), Jensen and Ruback (1983).

[b] *Source:* Hite and Owers (1983), Miles and Rosenfeld (1983), Schipper and Smith (1983), Rosenfeld (1984).

[c] *Source:* Alexander, Benson, and Kampmeyer (1984), Rosenfeld (1984), Hite and Owers (1985), Jain (1985), Klein (1985), Vetsuypens (1985).

[d] *Source:* Rosenfeld (1984), Hite and Owers (1985), Jain (1985), Klein (1985).

[e] *Source:* Schipper and Smith (1986).

[f] *Source:* McConnell and Nantell (1985).

[g] *Source:* DeAngelo, DeAngelo, and Rice (1984).

[h] *Source:* Kim and Schatzberg (1985).

[i] *Source:* Mayers and Smith (1985).

[j] *Source:* Masulis (1985).

[k] *Source:* Dodd and Warner (1983).

[l] *Source:* Bradley, Desai, and Kim (1985), Jensen and Ruback (1983).

[m] *Source:* Holderness and Sheehan (1985), Mikkelson and Ruback (1985).

[n] *Source:* Mikkelson and Partch (1985).

[o] *Source:* Dann and DeAngelo (1983), Bradley and Wakeman (1983).

*Interpreted by authors as not significantly different from zero.

3. Security Offerings by Public Corporations

After a firm decides on the security to issue, it must choose among a number of methods to market it. The firm can offer the securities on a pro rata basis to its own stockholders through a rights offering; it can hire an underwriter to offer the securities for sale to the public; or it can place the securities privately. If the firm uses an underwriter,[7] it can negotiate the offering terms with the underwriter, or it can structure the offering internally, then put it out for competitive bid. The underwriting contract can be a firm commitment or a best efforts offering. Finally, the issue can be registered with the Securities and Exchange Commission under its traditional registration procedures, or, if the firm qualifies, it can file a shelf registration in which the firm registers all securities it intends to sell over the next two years.

3.1. Rights versus Underwritten Offerings

The two most frequently employed methods by which public corporations market new securities are rights offerings and firm commitment underwritten offerings. In an underwritten offering, initial negotiation focuses on the amount of capital, the type of security, and the terms of the offering. If the firm and underwriter agree to proceed, the underwriter begins to assess the prospects. The investigation includes an audit by a public accounting firm and a legal opinion from a law firm. The issuing firm, the investment banker, the auditing firm, and the law firm all typically participate in filing the required registration statements with the Securities and Exchange Commission (as well as with the appropriate state securities commissions). The offering can proceed only when the registration statement becomes effective. Although oral sales efforts are permitted, any indications of interest are not legally enforceable commitments of customers. No written sales literature other than "red herring" prospectus and "tombstone advertisements" are permitted between the filing and offer date. The "Rules of Fair Practice" of the National Association of Security Dealers require that once the underwriters file the offer price with the SEC, the securities cannot be sold above this price, although they can be offered at a lower price if the syndicate "breaks."

In a rights offering, each stockholder receives options to buy newly issued securities. One right is issued for each share held. The contract states the number of rights required to purchase one unit of the newly issued security, the exercise price, and the expiration date. Rights offerings must be registered with the SEC. Rights typically trade on the exchange on which the stock is listed.

Smith (1977) documents that the out-of-pocket expenses of an equity issue underwritten by an investment banker are from three to thirty times higher than the costs of a non-underwritten rights offering. Yet over 80 percent of the equity offerings he examines employ underwriters.[8] Eckbo (1986) finds five percent of bond issues between 1964 and 1981 are sold through rights offers.

---

[7] Without exception, the analysis summarized here assumes effective competition within the investment banking industry. In fact, there are no effective barriers to entry in the industry. Effective competition provides strong incentives to supply efficient combinations of contractual provisions including services, fees, and underpricing.

[8] Hansen and Pinkerton (1982) document that firms which employ rights offerings have high ownership concentrations. Although they claim to resolve the paradox about the use of rights offerings, they ignore all costs except direct costs reported to the SEC and, as Smith and Dhatt (1984) indicate, overstate the significance of their statistical tests.

A number of authors have argued that investment bankers are effective in monitoring the firm's activities.[9] The monitoring is potentially valuable because of the differential information between managers and outside stockholders. Thus, in addition to a marketing function, the investment banker performs a monitoring function analogous to that of bond rating agencies (Wakeman [1981], Fama and Jensen [1985]), of independent auditing firms (Jensen and Meckling [1976], Watts [1977], DeAngelo [1981]),[10] of outside members of a firm's board of directors (Fama [1980]), and of insurance companies (Mayers and Smith [1982]). In each case, it is argued that while the activity is expensive, it is justified because periodic exposure of the firm's decision makers to effective monitoring raises the price external security holders are willing to pay for the firm.[11]

3.2. Negotiated versus Competitive Bid Contracts

Rule 50 of the Public Utilities Holding Company Act of 1935 requires registered public utility holding companies to sell securities through competitive bid, unless the firm obtains an exemption from the SEC. The Commission generally grants exemptions only if the firm cannot secure competitive bids or if it judges the market conditions to be "unsettled." Utilities not organized as holding companies are not affected by the Act.

Bhagat and Frost (1986) compare the issue costs for public utility firms that sell common stock using competitive bid and negotiated underwritten contracts. They measure total issue costs as the sum of underwriter's commissions, issuer-borne expenses, and underpricing. They examine a sample of 552 offerings between 1973 and 1980 in which 73 are competitive bid and 479 are negotiated. Of the 479 negotiated offerings, 28 are negotiated after obtaining an exemption from the Securities and Exchange Commission. Bhagat and Frost estimate that the total issue costs are higher for firms which use negotiated offerings by 1.2 percent of the proceeds. Moreover, they find each component of cost (commissions, issuer-borne expenses and underpricing) higher in negotiated offerings.

The Bhagat and Frost evidence is consistent with that of Logue and Jarrow (1978), Ederington (1976), and Dyl and Joehnk (1976). Logue and Jarrow find that for a sample of 122 utility common stock issues between 1963 and 1974, the average underwriting commissions are 1.2 percent higher for negotiated offerings than competitive bid. Ederington examines 1,081 issues of public utility

---

[9] See Rozeff (1982), Easterbrook (1984), Booth and Smith (1986), Heinkel and Schwartz (1985), and Schneller (1985).

[10] The monitoring hypothesis for both investment bankers and independent auditing firms is also suggested by the evidence in Burton and Roberts (1967) and Carpenter and Strawser (1971) that a significant fraction of changes in auditing firms is associated with new securities offerings.

[11] The major observation that seems inconsistent with the monitoring explanation of the investment banker's function is the evidence that Smith (1977) and Bhagat (1983) provide. They examine firms that eliminate the preemptive right from the corporate charter. If investment bankers provide a valuable monitoring function, the benefit should be forecast and impounded when firms change policies. Thus, examination of returns around the elimination of the preemptive right (which requires firms to offer new shares first on a pro rata basis to existing shareholders) should pick up the present value of the incremental benefit from increased use of underwriters. But Bhagat finds a significant negative stock return at the proxy mailing date. Neither Bhagat nor Smith find significant returns at the annual meeting date when the vote is taken. There are two important qualifications of the evidence from preemptive right elimination. First, given the evidence in Table 1 that the average response to new equity issues is negative, the negative effect observed by Bhagat could measure the higher probability of a stock offering. It is likely that firms only incur the expense to eliminate the preemptive right if they anticipate making an offering. Second, neither Smith nor Bhagat distinguish between firms who had used rights alone and firms that normally had their rights offerings underwritten. Neither the difference in monitoring nor out-of-pocket expenses are as great when comparing underwritten issues with underwritten rights offerings.

and industrial bond offerings between 1964 and 1971. He finds that the offering yields on negotiated issues are approximately seven to eight basis points higher than the yields on equivalent competitive bid issues offered at the same time. And although underwriter spreads are on average less
for competitive bid than negotiated issues, there are periods where negotiated bids are less expensive. Dyl and Joehnk examine a sample of 312 competitive bids and 71 negotiated new issues of
debt by public utilities between 1972 and 1974. They find that the average underwriters' commission as a fraction of proceeds is higher by 0.13 percent and the yield on the debt is higher by 36
basis points for negotiated than for competitive bid offers. These differences are evident across
bond rating classes. Moreover, the results occur despite the fact that the average negotiated offer
was approximately $10 million larger than the average competitive bid; with economies of scale in
the investment banking industry, larger issues are expected to receive lower percentage fees.

   Thus, the evidence suggests that competitive bid offerings involve lower total flotation costs
than negotiated offerings. Yet it appears that the major users of competitive bids are regulated firms
which are required to do so. Firms not facing a regulatory constraint overwhelmingly choose negotiated offers.

   Bhagat and Frost suggest that this behavior can be explained by differences in incentives between managers and shareholders and the costs of controlling the firm's managers. They conjecture
that managers might benefit from (1) side payments from investment bankers—especially those investment bankers who are members of the corporate board of directors, (2) increased compensation
if managerial compensation is tied to accounting profits,[12] and (3) less variation in cost (a benefit if
the managers are risk-averse) since they offer evidence that the variance of issuing costs is higher
for competitive bid offerings.

   An alternative explanation follows from the hypothesis that there is information asymmetry between managers and outside security holders that produces a derived demand for monitoring. In a
competitive bid offering, the issuing firm specifies the details of the offering—the type of security,
the issue date, and (if it is a bond) the covenants. Thus, differential information available to managers can be used in setting the terms of the offering without constraints from negotiation with investment bankers. And because the firm retains this additional flexibility, potential security holders
reduce the price they are willing to pay for the issue. Moreover, if it is difficult to control the use of
information received by investment bankers not awarded the contract, then companies with potentially sensitive information are likely to find competitive bids costly. If the effective monitoring provided through a competitively bid offering is less than that provided through a negotiated
underwritten issue, then firms would have incentives to employ negotiated offerings, even though
the flotation costs are higher.

   The monitoring hypothesis has implications for the cross-sectional distribution of competitive bid
versus negotiated offerings. Firms with smaller information asymmetry between outside security
holders and managers will more likely use competitive bids. Thus, if the rate regulation process
reduces the differential information, regulated utilities not subject to Rule 50 should use competitive
bids more frequently than unregulated firms. Similarly, since competitive bids allow the issuing firm's
management to specify the date of the offering, if the informational asymmetry problem is severe,

---

[12] Since future consulting services could be bundled into the underwriter's fee, and since costs of selling securities do not go
through the income statement but are charged directly to the capital account, accounting earnings are higher, though cash
flows are lower.

competitive bids will be expensive. Thus, firms with less discretion in the timing of security offerings should more frequently employ competitive bids. Finally, with more senior claims, the informational asymmetry problem is less severe because the value of the claim is less sensitive to firm value. Thus straight debt, secured debt, and non-convertible preferred stock should be sold through competitive bids more frequently than common stock, convertible preferred stock, or convertible bonds.

However, Bhagat (1985) finds evidence which is consistent with this monitoring hypothesis. He examines the price reaction of firms affected by the suspension of Rule 50, which requires public utilities holding companies to seek competitive bids. He finds that at the announcement, share prices fall, and on reinstatement of the rule, share prices rise. Since the SEC suspends the rule when market conditions are "unsettled," Bhagat's test may pick up adverse changes in underlying market conditions. However, that would require that the Commission either move very fast or have valuable information about the state of the market otherwise unavailable to security holders. Neither of these conditions seems plausible.

3.3. Shelf versus Traditional Registration

In March 1982, the SEC authorized Rule 415 on an experimental basis. It permitted certain firms to employ shelf registration for public security issues. Rule 415 was made permanent in November 1983. The procedure is called shelf registration because it allows companies to register securities, "put them on the shelf," and then issue the securities whenever they choose. It permits firms with more than $150 million of stock held by investors unaffiliated with the company to specify and register the total dollar amount of securities they expect to sell publicly over the next two years. After the securities are registered, the firm can then offer and sell them for up to two years on a continuous basis. Rule 415 also allows the firm to modify a debt instrument and sell it without first filing an amendment to the registration statement. Thus, shelf registration allows qualifying firms additional flexibility both in structuring debt issues and in timing for all security issues.

The shelf registration procedure has been employed more frequently with debt than equity offerings. However, if the problem of differential information between managers and potential shareholders is severe, fewer equity issues should be registered through shelf procedures. With the additional timing flexibility given management, there is an increased opportunity to exploit inside information. Potential security holders anticipating this problem would lower the amount they are willing to pay. Hence, stock price reactions to announcements of new equity offerings registered under Rule 415 should have more negative stock price reactions than if they were registered under traditional registration procedures.

Shelf registration procedures also should affect the structure of flotation costs. For example, shelf registration should lower fixed costs of public debt issues. This could lead qualified firms to change their practices with respect to debt offerings. Rather than use a line of credit at a bank until a large public issue can be made, firms could use the shelf registration process to place several smaller issues rather than having one large issue. Liquidity advantages with respect to secondary markets could be retained by having multiple issues with the same coupon rate, coupon dates, maturity dates, and covenants.

Kidwell, Marr, and Thompson (1984) and Rogowski and Sorensen (1985) examine the implications of allowing firms to choose between shelf and traditional registration procedures in issuing bonds. Both use regression techniques for a cross-section of issues to examine the alternative costs. They conclude that shelf registration lowers the interest rate by between 20 and 40 basis points.

4. Initial Public Equity Offerings

Privately owned corporations face two major alternatives: to remain private or to become a public corporation. A public corporation incurs a number of obligations not imposed on private firms.[13] For example, the SEC requires periodic filings which can be costly in three dimensions: (1) the out-of-pocket production costs, (2) the value of management's time, and (3) the reduction in firm value from disclosing valuable information otherwise unavailable to the firm's competitors.

Private firms that choose to go public typically obtain the services of an underwriter and have an initial public equity offering. Initial public equity offerings are an interesting special case of security offerings. They differ from offerings previously discussed in two important ways: (1) the uncertainty about the market clearing price of the offering is significantly greater than for public corporations with claims currently trading and (2) because the firm has no traded shares, examinations of stock price reactions to announcements (as in section 2) are impossible. The first difference affects the way these securities are marketed; the second limits the ways researchers can study the offerings.

4.1. Underpricing

Examination of the return behavior of initial public equity offerings from offer price to after-market indicates that the average issue is offered at a significant discount from the price expected in the after-market; however, after-market returns appear to be normal (Ibottson [1975]), Ibbotson and Jaffe [1975], Ritter [1984, 1985], and Chalk and Peavy [1985]). Table 5 summarizes the results from studies of offer prices for initial public equity offerings as well as new issues of seasoned equity and bonds. For initial public equity offerings, the average underpricing appears to exceed 15 percent.

Hypotheses have been offered to explain underpricing of new issues (Baron [1982], Ritter [1985], Chalk and Peavy [1985], Rock [1986], and Beatty and Ritter [1986]). Baron focuses on the asymmetry in information between the issuing firm and the investment banker. The other authors focus on the asymmetry of information between informed and uninformed potential security holders.

The Rock and the Ritter analyses of underpricing assume that markets are efficient in a very specific sense—that the marginal investment in information yields a normal expected return. Potential security-holders can be divided into three groups: (1) marginal investors who are indifferent about investing in information, (2) inframarginal investors who are better informed and thus earn abnormal returns, and (3) inframarginal investors who rationally choose (either because of the size of their portfolio or the opportunity cost of their time) not to invest in information.

In an offering, there is uncertainty about the market-clearing price. If the offer prices are set at their expected market-clearing price, uninformed investors systematically earn below normal returns; if an issue is underpriced, informed investors also submit bids and the issue is rationed; and if the issue is

---

[13] See DeAngelo, DeAngelo, and Rice (1984). Fairly strict limits control the maximum number of equity holders a firm may have and still remain private. This limitation implies that the larger the firm, the greater the underdiversification cost imposed on equity holders. The equity claims are also less liquid since some otherwise feasible transfers are restricted by regulation and would jeopardize the firm's private status. Note that since this constraint is on the ownership distribution of the firm, it generates a potential conflict among the stockholders of a private corporation. For example, if there can be no more than 20 equity holders to maintain private corporation status, but currently there are 15, a stockholder selling his shares to more than one person who is not currently a stockholder consumes degrees of freedom of the remaining equity holders.

Table 5   Summary of Estimated Underpricing of New Securities at Issuance by Type of Offering

Underpricing is measured by the average percentage change from offer prices to after-market price.

Type of Offering	Study	Sample Period	Sample Size	Estimated Underpricing
Initial public equity offering	Ibbotson (1974)	1960–1969	120	11.4%
Initial public equity offering	Ibbotson and Jaffe (1975)	1960–1970	2650	16.8
Initial public equity offering	Ritter (1984)	1960–1982	5162	18.8
		1977–1982	1028	26.5
		1980–1981	325	48.4
Initial public equity offering	Ritter (1985)	1977–1982		
firm commitment			664	14.8
best efforts			364	47.8
Initial public equity offering	Chalk and Peavy (1985)	1974–1982	440	13.8
firm commitment			415	10.6
best efforts			82	52.0
Equity carve-outs	Schipper and Smith (1986)	1963–1983	36	0.19
Seasoned new equity offering	Smith (1977)	1971–1975	328	0.6
Seasoned new utility equity offering	Bhagat and Frost (1986)	1973–1980	552	−0.30
negotiated			479	−0.25
competitive bid			73	−0.65
Primary debt issue	Weinstein (1978)	1962–1974	412	0.05

overpriced, informed investors are less likely to submit bids and the issue is more likely to be undersubscribed. Hence, uninformed investors systematically receive more of overpriced issues and less of underpriced issues. Uninformed investors anticipate this adverse selection and bid only if the offer price is below their expected after-market price by enough to compensate for their expected losses on overpriced issues. This implies that the average underpricing is greater for issues with greater price uncertainty.

Baron (1982) analyzes an optimal contract for advising and marketing services between a firm and its investment banker. He hypothesizes that the investment banker is better informed about the market demand for the firm's securities than is the firm. Since the firm must compensate the investment banker for providing advice in setting the offer price for the issue and for marketing the securities, the optimal offer price is a decreasing function of the uncertainty about the market demand for the issue, while the value of delegation to the underwriter is an increasing function of the uncertainty.

Thus, while the alternative hypotheses focus on different information problems—(1) between informed and uninformed potential security holders and (2) between the issuing firm and its investment banker—the two yield similar implications about which firms employ which contract for a given issue.

Beatty and Ritter (1986) attempt to test the underpricing hypotheses using data from initial public offerings. They argue that there is an equilibrium amount of underpricing. If an investment banker underprices too much, given the characteristics of the issue, the investment banker loses future offerings. If the investment banker underprices too little, he loses investors. Beatty and Ritter estimate an underpricing function and examine the average deviation of 49 investment bankers who handled four or more initial public offerings during the period 1977–1981. They compare subsequent performance of the 24 underwriters whose average deviation from their estimated normal underpricing is greatest with that of the remaining 25 underwriters whose average deviation is least. For the 24 with the greatest deviation, their market share goes from 46.6 to 24.5 percent and 5 of the 24 cease operations during 1981–1982. For the 25 with the smallest deviation, their market share goes from 27.2 to 21.0 percent and 1 of the 25 ceases operation.

Schipper and Smith find that for their sample of initial public offerings, which result from equity carve-outs, the average underpricing is only 0.19 percent. It seems plausible that potential asymmetric information problems are less severe for this subset of initial offerings than the average; thus, less underpricing is expected. Yet it is surprising that the measured underpricing is so similar to that of seasoned new issues.[14]

As Table 5 shows, security issues by public corporations are also underpriced. Smith finds seasoned equity issues underpriced by 0.6 percent, Bhagat and Frost find seasoned equity issues by utilities overpriced by 0.3 percent, and Weinstein finds new bonds underpriced by 0.05 percent. Parsons and Raviv (1985) extend Rock's analysis of underpricing initial public equity offerings to consider seasoned new equity offerings. In a seasoned offering, potential security holders have the option of buying after the announcement but before the offering, at the offering or in the aftermarket. Again, the asymmetry in information among investors implies that the offer price will be set systematically below both the security price between the announcement and the offer date as well as below the expected after-market price.[15] This hypothesis implies that underpricing should be greater with competitive bid than negotiated offerings, and with shelf than traditional registration procedures. (Unfortunately, this implication for shelf issues is somewhat more difficult to test because of the proximity of the announcement and issue dates.)

Smith and Chalk and Peavy indicate that the average measured underpricing could overstate the cost imposed on issuers if the underwriter can extract gains by rationing ex post underpriced issues. Then, competition among underwriters transfers the expected gains back to the issuer through the quoted offer fees.

4.2. Best Efforts versus Firm Commitment Contracts

Two alternative forms of underwriting contracts are typically employed in initial public equity offerings. The first is a firm commitment underwriting agreement under which the underwriter agrees to purchase the whole issue from the firm at a particular price for resale to the public. The second is

---

[14] This underpricing evidence combined with the clustering of event dates provides potential corroboration of the Ibbotson and Jaffe (1975) and Ritter (1984) hypotheses about the non-stationary time series behavior of underpricing.

[15] Note that the Bhagat and Frost evidence is potentially consistent with the Parsons and Raviv hypothesis if one recognizes the difference in transactions costs in the two transactions. The transaction generating the closing price will as frequently be initiated by a buy order as a sell order; on average, the closing price represents the midpoint of the bid–ask spread. Moreover, the transaction generating the closing price involves brokerage fees. There are no purchases-borne fees in a primary distribution. Phillips and Smith (1980) estimate the bid–ask spread at 0.6 percent and the brokerage fees for individuals at 0.4 percent. Thus, the purchaser's expenditure is the closing price plus half the bid–ask spread plus the brokerage fee. These adjustments exceed Bhagat and Frost's measured overpricing.

a best efforts underwriting agreement under which the underwriter acts only as a marketing agent for the firm.[16] The underwriter does not agree to purchase the issue at a predetermined price, but sells the security and takes a predetermined spread, with the firm taking the residual. The agreement generally specifies a minimum amount that must be sold within a given period of time; if this amount is not reached, the offering is canceled. Ritter (1985) reports that 35 percent of initial public equity offerings from 1977 to 1982 are sold with best efforts contracts, although they represent only 13 percent of the gross proceeds.

The information problem between informed and uninformed potential security holders, as well as the information and contracting problems between the issuing firm and its investment banker, influence the choice between firm commitment and best efforts contracts. Ritter (1985) contrasts the preceding argument for underpricing firm commitments with the incentives in a best efforts contract. He argues that in a best efforts contract, if the issue is overpriced and the issue falls short of the minimum specified in the underwriting contract, the offer is canceled and the losses to the uninformed investors are reduced. Structuring the contract in this manner reduces the problem faced by uninformed potential security holders, and thus reduces the discount necessary to induce them to bid.

Ritter argues that the relative attractiveness of the two contracts varies with changes in the amount of uncertainty associated with the issue. The prohibition against raising prices for an oversubscribed issue imposed by the Rules of Fair Practice of the National Association of Security Dealers is analogous to the firm giving a call option to potential stockholders [see Smith [1979]]. Thus, in a firm commitment offering, the expected proceeds to the firm are reduced if the uncertainty about after-market prices is higher. In a best efforts contract, the firm again gives the call because of the rule against raising the price, but the firm also gives an option to potential shareholders to put the shares back to the firm if the issue is undersubscribed. Thus, with more uncertainty about after-market prices, best efforts contracts become relatively more attractive.

Mandelker and Raviv (1977), Baron (1979, 1982), and Baron and Holmstrom (1980) hypothesize that there is uncertainty among the capital market participants about the market-clearing price for the securities. Furthermore, their models focus on the conflict of interest between the issuing firm and its underwriter. They derive optimal contracts, either best efforts or firm commitment, based on the uncertainty associated with the issue and the degree of risk aversion of the issuer and investment banker. Mandelker and Raviv assume symmetric information when the contract is negotiated between the firm and the investment banker. Baron (1979) also assumes symmetric information between the investment banker and the issuing firm but considers the potential conflict of interest because of the issuer's inability to observe the investment banker's marketing effort. Baron and Holmstrom assume symmetric information at the time of contracting but allow the investment banker to acquire information during the preselling period before the offering. Baron (1982) allows the investment banker to have better information about the market at the time the contract is negotiated. In their analyses a firm commitment offering is more likely to be optimal: (1) the more risk-averse the issuer, (2) the less risk-averse the investment banker, (3) the less the uncertainty about the market clearing price, (4) the less the asymmetry in information between the issuer and the investment banker, and (5) the more observable the investment banker's effort.

---

[16] Booth and Smith (1986) report that in non-initial offerings from 1977 to 1982, best efforts contracts are used in two percent of the equity offerings, two percent of convertible issues, no preferred stock issues, and eight percent of debt issues.

Therefore, both lines of analysis predict that best efforts contracts are more likely the greater the uncertainty of the after-market issue price. Ritter tests this hypothesis using the after-market standard deviation of returns as a proxy for ex ante uncertainty. He estimates the after-market standard deviation using the first 20 quoted bid prices after the offering. He finds that the average standard deviation for 285 best efforts offerings is 7.6 percent, and is statistically significantly above the 4.2 percent standard deviation of 641 firm commitment offerings. This is consistent with the hypothesis that issues with greater uncertainty are more likely to employ best efforts than firm commitment contracts.

5. Unresolved Issues

The growth of knowledge about the process of raising capital has been substantial. I believe that this area will continue to receive a great deal of attention, particularly because a number of interesting questions have been suggested by this examination of the capital acquisition process: (1) Do stock price reactions to announcements of new security sales differ between rights and underwritten offers? (2) Marsh (1979) reports that in 1975, 99 percent of the new equity in England was raised through rights offers. Why is there the dramatic difference in use of rights between the United States and the United Kingdom? (3) Researchers typically have contrasted underwritten offers with non-underwritten rights offers, yet in a significant fraction of rights offers, underwriters are retained on a standby basis. Under what circumstances are rights offering with standby underwriting contracts optimal? (4) Standby underwriting contracts typically are either single-fee agreements or two-fee agreements which specify both a "standby fee" and a "take-up fee" based on the number of rights handled. What determines the optimal fee structure? (5) Underwriters typically trade in the secondary market during and immediately after a security offering. Why is this "stabilization" activity beneficial? (6) Underwritten equity offers frequently include a "green shoe" option that gives the underwriter the right to buy additional shares from the firm at the offer price. For which offers is that provision optimal? (7) If we restrict ourselves to companies not constrained by Rule 50 of the Public Utilities Holding Company Act, how does frequency of use of competitive bids vary with the type of security? With the size of the offering? With the industry of the issuing firm? And with the ownership concentration of the firm? (8) Are convertible bonds and convertible preferred stock underpriced at issue? (9) Are there differences in underpricing between issues registered under Rule 415 versus traditional procedures?

References

Ahrony, Joseph, and Itzhak Swary, 1980. Quarterly dividend and earnings announcements and stockholder's returns: An empirical analysis. *The Journal of Finance* 35, 1–12.

Alexander, Gordon J., P. George Benson, and Joan M. Kampmeyer, 1984. Investigating the valuation effects of announcements of voluntary corporate selloffs. *The Journal of Finance* 39, 503–17.

Asquith, Paul, 1983. Merger bids, uncertainty, and stockholder returns. *Journal of Financial Economics* 11, 51–83.

Asquith, Paul, and David Mullins, 1983. The impact of initiating dividend payments on shareholder wealth. *Journal of Business* 56, 77–96.

Asquith, Paul, and David Mullins, 1986. Equity issues and offering dilution. *Journal of Financial Economics* 15, 61–89.

Baron, David P., 1979. The incentive problem and the design of investment banking contracts. *Journal of Banking and Finance* 3, 157–75.

Baron, David P., 1982. A model of the demand for investment banking advising and distribution services for new issues. *The Journal of Finance* 37, 955–76.

Baron, David P., and Bengt Holmstrom, 1980. The investment banking contract for new issues under asymmetric information: Delegation and the incentive problem. *The Journal of Finance* 35, 1115–38.

Beatty, Randolph P., and Jay R. Ritter, 1986. Investment banking, reputation, and the underpricing of initial public offerings. *Journal of Financial Economics* 15, 213–32.

Bhagat, Sanjai 1983. The effect of pre-emptive right amendments on shareholder wealth. *Journal of Financial Economics* 12, 289–310.

Bhagat, Sanjai, 1985. The effect of management's choice between negotiated and competitive equity offerings on shareholder wealth. *Journal of Financial and Quantitative Analysis*.

Bhagat, Sanjai, and Peter A. Frost. 1986, Issuing costs to existing shareholders in competitive and negotiated underwritten public utility equity offerings. *Journal of Financial Economics* 15, 233–59.

Booth, James R., and Richard L. Smith, III, 1986. Capital raising, underwriting and the certification hypothesis. *Journal of Financial Economics* 15, 261–81.

Bradley, Michael, Anand Desai, and E. Han Kim, 1983. The rationale behind interfirm tender offers: Information or synergy? *Journal of Financial Economics* 11, 183–206.

Bradley, Michael, and L. M. Wakeman, 1983. The wealth effects of targeted share repurchases. *Journal of Financial Economics* 11, 301–28.

Brennan, Michael, and Eduardo Schwartz, 1978. Corporate income taxes, valuation, and the problem of optimal capital structure. *Journal of Business* 51, 103–14.

Brickley, James, 1983. Shareholder wealth, information signaling and the specially designated dividend: An empirical study. *Journal of Financial Economics* 12, 187–209.

Burton, John C., and William Roberts, 1967. A study of auditor changes, *Journal of Accountancy*, 31–36.

Carpenter, Charles G., and Robert H. Strawser, 1971. Displacement of auditors when clients go public. *Journal of Accountancy,* 55–58.

Chalk, Andrew J., and John W. Peavy, III, 1985. Understanding the pricing of initial public offerings. Unpublished manuscript (Southern Methodist University, Dallas, TX).

Charest, Guy, 1978. Dividend information, stock returns, and market efficiency—II. *Journal of Financial Economics* 6, 297–330.

Dann, Larry, 1980. The effect of common stock repurchase on stockholder returns. Unpublished dissertation (University of California, Los Angeles, CA).

Dann, Larry, 1981. Common stock repurchases: An analysis of returns to bondholders and stockholders. *Journal of Financial Economics* 9, 113–38.

Dann, Larry, and Harry DeAngelo, 1983. Standstill agreements, privately negotiated stock repurchases and the market for corporate control. *Journal of Financial Economics* 11, 275–300.

Dann, Larry Y., David Mayers, and Robert J. Raab, Jr., 1977. Trading rules, large blocks and the speed of price adjustment. *Journal of Financial Economics* 4, 3–22.

Dann, Larry Y., and Wayne H. Mikkelson, 1984. Convertible debt issuance, capital structure change and financing-related information: Some new evidence. *Journal of Financial Economics* 13, 157–186.

Dealer's Digest Inc., 1985. Five year directory of corporate financing 1980–1984, Anthony V. Ricotta, ed. (Mason Slaine, New York).

DeAngelo, Harry, Linda DeAngelo, and Edward M. Rice, 1984. Going private: Minority freezeouts and shareholder wealth. *Journal of Law and Economics* 27, 367–401.

DeAngelo, Harry, and Ronald Masulis, 1980. Optimal capital structure under corporate and personal taxation. *Journal of Financial Economics* 8, 3–29.

DeAngelo, Linda, 1981. Auditor independence, "low balling," and disclosure regulation. *Journal of Accounting and Economics* 3, 113–27.

Dietrich, J. Richard, 1984. Effects of early bond refundings: An empirical investigation of security returns. *Journal of Accounting and Economics* 6, 67–96.

Dodd, Peter, 1980. Merger proposals, management discretion and stockholder wealth. *Journal of Financial Economics* 8, 105–38.

Dodd, Peter, and Richard S. Ruback, 1977. Tender offers and stockholder returns: An empirical analysis. *Journal of Financial Economics* 5, 351–74.

Dodd, Peter, and Jerold B. Warner, 1983. On corporate governance: A study of proxy contests. *Journal of Financial Economics* 11, 401–38.

Dyl, Edward, and Michael D. Joehnk, 1976. Competitive versus negotiated underwriting of public utility debt, *Bell Journal of Economics* 7, 680–89.

Easterbrook, Frank H., 1983. Two agency-cost explanations of dividends. *American Economic Review* 74, 650–59.

Eckbo, B. Espen, 1983. Horizontal mergers, collusion, and stockholder wealth. *Journal of Financial Economics* 11, 241–73.

Eckbo, B. Espen, 1986. Valuation effects of corporate debt offerings. *Journal of Financial Economics* 15, 119–51.

Ederington, Louis H., 1976. Negotiated versus competitive underwritings of corporate bonds. *The Journal of Finance* 31, 17–28.

Fama, Eugene F., 1978. The effect of a firm's investment and financing decisions. *American Economic Review* 68, 272–84.

Fama, Eugene F., 1980. Agency problems and the theory of the firm. *Journal of Political Economy* 88, 288–307.

Fama, Eugene F., and Michael C. Jensen, 1985. Residual claims and investment decisions. *Journal of Financial Economics* 14, 101–19.

Gilson, Ronald J., and Reinier H. Kraakman, 1984. The mechanisms of market efficiency. *Virginia Law Review* 70, 549–644.

Hansen, Robert S., and John M. Pinkerton, 1982. Direct equity financing: A resolution of a paradox. *The Journal of Finance* 37, 651–65.

Heinkel, Robert, and Eduardo S. Schwartz, 1984. Rights versus underwritten offerings: An asymmetric information approach. Unpublished manuscript (University of British Columbia, Vancouver).

Hite, Gailen, and James E. Owers, 1983. Security price reactions around corporate spin-off announcements. *Journal of Financial Economics* 12, 409–36.

Hite, Gailen, and James E. Owers, 1985. Sale divestitures: Implications for buyers and sellers. Unpublished manuscript (Southern Methodist University, Dallas, TX).

Holderness, Clifford G., and Dennis P. Sheehan, 1985. Raiders or saviors? The evidence on six controversial investors. *Journal of Financial Economics* 14, 555–79.

Ibbotson, Roger, 1975. Price performance of common stock new issues. *Journal of Financial Economics* 2, 235–72.

Ibbotson, Roger G., and Jeffrey F. Jaffe, 1975. "Hot issue" markets. *The Journal of Finance* 30, 1027–42.

Jain, Prem C., 1985. The effect of voluntary sell-off announcements on shareholder wealth. *The Journal of Finance* 40, 209–24.

Jensen, Michael C., and William H. Meckling, 1976. Theory of the firm: Managerial behavior agency costs and ownership structure. *Journal of Financial Economics* 3, 305–60.

Jensen, Michael C., and Richard S. Ruback, 1983. The market for corporate control: The scientific evidence. *Journal of Financial Economics* 11, 5–50.

Kidwell, David S., M. Wayne Marr, and G. Rodney Thompson, 1984. SEC Rule 415: The ultimate competitive bid. *Journal of Financial and Quantitative Analysis* 19, 183–95.

Kim, E. Han, and John D. Schatzberg, 1985. Voluntary liquidation and stockholder returns. Unpublished manuscript (University of Michigan, Ann Arbor, MI).

Klein, April, 1984. The effects of voluntary corporate divestitures on shareholders' wealth. Unpublished manuscript (University of Chicago, Chicago, IL).

Kolodny, Richard, and Diane Rizzuto Suhler, 1985. Changes in capital structure, new equity issues, and scale effects. *Journal of Financial Research* 8, 127–36.

Kraus, Alan, and Robert Litzenberger, 1973. A state preference model of optimal financial leverage. *The Journal of Finance* 28, 911–22.

Linn, Scott, and J. Michael Pinegar, 1985. The effect of issuing preferred stock on common stockholder wealth. Unpublished manuscript (University of Iowa, Iowa City, IA).

Logue, Dennis E., and Robert A. Jarrow, 1978. Negotiation vs. competitive bidding in the sale of securities by public utilities. *Financial Management* 7, 31–39.

Mandelker, Gershon, and Artur Raviv, 1977. Investment banking: An economic analysis of optimal underwriting contracts. *The Journal of Finance* 32, 683–94.

Marsh, Paul, 1979. Equity rights issues and the efficiency of the UK stock market. *The Journal of Finance* 34, 839–62.

Marsh, Paul, 1982. The choice between equity and debt: An empirical study. *The Journal of Finance* 37, 121–44.

Masulis, Ronald M., 1980. Stock repurchase by tender offer: An analysis of the causes of common stock price changes. *The Journal of Finance* 35, 305–19.

Masulis, Ronald, 1983. The impact of capital structure change on firm value: Some estimates. *The Journal of Finance* 37, 107–26.

Masulis, Ronald, 1985. Changes in ownership structure: Conversions of mutual savings and loans to stock charter. Unpublished manuscript (University of California, Los Angeles, CA).

Masulis, Ronald W., and Ashok Korwar, 1986. Seasoned equity offerings: An empirical investigation. *Journal of Financial Economics* 15, 91–118.

Mayers, David, and Clifford Smith, 1982. On the corporate demand for insurance. *Journal of Business* 55, 281–96.

Mayers, David, and Clifford Smith, 1985. Ownership structure and control: The mutualization of stock life insurance companies. *Journal of Financial Economics*.

McConnell, John, and Chris J. Muscarella, 1985. Corporate capital expenditure decisions and the market value of the firm. *Journal of Financial Economics* 14, 399–422.

McConnell, John, and Timothy Nantell, 1985. Corporate combinations and common stock returns: The case of joint ventures. *The Journal of Finance* 40, 519–36.

McConnell, John, and Gary Schlarbaum, 1981. Evidence on the impact of exchange offers on security prices: The case of income bonds. *Journal of Business* 54, 65–85.

Mikkelson, Wayne, 1981. Convertible calls and security returns. *Journal of Financial Economics* 9, 237–64.

Mikkelson, Wayne H., and M. Megan Partch, 1985. Stock price effects and costs of secondary distributions. *Journal of Financial Economics* 14, 165–94.

Mikkelson, Wayne H., and M. Megan Partch, 1986. Valuation effects of security offerings and the issuance process. *Journal of Financial Economics* 15, 31–61.

Mikkelson, Wayne H., and Richard S. Ruback, 1985. Corporate investments in common stock. *Journal of Financial Economics*.

Miles, J., and J. Rosenfeld, 1983. An empirical analysis of the effects of spin-off announcements on shareholder wealth. *The Journal of Finance* 38, 1597–1606.

Miller, Merton, 1977. Debt and taxes. *The Journal of Finance* 32, 261–76.

Miller, Merton, and Kevin Rock, 1985. Dividend policy under asymmetric information. *The Journal of Finance*.

Modigliani, Franco, and Merton Miller, 1958. The cost of capital, corporation finance and the theory of investment. *American Economic Review* 48, 261–97.

Modigliani, Franco, and Merton Miller, 1963. Corporate income taxes and the cost of capital: A correction. *American Economic Review* 53, 433–43.

Myers, Stewart, 1977. Determinants of corporate borrowing. *Journal of Financial Economics* 5, 147–75.

Myers Stewart, 1984. The capital structure puzzle, *The Journal of Finance* 39, 575–92.

Myers, Stewart C., and Nicholas S. Majluf, 1984. Corporate financing and investment decisions when firms have information that investors do not have. *Journal of Financial Economics* 13, 187–221.

Parsons, John, and Artur Raviv, 1985. Underpricing of seasoned issues. *Journal of Financial Economics* 14, 377–97.

Pettway, Richard H., and Robert C. Radcliffe, 1985. Impacts of new equity sales upon electric utility share prices. *Financial Management* 14, 16–25.

Phillips, Susan M., and Clifford W. Smith, Jr., 1980. Trading costs for listed options: The implications for market efficiency. *Journal of Financial Economics* 8, 179–201.

Ritter, Jay R., 1984. The "hot issue" market of 1980. *Journal of Business* 57, 215–40.

Ritter, Jay R., 1985. The choice between firm commitment and best efforts contracts. Unpublished manuscript (University of Pennsylvania, Philadelphia, PA).

Rock, Kevin, 1985. Why new issues are underpriced. *Journal of Financial Economics*, 187–212.

Rogowski, Robert J., and Eric H. Sorensen, 1985. Deregulation in investment banking: Shelf registrations, structure, and performance. *Financial Management* 14, 5–15.

Rosenfeld, Ahron, 1982. Repurchase offers: Information adjusted premiums and shareholders' response, MERC monograph series MT-82-01 (University of Rochester, Rochester, NY).

Rosenfeld, James D., 1984. Additional evidence on the relation between divestiture announcements and shareholder wealth. *The Journal of Finance* 39, 1437–48.

Rozeff, Michael S., 1982. Growth, beta and agency costs as determinants of dividend payout ratios. *Journal of Financial Research* 5, 249–59.

Schneller, Meir I., 1984. Dividend policy and the stockholders-management conflict. Unpublished manuscript (University of Pennsylvania, Philadelphia, PA).

Schipper, Katherine, and Abbie Smith, 1983. Effects of recontracting on shareholder wealth: The case of voluntary spin-offs. *Journal of Financial Economics* 12, 437–67.

Schipper, Katherine, and Abbie Smith, 1986. A comparison of equity carve-outs and seasoned equity offerings: Share price effects and corporate restructuring. *Journal of Financial Economics* 15, 153–86.

Scholes, Myron, 1972. Market for securities: Substitution versus price pressure and the effects of information on share prices. *Journal of Business* 45, 179–211.

Smith, Clifford, 1977. Alternative methods for raising capital: Rights versus underwritten offerings. *Journal of Financial Economics* 5, 273–307.

Smith, Clifford, 1979. Applications of option pricing analysis. In J. L. Bicksler, ed., Handbook of financial economics (North-Holland, Amsterdam), 80–121.

Smith, Clifford, and Jerold Warner, 1979. On financial contracting: An analysis of bond covenants. *Journal of Financial Economics* 7, 117–61.

Smith, Clifford, and Ross Watts, 1982. Incentive and tax effects of U.S. executive compensation plans. *Australian Journal of Management* 7, 139–57.

Smith, Clifford, and Ross Watts, 1984. The structure of executive compensation contracts and the control of management. Unpublished manuscript (University of Rochester, Rochester, NY).

Smith, Richard, and Manjeet Dhatt, 1984. Direct equity financing: A resolution of a paradox: A comment. *The Journal of Finance* 39, 1615–18.

Stultz, Rene M., and Herb Johnson, 1985. An analysis of secured debt. *Journal of Financial Economics* 14, 501–21.

Vermaelen, Theo, 1981. Common stock repurchases and market signalling. *Journal of Financial Economics* 9, 139–83.

Vetsuypens, Michel, 1985. Agency costs, asset substitution, and voluntary corporate divestitures: A test of bondholder wealth expropriation. Unpublished manuscript (University of Rochester, Rochester, NY).

Vu, Joseph D., 1986. An examination of corporate call behavior on nonconvertible bonds. *Journal of Financial Economics*.

Wakeman, Lee M., 1981. The real function of bond rating agencies. *Chase Financial Quarterly* 1, 18–26.

Watts, Ross L., 1977. Corporate financial statements, a product of the market and political processes. *Australian Journal of Management* 2, 53–75.

Weinstein, Mark, 1978. The seasoning process of new corporate bond issues. *The Journal of Finance* 33, 1343–54.

Discussion Questions

1. Given that abnormal returns were negative following the sale of each type of securities (Table 1), explain the following explanatory hypotheses:

   a. optimal capital structure and relative price effects.

   b. implied changes in expected net operative cash flows and relative price effects.

   c. unanticipated announcements and relative price effects.

   d. predictability of debt versus equity offers.

   e predictability of industrial versus utility offers.

   f. informational asymmetry and relative price effects.

   g. changes in ownership and relative price effects.

2 Explain what is meant by the high value of monitoring by outside concerns, such as investment bankers, and why this may help to justify the high costs of underwriters.

3. Cite what evidence exists that negotiated offerings are more costly than those using competitive bidding.

4. Explain what "shelf registration" is and the rationale for allowing it. Does evidence support the purpose?

5. Why is there such a systematic tendency for underpricing of new issues? Who pays the cost of underpricing?

Robert Rogowski and Eric Sorensen

The New Competitive Environment of Investment Banking: Transactional Finance and Concession Pricing of New Issues

Investment banking is the process by which firms needing funds for expansion can sell bonds or stocks in the securities market. Investment bankers, being very knowledgeable and having access to the ultimate purchasers of the securities, help issuers in this process. If the securities are under-written, the investment banker purchases them from the issuer and then sells them to the ultimate investors, but there are other procedures as well. This article discusses some of the trends in investment banking, especially as they relate to a relatively new process called shelf registration.

Investment banking, once a static tapestry of carefully cultivated relationships between banks and clients, seems to be displaying a new burst of competitive energy. Structural changes, the proliferation of new financial instruments to deal with increased price volatility, new competitors, and the increasing sophistication of issuers have altered cozy client-bank ties, transforming the industry. Issuers of new securities may now choose from a growing variety of issue structures promoted by domestic investment banks and overseas merchant banks. Innovative strategies for adapting to increased price volatility in new offerings have been devised. Investment banks, for example, now use futures, options, and futures options to lay off some of the price risks of holding securities in inventory. Also, market timing and foreign offerings intended to ensure favorable issue prices have become art forms with subjective claims of prowess abounding.

The single event which stands out most prominently amid this sea change in investment banking is, of course, the SEC's experimental introduction of Rule 415, or shelf registration. On March 16,

Source: Reprinted with permission from *Midland Corporate Finance Journal* (Spring 1986), pp. 64–71. Robert Rogowski is a former Professor of Finance at Washington State University and Principal, Alexander Hutton, Inc. Eric Sorensen is of Gould Research, Inc.

1982, the SEC allowed corporate issuers to register all the securities they expected to sell within the ensuing two years, and then sell the securities quickly when they so chose. This change in registration procedure has provided issuers much greater flexibility in structuring the terms of an issue to take advantage of rapidly changing market conditions.

Competition in investment banking has also intensified owing to the efforts of commercial and foreign banks to enter what they see as a very lucrative alternative to their traditional lending business. American money-center banks have aggressively entered Eurobond underwriting and are challenging the bounds of the Glass-Steagall Act in both the markets and the courts. And recognizing that all expertise hardly exists in the United States, foreign merchant banks have responded by entering American markets.

The greater sophistication of issuers has also contributed to this new era of competition. Today's chief financial officer has the skills to evaluate investment bank proposals and the techniques to minimize transaction costs while even perhaps earning a profit by adroitly managing corporate liabilities. As a result, the selection and evaluation of an investment banker's services are becoming increasingly more objective, quantitative tasks—in sharp contrast to the subjective and qualitative factors which dominated such decisions in the past.

Structural changes in the offering process, new entrants, and issuer awareness have all played roles in increasing competition and thus shrinking issue costs for new securities offerings. Academic evidence of reduced underwriter spreads, reoffering yields, and issue costs has generally corroborated the widespread belief that returns to investment banking have declined. Because little research to date has focused on the underpricing of new corporate bond issues, we recently performed a study which sheds some light on this issue. To illustrate how our study contributes to financial economists' understanding of capital markets, however, we think it would first be helpful to begin by surveying current investment banking practices to see how they have changed, and are continuing to change, in this era of greater competition. Following this survey, we discuss the findings of our own recent study of the underpricing of corporate bonds before and after the start of shelf registration.

New Securities Offerings

Once corporate management decides upon a debt or equity offering, it must choose the form of contract. Equity offerings may take the form of common stock, convertible preferred, or straight preferred stock. Debt offerings, of course, are much more protean. But even with the continuing proliferation of new debt instruments, the many shapes of debt can be reduced for our purposes to two forms: "inside" and "outside" debt. Because of the possibility that management as insiders can have a significantly different view of its company's prospects than outside investors, the choice between inside and outside often turns on how drastically such an "informational asymmetry" can affect the value of the security to be offered.[1] In the case of large, heavily traded companies, such a problem is less likely to be important than, say, in the case of small OTC firms. In the case of inside debt, the debtholder obtains access to private information about the firm's decision process before committing his funds. Outside debtholders, by contrast, rely on publicly available information generated internally or purchased by the firm in the form of bond ratings or audits.

---

[1] See E. Fama, "What's Different About Banks?" *Journal of Monetary Economics* (1985).

A company's choice between inside and outside debt thus depends on how great is the company's need for credit quality signals to persuade investors to buy its securities at (or near) current market prices. If a firm chooses inside debt, it may use either private placements or commercial bank loans. A bank loan indicates that the firm is willing to submit itself to periodic scrutiny by a bank in return for a short-term revolving credit with claims junior to most other fixed payment contracts.

The outside debt and equity alternatives usually entail a relationship with an investment bank. The issuer and investment bank negotiate an underwriting contract, sales method, and other features. Issuers typically refer an outright sale of an issue to an investment bank, which in turn resells the issue at a higher price to its investing clients. Similar to writing a put option, the investment bank faces a downside loss theoretically equal to the amount by which the price of the security can fall while the issue remains in syndication; its upside gain is limited by the amount of the spread. The underwriting syndicate formed by the lead underwriter sets a fixed offer price which remains in effect until the issue sells out or the syndicate dissolves.[2]

In contrast to the "firm commitment" arrangement described above, a best efforts offering is akin to a consignment sale. The investment bank acts simply as a sales agent for the issuer; there is no underwriting or "insurance" function. Uncertainty about the aftermarket issue price seems to determine the penchant for best efforts deals (which are used almost exclusively in IPOs), with greater uncertainty increasing the probability that the best efforts method will be chosen.[3]

Choice of the sales method, negotiated or competitive, is also a key decision. A competitive underwriting is a public auction in which the issue is sold to the underwriter whose bid results in the lowest interest cost to the issuer and meets all the conditions of the sale and bidding instructions. A negotiated sale is an exclusive contract giving an investment bank the right to package, underwrite, and distribute the new issue. If a negotiated sale is selected, the underwriter usually performs origination services and conducts pre-sale market tests to determine the demand for an issue. In a competitive sale, the issuer either purchases origination services separately or performs the function itself. Potential underwriters limit their pre-sale marketing activities because they only receive compensation for these activities if they win the bid.

Most studies of underwriting competition and the negotiated vs. competitive bid decision arrive at the same conclusion: Greater competition reduces borrowing costs for all save high-risk issues.[4] The search for investors willing to pay the highest price for securities seems to intensify as the number of bids rises (a negotiated offering can be viewed as a one-bid competitive offering). Monopsony bidding behavior is another possible explanation of the documented cost savings from using competitive bids. Issues receiving only one or two bids suggest the presence of monopsony bidding in which the conspiring bidder shares the profits with abstaining conspirators. A third possibility is that a bidder's price strategy is responsive to other bidders. The greater the uncertainty about competitors' bids, the larger must be the expected price concession to win the bid.[5]

---

[2] I. Giddy, "Is Equity Underwriting Risky for Commercial Bank Affiliates?" *Deregulating Wall Street* (1985).

[3] See D. Baron and B. Holmstrom, "The Investment Banking Contract for New Issues Under Asymmetric Information: Delegation and Incentive Problem," *Journal of Finance* (1980).

[4] Frank Fabozzi and Richard R. West, "Negotiated vs. Competitive Underwritings of Public Utility Bonds: Just One More Time," *Journal of Financial and Quantitative Analysis* (1981); R. Kessel, "A Study of the Effects of Competition on the Tax-Exempt Bond Market," *Journal of Political Economy* (1971): Richard R. West, "New Issue Concession on Municipal Bonds: A Case of Monopsony Pricing," *Journal of Business* (1965).

[5] Louis H. Ederington, "Uncertainty, Competition and Costs in Corporate Bond Underwriting," *Journal of Financial Economics* (1975).

In addition to the origination, risk-bearing, and distribution services provided by investment banks, the performance of "due diligence" (the underwriter requirement to investigate issuer disclosures made in the prospectus) provides a potentially valuable monitoring service on behalf of investors.[6] Due diligence exposes the firm's decision processes to outside scrutiny and helps overcome contracting problems between insiders and outside investors who may possess different information about the firm.

The Emergence of Eurosecurities Markets

An issuer may choose to offer securities in foreign markets. The appeal of issuing in foreign markets is fewer regulations, a different investor clientele (often seeking diversification into dollars), and more lenient investor tax treatment—all of which may lead to reductions in borrowing costs. For example, the option of the investor to evade taxes on bearer bonds may in large part explain lower Eurobond borrowing costs.

In the absence of structural barriers, however, arbitrage between markets should extinguish any interest rate differences, though persistent differences in taxes and regulations and diversification benefits could allow for market segmentation. A recent study of U.S. public utility firms selling Eurobonds over 1979–1983 shows that Eurobond underwriting spreads and reoffering yields were wider and lower, respectively, than those of comparable domestic issues.[7] Because the cost of the wider spread only partly offsets the benefit of the lower reoffering yield, the result suggests significant interest cost savings for Eurobond issuers. The trend in underwriting spreads, however, has been downward; spreads have declined approximately 25 percent over the past five years, which may reflect intensifying competition in this retail-oriented market. Such competition may in turn have forced domestic underwriting spreads lower to maintain parity

Shelf Registration and the Rise of the "Bought Deal"

Two structural changes, Rule 415 and bought deals, have significantly altered the provision of investment banking services. The advent of Rule 415 has provided issuers with a new sales method, one which enables issuers to reduce registration costs and to offer securities within minutes during a favorable market condition. Shelf registration also affords issuers and underwriters much greater flexibility in structuring as well as timing offerings. An issuer can now tailor its securities to attract the greatest number of investors without facing a 48-hour delay. Once the registration statement is filed, issuers may take down securities from the shelf either when solicited by an underwriter (or investor) or when they judge the market condition to be most favorable.[8]

---

[6] Cliff W. Smith, "Investment Banking and the Capital Acquisition Process" (1986).

[7] See David S. Kidwell, M. Wayne Marr, and G. R. Thompson, "Eurodollar Bonds: Alternative Financing for U.S. Companies," *Financial Management* (1985).

[8] To register under Rule 415, a firm may file form S-3 or F-3, which has the following requirements:
  (1) Annual trading volume is greater than 3 million shares,
  (2) Aggregate market value of voting stock is greater than $150 million,
  (3) No earnings requirement,
  (4) No firm commitment requirement for the underwriter,
  (5) Investment grade rating on bonds,
  (6) No default on dividends or sinking fund payments in the last three years, and
  (7) Disclosure rules stipulating adequate financial disclosure over the previous three years.

Several market conventions have already evolved under the reign of Rule 415. Issuers often agree not to offer securities within a period of 10–30 days after an initial shelf sale. This "blackout provision" provides the underwriters with time to distribute securities from the initial shelf offering if market conditions sour. Also, a variety of bidding arrangements have emerged, ranging from a fully competitive auction to a pre-arranged sale to a single lead underwriter. Some issuers choose the investment banks they prefer to bid on the shelf issue while others offer any underwriter access to the bidding process. For equity shelf offerings, some issuers have gravitated toward use of a "dribble" method, whereby an underwriter is appointed the sales agent to sell a small number of shares intermittently.

Shelf registration has also led to the emergence and growth of "bought deals" in lieu of syndicated offerings. Bought deals are those in which a single underwriter purchases an entire issue without any pre-selling activities. Investment bankers maintain that a broad syndicate has value generally for small, poorly followed companies which appeal to retail investors. With retail-oriented underwritings, the pre-selling activities require time before an issue is taken down. With Rule 415 some investment banks (and issuers) have chosen to forgo syndicates. Market conditions and investor mix may dictate which of these selling formats is most cost-effective.

Investment Bank Performance With Shelf Registration

The introduction of shelf registration and the concomitant growth of bought deals have accelerated the trend toward transactional finance, eroding institutional "loyalty" to the point that many issuers now select from a number of underwriters in awarding new issues. Such underwriters, in turn, may choose *not* to form the customary syndicate with a set membership to distribute the securities.

The potential economic effects of Rule 415 are several. First, Rule 415 simplifies and streamlines the registration process and reduces issue preparation costs. The preparation costs of a traditional negotiated offering exceed those of either a convenience or competitive shelf issue. Second, the issuer has increased flexibility in market timing and issue design. When interest rates are low relative to previous periods, the issuer can offer securities off the shelf within minutes rather than endure the 48-hour delay between filing and bringing the issue to market. An issuer may also adjust the issue design to fit market conditions with Rule 415 without the 48-hour amendment delay required with traditional offerings. Adroit adjustment of issue design may bring about lower interest costs due to changes in investor preference.

Shelf registration may also have the effect of stimulating competition due to the public display of securities on the shelf, and to the well-known propensity of investment banks to call on issuers to arrange deals. Prior to Rule 415, investment banks generally did not know which firms were contemplating entry in the primary market. The rise of the "telephone auction" (in which issuers ask for bids on new securities in very short time periods, sometimes within minutes) with competitive shelf issues may also signal an erosion of client loyalty for investment banks. Informal discussions with investment bankers suggest that they now feel themselves to be engaged in more heated competition for underwriting business. Such bankers have lamented especially the emergence of the "kamikaze" bid with narrow spreads and no syndicate. To the extent that a competitive shelf offering is giving rise to greater competition than a traditional negotiated or competitive offering, Rule 415 can be expected to reduce issue borrowing costs, all other things equal.

Academic research on these competitive effects suggests that underwriter spreads and/or reoffering yields have indeed been smaller for shelf issues.[9] Studies of the bond market show that both spread and reoffering yield have been significantly reduced in shelf issues. In fact, non-shelf as well as shelf issues experienced lower borrowing costs since the introduction of Rule 415, suggesting that the competitive effect of shelf registration has exerted pressure throughout all aspects of the underwriting industry. And even if underwriter spread were unchanged, the reduction in reoffering yields implies that the *risk-adjusted* returns to underwriting may have declined due to Rule 415; that is, those underwriters which appear to be earning the same returns as earlier are probably, in most cases, bearing significantly greater price risk.

Equity shelf issues have also displayed narrower spreads than non-shelf issues. The issuing cost savings from shelf issues have been estimated at 13 percent for comparable syndicated equity offerings, and at over 50 percent (!) for comparable nonsyndicated traditional offerings.

Such cost savings notwithstanding, there is a controversy over the price effect of equity shelf offerings. Some critics of shelf registration argue that a "market overhang" effect may depress current stock prices because the issuer has the option to bring the shares on the shelf to market at any time in the two years after registration. Such critics argue that, in all equity offerings, a price decline directly proportional to the relative issue size must occur to induce new investors to purchase additional shares, and that this effect is more pronounced in the case of shelf offerings than in traditional offerings. Proponents of modern finance, however, argue that the demand curve for equity securities is better approximated by a horizontal line, at least in the case of companies traded heavily on major stock exchanges. If the latter is the case, then there should be no major "market overhang" effect in response to shelf-registered equity offerings.

In support of financial economists' notion of a flat demand curve for securities, a recent study of stock price behavior around the announcement date of new shelf offerings failed to find any evidence of a market overhang effect.[10] No significant differences were found in price reactions to announcements of shelf and traditional offerings.

The trend toward bought deals, which may help investment bankers to recoup some of their losses from reductions in underwriting spreads, places greater emphasis on capital commitment and distribution capacity. This in turn may lead to greater industry concentration. Some observers have suggested that such pressures are likely to result in an oligopolistic industry structure in which a few large investment banks handle the bulk of financing volume. (A cursory view of this trend toward greater concentration is shown in Table 1, which shows that the largest five and ten investment banks have increased their collective market share in the 1980s.)

Concern has also been expressed about the quality of investment bankers' performance of due diligence under shelf registration. Because the period between the intention and the act of issuing has been drastically cut, the SEC has proposed anticipatory or continuous due diligence as a remedy. The cost of periodic meetings and the economic self-interest of underwriter counsel (which dictates putting underwriter before investor welfare) may reduce the effectiveness of the monitoring traditionally provided by due diligence. If this causes investors to lose confidence, companies' total issuing costs (in-

---

[9] See Sanjai Bhagat, M. Wayne Marr, and G. Rodney Thompson, "The Rule 415 Experiment: Equity Market," *Journal of Finance* (1985); David S. Kidwell, M. Wayne Marr, and G. R. Thompson. "SEC Rule 415: The Ultimate Competitive Bid," *Journal of Financial and Quantitative Analysis* (1984); Robert J. Rogowski and Eric H. Sorensen, "Deregulation in Investment Banking: Shelf Registrations, Structure, and Performance," *Financial Management* (1985).

[10] See Bhagat, Marr, and Thompson, previous citation.

Table 1   Total Corporate Securities Underwriting: Concentration of Ten Top Investment Banks

	Top Five (in Millions) Investment Banks		Top Ten Investment Banks	
	Amount[a]	Percentage	Amount	Percentage
1979	$22,730	62.1%	$30,358	82.9%
1980	35,623	59.1	50,166	83.2
1981	40,760	63.1	53,446	83.5
1982	42,782	54.1	55,637	70.5
1983	56,248	56.5	78,179	78.5
1984	58,363	70.8	75,335	91.4
1985[b]	66,375	70.1	85,645	90.5

[a]Full credit given to lead manager based on issue principal.
[b]January-September, 1985.
Source: Directory of Corporate Financing, *Investment Dealer Digest*, various issues.

cluding negative announcement effects on stock price) may actually rise as a result of the shelf procedure. Such a possibility, however, seems unlikely given that stringent SEC rules for shelf eligibility limit shelf to larger firms that are widely followed by the financial community. For many such companies, due diligence may be largely a perfunctory exercise necessary to satisfy regulators.

An Underpricing Experiment

The phenomenon of underpricing, selling securities to new investors at prices below equilibrium levels, may exist for several reasons. The fact that issuers can withhold negative insider information from their investment bankers during the pre-sale marketing period may cause underpricing.[11] As some academics have suggested, a sharp dichotomy between informed and less informed investor groups (corresponding, for example, to institutional and retail investors) may force underwriters to underprice in order to induce the less informed investors (who are aware of their own informational disadvantage) to bid on an issue.[12] A third possibility is that underwriters seek to limit their price risk by reducing their holding period with below-equilibrium prices.[13] Such underpricing, however, clearly represents a cost to issuing corporations which should be limited by competition among investment bankers for corporate clients.

Remember that investment banks earn their underwriting spreads by buying new securities from issuers at prices lower than what the final investors are willing to pay. In the case of a new bond offering, the issuer seeks the highest possible price (lowest yield) for an issue while investors search for the lowest price (highest yield) for a given risk level. Any imbalance in this pricing should affect the professional reputation of the banker and thus the number of offerings it will be asked to underwrite in the future.

[11] See David P. Baron and B. Holmstrom, previous citation.

[12] See Jay Ritter, "The Choice Between Firm Commitment and Best Efforts Contracts" (1986); Kevin Rock, "Why New Issues Are Underpriced" (1986).

[13] See Ian Giddy, previous citation.

At first glance, the existence of underpricing suggests that investors benefit directly at the issuer's expense. Further reflection suggests that, in the case of IPOs at least, issuers may be unable to detect systematic underpricing because of the inherent imprecision of the process of valuing unseasoned offerings. Alternatively, in the case of seasoned as well as unseasoned offerings, corporate issuers may be persuaded by their underwriters to view any post-offering price rise as evidence of effective secondary market "support" or "stabilization." With sufficient coaching, they may even come to welcome such strong aftermarket performance as providing a signal of quality to the market which will enable future issues to sell at higher prices.

Nevertheless, even if there is some economic justification for this systematic wealth transfer from issuers to investors via investment banker underpricing (such benefits also, of course, accrue to the investment banker in the form of client satisfaction), an increase in underwriter competition can be expected to reduce the tendency to underprice new issues. As more investment banks vie for an issue, the search for investors and pricing strategy should likely cause more aggressive pricing of new issues.

Discussions with investment bankers indicate that Eurobond offerings, for example, have recently become particularly competitive. Some issuers have even chosen negotiated over competitive offerings to avoid "overpricing" their issues. Eurobond underwriters have apparently been willing to absorb occasional losses just to maintain a market presence and, hence, have been pricing issues above market levels to win a bid. But issuers concerned about market acceptance of future offerings have, in some cases, been passing up overpriced bids to protect the perceived quality of their offerings.

Shelf registration, with the accompanying reduction of due diligence and the spur to competition, provides a unique test of underpricing. Because presale marketing activities are reduced, the potential problem of losses to the investment banker in traditional offerings from withheld insider information should be eliminated. However, underpricing designed to attract less sophisticated investors or to reduce investment bankers' price risk may increase because of foreshortened due diligence. Bought deals may also increase price risks and thus provide underwriters with even stronger incentives to underprice.

Academic studies have documented underpricing of new bond issues prior to the beginning of registration in March 1982.[14] In some of our recent work, we constructed an experimental test which compares the underpricing of shelf with non-shelf bond issues over the period 1981–1984.

Our analysis required two steps. First, we used multiple regression to "fit" yield data for a large sample of new corporate bonds to a group of variables such as issue size, risk rating, and market conditions. This allowed us to estimate the equilibrium yield (or price) for each bond based on key characteristics of comparable issues for each of the five weeks following the offering. This enabled us to compare actual and estimated equilibrium secondary market prices for shelf and non-shelf issues relative to general bond market movements, and thus to come to some conclusions about how shelf registration has affected initial underpricing.

To estimate the appropriate yields on the new bond issues and to track aftermarket price changes, we gathered data on all newly issued corporate utility and industrial bonds of par value of $1 million or greater and maturity 5 years or greater (as recorded by *Institutional Investor*) issued

---

[14] See Eric H. Sorensen, "On the Seasoning Process of New Bonds: Some Are More Seasoned Than Others," *Journal of Financial and Quantitative Analysis* (1982); Mark I. Weinstein, "The Seasoning Process of New Corporate Bond Issues," *Journal of Finance* (1978).

Table 2   Mean Price Changes and ANOVA F-Tests for Mean Differences between Shelf and Non-Shelf Issues

Variable	Shelf Mean Shelf	Non-Shelf Mean Non-Shelf	F-Statistic
	$(N = 176)$	$(N = 385)$	
PRICEX2	−.19%	.23%	9.96
PRICEX3	−.20	.27	5.61
PRICEX4	−.02	.35	2.23
PRICEX5	.06	.39	1.00

[a]Significant at .05 percent level or better.

over the interest rate cycle from January 1981 to January 1984. Eliminating issues with incomplete information, low or zero coupons, a put option, or a convertibility option, we ended up with a sample of approximately 630 issues. Price data were collected for each issue for five weeks following the offering from Salomon Brothers' Bond Market Roundup.

A multiple regression model of new issue pricing was estimated for both industrial and utility bonds (see Appendix A for the specifics of the model). These models provided equilibrium yields to which we compared the actual yield to estimate the amount of underpricing. Converting yields to prices, we measured the market-adjusted price change for each of five weeks following the offering. These price changes, labeled PRICEX2, PRICEX3, PRICEX4, and PRICEX5, are presented in Table 2 for shelf and non-shelf issues. The findings there demonstrate an interesting comparison between issues sold by shelf and non-shelf. The set of shelf bonds tends to fall slightly in price initially, and then returns to the original equilibrium price. This suggests that issues sold with Rule 415 have initial prices which in general are sufficiently high such that they would not be considered underpriced.

There are at least two explanations for the fact that the prices of shelf issues tend not to rise but, if anything, to fall in the aftermarket. First, there may be more heated competition among investment bankers for the purchase of shelf issues because these issues are placed very quickly with investors. Second, the timing is such that the underwriting risk is minimal; and lower underwriting risk, all else equal, leads to a higher reoffering price.

Table 2 reveals that non-shelf issues, in comparison to shelf issues, tend to rise in price by approximately 0.40 percent. For example, a bond initially sold at 100.00 is likely to rise to 100.40 (after adjusting for general market movements). PRICEX2 and PRICEX3 are also significantly different between the two groups, thus making the initial underpricing even larger.

We also conducted another test designed to compare the underpricing of all issues sold prior to the use of shelf (from January 1980 to March 1982) with all issues sold after shelf was in full swing (post March 1982). As displayed in Table 3, the results suggest that there was a general structural change in the pricing of new bonds associated with the introduction of Rule 415. After the change, new issue prices did not appear to depart, on average, from their original values. On the other hand, prior to shelf registration prices in general rose in the aftermarket, thus suggesting widespread underpricing.

One possible conclusion to be drawn from our study is that the new environment initiated (or perhaps just accompanied) by shelf registration has caused an end, or at least a temporary halt, to

Table 3   Mean Price Changes for Issues Sold Pre-Shelf and Post-Shelf

	Pre-Shelf	Post-Shelf	
Variable	Mean	Mean	F-Statistic
(N = 245)	(N = 315)		
PRICEX2	.27%	−.03%	5.52[a]
PRICEX3	.39	−.08	6.57[a]
PRICEX4	.52	−.03	6.12[a]
PRICEX5	.68	−.04	5.63[a]

[a]Significant at .05 percent level or better.

new issue underpricing. Our suspicion is that the direct supply of underwriting services, or the potential for it, has heightened competition and rewarded bond issuers as a group.

Concluding Comments

The business of investment banking has become a more lively competitive affair with greater emphasis on economical financing of new issues. Structural changes, new competition, and the growing level of issuer sophistication have all caused returns to traditional investment banking services to shrink. The movement to add or strengthen merger and acquisition services, mortgage securities, and junk bond groups is almost certainly a response to the decline of revenues from underwriting new issues.

Shelf registration and bought deals have replaced traditional offerings, customary banker-client relationships, and syndicate formations, particularly in the case of corporate bond issues. Academic research on the competitive effects of Rule 415 is virtually unanimous in reaching the conclusion that shelf registration has reduced new issue costs for qualified issuers. Our own recent study of bond underpricing suggests that a more competitive environment has emerged since the beginning of shelf registration in 1982. Under the pressure of such changes, investment banks have shown less willingness or ability to lower new issue prices.

Appendix A

Yield Estimators

The model for YIELD was estimated for the following samples:

Bond Type	1981	1982	1983
Industrial	N = 90	N = 123	N = 89
	$R^2 = .90$	$R^2 = .96$	$R^2 = .91$
Utility	N = 108	N = 105	N = 85
	$R^2 = .94$	$R^2 = .97$	$R^2 = .91$

YIELD	=	f(IRATE, TREND, SUPPLY, SIZELN, RATINGS, MATURE, CALLPRO, MATURE X CALLPRO) where:
YIELD	=	Planned reoffering yield
IRATE	=	The estimated interest rate for long term, AAA-rated new issues at the end of the day prior to the new sale issue, as reported by Salomon Brothers. An industrial bond estimate or utility bond estimate was used, whichever was appropriate.
TREND	=	The average daily change in IRATE over the 10 trading days prior to the sale date. A negative value for TREND represents a recent period of falling rates.
SIZELN	=	Natural log of issue size in \$1,000,000.
RATINGS	=	Zero-one dummy variables for Moody's credit ratings: AAA to BAA, with BA and lower the omitted class.
MATURE	=	A measure of expected maturity. It is the average of the length of the deferred call period (earliest possible maturity) and the stated term-to-maturity.
CALLPRO	=	(Yield – "refunding rate")/IRATE
	=	(Yield – coupon/call price)/IRATE. It is the approximate percentage amount that rates have to drop in order for refunding to be profitable. (See footnote 14.)
MATURE X CALLPRO	=	An interactive term to account for the joint influence of maturity and call price.

As an example of model results, the industrial bond sample of 1982 had the following estimate:

$$\text{YIELD} = +.350 + 1.145(\text{IRATE}) - 1.02(\text{TREND}) - .066(\text{SIZELN}) - 8.55(\text{AAA})$$
$$-2.20(\text{AA}) - 1.77(\text{A}) - 1.02(\text{BAA}) + .029(\text{MATURE}) + .095(\text{CALLPRO})$$
$$-.003(\text{MATURE X CALLPRO})$$

Selected Bibliography

Aharony, Joseph, and Itzhak Swary. Quarterly Dividend and Earnings Announcements and Stockholder's Returns: An Empirical Analysis. *Journal of Finance* 35 (1980), 1–12.

Alexander, Gordon J., P. George Benson, and Joan M. Kampmeyer. Investigating the Valuation Effects of Announcements of Voluntary Corporate Selloffs. *Journal of Finance* 39 (1984), 503–517.

Asquith, Paul. Merger Bids, Uncertainty, and Stockholder Returns. *Journal of Financial Economics* 11 (1983), 51–83.

Asquith, Paul, and David Mullins. The Impact of Initiating Dividend Payments on Shareholder Weaith. *Journal of Business* 56 (1983), 77–96.

Asquith, Paul, and David Mullins. Equity Issues and Offering Dilution. *Journal of Financial Economics* 15 (1986), 61–89.

Baron, David P. The Incentive Problem and the Design of Investment Banking Contracts. *Journal of Banking and Finance* 3 (1979), 157–75.

Baron, David P. A Model of the Demand for Investment Banking Advising and Distribution Services for New Issues. *Journal of Finance* 37 (1982), 955–76.

Baron, David P., and Bengt Holmstrom. The Investment Banking Contract for New Issues under Asymmetric Information: Delegation and the Incentive Problem. *Journal of Finance* 35 (1980), 1115–38.

Beatty, Randolph P., and Jay R. Ritter. Investment Banking, Reputation, and the Underpricing of Initial Public Offerings. *Journal of Financial Economics* 15 (1986), 213–32.

Bhagat, Sanjai. The Effect of Pre-Emptive Right Amendments on Shareholder Wealth. *Journal of Financial Economics* 12 (1983), 289–310.

Bhagat, Sanjai. The Effect of Management's Choice Between Negotiated and Competitive Equity Offerings on Shareholder Wealth. *Journal of Financial and Quantitative Analysis* 21 (1986).

Bhagat, Sanjai, M. Wayne Marr, and G. Rodney Thompson. The Rule 415 Experiment: Equity Markets. *Journal of Finance* (December 1985), 1385–1402.

Bhagat, Sanjai, and Peter A. Frost. Issuing Costs to Existing Shareholders in Competitive and Negotiated Underwritten Public Utility Equity Offerings. *Journal of Financial Economics* 15 (1986), 233–59.

Black, Fisher, and Myron Scholes. The Pricing of Options and Corporate Liabilities. *Journal of Political Economy* (1973), 637–54.

Booth, James R., and Richard L. Smith, III. Capital Raising, Underwriting and the Certification Hypothesis. *Journal of Financial Economics* 15 (1986), 261–81.

Bradley, Michael, Anand Desai, and E. Han Kim. The Rationale behind Interfirm Tender Offers: Information or Synergy? *Journal of Financial Economics* 11 (1983), 183–206.

Bradley, Michael, and L. M. Wakeman. The Wealth Effects of Targeted Share Repurchases. *Journal of Financial Economics* 11 (1983), 301–28.

Brennan, Michael, and Eduardo Schwartz. Corporate Income Taxes, Valuation, and the Problem of Optimal Capital Structure. *Journal of Business* 51 (1978), 103–14.

Brickley, James. Shareholder Wealth, Information Signaling and the Specially Designated Dividend: An Empirical Study. *Journal of Financial Economics* 12 (1983), 187–209.

Burton, John C., and William Roberts. A Study of Auditor Changes. *The Journal of Accountancy* (1967), 31–36.

Carpenter, Charles G., and Robert H. Strawser. Displacement of Auditors When Clients Go Public. *Journal of Accountancy* (1971), 55–58.

Chalk, Andrew J., and John W. Peavy, III. Understanding the Pricing of Initial Public Offerings. Southern Methodist University (1985), unpublished manuscript.

Charest, Guy. Dividend Information, Stock Returns, and Market Efficiency—II. *Journal of Financial Economics* 6 (1978), 297–330.

Dann, Larry. The Effect of Common Stock Repurchase on Stockholder Returns. Unpublished dissertation (University of California, Los Angeles, CA) (1980).

Dann, Larry. Common Stock Repurchasers: An Analysis of Returns to Bondholders and Stockholders. *Journal of Financial Economics* 9 (1981), 113–38.

Dann, Larry, and Harry DeAngelo. Standstill Agreements, Privately Negotiated Stock Repurchases and the Market for Corporate Control. *Journal of Financial Economics* 11 (1983), 275–300.

Dann, Larry Y., David Mayers, and Robert J. Raab, Jr. Trading Rules, Large Blocks and the Speed of Price Adjustment. *Journal of Financial Economics* 4 (1977), 3–22.

Dann, Larry Y., and Wayne H. Mikkelson. Convertible Debt Issuance, Capital Structure Change and Financing-Related Information: Some New Evidence. *Journal of Financial Economics* 13 (1984), 157–86.

Dealers' Digest Inc. *Five Year Directory of Corporate Financing 1980–1984*, Anthony V. Ricotta, editor. (Mason Slaine: New York) (1985).

DeAngelo, Harry, Linda DeAngelo, and Edward M. Rice. Going Private: Minority Freezeouts and Shareholder Wealth. *Journal of Law and Economics* 27 (1984), 367–401.

DeAngelo, Harry, and Ronald Masulis. Optimal Capital Structure under Corporate and Personal Taxation. *Journal of Financial Economics* 8 (1980), 3–29.

DeAngelo, Linda. Auditor Independence, "Low Balling," and Disclosure Regulation. *Journal of Accounting and Economics* 3 (1981), 113–27.

Dietrich, J. Richard. Effects of Early Bond Refundings: An Empirical Investigation of Security Returns. *Journal of Accounting and Economics* 6 (1984), 67–96.

Dodd, Peter. Merger Proposals, Management Discretion and Stockholder Wealth. *Journal of Financial Economics* 8 (1980), 105–38.

Dodd, Peter, and Richard S. Ruback. Tender Offers and Stockholder Returns: An Empirical Analysis. *Journal of Financial Economics* 5 (1977), 351–74.

Dodd, Peter, and Jerold B. Warner. On Corporate Governance: A Study of Proxy Contests. *Journal of Financial Economics* 11 (1983), 401–38.

Dyl, Edward A., and Michael D. Joehnk. Competitive versus Negotiated Underwriting of Public Utility Debt. *Bell Journal of Economics* 7 (1976), 680–89.

Easterbrook, Frank H. Two Agency-Cost Explanations of Dividends. *American Economic Review* 74 (1983), 650–59.

Eckbo, B. Espen. Horizontal Mergers, Collusion, and Stockholder Wealth. *Journal of Financial Economics* 11 (1983), 241–73.

Eckbo, B. Espen. Valuation Effects of Corporate Debt Offerings. *Journal of Financial Economics* 15 (1986), 119–51.

Ederington, Louis H. Uncertainty, Competition, and Costs in Corporate Bond Underwriting. *Journal of Financial Economics* (March 1975), 71–94.

Ederington, Louis H. Negotiated versus Competitive Underwritings of Corporate Bonds. *Journal of Finance* 31 (1976), 17–28.

Ederington, Louis H. The Yield Spread on New Issues of Corporate Bonds. *Journal of Finance* (December 1980), 1531–43.

Fabozzi, Frank J., and Richard West. Negotiated versus Competitive Underwritings of Public Utility Bonds: Just One More Time. *Journal of Financial and Quantitative Analysis* (September 1981), 323–39.

Fama, Eugene F. The Effect of a Firm's Investment and Financing Decisions. *American Economic Review* 68 (1978), 272–84.

Fama, Eugene F. Agency Problems and the Theory of the Firm. *Journal of Political Economy* 88 (1980), 288–307.

Fama, Eugene F. What's Different about Banks? *Journal of Monetary Economics* (January 1985), 28–39.

Fama, Eugene F., and Michael C. Jensen. Residual Claims and Investment Decisions. *Journal of Financial Economics* 14 (1985), 101–19.

Giddy, Ian H. Is Equity Underwriting Risky for Commercial Bank Affiliates? *Deregulating Wall Street: Commercial Bank Penetration of the Corporate Securities Market*, Ingo Walter, editor (New York: Wiley) (1985).

Gilson, Ronald J., and Reinier H. Kraakman. The Mechanisms of Market Efficiency. *Virginia Law Review* 70 (1984), 549–644.

Hansen, Robert S., and John M. Pinkerton. Direct Equity Financing: A Resolution of a Paradox. *Journal of Finance* 37 (1982), 651–65.

Hansen, Robert S. The Equity Financing Method Decision: Empirical Evidence from the Standy Underwritten Offering. Working Paper, Virginia Polytechnic Institute and State University (1985).

Heinkel, Robert, and Eduardo S. Schwartz. Rights versus Underwritten Offerings: An Asymmetric Information Approach. University of British Columbia (1984), unpublished manuscript.

Hite, Gailen L., and James E. Owers. Security Price Reactions around Corporate Spin-Off Announcements. *Journal of Financial Economics* 12 (1983), 409–36.

Hite, Gailen L., and James E. Owers. Sales Divestitures: Implications for Buyers and Sellers. Southern Methodist University (1985), unpublished manuscript.

Holderness, Clifford G., and Dennis P. Sheehan. Raiders or Saviors? The Evidence on Six Controversial Investors. *Journal of Financial Economics* 14 (1985), 555–79.

Ibbotson, Roger. Price Performance of Common Stock New Issues. *Journal of Financial Economics* 2 (1975), 235–72.

Ibbotson, Roger G., and Jeffrey F. Jaffe. "Hot Issue" Markets. *Journal of Finance* 30 (1975), 1027–42.

Jain, Prem C. The Effect of Voluntary Sell-off Announcements on Shareholder Wealth. *Journal of Finance* 40 (1985), 209–24.

Jensen, Michael C., and William H. Meckling. Theory of the Firm: Managerial Behavior Agency Costs and Ownership Structure. *Journal of Financial Economics* 3 (1976), 305–60.

Jensen, Michael C., and Richard S. Ruback. The Market for Corporate Control: The Scientific Evidence. *Journal of Financial Economics* 11 (1983), 5–50.

Kessel, Reuben. A Study of the Effects of Competition on the Tax-Exempt Bond Market. *Journal of Political Economy* (July/August 1971), 706–38.

Kidwell, David S., M. Wayne Marr, and G. Rodney Thompson. SEC Rule 415: The Ultimate Competitive Bid. *Journal of Financial and Quantitative Analysis* 19 (1984), 183–95.

Kim, E. Han, and John D. Schatzberg. Voluntary Liquidation and Stockholder Returns. University of Michigan (1985), unpublished manuscript.

Klein, April. The Effects of Voluntary Corporate Divestitures on Shareholders' Wealth. University of Chicago (1984), unpublished manuscript.

Kolodny, Richard, and Diane Rizzuto Suhler. Changes in Capital Structure, New Equity Issues, and Scale Effects. *Journal of Financial Research* 8 (1985), 127–36.

Kraus, Alan, and Robert Litzenberger. A State Preference Model of Optimal Financial Leverage. *Journal of Finance* 28 (1973), 911–22.

Linn, Scott, and J. Michael Pinegar. The Effect of Issuing Preferred Stock on Common Stockholder Wealth. University of Iowa (1986), unpublished manuscript.

Logue, Dennis E., and Robert A. Jarrow. Negotiation versus Competitive Bidding in the Sale of Securities by Public Utilities. *Financial Management* 7 (1978), 31–39.

Mandelker, Gershon, and Artur Raviv. Investment Banking: An Economic Analysis of Optimal Underwriting Contracts. *Journal of Finance* 32 (1977), 683–94.

Marsh, Paul. Equity Rights Issues and the Efficiency of the U.K. Stock Market. *Journal of Finance* 34 (1979), 839–62.

Marsh, Paul. The Choice Between Equity and Debt: An Empirical Study. *Journal of Finance* 37 (1982), 121–44.

Masulis, Ronald M. Stock Repurchase by Tender Offer: An Analysis of the Causes of Common Stock Price Changes. *Journal of Finance* 35 (1980), 305–19.

Masulis, Ronald. The Impact of Capital Structure Change on Firm Value: Some Estimates. *Journal of Finance* 38 (1983), 107–26.

Masulis, Ronald. Changes in Ownership Structure: Conversions of Mutual Savings and Loans to Stock Charter. University of California, Los Angeles (1986), unpublished manuscript.

Masulis, Ronald W., and Ashok Korwar. Seasoned Equity Offerings: An Empirical Investigation. *Journal of Financial Economics* 15 (1986), 91–118.

Mayers, David, and Clifford Smith. On the Corporate Demand for Insurance. *Journal of Business* 55 (1982), 281–96.

Mayers, David, and Clifford Smith. Ownership Structure and Control: The Mutualization of Stock Life Insurance Companies. *Journal of Financial Economics* (1986).

McConnell, John, and Chris J. Muscarella. Corporate Capital Expenditure Decisions and the Market Value of the Firm. *Journal of Financial Economics* 14 (1985), 399–422.

McConnell, John, and Timothy Nantell. Corporate Combinations and Common Stock Returns: The Case of Joint Ventures. *Journal of Finance* 40 (1985), 519–36.

McConnell, John, and Gary Schlarbaum. Evidence on the Impact of Exchange Offers on Security Prices: The Case of Income Bonds. *Journal of Business* 54 (1981), 65–85.

Mikkelson, Wayne. Convertible Calls and Security Returns. *Journal of Financial Economics* 9 (1981), 237–64.

Mikkelson, Wayne H., and M. Megan Partch. Stock Price Effects and Costs of Secondary Distributions. *Journal of Financial Economics* 14 (1985), 165–94.

Mikkelson, Wayne H., and M. Megan Partch. Valuation Effects of Security Offerings and the Issuance Process. *Journal of Financial Economics* 15 (1986), 31–60.

Mikkelson, Wayne H., and Richard S. Ruback. Corporate Investments in Common Stock. *Journal of Financial Economics* 14 (1985), 523–53.

Miles, J., and J. Rosenfeld. An Empirical Analysis of the Effects of Spin-Off Announcements on Shareholder Wealth. *Journal of Finance* 38 (1983), 1597–1606.

Miller, Merton. Debt and Taxes. *Journal of Finance* 32 (1977), 261–76.

Miller, Merton, and Kevin Rock. Dividend Policy under Asymmetric Information. *Journal of Finance* (1985), 1031–51.

Modigliani, Franco, and Merton Miller. The Cost of Capital, Corporation Finance and the Theory of Investment. *American Economic Review* 48 (1958), 261–97.

Modligliani, Franco, and Merton Miller. Corporate Income Taxes and the Cost of Capital: A Correction. *American Economic Review* 53 (1963), 433–43.

Myers, Stewart. Determinants of Corporate Borrowing. *Journal of Financial Economics* 5 (1977), 147–75.

Myers, Stewart. The Capital Structure Puzzle. *Journal of Finance* 39 (1984), 575–92.

Myers, Stewart C., and Nicholas S. Majluf. Corporate Financing and Investment Decisions When Firms Have Information That Investors Do Not Have. *Journal of Financial Economics* 13 (1984), 187–221.

Parsons, John and Artur Raviv. Underpricing of Seasoned Issues. *Journal of Financial Economics* 14 (1985), 377–97.

Pettway, Richard H., and Robert C. Radcliffe. Impacts of New Equity Sales upon Electric Utility Share Prices. *Financial Management* 14 (1985), 16–25.

Phillips, Susan M., and Clifford W. Smith, Jr. Trading Costs for Listed Options: The Implications for Market Efficiency. *Journal of Financial Economics* 8 (1980), 179–201.

Ritter, Jay R. The "Hot Issue" Market of 1980. *Journal of Business* 57 (1984), 215–40.

Ritter, Jay R. The Choice between Firm Commitment and Best Effort Contracts. University of Pennsylvania (1985), unpublished manuscript.

Rock, Kevin. Why New Issues Are Underpriced. *Journal of Financial Economics* 15 (1985), 187–272.

Rogowski, Robert J., and Eric H. Sorensen. Deregulation in Investment Banking: Shelf Registrations, Structure, and Performance. *Financial Management* 14 (1985), 5–15.

Rosenfeld, Ahron. Repurchase Offers: Information Adjusted Premiums and Shareholders' Response. University of Rochester, MERC Monograph Series MT-82-01 (1982).

Rosenfeld, James D. Additional Evidence on the Relation between Divestiture Announcements and Shareholder Wealth. *Journal of Finance* 39 (1984), 1437–48.

where $\lambda_i = (1 - d_i)e^{\text{cov}(l,\, y)}$, $\overline{d}_i$ is the expected rate of economic depreciation of leased asset i, and $\text{cov}(l, y)$ is the covariance between the log of one minus the random rate of economic depreciation of the asset l and a random "market factor" y.[2] In this analysis, the risk-free rate, the expected rate of economic depreciation, and the covariance term are assumed to be constant over time, so the time subscript can be omitted. Thus, as in the single-period case, risk enters into the determination of the equilibrium rental rate of a financial lease only because the end-of-lease residual value of the asset is uncertain. Furthermore, only the non-diversifiable risk associated with the asset's residual value is relevant to the determination of the rental payments on the lease. However, because the lessor bears the residual-value risk only at the termination of the lease, only the discounted value of residual-value risk is relevant to the determination of the rental payment L_i.

To calculate the yield of a multi-period lease, (3) can be written as

$$A_{i0} = \sum_{t=0}^{N-1} \frac{L_i}{(1+y)^t} + \frac{\overline{S}^N}{(1+y)^N}, \tag{5}$$

and solved iteratively for y, where $\overline{S}^N$ is the expected residual value of the leased asset at time N and the lease payment L_i is constant across time. Because L_i is a positive function of R_f, the yield on the lease is also a positive function of R_f. Futhermore, because L_i is a negative function of covariance risk, y is also a negative function of covariance risk. However, this term could have been stated in terms of capital appreciation, in which case L_i would be a positive function of non-diversifiable residual-value risk.

Our primary objective is to test the hypothesis of Miller/Upton and McConnell/Schallheim that yields of financial leases are a function of the risk-free interest rate and the discounted value of the covariance risk of the asset's residual value. However, other hypotheses are tested as well.

3. Other Hypotheses

Two important assumptions underlie the Miller and Upton and McConnell and Schallheim analyses. The first is that capital markets are perfect. The second is that financial leases are default-free. Once these assumptions are relaxed, the role of transaction costs, information asymmetries, and default risk must be considered.

In a lease, transaction costs are the per-unit costs of writing the contract, specifying the security agreement, identifying the asset, negotiating the terms of the lease, and so forth. Most of these costs are fixed and independent of the characteristics of the lessee, the lessor, and the leased asset. Hence, transaction costs decline proportionately with the cost of the asset. These costs are recaptured over time by the lessor through periodic (level) rental payments. Thus, we hypothesize that lease yields are an inverse function of the value of the leased asset. To illustrate, assume a perpetual lease so that

$$y = \frac{L_i}{A_{i0}} \tag{6}$$

is the lease's yield in the absence of transaction costs. With a fixed transaction cost that is recaptured through periodic (level) rental payments over the life of the lease,

---

[2]The term $\text{cov}(l, y)$ can be interpreted as $\text{cov}(l, y) \doteq \text{cov}(-\tilde{d}_i, -\tilde{R}_m) = \text{cov}(\tilde{a}_i, -\tilde{R}_M) = -\text{cov}(\tilde{a}_i, \tilde{R}_m)$, which is approximately equal to the negative of the traditional measure of an asset's systematic risk ($\tilde{a}$ represents random "appreciation").

$$y = \frac{L_i^*}{A_{i0}} = \frac{L_i + c}{A_{i0}} = \frac{L_i}{A_{i0}} + \frac{c}{A_{i0}}, \tag{7}$$

where L_i^* is total periodic lease payment and c is the (unobservable) transaction cost recovered per period in the rental payment. L_i increases proportionately as A_{i0} increases, so L_i/A_{i0} remains constant. However, because c is fixed, c/A_{i0} declincs as A_{i0} increases and, therefore, y declines as A_{i0} increases. Thus, we hypothesize that the lease yield is inversely related to the cost of the leased asset. Furthermore, because c/A_{i0} approaches zero as A_{i0} becomes large, for leases on higher-priced assets, transaction costs will be a less significant component of the lease yield, and, for leases on lower-priced assets, transaction costs will be a more significant component of the yield.

When the potential for default is admitted, information asymmetries also are relevant. When the lessor has perfect information about the financial condition of the lessee, lease yields accurately reflect lessees' default potential and lease yields will be related negatively to the lessee's financial condition. In the absence of perfect information, the lease yield will be a negative function of the lessee's financial condition, and it also will be related negatively to the quality of information about the lessee. In the spirit of Akerlof (1970), in the absence of reliable information, the lessor will assume the worst and the lease yield will be commensurately high. Thus, we hypothesize that lease yields will be related negatively to the financial condition of the lessee and to the quality of information about the lessee.

In our empirical analysis, we do not have a precise measure of information quality. However, assuming that the "size" of the firm is a reasonable proxy for "prominence," we employ the book value of the lessee's assets as a proxy for the availability of reliable information. Thus, we conjecture that lease yields will be related inversely to the book value of the lessee's assets.

We also do not have an accurate measure of the lessee's financial condition. However, as a proxy for this information, we employ several measures of default risk that prior literature reports to have predictive power in identifying corporate bankruptcies.

4. Sampling Procedure and Data Description

4.1. Sampling Procedure

To gather data for this study, we accessed the files of seven non-bank leasing companies and one bank-owned leasing company. Four of the companies have their headquarters in the Mountain West, two are located in the Midwest, one is located in the Southwest, and one is on the West Coast. These eight firms allowed their files to be inspected under the condition that their customers not be identified or contacted and that their names not be revealed. Both currently open (i.e., active) and closed (i.e., completed) leases were accessed.

A random sample of 453 contracts was drawn for evaluation. Because of certain data requirements, only 363 of these contracts are usable in our statistical analyses.[3] Of the 363 usable leases, 223 were open and 140 were closed contracts as of September 1982. All 363 usable leases are financial leases.

---

[3] Of the 453 contracts, 55 are deleted because we cannot identify the industry type of the leased asset and 35 are deleted because they are not financial leases. Of the 35 that are not financial leases, 21 are conditional sales contracts.

The information recorded for each lease includes the origination date of the contract, the geographic location of the lessee, the type and cost of the leased asset, the type and maturity of the lease, the date the lessor paid for the asset, the date and amount of any lease prepayments, the due dates and amounts of the periodic rental payments, the amount of any broker commissions paid to originate the lease, the residual value of the asset (as estimated by the lessor), and an indication as to whether the investment tax credit *(ITC)* was taken by the lessor or passed to the lessee. In addition, in those cases in which reliable financial information is available, various accounting data are taken from the lessee's application. Such data are available in reliable form for 82 of the 363 lease applications.

4.2. Data Description

Data describing the sample are displayed in Table 1. Panel A is a frequency distribution of the leases according to their contract initiation dates. The oldest lease was written in January 1973, and the most recent lease was written in June 1982. The lessees are located in at least 43 different states (for 41 leases, the state in which the lessee is located could not be identified). In each contract, the lessee is responsible for selection, acquisition, and maintenance of the asset and for paying associated property taxes and insurance premiums. All the leases are non-cancellable. At the maturity date of the lease, the residual value of the asset reverts to the lessor. If the lessee defaults, the lessor can repossess the asset, declare the remaining payments due and payable, and make claims for any deficiencies.

Frequency distributions of the leases categorized according to the cost of the leased asset and the term-to-maturity of the contract are contained in Panels B and C, respectively. A frequency distribution of leases according to the general type of asset is contained in Panel D. The assets are placed in 18 general categories. Panel E is a frequency distribution of the book values of the assets of the 258 lessee firms for which this statistic is available.

4.3. Covariance Risk

According to the Miller/Upton and McConnell/Schallheim analyses, lease yields are a function of the covariance risk between the leased asset's residual value and a market factor. If the rate of change in the asset's market value is expressed in terms of the rate of capital appreciation, the relationship between residual-value covariance risk and lease yield is positive. Ideally, this measure of market-value risk would be estimated with a time series of market prices of the leased asset. Unfortunately, consistent time series data on these asset prices are not available. As a consequence, in this study, two proxies for systematic residual-value risk are employed.

The first proxy (and the one on which we rely most heavily) uses a representative sample of firms whose primary (or exclusive) activity is manufacturing assets of the same general type as the leased asset. For example, for leases covering construction equipment, the representative sample includes American Hoist, Caterpillar Tractor, Clark Equipment, and Harnischfeger. The use of data from firms manufacturing the asset to estimate systematic risk assumes that the risk of the asset producer is closely linked with the risk of the asset being produced.[4]

For each representative firm, a market model beta is estimated as of the origination date of the corresponding lease using 60 previous monthly stock market returns taken from the Center for

---

[4]A list of the representative firms in each category is available from the authors upon request.

Table 1   Descriptive Statistics Characterizing the Sample of 363 Financial Leasing Contracts Originated over the Period 1973–1982

A. Frequency Distribution by Origination Date of the Lease Contract

Year of Origination	Number of Leases	Percent of Total
1973	9	2.5
1974	17	4.7
1975	7	1.9
1976	11	3.0
1977	46	12.7
1978	28	7.7
1979	65	17.9
1980	65	17.9
1981	82	22.6
1982	33	9.1

B. Frequency Distribution by Cost of Leased Asset

Cost of Asset	Number of Leases	Percent of Total
$10,000 or Less	134	36.9
$10,001 to $50,000	109	30.0
$50,001 to $100,000	25	6.9
$100,001 to $250,000	35	9.7
$250,001 to $500,000	18	14.9
Over $500,000	42	11.6

Maximum = $63,000,000   Mean = $636,690

Minimum = $1,000   Median = $19,396

C. Frequency Distribution by Term-to-Maturity of the Lease

Term-to-Maturity (in Months)	Number of Leases	Percent of Total
24 or fewer	9	2.5
25 to 26	89	24.5
37 to 48	28	7.7
49 to 60	151	41.6
61 to 72	8	2.2
73 to 84	42	11.6
85 to 96	18	4.9
97 to 108	1	0.3
109 to 120	10	2.8
Over 120	7	1.9

Maximum = 300 months   Mean = 61.3 months

Minimum = 11 months   Median = 60 months

D. Frequency Distribution by Type of Leased Asset

Type of Asset	Number of Leases	Percent of Total
Aircraft	10	2.8
Auto repair equipment	12	3.3

(*continued*)

Table 1 (*continued*)

D. Frequency Distribution by Type of Leased Asset

Type of Asset	Number of Leases	Percent of Total
Computers and processors	43	11.8
Construction equipment	35	9.6
Copy machines	30	8.3
Farm machinery	17	4.7
Food preparation equipment	16	4.4
Industrial laundry machines	8	2.2
Machine tools	28	7.7
Marine equipment	4	1.1
Medical equipment	19	5.2
Misc. electronic equipment	21	5.8
Motel & hotel furnishings	6	1.7
Office equipment	15	4.1
Office furniture	23	6.3
Railroad rolling stock	6	1.6
Telephone systems	20	5.5
Trucks and trailers	50	13.8

E. Frequency Distribution by Book Value of the Assets of the Lessee Firm for 258 Firms for which Data Are Available

Book Value of Lessee's Assets	Number of Leases	Percent of Total
$250,000 or less	76	29.5
$250,001 to $500,000	36	13.9
$500,001 to $1,000,000	24	9.3
$1,000,001 to $2,000,000	25	9.7
$2,000,001 to $5,000,000	24	9.3
$5,000,001 to $10,000,000	26	10.1
$10,000,001 to $25,000,000	11	4.2
$25,000,001 to $100,000,000	17	6.6
Over $100,000,000	19	7.4

Maximum = $8,972,000,000   Mean = $636,690

Minimum = $1,000   Median = $19,396

F. Frequency Distribution by Leased Asset's Unlevered Beta Estimated with Manufacturer Firms

Asset Beta	Number of Leases	Percent of Total
0.500 or less	48	13.2
0.501 to 0.600	61	16.8
0.601 to 0.700	61	16.8
0.701 to 0.800	60	16.5
0.801 to 0.900	69	19.0
0.901 to 1.000	29	8.0
1.001 to 1.100	23	6.3
1.101 to 1.200	7	6.3
1.201 to 1.300	5	1.4

Research in Security Prices (CRSP) returns file. The value-weighted market index from the CRSP file is used to represent the market return. The beta for each firm is then adjusted according to the procedure described by Hamada (1969) to remove the effect of financial leverage. Specifically, each levered beta is converted to an unlevered beta by dividing by one plus the debt/equity ratio as reported by *Value Line* for the year-end prior to the origination date of the relevant lease. Finally, for each asset in the sample, these unlevered betas are averaged across producer firms to obtain an estimate of the leased asset's systematic residual-value risk. This procedure yields one beta estimate for each lease in the sample. A frequency distribution of the unlevered betas is given in Panel F of Table 1.[5]

The second proxy measure of residual value covariance risk involves the estimation of a market model beta for a portfolio of asset-user firms whose primary line of business relies heavily on the use of a particular category of leased assets. The procedure involved in estimating this proxy is identical to the procedure used to estimate the first proxy, with the only difference being the representative firms employed. Further discussion of this proxy variable is contained in section 5.2.

4.4. The Calculation of Lease Yields and the Role of Taxes

In our statistical analysis, the dependent variable is the lease yield. In a competitive leasing market, the relevant yield to the lessor firm is the after-tax yield that is comparable to after-tax yields on alternative investment opportunities. A pragmatic argument against the use of after-tax yields is that it is not possible to estimate accurately the marginal tax rates of either lessee or lessor firms. Because of this limitation, each of the regressions is estimated with both a before- and an after-tax yield. The two yields are computed by solving the following equation iteratively for y:

$$\frac{Cost - ITC}{(1+y)^{t_1}} = \frac{P(1-\tau)+SD}{(1+y)^{t_2}} - \frac{Com(1-\tau)}{(1+y)^{t_3}} + \sum_{x=4}^{np} \frac{L(1-\tau)}{(1+y)^{t_x}} + \sum_{t=q_1}^{q_n} \frac{D_t(\tau)}{(1+y)^t} + \frac{RV - SD}{(1+y)^{t_n}}, \quad (8)$$

where *Cost* is the original cost of the leased asset; *ITC* is the investment tax credit if retained by the lessor; P is the amount of any prepayments made on the lease; *SD* is any security deposit required on the lease; *Com* is the amount of any broker commission paid on the lease;[6] L is the periodic lease payment; D_t is the depreciation on the leased asset in period t; *RV* is the residual value of the leased asset as estimated by the lessor; and τ is a corporate tax rate. The time components $t_1, \ldots, t_n$ are the number of days between time zero and the data of the respective cash flow. Time zero is either t_1 or t_2, depending on which cash flow occurs earliest. The time components $q_1, \ldots, q_n$ represent quarterly intervals. The symbol *np* represents the number of lease payments, and t_n is the number of days until the maturity date of the lease.

In calculating the before-tax yield, *ITC* and τ are both set equal to zero. In calculating the after-tax yield, *ITC* is set equal to the amount of the *ITC* if the investment tax credit is retained by the

[5]We recognize that our unlevered beta estimates are imperfect proxies for the asset's residual-value systematic risk. For example, we have not adjusted the unlevered beta for corporate taxes. We have not done so for two reasons. First, theoretically, the relationship between beta and taxes is unclear. Second, empirically, we are uncertain as to how to estimate each firm's marginal tax rate. Additionally, we have not adjusted unlevered beta for differing maturities of debt, nor have we incorporated the lease liabilities of the representative firms. The imperfect nature of this proxy means that, barring some unknown source of spurious correlation, the tests are biased against rejecting the null hypothesis.

[6]Six of the lessor firms in the sample recorded some form of brokerage commissions. For those leases on which a brokerage commission was paid, the average commission (i.e., finder's fee) was 1.6 percent of the cost of the leased asset.

Table 2   Frequency Distribution by Lease Yields for the Sample of 363 Leases Originated over the Period 1973–1982 Computed According to the Following Equation:[a]

$$\frac{Cost - ITC}{(1+y)^{t_1}} = \frac{P(1-\tau)+SD}{(1+y)^{t_2}} - \frac{Com(1-\tau)}{(1+y)^{t_3}} + \sum_{x=4}^{np} \frac{L(1-\tau)}{(1+y)^{t_x}} + \sum_{t=q_1}^{q_n} \frac{D_t(\tau)}{(1+y)^t} + \frac{RV-SD}{(1+y)^{t_n}}$$

Before-Tax Yield			After-Tax Yield		
Lease Yield (Percent per Year)	Number of Leases	Percent of Total	Lease Yield (Percent per Year)	Number of Leases	Percent of Total
9 or less	51	14.0			
9.1 to 12.0	37	10.2	6 or less	9	2.4
12.1 to 15.0	20	5.6	6.1 to 9.0	62	17.1
15.1 to 18.0	41	11.2	9.1 to 12.0	71	19.6
18.1 to 21.0	62	17.1	12.1 to 15.0	75	20.7
21.1 to 24.0	73	20.1	15.1 to 18.0	90	24.8
24.1 to 27.0	50	13.8	18.1 to 21.0	44	12.1
27.1 to 30.0	17	4.7	21.1 to 24.0	8	2.2
30.1 to 33.0	3	0.8	24.1 to 27.0	3	0.8
33.1 to 36.0	2	0.6	27.1 or more	1	0.3
36.1 to 39.0	3	0.8			
39.1 or more	4	1.1			
Minimum = 4.41%	Mean =	18.63%	Minimum = 3.49%	Mean =	13.40%
Maximum = 45.30%	Median =	19.57%	Maximum = 29.0%	Median =	13.89%

[a]Terms are defined as:

y: before- or after-tax lease yield,

Cost: original cost of the leased asset,

ITC: investment tax credit if retained by the lessee in the after-tax yield calculations, zero in before-tax yield calculations,

P: prepayments made on the lease,

SD: security-deposit on the lease,

Com: brokerage commission paid on the lease,

L: periodic lease payment

D_t: depreciation on the leased asset in period t,

RV: residual value of the leased asset as estimated by the lessor,

τ: corporate tax rate in after-tax yield calculations, zero in before-tax yield calculations,

$t_1, \ldots, t_n$: number of days between time zero and the date of the respective cash flow,

$q_1, \ldots, q_n$: quarterly intervals,

np: the number of lease payments,

t_n: the number of days until the maturity date of the lease.

lessor and τ is set equal to the maximum corporate tax rate in use when the lease was originated.[7] Frequency distributions of the annualized lease yields are displayed in Table 2.

[7]For leases initiated before 1979, the maximum corporate tax rate of 48 percent is used. For leases originated after January 1, 1979, the maximum corporate rate of 46 percent is used. In addition, in computing after-tax yields it is necessary to make some assumption about the appropriate depreciation schedule. For leases beginning prior to 1981, double-declining balance depreciation for the life of the lease is used. For leases initiated after January 1, 1981, the accelerated cost recovery system is used. The tax benefits of depreciation are assumed to occur quarterly.

The final data used in the analysis are government bond yields. As of the origination date of the lease, for each lease in the sample, the yield of the treasury bond with a maturity date closest to the maturity date of the lease was collected. This yield is used as a proxy for the risk-free rate of return.

5. Empirical Results

5.1. Yield Regressions

The results of the regressions are reported in Table 3. The two panels of the table contain parallel sets of regressions. Panel A contains the results when the dependent variable is the before-tax yield; Panel B contains the results when the dependent variable is the after-tax yield. The statistical results across the two panels are remarkably consistent.

In the first regression reported in each panel, the two independent variables are the yield of the treasury bond of the same maturity as the lease contract and the leased asset's discounted beta estimated with asset-manufacturing-firm stock returns. The discounted beta is calculated by discounting the asset's estimated beta with the yield of the treasury bond of the same maturity as the lease contract. In Panel B, the treasury bond yield is an after-tax yield calculated by multiplying the before-tax yield by one minus the maximum statutory corporate tax rate applicable at the origination date of the lease. This after-tax yield also is used to calculate the asset's discounted beta.

In each panel, the coefficient of the treasury bond yield is positive and statistically significant at the 0.01 level, with t-statistics of 11.45 and 9.99. In addition, in each panel, the coefficient of discounted beta is positive and statistically significant at the 0.01 level, with t-statistics of 9.05 and 6.45. These results are consistent with the predictions of Miller/Upton and McConnell/Schallheim.

It is also possible that discounted beta reflects a general risk measure associated with leases rather than a specific measure of non-diversifiable risk. To investigate this possibility, the variance of return is estimated for each leased asset's representative firms. The variance of return is estimated using the 60 monthly returns immediately preceding the origination date of the relevant lease. The variance of return is then entered as a third independent variable in the regressions. The results are reported as the second regression in the two panels of Table 3. In each case, the coefficients and t-statistics of the T-bond yield and discounted beta are virtually the same as those in the first regression. In no case, however, is the coefficient of the asset's estimated variance difference from zero at any reasonable level of significance.

It is also possible that the statistical significance of discounted beta is not due to the importance of beta per se, but rather to the fact that the beta discounting function uses the treasury bond yield of the same maturity as the lease. Independently, this variable is significant in explaining lease yields, and it may be that the discounting function merely captures an additional element of the effect of interest rates on lease yields. To examine this possibility, the regressions are re-estimated with two independent variables: the treasury bond yield and undiscounted beta. The results are reported as the third regression in each panel.

In both regressions, the magnitudes of the coefficients of the treasury bond yield are approximately the same as in the previous regressions, and they are significant at the 0.01 level. As might be anticipated, however, even if Miller/Upton and McConnell/Schallheim are correct, the coefficients and t-statistics of undiscounted beta are substantially attenuated in comparison with those estimated for discounted beta. However, in the two regressions, the coefficients continue to be

Table 3 Regressions of Lease Yields on Various Independent Variables for a Sample of 363 Leases Originated over the Period 1973–1982 (t-Statistics in Parentheses)[a]

	Intercept	T-Bond	D-Beta	Var	U-Beta	1/Cost	1/BV	Profit	Lev	Liquid	R^2	F	N
A. Regression Coefficients with the Before-Tax Lease Yield as the Dependent Variable													
1.	-2.89	1.19	19.55								0.33	89.6	363
	(-1.76)	(11.45)	(9.05)										
2.	-1.64	1.16	20.38	-105.79							0.34	60.5	363
	(-0.88)	(10.85)	(9.10)	(-1.40)									
3.	6.13	0.98			2.69						0.19	41.1	363
	(3.64)	(8.67)			(1.53)								
4.	-0.85	1.09	14.01			133.51					0.42	85.3	363
	(-0.55)	(11.09)	(6.47)			(7.18)							
5.	-0.96	1.05	12.60			153.79	77.39				0.46	53.5	258
	(-0.54)	(9.31)	(5.05)			(5.05)	(3.46)						
6.	-1.72	1.12	14.31			183.09	347.35	1.09	-2.72	-0.12	0.65	19.2	82
	(-0.51)	(6.28)	(3.97)			(1.76)	(3.22)	(0.37)	(-1.25)	(-4.34)			
B. Regression Coefficient with the After-Tax Lease Yield as the Dependent Variable													
1.	2.27	1.17	8.08								0.27	65.3	363
	(2.20)	(9.99)	(6.45)										
2.	1.92	1.19	7.85	30.44							0.27	43.6	363
	(1.64)	(9.81)	(6.02)	(0.63)									
3.	5.75	1.07			2.17						0.19	42.4	363
	(5.72)	(8.64)			(2.03)								
4.	3.24	1.08	5.20			100.99					0.40	80.8	363
	(3.46)	(10.14)	(4.43)			(7.07)							
5.	3.54	1.04	3.72			115.33	49.09				0.44	49.0	253
	(3.30)	(8.49)	(2.71)			(7.49)	(3.56)						
6.	4.34	1.08	4.49			144.10	212.74	0.79	-3.26	-0.06	0.61	16.3	82
	(1.98)	(5.30)	(2.17)			(5.90)	(3.03)	(0.42)	(-2.30)	(-3.42)			

[a]Independent variables are:

T-Bond: yield of the treasury bond with a maturity date closest to the maturity date of the lease, as of the initiation of the lease,

D-Beta: leased asset's estimated beta discounted at the corresponding treasury bond yield,

Var: variance of return estimated for each asset's representative firms,

U-Beta: leased asset's undiscounted beta,

1/Cost: inverse of the purchase price of the leased asset,

1/BV: inverse of the book value of the lessee's assets,

Profit: lessee's net income divided by total assets,

Lev: lessee's total debt divided by total assets,

Liquid: lessee's current assets divided by current liabilities.

positive and significant at the 0.15 and 0.05 levels, respectively. Although the statistics are not as strong as when discounted beta is employed, the evidence is consistent with the contention that residual-value covariance risk is a determinant of financial lease yields.

To this point, our results are consistent with the prediction that lease yields are a function of the risk-free rate of interest and the discounted value of the non-diversifiable residual-value risk of the leased asset. Beyond that, we have argued that once the assumptions of perfect capital markets and default-free leases are relaxed, lease yields also will be a function of the transaction costs associated with negotiating the lease, the availability of reliable information about the lessee, and the probability of default by the lessee. We further conjecture that the inverse of the value of the leased asset's purchase price can serve as a proxy for the transaction-cost effect in lease yields, that the inverse of the book value of the lessee firm's assets can serve as a proxy for the availability of reliable information about the lessee, and that various financial ratios of the lessee can serve as proxies for the probability of default by the lessee. The remaining regressions reported in Table 3 are aimed at exploring these conjectures.

In the fourth regression in each panel, the independent variables are the treasury bond yield, discounted beta, and the inverse of the purchase price of the leased asset. In the fifth regression, the independent variables are the same as those in the fourth regression plus the inverse of the book value of the lessee's assets. (In the fifth regression, the sample size declines to 258 because we are not able to identify the book value of the assets of 105 of the lessees in the sample.)

In each regression, the coefficients of the treasury bond yield and discounted beta are positive and significant at the 0.01 level. In addition, the coefficients of the inverse of the purchase price of the leased asset and the inverse of the book value of the lessee's assets are positive and significant at the 0.01 level in each regression. If we assume that these variables capture the effects of transaction costs and asymmetric information in lease yields, the results are consistent with our hypotheses that the yields of risky leases are a function of the fixed cost of negotiating the lease and of the availability of reliable information about the lessee firm.

To test our hypothesis that the yields of risky leases are also a function of the financial condition of the lessee firm, three financial ratios—a profitability ratio, a leverage ratio, and a liquidity ratio—are added to the regressions. The profitability ratio is net income divided by total assets, the leverage ratio is total liabilities divided by total assets, and the liquidity ratio is current assets divided by current liabilities.

In a recent study, Ohlson (1980) reviews studies prior to his and uses variables identified by others in constructing a bankruptcy prediction model. He identifies four factors that are useful in predicting corporate bankruptcies: (1) the log of the total assets of the firm, (2) a leverage measure (total liabilities divided by total assets), (3) a measure of performance (either net income divided by total assets or funds provided by operations divided by total liabilities), and (4) a measure of liquidity (either working capital divided by total assets or working capital divided by total assets and current liabilities divided by current assets jointly).

We have already used total assets of the lessee in the regressions. The other variables we employ are dictated largely by data availability. To include a firm in the regressions using financial ratios, we require that its financial statement be "reliable." Firms are omitted if their financial statements are incomplete or if data on the lease application are inconsistent with data on the firm's financial statements. Because of this requirement, the usable sample declines to 82 observations.

The sign of the coefficient of the profitability variable is predicted to be negative, the sign of the coefficient of the leverage variable is predicted to be positive, and the sign of the coefficient of the liquidity variable is predicted to be negative. The results of these regressions are reported in the sixth row in the two panels of Table 3.

Several aspects of the results merit comment. First, in each instance, the coefficients of the treasury bond yield, discounted beta, the inverse of the asset's purchase price, and the inverse of the book value of the lessee's assets continue to be positive and significantly different from zero. These results support our hypotheses because they are little changed even though the sample has declined by more than 75 percent. Second, there is some evidence of a relationship between lease yields and the financial condition of the lessee firm. The coefficient of the liquidity ratio is negative as predicted and significant at the 0.01 level with t-statistics of -4.34 and -3.42. However, the other financial variables do not enter as statistically significant (except in one case), and the signs of their coefficients are the opposite of those predicted. Overall, though, we view the results as being remarkably supportive of the predictions of Miller/Uptown and McConnell/Schallheim and of our ancillary hypotheses.

5.2. Regressions Estimated with an Alternative Proxy for Systematic Residual-Value Risk

One troublesome aspect of our empirical analysis is the measurement of the leased asset's residual-value risk using data from firms that manufacture the leased asset. An alternative procedure is to identify a portfolio of firms whose primary line of business involves the use of the leased asset. For example, it seems reasonable to argue that the market value of American Airlines is highly correlated with the market value of aircraft.

The major disadvantage in the use of asset-user firms to estimate asset betas is that it is more difficult to identify single-asset-user firms than to identify single-asset-manufacturer firms. Nevertheless, for seven of the categories of leased assets, we have identified firms whose values are likely to be tied closely to one of the categories. The seven categories are aircraft, construction equipment, marine equipment, medical equipment, motel and hotel furnishings, railroad rolling stock, and trucks and trailers. These seven categories encompass 130 leases.

For each category, a portfolio of representative asset-user firms is identified. For each of the 130 eligible leases, an unlevered beta is estimated following the same procedure used to estimate betas with asset-manufacturer firms.[8] The yield regressions are then reestimated. The results are reported in Table 4. As before, the table contains two panels that report parallel sets of regressions: Panel A employs before-tax yields; Panel B employs after-tax yields. In addition, within each panel, two parallel sets of regressions (labeled USER and MNFR) are reported. Those labeled USER

[8]Two tests were conducted to determine the degree of correspondence between asset-manufacturer and asset-user firms' betas. The first is a matched sample-test. In this test, unlevered betas were computed over four non-overlapping time intervals for each asset-manufacturer and asset-user firm in the sample. The average unlevered beta was computed for each category of leased assets, and the difference between the average unlevered betas estimated with the portfolios of asset-user and asset-producer firms was computed. A t-test indicates that the average difference in betas of 0.023 is not significant ($t = 0.048$). In the second test, a simple correlation was estimated between unlevered asset-user firms' betas and asset-manufacturer firms' betas. For $N = 26$, the simple correlation coefficient is 0.27 with $F = 1.89$. A list of the asset-user firms is available from the authors upon request.

Table 4   Regressions of Lease Yields on Various Independent Variables for a Sample of 130 Leases Originated over the Period 1973–1982 (*t*-Statistics in Parentheses)[a]

		Intercept	T-Bond	D-Beta	U-Beta	1/Cost	R^2	F	N
A. Regression Coefficients with the Before-Tax Lease Yield as the Dependent Variable									
1.	USER[b]	−10.68	1.63	24.62			0.36	36.1	130
		(−3.33)	(8.16)	(5.86)					
	MNFR[b]	−13.93	1.57	37.61			0.48	58.4	130
		(−5.00)	(9.21)	(8.40)					
2.	USER	0.05	1.15		6.00		0.20	16.1	130
		(0.01)	(5.67)		(1.43)				
	MNFR	0.71	1.05		6.93		0.21	16.6	130
		(0.23)	(5.26)		(1.69)				
3.	USER	−6.84	1.40	14.58		509.62	0.53	48.2	130
		(−2.44)	(8.01)	(3.75)		(6.83)			
	MNFR	−10.07	1.41	25.73		425.52	0.59	60.5	130
		(−3.92)	(9.15)	(5.75)		(5.85)			
B. Regression Coefficients with the After-Tax Lease Yield as the Dependent Variable									
1.	USER	−2.71	1.63	11.21			0.34	32.4	130
		(−1.40)	(7.89)	(4.72)					
	MNFR	−3.35	1.46	15.56			0.39	40.0	130
		(−1.92)	(7.89)	(5.85)					
2.	USER	1.95	1.29		4.05		0.24	19.9	130
		(0.94)	(6.29)		(1.71)				
	MNFR	3.23	1.19		3.11		0.23	19.2	130
		(1.89)	(5.82)		(1.33)				
3.	USER	−0.64	1.41	5.83		354.91	0.60	63.8	130
		(−0.42)	(8.72)	(3.01)		(9.18)			
	MNFR	−1.17	1.33	8.60		338.19	0.62	68.1	130
		(−0.83)	(9.07)	(3.82)		(8.76)			

[a]Independent variables are:

T-Bond: yield of the treasury bond with a maturity date closest to the maturity date of the lease, as of the initiation of the lease,

D-Beta: leased asset's estimated beta discounted at the corresponding treasury bond yield,

U-Beta: leased asset's undiscounted beta,

1/Cost: inverse of the purchase price of the leased asset.

[b]*USER* indicates regressions estimated with user-firm betas and MNFR those estimated with manufacturer-firm betas.

employ the asset-user betas; those labeled MNFR use asset-manufacturer betas. In each regression, the sample contains 130 leases.

The regressions are estimated with three sets of explanatory variables: (1) the treasury bond yield and discounted beta, (2) the treasury bond yield and undiscounted beta, and (3) the treasury bond yield, discounted beta, and the inverse of the purchase price of the leased asset.[9,10] First, in both panels, the coefficients, t-statistics and R^2's are similar between the pairs of USER and MNFR regressions. Second, in each case the coefficients of the treasury bond yield, discounted beta, and the inverse of the asset cost are positive and significant at the 0.01 level. Third, the coefficients, t-statistics and R^2's in Table 4 are similar to those for the corresponding regressions estimated with the full sample in Table 3. In sum, then, the regressions estimated with asset-user betas are consistent with our hypotheses.

5.3. A Further Look at the Data

The descriptive statistics in Table 2 indicate that the average before-tax lease yield of 18.63 percent is substantially above the yields of Aaa corporate bonds, which ranged from 7.15 percent to 15.49 percent over the period covered by this study. A natural question that arises is this: Why would corporations raise capital by means of leasing arrangements when borrowing appears to be a much less expensive form of financing? One hypothesis is that only the largest corporate borrowers are able to issue publicly traded debt. If so, our arguments suggest that the appropriate benchmarks are the yields on the largest leases issued by the largest lessees. Evidence on this point is presented in Table 5.

Table 5 is a cross-tabulation of the lease yields less Aaa corporate bond yields taken from the *Federal Reserve Bulletin*. The entries in the table are averages of individual lease yields less the Aaa corporate bond yields during the origination month of the lease. Row categories are the purchase prices of the leased asset by quartile. Column categories are the book values of the lessee's assets by quartile. Panels A and B contain average spreads for the before-tax and after-tax yields, respectively. In computing the yield spreads in Panel B, the Aaa bond yield was multiplied by one minus the maximum statutory corporate tax rate applicable at the origination of the corresponding lease.

In each panel, the largest yield spread is contained in the upper left-hand corner, which corresponds to the smallest assets leased by the smallest lessees. In both panels, the yield spread contained in the lower right-hand corner is the second smallest one in the panel. This cell corresponds to the largest assets leased by the largest lessees. (The smallest spread in each panel is contained in the lower left-hand corner, but this cell contains only one observation.) In addition, in each panel, the row marginals decline monotonically as the book value of the lessees' assets increases, and the column marginals decline monotonically as the purchase price of the leased assets increases. In short, these results indicate that the "cost" of leasing approaches the "cost" of issuing debt for large corporations that lease large assets. If small corporations that lease small assets also face significant fixed costs in borrowing to finance their assets, then leasing is no more costly than borrowing, once the "cost" of each is adjusted for transaction and information costs.

---

[9] As in Table 3, in the after-tax regressions the treasury bond yield is an after-tax yield, and this after-tax yield is used to compute discounted beta.

[10] Regressions are not estimated with the lessee's asset value and the various financial ratios because the already reduced sample becomes so small and so heavily concentrated in a few industries that the results become meaningless.

Table 5 Cross-Tabulations of Average Yield Spreads for a Sample of 258 Leases Originated over the Period 1973–1982

Cells contain the average of the individual lease yields less the yield of the Aaa corporate bond index as of the origination date of the lease (in each panel, the rows give the asset purchase price quartile and the columns give the book value of the lessee's assets quartile).

		Quartile of Book Value of Lessee's Assets[a]				Purchase Price Marginal[b]
		1	2	3	4	
A. Before-Tax Lease Yield Less the Aaa Corporate Bond Yield (Percent per Year)						
Quartile of purchase price of leased asset[c]	1	12.28	11.62	10.36	6.18	11.50
		(33)	(22)	(6)	(4)	(65)
	2	11.61	10.06	8.96	10.19	10.36
		(21)	(24)	(13)	(6)	(64)
	3	10.55	9.04	3.98	0.97	5.16
		(9)	(16)	(19)	(21)	(65)
	4	−3.76	0.10	−1.08	−1.27	−1.17
		(1)	(3)	(25)	(35)	(64)
Book value		11.57	9.88	3.61	0.94	
Marginal		(64)	(65)	(63)	(66)	
B. After-Tax Lease Yield Less the After-Tax Aaa Corporate Bond Yield (Percent per Year)						
Quartile of purchase price of leased asset[c]	1	10.87	9.74	10.71	6.20	10.19
		(33)	(22)	(6)	(4)	(65)
	2	9.61	8.64	9.24	7.38	8.96
		(21)	(24)	(13)	(6)	(64)
	3	9.00	7.90	4.41	3.10	5.48
		(9)	(16)	(19)	(21)	(65)
	4	2.33	3.40	2.70	2.80	2.78
		(1)	(3)	(25)	(35)	(64)
Book value		10.06	8.59	5.33	3.52	
Marginal		(64)	(65)	(63)	(66)	

[a]Numbers in parentheses are the number of observations in each cell.
[b]Purchase price marginals are calculated as the average of the yield spreads for each purchase price quartile, where the first quartile includes the 25 percent of the leases with the lowest asset purchase prices, the second quartile includes the 25 percent of the leases with the next lowest asset purchase prices, and so on.
[c]Book value marginals are calculated as the average of the yield spreads for each lessee size quartile, where the first quartile includes the 25 percent of the leases with the smallest book value of lessee's assets, the second quartile includes the 25 percent of the leases with the next lowest book value of lessee's assets, and so on.

5.4. Lease Yields and the Role of Taxes

One concern in the leasing literature has been whether the value associated with the tax shields generated by leasing arrangements accrues to the lessor or the lessee firm.[11] We have some indirect evidence on this point. For each of the leases in the sample, we determine whether the investment

---

[11]For discussions of the role of taxes in leasing, see, for example, Brealey and Young (1980); Lewellen, Long, and McConnell (1976); Miller and Upton (1976); Myers, Dill, and Bautista (1976); Schall (1974); and Smith and Wakeman (1985).

Table 6 Regressions of After-Tax Yields, with and without the *ITC*, on Five Independent Variables Plus an *ITC* Dummy Variable for a Sample of 82 Leases Originated over the Period 1973–1982 (*t*-Statistics in Parentheses)

Intercept	T-Bond	D-Beta	1/Cost	1/BV	Liquid	ITC	R^2	F	N
1. Regression with After-Tax Lease Yield as the Dependent Variable									
0.89	1.14	5.75	130.65	253.77	–0.05	0.91	0.58	17.6	82
(0.42)	(5.46)	(2.62)	(5.43)	(3.71)	(–3.06)	(1.42)			
2. Regression with After-Tax, but before ITC, Lease Yield as the Dependent Variable									
1.46	1.14	4.93	135.06	229.71	–0.06	–2.25	0.66	24.4	82
(0.74)	(5.86)	(2.42)	(6.03)	(3.61)	(–3.59)	(–3.78)			

[a]Independent variables are:

T-Bond: yield of the treasury bond with a maturity date closest to the maturity date of the lease, as of the initiation of the lease,
D-Beta: Leased asset's estimated beta discounted at the corresponding treasury bond yield,
1/Cost: inverse of the purchase price of the leased assets,
1/BV: inverse of the book value of the lessee's assets,
Liquid: lessee's current assets divided by current liabilities,
ITC: a zero-one dummy variable with the value of one if the lessor retains the investment tax credit.

tax credit is retained by the lessor or passed through to the lessee.[12] If the leasing market is perfectly competitive, the value of the tax shield should accrue to the lessee, and after-tax (and after-*ITC*) yields should be indistinguishable regardless of whether the *ITC* is retained by the lessor or passed through to the lessee. That is, in those cases in which the *ITC* is retained by the lessor, the lease payments should be commensurably lower than when it is passed through to the lessee, but the after-tax (and after-*ITC*) lease yields should be indistinguishable.

To examine this issue, we estimate a regression that includes the treasury bond yield, discounted beta (estimated with the portfolio of asset-manufacturing firms), the inverse of the purchase price of the leased asset, the inverse of the lessee's book value, and the lessee's current ratio as independent variables. In addition, a dummy variable that takes on the value of 1.0 when the *ITC* is retained by the lessor and a value of zero when the *ITC* is passed through to the lessee is included. The dependent variable in this regression is the after-tax lease yield. The results are presented in the first row of Table 6. Consistent with a perfectly competitive leasing market, the coefficient of the dummy variable is not significant at the 0.05 level. It is, however, significant at the 0.10 level ($t = 1.42$), and the magnitude of the coefficient indicates that the average difference in the yields of the two groups is almost 1 percent (after adjusting for other factors).

As a further consideration of this issue, after-tax lease yields are recomputed assuming that the *ITC* is always passed through to the lessee. If lease terms are not adjusted to reflect the retention of

---

[12]For 122 of the contracts (i.e., 33.6 percent of the sample), the *ITC* was passed through to the lessee. In 185 contracts (i.e., 51 percent of the sample), the *ITC* was retained by the lessor. In the remaining cases, the *ITC* was not available for either party, usually because the asset was not a new piece of equipment. Of the leases in which the *ITC* was available, it was retained by the lessor 60.3 percent of the time. Strickney, Weil, and Wolfson (1983) analyze the division of tax benefits associated with the purchase by General Electric Credit Corporation of over $1.5 billion in tax shields related to safe harbor leasing contracts in 1981.

the *ITC* by the lessor, these yields would be indistinguishable regardless of which party receives the credit. The second row of Table 6 reports the results when the regression is re-estimated with the same variables as before, except that the dependent variable is the after-tax yield computed ignoring the *ITC*. In this case, the coefficient of the dummy variable is significantly negative ($t = -3.78$). This result indicates that the terms of lease contracts are adjusted according to which party receives the *ITC*. Because of the marginal significance of the coefficient of the dummy variable in the first regression, however, there remains some ambiguity as to whether the full value of the tax shield is passed through to the lessee firm, as would be predicted in a perfectly competitive market.

6. Summary and Conclusion

Miller and Upton (1976) and McConnell and Schallheim (1983) present theoretical models of financial lease valuation in which the lease yield is a function of the risk-free rate of interest and the discounted value of the leased asset's residual-value covariance risk. To test this hypothesis, we compiled a sample of 363 financial leases originated over the period 1973 through 1982. Before- and after-tax lease yields are regressed against the yield of the treasury bond of the same maturity as the lease and a proxy for the discounted value of the leased asset's residual-value covariance risk. The coefficients of both variables are positive and statistically different from zero at conventional levels of significance. These results are consistent with the predictions of Miller/Upton and McConnell/Schallheim.

Additionally, we hypothesize that lease yields are a function of the transaction costs associated with negotiating and writing the lease, the quality and quantity of information about the lessee firm, and the default risk associated with the lessee firm. We further conjecture that (1) the transaction costs associated with negotiating and writing the lease decline proportionately as the dollar value of the leased asset increases so that the lease yield is an inverse function of the cost of the leased asset; (2) the availability of reliable information about the lessee firm increases as the "size" of the lessee increases so that lease yields are an inverse function of the book value of the lessee firm's assets; and (3) lease yields are a positive function of the default potential of the lessee firm. Three financial ratios are used as proxies for lessee default potential: (1) a profitability ratio, (2) a liquidity ratio, and (3) a leverage ratio. Additional regressions indicate that, in addition to the yield of the treasury bond of the same maturity as the lease and a proxy for the discounted residual-value covariance risk of the leased asset, lease yields are positively related to the inverse of the purchase price of the leased asset and the inverse of the book value of the lessee's assets and negatively related to the lessee's current ratio. We interpret these results as being consistent with our hypotheses. The failure of the other two financial ratios to enter significantly into the yield regression may be due to the inadequacy of the data or to the inability of these ratios to capture the default potential of lessee firms. These results do suggest that a further inquiry should investigate the predictability of lessee default.

References

Akerlof, George, 1970. The market for lemons: Qualitative uncertainty and the market mechanism. *Quarterly Journal of Economics* 89, 488–500.

Brealey, Richard A., and Charles M. Young, 1980. Debt, taxes and leasing: A note. *Journal of Finance* 35, 1245–50.

Crawford, Peggy J., Charles Harper, and John J. McConnell, 1981. Further evidence on the terms of financial leases. *Financial Management* 10, 7–14.

Geske, Robert, 1977. The valuation of corporate liabilities as compound options. *Journal of Financial and Quantitative Analysis* 12, 541–42.

Hamada, Robert, 1969. Portfolio analysis, market equilibrium, and corporation finance. *Journal of Finance* 24, 13–31.

Lewellen, W. G., Michael S. Long, and John J. McConnell, 1976. Asset leasing in competitive capital markets. *Journal of Finance* 31, 787–98.

McConnell, John J., and James S. Schallheim, 1983. Valuation of asset leasing contracts. *Journal of Financial Economics* 12, 237–261.

Miller, Merton H., and Charles Upton, 1976. Leasing, buying and the cost of capital services. *Journal of Finance* 31, 761–86.

Myers, S. C., D. A. Dill, and A. J. Bautista, 1976. Valuation of financial lease contracts. *Journal of Finance* 31, 799–819.

Ohlson, James, 1980. Financial ratios and the probabilistic prediction of bankruptcy. *Journal of Accounting Research* 18, 109–31.

Rubinstein, Mark, 1976. The value of uncertain income streams and the pricing of options. *Bell Journal of Economics* 7, 407–25.

Schall, Lawrence D., 1974. The lease-or-buy and asset acquisition decision. *Journal of Finance* 29, 1203–14.

Smith, Clifford W., and L. MacDonald Wakeman, 1985. Determinants of corporate leasing policy. *Journal of Finance* 40, 895–908.

Sorenson, Ivar, and Ramon Johnson, 1977. Equipment financial leasing practices and costs: An empirical study. *Financial Management* 6, 33–40.

Stickney, Clyde P., Roman L. Weil, and Mark A. Wolfson, 1983. Income taxes and tax transfer leases. *Accounting Review* 58, 439–59.

Discussion Questions

1. Rationalize the hypothesis that lease yields are an inverse function of the value of the leased assets.

2. Why should lease yields be positively related to the default potential of the lessee?

3. Why could it be expected that required lease yields would be greater the lower the quality of information about the lessee? Do you agree with the authors' use of company size to measure information quality?

4. The authors hypothesize that required lease yields would be greater as the risk of residual value increases. How do the authors measure the risk pertaining to the residual value of the asset leased?

5. Check Table 2's present value formula, which shows how to calculate the expected yield on a lease. Does it make sense?

6. How were required yields related to the cost of the asset(s) leased? How do the authors explain this?

7. Why should lease yields bear a positive association with interest rates on Treasury obligations?

John D. Finnerty *

Financial Engineering in Corporate Finance: An Overview

In the author's words, "Financial engineering involves the design, the development, and the implementation of innovative financial instruments and processes, and the formulation of creative solutions to problems in finance." To be successful, innovations need to reduce costs to issuers, increase returns to investors, or both.

Financial innovation over the past 13 years has accelerated because of rapid changes in interest rates, radical changes in regulation and taxation, and the emergence of greater capability for high-technology solutions due to computer, communication, data, and human capabilities.

Financial innovation over the past two decades has rapidly brought about revolutionary changes in financial instruments and processes. Almost daily the financial press carries yet another tombstone advertisement featuring a new security. A variety of factors, among the more important of which are increased interest rate volatility and the frequency of tax and regulatory changes, have stimulated the process of financial innovation. The deregulation of the financial services industry and increased competition within investment banking have undoubtedly placed increased emphasis on being able to design new products, develop better processes, and implement more effective solutions to increasingly complex financial problems. Financial engineering is the lifeblood of this activity.

Financial engineering involves the design, the development, and the implementation of innovative financial instruments and processes, and the formulation of creative solutions to problems in finance. The term *innovative* is used here to describe a solution that is nontrivial. Innovative financial solutions may involve a new consumer-type financial instrument, such as IRA and Keogh accounts; a new security, such as money market preferred stock; a new process, such as the shelf registration process; or a creative solution to a corporate finance problem, such as the design of customized security arrangements for a project financing or a leveraged buyout.

* The author would like to thank James Ang, Laurence Booth, Marek Borun, Dennis Logue, and the anonymous referees for helpful comments on earlier drafts of the paper. Earlier versions of the paper were presented at Florida State University, the University of Toronto, and the 18th Annual Meeting of the FMA in New Orleans, LA, October 22, 1988.

Source: Reprinted with permission from *Financial Management* (Winter 1988), pp. 14–33. John D. Finnerty is a Professor of Finance at Fordham University and is Executive Vice President and Chief Financial Officer of College Savings Bank.

453

I. Scope of Financial Engineering

The definition of corporate financial engineering distinguishes three types of activities. The first, securities innovation, involves the development of innovative financial instruments, including those developed primarily for consumer-type applications such as new types of bank accounts, new forms of mutual funds, new types of life insurance products, and new forms of residential mortgages. Innovative financial instruments also include those developed primarily for corporate finance applications such as new debt instruments; options, futures, and other new risk management vehicles; new types of preferred stock; new forms of convertible securities; and new types of common equity instruments.

The second branch of corporate financial engineering involves the development of innovative financial processes. These new processes reduce the cost of effecting financial transactions and are generally the result of legislative or regulatory changes (for example, the shelf registration process) or of technological developments (electronic security trading).

The third branch involves creative solutions to corporate finance problems. It encompasses innovative cash management strategies, innovative debt management strategies, and customized corporate financing structures such as those involved in various forms of asset-based financing.

II. The Process of Financial Innovation

Miller [38], Silber [46, 47, 48], and Van Horne [53] characterize the process of financial innovation in different terms.[1] Miller finds that regulatory and tax factors have provided the major impetus for financial innovation over the past 20 years. He describes financial innovations as "unforecastable improvements" in the array of available financial products and processes that came into being as a result of unexpected tax or regulatory impulses [38, p. 460]. Zero coupon bonds provide a good example of how a tax impulse led to innovation.

Prior to the passage of the Tax Equity and Fiscal Responsibility Act of 1982 (TEFRA), an issuer of zero coupon bonds could have amortized the original issue discount—the difference between the face amount of the bonds and their issue price—on a straight-line basis for tax purposes. Being able to deduct the interest expense faster than the interest implicitly compounded on the bonds produced significant tax benefits, which were greater the higher the bond's offering yield. And the higher the bond's offering yield, the deeper the discount. When interest rates rose sharply in 1981 and 1982, there was a flood of zero coupon bond issues to exploit this tax loophole. (See Fisher, Brick, and Ng [24] and Yawitz and Maloney [55].) Zero coupon bonds were not a new financial instrument; it took an external shock (rising interest rates that greatly enhanced the potential tax benefits) to spur their use.

Zero coupon bonds also illustrate the interaction between Kane's regulatory dialectic and financial engineering [31, 32, 33]. Kane defines the regulatory dialectic as a cyclical process in which the opposing forces of regulation and regulatee avoidance adapt continually to one another. Finnerty [19] describes how U.S. corporations responded to TEFRA's closing of the domestic tax loophole by their

---

[1]Other noteworthy contributions to the literature on financial innovations have been made by Atchison, DeMong, and Kling [4]; Black and Scholes [8]; Darrow and Mestres [17]; and Friedman [25].

issuing zero coupon bonds to Japanese investors in order to exploit a Japanese tax loophole. The Japanese regulatory authorities first responded to this activity by imposing quantitative restrictions on Japanese purchases, and then by threatening to close the tax loophole.

Silber [46, 47, 48] views the process of financial innovation differently from Miller. He characterizes innovative financial instruments and processes as attempts by corporations to lessen the financial constraints they face. In his view, firms maximize utility subject to a number of constraints, some of which are imposed by government regulation, and the balance of which are imposed either by the marketplace or by the firm itself. Innovative activity responds to economic impulses that increase the cost of adhering to a particular constraint. The increased cost stimulates innovative activity to relax the constraint and thereby reduce the cost of adhering to it. For example, banks are capital-constrained. Considerable effort has gone into designing capital notes, which are debt instruments that qualify as "capital" for bank regulatory purposes. Issuing capital notes enables banks to increase the degree of leverage any particular amount of common equity would otherwise support. As a second example, increasingly volatile interest rates raised the cost of adhering to a policy of investing in fixed-dividend-rate preferred stock, which stimulated the innovative activity that led to the development of various forms of adjustable rate preferred stock.

Both Ben-Horim and Silber [5] and Silber [48] report that Silber's constraint-induced model of innovation explains a large percentage of new commercial bank products introduced during the 1952–1982 period. Nevertheless, Silber's model provides only a partial explanation of the process of financial innovation because it focuses almost exclusively on the securities issuer and leaves investors with an essentially passive role.

Van Horne takes a more critical view of the process of financial innovation than either Miller or Silber. In his 1984 presidential address to the American Finance Association, Van Horne [53] argues that in order for a new financial instrument or process to be truly innovative, it must enable the financial markets to operate more efficiently or make them more complete. If the financial markets were perfect and complete, there would be no opportunities for (nontrivial) financial innovation. Greater efficiency can be achieved by reducing transaction costs, which innovations such as the shelf registration process and electronic funds transfer have accomplished, or by reducing differential taxes and other "deadweight" losses. The financial markets can be made more complete by designing a new security whose contingent after-tax returns cannot be replicated by any combination of existing securities.

Van Horne also notes the excesses that have resulted from the innovative process, citing "innovations" whose only apparent benefit is some sort of desirable accounting treatment (for example, in-substance defeasance) and pointing out the apparently substantial fees that investment bankers and other promoters of financial innovations have reaped.[2] How the innovator shares in the rewards to innovation is an interesting empirical question that deserves careful study. In particular, how do the underwriting spreads on innovative securities vary as additional issuers enter the market? How is the net advantage of financial innovation allocated among the various parties to the transaction, and how does this allocation change as the innovative security becomes seasoned and as imitators

---

[2]Ricks [43] notes that the SEC is concerned that certain innovative financial products have been misrepresented to investors; for example, the index option has been marketed to retail investors as a conservative hedging product. Ricks raises an interesting issue—whether the evolution of financial instruments has outstripped the ability of brokers to understand what they are selling and of brokerage firms to provide adequate supervision.

enter the market? On this last point, Winger et al. [54] found that in the case of adjustable rate preferred stock, later issuers achieved more favorable terms than the initial issuers.

The Miller, Silber, and Van Horne papers suggest that the factors responsible for financial innovation can be classified into 11 categories: (*i*) tax asymmetries that can be exploited to produce tax savings for the issuer, investors, or both, that are not offset by the added tax liabilities of the other; (*ii*) transaction costs; (*iii*) agency costs; (*iv*) opportunities to reduce some form of risk or to reallocate risk from one market participant to another who is either less risk averse or else willing to bear the risk at a lower cost; (*v*) opportunities to increase an asset's liquidity; (*vi*) regulatory or legislative change; (*vii*) level and volatility of interest rates; (*viii*) level and volatility of prices; (*ix*) academic work that resulted in advances in financial theories or better understanding of the risk-return characteristics of existing classes of securities; (*x*) accounting benefits (which may, and often do, have at best an ephemeral effect on shareholder wealth); and (*xi*) technological advances and other factors. Exhibit 1 lists a broad variety of financial innovations and identifies the factors primarily responsible for each.

III. Consumer-Type Financial Instruments

Exhibit 1 lists 14 innovative consumer-type financial instruments introduced within the past 20 years. Broker cash management accounts, which permit individuals to earn money market rates of interest on funds not currently invested in securities; money market mutual funds and money market accounts offered by banks, which pay current market interest rates on invested cash balances; NOW accounts, which are interest bearing checking accounts; and debit cards, which enable bank depositors to shift money between accounts or withdraw cash from accounts at remote teller stations; all owe their existence at least partly to rising interest rates, which increased the opportunity cost of maintaining funds in non-interest-bearing checking or passbook accounts. In particular, money market mutual funds circumvented the outmoded Regulation Q interest rate ceilings. Money market accounts and NOW accounts resulted also from relaxed regulatory restrictions on the types of accounts banks could offer.

Municipal bond funds, IRA/Keogh accounts, and all-saver certificates were initiated by legislation. Municipal bond funds enable smaller individual investors to achieve a degree of portfolio diversification more cheaply than they could on their own. IRA/Keogh accounts conveyed special tax advantages to self-directed retirement accounts. All-saver certificates provided a tax incentive to depositing funds in thrifts, which faced funding problems at least partly brought on by high interest rates.

The equity access account was designed to enable individuals to borrow against the equity built up in their own homes. The Tax Reform Act of 1986 limited full interest deductions to mortgage interest, which stimulated the use of this vehicle. Bull and bear CDs pay a variable interest rate that is tied to changes in the Standard & Poor's 500 Index. They give individuals an indirect way of participating in the market for options on the S&P 500 Index. Tuition futures enable families to prepay the future cost of an undergraduate education, which transfers college cost inflation risk to the seller of the tuition futures contract.

The remaining three products are all by-products of the higher level and volatility of interest rates. Universal life insurance and variable life insurance provide a wider choice of investment options than traditional whole life insurance, while retaining the tax deferral of investment earnings that life insurance products provide. Universal life insurance policies build cash value at a stated

Exhibit 1   Factors Primarily Responsible for Financial Innovations

Innovation	Factors Primarily Responsible*	Innovation	Factors Primarily Responsible*
Consumer-Type Financial Instruments			
Broker cash management accounts	7	Money market mutual funds	6, 7
Municipal bond funds	2, 4, 6	Money market accounts	6, 7
All-saver certificates	6, 7	NOW accounts	6, 7
Equity access account	1, 6, 8	Bull/Bear CDs	2
Debit card	2, 7, 11	IRA/Keogh accounts	1, 6
Tuition futures	4, 8	Universal or variable life insurance	1, 7, 8
Variable or adjustable rate mortgages	7	Convertible mortgages or reduction option loans	2, 7
Securities			
Deep discount/zero coupon bonds	1, 4, 7	Stripped debt securities	1, 4, 7
Floating rate notes	4, 5, 7	Floating rate, rating sensitive notes	3, 4, 5, 7
Floating rate tax-exempt notes	4, 5, 7	Auction rate notes/debentures	2, 3, 4, 7
Real yield securities	2, 4, 5, 8	Dollar BILS	4, 7
Puttable-extendible notes	2, 3, 4	Increasing rate notes	3
Interest rate reset notes	3	Annuity notes	11
Extendible notes	2, 4	Variable coupon/rate renewable notes	2, 4, 6
Puttable/adjustable tender bonds	2, 4, 7	Variable duration notes	4, 7
Euronotes/Euro-commercial paper	2, 4	Universal commercial paper	4
Medium term notes	2	Negotiable CDs	2, 5
Mortgage-backed bonds	4	Mortgage pass-throughs	2, 4, 5
Collateralized mortgage obligations	2, 4, 5	Stripped mortgage-backed securities	4
Receivable-backed securities	4, 5	Real estate-backed bonds	4, 5
Letter of credit/surety bond credit support	4, 11	Yield curve/maximum rate notes	4, 6, 7
Interest rate swaps	4, 6, 7	Currency swaps	4, 6
Interest rate caps/floors/collars	4, 7	Remarketed reset notes	2, 3, 4
Foreign-currency-denominated bonds	4, 7	Eurocurrency bonds	7
Dual currency bonds	4, 6	Indexed currency option notes/principal exchange rate linked securities	4, 6, 7
Commodity-linked bonds	4, 6, 8	High-yield (junk) bonds	2, 5, 7, 9
Gold loans	4, 8	Foreign currency futures	4, 9, 11
Exchange-traded options	4, 9	Stock index futures	4, 8, 9
Interest rate futures	4, 7, 9	Forward rate agreements	4, 7
Options on futures contracts	4, 7, 9	Adjustable rate preferred stock	1, 4, 5, 6, 7
Warrants to purchase bonds	4, 7	Auction rate preferred stock	1, 4, 5, 7
Convertible adjustable preferred stock	1, 4, 5, 7	Indexed floating rate preferred stock	1, 4, 5, 7
Remarketed preferred stock	1, 4, 5, 7, 11	Stated rate auction preferred stock	1, 3, 4, 5, 7
Single point adjustable rate stock	1, 2, 4, 5, 7	Convertible exchangeable preferred	1, 2, 10
Variable cumulative preferred stock	1, 2, 3, 4, 5, 7	Zero coupon convertible debt	1, 11
Adjustable rate convertible debt	1, 10	Mandatory convertible/equity contract notes	1, 6
Puttable convertible bonds	3, 4, 7	Exchangeable auction preferred	1, 2, 4, 5, 7
Synthetic convertible debt	1, 10	Participating bonds	3, 4
Convertible reset debentures	3	Additional class(es) of common stock	11
Master limited partnership	1	Paired common stock	4
Americus trust	4, 6		
Puttable common stock	3, 4, 10		
Financial Processes			
Shelf registration	2, 6, 7	Direct public sale of securities	2, 6
Discount brokerage	2, 6	Automated teller machines	2, 11
Point-of-sale terminals	11	Electronic security trading	2, 11
Electronic funds transfer/automated clearing houses	7, 11	CHIPS (same day settlement)	7, 11
		Cash management/sweep accounts	7, 11
Financial Strategies/Solutions			
More efficient bond call strategies	7, 9	Debt-for-debt exchanges	1, 7, 10
Stock-for-debt swaps	1, 7, 10	In-substance defeasance	1, 7, 10
Preferred dividend rolls	1	Hedged divided capture	1
Leveraged buyout structuring	1, 9, 11	Corporate restructuring	1, 9, 11
Project finance/lease/asset-based financial structuring	4		

Note: 1, tax advantages; 2, reduced transaction costs; 3, reduced agency costs; 4, risk reallocation; 5, increased liquidity; 6, regulatory or legislative factors; 7, level and volatility of interest rates; 8, level and volatility of prices; 9, academic work; 10, accounting benefits; and 11, technological developments and other factors.

fixed rate, or according to a stated interest rate formula that the insurance company guarantees. Variable life insurance policies are really families of mutual funds wrapped within a life insurance contract. Current yield and redemption value are tied directly to the particular mutual fund around which the policy is wrapped. Variable rate and adjustable rate mortgages allow the mortgage interest rate to adjust over time, which facilitates thrift asset-liability management in a volatile interest rate environment. Convertible mortgages (also referred to as reduction option loans) give borrowers the option to fix the interest rate on a variable rate or adjustable rate mortgage on one or more specified mortgage rate reset dates, provided the "index" rate has fallen more than two percentage points since the mortgage's issue date. To exercise the option, the borrower pays a fee which is typically smaller than the cost of refunding the original mortgage.

IV. Securities Innovation

There has been a more or less steady flow of security innovations in recent years. The investment banks who develop the new securities herald each new product's introduction along with its advantages, and the financial press dutifully reports them [18, 37]. However, the process is not without its detractors [45, 53].

In addition to the factors discussed in Section II, a change in the industry environment helps account for the revolution in securities innovation. In recent years, the investment banking business has shifted away from what is known as "relationship banking" and become more competitive, hence more transactional. Developing an innovative security provides an opportunity for the financial engineer to solicit business from companies that have traditionally used other investment bankers. A successful innovator is usually awarded a mandate to sell the new security on a negotiated basis, rather than having to bid for securities "off the shelf" as is the case with conventional debt instruments. Investment banks therefore have a strong financial incentive to engineer innovative securities [26, 34].

A new security is truly "innovative" only if it (*i*) enables an investor to realize a higher after-tax risk-adjusted rate of return without adversely affecting the issuer's after-tax cost of funds, and/or (*ii*) enables an issuer to realize a lower after-tax cost of funds without adversely affecting investors than had been possible prior to the introduction of the new security. A new security can accomplish this only if it makes the markets more efficient or more complete. It is not enough for a new security just to be different; there must be some real value added to the issuing company's shareholders.

A. Sources of Value Added

The purpose of securities innovation is to develop positive net present value financing mechanisms [44]. Finnerty [22] develops an analytical framework that indicates three principal sources of value added through securities innovation: features that reallocate or reduce risk and in so doing reduce the required offering yield, characteristics that lead to lower issuance expenses during the period the financial obligation is intended to remain outstanding, and features that create a tax arbitrage for the issuer and investors (at the expense of the Internal Revenue Service). The resulting value added will be allocated among the company's shareholders, the purchasers of the innovative security, and the underwriters through the pricing of the innovative security and the setting of underwriting commissions.

If a company can repackage a security's payment stream so that it either involves less risk or reallocates risk from one class of investors to one that is less risk-sensitive and thus requires a smaller risk premium, and does so in a manner that investors cannot duplicate as cheaply by utilizing existing securities, then shareholder value will be enhanced. Collateralized mortgage obligations (CMOs) and stripped mortgage-backed securities are examples. If a company can issue a security against a diversified portfolio of assets, it can reduce the investor's risk and hence the required yield. If the issuer can accomplish this more cheaply than the investor can by himself, there is opportunity for gain. Some examples are mortgage pass-through securities and debt backed by a portfolio of automobile receivables. If a company can securitize a loan so that it becomes publicly tradable, the lender's liquidity risk is reduced, resulting in a lower required yield. Negotiable certificates of deposit and nonrecourse notes (i.e., mortages) secured by commercial real estate are examples. Both can be traded in the public securities markets, unlike conventional certificates of deposit and most commercial mortgages. If a company can design a security that reduces the agency costs that would normally arise in connection with a conventional financing—for example, costs due to informational asymmetries between the issuer and investors—a lower offering yield can result. Floating rate, rating sensitive notes, whose interest rate increases when the issuer's debt rating decreases, are an example.

Second, if a company can structure a securities issue so that underwriting commissions are reduced, shareholder value will be enhanced. Extendible notes are an example. Their maturity can be extended by mutual agreement between the insuer and investors, effectively rolling over the notes without additional underwriting commissions. Third, if a company can structure a new security so as to reduce investor taxes without increasing corporate income taxes, shareholder value will be enhanced as a result of this tax arbitrage. For example, a company that is not currently a taxpayer can create such an arbitrage by issuing auction rate preferred stock to fully taxable corporate investors in lieu of commercial paper [1, 54]. Fourth, if a company can structure a new security so as to increase the present value tax shields available to the issuer without increasing the investor's tax liabilities, shareholder value can again be enhanced through tax arbitrage. For example, the selling of zero coupon notes to tax-emempt investors before TEFRA resulted in such an arbitrage because the issuer could deduct the original issue discount on a straight-line basis. This tax treatment did not adversely affect tax-exempt investors. The balance of this section describes a number of innovative securities listed in Exhibit 1 in greater detail.

B. Debt Innovations

Most of the financial innovations in recent years have involved debt securities. Some, such as zero coupon bonds, were issued in large volume for a period of time but have become very rare, either because changes in tax law eliminated their advantages or because more recent innovations superseded them. Other debt innovations such as extendible notes, medium-term notes, and collateralized mortgage obligations have had a more lasting impact. Yet others, such as indexed currency option notes, variable duration notes, certain commodity-linked bonds, and annuity notes, have been introduced and disappeared quickly, in some cases after just a single issue. Exhibit 2 lists several of the more significant debt innovations and classifies each innovation's value-enhancing features.

Risk Reallocation/Yield Reduction. Most of the debt innovations in Exhibit 2 involve some form of risk reallocation as compared to conventional debt instruments or some other form of yield reduction mechanism. Involving the reapportioning of interest rate risk, credit risk, or some other

Exhibit 2 Selected Debt Innovations

Security	Distinguishing Characteristics	Risk Reallocation/ Yield Reduction	Enhanced Liquidity	Reduction in Agency Costs	Reduction in Transaction Costs	Tax Arbitrage	Other Benefits
Adjustable rate notes and floating rate	Coupon rate floats with some index, such as the 91-day Treasury bill rate	Issuer exposed to floating interest rate risk, but initial rate is lower than for fixed-rate issue.	Price remains closer to par than the price of a fixed-rate note of the same maturity.				
Auction rate notes and debentures	Interest rate reset by Dutch auction at the end of each interest period.	Coupon based on length of interest period, not on final maturity.	Designed to trade closer to par value than a floating rate note with a fixed interest rate formula.	Interest rate each period is determined in the marketplace, rather than by the issuer or the issuer's investment banker.	Intended to have lower transaction costs than repeatedly rolling over shorter maturity securities.		
Bonds linked to commodity price or index	Interest and/or principal linked to a specified commodity price or index.	Issuer assumes commodity price or index risk in return for lower (minimum) coupon. Can serve as a hedge if the issuer produces the particular commodity.					Attractive to investors who would like to speculate in commodity options but cannot, for regulatory or other reasons, purchase commodity options directly.
Collateralized Mortgage Obligations (CMOs) and Real Estate Mortgage Investment Conduits (REMICs)	Mortgage payment stream is divided into several classes which are prioritized in terms of their right to receive principal payments.	Reduction in prepayment risk to classes with prepayment priority. Designed to appeal to different classes of investors; sum of the parts can exceed the whole.	More liquid than individual mortgages.		Most investors could not achieve the same degree of prepayment risk reduction as cheaply on their own.		
Commercial real estate-backed bonds	Nonrecourse bonds serviced and backed by a specified piece (or portfolio) of real estate.	Reduced yield due to greater liquidity.	More liquid than individual mortgages.				Appeals to investors who like to lend against real estate properties.
Credit-enhanced debt securities	Issuer's obligation to pay is backed by an irrevocable letter of credit or a surety bond.	Stronger credit rating of the letter of credit or surety bond issuer leads to lower yield, which can more than offset letter of credit/surety bond fees.					Enables a privately held company to borrow publicly while preserving confidentiality of financial information.

Exhibit 2 (*continued*)

Security	Distinguishing Characteristics	Risk Reallocation/ Yield Reduction	Enhanced Liquidity	Reduction in Agency Costs	Reduction in Transaction Costs	Tax Arbitrage	Other Benefits
Dollar BILS	Floating rate zero coupon note the effective interest rate on which is determined retrospectively based on the change in the value of a specified index that measures the total return on long-term, high-grade corporate bonds.	Issuer assumes reinvestment risk.					Useful for hedging and immunization purposes because Dollar BILSs have a zero duration when duration is measured with respect to the specified index.
Dual currency bonds	Interest payable in U.S. dollars but principal payable in a currency other than U.S. dollars.	Issuer has foreign currency risk with respect to principal repayment obligation. Currency swap can hedge this risk and lead, in some cases, to yield reduction.					Euroyen-dollar dual currency bonds popular with Japanese investors who are subject to regulatory restrictions and desire income in dollars without principal risk.
Euronotes and Euro-commercial paper	Euro-commercial paper is similar to U.S. commercial paper.	Elimination of intermediary brings savings that lender and borrower can share.			Corporations invest in each other's paper directly rather than through an intermediary.		
Extendible notes	Interest rate adjusts every 2–3 years to a new interest rate the issuer establishes, at which time note holder has the option to put the notes back to the issuer if the new rate is unacceptable.	Coupon based on 2–3 year put date, not on final maturity.		Investor has put option, which provides protection against deterioration in credit quality or below-market coupon rate.	Lower transaction costs than issuing 2- or 3-year notes and rolling them over.		
Floating rate, rating sensitive notes	Coupon rate resets quarterly based on a spread over LIBOR. Spread increases if the issuer's debt rating declines.	Issuer exposed to floating interest rate risk, but initial rate is lower than for fixed-rate issue.	Price remains closer to par than the price of a fixed-rate note of the same maturity.	Investor protected against deterioration in the issuer's credit quality because of increase in coupon rate when rating declines.			
Floating rate tax-exempt revenue bonds	Coupon rate floats with some index, such as the 60-day high-grade commercial paper rate.	Issuer exposed to floating interest rate risk, but initial rate is lower than for fixed-rate issue. Effectively, tax-exempt commercial paper.				Investor does not have to pay income tax on the interest payments but issuer gets to deduct them.	

Exhibit 2 (*continued*)

Security	Distinguishing Characteristics	Risk Reallocation/ Yield Reduction	Enhanced Liquidity	Reduction in Agency Costs	Reduction in Transaction Costs	Tax Arbitrage	Other Benefits
Increasing rate notes	Coupon rate increases by specified amounts at specified intervals.	Defers portion of interest expense to later years, which increases duration.		When such notes are issued in connection with a bridge financing, the step-up in coupon rate compensates investors for the issuer's failure to redeem the notes on schedule.			
Indexed currency option notes/Principal exchange rate linked securities	Issuer pays reduced principal at maturity if specified foreign currency appreciates sufficiently relative to the U.S. dollar.	Investor assumes foreign currency risk by effectively selling the issuer a call option denominated in the foreign currency.					Attractive to investors who would like to speculate in foreign currencies but cannot, for regulatory or other reasons, purchase or sell currency options directly.
Interest rate caps, floors, and collars	Investor who writes an interest rate cap (floor/collar) contract agrees to make payments to the contract purchaser when a specified interest rate exceed the specified cap (falls below the floor/falls outside the collar range).	Seller assumes the risk that interest rates may rise above the cap (fall below the floor/fall outside the collar range.)					
Interest rate reset notes	Interest rate is reset 3 years after issuance to the greater of (*i*) the initial rate and (*ii*) a rate sufficient to give the notes a market value equal to .01 percent of their face amount.	Reduced (initial) yield due to the reduction in agency costs.		Investor is compensated for a deterioration in the issuer's credit standing within 3 years of issuance.			
Interest rate swaps.	Two entities agree to swap interest rate payment obligations, typically fixed rate for floating rate.	Effective vehicle for transferring interest rate risk from one party to another. Also, parties to a swap can realize a net benefit if they enjoy comparative advantages in different international credit markets.					Interest rate swaps are often designed to take advantage of special opportunities in particular markets outside the issuer's traditional market or to circumvent regulatory restrictions.
Medium-term notes	Notes are sold in varying amounts and in varying	Issuer bears market price during the marketing			Agent's commissions are lower than underwriting		

Exhibit 2 (*continued*)

Security	Distinguishing Characteristics	Risk Reallocation/ Yield Reduction	Enhanced Liquidity	Reduction in Agency Costs	Reduction in Transaction Costs	Tax Arbitrage	Other Benefits
	maturities on an agency basis.	process.			spreads.		
Mortgage pass-through certificates	Investor buys an undivided interest in a pool of mortgages.	Reduced yield due to the benefit to the investor of diversification and greater liquidity.	More liquid than individual mortgages.		Most investors could not achieve the same degree of diversification as cheaply on their own.		
Negotiable certificates of deposit	Certificates of deposit are registered and sold to the public on an agency basis.	Issuer bears market price risk during the marketing process.	More liquid than nonnegotiable CDs.		Agents' commissions are lower than underwriting spreads.		
Puttable bonds and adjustable tender securities	Issuer can periodically reset the terms, in effect rolling over debt without having to redeem it until the final maturity.	Coupon based on whether fixed or floating rate and on the length of the interest rate period selected, not on final maturity.		Investor has a put option which provides protection against deterioration in credit quality or below-market coupon rate.	Lower transaction costs than having to perform a series of refundings.		
Puttable-extendible notes	At the end of each interest period, the issuer may elect to redeem the notes at par or to extend the maturity on terms the issuer proposes, at which time the note holder can put the notes back to the issuer if the new terms are unacceptable. Investors also have series of put options during initial interest period.	Coupon based on length of interest interval, not on final maturity.		Put options protect against deterioration in issuer's credit standing and also against issuer setting below-market coupon rate or other terms that might work to investor's disadvantage.			
Real yield securities	Coupon rate resets quarterly to the greater of (*i*) change in consumer price index plus the "Real Yield Spread" (3.0 percent in the first such issue) and (*ii*) the Real Yield Spread, in each case on a semi-annual-equivalent basis.	Issuer exposed to inflation risk, which may be hedged in the CPI futures market.	Real yield securities could become more liquid than CPI futures, which tend to trade in significant volume only around the monthly CPI announcement date.		Investors obtain a long-dated inflation hedging instrument that they could not create as cheaply on their own.		Real yield securities have a longer duration than alternative inflation hedging instruments.

Exhibit 2 (*continued*)

Security	Distinguishing Characteristics	Risk Reallocation/ Yield Reduction	Enhanced Liquidity	Reduction in Agency Costs	Reduction in Transaction Costs	Tax Arbitrage	Other Benefits
Receivable pay-through securities	Investor buys an undivided interest in a pool of receivables	Reduced yield due to the benefit of the investor of diversification and greater liquidity. Significantly cheaper for issuer than pledging receivables to a bank.	More liquid than individual receivables.		Security purchasers could not achieve the same degree of diversification as cheaply on their own.		
Remarketed reset notes	Interest rate reset at the end of each interest period to a rate the remarketing agent determines will make the notes worth par. If issuer and remarketing agent can not agree on rate, then the coupon rate is determined by formula which dictates a higher rate the lower the issuer's credit standing.	Coupon based on length of interest period, not on final maturity.	Designed to trade closer to par value than a floating-rate note with a fixed interest rate formula.	Investors have a put option, which protects against the issuer and remarketing agent agreeing to set a below-market coupon rate, and the flexible interest rate formula protects investors against deterioration in the issuer's credit standing.	Intended to have lower transaction costs than auction rate notes and debentures, which require periodic Dutch auctions.		
Stripped mortgage-backed securities	Mortgage payment stream subdivided into two classes: (*i*) one with below-market coupon and the other with above-market coupon or (*ii*) one receiving interest only and the other receiving principal only from mortgage pools.	Securities have unique option characteristics that make them useful for hedging purposes. Designed to appeal to different classes of investors; sum of the parts can exceed the whole.					
Stripped treasury or municipal securities	Coupons separated from corpus to create a series of zero coupon bonds that can be sold separately.	Yield curve arbitrage; sum of the parts can exceed the whole.					

Exhibit 2 (*continued*)

Security	Distinguishing Characteristics	Risk Reallocation/ Yield Reduction	Enhanced Liquidity	Reduction in Agency Costs	Reduction in Transaction Costs	Tax Arbitrage	Other Benefits
Variable coupon renewable notes	Coupon rate varies weekly and equals a fixed spread over the 91-day T-bill rate. Each 91 days the maturity extends another 91 days. If put option exercised, spread is reduced.	Coupon based on 1-year termination date, not on final maturity.			Lower transaction costs than issuing 1-year note and rolling it over.		Designed to appeal to money market mutual funds, which face tight investment restrictions, and to discourage put to issuer.
Variable rate renewable notes	Coupon rate varies monthly and equals a fixed spread over the 1-month commercial paper rate. Each quarter the maturity automatically extends an additional quarter unless the investor elects to terminate the extension.	Coupon based on 1-year termination date, not on final maturity.			Lower transaction costs than issuing 1-year note and rolling it over.		Designed to appeal to money market mutual funds, which face tight investment restrictions.
Warrants to purchase debt securities	Warrant with 1–5 years to expiration to buy intermediate-term or long-term bonds.	Issuer is effectively selling a covered call option, which can afford investors opportunities not available in the traditional options markets.					
Yield curve notes and maximum rate notes	Interest rate equals a specified rate minus LIBOR.	Might reduce yield relative to conventional debt when coupled with an interest rate swap against LIBOR.					
Zero coupon bonds (sometimes issued in series)	Non-interest-bearing. Payment in one lump sum at maturity.	Issuer assumes reinvestment risk. Issues sold in Japan carried below-taxable-market yields reflecting their tax advantage over conventional debt issues.				Straight-line amortization of original issue discount pre-TEFRA. Japanese investors realize significant tax savings.	Useful for hedging and immunization purposes because of very long duration.

form of risk, risk reallocation is beneficial when it transfers risk from those who are less willing to bear it to those who are more willing to bear it, in the sense that they require a smaller yield premium to compensate them for bearing the risk. A yield reduction (or equivalently, an increase in the net proceeds that can be realized from the sale of a given debt service stream) results when repackaging a particular debt service stream and selling the component parts yields greater proceeds than selling the original debt service stream intact.

Serial zero coupon bonds, stripped U.S. Treasury securities, and stripped municipal securities illustrate that the sum of the parts can exceed the whole when a particular debt service stream is subdivided and its constituent parts are sold separately. For example, stripping a bearer U.S. Treasury bond creates a serial zero coupon issue. Each zero coupon bond in the series can be sold to the highest bidder. Because the U.S. Treasury did not issue zero coupon bonds, securities firms created them by stripping bearer Treasury securities and earned an arbitrage profit for their effort. As one would expect, the substantial arbitrage profits earned by the securities firms initially involved in stripping were eliminated over time as competitors entered the market.

Mortgage pass-through certificates and receivable-backed securities can be sold in the marketplace at a lower yield than the assets that back them because they provide investors a degree of diversification that many (smaller) investors could not achieve as cheaply on their own. In addition, the issuer often retains a subordinated interest in the collateral pool so that much of the apparent yield reduction results from the investors' senior position with respect to mortgage or receivable pool cash flows. Collateralized mortgage obligations (CMOs) and stripped mortgage-backed securities illustrate the benefits that can result from repackaging mortgage payement streams [50]. Most mortgages are prepayable at par at the option of the mortgagor after some brief period. This creates significant prepayment risk for lenders. CMOs package the mortgage payement stream from a portfolio of mortgages into several series of debt instruments—sometimes more than a dozen—which are prioritized in terms of their right to receive principal payments. In the simplest form of CMO, each series must be repaid in full before any principal payments can be made to the holders of the next series in order to reduce prepayment uncertainty. Thus, CMOs may serve to make the capital market more complete by producing specific payoff streams that were previously unavailable. This occurs especially by achieving a specific allocation of prepayment risk across the different tranches. Stripped mortgage-backed securities divide the mortgage payment stream into two separate streams of claims, in the extreme case, one involving interest payments exclusively and the other involving principal repayments exclusively. The introduction of these securities also enhanced market completeness because of their duration and convexity characteristics. The apparent failure to understand fully the riskiness of these securities led to a substantial and highly publicized financial loss by a major brokerage house [51].

Adjustable rate notes and floating rate notes expose the issuer to floating interest rate risk but reduce the investor's principal risk. This interest rate risk reallocation can be of mutual benefit to issuers whose assets are interest-rate sensitive, such as banks, credit companies, and certain types of investors. Dollar BILS are a special type of floating rate note, one that has zero duration when duration is measured with respect to the specified index to which the floating rate is tied.

A recently introduced mechanism for transferring interest rate risk goes by two different names because it has two different sponsoring securities firms. Yield curve notes and maximum rate notes, collectively "inverse floaters," carry an interest rate that increases (decreases) as interest rates fall (rise) [28, 39, 49]. Typically, the incentive in issuing an inverse floater is to fix the coupon by entering into an interest rate swap agreement. The two transactions together benefit the issuer when they result in a lower cost of funds than a conventional fixed-rate issue. Investors find inverse floaters useful for immunization purposes because of their very long duration, which may exceed the maturity of the security [28, 39, 49].

Three other classes of debt innovations in Exhibit 2 also involve some form of risk reallocation. Credit-enhanced debt securities involve credit risk reallocation through bank letters of credit or insurance company surety bonds. When the letter of credit or surety bond fee is less than the resulting reduction in the yield required to sell the securities, the credit risk reallocation is beneficial to the issuer. Dual currency bonds, indexed currency option notes, and principal exchange rate linked securities illustrate two forms of currency risk reallocation. Bonds that make interest and/or principal payments that are linked to a specified index or commodity, such as the price of oil or the price of silver, are attractive to institutions that are not permitted to invest directly in commodity options and can serve as a hedge for an issuer who is a producer of the commodity.

Reduced Agency Costs.   Five of the debt innovations in Exhibit 2 are designed at least partly to reduce agency costs. Increasing rate notes, when used in connection with a bridge financing, provide an incentive for the issuer to redeem the notes (out of the proceeds of a permanent financing) on schedule. Interest rate reset notes protect against deterioration in the issuer's credit standing prior to the reset date. Puttable-extendible notes provide a series of put options which protect against deterioration in the issuer's credit standing. The protection that such an option affords investors is not readily available in the options markets because there currently does not exist a well-organized market for long-term corporate bond options. Remarketed reset notes include a put option, which protects against the issuer and remarketing agent conspiring to set a below market coupon rate, and a flexible interest rate formula (in the event the issuer and the remarketing agent cannot agree on a rate), which provides for a higher interest rate the lower the issuer's credit standing. Similarly, floating rate, rating sensitive notes bear a coupon rate that varies inversely with the issuer's credit standing.

Reduced Issuance Expenses.   Extendible notes, variable coupon renewable notes, puttable bonds, adjustable tender securities, remarketed reset notes, and euronotes and euro-commercial paper are all designed to reduce issuance expenses and other forms of transaction costs. Extendible notes typically provide for an interest rate adjustment every 2 or 3 years, although other adjustment intervals are possible, and thus represent an alternative to rolling over 2- or 3-year note issues without incurring additional issuance expenses.

Variable coupon renewable notes represent a refinement of the extendible note concept. The maturity of the notes automatically extends 91 days at the end of each quarter—unless the holder elects to terminate the automatic extension, in which case the interest rate spread decreases. A holder wishing to terminate the investment would avoid the reduction in spread by selling the notes in the marketplace. Goodman and Yawitz [28] explain how these features were designed to meet regulatory investment restrictions that money market mutual funds face.[3] In another refinement of the extendible note concept, puttable bonds, adjustable tender securities, and remarketed reset notes give the issuer the flexibility to

---

[3]Variable coupon renewable notes have a nominal maturity of one year, which is the maximum maturity permitted money market mutual fund investments. Also, because of the weekly rate reset, variable coupon renewable notes count as 7-day assets in meeting the 120-day upper limit on a money market mutual fund's dollar-weighted average portfolio maturity.

reset the terms of the security periodically. These securities offer the issuer greater flexibility than extendible notes in the choice of terms on which to extend the maturity of the debt issue.

Euronotes and euro-commercial paper represent the extension of commercial paper to the Euromarket [42]. Transaction cost savings result because corporations invest directly in one another's securities, rather than through banks and other intermediaries, as was the case previously.

Tax Arbitrage.   Zero coupon bonds, as previously noted, provided a form of tax arbitrage prior to the passage of TEFRA. In addition, the investor bears no reinvestment risk, because interest is compounded over the life of the debt issue at the yield at which the investor purchased the bond.

C. Options, Futures, and Other Interest Rate Risk Management Vehicles

Options, futures, and other interest rate risk management vehicles enable market participants who are averse to certain risks (such as foreign currency risk, interest rate risk, or stock market risk) to transfer that risk to others who are less risk averse, on certain specified terms in exchange for a fee. Miller [38] cites financial futures as the most significant financial innovation of the past 20 years. Block and Gallagher [9] and Booth, Smith, and Stolz [10] catalog the many uses to which interest rate futures may be put for risk management purposes.

Warrants to purchase debt securities, an innovative form of debt option, have been more popular in the Euromarket than in the domestic market. They typically take the form of an option to buy an intermediate-term or long-term bond, and generally have a term of expiration between 1 and 5 years. The warrant issuer is effectively writing a covered call option on the issuer's own debt. Issuing the warrant represents a form of hedging by the debt issuer, and it affords investors opportunities not available in the traditional options markets.

Interest rate risk management vehicles include interest rate futures, options on interest rate futures, forward rate agreements, interest rate swaps, interest rate caps, interest rate floors, and interest rate collars [3, 6, 13]. The interest rate swap market has exploded within the past five years, and swap activity currently exceeds $400 billion per year. Bicksler and Chen [6] describe the market imperfections that can create comparative advantages among different borrowers in the fixed rate debt and floating-rate debt markets and across national boundaries, and thereby provide economic incentives to engage in interest rate swaps. Arak et al. [3] provide an alternative rationale for swaps. They state that swaps enable borrowers to fix the risk-free rate so that borrowers who believe their credit standing is about to improve have an incentive to borrow short-term funds and swap into fixed payments. Brown and Smith [13] describe the innovative nature of interest rate caps, floors, and collars, all of which impose limits on an entity's exposure to floating-interest-rate risk.

Miller [38] questions whether diminishing returns to financial innovation have already set in. Much of the innovative activity in recent years has involved the development of new futures products. Reports in the financial press have stated that 80 percent to 90 percent of new futures products fail and argued that the financial futures industry has already developed perhaps as much as 90 percent of the potentially useful futures products [41]. Miller notes that the Chicago Board of Trade and the Chicago Mercantile Exchange spent a combined total of $5 to $6 million developing two distinct futures contracts for over-the-counter stocks, both of which failed in the marketplace. The economics of futures innovation is one area of investigation that might yield at least a partial answer to Miller's question.

D. Preferred Stock Innovations

Preferred stock offers a tax advantage over debt to corporate investors, who are permitted to deduct from their taxable income 70 percent of the dividends they receive from unaffiliated corporations. Corporate money managers have a tax incentive to purchase preferred stock rather than commercial paper or other short-term debt instruments with fully taxable interest. However, the purchasing of long-term fixed-dividend-rate preferred stock exposes the purchaser to the risk that rising interest rates could lead to a fall in the price of the preferred stock that would more than offset the tax saving. Exhibit 3 lists a variety of new securities designed to deal with this problem.

Adjustable rate preferred stock was designed to lessen the investor's principal risk by having the dividend rate adjust as interest rates change. The dividend rate adjusts based on a formula. At times the spread investors have required to value the securities at par has differed significantly from the fixed spread specified in the formula, causing the value of the security to deviate significantly from its face amount. Winger et al. [54] document the high volatility of adjustable rate preferred stock holding-period returns relative to those of alternative money market investments.

Convertible adjustable preferred stock (CAPS) was designed to eliminate this deficiency. CAPS have traded closer to their respective face amounts than adjustable rate preferred stocks. However, there have only been a few CAPS issues, probably because prospective issuers have objected possibly to having to issue common stock or raise a large amount of cash on short notice.

Auction rate preferred stock carried the evolutionary process a step further. The dividend rate is reset by Dutch auction every 49 days, which represents just enough weeks to meet the 46-day holding period required to qualify for the 70 percent dividends received deduction. (One variation of this security, stated rate auction preferred stock, fixes the dividend rate for several years before the regular Dutch auctions commence.) Alderson, Brown, and Lummer [1] document the tax arbitrage that auction rate preferred stock affords under current tax law. There are various versions of auction rate preferred stock that are sold under different acronyms (MMP, Money Market Preferred; AMPS, Auction Market Preferred Stock; DARTS, Dutch Auction Rate Transferable Securities; STAR, Short-Term Auction Rate; etc.) coined by the different securities firms that offer the product. The names may differ, but the securities are the same.

In an effort to refine the adjustable rate preferred stock concept further, there have been at least two attempts to design a superior security, but only one was successful. Single point adjustable rate stock (SPARS) has a dividend rate that adjusts automatically every 49 days to a specified percentage of the 60-day high-grade commercial paper rate. The security is designed so as to afford the same degree of liquidity as auction rate preferred stock, but with lower transaction costs since no auction need be held. However, the fixed dividend rate formula involves a potential agency cost that auction rate preferred stock does not. Investors will suffer a loss if the issuer's managers take actions that cause the issuer's credit standing to deteriorate, because the dividend formula is fixed. Primarily for this reason, there have been at most only a few SPARS issues.

Remarketed preferred stock has a dividend rate that is reset at the end of each dividend period to a dividend rate that a specified remarketing agent determines will make the preferred stock worth par. Such issues permit the issuer considerable flexibility in selecting the length of the dividend period, which may be of any length, even 1 day. Remarketed preferred also offers greater flexibility in selecting the other terms of the issue; in fact, each share of an issue could have different maturity, dividend rate, or other terms, provided the issuer and holders so agree. Remarketed preferred has

Exhibit 3   Selected Preferred Stock Innovations

Security	Distinguishing Characteristics	Risk Reallocation/ Yield Reduction	Enhanced Liquidity	Reduction in Agency Costs	Reduction in Transaction Costs	Tax Arbitrage	Other Benefits
Adjustable rate preferred stock	Quarterly dividend rate reset each quarter based on maximum 3-month T-bill, 10-year Treasury, and 20-year Treasury rates plus or minus a specified spread.	Issuer bears more interest rate risk than a fixed-rate preferred would involve. Lower yield than commercial paper.	Security is designed to trade near its par value.			Designed to enable short-term corporate investors to take advantage of 70 percent dividends received deduction.	
Auction rate preferred stock (MMP/DARTS/ AMPS/STAR)	Dividend rate reset by Dutch auction every 49 days (subject to a maximum rate of 110 percent, or under certain circumstances 125 percent, of the 60-day "AA" Composite Commercial Paper Rate). Dividend is paid at the end of each dividend period.	Issuer bears more interest rate risk than a fixed-rate preferred would involve. Lower yield than commercial paper.	Security is designed to provide greater liquidity than convertible adjustable preferred stock.	Dividend rate each period is determined in the marketplace, which provides protection against deterioration in issuer's credit standing (protection is limited by the dividend rate cap).		Designed to enable short-term corporate investors to take advantage of 70 percent dividends received deduction.	
Convertible adjustable preferred stock	Issue convertible on dividend payment dates into variable number of the issuer's common shares, subject to a cap, equal in market value to the par value of the preferred.	Issuer bears more interest rate risk than a fixed-rate preferred would involve. Lower yield than commercial paper.	Security is designed to provide greater liquidity than adjustable rate preferred stock (due to the conversion feature).			Designed to enable short-term corporate investors to take advantage of 70 percent dividends received deduction.	
Remarketed preferred stock (SABRES)	Perpetual preferred stock with a dividend rate that resets at the end of each dividend period to a rate the remarketing agent determines will make the preferred stock worth par (subject to a maximum rate of 110 percent, or under certain circumstances 125 percent, of the 60-day "AA" Composite Commercial Paper Rate). Dividend periods may be of any length, even 1 day. Different shares of a single issue may have different periods and different dividend rates.	Issuer bears more interest rate risk than a fixed-rate preferred would involve. Lower yield than commercial paper.	Security is designed to trade near its par value.			Designed to enable short-term corporate investors to take advantage of 70 percent dividends received deduction.	Remarketed preferred stock offers greater flexibility in setting the terms of the issue than auction rate preferred stock, which requires a Dutch auction for potentially the entire issue once every 49 days.

Exhibit 3 *(continued)*

Security	Distinguishing Characteristics	Risk Reallocation/ Yield Reduction	Enhanced Liquidity	Reduction in Agency Costs	Reduction in Transaction Costs	Tax Arbitrage	Other Benefits
Single point adjustable rate stock	Dividend rate reset every 49 days as specified percentage of the high-grade commercial paper rate.	Issuer bears more interest rate risk than a fixed-rate preferred would involve. Lower yield than commercial paper.	Security is designed to trade near its par value.		Security is designed to save on recurring transaction costs associated with auction rate preferred stock.	Designed to enable short-term corporate investors to take advantage of 70 percent dividends received deduction.	
Stated rate auction preferred stock	Initial dividend period of several years during which the dividend rate is fixed. Thereafter the issuer can elect to have the dividend rate reset every 49 days by Dutch auction.	Issuer bears more interest rate risk than a fixed-rate preferred would involve.	Security is designed to trade near its par value after initial dividend period has elapsed and the Dutch auctions determine the dividend rate.	The maximum permitted dividend rate, expressed as a percentage of the 60-day "AA" Composite Commercial Paper Rate, increases according to a specified schedule if the preferred stock's credit rating falls.		Designed so as eventually to enable short-term corporate investors to take advantage of 70 percent dividends received deduction.	
Variable cumulative preferred stock	At the end of any dividend period the issuer can select between the auction method and the remarketing method to have the dividend rate reset.	Issuer bears more interest rate risk than a fixed-rate preferred would involve. Lower yield than commercial paper.	Security is designed to trade near its par value.	The maximum permitted dividend rate, expressed as a percentage of the 60-day "AA" Composite Commercial Paper Rate, increases according to a specified schedule if the preferred stock's credit rating falls.	Security is designed to save on transaction costs the issuer would otherwise incur if it wanted to change from auction reset to remarketing reset or vice versa.	Designed to enable short-term corporate investors to take advantage of 70 percent dividends received deduction.	Security is designed to enable the issuer to select at the end of each dividend period the method of rate reset it prefers.

not proven as popular with issuers as auction rate preferred stock, but that could change due to the greater flexibility remarketed preferred affords.

As a result of the controversy over whether auction rate preferred stock or remarketed preferred stock results in more equitable pricing, variable cumulative preferred stock was invented in order to let the issuer decide at the end of each dividend period which of the two reset methods will determine the dividend rate for the following dividend period.

E. Convertible Debt/Preferred Stock Innovations

Convertible debt innovations share a dominant theme: the creation of additional tax deductions (while preserving the amelioration of moral hazard, which conventional convertible bonds achieve). The creation of additional tax deductions involves a form of tax arbitrage because 80–90 percent of convertible bond investors are tax exempt [21]. Exhibit 4 describes seven recent innovations involving convertible securities.

Convertible exchangeable preferred stock consists of convertible perpetual preferred stock that the issuer is permitted to exchange for an issue of convertible subordinated debt, having the same conversion terms and an interest rate that equals the dividend rate on the convertible preferred. The exchange feature enables the issuer to reissue the convertible preferred as convertible debt should it become taxable in the future, but without having to pay additional underwriting commissions. A large volume of such securities has been issued by companies that were not currently taxpayers for federal income tax purposes. Similarly, exchangeable auction preferred stock permits the issuer to exchange auction rate notes for auction rate preferred stock on any dividend payment date.

Adjustable rate convertible debt is a security with a purported tax advantage. The security represented an attempt to package equity as debt. The Internal Revenue Service has ruled that the security is equity for tax purposes, thereby denying the interest deductions and rendering the security unattractive. Zero coupon convertible debt reflects a similar theme [36]. If the issue is converted, both interest and principal are converted to common equity, in which case the issuer will have effectively sold common equity with a tax deductibility feature.

Debt with mandatory common stock purchase contracts represents debt that qualifies as primary capital for bank regulatory purposes because conversion is mandatory. In the meantime, the issuer gets a stream of interest tax deductions that simply selling common stock would not afford. Finnerty [21] and Jones and Mason [30] describe how to package a unit consisting of debt and warrants into synthetic convertible debt, the features of which mirror the features of conventional convertible debt. Synthetic convertible bonds enjoy a tax advantage relative to a comparable convertible debt issue because, in effect, the warrant proceeds are deductible for tax purposes over the life of the debt issue. Lastly, convertible reset debentures protect holders against deterioration in the issuer's financial prospects within two years of issuance through an interest rate reset mechanism.

Common Equity Innovations

There are four principal common equity innovations: additional class(es) of common stock whose dividends are tied to the earnings of a specified subsidiary of the issuer, the Americus Trust, the master limited partnership, and puttable common stock. Exhibit 5 indicates the principal benefits resulting from these innovations.

Exhibit 4   Selected Convertible Debt/Preferred Stock Innovations

Security	Distinguishing Characteristics	Risk Reallocation/ Yield Reduction	Enhanced Liquidity	Reduction in Agency Costs	Reduction in Transaction Costs	Tax Arbitrage	Other Benefits
Adjustable rate convertible debt	Debt, the interest rate on which varies directly with the dividend rate on the underlying common stock. No conversion premium.					Effectively, tax deductible common equity. Security has since been ruled equity by the IRS.	Portion of the issue carried as equity on the issuer's balance sheet.
Convertible exchangeable preferred stock	Convertible preferred stock that is exchangeable, at the issuer's option, for convertible debt with identical rate and identical conversion terms.				No need to reissue convertible security as debt—just exchange it—when the issuer becomes a taxpayer.	Issuer can exchange debt for the preferred when it becomes taxable with interest rate the same as the dividend rate and without any change in conversion features.	Appears as equity on the issuer's balance sheet until it is exchanged for convertible debt.
Convertible reset debentures	Convertible bond, the interest rate on which must be adjusted upward, if necessary, by an amount sufficient to give the debentures a market value equal to their face amount 2 years after issuance.			Investor is protected against a deterioration in the issuer's financial prospects within 2 years of issuance.			
Debt with mandatory common stock purchase contracts	Notes with contracts that obligate note purchasers to buy sufficient common stock from the issuer to retire the issue in full by its scheduled maturity date.					Notes provide a stream of interest tax shields, which (true) equity does not.	Commercial bank holding companies have issued it because it counted as "primary capital" for regulatory purposes.
Exchangeable auction preferred stock	Auction rate preferred stock that is exchangeable on any dividend payment date, at the option of the issuer, for auction rate notes, the interest rate on which is reset by Dutch auction every 35 days.	Issuer bears more interest rate risk than a fixed-rate instrument would involve.	Security is designed to trade near its par value.		Issuance of auction rate notes involves no underwriting commissions.	Issuer can exchange notes for the preferred when it becomes taxable.	Appears as equity on the issuer's balance sheet until it is exchanged for auction rate notes.
Synthetic convertible debt	Debt and warrants package structured in such a way as to mirror a traditional convertible debt issue.					In effect, warrant proceeds are tax deductible.	Warrants go on the balance sheet as equity.
Zero coupon convertible debt	Non-interest-bearing convertible debt issue.					If issue converts, the issuer will have sold, in effect, tax deductible equity.	If holders convert, entire debt service stream is converted to common equity.

Exhibit 5 Selected Common Equity Innovations

Security	Distinguishing Characteristics	Risk Reallocation/ Yield Reduction	Enhanced Liquidity	Reduction in Agency Costs	Reduction in Transaction Costs	Tax Arbitrage	Other Benefits
Additional class(es) of common stock	A company issues a second class of common stock, the dividends on which are tied to the earnings of a specified subsidiary.						Establishes separate market value for the subsidiary while assuring the parent 100 percent voting control. Useful for employee compensation programs for subsidiary.
Americus trust	Outstanding shares of a particular company's common stock are contributed to a five-year unit investment trust. Units may be separated into a PRIME component, which embodies full dividend and voting rights in the underlying share and permits limited capital appreciation, and a SCORE component, which provides full capital appreciation above a stated price.	Stream of annual total returns on a share of stock is separated into (i) a dividend stream (with limited capital appreciation potential) and (ii) a (residual) capital appreciation stream.				PRIME component would appeal to corporate investors who can take advantage of the 70 percent dividends received deduction. SCORE component would appeal to capital-gain-oriented individual investors.	PRIME component resembles participating preferred stock if the issuer's common stock dividend rate is stable. SCORE component is a longer-dated call option than the ones customarily traded in the options market.
Master limited partnership	A business is given the legal form of a partnership but is otherwise structured, and is traded publicly, like a corporation.					Eliminates a layer of taxation because partnerships are not taxable entities.	
Puttable common stock	Issuer sells a new issuance of common stock along with rights to put the stock back to the issuer on a specified date at a specified price.	Issuer sells investors a put option, which investors will exercise if the company's share price decreases.		The put option reduces agency costs associated with a new share issue that are brought on by informational asymmetries.			Equivalent under certain conditions to convertible bonds but can be recorded as equity on the balance sheet so long as the company's payment obligation under the put option can be settled in common stock.

The creation of a new class of common stock that reflects the financial condition and operating performance of a subsidiary is best illustrated by the General Motors Corporation Class E Common Stock. Class E Stock holders are entitled to only one-half a vote per share, and their dividends are dependent on the paid-in surplus attributable to that particular class of stock and to the separate net income of General Motors' Electronic Data Systems Corporation subsidiary. Such a class of stock enables the marketplace to establish a separate market value for the subsidiary while ensuring that the parent company retains 100 percent voting control and thus the right to consolidate the subsidiary for federal income tax purposes. It can also prove useful for an employee stock option plan or other incentive compensation schemes for employees of the subsidiary.

The first Americus Trust was offered to owners of American Telephone & Telegraph Company common stock on October 25, 1983 [2]. Since then, more than two dozen other Americus Trusts have been formed. An Americus Trust offers the common stockholders of a company the opportunity to strip each of their common shares into a PRIME Component, which carries full dividend and voting rights and limited capital appreciation rights, and a SCORE Component, which carries full capital appreciation rights above a threshold price. PRIMES and SCORES appear to expand the range of securities available for inclusion in investment portfolios.[4]

Master limited partnerships are publicly traded limited partnerships that operate much like corporations except for their legal status, and many are listed on the New York Stock Exchange. The partnership structure eliminates a layer of taxation. However, if an entity is profitable and needs to retain the bulk of its earnings, the limited partners will owe tax on their respective pro rata shares of the partnership's income. Collins and Bey [16] show that the master limited partnership structure is best suited for companies with high tax rates and low retention rates, i.e., companies in "mature" industries, but is poorly suited for companies in "growth" industries.

Puttable common stock involves the sale of put options along with a new issue of common stock. The package of securities is comparable to a convertible bond [15]. The put option reduces the agency costs associated with a new share issue and could prove useful in reducing, or perhaps even eliminating, the underpricing of initial public offerings.

V. Innovative Financial Processes

The innovative financial processes listed in Exhibit 1 reflect three basic causal factors: (*i*) efforts aimed at reducing transaction costs, (*ii*) steps taken to reduce idle cash balances in response to higher interest rates, and (*iii*) the availability of relatively inexpensive computer technology to facilitate quicker financial transactions. The shelf registration process, extended to a broad range of corporate issuers by the Securities and Exchange Commission in 1982, has streamlined the process of issuing corporate securities. Kidwell, Marr, and Thompson [34] document the reduction in flotation costs that has resulted from this innovative offering process. Similarly, the direct sale of securities to the public, as evidenced by Green Mountain Power Company's sale of debt securities to its ratepayers beginning in 1970 and Virginia Electric and Power Company's sale of common stock to its ratepayers beginning some ten years later, also reduces transaction costs because the securities

---

[4]The AT&T Americus Trust was formed prior to the breakup of AT&T. The trust therefore provided an opportunity for investors to acquire units representing shares in pre-reorganization AT&T (i.e., proportionate interests in post-reorganization AT&T and in the seven regional holding companies AT&T spun off) perhaps more cheaply than they could by accumulating the shares of the different entities on their own.

are not sold through securities firms. Such offering methods have the potential for reducing a company's cost of capital by appealing to a natural clientele for the company's securities.

Discount brokerage, which resulted from the elimination of fixed commission rates by the Securities and Exchange Commission on May 1, 1975, has substantially reduced brokerage commission charges below the commission rates the "full service" brokerage houses charge. Essentially, brokerage services have become unbundled. As a result of discount brokerage, individuals can pay separately for transaction execution. Electronic security trading and automated teller machines were also intended to reduce transaction costs.

Electronic security trading, automated teller machines, point-of-sale terminals, electronic funds transfer, CHIPS (Clearinghouse Interbank Payment System), and cash management/sweep accounts have all been made possible by the availability of inexpensive computer technology. The last three were also motivated by a desire to speed cash collection, to speed check processing, and to ensure the investment of excess cash balances, respectively, all in order to reduce idle cash balances, whose opportunity cost increases with rising interest rates. Gentry [27] provides a comprehensive review of recent developments in corporate cash management. It seems likely that further technological advances will lead to more efficient systems for effecting financial transactions and for managing cash balances.

VI. Creative Solutions to Corporate Finance Problems

Although it does not seem reflected in the relatively small number of items listed in that category in Exhibit 1, finding creative solutions to corporate finance problems is an important undertaking. For example, considerable practitioner and academic effort has been expended trying to develop the most efficient strategy for calling high-coupon debt when interest rates decline [11]. Volatile interest rates have also created opportunities for companies to extinguish debt at a discount from its face amount, which produces accounting benefits. Developing techniques for accomplishing this tax-free illustrates the interaction between financial engineering and Kane's regulatory dialectic. The Bankruptcy Tax Act of 1980 eliminated several widely used strategies for obtaining the gain tax-free. Such a gain is the difference between the face amount of the debt and the repurchase price. Investment bankers first developed debt-for-lower-coupon-debt exchanges, and later developed stock-for-debt swaps, in order to achieve tax-free treatment. But the Tax Reform Act of 1984 made the gain realized in such transactions taxable and thereby virtually eliminated all remaining possibilities for refunding discounted debt profitably [20]. Nevertheless, investment bankers came up with in-substance defeasance as a means for extinguishing discounted debt in a tax-free manner. However, Peterson, Peterson, and Ang [40] correctly point out that such transactions are unlikely to enhance shareholder wealth.

Bankers and corporate treasurers have also expended considerable effort to come up with more tax-effective cash management strategies, including preferred dividend rolls (see Joehnk, Bowlin, and Petty [29]) and hedged dividend capture (see Brown and Lummer [12] and Zivney and Alderson [56] and references therein), in addition to the new forms of floating-rate preferred stock discussed earlier.

The third major area of activity encompasses leveraged buyout structuring, corporate restructuring, and project finance/lease/asset-based financial structurings. All involve, among other things, the crafting of contractual and other security arrangements that allocate financial risks and rewards among shareholders and one or more classes of creditors. For example, a leveraged buyout typically involves multiple layers of equity and multiple layers of debt, each with its own particular security arrangements. The capital structure must be engineered to suit the risk-return characteristics of the portfolio of operating assets, to satisfy the risk-return preferences of the various classes of investors, and to minimize potential agency costs.

Recent research has documented the substantial increases in shareholder wealth—on the order of 30 percent—accompanying the announcements of leveraged buyouts and leveraged recapitalizations [7, 35, 52]. Financial engineering in such cases involves estimating the cash flow stream available to service debt and preferred stock, determining the most appropriate capital structure (including the examining of the advantages of using employee stock ownership plans or other specialized forms of financing to effect the transaction [14]), designing the terms of each issue of securities so as to allocate risks and returns appropriately and minimize potential agency costs, and crafting incentive compensation arrangements for managers to ensure shareholder-wealth-maximizing behavior. Most attention in the financial press has been focused on the restructuring of financially healthy companies, but the same issues arise, and are potentially more challenging, when a troubled company is involved (as for example in the reorganization of First City Bancorporation of Texas into a recapitalized bank holding company and a collecting bank, the latter being given $1.79 billion of nonperforming, past due, and other lesser quality assets that were removed from First City Bancorporation's books [23]).

VII. Conclusion

One of the more important questions raised by Miller is whether the process of financial innovation has reached the point of diminishing returns. If the tax regime remains static, if interest rates stabilize, if the regulatory landscape solidifies, and so on, diminishing returns to financial innovation are bound to set in eventually. But to the extent that financial innovation occurs in response to unexpected economic, tax, and regulatory shocks, such shocks can keep the process of financial innovation going indefinitely without diminishing returns necessarily setting in. Financial innovations symbolize the profit-driven response to the changes in the economic, tax, and regulatory environment. As this environment changes, and as consolidation within the financial services industry intensifies competition, market participants will seek out new ways to conduct financial transactions more efficiently. The rapid pace of financial innovation therefore seems likely to continue.

While much has been written about the process of financial innovation, there has been little empirical analysis of the process. Future research might fruitfully pursue either of two basic lines of inquiry: possible further financial innovations and the economics of financial innovation. With regard to the first line of inquiry, one area that seems particularly fruitful for further investigation is that of mortgage-related securities—specifically, developing the means for further reducing the investor's prepayment risk, and perhaps eventually combining a portfolio of mortgages with options and/or futures and/or interest rate swaps so as to eliminate prepayment risk entirely. Other areas include the securitization of additional classes of assets and further applications of futures and options to customize securities issues to suit issuer and investor preferences better.

With regard to the economics of financial innovation, the principal issues concern the profitability of securities innovation and how the process of financial innovation operates. In particular, how are the rewards to securities innovation allocated among the financial institution that develops the innovative security, the issuer, and investors? Are the innovator's profits excessive, as Van Horne seems to suggest they might have been in some cases, or are they commensurate with the costs and risks of the process that Miller and others have noted? How are the rewards to the innovator affected as competitors introduce similar products or refinements? Who are the principal innovators: securities firms, banks, securities issuers, the academic community, or others? The answers to these and related questions will promote our understanding of financial engineering, an activity that plays a crucial role in promoting market efficiency.

References

1. M. J. Alderson, K. C. Brown, and S. L. Lummer. "Dutch Auction Rate Preferred Stock." *Financial Management* (Summer 1987), 68–73.
2. Americus Trust for AT&T Common Shares, Series A. Prospectus, October 25, 1983.
3. M. Arak, A. Estrella, L. Goodman, and A. Silver. "Interest Rate Swaps: An Alternative Explanation." *Financial Management* (Summer 1988), 12–18.
4. M. D. Atchison, R. F. DeMong, and J. L. Kling. *New Financial Instruments: A Descriptive Guide.* Charlottesville, VA, Financial Analysts Research Foundation, 1985.
5. M. Ben-Horim and W. Silber. "Financial Innovation: A Linear Programming Approach." *Journal of Banking and Finance* (September 1977), 277–96.
6. J. Bicksler and A. H. Chen. "An Economic Analysis of Interest Rate Swaps." *Journal of Finance* (July 1986), 645–55.
7. B. S. Black and J. A. Grundfest. "Shareholder Gains from Takeovers and Restructurings between 1981 and 1986: $162 Billion Is a Lot of Money." *The Continental Bank Journal of Applied Corporate Finance* (Spring 1988), 5–15.
8. F. Black and M. Scholes. "From Theory to a New Financial Product." *Journal of Finance* (May 1974), 399–412.
9. J. D. Block and T. J. Gallagher. "The Use of Interest Rate Futures and Options by Corporate Financial Managers." *Financial Management* (Autumn 1986), 73–78.
10. J. R. Booth, R. L. Smith, and R. W. Stolz. "The Use of Interest Futures by Financial Institutions." *Journal of Bank Research* (Spring 1984), 15–20.
11. W. M. Boyce and A. J. Kalotay. "Optimum Bond Calling and Refunding." *Interfaces* (November 1979), 36–49.
12. K. C. Brown and S. L. Lummer. "A Reexamination of the Covered Call Option Strategy for Corporate Cash Management." *Financial Management* (Summer 1986), 13–17.
13. K. C. Brown and D. J. Smith. "Recent Innovations in Interest Rate Risk Management and the Reintermediation of Commercial Banking." *Financial Management* (Winter 1988).
14. R. F. Bruner. "Leveraged ESOPs and Corporate Restructuring." *The Continental Bank Journal of Applied Corporate Finance* (Spring 1988), 54–66.
15. A. H. Chen and J. W. Kensinger. "Puttable Stock: A New Innovation in Equity Financing." *Financial Management* (Spring 1988), 27–37.
16. J. M. Collins and R. P. Bey. "The Master Limited Partnership: An Alternative to the Corporation." *Financial Management* (Winter 1986), 5–14.
17. P. H. Darrow and R. A. Mestres, Jr. *Creative Financing in the 1980s.* New York, Practising Law Institute, 1983.
18. J. Dutt. "What's Hot, What's Not." *Investment Dealers' Digest* (March 17, 1986), 20–28.
19. J. D. Finnerty. "Zero Coupon Bond Arbitrage: An Illustration of the Regulatory Dialectic at Work." *Financial Management* (Winter 1985), 13–17.
20. ———. "Refunding Discounted Debt: A Clarifying Analysis." *Journal of Financial and Quantitative Analysis* (March 1986), 95–106.
21. ———. "The Case for Issuing Synthetic Convertible Bonds." *Midland Corporate Finance Journal* (Fall 1986), 73–82.
22. ———. "An Analytical Framework for Evaluating Securities Innovations." *Journal of Corporate Finance* (Winter 1987), 3–18.

23. First City Bancorporation of Texas, Inc. Proxy Statement, January 26, 1988.

24. L. Fisher, I. E. Brick, and F. K. W. Ng. "Tax Incentives and Financial Innovation: The Case of Zero-Coupon and Other Deep-Discount Corporate Bonds." *Financial Review* (November 1983), 292–305.

25. B. Friedman. "Postwar Changes in the American Financial Markets." In M. Feldstein (ed.), *The American Economy in Transition*. Chicago, University of Chicago Press, 1980.

26. W. K. H. Fung and A. Rudd. "Pricing New Corporate Bond Issues: An Analysis of Issue Cost and Seasoning Effects." *Journal of Finance* (July 1986), 633–43.

27. J. A. Gentry. "State of the Art of Short-Run Financial Managment." *Financial Management* (Summer 1988), 41–57.

28. L. S. Goodman and J. B. Yawitz. "Innovation in the U.S. Bond Market." *Institutional Investor Money Management Forum* (December 1987), 102–04.

29. M. D. Joehnk, O. D. Bowlin, and J. W. Petty. "Preferred Dividend Rolls: A Viable Strategy for Corporate Money Managers?" *Financial Management* (Summer 1980), 78–87.

30. E. P. Jones and S. P. Mason. "Equity-Linked Debt." *Midland Corporate Finance Journal* (Winter 1986), 47–58.

31. E. J. Kane. "Good Intentions and Unintended Evil: The Case Against Selective Credit Allocation." *Journal of Money, Credit and Banking* (February 1977), 55–69.

32. ———. "Accelerating Inflation, Technological Innovation, and the Decreasing Effectiveness of Banking Regulation." *Journal of Finance* (May 1981), 355–67.

33. ———. "Technological and Regulatory Forces in the Developing Fusion of Financial—Services Competition." *Journal of Finance* (July 1984), 759–72.

34. D. S. Kidwell, M. W. Marr, and G. R. Thompson. "SEC Rules 415: The Ultimate Competitive Bid." *Journal of Financial and Quantitative Analysis* (June 1984), 183–95.

35. R. T. Kleiman. "The Shareholder Gains from Leveraged Cashouts: Some Preliminary Evidence." *The Continental Bank Journal of Applied Corporate Finance* (Spring 1988), 46–53.

36. J. J. McConnell and E. S. Schwartz. "LYON Taming." *Journal of Finance* (July 1986), 561–76.

37. G. Miller. "The Knockoff Artists." *Institutional Investor* (May 1986), 8lff.

38. M. H. Miller. "Financial Innovation: The Last Twenty Years and the Next." *Journal of Financial and Quantitative Analysis* (December 1986), 459–71.

39. J. P. Ogden. "An Analysis of Yield Curve Notes." *Journal of Finance* (March 1987), 99–110.

40. P. Peterson, D. Peterson, and J. Ang. "The Extinguishment of Debt through In-Substance Defeasance." *Financial Management* (Spring 1985), 59–67.

41. W. Power. "Many of 1987's New Trading Products Are Failing Despite Spirited Marketing." *Wall Street Journal* (January 4, 1988), 26.

42. *Recent Innovations in International Banking*. Bank for International Settlements, April 1986.

43. T. E. Ricks. "SEC Chief Calls Some Financial Products 'Too Dangerous' for Individual Investors." *Wall Street Journal* (January 7, 1988), 46.

44. A. C. Shapiro. "Guidelines for Long-Term Corporate Financing Strategy." *Midland Corporate Finance Journal* (Winter 1986), 6–19.

45. D. Shirreff. "Down with Innovation!" *Euromoney* (August 1986), 23ff.

46. W. L. Silber (ed.). *Financial Innovation*. Lexington MA, Lexington Books, 1975.

47. ———. "Innovation, Competition, and New Contract Design in Futures Markets." *Journal of Futures Markets* (No. 2, 1981), 123–56.

48. ———. "The Process of Financial Innovation." *American Economic Review* (May 1983), 89–95.

49. D. J. Smith. "The Pricing of Bull and Bear Floating Rate Notes: An Application of Financial Engineering." *Financial Management* (Winter 1988).

50. J. Spratlin and P. Vianna. *An Investor's Guide to CMOs*. New York, Salomon Brothers, May 1986.

51. J. Sterngold. "Anatomy of a Staggering Loss." *New York Times* (May 11, 1987), D1ff.

52. K. Torabzadeh and W. Bertin. "Leveraged Buyouts and Stockholder Wealth." *Journal of Financial Research* (Winter 1987), 313–21.

53. J. C. Van Horne. "Of Financial Innovations and Excesses." *Journal of Finance* (July 1985), 621–31.

54. B. J. Winger, C. R. Chen, J. D. Martin, J. W. Petty, and S. C. Hayden. "Adjustable Rate Preferred Stock." *Financial Management* (Spring 1986), 48–57.

55. J. B. Yawitz and K. J. Maloney. "Evaluating the Decision to Issue Original Issue Discount Bonds: Term Structure and Tax Effects." *Financial Management* (Winter 1983), 36–46.

56. T. L. Zivney and M. J. Alderson. "Hedged Dividend Capture with Stock Index Options." *Financial Managment* (Summer 1986), 5–12.

Discussion Questions

1. In what way did the tax laws provide the stimulation for creating zero coupon bonds?

2. Compare Kane's regulatory dialectic with the relationship between universities and students.

3. What are the conditions necessary for a new security to be considered truly "innovative"?

4. Explain why securitizing loans can be of benefit to the lender (the bank)?

5. Explain how securities firms created zero coupon bonds from bearer Treasury securities.

6. How does adjustable rate preferred stock lessen investors' risk?

7. What regulatory and economic conditions are necessary for financial innovation to continue? Explain.

part **VI**

Short-Term Financial Management

Short-term financial management (or short-run financial management) refers to the management of short-term assets and liabilities or to the daily operations of receiving funds and paying bills.

The article by Lewellen and Johnson shows a dynamic approach to the monitoring of accounts receivable, and Gentry provides a comprehensive overview of the dimensions of short-run financial management.

Wilbur G. Lewellen and Robert W. Johnson

Better Way to Monitor Accounts Receivable

Once a firm has established its credit policy, the financial manager must constantly monitor his or her credit operations to ensure that the policy is being followed and that satisfactory results are being achieved. This monitoring process is extremely important for a firm's long-run viability, yet many firms' credit feedback mechanisms are inadequate. Lewellen and Johnson present a monitoring technique that is better than many currently available methods. They point out that when sales are rising or falling, other monitoring techniques can give misleading signals. The superiority of the Lewellen-Johnson method is that it separates the accounts receivables originating in different periods, thus avoiding timing overlays.

When a warning signal flashes on the instrument panel of his aircraft, the skilled pilot immediately questions whether the signal mechanism is faulty or whether the airplane is indeed in trouble. The financial executive charged with overseeing the management of accounts receivable for his company faces a similar problem. When the reporting device he uses to monitor collection experience flashes a warning, he confronts a dilemma: Is the monitoring device defective, or are accounts receivable in fact moving out of control? Just as the pilot may endanger his passengers if he responds to a false signal light, so may the financial executive compromise the profitability of his company by his reactions to an erroneous credit indicator. Equally dangerous, of course, is the warning signal that fails to operate when it should.

It is our contention that most of the procedures now widely used for monitoring the management of accounts receivable are, by their very nature, misleading and capable of frequent errors—of both omission and commission. We shall show how commonly used control mechanisms may signal improvement or deterioration in the status of accounts receivable when there actually has been no change in the rate of customer payments. We will also show that the same faulty control mechanism

Source: Reprinted by permission of *Harvard Business Review*. "Better Way to Monitor Accounts Receivable" by Wilbur C. Lewellen and Robert W. Johnson. May–June 1972, pp. 101–109. Wilbur G. Lewellen is Professor of Finance and Robert W. Johnson is Professor Emeritus of Management at Purdue University.

which permits such false signals can also fail to flash a warning when one *is* needed. We shall then go on to suggest an alternative analytical framework that does provide meaningful and reliable information for managers.

Collection Experience

As a starting point, it is necessary to specify exactly what is meant by the term *collection experience* as it applies to an enterprise that sells to customers on credit. It seems to us logical to define that notion simply as the rate at which remittances for credit sales are received over time—that is, the chronological pattern according to which the receivables created during a given interval are converted into cash. If we take a month to be our standard unit of account, the issue is the liquidation rate for each month's new credit sales. A *constant* collection experience—receivables "in control"—denotes a situation wherein the fractions of credit sales still uncollected as time passes follow a stable and predictable pattern from month to month. To illustrate:

Suppose a company finds that, say, 90 percent of the credit sales made during a month always remain outstanding at the end of that month, 60 percent always remain outstanding at the end of the following month, and 20 percent always are still uncollected at the end of an additional month, but all are liquidated within the succeeding 30 days. If, for instance, we assume that the company in question has $100,000 of credit sales in January of a particular year, the receivables—and collections—generated by those sales would be as shown in Exhibit 1. Likewise, another $100,000 of credit sales in February would give rise to a set of collections and receivables running from February to May; March's sales would affect events until June; and so on throughout the year. The total of collections and receivables attributable to the various individual months would combine to produce, at any stage, aggregates for the company as a whole.

Reasons for Failure

The concept of collection experience, therefore, refers to nothing more than this standard notion of the rate of account conversion into cash—and will be used in just that sense here as we consider whether the usual techniques for assessing a company's receivables provide accurate signals about customer payment patterns. We shall examine with some care the two most common criteria—days' sales outstanding and aging of accounts receivable.

(A critical discussion of other systems may be found in the Appendix to this article.)

Days' Sales Outstanding

A widely used index of the efficiency of credit and collections is the collection period, or number of days' sales outstanding in receivables (DSO). It is calculated for any point in time by dividing the recent average dollar sales volume per day into the dollar amount of receivables outstanding at that time. The equivalent reciprocal index, called receivables turnover, is simply DSO divided into 360 days. Thus, if receivables "turn over" six times a year, the collection period is necessarily 60 days. Our comments therefore apply to both measures of credit circumstances.

The manifest unreliability of these measures can be seen by examining the signals flashed to the credit manager of a company whose collection experience is stable, but whose monthly sales vary over time. Consider the hypothetical case earlier described, wherein the percentages of receiv-

Exhibit 1   Collection Experience of Hypothetical Company for January Sales (in Thousands of Dollars)

Month	Collections During Month	Receivables Outstanding at End of Month
January	$10	$90
February	30	60
March	40	20
April	20	0

ables still uncollected for a given month's credit sales consistently follow a 90 percent/60 percent/20 percent sequential end-of-month pattern—in short, a fixed and definite rate of customer payments. Exhibit 2 indicates the effect on the DSO calculation of three sales profiles under this steady collection experience:

1. Level sales for three months at $60,000 per month.

2. Rising sales for the next three months at $30,000, $60,000, and $90,000, respectively.

3. A declining sales profile of $90,000, $60,000, and $30,000.

Thus, in all three situations, *total* sales for the calendar quarter are identical. Only their distribution differs.

Exhibit 2 reveals the collection period the credit manager would record at the *end* of each of the three quarters. Clearly, the signals are both misleading and capricious. They are sensitive not only to the sales pattern observed but also to the sales-averaging period selected. Indeed, the choice of averaging period virtually determines the nature of the signals.

If, for example, the most recent 30 days were chosen for computing average daily sales, then it would appear that collection experience had improved for the company during April through June, as compared with January through March, because the collection period had fallen from 51 to 41 days. Similarly, as the sales pattern of July through September unfolded, the DSO figure would climb to 81 days and generate concern that remittances were slowing significantly. Throughout, however, the rate of customer payments is *invariant,* by stipulation. The problem lies entirely with the monitoring device.

Comparable ambiguities prevail for any averaging period. If 90 days were selected instead, the chronological sequence of erroneous signals would simply be reversed. Balances at the end of the second quarter would indicate 62 days' sales outstanding and imply a deterioration in collections, but, by the end of the third quarter, an apparent improvement to 41 days would be reported.

Thus, no single averaging period will consistently yield a correct appraisal where there are fluctuations in sales. In fact, within any given sales interval, even the *direction* of the signal depends on the averaging period chosen.

It should be emphasized that these observations do not rely for their validity on sales variations as sharp as those depicted in Exhibit 2. Milder increases and decreases in volume would merely moderate—not eliminate—the discrepancies identified. Moreover, 60 days cannot be recommended

Exhibit 2 Days' Sales Outstanding (DSO) with Varying Sales Patterns and Varying Averaging Periods (Dollar Figures in Thousands)

Month	Sales	Receivables Outstanding at End of Quarter		Sales per Day if Averaging Period Is Most Recent			Reported End-of-Quarter Collection Period, if Averaging period Is:		
		Percent of Sales	Dollar Amount	30 Days	60 Days	90 Days	30 Days	60 Days	90 Days
January	$60	20%	$ 12						
February	60	60	36						
March	60	90	54						
			$102	$2	$2.0	$2	51 days	51 days	51 days
April	$30	20%	$ 6						
May	60	60	36						
June	90	90	81						
			$123	$3	$2.5	$2	41 days	49 days	62 days
July	$90	20%	$ 18						
August	60	60	36						
September	30	90	27						
			$ 81	$	$1.5	$2	81 days	54 days	41 days

as a kind of "happy medium" averaging period that can be counted on to minimize the extent of potential errors. This interval looks relatively good here only by accident. Consider, for example, the DSO figures based on the most recent 60 days' sales that would emerge if the sales for April and May, or July and August, were reversed.

Insuperable Difficulties. Despite a vague awareness of the existence of problems of this sort, it has been argued in the literature that valid comparisons of DSO figures may be made if the calculations pertain to the same point in a company's seasonal sales cycle from year to year, or that comparisons among companies are legitimate so long as the same date is utilized in the computations for each.[1] We cannot agree. Intertemporal or intercorporate reliability of such an index can be counted on only if the credit sales patterns involved for the months preceding the analysis point are *literally* identical. This condition is, of course, unlikely.

An added difficulty is the fact that a mechanism which transmits false signals about nonexistent changes in collection experience may also fail to send the *true* warning when needed. To illustrate:

Suppose that during the April to June period in Exhibit 2, customer payments slow down in such a way that the pattern of successive end-of-month uncollected balances becomes 60 percent/80 percent/95 percent instead of 20 percent/60 percent/90 percent. Receivables at the end of June would then amount to $152,000. A 30-day sales averaging period for the DSO calculation would suggest 51 days' sales outstanding—matching the value for the end of March and concealing the underlying deterioration in payment patterns. The financial executive would be lulled into believing that credits and collections are in control when actually they are not.

Aging of Receivables

Another common device for monitoring receivables is the "aging" criterion. Again, however, we must ask how dependable this monitoring method is when sales can vary from month to month.

The aging schedules in Exhibit 3—derived as of the end of each calendar quarter from the data in Exhibit 2—show that rising sales (Quarter 2) create an impression of improved customer payment patterns, whereas falling sales (Quarter 3) produce a schedule that suggests a deterioration in collections. This is understandable when one recognizes that the most recent month's sales always dominate the calculations. Thus, the proportion of total receivables in accounts less than 30 days old will naturally be relatively high in a period of rising sales, and low in a period of falling sales—even when, as is the case here, the payment profile is completely stable.

This will result in a continual series of spurious warning signals being flashed to the credit manager simply in response to normal sales fluctuations. Only during the unusual intervals when sales are level from month to month will the indicator be of any potential use.

Even at that, the aging schedule suffers from an inherent deficiency. It is difficult to interpret meaningfully any figures that are contributed from differing sources but are constrained to add up to 100 percent. The fact that, say, 30 percent of a company's receivables outstanding at a point in time are under 30 days old, and 70 percent are 30–60 days old, may not mean that there is an extraordinarily large

---

[1] See, for example, Pearson Hunt, Charles Williams, and Gordon Donaldson, *Basic Business Finance,* 4th Edition (Homewood, Illinois, Irwin, 1971), p. 62.

Exhibit 3   Reported Receivables Aging Schedules (Dollar Figures in Thousands)

Age of Account	Receivables Outstanding at End of Quarter[a]	Percent of Total
End of Quarter 1		
(March 31):		
60–90 days	$ 12	12%
30–60 days	36	35
0–30 days	54	53
	$102	100%
End of Quarter 2		
(June 30):		
60–90 days	$ 6	5%
30–60 days	36	29
0–30 days	81	66
	$123	100%
End of Quarter 3		
(September 30):		
60–90 days	$ 18	22%
30–60 days	36	45
0–30 days	27	33
	$ 81	100%

[a] Figures from Exhibit 2.

number of overdue accounts and that receivables are out of control. It could merely be that an unusually—and desirably—high percentage of rapid payments were made on the most recent month's sales, leaving very few of them outstanding and raising the apparent weight of old accounts. The latter, however, may be no greater than normal in relation to the original sales that created them.

From the aging proportions per se there is no way of detecting this phenomenon, and erroneous conclusions could easily be drawn by management. Any criterion according to which the role of one element is automatically affected by changes in the others embodies this defect.

Adjusting for the Biases

One response to the foregoing observations might be that it would be possible to live with the distortions inherent in the various procedures described, so long as the credit manager is aware of the general nature and direction of the relevant biases. Again, we would demur.

In the illustrations cited, we have employed rather basic patterns of progressive increases and decreases in sales. While one might conceivably develop some rule-of-thumb adjustment allowances to handle the effects of such simple changes in volume, it would be much more difficult— if not impossible—to compensate correctly for all the peculiar, nonsystematic variations in sales confronted in actual practice. Even if the *direction* of the distortion were known, the *extent* would still be an issue—and would still be obscured. For example:

**Exhibit 4   Uncollected Balances as Percentages of Original Sales
(Dollar Figures in Thousands)**

Month of Origin	Sales During That Month	Receivables Outstanding at End of Quarter	Percentage Outstanding (Receivables/Sales)
January	$60	$ 12	20%
February	60	36	60
March	60	54	90
		$102	
April	$30	$ 6	20%
May	60	36	60
June	90	81	90
		$123	
July	$90	$ 18	20%
August	60	36	60
September	30	27	90
		$81	

Suppose that in a period of rising sales it turns out that the collection period has lengthened from 40 days to 50 days. The financial executive would have to know whether that is more or less than the "normal" result for the specific monthly sales growth rate being experienced.

An Effective Tool

The central difficulty with the two most commonly used monitoring devices (as well as those discussed in the Appendix) is that, in one form or another, the view taken of collection experience is conceptually inappropriate. Either collections or balances are *aggregated* in the calculations, making it impossible to detect changes in remittance rates for particular components of credit sales.

If aggregation is the problem, *disaggregation* is the key to its solution. The remittance rates for each individual component of sales should be identified and separated out if the data are not to be confounded by external influences, such as sales variations.

Can this be done? Fortunately, there is an analytical technique that meets the need. It involves nothing more than casting up the periodic receivables status report in the same form as the basic definition of "collection experience" with which we began our discussion, i.e., balances outstanding as a percentage of the respective *original* sales that gave rise to those balances. In this fashion, customer payment rates are automatically traced to their source, and the appraisal of collection success is rendered independent of sales patterns and of the impact of changes in relative account composition. A typical report—prepared as of the end of each calendar quarter for our illustrative situation—is offered in Exhibit 4.

Not surprisingly, this record of the ratio of receivables balances to original sales indicates that the collection rate on accounts has been perfectly stable throughout the period in question. Exactly 90 percent of the most recent month's, 60 percent of the next most recent month's, and 20 percent of the third most recent month's credit sales show up as outstanding at each point in time examined.

Exhibit 5   Effect on Percentages Outstanding of Slow Payment on February Sales (Dollar Figures in Thousands)

Month	Sales During Month	Receivables Outstanding at End of Quarter	Percentage Outstanding (Receivables/Sales)
January	$60	$ 12	20%
February	60	45	75
March	60	_54_	90
		$111	

(These figures do not—and will not, except by accident—sum to 100 percent, since they do not purport to describe the makeup of a fixed total. Each is calculated according to a *different* sales base.)

The same answer would emerge at the end of every one of the nine months tabulated, and will persist under any conceivable sales pattern we might stipulate, so long as customer payment rates are in fact stable. Conversely, any deviation in those rates for any of the relevant sales intervals would be immediately detected and would not be concealed by aggregation or changes in other collections.

Accurate Analysis

To illustrate the improvement from a management standpoint, consider a simple example:

Suppose the customers to whom merchandise was sold during February happen to be slow payers and remit for only 15 percent of their purchases during the month following the month of sale, rather than the 30 percent figure which has been normal. In that case, balances at the end of March would be as shown in Exhibit 5, instead of as portrayed in Exhibit 4. Since only the figure for February would show up as out of line with past experience in the status report, the problem could be tracked to its source without difficulty.

Of equal importance, an acceleration of the payments on other months' sales would not obscure the analysis by exerting offsetting effects. Assume, for instance, that collections on credit sales originally made during January are simultaneously higher than normal, amounting to fully 55 percent of original balances during March rather than the usual 40 percent. Those extra receipts would neutralize the concurrent decline attributable to the customers from February, and put total receivables back at $102,000 as of the end of March (Exhibit 6).

Nonetheless, the credit executive could see from the report that changes *have* occurred even though the totals are "normal." He would not be lulled into thinking that payment patterns have remained stable—as would be indicated by, say, a DSO calculation—and could institute policy changes before it is too late to prevent some unpleasant surprises. In particular, if the shift in collection rates persists, then, as sales begin to rise, the increase in the funds commitment necessary to support receivables could be anticipated.

Value in Forecasting

The virtues of the framework we propose are, in fact, as notable in the context of forecasting funds requirements as in the contemplation of changes in policy. It may often be that the financial execu-

Exhibit 6   The Combined Effect of Fast Payment on January Sales and Slow Payment on February Sales (Dollar Figures in Thousands)

Month	Sales During Month	Receivables Outstanding at End of Quarter	Percentage Outstanding (Receivables/Sales)
January	$60	$ 3	5%
February	60	45	75
March	60	54	90
		$102	

tive cannot do much about a slowdown in customer payment patterns without adversely affecting profitability. Competitive conditions—or the simple undercapitalization of many customers—may render it impossible to tighten terms and raise standards of acceptability without a substantial loss of revenue. Whatever the constraints, the need to project receivables balances for budgeting purposes is always present, and it is clear that the usual techniques leave a great deal to be desired. To illustrate:

Consider the forecasts that would be made by the credit manager of a company whose sales and collection experience has for some time been steady, as in the January–March period in Exhibit 2. Assume that total sales in the upcoming calendar quarter are predicted to be $180,000 again, but that they follow the monthly pattern of April through June.

If the executive were monitoring receivables in terms of DSO—with a 90-day sales averaging period—he would see 51 days' sales outstanding consistently, and would therefore use that standard to forecast balances. Because total sales anticipated for the next 90 days just match those experienced during the most recent 90, the DSO prediction would simply be for $102,000 in receivables outstanding as of the end of June. Given the 90 percent/60 percent/20 percent uncollected balance sequence that actually prevails, however, receivables would turn out to be $123,000 instead—an error that could be uncomfortable.

If sales of $180,000 were then forecasted for the third quarter, $102,000 in outstanding accounts would once more be the DSO-based estimate for the end of September, but $81,000 would turn out to be the actual figure. Comparable mistakes would—or could, depending on the circumstances—occur from use of the other techniques described earlier and in the Appendix, since none really gets at the rate of customer payments in a meaningful way.

Only by ascertaining that the normal uncollected balance profile is 90 percent/60 percent/ 20 percent (that is, collections are 10 percent/30 percent/40 percent/20 percent) can one disentangle the independent effects of remittance rates and sales patterns and thereby achieve an accurate forecast. Accuracy, of course, is important not only to the credit executive but also to the company's banker, who may be confronted with a working-capital loan request based in large part on receivables predictions.

Tracking Flows over Time

The parameters of the model, for forecasting purposes, are easily obtained from past data. Ordinarily, a simple record of historical end-of-month balances (like that shown in Exhibit 4), broken down into percentages of original monthly sales for, say, the most recent two years, will suffice. This number of observations should provide a reasonably good indication of the trend, or lack thereof, of payment patterns.

The analysis might resemble the one presented in Exhibit 7, where it appears that the fraction of sales made in a given month which are uncollected at the end of that same month has varied from 86 percent to 97 percent during the year considered; the fraction still on the books 30 days later has ranged from 54 percent to 73 percent; and the proportion after another 30 days has been between 17 percent and 39 percent. (Balances for four, five, or more months might also be shown if customers took longer to pay.)

Whether tabulated in this manner or plotted on a graph, the indicated percentages summarize very quickly and conveniently for management the company's ongoing collection experience. A continual updating of the record will then keep the appraisal current.

It would appear, in the situation shown in Exhibit 7, that remittance rates *are* fairly stable; no secular trend is evident in the 24 months examined. On the other hand, it seems characteristic for payments to slow down during April, May, and June of each year before returning to the "normal" pattern of roughly 90 percent/60 percent/20 percent. Additional data for earlier years might be collected to confirm this interpretation. Various standard statistical techniques, including regression analysis, could be applied to test rigorously whether a trend is present, as judged by whether the more recent percentages tabulated differ significantly—in the statistical sense—from those of earlier periods.

Alternatively, and less formally, a simple moving average of perhaps the last six months' percentages at each of the three levels could be maintained and compared with the corresponding averages for the same intervals one and two years earlier. Or, if no seasonal variations were apparent, a comparison of *any* successive six-month intervals would do. Note that seasonality in *sales* is not the issue. That effect has been factored out by the percentage calculations. Indeed, as is obvious, the volume of sales need not be recorded in the receivables status report. Only payment patterns are of concern.

The average collection experience suggested by these calculations would then be used in forecasting receivables balances, given monthly sales estimates from the company's marketing department. Thus, the average end-of-month outstanding balance percentages listed in Exhibit 7 for July through December of 1970 and 1971 are 90 percent, 60 percent, and 20 percent; and for April through June of both years, 95 percent, 70 percent, and 35 percent. Projections of balances for 1972 would logically be based on these relationships.

Whatever the evidence for the particular company involved, and whatever the preferred averaging technique, the percentages displayed provide the financial executive with an effective tool *both* for detecting changes in remittance rates and for forecasting.

Control Limits

As far as policy is concerned, the signal to management that something has happened with customer payments would be either an affirmative statistical significance test of the kind just described or a deviation of the moving average greater than a specified tolerance limit. To illustrate:

The credit manager might establish a rule that a 5 percent change in the most recent six-month outstanding balance averages in comparison with the averages for the preceding six months, or for

Exhibit 7 Status Report on Receivables Outstanding as a Percent of Original Sales

					Month							
	J	F	M	A	M	J	J	A	S	O	N	D
Percentages outstanding for 1970 from sales of:												
Same month	90%	89%	91%	95%	97%	93%	86%	92%	91%	90%	91%	90%
One month before	60	62	59	68	73	69	59	54	62	63	61	60
Two months before	20	19	18	35	37	33	23	20	17	21	22	20
Percentages outstanding for 1971 from sales of:												
Same month	90%	91%	90%	93%	96%	96%	89%	91%	90%	88%	89%	90%
One month before	60	61	59	70	72	68	57	62	59	61	61	60
Two months before	20	22	21	33	39	33	19	18	21	20	19	20

Note: To ascertain the payment flow for one month's original sales, see the numbers in a descending left-to-right diagonal pattern. Thus the sequence 89 per-cent/62 percent/21 percent singled out for July–August–September of 1971 refers to balances originating in July's sales as they remain outstanding as of the end of three successive months.

the corresponding period a year earlier, would be reason to consider a revision in credit policy. Thus, if the July–December 1971 end-of-month receivables averages come out to a 95 percent/ 65 percent/25 percent profile, whereas 1970's July–December figures were 90 percent/60 percent/ 20 percent, that might well be grounds for reexamining sales terms and credit standards. In fact, a 5 percent increase or decrease even in *one* of the three percentages in the profile could suggest the need for action. Alternatively, an observation of three consecutive monthly percentage deviations (other than seasonal) of 5 percent above or below the average at that position in the profile over the preceding 6 or 12 months might trigger the manager's attention.

A potential increase in bad debts in particular might be foreshadowed by a rise in the percentages at the tail end of the receivables schedule, or the appearance of balances for an additional end-of-month interval. For instance, the profile might begin to change to 90 percent/60 percent/20 percent/3 percent; the last figure could represent not merely slow payers, but prospective default cases.

It should be emphasized that a below-average outstanding balance tendency can be as important to management as an upward shift. A general acceleration in remittance rates may indicate that credit guidelines or collection practices are becoming *too* stringent, and that many legitimate customers are in fact being excluded.

Concluding Note

No single measure of deviation will fit every company's circumstances and tastes for "fine tuning" credit policy. Purely random fluctuations in the relevant percentages may be much larger for one company than for another. The important thing is to organize the detection and control of collection experience around an analytical framework that provides input information useful to the decision process.

We believe the scheme outlined in this article meets that requirement far better than any other currently available. It does not mix together receivables originating in different sales periods, and it is the only procedure which is not distorted by changes in sales patterns.

Appendix—Deficiencies of Other Systems

In this article we have described the shortcomings of the best-known approaches used by management to monitor accounts receivable. Here we describe some variations of these approaches that are familiar to many businessmen, and point out their deficiencies.

Average Age of Receivables

Some companies employ a receivables-monitoring device which summarizes, in a single number, the information contained in the aging schedule. This number or index is the so-called "average age of receivables." It is typically calculated with the assumption that the average duration of outstanding accounts that are less than 30 days old is exactly 15 days, that the average for those 30 to 60 days old is 45 days, and so on, for as many categories as are relevant. The product of these figures times the proportions of each age segment in the total, when summed, yields a global average age measure of overall balances. By this criterion, the schedules depicted in Exhibit 3 would imply that an average account was 32.8 days old as of the end of Quarter 1. The computation would be:

$$.12 \times 75 \text{ days} = 9.0 \text{ days}$$
$$+ \quad .35 \times 45 \text{ days} = 15.8 \text{ days}$$
$$+ \quad .53 \times 15 \text{ days} = 8.0 \text{ days}$$

| Total | = 32.8 days |

Similarly, an average account would be 26.8 and 41.8 days old, respectively, as of the close of Quarters 2 and 3.

The signals given by "average age" must, of course, coincide with those given by the complete aging schedule—and can only incorporate the same shortcomings.

Relative Changes

Another technique often followed compares the periodic changes in the level of receivables to the concurrent changes in the level of sales. The misleading signals that result are in the same direction as those generated by collection period methods, and they occur for the same reason: rising (falling) sales necessarily produce quarter-end receivables that are large (small) relative to the sales for the entire quarter, despite a constant collection experience for each individual monthly bloc of credit sales.

Percentage Collections

It has also been argued that the collection/balance ratio should be used by management. For example:

> A further means of checking upon the quality of a firm's credit and collections policies is the preparation of periodic reports to show what percentage of customers' balances on the books at the beginning of each period is collected during that period.[2]

The reliability of this scheme can be tested by comparing the results it would show for the nine-month sales pattern of our standard illustration. If we assume that the company's sales for the last several months of the preceding fiscal year were steady at $60,000 per month, the ratio of monthly collections to beginning-of-month receivables for January through September would vary from 54 percent to 68 percent. Since these indexes can fluctuate so widely even under conditions of no change in customer payment rates, their usefulness as inputs to credit policy decisions is in serious question.

Aging of Collections

Finally, the distribution of monthly collections by age of account involved has been suggested as a possible monitoring device.[3] Table 1 presents such a breakdown for March, June, and September of our example. Examination of the data would lead the credit manager to believe that collections were speeding up in the vicinity of June, since a larger percentage of collections are in the 0–30 day and

---

[2] R. P. Kent, *Corporate Financial Management*, 3rd Edition (Homewood, Illinois, Irwin, 1969), p. 194.

[3] H. Benishay, "Managerial Controls of Accounts Receivable: A Deterministic Approach," *Journal of Accounting Research*, Spring 1965, p. 114.

**Table 1   Distribution of Collections by Age of Account
(Dollar Figures in Thousands)**

Age of Account (in Days)	March		June		September	
	Collections	Percent of Total	Collections	Percent of Total	Collections	Percent of Total
0–30	$ 6	10.0%	$ 9	17.7%	$ 3	4.0%
30–60	18	30.0	18	35.3	18	24.0
60–90	24	40.0	12	23.5	36	48.0
90–120	12	20.0	12	23.5	18	24.0
	$60	100.0%	$51	100.0%	$75	100.0%

30–60 day age groups than was true three months earlier. Similarly, he would become concerned that collections were slowing in September because the percentage distribution of receipts shifted back toward the 60–90 day and 90–120 day categories.

This distortion, of course, is nothing more than the normal result of rising and falling monthly sales volumes. Payment rates being stable, the higher the proportion of more recent sales, the heavier will be the weight of collections on recent accounts compared to total collections—and vice versa for a declining sales pattern. The financial executive might, in consequence, be led to undertake "remedial" action that could be detrimental to profitability, when in fact no revisions are warranted.

Discussion Questions

1. Explain why accounts receivable (A/R) aging will indicate an "improvement" (deterioration) in the quality of accounts receivable if sales have been increasing (decreasing).

2. Explain why the averaging period used for day's sales outstanding (DSO) may influence the signal received regarding the quality of accounts receivable.

3. What is meant by the term "collection experience," and what does a constant collection experience denote?

4. A valid comparison of DSO figures may be made if the calculations pertain to the same point in a company's seasonal sales cycle from year to year—do you agree? Discuss why or why not.

5. Assume that your firm is using the monitoring system advocated by Lewellen and Johnson. The control limits could be pierced because of internal problems associated with easing of credit standards, or departure from norms could result from fundamental changes in the economic environment. Explain how departures from norms might be caused by (a) an economic recession, (b) tight money, (c) excess capacity in your industry. Should your credit policy and enforcement *always* be adjusted to keep within the control limits?

Problem

1. The Wilbob Corporation is uncertain whether their growing A/R balance is a warning flash or not. Its business has been profitable, but A/R increased almost six times, while sales increased only about four times over the period January 31 to April 30, 1976. Records of their collection experience show the following information:

Month of Sale	Sales for Month	Collected in January	Collected in February	Collected in March	Collected in April
January	25	5.0	7.5	10.0	2.5
February	45	—	9.0	13.5	18.0
March	80	—	—	16.0	24.0
April	100	—	—	—	20.0
A/R balance		22.2	48.9	89.0	124.5

a. Analyze the firm's collection experience using at least two different methods suggested in this article. If an average period is used, use ninety days. Sales for November and December were 2 and 4, respectively.
b. What is the status of the "collection experience"?
c. Sales for the next four months are forecasted to be $90, 75, 60, and 50, respectively. What will receivables be on August 31, 1976?

James A. Gentry *

State of the Art of Short-Run Financial Management

Short-run financial management (SRFM) encompasses not only working capital management but also a system of operations-related functions dealing with the daily problems of paying and getting paid, or getting through the short run so that there is a satisfactory long run. There are many conceptual and analytical issues embodied in SRFM. Professor Gentry outlines the issues and what is known about them in a comprehensive manner. Importantly, this article integrates these topics very well.

In 1973, Smith [170] presented the state of the art of, and traced the development of research in, working capital management (WCM), thereby providing an anchor for measuring future research productivity. Since the early 1970s, the development of substantive WCM research has expanded dramatically. Thus, it seems appropriate to now update the state of the art of short-run financial management (SRFM). SRFM reflects a broad, dynamic perspective, in contrast with WCM, which connotes a static view with a balance sheet orientation. Therefore, in this paper SRFM is used to encompass all of the components that affect the inflow and/or outflow of cash through a firm. The objectives of this paper are to interpret the major directions of SRFM research in recent years and present a critical review of the SRFM literature, and, finally, to hypothesize various paths that future SRFM research might follow.

Before evaluating the recent contributions to the SRFM literature, it is useful to identify major SRFM research themes. Exhibit 1 presents a three dimensional framework developed by Howard [88] that characterizes decision problems by their underlying structure. The three dimensions of the problem space are degrees of uncertainty, time dependence, and complexity. The degree of uncertainty ranges from deterministic situations where all variables are known, to highly probabilistic situations where little information is available about any variable. The time dimension ranges from a static condition of no change at a specific moment, to a dynamic condition that reflects changes occurring in future time periods. The complexity dimension is measured in terms of the number of

* The author is grateful to W. Beranek, G. Emery, G. Gallinger, N. Hill, Y. Kim, J. Lakonishok, H. W. Lee, D. McCarty, A. Rappaport, V. Srinivasan, B. K. Stone, and D. T. Whitford for the numerous insights, suggestions, and encouragement.

Source: Reprinted with permission from *Financial Management* (Summer 1988), pp. 41–57. James A. Gentry is the IBE Distinguished Professor of Finance at University of Illinois—Urbana-Champaign.

Exhibit 1 The Problem Space—Models, Authors, and Accounting Information

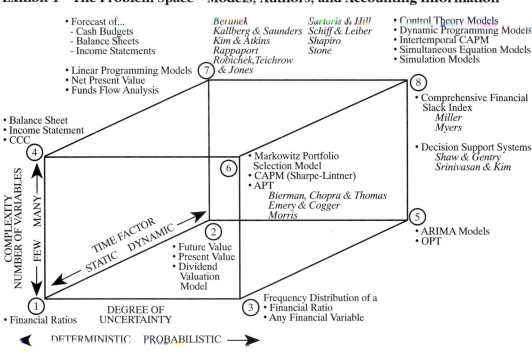

variables required, where the more variables involved in the analysis, the greater the complexity [88, p. 212].

Each corner of the problem space corresponds to the specific types of financial information or models. Corner 1 depicts information for a single variable that is deterministic and static. Financial ratios would be an example of Corner 1 information. Moving up the plane to Corner 4, the number of variables is increased, but the deterministic and static constraints are still present. From a financial perspective, Corner 4 corresponds to balance sheet or income statement information.

Corner 2 reflects a deterministic, single variable problem with a changing (dynamic) orientation. Examples of Corner 2 information would be the calculation of future value or present value of an investment. The dividend valuation model is another example of a Corner 2 model. Corner 7 represents several variables that are changing over time. SRFM examples would be a forecast of monthly cash budgets, monthly pro forma balance sheets, and income statements. Also located at Corner 7 are linear programming models and the net present value (NPV) model, i.e., the discounted cash flow model (DCF).

Corner 3 represents a probabilistic, static, single variable set of information such as the frequency distribution of a financial ratio, funds flow component, or any financial variable. Corner 6 is a probabilistic, static, multivariable problem that resembles Markowitz's portfolio selection model [127]. Exhibit 1 shows that Markowitz added a new plane of thought to financial theory that encompasses the area bounded by Corners 1, 3, 4 and 6. Located at Corner 6 are leading financial theory models, such as the Sharpe-Lintner capital asset pricing model (CAPM), and arbitrage pricing theory (APT).

Uncertainty and dynamic dimensions for a single variable are introduced in Corner 5. Option pricing theory (OPT) is a classic example of a Corner 5 model. Also exemplifying a Corner 5 analysis is the use of past daily cash flow information in an ARIMA model to predict a firm's cash flow position.

SRFM involves the management of real cash flows, assets, and liabilities, and includes many variables that cause a firm's daily flow of cash to change continuously. These characteristics of SRFM are best represented at either Corners 7 or 8 of the Problem Space. The CAPM, APT, and OPT do not focus on the management of real cash flows, assets, and liabilities, and unless modified the CAPM and APT do not possess the dynamic features that are needed to integrate the flows related to SRFM into a total financial planning model.

Corner 8 is the most complex corner location in the problem space. All decision problems could be at Corner 8, because it incorporates all three factors that are indispensable for a meaningful analysis [88, p. 214]. The five classes of models that incorporate all three dimensions are control theory, dynamic programming, intertemporal CAPM, simulation, and simultaneous equations. The problem space provides a structure for classifying contributions to the SRFM literature.

I. A Critical Review of SRFM Literature

Because of several substantive research developments during the past 15 years, a critical review of the major research themes will set the stage for projecting future directions in SRFM.

A. From Simple to Complex Models

Prior to the early 1970s, SRFM was identified with the management of individual current assets or liabilities. Early research used accounting information to model or focus on specific activities such as cash management, accounts receivable management, inventory management, short-term borrowing, and cash budgeting.[1]

As the knowledge base grew, more complex models were developed, linking together two or more SRFM components. Stone identified the natural integration of cash and credit management [183], and the design of a firm's banking system [184, 188]. Schiff and Lieber [162] and Shapiro [165] developed interrelationships that exist between receivables and inventories, while Bierman, Chopra, and Thomas [15] focused on the linkage between optimal working capital and capital structure. The authors of the more advanced models are located at Corners 6 or 7 in Exhibit 1. These models highlight the evolution of SRFM research during the past 15 years.

The early research in SRFM created generally unrelated pockets of knowledge and was conceptually based on balance sheet information. Early research efforts did not create a theory that integrated the cash flow contributions of the SRFM variables into the total value of the firm.

---

[1] For information on each activity, see (respectively) Baumol [4] and Miller and Orr [131]; Cyert, Davidson, and Thompson [36], Cyert and Thompson [37], Benishay [8], Levy [113], Mehta [128, 129], and Greer [78]; Beranek [10], Magee [118], and Snyder [172]; Robichek, Teichroew, and Jones [157]; and Lerner [110].

Monitoring the performance of receivables is the area that has received the greatest attention by researchers.[13] Several authors have shown that DSO (days' sales outstanding in account receivables) is driven by a sales effect and is, therefore, a biased measure. Stone [185] was most lucid in showing that a payment pattern effect was responsible for changes in receivables. Carpenter and Miller (CM) [26] developed an algorithm that measured the changes in receivables caused by sales and collection effects. Gentry and De La Garza (GD) [64, 65] refined the CM algorithm, added a joint effect, and used the trend in sales and collection patterns to measure the receivable strategy employed by management. Gallinger and Ifflander (GI) [61] suggested using the difference between actual and budgeted receivables in a single time period as a technique to measure the factors that cause receivables to change.

Customer payment behavior is crucial in explaining changes in accounts receivable. The standard textbook example assumes collection patterns are stable in the preparation of a cash budget. Kallberg and Saunders (KS) [96] tested the stability of the payment behavior of retail customers and found that when economic conditions worsen, customers accelerate their payments in order to preserve their financial credibility with the retailers. Although untested, discovering if the payment behavior of corporate industrial customers is stable during a recession will be a significant contribution to the credit literature. Finally, evaluating the effect that changes in credit policy have on the level and flow of accounts receivable is a valuable research area in corporate finance.[14]

Why do nonfinancial firms extend credit to their customers, and how do they establish the terms of sale?[15] Emery [44] focused on several financial market imperfections in explaining why firms extend trade credit and how they establish the terms of sale, i.e., a pure financial explanation, a pure operating flexibility motive, and a pure financial intermediary motive. Emery showed that a trade credit lender is familiar with the payment behavior of its customers and can economize on lending transaction costs when extending trade credit. Additionally, the trade credit lender has an advantage over financial intermediaries as related to collection costs. Finally, Emery showed there are increasing opportunity costs to the firm for not extending trade credit and that there are financial market imperfections in the extension of trade credit. These factors establish the limits on credit

---

[13] For example, Freitas [57], Levy [113], Lewellen and Edmister [114], and Stone [185].

[14] Greer [78] developed two normative, analytical models to determine the optimal number of credit applicants to accept. Halloran and Lanser [81] showed that credit policy adjustments in response to anticipated inflation does affect the value of the firm. Hill and Riener [84] used a discounted cash flow model to measure the cost/benefit tradeoffs related to a cash discount decision. Weston and Tuan [201] verified the optimizing methodology of Hill and Riener and found it produced the same results as a generalized approximation method. Mehta [128] derived operating decision rules for credit extension by examining past bad debt levels, credit period length, collection activities, and lost sales levels. Srinivasan and Kim [175], with a comment by Eisenbeis [41], focus on a credit granting classification model.

[15] Bierman and Hausman (BH) [16] offer a set of credit granting models that quantify the expected value of future credit extension opportunities. BH capture an important dimension concerning why firms extend credit. Credit scoring models discriminate between good and bad credit risks, and generate weights for various characteristics of the credit applicant. The total weighted score is used to estimate creditworthiness, which provides a foundation for establishing credit terms [155, 176]. Schwartz [163] concluded that a seller with easy access to capital markets may benefit by extending trade credit to customers who do not have easy access to capital. Lewellen, McConnell, and Scott [116] showed that trade credit cannot be used to increase firm value when financial markets are perfect. Under these circumstances, all acceptable credit terms to sellers and buyers are the present value equivalent of cash terms. They did indicate imperfections in the financial markets may exist which would explain the presence of accounts receivable.

policy and provide the rationale for extending trade. Based on the preceding assumptions, Emery derived an optimal level of accounts receivable for the firm.[16]

Recently, Mian and Smith [130] analyzed the implications of the choice of accounts receivable financing policy that ranged from internal management to subcontracted financing through a factor. They presented seven alternate trade credit administration policies that are used to finance receivables.[17] They found that the larger, more creditworthy firms established captives, while the smaller, riskier firms issued debt secured by accounts receivable.

The literature related to inventories is voluminous. In general, the inventory literature is not found in finance related journals, but rather is located in three separate areas. Topics related to inventory valuation are in the accounting related journals. Inventory planning and control models are in the management science literature, while the effect that inventories have on the aggregate economy is found in the economics literature. From a financial perspective Hall's concept of a stockless production strategy [80] not only stands in sharp contrast to the traditional view of an optimal level of inventory, but it has profound implications on cash flow performance. Stockless production reduces work in process inventory and space needed for production, plus eliminates problems related to quality, production bottlenecks, coordination, obsolescence, shrinkage, and supplier unreliability [94]. The financial benefit of stockless production is an increase in profitability and liquidity, and a decrease in financial leverage. Likewise, the growth of global competition [87, 112] has changed the competitive environment and created a revolution in manufacturing operations. Johnson and Kaplan [94] point out that the revolution was led by new practices emphasizing total quality control, just-in-time inventory systems, and computer integrated manufacturing systems. The result is a change in inventory systems that have a direct effect on financial performance. Johnson and Kaplan emphasize that the challenge for today is to develop new and more flexible approaches to the design of effective cost accounting, management control, and performance measurement systems. The development of these systems highlights the contribution that SRFM has on the total value of the firm.

Robichek, Teichroew, and Jones [157] developed the importance of accounts payable as a primary source of short-run financing in a linear programming model. Gentry and De La Garza [65] have developed algorithms for monitoring payables and receivables. Their model shows payables change because of purchasing, payment, and joint effects. A weighted cash conversion cycle (WCCC) [71] introduces a payables effect that takes into account the relative financing contribution provided by payables in the cash conversion cycle. The payable effect causes the WCCC to be longer than the original CCC.

F. Related Research

Decision makers gain substantive insights from accounting and financial information used in multivariate models [1, 56, 111]. In 14 major studies that predicted corporate bankruptcy, slightly over

---

[16] In another article, Emery [45] discusses the four incentives for trade credit. The incentives are financial, operating, contracting cost, and pricing motives. The theories described provided explanations concerning why and when nonfinancial firms lend money to their customers. Emery [47] develops a positive theory of trade credit based on its use as a financial response to deterministic variations in demand. The operating alternatives to demand are modeled using results from the peak-load pricing literature [47].

[17] They were financing through general corporate credit, establishing a captive finance subsidiary, financing through accounts receivable secured debt (using a credit reporting agency, a credit collection agency, or a credit insurance company), or using a factoring agent.

one-fourth of the significant ratios were related to working capital components [67]. In a study using cash flow components to predict financial failures, the receivables component was one of three significant variables [67, 69]. In a similar study using cash flow components to predict the ratings of bonds that had been reclassified, two of the five significant components were SRFM variables [70]—i.e., inventories and other current liabilities.[18] Financial ratios related to SRFM were used in two major studies to classify loan risk [38, 126], but none were found to be significant.

In determining the major financial characteristics that existed in a set of companies, Chen and Shimerda [29] and Pinches et al. [145] found seven principal components that emerged from a cross-section of companies. Four of the components were SRFM variables: short-term liquidity, cash position, inventory, and receivables turnover. In explaining the differences between large and small companies, Walker and Petty [199] found dividend policy, relative liquidity, and profitability emerged as the three most significant discriminators. Stoll and Curley [181] found the current ratio and the quick ratio increased as the firm size became larger. These two studies support the general belief that a shortage of working capital is a problem for small firms. Recent studies [23, 58, 124] have developed a theoretical link between market determined risk, beta, and the degree of operating and financial leverage. These studies show that SRFM policies and practices affect cash inflow and outflow results, which are highly correlated to the variance of market rates of return on a firm's common stock.

II. Future Directions

A. Perspectives

In 1973, Smith [170] presented a forecast that focused on future directions and developments in working capital management research. He envisioned a dynamic model that would incorporate the tradeoffs between liquidity and profitability and that would reflect the interrelationships among the management of current assets and current liabilities. Smith advocated the development of a model that simulated various financial strategies and generated cash budgets, pro forma balance sheets, and income statements. Finally, he saw the availability of better data bases and the spirit of cooperation between academics and business executives as a motivating force that would integrate short and long-run issues into a common theoretical framework. It has taken more than a decade for Smith's early insights to materialize.

In 1986, Srinivasan and Kim (S&K) [174] suggested that cash management decisions be grouped as operational and infrastructural, and that research should be directed toward developing control measures for each major group of decisions. The operational decisions are related to cash forecasting, investing, borrowing. and cash position. Infrastructure decisions relate to building support systems for collecting deposits, controlling disbursements, determining target balances, transferring cash, and establishing credit lines.

Porter [152, 153] and Rappaport [154] have developed a solid structure that will motivate future research in the SRFM area. Porter's competitive analysis model provides a solid anchor for

---

[18] SRFM ratios were included in all of the following studies designed to predict bond ratings [3, 6, 7, 86, 98, 144, 146, 147, 148, 151, 200].

designing and evaluating strategic plans. In concert, Porter's value chain and Rappaport's discounted cash flow information system show how value is created in a company and, thereby, make it possible to determine if a chosen strategy will result in a company achieving a competitive advantage. The shareholder value approach shows that SRFM decisions related to operating inflows, operating outflows, and working capital are major contributors to the value creation process. During the next decade, research that focuses on the understanding of the linkage between SRFM decisions and shareholders' value creation will provide new discoveries, insights, and enlightenment.

B. Valuation Models

Earlier we observed that the cash flow components contributing directly to the value of the firm have been integrated into the discounted cash flow model (DCF) and the CAPM. However, the CAPM is unable to capture the dynamics of the intertemporal changes that are pervasive among the SRFM cash flow components, and the DCF model does not provide a direct measure of the risk-return tradeoff that is present in the CAPM. Ideally, what is needed is a valuation model that incorporates the nonlinear dynamics of the cash flow components, accommodates the simultaneous interaction effects among these components, and captures the risk/return tradeoff perspective.

There are several possible paths concerning valuation models which future research may follow. Two approaches that offer promise are simultaneous equations [59] and control theory models [30]. Brealey and Myers [21, p. 789] are optimistic that the option pricing theory may provide fresh insight into the unraveling of this highly complex valuation process. Lam and Chen [106] provide a contingent chain approach related to credit policy. Jackson [89] has developed a nonlinear dynamics approach that appears to have significant potential for integrating cash inflows and outflows from several sectors into a total valuation model. The literature on fluid dynamics [195] may provide another theoretical approach for building a complete valuation model [123]. Finally, it may be that the SRFM process is too complex to be integrated realistically into a total valuation model. In that event the development of partial valuation models that focus on lowering cost or reducing risk may be more achievable.

C. Positive Research

In the future more attention will be devoted to developing positive theories of working capital management. Many descriptive contributions have been the result of examining trade credit or cash management behavior under the economic conditions of imperfect markets.[19] One approach to a positive theory of why firms extend trade credit is that the firm extending credit has more information than the buyer of the product. This concept is referred to as the asymmetry of information and has provided unique insight in explaining the implications of trade credit behavior [169].

Emery [46] suggests the need to stop explaining the size of cash balances and to start explaining the utilization of cash management services. Emery's approach focuses attention on the information used for decision making and on the costs associated with collecting the amounts receivable. Porter [152, 153] advocates analyzing the competitive position of the buyer and seller in evaluating the competitive position of a firm. Determining the bargaining power of the buyer and the seller

---

[19] For example, see Beranek [11], Bierman and Hausman [16], Dirick and Wakeman [39], Ferris [52], Greer [78], Smith [169], Schwartz [163], and Schwartz and Whitcomb [164].

provides a fruitful approach for explaining collection and payment behavior and the rationale for existing credit terms.[20]

An undeveloped area in financial management is the management and control of inventory. The accounting literature provides the best source of information for explaining the valuation of inventories. Equally important is understanding the efficiency involved in managing and controlling inventory. One of the most critical problems facing management is predicting and controlling inventory when there are errors in forecasting the demand for a product, In turn, these forecasting errors create uncertainty in purchasing and production, which results in inefficiencies in managing inventories.

By examining decision making under conditions of uncertainty, we may be able to build a framework for enhancing our understanding of collection and payment behavior. The positive theorist is interested in what causes risk and how firms try to control the risks that are present in a credit granting environment.[21] Additionally, credit is considered a marketing tool that directly affects the price of the product. Thus, exploring, creating, controlling, or avoiding risk appears to be a productive approach to developing positive theories related to cash and credit management.

Kaplan [97] observes that cost systems are designed to value inventory for financial and tax statements. He believes these systems are not giving managers accurate and timely information needed to promote operating efficiencies to measure product cost. A valuable contribution to the SRFM literature would be the development of positive theories that explain the financial implications of inventory on firm valuation.

D. Financial Slack

What is the value of liquidity? According to Brealey and Myers [21, pp. 790–791], determining the value of liquidity is one of the ten unsolved problems in finance. They indicate that liquidity is a matter of degree and that the relevant strategic question for management is "How should it divide its total investment between relatively liquid assets?" We do not have a theory that explains how much cash a firm should hold or be able to acquire quickly without affecting its cost. In an anecdotal sense, we observe that liquidity is most appreciated during a financial crisis and is not as important when financial stress is relatively low.

Future research efforts should focus on creating a comprehensive financial slack index. A liquidity system measure should take into account the relative liquidity of each asset class (e.g., receivables, raw materials, finished goods), and the ability to access capital or money markets [14, 189]. Liquidity should be judged on a continuum and each asset or source of funds rank ordered according to its liquidity characteristics, Additionally, an analysis of daily cash inflow and outflow patterns provides separate components for a liquidity measure. The qualitative characteristics of a firm's assets, liabilities, and cash flows supply another component for a liquidity measure. Combining the qualitative and quantitative components would provide the information needed to create a comprehensive financial slack index (CFSI) (Miller [132] and Myers [135]). Exhibit 1 shows the CFSI incorporates all three dimensions of the problem space and is located at Corner 8. The development of

---

[20] See Beranek [11] for a series of hypothesized relationships that serve as the basis of future research topics in the area of positive theory building.

[21] Norgaard [140] focused on building a positive theory that would have zero working capital in the firm.

a comprehensive financial slack index should lead to the evolution of a theory that integrates the dimension of liquidity into the value of the firm.

E. Technology and Information Effects

During the last decade electronic technology has created a revolution in activities related to managing the inflows and outflows of cash and controlling inventories [83]. There is little doubt that future growth and refinement of decision-support systems and management of information will result in changes in operating management achievements that are currently unimaginable. Corporate strategy will focus on using capital resources to improve the decision support systems and the management of information in order to gain a competitive advantage and improve operating performance [63]. Firm value is created through the building of these systems, and thus short-run financial management research is directly connected to the evolution of the information age. New technology and data bases [83] will be at the forefront of advances in short-run financial management research in the next decade, since a natural interrelationship exists between SRFM and corporate strategic management based on the substantive contributions that operating cash flows make to firm value. In the future there should be significant growth in research that explores the connection among financial information systems, financial management activities related to operations, and strategic management of the firm.

Daily cash flow information is the cornerstone for building a deeper understanding of SRFM. Cash flow data files explicitly show the patterns of cash inflows and outflows, which are the foundation for determining what causes cash flow components to change, and for analyzing the intertemporal relationships among the inflow and outflow components [76, 77]. Although currently these cash flow data bases are not easily accessed, they are the ultimate information source for developing theoretical relationships and testing hypotheses related to SRFM. Perhaps in the future there will be an institutionalized cash flow data base equivalent to CRSP or Compustat. The availability of cash flow data bases will stimulate new research efforts and provide fresh insights and new theoretical developments into SRFM.

In preparing cash budgets and in monitoring receivables and payables, a major problem is predicting the timing of cash inflows and outflows.[22] The timing of cash inflows and outflows is closely related to the payment behavior of the customers and to the firm's disbursement behavior to suppliers. Corporate software programs for managing and controlling receivables and payables make it possible to measure and evaluate the stability of customer payment behavior and the supplier disbursement patterns. The profiles of payment and disbursement patterns are affected by competitive factors in the industry and firm, as well as seasonal and random effects. The study of payment and disbursement behavior should lead to improved techniques and models for predicting cash inflows and outflows. One natural outgrowth of this research should be a better understanding of the relationships among customer payment behavior, disbursement behavior to suppliers, and a firm's value creation process.

Porter and Rappaport provide an economic framework for evaluating the contribution of various SRFM cash flow effects to the value creation process. Quarterly financial statement information

---

[22] For example, see Bowen, Burgstahler, and Daley [19], Emery [42], Ferguson and Hill [50], Lewellen and Edmister [114], Lewellen and Johnson [115], and Stone [188].

in Compustat II is ideal for analyzing relationships among key SRFM variables and discovering how they contribute to the value of a firm.[23] Additionally, Compustat II makes possible the study of intertemporal value chain-cash flow relationships that exist among cash based funds flow components for firms in different competitive environments.[24]

Since managing receivables and payables is a massive task for larger companies, a few firms are experimenting with new procedures related to purchases and payments. Where the customer and supplier have a well-established relationship, and the supplier has a record of delivering quality goods, the customer places an order with the supplier and simultaneously encloses payment without receiving an invoice. The result of this action is a substantive reduction in operating costs. Additionally, a few large corporations have changed to an electronic disbursement system for paying their suppliers [83]. If these procedures are followed by large and/or mid-size companies, then there may be dramatic changes in cash receipt management in the next decade. These and other changes in SRFM procedures can cause substantive changes in value. Compustat II information may be used in the future to evaluate these changes in accounting procedures and will develop the effect of these changes on the creation of value.

In summary, there are several new research developments on the horizon that should lead to a better understanding of the linkage between SRFM and the value creation process. As these linkages are developed, SRFM will be naturally integrated into valuation models of the firm. The ultimate goal is the development of Corner 8 valuation models that incorporate key theoretical relationships among long and short-run variables.

F. Artificial Intelligence

Several SRFM activities are natural applications for artificial intelligence (AI) systems [166, 173, 174]. These include credit analysis and management, credit scoring, cash management coupled with short-term lending and borrowing decisions, management and control of inventories, and production planning and control. The information used in the knowledge-based system is frequently acquired by the method of learning by being told. The system acquires its domain knowledge from experienced decision makers in the field, such as experienced credit or cash managers, and transforms the knowledge into the appropriate form.

Due to the fact that learning is an important feature of any intelligent system, more advanced AI systems are equipped with learning capabilities. This learning dimension comes into play when the system (1) learns decision rules from the knowledge base and (2) refines existing rules by observing prior problem solving experience. To achieve these learning functions poses an important design issue related to the inductive inference techniques used in rule learning and knowledge acquisition.

---

[23] Studying the interrelationships among the leading working capital components offers unique promise toward building new theoretical understanding of cash inflows and outflows. Only a few researchers have pursued this topic. Haley and Higgins [79] analyze the relationship between inventory policy (order time) and trade credit policy (order quantity and payment time). Schiff and Lieber [162] present an integrated dynamic model for receivables and inventory management. The model optimizes credit and inventory policy. Shapiro [166] discusses inventory purchase strategies and credit granting policies in soft currency countries. Refer to footnote 3 for additional information.

[24] The "Statement of Cash Flows" based on the direct method recognizes that cash inflows and outflows are generated through the interaction of all major balance sheet and income statement components. The data from the Statement of Cash Flows supplies the necessary information for modeling the cash flow process in a simultaneous equation framework. In the future, a simultaneous equation approach can be used to determine the complex relationships that exist among the various cash flow components.

The models developed for SRFM will employ production rules that represent basic knowledge of the system being created. The success of the AI models for SRFM will rest on the ability to structure the decision process being created and to design appropriate production rules that correctly represent the system being created. The economic payoff for creating AI systems is quite high in areas related to credit and/or cash management and in production and/or inventory management. Within the next five years, the development of these AI systems will provide fresh insight and new perspectives related to SRFM.

G. Financial Instruments and Other Topics

The need to shift risk via financial futures or options will experience substantial growth in the next decade. Emerging financial strategies create new financial contracts that shift a firm's risk exposure to the marketplace. The growth of the derivative securities market is closely related to SRFM, and it provides a natural base for growth and development, e.g., financial futures and options [17, 18, 101, 105, 149, 167, 196], and swaps [168, 197]. An interest rate swap occurs when a company with one type of debt instrument agrees to swap interest payments with a firm that has issued a different type of debt instrument. Additionally, investment banking firms are creating new financial instruments to meet specialized corporate needs and extend the rate of return effects on the short-run portfolio [207, 108]. These new instruments are providing new sources of cash as well as opportunities to meet SRFM investment and borrowing needs. During the next decade, these new instruments will provide numerous directions for future SRFM research.

There are a variety of changes occurring in the business environment that will significantly affect future developments related to SRFM. The globalization of markets [87, 94, 112] introduces new control and management systems that directly change the in and out-flow of cash, the allocation of costs, and the level of inventories, receivables, and payables. The long-run impacts of financial and organizational restructuring are not understood, but they will introduce significant changes in SRFM [40]. The need to devise short-run performance measures that are consistent with a firm's strategies and its product and process technologies [94] will have a profound effect on the future directions of SRFM. The change to a statement of cash flows [49, 55] introduces a new measurement system which will significantly enhance the contributions of SRFM to the value creation process.

III. Conclusion

SRFM is closely related to the operations management of a firm and plays a key role in creating stockholder value. The theoretical linkage between cash flows generated from SFRM and strategic financial management decision making is well-established. Because SRFM is associated with operations, it does not possess the romance of financial restructuring or the deal making related to a takeover. Nevertheless, the creation of net cash flows through SRFM decision making is how long-run value is created for stockholders.

Future research will focus on the creation of valuation models that incorporate the nonlinear dynamics of the cash flow components, accommodate the simultaneous interaction effects among the components, and capture the risk return perspective. Liquidity is another area where future research will produce a comprehensive index that will measure financial slack. Furthermore, linking liquidity to valuation theory will be a substantive contribution to the SRFM literature. Corporate decision support systems and the management of financial information form a new research centerpiece for SRFM.

Daily or weekly cash flow data files will serve to enhance our knowledge of the liquidity system. The foundation for future directions of SRFM research is built on artificial intelligence model building, information technology expansion, risk shifting through derivative securities, the globalization of markets and devising short-run performance measures that are consistent with a firm's strategies, and product and process technologies.

Financial research has not yet focused on SRFM behavioral dimensions that cause the creation or destruction of shareholder value. e.g., cash flow forecasting errors, customer payment patterns, supplier disbursement patterns, or inventory cost patterns. Behavioral research related to SRFM may grow rapidly in the future and provide an entirely new set of issues.

References

1. E. I. Altman, R. B. Avery, R. A. Eisenbeis, and J. F. Sinkey, Jr. *Application of Classification Techniques in Business, Banking and Finance.* Greenwich, CT, JAI Press, 1981.

2. Y. Amihud and H. Mendelson. "Liquidity and Asset Prices: Financial Management Implications." *Financial Management* (Spring 1988), 5–15.

3. J. S. Ang and K. A. Patel. "Bond Rating Methods: Comparison and Validation." *Journal of Finance* (May 1975), 631–40.

4. W. J. Baumol. "The Transactions Demand for Cash: An Inventory Theoretic Approach." *Quarterly Journal of Economics* (November 1952), 545–56.

5. P. Beehler. *Contemporary Cash Management.* New York, Irwin, 1983.

6. A. Belkaoui. "Industrial Bond Ratings: A New Look." *Financial Management* (Autumn 1980), 44–51.

7. ———. *Industrial Bonds and the Rating Process.* Westport, CT, Quorum Books, 1983.

8. H. Benishay. "A Stochastic Model of Credit Sales Debt." *Journal of the American Statistical Association* (December 1966), 1010–28.

9. W. Beranek. *Analysis for Financial Decisions.* Homewood, IL, Irwin, 1963.

10. ———. "Financial Implications of Lot Size Inventory Models." *Management Science* (April 1967), B401–B408.

11. ———. "Towards a Positive Theory of Working Capital." Working Paper, September 1986.

12. ———. "An Historical Perspective of Research and Practice in Working Capital Management." In *Advances in Working Capital Management,* Y. H. Kim (ed.). Reading, MA, Addison-Wesley, 1987.

13. R. A. Bettis. "Modern Theory, Corporate Strategy and Public Policy: Three Conundrums." *Academy of Management Review* (1983), 406–15.

14. A. K. Bhattacharya and G. W. Gallinger. "The Relationship between Firm Value, Capital Structure and Liquidity: A Simulation." Working Paper, 1987.

15. H. K. Bierman, K. Chopra, and L. J. Thomas. "Ruin Consideration: Optimal Working Capital and Capital Structure." *Journal of Financial and Quantitative Analysis* (March 1975), 119–28.

16. H. Bierman, Jr. and W. H. Hausman. "The Credit Granting Decision." *Management Science* (April 1970), B519–B532.

17. S. J. Block and T. S. Gallagher. "The Use of Interest Rate Futures and Options by Corporate Financial Managers." *Financial Management* (Autumn 1986), 73–78.

18. R. Bookstabler. "The Valuation and Exposure Management of Bonds with Imbedded Options." In *The Handbook of Fixed Income Securities,* Second Edition. F. J. Fabozzi and I. M. Pollack (eds.). Homewood, IL, Dow Jones-Irwin, 1987, 856–90.

19. R. M. Bowen, D. Burgstahler, and L. A. Daley. "Evidence on the Relationships between Earnings and Various Measures of Cash Flow." *Accounting Review* (October 1986), 713–25.

20. K. Boyd and V. A. Mabert. "A Two Stage Forecasting Approach at Chemical Bank of New York for Check Processing." *Journal of Bank Research* (1977), 101–07.

21. A. Brealey and S. Myers. *Principles of Corporate Finance.* Third Edition, New York, McGraw-Hill, 1988.

22. M. J. Brennan and E. S. Schwarz. "Optimal Financial Policy and Firm Valuation." *Journal of Finance* (July 1984), 593–609.

23. M. Brenner and S. Schmidt. "Asset Characteristics and Systematic Risk." *Financial Management* (Winter 1978), 33–39.

24. K. C. Brown and S. L. Lummer. "The Cash Management Implications of a Hedged Dividend Capture Strategy." *Financial Management* (Winter 1984), 7–17.

25. ———. "A Re-Examination of the Covered Call Option Strategy for Corporate Cash Management." *Financial Management* (Summer 1986), 13–17.

26. M. D. Carpenter and J. E. Miller. "A Reliable Framework for Monitoring Accounts Receivable." *Financial Management* (Winter 1979), 37–40.

27. C. J. Casey and N. J. Bartczak. "Cash Flow—It's Not the Bottom Line." *Harvard Business Review* (July/August 1984), 60–66.

28. ———. "Operating Cash Flow Data and Financial Distress: Some Empirical Evidence." *Journal of Accounting Research* (Spring 1985), 384–401.

29. K. H. Chen and T. A. Shimerda. "An Empirical Analysis of Useful Ratios." *Financial Management* (Spring 1981), 51–60.

30. G. C. Chow. "Analyzing Econometric Models by Control Methods." In *Evaluating the Reliability of Macroeconomic Models,* G. C. Chow and P. Corti (eds.). Chicester, U.K., Wiley, 1982.

31. R. A. Cohn and J. J. Pringle. "Steps Toward an Integration of Corporate Financial Theory." In *Readings on the Management of Working Capital,* Keith V. Smith (ed.). St. Paul, West Publishing Company, 1980, 35–42.

32. I. Cooper and J. Franks. "Treasury Performance Measurement." *Midland Corporate Finance Journal* (Winter 1987), 29–43.

33. T. Copeland and S. Khourg. "A Theory of Credit Extension with Default Risk and Systematic Risk." *Engineering Economist* (Fall 1979), 35–51.

34. G. Cornuejols, M. L. Fisher, and G. L. Nemhauser. "Location of Bank Accounts to Optimize Float: An Analytical Study of Exact and Approximate Algorithms." *Management Science* (1977), 780–810.

35. D. Cox and H. Miller. *The Theory of Stochastic Processes.* New York, Wiley, 1965.

36. R. M. Cyert, H. J. Davidson, and G. L. Thompson. "Estimation of the Allowance for Doubtful Accounts by Markov Chains." *Management Science* (April 1962), 287–303.

37. R. M. Cyert and G. L. Thompson. "Selecting a Portfolio of Credit Risks by Markov Chains." *The Journal of Business* (January 1968), 39–46.

38. J. R. Dietrich and R. S. Kaplan. "Empirical Analysis of the Commercial Loan Classification Decision." *Accounting Review* (January 1982), 18–38.

39. Y. M. Dirick and L. Wakeman. "An Extension of the Bierman-Hausman Model for Credit Granting." *Management Review* (1976), 1229–37.

40. P. F. Drucker. "The Coming of the New Organization." *Harvard Business Review* (January/February 1988), 45–53.

41. R. A. Eisenbeis. "Discussion." *Journal of Finance* (July 1987), 681–83.

42. G. W. Emery. "Some Empirical Evidence on the Properties of Daily Cash Flow." *Financial Management* (Spring 1981), 21–28.

43. ———. "Discussion: The Design of a Company's Banking System." *Journal of Finance* (May 1983), 387–89.

44. ———. "A Pure Financial Explanation for Trade Credit." *Journal of Financial and Quantitative and Financial Analysis* (September 1984), 271–85.

45. ———. "Positive Theories of Trade Credit." Working Paper, Indiana University, January 1986.

46. ———. "Discussion of: 'Towards a Positive Theory of Working Capital,' by William Beranek." Presented at Financial Management Association Meetings, October 1986.

47. ———. "An Optimal Response to Variable Demand." *Journal of Financial and Qualitative Analysis* (June 1987), 209–25.

48. G. W. Emery and K. O. Cogger. "The Measurement of Liquidity." *Journal of Accounting Research* (Autumn 1982), 290–303.

49. FASB Exposure Draft. *Statement of Cash Flows.* Ernst & Whinney, October 1986.

50. D. M. Ferguson and N. C. Hill. "Cash Flow Timeline Management: The Next Frontier of Cash Management." *Journal of Cash Management* (May/June 1985), 12–22.

51. D. M. Ferguson and S. F. Mairer. "Disbursement Design for the 1980's." *Journal of Cash Management* (November 1982), 56–69.

52. J. S. Ferris. "A Transaction Theory of Trade Credit Use." *Quarterly Journal of Economics* (May 1981), 243–70.

53. B. D. Fielitz and D. L. White. "A Two Stage Solution Procedure for the Lockbox Problem." *Management Science* (August 1981), 881–86

54. ———. "An Evaluation and Linking of Alternative Solution Procedures for the Lock Box Location Problem." *Journal of Bank Research* (1982), 17–27.

55. Financial Accounting Series. *Statement of Cash Flows.* Exposure Draft of a Proposed Statement of Financial Accounting Standards. Stamford, CT, Financial Accounting Standards Board, July 31, 1986.

56. G. Foster. *Financial Statement Analysis,* Second Edition. Englewood Cliffs, NJ, Prentice Hall, 1986.

57. L. Freitas. "Monitoring Accounts Receivable." *Management Accounting* (September 1973), 18–21.

58. J. M. Gahlon and J. A. Gentry. "On the Relationship between Systematic Risk and the Degrees of Operating and Financial Leverage." *Financial Management* (Summer 1982), 15–23.

59. A. R. Gallant. "Three Stage Least Squares and Estimation for a System of Simultaneous, Nonlinear, Implicit Equations." *Journal of Econometrics* (1974), 71–88.

60. G. W. Gallinger and P. B. Healey. *Liquidity Analysis and Management.* Reading, MA, Addison-Wesley, 1987.

61. G. W. Gallinger and A. J. Ifflander. "Monitoring Accounts Receivable Using Variance Analysis." *Financial Management* (Winter 1986), 69–76.

62. J. A. Gentry. "Integrating Working Capital and Capital Investment Processes." In *Readings on the Management of Working Capital,* Keith V. Smith (ed.). West Publishing Company, 1980, 585–608.

63. ———. "Management of Information, Competitive Advantages and Short-Run Financial Management Systems." In *Advances in Working Capital Management,* Y. H. Kim (ed.). Reading, MA, Addison-Wesley, 1988.

64. J. A. Gentry and J. M. De La Garza. "A Generalized Model for Monitoring Accounts Receivable." *Financial Management* (Winter 1985), 28–38.

65. ———. "Monitoring Payables and Receivables." Faculty Working Paper No. 1358, College of Commerce and Business Administration, University of Illinois, May 1987.

66. J. A. Gentry and H. W. Lee. "An Integrated Cash Flow Model of the Firm." Faculty Working Paper No. 1314, College of Commerce and Business Administration, University of Illinois, December 1986.

67. J. A. Gentry, P. Newbold, and D. T. Whitford. "Bankruptcy, Working Capital and Funds Flow Components." *Managerial Finance: Key Issues in Working Capital Management* (1984), 26–39.

68. ———. "Classifying Bankrupt Firms with Funds Flow Components." *Journal of Accounting Research* (Spring 1985a), 140–60.

69. ———. "Predicting Bankruptcy: If Cash Flow's Not the Bottom Line, What Is?" *Financial Analysts Journal* (September/October 1985b), 47–56.

70. ———. "Predicting Industrial Bond Ratings with a Probit Model and Funds Flow Components." *Financial Review* (Summer 1988), 269–86.

71. J. A. Gentry, R. Vaidyananthan, and H. W. Lee. "A Weighted Cash Conversion Cycle." Faculty Working Paper No. 1315, College of Commerce and Business Administration, University of Illinois, December 1986, revised March 1988.

72. R. H. Gilmer. "The Optimal Level of Liquid Assets: An Empirical Test." *Financial Management* (Winter 1985), 39–43.

73. L. J. Gitman, D. K. Forrester, and J. R. Forrester. "Maximizing Cash Disbursement Float." *Financial Management* (Summer 1976), 15–24.

74. L. J. Gitman, E. R. Moses, and J. T. White. "An Assessment of Corporate Cash Management Practices." *Financial Management* (Spring 1979), 32–41.

75. M. J. Gombola, M. E. Haskins, J. E. Ketz, and D. D. Williams. "Cash Flow in Bankruptcy Prediction." *Financial Management* (Winter 1987), 55–65.

76. M. J. Gombola and J. E. Ketz. "A Note on Cash Flow and Classification Patterns of Financial Ratios." *The Accounting Review* (January 1983a), 105–14.

77. ———. "Financial Ratio Patterns in Retail and Manufacturing Organizations." *Financial Management* (Summer 1983b), 45–56.

78. C. C. Greer. "The Optimal Credit Acceptance Policy." *Journal of Financial and Quantitative Analysis* (December 1967), 399–416.

79. C. W. Haley and R. G. Higgins. "Inventory Control Theory and Trade Credit Financing." *Management Science,* Vol. 20 (December 1973), 964–71.

80. R. W. Hall. *Zero Inventories.* Homewood, IL, Dow Jones-Irwin, 1983.

81. J. A. Halloran and H. P. Lanser. "The Credit Policy Decision in an Inflationary Environment." *Financial Management* (Winter 1981), 31–38.

82. E. A. Helfert. *Techniques of Financial Analysis,* Fifth Edition. Homewood, IL, Irwin, 1982.

83. N. C. Hill, D. M. Ferguson, and B. K. Stone. "Electronic Data Interchange: An Introduction and Status Report." Working Paper presented at Financial Management Association Meetings, October 13, 1987.

84. N. C. Hill and K. D. Riener. "Determining the Cash Discount on the Firm's Credit Policy." *Financial Management* (Spring 1979), 68–73.

85. R. Homonoff and D. W. Mullins, Jr. *Cash Management.* Lexington, MA, Lexington Books, 1975.

86. J. D. Horrigan. "The Determination of Long-Term Credit Standing with Financial Ratios." *Empirical Research in Accounting: Selected Studies, 1966* (1966), 44–62.

87. T. Hout, M. E. Porter, and E. Rudden. "How Global Companies Win Out." *Harvard Business Review* (September/October 1982), 98–108.

88. R. A. Howard. "The Foundations of Decision Analysis." *IEEE Transactions on Systems Sciences and Cybernetics* (September 1968), 212–13.

89. E. A. Jackson. *Perspectives on Nonlinear Dynamics,* Volumes 1 and 2. London, Cambridge University Press, 1988.

90. M. J. Jensen. "Takeovers: Folklore and Science." *Harvard Business Review* (November/December 1984).

91. ———. "The Takeover Controversy: Analysis and Evidence." *Midland Corporate Finance Journal* (Summer 1986), 6–32.

92. M. J. Jensen and R. S. Ruback. "The Market for Corporate Control: The Scientific Evidence." *Journal of Financial Economics* (April 1983), 5–50.

93. M. Joehnk, O. Bowlin, and J. Petty. "Preferred Dividend Rolls: A Viable Strategy for Corporate Money Managers." *Financial Management* (Summer 1980), 78–87.

94. H. T. Johnson and R. S. Kaplan. *Relevance Lost.* Boston, MA, Harvard Business School Press, 1987.

95. J. G. Kallberg and K. Parkinson. *Current Asset Management,* New York, Wiley, 1984.

96. J. G. Kallberg and A. Saunders. "Market Chain Approaches to the Analysis of Payment Behavior of Retail Credit Customers." *Financial Management* (Summer 1983), 5–14.

97. R. S. Kaplan. "One Cost System Isn't Enough." *Harvard Business Review* (January/February 1988), 61–66.

98. R. S. Kaplan and G. Urwitz. "Statistical Model of Bond Ratings: A Methodological Inquiry." *Journal of Business* (April 1979), 231–61.

99. P. Katz and S. Katz. "The Differential Effect of Bond Rating Changes Among Industrial and Public Utility Bonds by Maturity." *Journal of Business* (April 1976), 226–39.

100. S. Katz. "The Price Adjustment Process of Bonds to Rating Reclassifications: A Test of Market Efficiency." *Journal of Finance* (May 1974), 551–59.

101. I. J. Kawaller. "How and Why to Hedge a Short-Term Portfolio." *Journal of Cash Management* (January/February 1985), 26–30.

102. Y. H. Kim and J. C. Atkins. "Evaluating Investments in Accounts Receivable: A Wealth Maximization Framework." *Journal of Finance* (May 1978), 403–12.

103. Y. H. Kim and V. Srinivasan. "Deterministic Cash Flow Management: State of the Art and Research Directions." *Omega* (1986), 145–66.

104. W. D. Knight. "Working Capital Management—Satisfying vs. Optimization." *Financial Management* (Spring 1972), 33–40.

105. R. W. Kopprasch and V. J. Haghani. "Exchange-Traded Options on Fixed Income Securities." In *The Handbook of Fixed Income Securities,* Second Edition. F. J. Fabozzi and L. M. Pollack (eds.). Homewood, IL, Dow Jones-Irwin, 1987, 809–55.

106. C. H. Lam and A. H. Chen. "A Note on Optimal Credit and Pricing Policy Under Uncertainty: A Contingent Claims Approach." *Journal of Finance* (December 1986), 1141–48.

107. M. L. Leibowitz. "Horizon Analysis: An Analytical Framework for Managed Bond Portfolios." In *The Handbook of Fixed Income Securities,* Second Edition. F. J. Fabozzi and L. M. Pollack (eds.). Homewood, IL, Dow Jones-Irwin, 1987a, 633–45.

108. ———. "Analysis of Yield Curves." In *The Handbook of Fixed Income Securities,* Second Edition. F. J. Fabozzi and L. M. Pollack (eds.). Homewood, IL, Dow Jones-Irwin, 1987b, 654–75.

109. K. W. Lemke. "The Evaluation of Liquidity: An Analytical Study." *Journal of Accounting Research* (Spring 1980), 47–77.

110. E. M. Lerner. "Simulating a Cash Budget." *California Management Review* (Winter 1968), 79–86.

111. B. Lev. *Financial Statement Analysis.* Englewood Cliffs, NJ, Prentice Hall, 1974.

112. T. Levitt. "The Globalization of Markets." *Harvard Business Review* (May-June 1983), 92–102.

113. F. K. Levy. "An Application of Heuristic Problem Solving to Accounts Receivable Management." *Management Science* (February 1966), B236–B244.

114. W. G. Lewellen and R. O. Edmister. "A General Model for Accounts Receivable and Control." *Journal of Financial and Quantitative Analysis* (March 1973), 145–206.

115. W. G. Lewellen and R. W. Johnson. "Better Way to Monitor Accounts Receivable." *Harvard Business Review* (May/June 1972), 101–09.

116. W. G. Lewellen, J. J. McConnell, and J. A. Scott. "Capital Market Influences on Trade Credit Policies." *Journal of Financial Research* (Summer 1980), 105–13.

117. Z. Lieber and Y. E. Orgler. "An Integrated Model for Accounts Receivable." *Management Science* (October 1975), 212–19.

118. J. F. Magee. "Guides to Inventory Policy: Problems of Uncertainty." *Harvard Business Review* (March/April 1956), 103–16.

119. S. F. Maier and J. A. Vander Weide. "A Unified Location Model for Cash Disbursement and Lockbox Collections." *Journal of Bank Research* (1976–1977), 166–72.

120. ———. "A Practical Approach to Short-Run Financial Planning." *Financial Management* (Winter 1978), 10–16.

121. ———. "What Lock Box and Disbursement Models Really Do." *Journal of Finance* (May 1983), 361–71.

122. ———. *Managing Corporate Liquidity: An Introduction to Working Capital Management.* New York, Wiley, 1985.

123. P. Mampilly. "Pipe Line Theory on Working Capital." *Vikalpa* (July 1976), 7–21.

124. G. N. Mandelker and S. G. Rhee. "The Impact of the Degrees of Operating Leverage and Financial Leverage on Systematic Risk of Common Stock." *Journal of Financial and Quantitative Analysis* (March 1984), 45–57.

125. J. C. T. Mao. "Application of Linear Programming to the Short Term Financing Decision." *Engineering Economist* (1968), 221–41.

126. M. L. Marais, J. M. Patell, and M. A. Wolfson. "The Experimental Design of Classification Models: An Application of Recursive Partitioning and Bootstrapping to Commercial Bank Loan Classifications." *Studies on Current Econometric Issues in Accounting Research,* supplement to *Journal of Accounting Research* (1984), 87–114.

127. H. M. Markowitz. *Portfolio Selection.* New York, Wiley, 1959.

128. D. Mehta. "The Formulation of Credit Policy Models." *Management Science* (October 1968), B30–B50.

129. ———. "Optimal Credit Policy Selection: A Dynamic Approach." *Journal of Financial and Quantitative Analysis* (December 1970), 421–44.

130. S. L. Mian and C. W. Smith, Jr. "Accounts Receivable Management." Working Paper presented at 1987 Financial Management Association Meetings, October 14, 1987.

131. M. H. Miller and D. Orr. "A Model of the Demand for Money by Firms." *Quarterly Journal of Economics* (August 1966), 413–35.

132. T. W. Miller. "A Systems View of Short-Term Investment Management." Working Paper, December 1986.

133. T. W. Miller and B. K. Stone. "Daily Cash Forecasting and Seasonal Resolution: Alternative Models and Techniques for Using the Distribution Approach." *Journal of Financial and Quantitative Analysis* (September 1985), 335–51.

134. J. R. Morris. "The Role of Cash Balances in Firm Valuation." *Journal of Financial and Quantitative Analysis* (December 1983), 533–45.

135. S. C. Myers. "The Capital Structure Puzzle." *Journal of Finance* (July 1984), 575–92.

136. S. C. Myers and N. Majluf. "Corporate Financing and Investment Decisions When Firms Have Information Investors Do Not Have." *Journal of Financial Economics* (1984), 187–221.

137. "Finance Theory and Financial Strategy." *Midland Corporate Finance Journal* (Spring 1987), 5–13.

138. R. M. Nauss and R. E. Markland. "Theory and Application of an Optimizing Procedure for Lock Box Location Analysis." *Management Science* (1974), 855–65.

139. ———. "Solving the Lockbox Location Problem." *Financial Management* (Spring 1979), 21–31.

140. R. Norgaard. "Working Capital Research and Theory." Working Paper, presented at the Third Symposium on Cash, Treasury and Working Capital, October 14, 1987.

141. Y. Orgler. *Cash Management: Methods and Models.* Belmont, CA, Wadsworth, 1970.

142. ———. "An Unequal Period Model for Cash Management Decisions." *Management Science* (1974), 1350–63.

143. J. W. Peavy, III. "Modern Financial Theory, Corporate Strategy, and Public Policy: Another Perspective." *Academy of Management Review* (1984), 152–57.

*Edward I. Altman**

Financial Ratios, Discriminant Analysis, and the Prediction of Corporate Bankruptcy

This paper evaluates the analytical quality of ratio analysis for its potential as a tool in predicting corporate bankruptcy. Professor Altman was one of the first to use multiple discriminant analysis in financial management. The approach uses various ratios as the variables in a discriminant function to categorize borrowers into two groups—those who did and those who did not go bankrupt.

Similar methodology has subsequently been used in the analysis of granting bank loans, trade credit, consumer loans, and issuance of credit cards. Many of these have been proprietary studies for individual companies, and they are not available in the published media.

Academicians seem to be moving toward the elimination of ratio analysis as an analytical technique in assessing the performance of the business enterprise. Theorists downgrade arbitrary rules of thumb, such as company ratio comparisons, widely used by practitioners. Since attacks on the relevance of ratio analysis emanate from many esteemed members of the scholarly world, does this mean that ratio analysis is limited to the world of "nuts and bolts"? Or has the significance of such an approach been unattractively garbed and therefore unfairly handicapped? Can we bridge the gap, rather than sever the link, between traditional ratio "analysis" and the more rigorous statistical techniques which have become popular among academicians in recent years?

The purpose of this paper is to attempt an assessment of this issue—the quality of ratio analysis as an analytical technique The prediction of corporate bankruptcy is used as an illustrative case.[1]

* The author acknowledges the helpful suggestions and comments of Keith V. Smith, Edward F. Renshaw, Lawrence S. Ritter, and the *Journal's* reviewer. The research was conducted while under a Regents Fellowship at the University of California, Los Angeles.

Source: Reprinted with permission, from *The Journal of Finance* (September 1968), pp. 589–609. Edward I. Altman is the Max L. Heine Professor of Finance at New York University.

[1] In this study the term *bankruptcy* will, except where otherwise noted, refer to those firms that are legally bankrupt and either placed in receivership or have been granted the right to reorganize under the provisions of the National Bankruptcy Act.

Specifically, a set of financial and economic ratios will be investigated in a bankruptcy prediction context wherein a multiple discriminant statistical methodology is employed. The data used in the study are limited to manufacturing corporations.

A brief review of the development of traditional ratio analysis as a technique for investigating corporate performance is presented in Section I. In Section II the shortcomings of this approach are discussed, and multiple discriminant analysis is introduced, with the emphasis centering on its compatibility with ratio analysis in a bankruptcy prediction context. The discriminant model is developed in Section III, where an initial sample of sixty-six firms is utilized to establish a function which best discriminates between companies in two mutually exclusive groups: bankrupt and non-bankrupt firms. Section IV reviews empirical results obtained from the initial sample and several secondary samples, the latter being selected to examine the reliability of the discriminant model as a predictive technique. In Section V the model's adaptability to practical decision-making situations and its potential benefits in a variety of situations are suggested. The final section summarizes the findings and conclusions of the study, and assesses the role and significance of traditional ratio analysis within a modern analytical context.

I. Traditional Ratio Analysis

The detection of company operating and financial difficulties is a subject which has been particularly susceptible to financial ratio analysis. Prior to the development of quantitative measures of company performance, agencies were established to supply a qualitative type of information assessing the creditworthiness of particular merchants.[2] Formal aggregate studies concerned with portents of business failure were evident in the 1930s. A study at that time[3] and several later ones concluded that failing firms exhibit significantly different ratio measurements than continuing entities.[4] In addition, another study was concerned with ratios of large asset-size corporations that experienced difficulties in meeting their fixed indebtedness obligations.[5] A recent study involved the analysis of financial ratios in a bankruptcy-prediction context.[6] This latter work compared a list of ratios individually for failed firms and a matched sample of non-failed firms. Observed evidence for five years prior to failure was cited as conclusive that ratio analysis can be useful in the prediction of failure.

The aforementioned studies imply a definite potential of ratios as predictors of bankruptcy. In general, ratios measuring profitability, liquidity, and solvency prevailed as the most significant indicators. The order of their importance is not clear since almost every study cited a different ratio as being the most effective indication of impending problems.

---

[2] For instance, the forerunner of well-known Dun & Bradstreet, Inc. was organized in 1849 in Cincinnati, Ohio, in order to provide independent credit investigations. For an interesting and informative discussion on the development of credit agencies and financial measures of company performance, see Roy A. Foulke, *Practical Financial Statement Analysis,* 5th Ed. (New York: McGraw-Hill, 1961).

[3] R. F. Smith and A. H. Winakor, *Changes in the Financial Structure of Unsuccessful Corporations* (University of Illinois: Bureau of Business Research, 1935).

[4] For instance, a comprehensive study covering over 900 firms compared discontinuing firms with continuing ones. See C. Merwin, *Financing Small Corporations* (New York: Bureau of Economic Research, 1942).

[5] W. B. Hickman, *Corporate Bond Quality and Investor Experience* (Princeton, NJ: Princeton University Press, 1958).

[6] W. H. Beaver, "Financial Ratios as Predictors of Failure," *Empirical Research in Accounting, Selected Studies, 1966* (Institute of Professional Accounting, January 1967), pp. 71–111. Also, a recent attempt was made to weight ratios arbitrarily; see M. Tamari, "Financial Ratios as a Means of Forecasting Bankruptcy," *Management International Review,* vol. 4 (1966), pp. 15–21.

II. Multiple Discriminant Analysis

The previous section cited several studies devoted to the analysis of a firm's condition prior to financial difficulties. Although these works established certain important generalizations regarding the performance and trends of particular measurements, the adaptation of their results for assessing bankruptcy potential of firms, both theoretically and practically, is questionable.[7] In almost every case, the methodology was essentially univariate in nature and emphasis was placed on individual signals of impending problems.[8] Ratio analysis presented in this fashion is susceptible to faulty interpretation and is potentially confusing. For instance, a firm with a poor profitability and/or solvency record may be regarded as a potential bankrupt. However, because of its above average liquidity, the situation may not be considered serious. The potential ambiguity as to the relative performance of several firms is clearly evident. The crux of the shortcomings inherent in any univariate analysis lies therein. An appropriate extension of the previously cited studies, therefore, is to build upon their findings and to combine several measures into a meaningful predictive model. In so doing, the highlights of ratio analysis as an analytical technique will be emphasized rather than downgraded. The question becomes which ratios are most important in detecting bankruptcy potential, what weights should be attached to those selected ratios, and how should the weights be objectively established.

After careful consideration of the nature of the problem and of the purpose of the paper, a multiple discriminant analysis (MDA) was chosen as the appropriate statistical technique. Although not as popular as regression analysis, MDA has been utilized in a variety of disciplines since its first application in the 1930s.[9] During those earlier years MDA was used mainly in the biological and behavioral sciences.[10] More recently this method had been applied successfully to financial problems such as consumer credit evaluation[11] and investment classification. For instance, in the latter area, Walter utilized a MDA model to classify high and low price earnings rated firms,[12] and Smith applied the technique in the classification of firms into standard investment categories.[13]

MDA is a statistical technique used to classify an observation into one of several *a priori* groupings dependent upon the observation's individual characteristics. It is used primarily to classify and/or make predictions in problems where the dependent variable appears in qualitative form,

---

[7] At this point bankruptcy is used in its most general sense, meaning simply business failure.

[8] Exceptions to this generalization were noted in works where there was an attempt to emphasize the importance of a group of ratios as an indication of overall performance. For instance, see Foulke, op. cit., Chapters XIV and XV, and A. Wall and R. W. Duning, *Ratio Analysis of Financial Statements* (New York: Harper and Row, 1928), p. 159.

[9] R. A. Fisher, "The Use of Multiple Measurements in Taxonomic Problems," *Annals of Eugenics,* No. 7 (September 1936), pp. 179–88.

[10] For a comprehensive review of studies using MDA, see W. G. Cochran, "On the Performance of the Linear Discriminant Function." *Technometrics,* vol. 6 (May 1964), pp. 179–90.

[11] The pioneering work utilizing MDA in a financial context was performed by Durand in evaluating the creditworthiness of used car loan applicants. See D. D. Durand, *Risk Elements in Consumer Installment Financing,* Studies in Consumer Installment Financing (New York: National Bureau of Economic Research, 1941), pp. 105–42. More recently, Myers and Forgy analyzed several techniques, including MDA, in the evaluation of good and bad installment loans. See H. Myers and E. W. Forgy, "Development of Numerical Credit Evaluation Systems," *Journal of American Statistical Association,* vol. 50 (September 1963), pp. 797–806.

[12] J. E. Walter, "A Discriminant Function for Earnings Price Ratios of Large Industrial Corporations," *Review of Economics and Statistics,* vol. XLI (February 1959), pp. 44–52.

[13] K. V. Smith, *Classification of Investment Securities Using MDA,* Institute Paper #101 (Purdue University, Institute for Research in the Behavioral, Economic, and Management Sciences, 1965).

e.g., male or female, bankrupt or non-bankrupt. Therefore, the first step is to establish explicit group classifications. The number of original groups can be two or more.

After the groups are established, data are collected for the objects in the groups; MDA then attempts to derive a linear combination of these characteristics which "best" discriminates between the groups. If a particular object, for instance a corporation, has characteristics (financial ratios) which can be quantified for all of the companies in the analysis, the MDA determines a set of discriminant coefficients. When these coefficients are applied to the actual ratio, a basis for classification into one of the mutually exclusive groupings exists. The MDA technique has the advantage of considering an entire profile of characteristics common to the relevant firms, as well as the interaction of these properties. A univariate study, on the other hand, can only consider the measurements used for group assignments one at a time.

Another advantage of MDA is the reduction of the analyst's space dimensionality, i.e., from the number of different independent variables to $G - 1$ dimensions (s), where G equals the number of original *a priori* groups.[14] This paper is concerned with two groups, consisting of bankrupt firms on the one hand, and of non-bankrupt firms on the other. Therefore, the analysis is transformed into its simplest form: one dimension. The discriminant function of the form $Z = v_1 x_1 + v_2 x_2 + \ldots + v_n x_n$ transforms individual variable values to a single discriminant score or Z value, which is then used to classify the object

$$\text{where} \quad v_1, v_2, \ldots, v_n \quad = \quad \text{Discriminant coefficients}$$

$$x_1, x_2, \ldots, x_n \quad = \quad \text{Independent variables.}$$

The MDA computes the discriminant coefficients, v_j, while the independent variables x_j are the actual values

$$\text{where } j = 1, 2, \ldots, n.$$

When utilizing a comprehensive list of financial ratios in assessing a firm's bankruptcy potential there is reason to believe that some of the measurements will have a high degree of correlation or collinearity with each other. While this aspect necessitates careful selection of the predictive variables (ratios), it also has the advantage of yielding a model with a relatively small number of selected measurements which has the potential of conveying a great deal of information. This information might very well indicate differences between groups, but whether or not these differences are significant and meaningful is a more important aspect of the analysis. To be sure, there are differences between bankrupt firms and healthy ones; but are these differences of a magnitude to facilitate the development of an accurate prediction model?

Perhaps the primary advantage of MDA in dealing with classification problems is the potential of analyzing the entire variable profile of the object simultaneously rather than sequentially examining its individual characteristics. Just as linear and integer programming have improved upon traditional techniques in capital budgeting,[15] the MDA approach to traditional ratio analysis has the

---

[14] For a formulation of the mathematical computations involved in MDA, see J. G. Bryan, "The Generalized Discriminant Function, Mathematical Foundation & Computational Routine," *Harvard Educational Review,* vol. XXI, no. 2 (Spring 1951), pp. 90–95; and C. R. Rao, *Advanced Statistical Methods in Biometric Research* (New York: John Wiley, 1952).

[15] H. M. Weingartner, *Mathematical Programming and the Analysis of Capital Budgeting, Budgeting Problems* (Englewood Cliffs, NJ: Prentice-Hall, 1963).

potential to reformulate the problem correctly. Specifically, combinations of ratios can be analyzed together in order to remove possible ambiguities and misclassifications observed in earlier traditional studies.

Given the above descriptive qualities, the MDA technique was selected as most appropriate for the bankruptcy study. A carefully devised and interpreted multiple regression analysis methodology conceivably could have been used in this two group case.

III. Development of the Model

Sample Selection

The initial sample is composed of sixty-six corporations, with thirty-three firms in each of the two groups. The bankrupt group (1) are manufacturers that filed a bankruptcy petition under Chapter X of the National Bankruptcy Act during the period 1946–1965.[16] The mean asset size of these firms is $6.4 million, with a range of between $0.7 million and $25.9 million. Recognizing that this group is not completely homogeneous, due to industry and size differences, a careful selection of non-bankrupt firms was attempted. Group 2 consisted of a paired sample of manufacturing firms chosen on a stratified random basis. The firms are stratified by industry and by size, with the asset range restricted to between $1–$25 million.[17] Firms in Group 2 were still in existence in 1966. Also, the data collected are from the same years as those compiled for the bankrupt firms. For the initial sample test, the data are derived from financial statements one reporting period prior to bankruptcy.[18]

An important issue is to determine the asset-size group to be sampled. The decision to eliminate both the small firms (under $1 million in total assets) and the very large companies from the initial sample essentially is due to the asset range of the firms in Group 1. In addition, the incidence of bankruptcy in the large asset-size firm is quite rare today while the absence of comprehensive data negated the representation of small firms. A frequent argument is that financial ratios, by their very nature, have the effect of deflating statistics by size, and therefore a good deal of the size effect is eliminated. To choose Group 1 firms in a restricted size range is not feasible, while selecting firms for Group 2 at random seemed unwise. However, subsequent tests to the original sample do not use size as a means of stratification.[19]

After the initial groups are defined and firms selected, balance sheet and income statement data are collected. Because of the large number of variables found to be significant indicators of corporate problems in past studies, a list of twenty-two potentially helpful variables (ratios) is compiled for evaluation. The variables are classified into five standard ratio categories, including liquidity, profitability, leverage, solvency, and activity ratios. The ratios are chosen on the basis of their

---

[16] The choice of a twenty year period is not the best procedure since average ratios do shift over time. Ideally we would prefer to examine a list of ratios in time period t in order to make predictions about other firms in the following period ($t + 1$). Unfortunately, it was not possible to do this because of data limitations. However, the number of bankruptcies were approximately evenly distributed over the twenty year period in both the original and the secondary samples.

[17] The mean asset size of the firms in Group 2 ($9.6 million) was slightly greater than that of Group 1, but matching exact asset size of the two groups seemed unnecessary.

[18] The data was derived from Moody's Industrial Manuals and selected Annual Reports. The average lead time of the financial statements was approximately seven and one-half months prior to bankruptcy.

[19] One of the tests included only firms that experienced operating losses (secondary sample of non-bankrupt firms).

(1) popularity in the literature,[20] (2) potential relevancy to the study, and a few "new" ratios initiated in this paper.

From the original list of variables, five variables are selected as doing the best overall job together in the prediction of corporate bankruptcy.[21] In order to arrive at a final profile of variables, the following procedures are utilized: (1) observation of the statistical significance of various alternative functions including determination of the relative contributions of each independent variable; (2) evaluation of inter-correlations between the relevant variables; (3) observation of the predictive accuracy of the various profiles; and (4) judgment of the analyst.

The variable profile finally established did not contain the most significant variables amongst the twenty-two original ones, measured independently. This would not necessarily improve upon the univariate, traditional analysis described earlier. The contribution of the entire profile is evaluated, and since this process is essentially iterative, there is no claim regarding the optimality of the resulting discriminant function. The function, however, does the best job among the alternatives which include numerous computer runs analyzing different ratio-profiles. The final discriminant function is as follows:

$$Z = .012X_1 + .014X_2 + .033X_3 + .006X_4 + .999X_5$$

where $\quad X_1 \quad = \quad$ Working capital/Total assets

$\qquad X_2 \quad = \quad$ Retained earnings/Total assets

$\qquad X_3 \quad = \quad$ Earnings before interest and taxes/Total assets

$\qquad X_4 \quad = \quad$ Market value equity/Book value of total debt

$\qquad X_5 \quad = \quad$ Sales/Total assets

$\qquad Z \quad = \quad$ Overall Index. $\hfill (1)$

X_1—Working Capital/Total Assets

The Working capital/Total assets ratio, frequently found in studies of corporate problems, is a measure of the net liquid assets of the firm relative to the total capitalization. Working capital is defined as the difference between current assets and current liabilities. Liquidity and size characteristics are explicitly considered. Ordinarily, a firm experiencing consistent operating losses will have shrinking current assets in relation to total assets. Of the three liquidity ratios evaluated, this one proved to be the most valuable.[22] Inclusion of this variable is consistent with the Merwin study, which rated the net working capital to total asset ratio as the best indicator of ultimate discontinuance.[23]

---

[20] The Beaver study (cited earlier) concluded that the cash flow to debt ratio was the best single ratio predictor. This ratio was not considered here because of the lack of consistent appearance of precise depreciation data. The results obtained, however (see section IV), are superior to the results Beaver attained with his single best ratio. See Beaver, op. cit., p. 89.

[21] The MDA computer program used in this study was developed by W. Cooley and P. Lohnes. The data are organized in a blocked format, the bankrupt firms' data first followed by the non-bankrupt firms'.

[22] The other two liquidity ratios were the current ratio and the quick ratio. The Working capital/Total assets ratio showed greater statistical significance both on a univariate and multivariate basis.

[23] Merwin, op. cit., p. 99.

X_2—Retained Earnings/Total Assets[24]

This measure of cumulative profitability over time was cited earlier as one of the "new" ratios. The age of a firm is implicitly considered in this ratio. For example, a relatively young firm will probably show a low RE/TA ratio because it has not had time to build up its cumulative profits. Therefore, it may be argued that the young firm is somewhat discriminated against in this analysis, and its chance of being classified as bankrupt is relatively higher than another, older firm, *ceteris paribus.* But, this is precisely the situation in the real world. The incidence of failure is much higher in a firm's earlier years.[25]

X_3—Earnings before Interest and Taxes/Total Assets

This ratio is calculated by dividing the total assets of a firm into its earnings before interest and tax reductions. In essence, it is a measure of the true productivity of the firm's assets, abstracting from any tax or leverage factors. Since a firm's ultimate existence is based in the earning power of its assets, this ratio appears to be particularly appropriate for studies dealing with corporate failure. Furthermore, insolvency in a bankruptcy sense occurs when the total liabilities exceed a fair valuation of the firm's assets with value determined by the earning power of the assets.

X_4—Market Value of Equity/Book Value of Total Debt

Equity is measured by the combined market value of all shares of stock, preferred and common, while debt includes both current and long-term. The measure shows how much the firm's assets can decline in value (measured by market value of equity plus debt) before the liabilities exceed the assets and the firm becomes insolvent. For example, a company with a market value of its equity of $1,000 and debt of $500 could experience a two-thirds drop in asset value before insolvency. However, the same firm with $250 in equity will be insolvent if its drop is only one-third in value. This ratio adds a market value dimension which other failure studies did not consider.[26] It also appears to be a more effective predictor of bankruptcy than a similar, more commonly used ratio: Net worth/Total debt (book values).

X_5—Sales/Total Assets

The capital/turnover ratio is a standard financial ratio illustrating the sales generating ability of the firm's assets. It is one measure of management's capability in dealing with competitive conditions.

---

[24] Retained earnings is the account which reports the total amount of reinvested earnings and/or losses of a firm over its entire life. The account is also referred to as Earned Surplus. It should be noted that the Retained Earnings account is subject to manipulation via corporate quasi-reorganizations and stock dividend declarations. While these occurrences are not evident in this study, it is conceivable that a bias would be created by a substantial reorganization or stock dividend.

[25] In 1965, over 50 percent of all manufacturing firms that failed did so in the first five years of their existence. Over 31 percent failed within three years. Statistics are taken from *The Failure Record, Through 1965* (New York: Dun & Bradstreet, 1966), p. 10.

[26] The reciprocal of X_4 is the familiar Debt/Equity ratio often used as a measure of financial leverage. X_4 is a slightly modified version of one of the variables used effectively by Fisher in a study of corporate bond interest rate differentials. See Lawrence Fisher, "Determinants of Risk Premiums on Corporate Bonds," *Journal of Political Economy,* LXVII, No. 3 (June 1959), pp. 217–37.

Table 1   Variable Means and Test of Significance

Variable	Bankrupt Group Mean	Non-Bankrupt Group Mean	F Ratio
	$n = 33$	$n = 33$	
X_1	−6.1%	41.4%	32.60[a]
X_2	−62.6	35.5	58.86[a]
X_3	−31.8	15.3	26.56[a]
X_4	40.1	247.7	33.26[a]
X_5	1.5	1.9	2.84

[a]Significant at the .001 level.

$F_{1 \cdot 60}(.001) = 12.00$

$F_{1 \cdot 60}(.01) = 7.00$

$F_{1 \cdot 60}(.05) = 4.00$

This final ratio is quite important because, as indicated below, it is the least significant ratio on an individual basis. In fact, based on the statistical significance measure, it would not have appeared at all. However, because of its unique relationship to other variables in the model, the Sales/Total assets ratio ranks second in its contribution to the overall discriminating ability of the model.

To test the individual discriminating ability of the variables, an "F" test is performed. This test relates the difference between the average values of the ratios in each group to the variability (or spread) of values of the ratios within each group. Variable means one financial statement prior to bankruptcy, and the resulting "F" statistics are presented in Table 1.

Variables X_1 through X_4 are all significant at the .001 level, indicating extremely significant differences in these variables between groups. Variable X_5 does not show a significant difference between groups, and the reason for its inclusion in the variable profile is not apparent as yet. On a strictly univariate level, all of the ratios indicate higher values for the non-bankrupt firms. Also, the discriminant coefficients of equation (1) display positive signs, which is what one would expect. Therefore, the greater a firm's bankruptcy potential, the lower its discriminant score.

One useful technique in arriving at the final variable profile is to determine the relative contribution of each variable to the total discriminating power of the function, and the interaction between them. The relevant statistic is observed as a scaled vector which is computed by multiplying corresponding elements by the square roots of the diagonal elements of the variance-covariance matrix.[27] Since the actual variable measurement units are not all comparable to each other, simple observation of the discriminant coefficients is misleading. The adjusted coefficients shown in Table 2 enable us to evaluate each variable's contribution on a relative basis.

The scaled vectors indicate that the large contributors to group separation of the discriminant function are X_3, X_5, and X_4, respectively. The profitability ratio contributes the most, which is not surprising if one considers that the incidence of bankruptcy in a firm that is earning a profit is almost

---

[27] For example, the square root of the appropriate variance-covariance figure (standard deviation) for X_1 is approximately 275 and when multiplied by the variable's coefficient (.012) yields a scaled vector of 3.29.

Table 2   Relative Contribution of the Variables

Variable	Scaled Vector	Ranking
X_1	3.29	5
X_2	6.04	4
X_3	9.89	1
X_4	7.42	3
X_5	8.41	2

nil. What is surprising, however, is the second highest contribution of X_5 (Sales/Total assets). Recalling that this ratio was insignificant on a univariate basis, the multivariate context is responsible for illuminating the importance of X_5.[28] A probable reason for this unexpected result is the high negative correlation (−.78) we observe between X_3 and X_5 in the bankruptcy group. The negative correlation is also evident in subsequent bankrupt group samples.

In a recent evaluation of the discriminate function, Cochran concluded that most correlations between variables in past studies were positive and that, by and large, negative correlations are more helpful than positive correlations in adding new information to the function.[29] The logic behind the high negative correlation in the bankrupt group is that as firms suffer losses and deteriorate toward failure, their assets are not replaced as much as in healthier times, and also the cumulative losses have further reduced the asset size through debits to Retained Earnings. The asset size reduction apparently dominates any sales movements.

A different argument, but one not necessarily inconsistent with the above, concerns a similar ratio to X_5, Net Sales to Tangible Net Worth. If the latter ratio is excessive, the firm is often referred to as a poor credit risk due to insufficient capital to support sales. Companies with moderate or even below average sales generating lower (low asset turnover, X_5) might very well possess an extremely high Net Sales/Net Worth ratio if the Net Worth has been reduced substantially due to cumulative operating losses. This ratio, and other net worth ratios, are not considered in the paper because of computational and interpretive difficulties arising when negative net worth totals are present.

It is clear that four of the five variables display significant differences between groups, but the importance of MDA is its ability to separate groups using multivariate measures. A test to determine the overall discriminating power of the model is the common F-value, which is the ratio of the sums-of-squares between-groups to the within-groups sums-of-squares. When this ratio of the form,

$$\lambda = \frac{\sum\limits_{g=1}^{G} N_g \, [\bar{y}_g - \bar{y}]^2}{\sum\limits_{g=1}^{G} \sum\limits_{p=1}^{N_g} [y_{pg} - \bar{y}_g]^2}$$

---

[28] For an excellent discussion of how a seemingly insignificant variable on a univariate basis can supply important information in a multivariate context, see W. W. Cooley and P. R. Lohnes, *Multivariate Procedures for the Behavioral Sciences* (New York: Wiley, 1962), p. 121.

[29] Cochran, op. cit., p. 182.

where G = Number of groups

  g = Group g, $g = 1 \ldots G$

  N_g = Number of firms in group g

  y_{pg} = Firm p in group g, $p = 1 \ldots N_g$

  $\bar{y}_g$ = Group mean (centroid)

  $\bar{y}$ = Overall sample mean,

is maximized, it has the effect of spreading the means (centroids) of the G groups apart and, simultaneously, reducing dispersion of the individual points (firm Z values, y_{pg}) about their respective group means. Logically, this test (commonly called the "F" test) is appropriate because one of the objectives of the MDA is to identify and to utilize those variables which best discriminate *between* groups and which are most similar *within* groups.

The group means, or centroids, of the original two-group sample of the form

$$\bar{y}_g = \frac{1}{N_g} \sum_{p=1}^{Ng} y_{pg}$$

are

Group 1 = -0.29 $F = 20.7$

Group 2 = $+5.02$ $F_{5.60}(.01) = 3.34.$

The significance test therefore *rejects* the null hypothesis that the observations come from the same population. With the conclusion that *a priori* groups are significantly different, further discriminatory analysis is possible.

Once the values of the discriminant coefficients are estimated, it is possible to calculate discriminant scores for each observation in the sample, or any firm, and to assign the observations to one of the groups based on this score. The essence of the procedure is to compare the profile of an individual firm with that of the alternate groupings. In this manner the firm is assigned to the group it most closely resembles. The comparisons are measured by a chi-square value, and assignments are made based upon the relative proximity of the firm's score to the various group centroids.

IV. Empirical Results

At the outset, it might be helpful to illustrate the format for presenting the result. In the multi-group case, results are shown in a classification chart or "accuracy-matrix." The chart is set up as follows:

	Predicted Group Membership	
Actual Group Membership	**Bankrupt**	**Non-Bankrupt**
Bankrupt	H	M_1
Non-Bankrupt	M_2	H

The actual group membership is equivalent to the *a priori* groupings, and the model attempts to classify correctly these firms. At this stage, the model is basically explanatory. When new companies are classified, the nature of the model is predictive.

The H's stand for correct classifications (Hits) and the M's stand for misclassifications (Misses). M_1 represents a Type I error and M_2 a Type II error. The sum of the diagonal elements equals the total correct "hits," and when divided into the total number of firms classified (sixty-six in the case of the initial sample), yields the measure of success of the MDA in classifying firms, that is, the percent of firms correctly classified. This percentage is analogous to the coefficient of determination (R_2) in regression analysis, which measures the percent of the variation of the dependent variable explained by the independent variables.

The final criterion used to establish the best model was to observe its accuracy in predicting bankruptcy. A series of six tests were performed.

(1) Initial Sample (Group 1)

The initial sample of 33 firms in each of the two groups is examined using data one financial statement prior to bankruptcy. Since the discriminant coefficients and the group distributions are derived from this sample, a high degree of successful classification is expected. This should occur because the firms are classified using a discriminant function which, in fact, is based upon the individual measurements of these same firms. The classification matrix for the initial sample is as follows:

	Predicted	
Actual	**Group 1**	**Group 2**
Group 1	31	2
Group 2	1	32

	Number Correct	**Percent Correct**	**Percent Error**	***n***
Type I	31	94	6	33
Type II	32	97	3	33
Total	63	95	5	66

The model is extremely accurate in classifying 95 percent of the total sample correctly. The *Type I error* proved to be only 6 percent, while the *Type II error* was even better at 3 percent. The results, therefore, are encouraging, but the obvious upward bias should be kept in mind, and further validation techniques are appropriate.

(2) Results Two Years Prior to Bankruptcy

The second test is made to observe the discriminating ability of the model for firms using data from two years prior to bankruptcy. The two year period is an exaggeration since the average lead time for the correctly classified firms is approximately twenty months with two firms having a thirteen month lead. The results are

Table 4   Five Year Predictive Accuracy of the MDA Model (Initial Sample)

Year Prior to Bankruptcy	Hits	Misses	Percent Correct
1st n = 33	31	2	95
2nd n = 32	23	9	72
3rd n = 29	14	15	48
4th n = 28	8	20	29
5th n = 25	9	16	36

the overall effectiveness of the discriminant model for a longer period of time prior to bankruptcy. Several studies, e.g., Beaver and Merwin, indicated that their analyses showed firms exhibiting failure tendencies as much as five years prior to the actual failure. Little is mentioned, however, of the true significance of these earlier year results. Is it enough to show that a firm's position is deteriorating, or is it more important to examine when in the life of a firm does its eventual failure, if any, become an acute possibility? Thus far, we have seen that bankruptcy can be predicted accurately for two years prior to failure. What about the more remote years?

To answer this question, data are gathered for the thirty-three original firms from the third, fourth, and fifth year prior to bankruptcy. The reduced sample is due to the fact that several of the firms were in existence for less than five years. In two cases data were available for the more remote years. One would expect on an *a priori* basis that, as the lead time increases, the relative predictive ability of any model would decrease. This was true in the univariate studies cited earlier, and it is also quite true for the multiple discriminant model. Table 4 summarizes the predictive accuracy for the total five year period.

It is obvious that the accuracy of the model falls off consistently with the one exception of the fourth and fifth years, when the results are reversed from what would be expected. The most logical reason for this occurrence is that after the second year, the discriminant model becomes unreliable in its predictive ability and, also, that the change from year to year has little or no meaning.

Implications

Based on the above results, it is suggested that the bankruptcy prediction model is an accurate forecaster of failure up to two years prior to bankruptcy and that the accuracy diminishes substantially as the lead time increases. In order to investigate the possible reasons underlying these findings, the trend in the five predictive variables is traced on a univariate basis for five years preceding bankruptcy. The ratios of four other important but less significant ratios are also listed in Table 5.

The two most important conclusions of this trend analysis are (1) that all of the observed ratios show a deteriorating trend as bankruptcy approached, and (2) that the most serious change in the majority of these ratios occurred between the third and the second years prior to bankruptcy. The degree of seriousness is measured by the yearly change in the ratio values. The latter observation is extremely significant as it provides evidence consistent with conclusions derived from the discriminant model. Therefore, the important information inherent in the individual ratio measurement trends takes on deserved significance only when integrated with the more analytical discriminant analysis findings.

Table 5 Average Ratios of Bankrupt Group Prior to Failure—Original Sample

Ratio	Fifth Year		Fourth Year		Third Year		Second Year		First Year	
	Ratio	Change[a]	Ratio	Change[a]	Ratio	Change[a]	Ratio	Change[a]	Ratio	Change[a]
Working capital/total assets (%) (X_1)	19.5		23.2	+3.6	17.6	−5.6	1.6	−16.0[b]	(6.1)	−7.7
Retained earnings/total assets (%) (X_2)	4.0		(0.8)	−4.8	(7.0)	−6.2	(30.1)	−23.1	(62.6)	−32.5[b]
EBIT/total assets (%) (X_3)	7.2		4.0	−3.2	(5.8)	−9.8	(20.7)	−14.9[b]	(31.8)	−11.1
Market value equity/total debt (%) (X_4)	180.0		147.6	−32.4	143.2	−4.4	74.2	−69.0[b]	40.1	−34.1
Sales/total assets (%) (X_5)	200.0		200.0	0.0	166.0	−34.0[b]	150.0	−16.0	150.0	0.0
Current ratio (%)	180.0		187.0	+7.0	162.0	−25.0	131.0	−31.0[b]	133.0	+2.0
Years of negative profit (years)	0.8		0.9	+0.1	1.2	+0.3	2.0	+0.8[b]	2.5	+0.5
Total debt/total assets (%)	54.2		60.9	+6.7	61.2	+0.3	77.0	+15.8	96.4	+19.4[b]
Net worth/total debt (%)	123.2		75.2	−28.0	112.6	+17.4	70.5	−42.1[b]	49.4	−21.1

[a] Change from previous year.
[b] Largest yearly change in the ratio.

Table 6 **Firm Whose Z Score Falls within Gray Area**

Firm Number Non Bankrupt	Z Score	Firm Number Bankrupt
2019[a]	1.81	
	1.98	1026
	2.10	1014
	2.67	1017[a]
2033	2.68	
2032	2.78	
	2.99	1025[a]

[a] Misclassified by the MDA model—for example, firm "19" in Group 2.

V. Applications

The use of a multiple discriminant model for predicting bankruptcy has displayed several advantages, but bankers, credit managers, executives, and investors will typically not have access to computer procedures such as the Cooley-Lohnes MDA program. Therefore, it will be necessary to investigate the results presented in Section IV closely and to attempt to extend the model for more general application. The procedure described below may be utilized to select a "cut-off" point, or optimum Z value, which enables predictions without computer support.[33]

By observing those firms which have been misclassified by the discriminant model in the initial sample, it is concluded that all firms having a Z score of greater than 2.99 clearly fall into the "non-bankrupt" sector, while those firms having a Z below 1.81 are all bankrupt. The area between 1.81 and 2.99 will be defined as the "zone of ignorance" or "gray area" because of the susceptibility to error classification (see Chart 1). Since errors are observed in this range of values, we will be uncertain about a *new* firm whose Z value falls within the "zone of ignorance." Hence, it is desirable to establish a guideline for classifying firms in the "gray area."

The process begins by identifying sample observations which fall within the overlapping range. These appear as in Table 6. The first digit of the firm number identifies the group, with the last two digits locating the firm within the group.

Next, the range of values of Z that results in the *minimum number of misclassifications* is found. In the analysis, Z's between (but not including) the indicated values produce the following misclassifications as shown in Table 7.

The best critical value conveniently falls between 2.67–2.68, and therefore 2.675, the midpoint of the interval, is chosen as the Z value that discriminates best between the bankrupt and non-bankrupt firms.

Of course, the real test of this "optimum" Z value is its discriminating power not only with the initial sample, but also with the secondary samples. The results of these tests are even slightly superior to the job done by the computer assignments, with the additional benefit of practical applicability.

---

[33] A similar method proved to be useful in selecting cut-off points for marketing decisions. See R. E. Frank, A. A. Kuehn, W. F. Massy, *Quantitative Techniques in Marketing Analysis* (Homewood, IL: Irwin, 1962), pp. 95–100.

Table 7 Number of Misclassifications Using Various Z Score Criterions

Range of Z	Number Misclassified	Firms
1.81–1.98	5	2019, 1026, 1014, 1017, 1025
1.98–2.10	4	2019, 1014, 1017, 1025
2.10–2.67	3	2019, 1017, 1025
2.67–2.68	2	2019, 1025
2.68–2.78	3	2019, 2033, 1025
2.78–2.99	4	2019, 2033, 2032, 1025

Business-Loan Evaluation

Reference was made earlier to several studies which examined the effectiveness of discriminant analysis in evaluating *consumer-loan* applications, and, perhaps, these suggest a useful extension of the bankruptcy-prediction model. The evaluation of *business loans* is an important function in our society, especially to commercial banks and other lending institutions. Studies have been devoted to the loan offer function[34] and to the adoption of a heuristic-bank-loan-officer model whereby a computer model was developed to simulate the loan officer function.[35] Admittedly, the analysis of the loan applicant's financial statements is but one section of the entire evaluation process, but it is a very important link. A fast and efficient device for detecting unfavorable credit risks might enable the loan officer to avoid potentially disastrous decisions. The significant point is that the MDA model contains many of the variables common to business-loan evaluation, and discriminant analysis has been used for consumer-loan evaluation. Therefore, the potential presents itself for utilization in the business sector.

Because such important variables as the purpose of the loan, its maturity, the security involved, the deposit status of the applicant, and the particular characteristics of the bank are not explicitly considered in the model, the MDA should probably not be used as the only means of credit evaluation. The discriminant Z score index can be used, however, as a guide in efforts to lower the costs of investigation of loan applicants. Less time and effort would be spent on companies whose Z score is very high, i.e., above 3.0, while those with low Z scores would signal a very thorough investigation. This policy would be advisable to the loan officer who had some degree of faith in the discriminant analysis approach, but who did not want his final decision to depend solely on a numerical score. Also, the method would be particularly efficient in the case of short-term loans or relatively small loans where the normal credit evaluation process is very costly relative to the expected income from the loan. Herein lie important advantages of the MDA model—its simplicity and low cost.

Internal Control Considerations and Investment Criteria

An extremely important, but often very difficult, task of corporate management is to periodically assess honestly the firm's present condition. By doing so, important strengths and weaknesses may

---

[34] D. D. Hester, "An Empirical Examination of a Commercial Loan Offer Function," *Yale Economic Essays,* vol. 2, no. 1 (1962), pp. 3–57.

[35] K. Cohen, T. Gilmore, and F. Singer, "Banks Procedures for Analyzing Business Loan Applications," *Analytical Methods in Banking,* K. Cohen and F. Hammer, eds. (Homewood, IL: Irwin, 1966), pp. 218–51.

be recognized, and, in the latter case, changes in policies and actions will usually be in order. The suggestion here is that the discriminant model, if used correctly and periodically, has the ability to predict corporate problems early enough so as to enable management to realize the gravity of the situation in time to avoid failure. If failure is unavoidable, the firm's creditors and stockholders may be better off if a merger with a stronger enterprise is negotiated before bankruptcy.

The potentially useful applications of an accurate bankruptcy predictive model are not limited to internal considerations or to credit evaluation purposes. An efficient predictor of financial difficulties could also be a valuable technique for screening out undesirable investments. On the more optimistic side it appears that there are some very real opportunities for benefits. Since the model is basically predictive, the analyst can utilize these predictions to recommend appropriate investment policy. For instance, observations suggest that while investors are somewhat capable of anticipating declines in operating results of selective firms, there is an overwhelming tendency to underestimate the financial plight of the companies which eventually go bankrupt. Firms in the original sample whose Z scores were below the so-called "zone of ignorance" experienced an average decline in the market value of their common stock of 45 percent from the time the model first predicted bankruptcy until the actual failure date (an average period of about 15 months).

While the above results are derived from an admittedly small sample of very special firms, the potential implications are of interest. If an individual already owns stock in a firm whose future appears dismal, according to the model, he should sell in order to avoid further price declines. The sale would prevent further loss and provide capital for alternative investments. A different policy could be adopted by those aggressive investors looking for short-sale opportunities. An investor utilizing this strategy would have realized a 26 percent gain on those listed securities eligible for short-sales in the original sample of bankrupt firms. In the case of large companies, where bankruptcy occurs less frequently, an index which has the ability to forecast downside movements appears promising. This could be especially helpful in the area of efficient portfolio selection. That is, firms which appear to be strongly susceptible to downturns, according to the discriminant model, would be rejected regardless of any positive potential. Conversely, firms exhibiting these same downside characteristics could be sold short, thereby enabling the portfolio manager to be more aggressive in his other choices.

VI. Concluding Remarks

This paper seeks to assess the analytical quality of ratio analysis. It has been suggested that traditional ratio analysis is no longer an important analytical technique in the academic environment due to the relatively unsophisticated manner in which it has been presented. In order to assess its potential rigorously, a set of financial ratios was combined in a discriminant analysis approach to the problem of corporate bankruptcy prediction. The theory is that ratios, if analyzed within a multivariate framework, will take on greater statistical significance than the common technique of sequential ratio comparisons. The results are very encouraging.

The discriminant-ratio model proved to be extremely accurate in predicting bankruptcy correctly in 94 percent of the initial sample, with 95 percent of all firms in the bankrupt and non-bankrupt groups assigned to their actual group classification. Furthermore, the discriminant function was accurate in several secondary samples introduced to test the reliability of the model. Investigation of the individual ratio movements prior to bankruptcy corroborated the model's findings that bankruptcy can be accurately predicted up to two years prior to actual failure, with the accuracy diminishing rapidly after the second year. A limitation of the study is that the firms examined were all publicly held manufacturing corporations for which comprehensive financial data were obtainable, including market price quotations. An area for future research, therefore, would be to extend the analysis to relatively smaller asset-sized firms and unincorporated entities where the incidence of business failure is greater than with larger corporations.

Several practical and theoretical applications of the model were suggested. The former include business credit evaluation, internal control procedures, and investment guidelines. Inherent in these applications is the assumption that signs of deterioration, detected by a ratio index, can be observed clearly enough to take profitable action. A potential theoretical area of importance lies in the conceptualization of efficient portfolio selection. One of the current limitations in this area is in a realistic presentation of those securities and the types of investment policies which are necessary to balance the portfolio and avoid downside risk The ideal approach is to include those securities possessing negative co-variance with other securities in the portfolio. However, these securities are not likely to be easy to locate, if at all. The problem becomes somewhat more soluble if a method is introduced which rejects securities with high downside risk or includes them in a short-selling context. The discriminant-ratio model appears to have the potential to ease this problem. Further investigation, however, is required on this subject.

Discussion Questions

1. Examine the five variables (ratios) included in the Altman model and their respective coefficients. Do each variable and the sign of the coefficient make sense to you? Explain.

2. What is multiple discriminant analysis? What are some of its advantages over informal methods?

3. Regression lines are those which produce the smallest sum of the squared deviations from the regression line. Contrast the discriminant analysis objective to that of the regression lines.

4. If your firm were using the Altman model for decision making regarding trade credit, what would your decision be if the score for the credit applicant were

   a.   above 2.99?
   b.   below 1.81?
   c.   between 1.81 and 2.99?

5. What is meant by the "zone of ignorance"?

6. The data base for this study was industrial firms. Is the applicability of the results limited to industrial firms? Discuss.

7. Do you think that the determinants of corporate bankruptcy might change over time? Describe how you could find out.

part VIII

Special Topics

This section is devoted to important topics not necessarily falling under previous headings. They are efficient market, the pricing of options, mergers, international diversification, and dealing with financial distress.

Eugene Fama, in his 1965 *Financial Analysts Journal* article, develops the definitions and tests of the efficient markets hypothesis for the practitioner audience. This article, written for practitioners, was based on Fama's earlier works, which were milestones in this area.

No serious discussion of the pricing of options or of the marriage of theory and practice will fail to reference the classic article by Fischer Black and Myron Scholes. The Black and Scholes model is described in almost every textbook in financial management, and it is also used by practitioners.

Another issue deals with mergers and acquisitions, and what drives them. Michael Jensen and Richard Ruback present an important discussion of the merger phenomenon and who gains and loses.

One of the dominant themes of portfolio investing over the past 15 years has been international diversification. The 1974 article by Bruno Solnik was one of the earliest to show the impressive implications of including foreign stocks in the portfolio.

Some firms get into financial difficulty and need informal and formal procedures for solving their problems. Solutions range from asset or liability restructuring to formal bankruptcy declarations. The book ends with an excellent survey treatise on financial distress by Kose John.

*Eugene F. Fama**

Random Walks in
Stock Market Prices

Another important phenomenon of the 1950s and 1960s was the development of efficient market concepts. Tests of the notion that past changes in securities prices contain no information as to future changes were performed by a number of investigators. Professor Fama published a classic work on this subject titled "The Behavior of Stock Market Prices," which first appeared in the Journal of Business *in January 1965. This article from the* Financial Analysts Journal *was written for practitioners and was derived from the* Journal of Business *article.*

For many years economists, statisticians, and teachers of finance have been interested in developing and testing models of stock price behavior. One important model that has evolved from this research is the theory of random walks. This theory casts serious doubt on many other methods for describing and predicting stock price behavior—methods that have considerable popularity outside the academic world. For example, we shall see later that if the random walk theory is an accurate description of reality, then the various "technical" or "chartist" procedures for predicting stock prices are completely without value.

In general, the theory of random walks raises challenging questions for anyone who has more than a passing interest in understanding the behavior of stock prices. Unfortunately, however, most discussions of the theory have appeared in technical academic journals and in a form which the non-mathematician would usually find incomprehensible. This article describes, briefly and simply, the theory of random walks and some of the important issues it raises concerning the work of market analysts. To preserve brevity some aspects of the theory and its implications are omitted. More complete (and also more technical) discussions of the theory of random walks are available elsewhere; hopefully, the introduction provided here will encourage the reader to examine one of the more rigorous and lengthy works listed at the end of this article.

* The author is indebted to his colleagues William Alberts, David Green, Merton Miller, and Harry Roberts for their helpful comments and criticisms.

Source: Reprinted with permission from *Financial Analysts Journal,* September/October 1965. Copyright 1965, The Financial Analysts Federation, Charlottesville, Va. All rights reserved. Eugene F. Fama is Professor of Finance at the University of Chicago.

Common Techniques for Predicting Stock Market Prices

In order to put the theory of random walks into perspective we first discuss, in brief and general terms, the two approaches to predicting stock prices that are commonly espoused by market professionals. These are (1) "chartist" or "technical" theories and (2) the theory of fundamental or intrinsic value analysis.

The basic assumption of all the chartist or technical theories is that history tends to repeat itself; i.e., past patterns of price behavior in individual securities will tend to recur in the future. Thus the way to predict stock prices (and, of course, increase one's potential gains) is to develop a familiarity with past patterns of price behavior in order to recognize situations of likely recurrence.

Essentially, then, chartist techniques attempt to use knowledge of the past behavior of a price series to predict the probable future behavior of the series. A statistician would characterize such techniques as assuming that successive price changes in individual securities are dependent. That is, the various chartist theories assume that the *sequence* of price changes prior to any given day is important in predicting the price change for that day.[1]

The techniques of the chartist have always been surrounded by a certain degree of mysticism, however, and as a result most market professionals have found them suspect. Thus it is probably safe to say that the pure chartist is relatively rare among stock market analysts. Rather, the typical analyst adheres to a technique known as fundamental analysis or the intrinsic value method. The assumption of the fundamental analysis approach is that at any point in time an individual security has an intrinsic value (or in the terms of the economist, an equilibrium price) which depends on the earning potential of the security. The earning potential of the security depends in turn on such fundamental factors as quality of management, outlook for the industry and the economy, etc.

Through a careful study of these fundamental factors the analyst should, in principle, be able to determine whether the actual price of a security is above or below its intrinsic value. If actual prices tend to move toward intrinsic values, then attempting to determine the intrinsic value of a security is equivalent to making a prediction of its future price; and this is the essence of the predictive procedure implicit in fundamental analysis.

The Theory of Random Walks

Chartist theories and the theory of fundamental analysis are really the province of the market professional and to a large extent teachers of finance. Historically, however, there has been a large body of academic people, primarily economists and statisticians, who adhere to a radically different approach to market analysis—the theory of random walks in stock market prices. The remainder of this article will be devoted to a discussion of this theory and its major implications.

Random walk theorists usually start from the premise that the major security exchanges are good examples of "efficient" markets. An "efficient" market is defined as a market where there are large numbers of rational, profit-maximizers actively competing, with each trying to predict future market values of individual securities, and where important current information is almost freely available to all participants.

---

[1] Probably the best known example of the chartist approach to predicting stock prices is the Dow Theory.

In an efficient market, competition among the many intelligent participants leads to a situation where, at any point in time, actual prices of individual securities already reflect the effects of information based both on events that have already occurred and on events which, as of now, the market expects to take place in the future. In other words, in an efficient market at any point in time the actual price of a security will be a good estimate of its intrinsic value.

Now in an uncertain world the intrinsic value of a security can never be determined exactly. Thus there is always room for disagreement among market participants concerning just what the intrinsic value of an individual security is, and such disagreement will give rise to discrepancies between actual prices and intrinsic values. In an efficient market, however, the actions of the many competing participants should cause the actual price of a security to wander randomly about its intrinsic value. If the discrepancies between actual prices and intrinsic values are systematic rather than random in nature, then knowledge of this should help intelligent market participants to better predict the path by which actual prices will move towards intrinsic values. When the many intelligent traders attempt to take advantage of this knowledge, however, they will tend to neutralize such systematic behavior in price series. Although uncertainty concerning intrinsic values will remain, actual prices of securities will wander randomly about their intrinsic values.

Of course, intrinsic values can themselves change across time as a result of new information. The new information may involve such things as the success of a current research and development project, a change in management, a tariff imposed on the industry's product by a foreign country, an increase in industrial production or any other *actual* or *anticipated* change in a factor which is likely to affect the company's prospects.

In an efficient market, *on the average,* competition will cause the full effects of new information on intrinsic values to be reflected "instantaneously" in actual prices. In fact, however, because there is vagueness or uncertainty surrounding new information, "instantaneous adjustment" really has two implications. First, actual prices will initially overadjust to changes in intrinsic values as often as they will underadjust. Second, the lag in the complete adjustment of actual prices to successive new intrinsic values will itself be an independent, random variable with the adjustment of actual prices sometimes preceding the occurrence of the event which is the basis of the change in intrinsic values (i.e., when the event is anticipated by the market before it actually occurs) and sometimes following.

This means that the "instantaneous adjustment" property of an efficient market implies that successive price changes in individual securities will be independent. A market where successive price changes in individual securities are independent is, by definition, a random walk market. Most simply, the theory of random walks implies that a series of stock price changes has no memory—the past history of the series cannot be used to predict the future in any meaningful way. The future path of the price level of a security is no more predictable than the path of a series of cumulated random numbers.

It is unlikely that the random walk hypothesis provides an exact description of the behavior of stock market prices. For practical purposes, however, the model may be acceptable even though it does not fit the facts exactly. Thus although successive price changes may not be strictly independent, the actual amount of dependence may be so small as to be unimportant.

What should be classified as unimportant depends, of course, on the questions at hand. For the stock market trader or investor the criterion is obvious: The independence assumption of the random walk model is valid as long as knowledge of the past behavior of the series of price changes cannot be used to increase expected gains. More specifically, if successive price changes for a given security are independent, there is no problem in timing purchases and sales of that security. A simple policy of buying and holding the security will be as good as any more complicated mechanical procedure for timing purchases and sales. This implies that, for investment purposes, the independence assumption of the random walk model is an adequate description of reality as long as the actual degree of dependence in series of price changes is not sufficient to make the expected profits of any more "sophisticated" mechanical trading rule or chartist technique greater than the expected profits under a naive buy-and-hold policy.

Empirical Evidence on Independence

Over the years, a number of empirical tests of the random walk theory have been performed—indeed, so many that it is not possible to discuss them adequately here. Therefore, in describing the empirical evidence we limit ourselves to a brief discussion of the different approaches employed and the general conclusions that have evolved.

The main concern of empirical research on the random walk model has been to test the hypothesis that successive price changes are independent. Two different approaches have been followed. First there is the approach that relies primarily on common statistical tools such as serial correlation coefficients and analyses of runs of consecutive price changes of the same sign. If the statistical tests tend to support the assumption of independence, one then *infers* that there are probably no mechanical trading rules or chartist techniques, based solely on patterns in the past history of price changes, which would make the expected profits of the investor greater than they would be with a simple buy-and-hold policy. The second approach to testing independence proceeds by testing directly different mechanical trading rules to see whether or not they provide profits greater than buy-and-hold.

Research to date has tended to concentrate on the first or statistical approach to testing independence; the results have been consistent and impressive. I know of no study in which standard statistical tools have produced evidence of *important* dependence in series of successive price changes. In general, these studies (and there are many of them) have tended to uphold the theory of random walks. This is true, for example, of the serial correlation tests of Cootner [4],[2] Fama [5], Kendall [9], and Moore [10]. In all of these studies, the sample serial correlation coefficients computed for successive price changes were extremely close to zero, which is evidence against important dependence in the changes. Similarly, Fama's [5] analysis of runs of successive price changes of the same sign, and the spectral analysis techniques of Granger and Morgenstern [8], and Godfrey, Granger, and Morgenstern [7] also support the independence assumption of the random walk model.

We should emphasize, however, that although the statistical techniques mentioned above have been the common tools used in testing independence, the chartist or technical theorist probably would not consider them adequate. For example, he would not consider either serial correlations or runs analyses as adequate tests of whether the past history of series of price changes can be used to increase the investor's expected profits. The simple linear relationships that underlie the serial

[2] See References at article's end.

correlation model are much too unsophisticated to pick up the complicated "patterns" that the chartist sees in stock prices. Similarly, the runs tests are much too rigid in their manner of determining the duration of upward and downward movements in prices. In particular: in runs-testing, a run is considered as terminated whenever there is a change in sign in the sequence of successive price changes, regardless of the size of the price change that causes the change in sign. The chartist would like to have a more sophisticated method for identifying movements—a method which does not always predict the termination of the movement simply because the price level has temporarily changed direction.

These criticisms of common statistical tools have not gone unheeded, however. For example, Alexander's filter technique [1, 2] is an attempt to apply more sophisticated criteria to the identification of moves. Although the filter technique does not correspond exactly to any well-known chartist theory, it is closely related to such things as the Dow Theory. Thus, the profitability of the filter technique can be used to make inferences concerning the potential profitability of other mechanical trading rules.

A filter of, say, 5 percent is defined as follows: If the daily closing price of a particular security moves up at least 5 percent, buy and hold the security until its price moves down at least 5 percent from a subsequent high, at which time simultaneously sell and go short. The short position is maintained until the daily closing price rises at least 5 percent above a subsequent low, at which time one should simultaneously cover and buy. Moves less than 5 percent in either direction are ignored.

It is, of course, unnecessary to limit the size of the filter to 5 percent. In fact, Professor Alexander has reported tests of the filter technique for filters ranging in size from 1 percent to 50 percent. The tests cover different time periods from 1897 to 1959 and involve daily closing prices for two indices, the Dow-Jones Industrials from 1897 to 1929 and Standard and Poor's Industrials from 1929 to 1959. In Alexander's latest work [2], it turns out that even when the higher broker's commissions incurred under the filter rule are ignored, the filter technique cannot consistently beat the simple policy of buying and holding the indices for the different periods tested. Elsewhere I have tested the filter technique on individual securities. Again the simple buy-and-hold method consistently beats the profits produced by different size filters. It seems, then, that at least for the purposes of the individual trader or investor, tests of the filter technique also tend to support the random walk model.

Implications of the Random Walk Theory for Chartist and Intrinsic Value Analysis

As stated earlier, chartist theories implicitly assume that there is dependence in series of successive price changes. That is, the history of the series can be used to make meaningful predictions concerning the future. On the other hand, the theory of random walks says that successive price changes are independent; i.e., the past cannot be used to predict the future. Thus the two theories are diametrically opposed, and if, as the empirical evidence seems to suggest, the random walk theory is valid, then chartist theories are akin to astrology and of no real value to the investor.

In an uncertain world, however, no amount of empirical testing is sufficient to establish the validity of a hypothesis beyond any shadow of doubt. The chartist or technical theorist always has the option of declaring that the evidence in support of the random walk theory is not sufficient to validate the theory. On the other hand, the chartist must admit that the evidence in favor of the random walk model is both consistent and voluminous, whereas there is precious little published discussion of rigorous empirical tests of the various technical theories. If the chartist rejects the evidence in favor of the random walk model, his position is weak if his own theories have not been subjected to equally rigorous tests. This, I believe, is the challenge that the random walk theory makes to the technician.

There is nothing in the above discussion, however, which suggests that superior fundamental or intrinsic value analysis is useless in a random walk-efficient market. In fact the analyst will do better than the investor who follows a simple buy-and-hold policy as long as he can more quickly identify situations where there are non-negligible discrepancies between actual prices and intrinsic values than other analysts and investors, and if he is better able to predict the occurrence of important events and evaluate their effects on intrinsic values.

If there are many analysts who are pretty good at this sort of thing, however, and if they have considerable resources at their disposal, they help narrow discrepancies between actual prices and intrinsic values and cause actual prices, on the average, to adjust "instantaneously" to changes in intrinsic values. That is, the existence of many sophisticated analysts helps make the market more efficient, which in turn implies a market which conforms more closely to the random walk model. Although the returns to these sophisticated analysts may be quite high, they establish a market in which fundamental analysis is a fairly useless procedure both for the average analyst and the average investor. That is, in a random walk-efficient market, on the average, a security chosen by a mediocre analyst will produce a return no better than that obtained from a randomly selected security of the same general riskiness.

There probably aren't many analysts (in fact, I know of none) who would willingly concede that they are no better than the "average" analyst. If all analysts think they are better than average, however, this only means that their estimate of the average is biased downward. Fortunately, it is not necessary to judge an analyst solely by his claims. The discussion above provides a natural benchmark with which we can evaluate his performance.

In a random walk-efficient market at any point in time the market price of a security will already reflect the judgments of many analysts concerning the relevance of currently available information to the prospects of that security. Now an individual analyst may feel that he has better insights than those that are already implicit in the market price. For example, he may feel that a discrepancy between market price and intrinsic value exists for some security, or he may think the intrinsic value of the security is itself about to change because of some impending piece of new information which is not yet generally available.

These "insights" of the analyst are of no real value, however, unless they are eventually borne out in the market, that is, unless the actual market price eventually moves in the predicted direction. In other words, if the analyst can make meaningful judgments concerning the purchase and sale of individual securities, his choices should consistently outperform randomly selected securities of the same general riskiness. It must be stressed, however, that the analyst must *consistently* produce results better than random selection, since, by the nature of uncertainty, for any given time period he has about a 50 percent chance of doing better than random selection even if his powers of analysis are completely nonexistent. Moreover, not only must the analyst do consistently better than random selection, but he must beat random selection by an amount which is at least sufficient to cover the cost of the resources (including his own time) which are expended in the process of carrying out his more complicated selection procedures.

What we propose, then, is that the analyst subject his performance to a rigorous comparison with a random selection procedure. One simple practical way of comparing the results produced by an analyst with a random selection procedure is the following: Every time the analyst recommends a security for purchase (or sale), another security of the same general riskiness is chosen randomly. A future date is then chosen at which time the results produced by the two securities will be compared. Even if the analyst is no better than the random selection procedure, in any given comparison there is still a 50 percent chance that the security he has chosen will outperform the randomly selected security. After the game has been played for a while, however, and the results of many different comparisons are accumulated, then it will become clear whether the analyst is worth his salt or not.

In many circumstances, however, the primary concern is with the performance of a portfolio rather than with the performance of individual securities in the portfolio. In this situation one would want to compare the performance of the portfolio in question with that of a portfolio of randomly selected securities. A useful benchmark for randomly selected portfolios has been provided by Fisher and Lorie [6]. They computed rates of return for investments in common stocks on the New York Stock Exchange for various time periods from 1926 to 1960. The basic assumption in all of their computations is that at the beginning of each period studied the investor puts an equal amount of money in each common stock listed at that time on the Exchange. This amounts to random sampling where the sampling is, of course, exhaustive. Different rates of return are then computed for different possible tax brackets of the investor, first under the assumption that all dividends are reinvested in the month paid, and then under the assumption that dividends are not reinvested.

A possible procedure for the analyst is to compare returns for given time periods earned by portfolios he has managed with the returns earned for the same time periods by the Fisher-Lorie "randomly selected" portfolios. It is important to note, however, that this will be a valid test procedure only if the portfolios managed by the analyst had about the same degree of riskiness as the Fisher-Lorie "market" portfolios. If this is not the case, the Fisher-Lorie results will not provide a proper benchmark. In order to make a proper comparison between the results produced by the analyst and a random selection policy, it will be necessary to define and study the behavior of portfolios of randomly selected securities, where these portfolios are selected in such a way that they have about the same degree of riskiness as those managed by the analyst.

If the claims of analysts concerning the advantages of fundamental analysis have any basis in fact, the tests suggested above would seem to be easy to pass. In fact, however, the only "analysts" that have so far undergone these tests are open end mutual funds. In their appeals to the public, mutual funds usually make two basic claims: (1) because it pools the resources of many individuals, a fund can diversify much more effectively than the average, small investor; and (2) because of its management's closeness to the market, the fund is better able to detect "good buys" in individual securities. In most cases the first claim is probably true. The second, however, implies that mutual funds provide a higher return than would be earned by a portfolio of randomly selected securities. In a separate paper [5] I reported the results of a study which suggest that if the initial loading charges of mutual funds are ignored, on the average the funds do about as well as a randomly selected portfolio. If one takes into account the higher initial loading charges of the funds, however, on the average the random investment policy outperforms the funds. In addition, these results would seem to be consistent with those of the now famous Wharton study of mutual funds [11].

These adverse results with respect to mutual funds have tended to lead random walk theorists to feel that other financial institutions, and most professional investment advisers as well, probably do no better than random selection. Institutions and analysts can only dispel such doubts by submitting their performance to a rigorous comparison with a random selection procedure.

Conclusion

In sum, the theory of random walks in stock market prices presents important challenges to both the chartist and the proponent of fundamental analysis. For the chartist, the challenge is straightforward. If the random walk model is a valid description of reality, the work of the chartist, like that of the astrologer, is of no real value in stock market analysis. The empirical evidence to date provides strong support for the random walk model. In this light the only way the chartist can vindicate his position is to *show* that he can *consistently* use his techniques to make better than chance predictions of stock prices. It is not enough for him to talk mystically about patterns that he sees in the data. He must show that he can consistently use these patterns to make meaningful predictions of future prices.

The challenge of the theory of random walks to the proponent of fundamental analysis, however, is more involved. If the random walk theory is valid and if security exchanges are "efficient" markets, then stock prices at any point in time will represent good estimates of intrinsic or fundamental values. Thus, additional fundamental analysis is of value only when the analyst has new information which was not fully considered in forming current market prices, or has new insights concerning the effects of generally available information which are not already implicit in current prices. If the analyst has neither better insights nor new information, he may as well forget about fundamental analysis and choose securities by some random selection procedure.

In essence, the challenge of the random walk theory to the proponent of fundamental analysis is to show that his more complicated procedures are actually more profitable than a simple random selection policy. As in the case of the chartist, the challenge is an empirical one. The analyst cannot merely protest that he thinks the securities he selects do better than randomly selected securities; he must demonstrate that this is in fact the case.

References

1. Alexander, Sidney S. "Price Movements in Speculative Markets: Trends or Random Walks." *Industrial Management Review* II (May 1961), 7–26.
2. Alexander, Sidney S. "Price Movements in Speculative Markets: Trends or Random Walks, Number 2." *Industrial Management Review* V (Spring 1964), 25–46.
3. Cootner, Paul H. (editor). *The Random Character of Stock Market Prices.* Cambridge: M.I.T. Press, 1964. An excellent compilation of research on the theory of random walks completed prior to mid-1963.
4. Cootner, Paul H. "Stock Prices: Random versus Systematic Changes." *Industrial Management Review* III (Spring 1962), 24–45.
5. Fama, Eugene F. "The Behavior of Stock Market Prices." *Journal of Business* XXXVIII (January 1965), 34–105.
6. Fisher, L., and Lorie, J. H. "Rates of Return on Investments in Common Stocks." *Journal of Business* (January 1964), 1–21.
7. Godfrey, Michael D., Granger, Clive W. J., and Morgenstern, Oskar. "The Random Walk Hypothesis of Stock Market Behavior." *Kyklos* XVII (January 1964), 1–30.

8. Granger, Clive W. J., and Morgenstern, O. "Spectral Analysis of New York Stock Market Prices." *Kyklos* XVI (January 1963), 1–27.

9. Kendall, M. G. "The Analysis of Economic Time Series." *Journal of the Royal Statistical Society* (Series A) XCVI (1953), 11–25.

10. Moore, Arnold. "A Statistical Analysis of Common Stock Prices." Unpublished Ph.D. dissertation, Graduate School of Business, University of Chicago (1962).

11. "A Study of Mutual Funds." Prepared for the Securities and Exchange Commission by the Wharton School of Finance and Commerce, Report of the Committee on Interstate and Foreign Commerce. Washington: U.S. Government Printing Office, 1962.

Discussion Questions

1. Describe an efficient market.

2. What does the random walk theory say regarding successive price changes in stock price?

3. In an efficient market, what should be the relationship between stock prices and their intrinsic values?

4. In an efficient market, how well will securities perform for the gifted securities analyst? Why?

5. Specify the design for a test of an efficient market.

*Fischer Black and Myron Scholes**

The Pricing of Options and Corporate Liabilities

The Black-Scholes option pricing model (formula) is one of the most important contributions to the study of finance. It is essential in many academic and practical arenas. According to Bernstein

> The important observation here is that "people had no choice." The options traders who ignored the Black-Scholes model and its variants did so at their peril: without it, they were destined to get the short end of the stick. Soon people were going about with little hand-held calculators that had been programmed to perform the necessary calculations once the inputs had been punched in. Many options traders operate with powerful computers at their beck and call.†

Reproduced below is the original paper in which Fischer Black and Myron Scholes described and developed their now famous model.

Abstract

If options are correctly priced in the market, it should not be possible to make sure profits by creating portfolios of long and short positions in options and their underlying stocks. Using this principle, a theoretical valuation formula for options is derived. Since almost all corporate liabilities can be viewed as combinations of options, the formula and the analysis that led to it are also applicable to corporate liabilities such as common stock, corporate bonds, and warrants. In particular, the formula can be used to derive the discount that should be applied to a corporate bond because of the possibility of default.

* The inspiration for this work was provided by Jack L. Treynor (1961a, 1961b). We are grateful for extensive comments on earlier drafts by Eugene F. Fama, Robert C. Merton, and Merton H. Miller. This work was supported in part by the Ford Foundation.

† Peter Bernstein, *Capital Ideas* (New York: The Free Press, 1992), p. 227.

Source: Reprinted with permission from Fischer Black, "The Pricing of Options and Corporate Liabilities," *Journal of Political Economy* (May/June 1973), pp. 637–654. Fischer Black is a Partner at Goldman, Sachs and Company, New York, New York. Myron Scholes is the Frank E. Buck Professor of Finance at Stanford University.

Introduction

An option is a security giving the right to buy or sell an asset, subject to certain conditions, within a specified period of time. An "American option" is one that can be exercised at any time up to the date the option expires. A "European option" is one that can be exercised only on a specified future date. The price that is paid for the asset when the option is exercised is called the "exercise price" or "striking price." The last day on which the option may be exercised is called the "expiration date" or "maturity date."

The simplest kind of option is one that gives the right to buy a single share of common stock. Throughout most of the paper, we will be discussing this kind of option, which is often referred to as a "call option."

In general, it seems clear that the higher the price of the stock, the greater the value of the option. When the stock price is much greater than the exercise price, the option is almost sure to be exercised. The current value of the option will thus be approximately equal to the price of the stock minus the price of a pure discount bond that matures on the same date as the option, with a face value equal to the striking price of the option.

On the other hand, if the price of the stock is much less than the exercise price, the option is almost sure to expire without being exercised, so its value will be near zero.

If the expiration date of the option is very far in the future, then the price of a bond that pays the exercise price on the maturity date will be very low, and the value of the option will be approximately equal to the price of the stock.

On the other hand, if the expiration date is very near, the value of the option will be approximately equal to the stock price minus the exercise price, or zero, if the stock price is less than the exercise price. Normally, the value of an option declines as its maturity date approaches, if the value of the stock does not change.

These general properties of the relation between the option value and the stock price are often illustrated in a diagram like Figure 1. Line A represents the maximum value of the option, since it cannot be worth more than the stock. Line B represents the minimum value of the option, since its value cannot be negative and cannot be less than the stock price minus the exercise price. Lines T_1, T_2, and T_3 represent the value of the option for successively shorter maturities.

Normally the curve representing the value of an option will be concave upward. Since it also lies below the 45° line, A, we can see that the option will be more volatile than the stock. A given percentage change in the stock price, holding maturity constant, will result in a larger percentage change in the option value. The relative volatility of the option is not constant, however. It depends on both the stock price and maturity.

Most of the previous work on the valuation of options has been expressed in terms of warrants. For example, Sprenkle (1961), Ayres (1963), Boness (1964), Samuelson (1965), Baumol, Malkiel, and Quandt (1966), and Chen (1970) all produced valuation formulas of the same general form. Their formulas, however, were not complete, since they all involved one or more arbitrary parameters.

For example, Sprenkle's formula for the value of an option can be written as follows:

$$kxN(b_1) - k^*cN(b_2)$$

$$b_1 = \frac{\ln kx/c + \frac{1}{2}v^2(t^* - t)}{v\sqrt{(t^* - t)}}$$

Figure 1   The Relation between Option Value and Stock Price

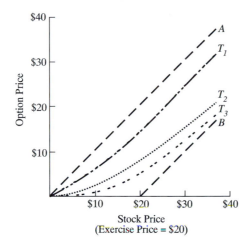

Stock Price
(Exercise Price = $20)

$$b_2 = \frac{\ln kx/c - \frac{1}{2} v^2(t^* - t)}{v\sqrt{(t^* - t)}}$$

In this expression, x is the stock price, c is the exercise price, t^* is the maturity date, t is the current date, v^2 is the variance rate of the return on the stock,[1] ln is the natural logarithm, and $N(b)$ is the cumulative normal density function. But k and k^* are unknown parameters. Sprenkle (1961) defines k as the ratio of the expected value of the stock price at the time the warrant matures to the current stock price, and k^* as a discount factor that depends on the risk of the stock. He tries to estimate the values of k and k^* empirically, but finds that he is unable to do so.

More typically, Samuelson (1965) has unknown parameters α and β, where α is the rate of expected return on the stock and β is the rate of expected return on the warrant or the discount rate to be applied to the warrant.[2] He assumes that the distribution of possible values of the stock when the warrant matures is log-normal and takes the expected value of this distribution, cutting it off at the exercise price. He then discounts this expected value to the present at the rate β. Unfortunately, there seems to be no model of the pricing of securities under conditions of capital market equilibrium that would make this an appropriate procedure for determining the value of a warrant.

In a subsequent paper, Samuelson and Merton (1969) recognize the fact that discounting the expected value of the distribution of possible values of the warrant when it is exercised is not an

---

[1] The variance rate of the return on a security is the limit, as the size of the interval of measurement goes to zero, of the variance of the return over that interval divided by the length of the interval.

[2] The rate of expected return on a security is the limit, as the size of the interval of measurement goes to zero, of the expected return over that interval divided by the length of the interval.

appropriate procedure. They advance the theory by treating the option price as a function of the stock price. They also recognize that the discount rates are determined in part by the requirement that investors be willing to hold all of the outstanding amounts of both the stock and the option. But they do not make use of the fact that investors must hold other assets as well, so that the risk of an option or stock that affects its discount rate is only that part of the risk that cannot be diversified away. Their final formula depends on the shape of the utility function that they assume for the typical investor.

One of the concepts that we use in developing our model is expressed by Thorp and Kassouf (1967). They obtain an empirical valuation formula for warrants by fitting a curve to actual warrant prices. Then they use this formula to calculate the ratio of shares of stock to options needed to create a hedged position by going long in one security and short in the other. What they fail to pursue is the fact that in equilibrium, the expected return on such a hedged position must be equal to the return on a riskless asset. What we show below is that this equilibrium condition can be used to derive a theoretical valuation formula.

The Valuation Formula

In deriving our formula for the value of an option in terms of the price of the stock, we will assume "ideal conditions" in the market for the stock and for the option:

a. The short-term interest rate is known and is constant through time.

b. The stock price follows a random walk in continuous time with a variance rate proportional to the square of the stock price. Thus the distribution of possible stock prices at the end of any finite interval is log-normal. The variance rate of the return on the stock is constant.

c. The stock pays no dividends or other distributions.

d. The option is "European"; that is, it can be exercised only at maturity.

e. There are no transaction costs in buying or selling the stock or the option.

f. It is possible to borrow any fraction of the price of a security to buy it or to hold it, at the short-term interest rate.

g. There are no penalties to short selling. A seller who does not own a security will simply accept the price of the security from a buyer, and will agree to settle with the buyer on some future date by paying him an amount equal to the price of the security on that date.

Under these assumptions, the value of the option will depend only on the price of the stock and time and on variables that are taken to be known constants. Thus, it is possible to create a hedged position, consisting of a long position in the stock and a short position in the option, whose value will not depend on the price of the stock, but will depend only on time and the values of known constants. Writing $w(x,t)$ for the value of the option as a function of the stock price x and time t, the number of options that must be sold short against one share of stock long is:

$$1/w_1(x,t). \tag{1}$$

In expression (1), the subscript refers to the partial derivative of $w(x,t)$ with respect to its first argument.

To see that the value of such a hedged position does not depend on the price of the stock, note that the ratio of the change in the option value to the change in the stock price, when the change in the stock price is small, is $w_1(x,t)$. To a first approximation, if the stock price changes by an amount

Δx, the option price will change by an amount $w_1(x,t) \Delta x$, and the number of options given by expression (1) will change by an amount Δx. Thus, the change in the value of a long position in the stock will be approximately offset by the change in value of a short position in $1/w_1$ options.

As the variables x and t change, the number of options to be sold short to create a hedged position with one share of stock changes. If the hedge is maintained continuously, then the approximations mentioned above become exact, and the return on the hedged position is completely independent of the change in the value of the stock. In fact, the return on the hedged position becomes certain.[3]

To illustrate the formation of the hedged position, let us refer to the solid line (T_2) in Figure 1 and assume that the price of the stock starts at \$15.00, so that the value of the option starts at \$5.00. Assume also that the slope of the line at that point is 1/2. This means that the hedged position is created by buying one share of stock and selling two options short. One share of stock costs \$15.00, and the sale of two options brings in \$10.00, so the equity in this position is \$5.00.

If the hedged position is not changed as the price of the stock changes, then there is some uncertainty in the value of the equity at the end of a finite interval. Suppose that two options go from \$10.00 to \$15.75 when the stock goes from \$15.00 to \$20.00, and that they go from \$10.00 to \$5.75 when the stock goes from \$15.00 to \$10.00. Thus, the equity goes from \$5.00 to \$4.25 when the stock changes by \$5.00 in either direction. This is a \$.75 decline in the equity for a \$5.00 change in the stock in either direction.[4]

In addition, the curve shifts (say from T_2 to T_3 in Figure 1) as the maturity of the options changes. The resulting decline in value of the options means an increase in the equity in the hedged position and tends to offset the possible losses due to a large change in the stock price.

Note that the decline in the equity value due to a large change in the stock price is small. The ratio of the decline in the equity value to the magnitude of the change in the stock price becomes smaller as the magnitude of the change in the stock price becomes smaller.

Note also that the direction of the change in the equity value is independent of the direction of the change in the stock price. This means that under our assumption that the stock price follows a continuous random walk and that the return has a constant variance rate, the covariance between the return on the equity and the return on the stock will be zero. If the stock price and the value of the "market portfolio" follow a joint continuous random walk with constant covariance rate, it means that the covariance between the return on the equity and the return on the market will be zero.

Thus the risk in the hedged position is zero if the short position in the option is adjusted continuously. If the position is not adjusted continuously, the risk is small, and consists entirely of risk that can be diversified away by forming a portfolio of a large number of such hedged positions.

In general, since the hedged position contains one share of stock long and $1/w_1$ options short, the value of the equity in the position is:

$$x - w/w_1. \tag{2}$$

The change in the value of the equity in a short interval Δt is:

$$\Delta x - \Delta w/w_1. \tag{3}$$

---

[3] This was pointed out to us by Robert Merton.

[4] These figures are purely for illustrative purposes. They correspond roughly to the way Figure 1 was drawn, but not to an option on any actual security.

Assuming that the short position is changed continuously, we can use stochastic calculus[5] to expand Δw, which is $w(x + \Delta x, \, t + \Delta t) - w(x,t)$, as follows:

$$\Delta w = w_1 \Delta x + \frac{1}{2} w_{11} v^2 x^2 \Delta t + w_2 \Delta t. \tag{4}$$

In equation (4), the subscripts on w refer to partial derivatives, and v^2 is the variance rate of the return on the stock.[6] Substituting from equation (4) into expression (3), we find that the change in the value of the equity in the hedged position is:

$$-\left(\frac{1}{2} w_{11} v^2 x^2 + w_2 \right) \Delta t / w_1. \tag{5}$$

Since the return on the equity in the hedged position is certain, the return must be equal to $r\Delta t$. Even if the hedged position is not changed continuously, its risk is small and is entirely risk that can be diversified away, so the expected return on the hedged position must be at the short term interest rate.[7] If this were not true, speculators would try to profit by borrowing large amounts of money to create such hedged positions, and would in the process force the returns down to the short term interest rate.

Thus the change in the equity (5) must equal the value of the equity (2) times $r\Delta t$.

$$-\left(\frac{1}{2} w_{11} v^2 x^2 + w^2 \right) \Delta t / w_1 = (x - w/w_1) r\Delta t. \tag{6}$$

Dropping the Δt from both sides, and rearranging, we have a differential equation for the value of the option,

$$w_2 = rw - rxw_1 - \frac{1}{2} v^2 x^2 w_{11}. \tag{7}$$

Writing t^* for the maturity date of the option and c for the exercise price, we know that:

$$
\begin{aligned}
w(x,t^*) \quad &= \quad x - c, \quad x \geq c \\[2mm]
&= \quad 0, \quad\quad x < c.
\end{aligned}
\tag{8}
$$

There is only one formula $w(x,t)$ that satisfies the differential equation (7) subject to the boundary condition (8). This formula must be the option valuation formula.

---

[5] For an exposition of stochastic calculus, see McKean (1969).

[6] See footnote 1.

[7] For a thorough discussion of the relation between risk and expected return, see Fama and Miller (1972) or Sharpe (1970). To see that the risk in the hedged position can be diversified away, note that if we don't adjust the hedge continuously, expression (5) becomes:

$$-\left(\frac{1}{2} w_{11} \Delta x^2 + w_2 \Delta t \right) / w_1. \tag{5'}$$

Writing Δm for the change in the value of the market portfolio between t and $t + \Delta t$, the "market risk" in the hedged position is proportional to the covariance between the change in the value of the hedged portfolio, as given by expression (5'), and Δm: $-\frac{1}{2} w_{11} \operatorname{cov}(\Delta x^2, \Delta m)$. But if Δx and Δm follow a joint normal distribution for small intervals Δt, this covariance will be zero. Since there is no market risk in the hedged position, all of the risk due to the fact that the hedge is not continuously adjusted must be risk that can be diversified away.

To solve this differential equation, we make the following substitution:

$$w(x,t) = e^{r(t-t^*)}y \quad \left[(2/v^2)\left(r - \frac{1}{2}v^2\right) \right.$$

$$\left[\ln x/c - \left(r - \frac{1}{2}v^2\right)(t - t^*) \right],$$

$$\left. - (2/v^2)\left(r - \frac{1}{2}v^2\right)^2(t - t^*) \right]. \tag{9}$$

With this substitution, the differential equation becomes:

$$y_2 = y_{11}, \tag{10}$$

and the boundary condition becomes:

$$y(u,0) \quad = \quad 0, \qquad\qquad\qquad u < 0$$

$$= \quad c\left[e^{u\left(\frac{1}{2}v^2\right)/\left(r - \frac{1}{2}v^2\right)} - 1 \right], \qquad u \geq 0. \tag{11}$$

The differential equation (10) is the heat-transfer equation of physics, and its solution is given by Churchill (1963, p. 155). In our notation, the solution is:

$$y(u,s) = 1/\sqrt{2\pi} \int_{-u/\sqrt{2s}}^{\infty}$$

$$c\left[e^{(u + q\sqrt{2s})\left(\frac{1}{2}v^2\right)/\left(r - \frac{1}{2}v^2\right)} - 1 \right] e^{-q^2/2} \, dq. \tag{12}$$

Substituting from equation (12) into equation (9), and simplifying, we find:

$$w(x,t) \quad = \quad xN(d_1) - ce^{r(t-t^*)}N(d_2)$$

$$d_1 \quad = \quad \frac{\ln x/c + (r + \frac{1}{2}v^2)(t^* - t)}{v\sqrt{t^* - t}}$$

$$d_2 \quad = \quad \frac{\ln x/c + (r - \frac{1}{2}v^2)(t^* - t)}{v\sqrt{t^* - t}} \tag{13}$$

In equation (13), $N(d)$ is the cumulative normal density function.

Note that the expected return on the stock does not appear in equation (13). The option value as a function of the stock price is independent of the expected return on the stock. The expected return on the option, however, will depend on the expected return on the stock. The faster the stock price rises, the faster the option price will rise through the functional relationship (13).

Note that the maturity $(t^* - t)$ appears in the formula only multiplied by the interest rate r or the variance rate v^2. Thus, an increase in maturity has the same effect on the value of the option as an equal percentage increase in both r and v^2.

Merton (1973) has shown that the option value as given by equation (13) increases continuously as any one of t^*, r, or v^2 increases. In each case, it approaches a maximum value equal to the stock price.

The partial derivative w_1 of the valuation formula is of interest, because it determines the ratio of shares of stock to options in the hedged position as in expression (1). Taking the partial derivative of equation (13), and simplifying, we find that:

$$w_1(x,t) = N(d_1). \tag{14}$$

In equation (14), d_1 is as defined in equation (13).

From equations (13) and (14), it is clear that xw_1/w is always greater than one. This shows that the option is always more volatile than the stock.

An Alternative Derivation

It is also possible to derive the differential equation (7) using the "capital asset pricing model." This derivation is given because it gives more understanding of the way in which one can discount the value of an option to the present, using a discount rate that depends on both time and the price of the stock.

The capital asset pricing model describes the relation between risk and expected return for a capital asset under conditions of market equilibrium.[8] The expected return on an asset gives the discount that must be applied to the end-of-period value of the asset to give its present value. Thus, the capital-asset pricing model gives a general method for discounting under uncertainty.

The capital-asset pricing model says that the expected return on an asset is a linear function of its β, which is defined as the covariance of the return on the asset with the return on the market, divided by the variance of the return on the market. From equation (4) we see that the covariance of the return on the option $\Delta w/w$ with the return on the market is equal to xw_1/w times the covariance of the return on the stock $\Delta x/x$ with the return on the market. Thus, we have the following relation between the option's β and the stock's β:

$$\beta_w = (xw_1/w)\beta_x. \tag{15}$$

The expression xw_1/w may also be interpreted as the "elasticity" of the option price with respect to the stock price. It is the ratio of the percentage change in the option price to the percentage change in the stock price, for small percentage changes, holding maturity constant.

To apply the capital-asset pricing model to an option and the underlying stock, let us first define a as the rate of expected return on the market minus the interest rate.[9] Then the expected return on the option and the stock are:

$$E(\Delta x/x) = r\Delta t + a\beta_x\Delta t, \tag{16}$$

$$E(\Delta w/w) = r\Delta t + a\beta_w\Delta t. \tag{17}$$

Multiplying equation (17) by w, and substituting for β_w from equation (15), we find:

$$E(\Delta w) = rw\Delta t + axw_1\beta_x\Delta t. \tag{18}$$

[8] The model was developed by Treynor (1961b), Sharpe (1964), Lintner (1965), and Mossin (1966). It is summarized by Sharpe (1970), and Fama and Miller (1972). The model was originally stated as a single-period model. Extending it to a multi-period model is, in general, difficult. Fama (1970), however, has shown that if we make an assumption that implies that the short-term interest rate is constant through time, then the model must apply to each successive period in time. His proof also goes through under somewhat more general assumptions.

[9] See footnote 2.

Using stochastic calculus,[10] we can expand Δw, which is $w(x + \Delta x, t + \Delta t) - w(x,t)$, as follows:

$$\Delta w = w_1 \Delta x + \frac{1}{2} w_{11} v^2 x^2 \Delta t + w_2 \Delta t. \tag{19}$$

Taking the expected value of equation (19), and substituting for $E(\Delta x)$ from equation (16), we have:

$$E(\Delta w) = rx w_1 \Delta t + ax w_1 \beta_x \Delta t + \frac{1}{2} v^2 x^2 w_{11} \Delta t + w_2 \Delta t. \tag{20}$$

Combining equations (18) and (20), we find that the terms involving a and β_x cancel, giving:

$$w_2 = rw - rx w_1 - \frac{1}{2} v^2 x^2 w_{11}. \tag{21}$$

Equation (21) is the same as equation (7).

More Complicated Options

The valuation formula (13) was derived under the assumption that the option can only be exercised at time t^*. Merton (1973) has shown, however, that the value of the option is always greater than the value it would have if it were exercised immediately $(x - c)$. Thus, a rational investor will not exercise a call option before maturity, and the value of an American call option is the same as the value of a European call option.

There is a simple modification of the formula that will make it applicable to European put options (options to sell) as well as call options (options to buy). Writing $u(x,t)$ for the value of a put option, we see that the differential equation remains unchanged.

$$u_2 = ru - rx u_1 - \frac{1}{2} v^2 x^2 u_{11}. \tag{22}$$

The boundary condition, however, becomes

$$u(x,t^*) \;=\; 0, \qquad x \geq c$$

$$\;=\; c - x, \;\; x < c. \tag{23}$$

To get the solution to this equation with the new boundary condition, we can simply note that the difference between the value of a call and the value of a put on the same stock, if both can be exercised only at maturity, must obey the same differential equation, but with the following boundary condition:

$$w(x,t^*) - u(x,t^*) = x - c. \tag{24}$$

The solution to the differential equation with this boundary condition is

$$w(x,t) - u(x,t) = x - ce^{r(t - t^*)}. \tag{25}$$

---

[10] For an exposition of stochastic calculus, see McKean (1969).

Thus the value of the European put option is

$$u(x,t) = w(x,t) - x + ce^{r(t-t^*)}. \tag{26}$$

Putting in the value of $w(x,t)$ from (13), and noting that $1 - N(d)$ is equal to $N(-d)$, we have

$$u(x,t) = -xN(-d_1) + ce^{-rt^*}N(-d_2). \tag{27}$$

In equation (27), d_1 and d_2 are defined as in equation (13).

Equation (25) also gives us a relation between the value of a European call and the value of a European put.[11] We see that if an investor were to buy a call and sell a put, his returns would be exactly the same as if he bought the stock on margin, borrowing $ce^{r(t-t^*)}$ toward the price of the stock.

Merton (1973) has also shown that the value of an American put option will be greater than the value of a European put option. This is true because it is sometimes advantageous to exercise a put option before maturity, if it is possible to do so. For example, suppose the stock price falls almost to zero and that the probability that the price will exceed the exercise price before the option expires is negligible. Then it will pay to exercise the option immediately, so that the exercise price will be received sooner rather than later. The investor thus gains the interest on the exercise price for the period up to the time he would otherwise have exercised it. So far, no one has been able to obtain a formula for the value of an American put option.

If we relax the assumption that the stock pays no dividend, we begin to get into some complicated problems. First of all, under certain conditions it will pay to exercise an American call option before maturity. Merton (1973) has shown that this can be true only just before the stock's ex-dividend date. Also, it is not clear what adjustment might be made in the terms of the option to protect the option holder against a loss due to a large dividend on the stock and to ensure that the value of the option will be the same as if the stock paid no dividend. Currently, the exercise price of a call option is generally reduced by the amount of any dividend paid on the stock. We can see that this is not adequate protection by imagining that the stock is that of a holding company and that it pays out all of its assets in the form of a dividend to its shareholders. This will reduce the price of the stock and the value of the option to zero, no matter what adjustment is made in the exercise price of the option. In fact, this example shows that there may not be any adjustment in the terms of the option that will give adequate protection against a large dividend. In this case, the option value is going to be zero after the distribution, no matter what its terms are. Merton (1973) was the first to point out that the current adjustment for dividends is not adequate.

Warrant Valuation

A warrant is an option that is a liability of a corporation. The holder of a warrant has the right to buy the corporation's stock (or other assets) on specified terms. The analysis of warrants is often much more complicated than the analysis of simple options, because

a. The life of a warrant is typically measured in years, rather than months. Over a period of years, the variance rate of the return on the stock may be expected to change substantially.

---

[11] The relation between the value of a call option and the value of a put option was first noted by Stoll (1969). He does not realize, however, that his analysis applies only to European options.

b. The exercise price of the warrant is usually not adjusted at all for dividends. The possibility that dividends will be paid requires a modification of the valuation formula.

c. The exercise price of a warrant sometimes changes on specified dates. It may pay to exercise a warrant just before its exercise price changes. This too requires a modification of the valuation formula.

d. If the company is involved in a merger, the adjustment that is made in the terms of the warrant may change its value.

e. Sometimes the exercise price can be paid using bonds of the corporation at face value, even though they may at the time be selling at a discount. This complicates the analysis and means that early exercise may sometimes be desirable.

f. The exercise of a large number of warrants may sometimes result in a significant increase in the number of common shares outstanding.

In some cases, these complications can be treated as insignificant, and equation (13) can be used as an approximation to give an estimate of the warrant value. In other cases, some simple modifications of equation (13) will improve the approximation. Suppose, for example, that there are warrants outstanding, which, if exercised, would double the number of shares of the company's common stock. Let us define the "equity" of the company as the sum of the value of all of its warrants and the value of all of its common stock. If the warrants are exercised at maturity, the equity of the company will increase by the aggregate amount of money paid in by the warrant holders when they exercise. The warrant holders will then own half of the new equity of the company, which is equal to the old equity plus the exercise money.

Thus, at maturity, the warrant holders will either receive nothing, or half of the new equity, minus the exercise money. Thus, they will receive nothing or half of the difference between the old equity and half the exercise money. We can look at the warrants as options to buy shares in the equity rather than shares of common stock, at half the stated exercise price rather than at the full exercise price. The value of a share in the equity is defined as the sum of the value of the warrants and the value of the common stock, divided by twice the number of outstanding shares of common stock. If we take this point of view, then we will take v_2 in equation (13) to be the variance rate of the return on the company's equity, rather than the variance rate of the return on the company's common stock.

A similar modification in the parameters of equation (13) can be made if the number of shares of stock outstanding after exercise of the warrants will be other than twice the number of shares outstanding before exercise of the warrants.

Common Stock and Bond Valuation

It is not generally realized that corporate liabilities other than warrants may be viewed as options. Consider, for example, a company that has common stock and bonds outstanding and whose only asset is shares of common stock of a second company. Suppose that the bonds are "pure discount bonds" with no coupon, giving the holder the right to a fixed sum of money, if the corporation can pay it, with a maturity of 10 years. Suppose that the bonds contain no restrictions on the company except a restriction that the company cannot pay any dividends until after the bonds are paid off. Finally, suppose that the company plans to sell all the stock it holds at the end of 10 years, pay off the bondholders if possible, and pay any remaining money to the stockholders as a liquidating dividend.

Under these conditions, it is clear that the stockholders have the equivalent of an option on their company's assets. In effect, the bondholders own the company's assets, but they have given options to the stockholders to buy the assets back. The value of the common stock at the end of 10 years will be the value of the company's assets minus the face value of the bonds, or zero, whichever is greater.

Thus, the value of the common stock will be $w(x,t)$, as given by equation (13), where we take v^2 to be the variance rate of the return on the shares held by the company, c to be the total face value of the outstanding bonds, and x to be the total value of the shares held by the company. The value of the bonds will simply be $x - w(x,t)$.

By subtracting the value of the bonds given by this formula from the value they would have if there were no default risk, we can figure the discount that should be applied to the bonds due to the existence of default risk.

Suppose, more generally, that the corporation holds business assets rather than financial assets. Suppose that at the end of the 10 year period, it will recapitalize by selling an entirely new class of common stock, using the proceeds to pay off the bondholders, and paying any money that is left to the old stockholders to retire their stock. In the absence of taxes, it is clear that the value of the corporation can be taken to be the sum of the total value of the debt and the total value of the common stock.[12] The amount of debt outstanding will not affect the total value of the corporation, but will affect the division of that value between the bonds and the stock. The formula for $w(x,t)$ will again describe the total value of the common stock, where x is taken to be the sum of the value of the bonds and the value of the stock. The formula for $x - w(x,t)$ will again describe the total value of the bonds. It can be shown that, as the face value c of the bonds increases, the market value $x - w(x,t)$ increases by a smaller percentage. An increase in the corporation's debt, keeping the total value of the corporation constant, will increase the probability of default and will thus reduce the market value of one of the corporation's bonds. If the company changes its capital structure by issuing more bonds and using the proceeds to retire common stock, it will hurt the existing bondholders, and help the existing stockholders. The bond price will fall, and the stock price will rise. In this sense, changes in the capital structure of a firm may affect the price of its common stock.[13] The price changes will occur when the change in the capital structure becomes certain, not when the actual change takes place.

Because of this possibility, the bond indenture may prohibit the sale of additional debt of the same or higher priority in the event that the firm is recapitalized. If the corporation issues new bonds that are subordinated to the existing bonds and uses the proceeds to retire common stock, the price of the existing bonds and the common stock price will be unaffected. Similarly, if the company issues new common stock and uses the proceeds to retire completely the most junior outstanding issue of bonds, neither the common stock price nor the price of any other issue of bonds will be affected.

---

[12] The fact that the total value of a corporation is not affected by its capital structure, in the absence of taxes and other imperfections, was first shown by Modigliani and Miller (1958).

[13] For a discussion of this point, see Fama and Miller (1972, pp. 151–52).

The corporation's dividend policy will also affect the division of its total value between the bonds and the stock.[14] To take an extreme example, suppose again that the corporation's only assets are the shares of another company, and suppose that it sells all these shares and uses the proceeds to pay a dividend to its common stockholders. Then the value of the firm will go to zero, and the value of the bonds will go to zero. The common stockholders will have "stolen" the company out from under the bondholders. Even for dividends of modest size, a higher dividend always favors the stockholders at the expense of the bondholders. A liberalization of dividend policy will increase the common stock price and decrease the bond price.[15] Because of this possibility, bond indentures contain restrictions on dividend policy, and the common stockholders have an incentive to pay themselves the largest dividend allowed by the terms of the bond indenture. However, it should be noted that the size of the effect of changing dividend policy will normally be very small.

If the company has coupon bonds rather than pure discount bonds outstanding, then we can view the common stock as a "compound option." The common stock is an option on an option on . . . an option on the firm. After making the last interest payment, the stockholders have an option to buy the company from the bondholders for the face value of the bonds. Call this "option 1." After making the next-to-the-last interest payment, but before making the last interest payment, the stockholders have an option to buy option 1 by making the last interest payment. Call this "option 2." Before making the next-to-the-last interest payment, the stockholders have an option to buy option 2 by making that interest payment. This is "option 3." The value of the stockholders' claim at any point in time is equal to the value of option $n + 1$, where n is the number of interest payments remaining in the life of the bond.

If payments to a sinking fund are required along with interest payments, then a similar analysis can be made. In this case, there is no "balloon payment" at the end of the life of the bond. The sinking fund will have a final value equal to the face value of the bond. Option 1 gives the stockholders the right to buy the company from the bondholders by making the last sinking fund and interest payment. Option 2 gives the stockholders the right to buy option 1 by making the next-to-the-last sinking fund and interest payment. And the value of the stockholders' claim at any point in time is equal to the value of option n, where n is the number of sinking fund and interest payments remaining in the life of the bond. It is clear that the value of a bond for which sinking fund payments are required is greater than the value of a bond for which they are not required.

---

[14] Miller and Modigliani (1961) show that the total value of a firm, in the absence of taxes and other imperfections, is not affected by its dividend policy. They also note that the price of the common stock and the value of the bonds will not be affected by a change in dividend policy if the funds for a higher dividend are raised by issuing common stock or if the money released by a lower dividend is used to repurchase common stock.

[15] This is true assuming that the liberalization of dividend policy is not accompanied by a change in the company's current and planned financial structure. Since the issue of common stock or junior debt will hurt the common shareholders (holding dividend policy constant), they will normally try to liberalize dividend policy without issuing new securities. They may be able to do this by selling some of the firm's financial assets, such as ownership claims on other firms. Or they may be able to do it by adding to the company's short-term bank debt, which is normally senior to its long-term debt. Finally, the company may be able to finance a higher dividend by selling off a division. Assuming that it receives a fair price for the division, and that there were no economies of combination, this need not involve any loss to the firm as a whole. If the firm issues new common stock or junior debt in exactly the amounts needed to finance the liberalization of dividend policy, then the common stock and bond prices will not be affected. If the liberalization of dividend policy is associated with a decision to issue more common stock or junior debt than is needed to pay the higher dividends, the common stock price will fall and the bond price will rise. But these actions are unlikely, since they are not in the stockholders' best interests.

If the company has callable bonds, then the stockholders have more than one option. They can buy the next option by making the next interest or sinking fund and interest payment, or they can exercise their option to retire the bonds before maturity at prices specified by the terms of the call feature. Under our assumption of a constant short-term interest rate, the bonds would never sell above face value, and the usual kind of call option would never be exercised. Under more general assumptions, however, the call feature would have value to the stockholders and would have to be taken into account in deciding how the value of the company is divided between the stockholders and the bondholders.

Similarly if the bonds are convertible, we simply add another option to the package. It is an option that the bondholders have to buy part of the company from the stockholders.

Unfortunately, these more complicated options cannot be handled by using the valuation formula (13). The valuation formula assumes that the variance rate of the return on the optioned asset is constant. But the variance of the return on an option is certainly not constant: it depends on the price of the stock and the maturity of the option. Thus the formula cannot be used, even as an approximation, to give the value of an option on an option. It is possible, however, that an analysis in the same spirit as the one that led to equation (13) would allow at least a numerical solution to the valuation of certain more complicated options.

Empirical Tests

We have done empirical tests of the valuation formula on a large body of call-option data (Black and Scholes 1972). These tests indicate that the actual prices at which options are bought and sold deviate in certain systematic ways from the values predicted by the formula. Option buyers pay prices that are consistently higher than those predicted by the formula. Option writers, however, receive prices that are at about the level predicted by the formula. There are large transaction costs in the option market, all of which are effectively paid by option buyers.

Also, the difference between the price paid by option buyers and the value given by the formula is greater for options on high-risk stocks than for options on high-risk stocks. The market appears to underestimate the effect of differences in variance rate on the value of an option. Given the magnitude of the transaction costs in this market, however, this systematic misestimation of value does not imply profit opportunities for a speculator in the option market.

References

Ayres, Herbert F. "Risk Aversion in the Warrants Market." *Indus. Management Rev.* 4 (Fall 1963): 497–505. Reprinted in Cootner (1967), pp. 497–505.

Baumol, William J., Malkiel, Burton G., and Quandt, Richard E. "The Valuation of Convertible Securities." *Q.J.E.* 80 (February 1966): 48–59.

Black, Fischer, and Scholes, Myron. "The Valuation of Option Contracts and a Test of Market Efficiency." *J. Finance* 27 (May 1972): 399–417.

Boness, A. James. "Elements of a Theory of Stock-Option Values." *J.P.E.* 72 (April 1964): 163–75.

Chen, Andrew H. Y. "A Model of Warrant Pricing in a Dynamic Market." *J. Finance* 25 (December 1970): 1041–60.

Churchill, R. V. *Fourier Series and Boundary Value Problems,* 2d ed. New York: McGraw-Hill, 1963.

Cootner, Paul A. *The Random Character of Stock Market Prices.* Cambridge, Mass.: M.I.T. Press, 1967.

Fama, Eugene F. "Multiperiod Consumption-Investment Decisions." *A.E.R.* 60 (March 1970): 1963–74.

Fama, Eugene F., and Miller, Merton H. *The Theory of Finance.* New York: Holt, Rinehart & Winston, 1972.

Lintner, John. "The Valuation of Risk Assets and the Selection of Risky Investments in Stock Portfolios and Capital Budgets." *Rev. Econ. and Statis.* 47 (February 1965): 768–83.

McKean H. P., Jr. *Stochastic Integrals.* New York: Academic Press. 1969.

Merton, Robert C. "Theory of Rational Option Pricing." *Bell J. Econ. and Management Sci.* (1973).

Miller, Merton H., and Modigliani, Franco. "Dividend Policy, Growth, and the Valuation of Shares." *J. Bus.* 34 (October 1961): 411–33.

Modigliani, Franco, and Miller, Merton H. "The Cost of Capital, Corporation Finance, and the Theory of Investment." *A.E.R.* 48 (June 1958): 261–97.

Mossin, Jan. "Equilibrium in a Capital Asset Market." *Econometrica* 34 (October 1966): 768–83.

Samuelson, Paul A. "Rational Theory of Warrant Pricing." *Indus. Management Rev.* 6 (Spring 1965): 13–31. Reprinted in Cootner (1967), pp. 506–32.

Samuelson, Paul A., and Merton, Robert C. "A Complete Model of Warrant Pricing that Maximizes Utility." *Indus. Management Rev.* 10 (Winter 1969): 17–46.

Sharpe, William F. "Capital Asset Prices: A Theory of Market Equilibrium under Conditions of Risk." *J. Finance* 19 (September 1964): 425–42.

———. *Portfolio Theory and Capital Markets:* New York: McGraw-Hill, 1970.

Sprenkle, Case. "Warrant Prices as Indications of Expectations." *Yale Econ. Essays* 1 (1961): 179–232. Reprinted in Cootner (1967), 412–74.

Stoll, Hans R. "The Relationship between Put and Call Option Prices." *J. Finance* 24 (December 1969): 802–24.

Thorp, Edward O., and Kassouf, Sheen T. *Beat the Market.* New York: Random House, 1967.

Treynor, Jack L. "Implications for the Theory of Finance." Unpublished memorandum, 1961(a).

———. "Toward a Theory of Market Value of Risky Assets." Unpublished memorandum, 1961(b).

Discussion Questions

1. What five factors determine the value of a call option for a common stock?

2. What assumptions were made by the authors in deriving their model?

3. What are some examples of options that are embedded in other investments?

4. What is the difference between an American and a European option?

5. If the risk of the stock increases, what happens to the value of a call option? Why?

6. As the expiration date moves more closely to the present, what happens to the value of a call option? Explain.

7. Of the variables or factors needed to value a call option, which are observable, and which require estimation?

Michael C. Jensen and Richard S. Ruback*

The Market for Corporate Control: The Scientific Evidence

This paper reviews much of the scientific literature on the market for corporate control. The evidence indicates that corporate takeovers generate positive gains, that target firm shareholders benefit, and that bidding firm shareholders do not lose. The gains created by corporate takeovers do not appear to come from the creation of market power. With the exception of actions that exclude potential bidders, it is difficult to find managerial actions related to corporate control that harm shareholders. Finally, it is argued that the market for corporate control is best viewed as an arena in which managerial teams compete for the rights to manage corporate resources.

1. The Analytical Perspective

1.1. Definition

Corporate control is frequently used to describe many phenomena ranging from the general forces that influence the use of corporate resources (such as legal and regulatory systems and competition in product and input markets) to the control of a majority of seats on a corporation's board of directors. We define corporate control as the rights to determine the management of corporate resources—that is, the rights to hire, fire and set the compensation of top-level managers (Fama and Jensen [1983a, b]). When a bidding firm acquires a target firm, the control rights to the target firm are transferred to the board of directors of the acquiring firm. While corporate boards always retain the top-level control rights, they

*We have benefited from the comments of Paul Asquith, Fischer Black, Michelle Bonnice, Michael Bradley, Andrew Christie, Frank Easterbrook, Richard Leftwich, Paul Malatesta, Terry Marsh, Robert Merton, Wayne Mikkelson, Walter Oi, Charles Plosser, Katherine Schipper, G. William Schwert, Clifford Smith, René Stulz, Jerold Warner, Martin Zimmerman, and especially Harry DeAngelo, Linda DeAngelo, and John Long. This research is sponsored by the Managerial Economics Research Center of the University of Rochester, Graduate School of Management.

Source: Reprinted with permission from the *Journal of Financial Economics* (April 1983) pp. 5–50, "The Market for Corporate Control: The Scientific Evidence" by Michael C. Jensen and Richard S. Ruback. Elsevier Science B.V., Amsterdam, The Netherlands. Michael C. Jensen is the Edsel Bryant Ford Professor of Business Administration at Harvard Business School. Richard S. Ruback is the Willard Prescott Smith Professor of Corporate Finance at Harvard University.

normally delegate the rights to manage corporate resources to internal managers. In this way the top management of the acquiring firm acquires the rights to manage the resources of the target firm.

1.2. Managerial Competition

We view the market for corporate control, often referred to as the takeover market, as a market in which alternative managerial teams compete for the rights to manage corporate resources. Hence, the takeover market is an important component of the managerial labor market; it complements the internal and external managerial labor markets discussed by Fama (1980). Viewing the market for corporate control as the arena in which management teams compete is a subtle but substantial shift from the traditional view, in which financiers and activist stockholders are the parities who (alone or in coalition with others) buy control of a company and hire and fire management to achieve better resource utilization. The managerial competition model instead views competing management teams as the primary activist entities, with stockholders (including institutions) playing a relatively passive, but fundamentally important, judicial role. Arbitrageurs and takeover specialists facilitate these transactions by acting as intermediaries to value offers by competing management teams, including incumbent managers. Therefore, stockholders in this system have relatively little use for detailed knowledge about the firm or the plans of competing management teams beyond that normally used for the market's price setting function. Stockholders have no loyalty to incumbent managers; they simply choose the highest dollar value offer from those presented to them in a well-functioning market for corporate control, including sale at the market price to anonymous arbitrageurs and takeover specialists. In this perspective, competition among managerial teams for the rights to manage resources limits divergence from shareholder wealth maximization by managers and provides the mechanism through which economies of scale or other synergies available from combining or reorganizing control and management of corporate resources are realized.

Takeovers can occur through merger, tender offer, or proxy contest, and sometimes elements of all three are involved. In mergers or tender offers the bidding firm offers to buy the common stock of the target at a price in excess of the target's previous market value. Mergers are negotiated directly with target managers and approved by the target's board of directors before going to a vote of target shareholders for approval. Tender offers are offers to buy shares made directly to target shareholders, who decide individually whether to tender their shares for sale to the bidding firm. Proxy contests occur when an insurgent group, often led by a dissatisfied former manager or large stockholder, attempts to gain controlling seats on the board of directors.

1.3. Overview of the Issues and Evidence

Manne's (1965) seminal article initiated an interest in how the market for control influences large corporations, and knowledge about many facets of the market for corporate control has recently increased considerably. This body of scientific knowledge about the corporate takeover market provides answers to the following questions:

1. How large are the gains to shareholders of bidding and target firms?
2. Does opposition to takeover bids by the managers of target firms reduce shareholder wealth?
3. Do takeovers create market power in product markets?
4. Does antitrust opposition to takeovers impose costs on merging firms?

5. Is shareholder wealth affected by proxy contests?

6. Are corporate voting rights valuable?

A brief overview of the evidence provides a useful guide to the more detailed discussion that follows. Numerous studies estimate the effects of mergers and tender offers on the stock prices of the participating firms. Tables 1 and 2 present a summary of stock price changes (measured net of marketwide price movements) for successful and unsuccessful takeovers in these studies. The returns in the tables represent our synthesis of the evidence. Discussion of the details of the studies and the issues that lie behind the estimates in the tables is contained in Section 2, "The Wealth Effects of Takeover Activities."

Table 1 shows that target firms in successful takeovers experience statistically significant abnormal stock price changes of 20 percent in mergers and 30 percent in tender offers. Bidding firms realize statistically abnormal gains of 4 percent in tender offers and zero in mergers. Table 2 shows that both bidders and targets suffer small negative abnormal stock price changes in unsuccessful merger and tender offer takeovers, although only the −5 percent return for unsuccessful bidders in mergers is significantly different from zero. Stockholders in companies that experience proxy contests earn statistically significant average abnormal returns of about 8 percent. Somewhat surprisingly, these returns are not substantially lower when the insurgent group loses the contest.

The contrast between the large stock price increases for successful target firms and the insignificant stock price changes for unsuccessful targets indicates that the benefits of mergers and tender offers are realized only when control of the target firm's assets is transferred to a bidding firm. This suggests that stockholders of potential target firms are harmed when target managers oppose takeover bids or take other actions that reduce the probability of a successful acquisition. Moreover, since target managers replaced after takeovers lose power, prestige, and the value of organization-specific human capital, they have incentives to oppose a takeover bid even though shareholders might benefit substantially from acquisition. However, management opposition to a takeover bid will benefit stockholders if it leads to a higher takeover price or otherwise increased stock prices. Thus, the effect of management opposition on shareholder wealth is an empirical matter.

The evidence indicates that the effect of unsuccessful takeover attempts varies across takeover techniques, and the reasons for these differences are not currently known. In unsuccessful mergers the target's stock price falls to about its pre-offer level. In unsuccessful tender offers the target's stock price remains substantially above its pre-offer level, unless a subsequent bid does not occur in the two years following the initial offer. If such a subsequent bid does not occur, the target's stock

---

Table 1   Abnormal Percentage Stock Price Changes Associated with Successful Corporate Takeovers[a]

Takeover Technique	Target	Bidders
Tender offers	30%	4%
Mergers	20	0
Proxy contests	8	n.a.[b]

[a]Abnormal price changes are price changes adjusted to eliminate the effects of marketwide price changes.
[b]Not applicable.

Table 2   Abnormal Percentage Stock Price Changes Associated with Unsuccessful Corporate Takeover Bids[a]

Takeover Technique	Target	Bidders
Tender offers	–3%	–1%
Mergers	–3	–5
Proxy contests	8	n.a.[b]

[a]Abnormal price changes are price changes adjusted to eliminate the effects of marketwide price changes.
[b]Not applicable.

price reverts to its pre-offer level. Finally, in proxy contests the 8 percent increase in equity values does not depend on the outcome of the contest.

The abnormal stock price changes summarized in Tables 1 and 2 indicate that transfer of the target-firm control rights produces gains. The evidence reviewed in Section 3, "Antitrust and the Source of Merger Gains," indicates that the merger gains do not come from the creation of product market power. This is an important finding since the evidence also indicates antitrust opposition to takeovers imposes costs on the merging firms by restricting transfers of corporate control. The takeover gains apparently come from the realization of increased efficiencies or synergies, but the evidence is not sufficient to identify their exact sources.

Section 4 contains a discussion of conflicts of interest between management and stockholders as well as estimates of the effects on stock prices of various managerial actions and proxy contests, and estimates of the value of corporate voting rights. Evidence presented in Section 4 indicates that some actions that reduce the probability of takeovers, such as corporate charter changes, do not reduce shareholder wealth. In contrast, managerial actions that eliminate potential bidders, such as targeted large-block repurchases or standstill agreements, apparently are costly to shareholders. Section 5 discusses unsettled issues and suggests directions for future research.

2. The Wealth Effects of Takeover Activities

Numerous studies estimate the effects of takeovers on stock prices of bidder and target firms around the time of announcement of takeover attempts. Such "event studies" use estimates of the abnormal stock price changes around the offer announcement date as a measure of the economic effects of the takeover. Abnormal returns are measured by the difference between actual and expected stock returns. The expected stock return is measured conditional on the realized return on a market index to take account of the influence of marketwise events on the returns of individual securities.[1]

---

[1] Fama, Fisher, Jensen, and Roll (1969) first used this methodology in their study of the price effects of stock splits. Brown and Warner (1980, 1983) provide a detailed discussion of the techniques and various methodological issues regarding their use and interpretation. For simplicity we avoid discussing the details of the abnormal return estimation technique used in each of the studies summarized here. The techniques used in the papers to calculate the abnormal returns are generally similar and, more importantly, the results appear robust with respect to the various estimation techniques used, although Malatesta (1983) raises some interesting questions regarding the effects of the use of constrained estimation techniques. The methodologically oriented reader is referred to the original studies for details on these matters.

Early event studies of takeovers, including Mandelker (1974), Ellert (1976), and Langetieg (1978), use the effective date of merger (the date of final approval by target shareholders) as the event date. The expected price effects will occur on or before the first public announcement of a takeover. Therefore, because the announcement date occurs at random times prior to the effective date, using the latter as the event date makes it difficult to identify changes in security prices that are due to the takeover event itself. (See Dodd and Ruback [1977].) Because of this difficulty, we focus on studies that, following Dodd and Ruback, analyze abnormal returns around the time of the first public announcement of a takeover.

Table 3 summarizes the estimated abnormal returns for successful and unsuccessful bidding and target firms around announcements of tender offers and mergers. Panel A of Table 3 reports the results of the tender offer studies. The results of the merger studies are contained in Panels B.1 through B.3 of Table 3, which provide measures of abnormal price changes for different time periods around the merger offer announcement. The table identifies the author(s) and year of publication of each study, the time period of the sample, the timing of the event period over which the abnormal returns are estimated, the sample size and t-statistic. In some cases the abnormal returns are obtained from studies whose primary purpose is to examine other issues,[2] for example, the antitrust implications of mergers. In some of these cases the numbers of interest for Table 3 are not directly presented and we have calculated the relevant abnormal returns and statistics from data in the articles. In several cases authors have provided estimates not published in the study. Italicized t-values are calculated by us using the methods described in footnote a to Table 3. Unavailable data are denoted by "n.a."

2.1. Target-Firm Stockholder Returns

Successful Target Returns. The thirteen studies summarized in Table 3 indicate that targets of successful takeover attempts realize substantial and statistically significant increases in their stock prices. The estimates of positive abnormal returns to targets of *successful tender offers*[3] in the month or two surrounding the offer shown in Table 3, Panel A, are uniformly positive ranging from 16.9 percent to 34.1 percent, and the weighted average abnormal return across the seven studies is 29.1 percent.[4]

For targets of *successful mergers,* the estimated abnormal returns immediately around the merger announcement in Panel B.1 of Table 3 range from 6.2 percent to 13.4 percent, and the weighted average abnormal return is 7.7 percent.[5] Abnormal returns measured over holding periods of approximately one month surrounding the merger announcement are presented in Panel B.2. The weighted average one-month return is 15.9 percent, which is about twice the magnitude of the two-day abnormal returns. This

---

[2] Eckbo (1983), Malatesta (1983), Wier (1983), Ruback (1983a), Bradley (1980), Bradley, Desai and Kim (1982, 1983), and Jarrell and Bradley (1980).

[3] Various definitions of a successful offer are used by the authors. Generally an offer is considered successful if the bidder acquires a substantial fraction of the number of shares initially sought.

[4] The weighted average abnormal return uses sample sizes as weights and ignores the issues associated with overlapping samples. Available data do not allow the calculation of t-values for any of the weighted averages.

[5] *The Wall Street Journal* publication date is conventionally used as the announcement date even though the actual announcement of the offers often occurs on the day prior to the publication date.

Table 3 Abnormal Returns Associated with Mergers and Tender Offers (Sample Size and *t*-Statistic[a*] Are Given in Parentheses)

Study	Sample Period	Event Period	Bidding Firms		Target Firms	
			Successful (Percent)	Unsuccessful (Percent)	Successful (Percent)	Unsuccessful (Percent)
Panel A. Tender Offers: Announcement Effects						
Dodd and Ruback (1977)	1958–1978	Offer announcement month	+2.83 (124, 2.16)	+0.58 (48, 1.19)	+20.58 (133, 25.81)	+18.96 (36, 12.41)
		The month of and month following offer announcement	+3.12 (124, 2.24)	–1.71 (48, –0.76)	+21.15 (133, 15.75)	+16.31 (36, 5.32)
Kummer and Hoffmeister (1978)	1956–1974	Offer announcement month	+5.20 (17, 1.96)	n.a.	+16.85 (50, 10.88)	+21.09 (38, 1.87)
Bradley[b] (1980)	1962–1977	Twenty days before through twenty days after the offer announcement	+4.36 (88, 2.67)	–2.96 (46, –1.31)	+32.18 (161, 26.68)	+47.26 (97, 30.42)
Jarrell and Bradley (1980)	1962–1977	Forty days before through twenty days after the offer announcement	+6.66 (88, 3.35)	n.a.	+34.06[c] (147, 25.48)	n.a.
Bradley, Desai, and Kim (1993)	1963–1980	Ten days before through ten days after the offer announcement	n.a.	–0.27 (94, 0.24)	n.a.	+35.55[d] (112, 36.61)
Bradley, Desai, and Kim (1982)	1962–1980	Ten days before through ten days after the offer announcement	+2.35 (161, 3.02)	n.a.	+31.80 (162, 36.52)	n.a.
Ruback (1983a)	1962–1981	Five days before through the offer announcement	n.a.	–0.38 (48, –0.63)	n.a.	n.a.
Weighted average abnormal return[e, h]			+3.81 (478, n.a.)	–1.11 (236, n.a.)	+29.09 (653, n.a.)	+35.17 (283, n.a.)

Table 3 (*continued*)

Study	Sample Period	Event Period	Bidding Firms		Target Firms	
			Successful (Percent)	Unsuccessful (Percent)	Successful (Percent)	Unsuccessful (Percent)
Panel B.1 Mergers: Two-Day Announcement Effects						
Dodd (1980)	1970–1977	The day before and day of the offer announcement	−1.09 (60, −2.98)	−1.24 (66, −2.63)	+13.41 (71, 23.80)	+12.73 (80, 19.08)
Asquith (1983)	1962–1976	The day before and day of the offer announcement	+0.20 (196, 0.78)	+0.50 (89, 1.92)	+6.20 (211, 23.07)	+7.00 (91, 12.83)
Eckbo (1983)	1963–1978	The day before through the day after the offer announcement	+0.07[f] (102, −0.12)	+1.20[g] (57, 2.98)	+6.24[f] (57, 9.97)	+10.20[g] (29, 15.22)
Weighted average abnormal return[b]			−0.05 (358, n.a.)	+0.15 (212, n.a.)	+7.72 (339, n.a.)	+9.76 (200, n.a.)
Panel B.2 Mergers: One-month Announcement Effects						
Dodd (1980)	1970–1977	Twenty days before through the first public announcement	+0.80 (60, 0.67)	+3.13 (66, 2.05)	+21.78 (71, 11.93)	+22.45 (80, 10.38)
Asquith (1983)	1962–1976	Nineteen days before through the first public announcement day	+0.20 (196, 0.25)	+1.20 (87, 1.49)	+13.30 (211, 15.65)	+11.70 (91, 6.71)
Eckbo (1983)	1963–1978	Twenty days before through ten days after the public announcement	+1.58[f] (102, 1.48)	+4.85[g] (57, 3.43)	+14.08[f] (57, 6.97)	+25.03[g] (29, 12.61)
Asquith,[i] Bruner, and Mullins (1983)	1963–1979	Twenty days before the announcement day through the announcement	+3.48 (170, 5.30)	+0.70 (41, 0.41)	+20.5 (35, 9.54)	+10.0 (19, 3.45)
Malatesta (1983)	1969–1974	Public announcement month	+0.90 (256, 1.53)	n.a.	+16.8 (83, 17.57)	n.a.
Weighted average abnormal return[h]			+1.37 (784, n.a.)	+2.45 (251, n.a.)	+15.90 (457, n.a.)	+17.24 (219, n.a.)

Table 3 *(continued)*

Panel B.3 Mergers: Total Abnormal Returns from Offer Announcement through Outcome

Study	Sample Period	Event Period	Bidding Firms		Target Firms	
			Successful (Percent)	Unsuccessful (Percent)	Successful (Percent)	Unsuccessful (Percent)
Dodd (1980)	1970–1977	Ten days before offer announcement through ten days after outcome date	−7.22 (60, −2.50)	−5.50 (66, −2.05)	+33.96 (71, 7.66)	+3.68 (80, 0.96)
Asquith (1983)	1962–1976	The day before offer announcement outcome date	−0.10 (196, −0.05)	−5.90 (89, −3.15)	+15.50 (211, 6.01)	−7.50 (91, −1.54)
Wier[f] (1983)	1962–1979	Ten days before offer announcement through ten days after cancellation date	n.a.	+3.99 (16, 0.89)	n.a.	−9.02 (17, −1.82)
Weighted average abnormal return[h]			−1.77 (256, n.a.)	−4.82 (171, n.a.)	+20.15 (282, n.a.)	−2.88 (188, n.a.)

[a]n.a. = Not available.

The non-italicized t-statistics were obtained directly from the cited study or calculated using standard errors reported in the study. In the absence of this information, we have approximated the t-statistics. The italicized t-statistics in panel A are calculated as: $t = \bar{X} \sqrt{N}/S \sqrt{T}$, where $\bar{X}$ is the reported abnormal return, N is the number of observations in the sample, T is the number of days over which the abnormal returns are cumulated, and S is the per day per observation standard deviation. $S = 2.39$ percent and is calculated as the average of the implied per day observation standard deviation in all of the studies. The italicized t-statistics in panel B.3 were calculated as $t = \bar{X} \sqrt{N}/S \sqrt{\bar{T}}$, where $\bar{T}$ is the average number of days in the average cumulative return, and the standard deviation is from the original study.

[b]These data are plotted in Bradley (1980). Bradley provided the numerical values in private correspondence.

[c]The abnormal return for successful targets is measured over the period forty days before through five days after the offer announcement.

[d]The abnormal return for unsuccessful targets in the announcement month.

[e]The weighted average excludes the announcement month results of Dodd and Ruback (1977) and includes their results for the month of and month following the announcement.

[f]Includes mergers which were not challenged by antitrust authorities.

[g]Sample consists of mergers that were challenged by antitrust authorities. Eckbo (1983) reports that most of these acquisitions were not completed.

[h]The abnormal returns are weighted by samples in calculating the weighed average. Overlapping sample problems are ignored.

[i]Asquith, Bruner, and Mullins (1983) provided the data for successful and unsuccessful target firms in private correspondence.

[j]Sample includes only mergers that are cancelled after antitrust complaints under Section 7 of the Clayton Act.

comparison suggests that almost half of the abnormal returns associated with the merger announcements occur prior to their public announcement.[6]

Panel B.3 presents abnormal returns from the first public announcement through the outcome day that incorporate all effects of changing information regarding the offer that occur after the initial announcement. These returns are the most complete measures of the profitability of the mergers to target shareholders in Table 3,[7] but they underestimate the gains to target shareholders because they do not include the premium on shares purchased by the bidder prior to the completion of the merger.[8] Dodd (1980) and Asquith (1983) report these total abnormal returns for successful targets as 34 percent and 15.5 percent respectively, and the weighted average of the two estimates is 20.2 percent.

Unsuccessful Target Returns. The weighted average abnormal returns to stockholders of target firms involved in *unsuccessful tender offers* shown in Table 3, Panel A, is 35.2 percent. The comparable one-month abnormal return for targets of *unsuccessful mergers* in Panel B.2 is 17.2 percent. As Panels A, B.1 reveal, these weighted average abnormal returns for targets of unsuccessful takeover attempts are approximately equal to those for targets of successful takeovers. Hence, on average the market appears to reflect approximately equal expected gains for both successful and unsuccessful takeovers at the time of the first public announcement. However, one-month announcement abnormal returns are an insufficient measure of stock price changes associated with unsuccessful takeover attempts because they do not include the stock price response to the information that the offer failed. The correct measure of the wealth effects, therefore, is the cumulative return from the offer through the termination announcement. The weighted average return to *unsuccessful merger* targets from the initial announcement through the outcome date presented in Panel B.3 is −2.9 percent. Thus, all of the announcement gains are lost over the time that the merger failure becomes known.

In contrast to the behavior of stock prices of targets of unsuccessful mergers, stock prices of targets of *unsuccessful tender offers* remain substantially above their pre-offer level even after the failure of the offer. Unfortunately, the tender offer studies do not present data on the cumulative abnormal return for unsuccessful tender offers from the initial announcement through the outcome date. Nevertheless, some information can be extracted from the abnormal returns following the initial announcement. Dodd and Ruback (1977) find an abnormal return of −2.65 percent for targets of unsuccessful tender offers in the month following the initial announcement, but the cumulative abnormal return over the entire year following the announcement is only −3.25 percent ($t = 0.90$).

---

[6] Keown and Pinkerton (1981) also find that roughly half of the price adjustment occurs prior to the public announcement date. They incorrectly conclude that "impending merger announcements are poorly held secrets" and that the pre-announcement price adjustments reflect insider trading and the leakage of inside information. They provide no tests of the plausible alternative hypothesis that the price adjustments prior to the "announcement day" are unbiased responses to public information that increases the probability of a takeover. For many purposes the relatively crude characterization of an event as *The Wall Street Journal* announcement date or the company's formal announcement date is satisfactory. However, for many events there is literally no single "event day," only a series of occurrences that increase or decrease the probability of an outcome such as a takeover. Inferences about insider trading or leakage require careful consideration of these issues.

[7] Interestingly, the target stock price changes appear to capture all of the target value changes associated with the merger. See Kim and McConnell (1977) and Asquith and Kim (1982), who find no merger announcement effects on publicly traded bond prices.

[8] See Ruback (1982) for calculation of gains to target shareholders that appropriately includes the proceeds to the tendering shareholders on repurchased shares.

Bradley, Desai, and Kim (1983) analyze the post-failure price behavior of a sample of 112 targets of *unsuccessful tender offers* that they segment into two categories: 86 targets that received subsequent takeover offers and 26 targets that did not receive such offers.[9] Returns in the announcement month for the two subsamples are 29.1 percent and 23.9 percent, respectively, and both are statistically significant. From the announcement month of the initial unsuccessful offer through the following two years, the average abnormal return for the targets that *received* subsequent offers is 57.19 percent ($t = 10.39$). In contrast, the average abnormal return over the same two-year period for targets that *did not receive* subsequent offers is an insignificant −3.53 percent ($t = −0.36$), and recall this return includes the announcement effects. Thus, the positive abnormal returns associated with unsuccessful tender offers appear to be due to the anticipation of subsequent offers; target shareholders realize additional positive abnormal returns when a subsequent offer is made, but lose the initial announcement gains if no subsequent offer occurs.[10]

Summary: The Returns to Targets.   In summary, the evidence indicates that targets of *successful tender offers* and *mergers* earn significantly positive abnormal returns on announcement of the offers and through completion of the offers. Targets of *unsuccessful tender offers* earn significantly positive abnormal returns on the offer announcement and through the realization of failure. However, those targets of unsuccessful tender offers that do not receive additional offers in the next two years lose all previous announcement gains, and those targets that do receive new offers earn even higher returns. Finally, targets of *unsuccessful mergers* appear to lose all positive returns earned in the offer announcement period by the time failure of the offer becomes known.

2.2. Bidding-Firm Stockholder Returns

Successful Bidders. The abnormal returns for bidders in *successful tender offers* summarized in Panel A of Table 3 are all significantly positive and range from 2.4 percent to 6.7 percent, with a weighted average return of 3.8 percent. Thus, bidders in successful tender offers realize significant percentage increases in equity value, although this increase is substantially lower than the 29.1 percent return to targets of successful tender offers.

The evidence on bidder returns in *mergers* is mixed and therefore more difficult to interpret than that for bidders in tender offers. On the whole it suggests that returns to bidders in mergers are approximately zero. The two-day abnormal returns associated with the announcement of a merger proposal summarized in Panel B.1 of Table 3 differ considerably across studies. Dodd (1980) finds a significant abnormal return of −1.09 percent for 60 successful bidders on the day before and the day of the first public announcement of the merger—indicating that merger bids are, on average, negative net present value investments for bidders. However, over the same two-day period, Asquith (1983) and Eckbo (1983) report slightly positive, but statistically insignificant, abnormal

---

[9] These data seem to indicate that the probability of becoming a takeover target rises substantially after an initial unsuccessful offer occurs.

[10] This evidence casts doubt in the earlier conjectures by Dodd and Ruback (1977) that unsuccessful tender offers lead to target shareholder gains through the disciplining of existing inefficient managers. It is also inconsistent with the argument made by DeAngelo, DeAngelo, and Rice (1982), that part of the target price change in takeover offers represents the value of implicit information about target profitability that is revealed by the offer announcement.

returns—suggesting that merger bids are zero net present value investments. In contrast to the mixed findings for the immediate announcement effects, all five estimates of the one-month announcement effects in Panel B.2 of Table 3 are positive, but only the estimate of 3.48 percent by Asquith, Bruner, and Mullins (1983) is significantly different from zero. The weighted averages are 1.37 percent for the one-month announcement effects and −0.05 percent for the two-day announcement effects.

Panel B.3 of Table 3 contains the results of two studies that report the total abnormal return for successful bidding firms from the initial announcement day through the outcome announcement day. If the initial announcement is unanticipated and there are no other information effects, this cumulative abnormal return includes the effects of all revisions in expectations and offer prices and therefore is a complete measure of the equity value changes for successful bidders. The weighted average of the two estimates is −1.77 percent, and the individual estimates are −7.22 percent for 60 successful bidders and −0.1 percent for 196 successful bidders.

The estimated abnormal returns to successful bidding firms in all the studies summarized in Panels B.1 through B.3 of Table 3 suggest that mergers are zero net present value investments for bidders[11]—except for the Dodd (1980) estimates in Panels B.1 and B.3. It is difficult to understand the reason for the substantial difference between Dodd's estimates and the others. His sample period and methodology are similar to those of the other studies, although his sample is restricted to acquisition proposals for NYSE firms that "are initially announced in the form of a merger" and is therefore somewhat more restrictive than others. His sample "does not include merger proposals that were preceded by a tender offer and does not include 'defensive mergers' where a target firm finds a merger partner in response to a tender offer by a third firm" (Dodd [1980, p. 107]). Lacking obvious clues to explain the difference in Dodd's estimates, we're left with the conjecture that his results are sample specific even though there is no apparent reason why this should be induced by his sample selection criteria.[12]

Malatesta (1983) provides estimates of total abnormal *dollar* returns to the equity holders of successful bidding firms in the period 1969–1974 that are consistent with Dodd's results. He reports an average loss of about $28 million ($t = −1.85$) in the period four months before through the month of announcement of the merger outcome (indicated by announcement of board/management approval) of the merger.

Unsuccessful Bidders. Inferences about the profitability of takeover bids can also be made from the behavior of bidding-firm stock prices around the time of termination announcements for unsuccessful acquisition attempts. Positive abnormal returns to a bidding firm in response to the announcement that a takeover attempt is unsuccessful (for reasons other than bidder cancellation) are inconsistent with the hypothesis that takeovers are positive net present value investments. Dodd reports insignificant average abnormal returns of 0.9 percent for 19 bidders on the day before and day

---

[11] There are, however, classic examples which seem to contradict the conclusion that merger bids are zero net present value investments. For example, see the detailed examination of the 1981 DuPont-Conoco merger by Ruback (1982) in which DuPont paid $7.54 billion, the largest takeover in U.S. corporate history. The value of DuPont fell by $789 million (−9.9 percent) over the takeover period, and $641 million of the decline occurred on the day of the announcement of DuPont's first offer.

[12] After discussing the issues with us, Dodd was kind enough to recheck and replicate his results—no data or computer programming errors were found.

of announcement of merger termination initiated by targets. If mergers are positive net return projects, these target-termination announcement returns should be negative. Dodd also reports positive termination announcement returns of 1.38 percent for 47 bidders in his bidder-termination subsample. These positive returns are consistent with the hypothesis that bidders maximize shareholder wealth and cancel mergers after finding out they overvalued the target on the initial offer.

Ruback (1983a) uses data on unsuccessful bidders to test directly for value-maximizing behavior of bidders. He argues that wealth-maximizing bidders will abandon takeover attempts when increments in the offer price would make the takeover a negative net present value investment. For 48 bidders in competitive tender offers (defined by the presence of multiple bidders), he finds the average potential gain to the unsuccessful bidder from matching the successful offer price is −$91 million ($t = -4.34$). The potential gain is calculated as the abnormal bidder equity value change associated with the original announcement of the unsuccessful bid minus the additional cost if the higher successful bid were matched. Furthermore, 41 bidders did not match higher offer prices that would have resulted in a negative net present value acquisition.[13] These results are consistent with value-maximizing behavior by bidding firms.

Problems in Measuring Bidder Returns. There is reason to believe the estimation of returns is more difficult for bidders than for targets. Since stock price changes reflect changes in expectations, a merger announcement will have no effect if its terms are fully anticipated in the market. Furthermore, targets are acquired once at most, whereas bidders can engage in prolonged acquisition programs. Malatesta (1981, 1983) and Schipper and Thompson (1983a) point out that the present value of the expected benefits of a bidder's acquisition program is incorporated into the share price when the acquisition program is announced or becomes apparent to the market. Thus, the gain to bidding firms is correctly measured by the value change associated with the initial information about the acquisition program and the incremental effect of each acquisition. The abnormal returns to bidding firms associated with mergers reported in Table 3 measure only the incremental value change of each acquisition and are therefore potentially incomplete measures of merger value to successful bidders.

Bidding firms do not typically announce acquisition programs explicitly; this information is generally revealed as the bidders pursue takeover targets. However, Schipper and Thompson (1983a) find that for some firms the start of a takeover program can be approximately determined. They examine the stock price behavior of 30 firms that announced acquisition programs during the period 1953 through 1968. The information that these firms intended to pursue an acquisition program was revealed either in annual reports or specific announcements to the financial press, or in association with other corporate policy changes. For 13 firms in their sample, Schipper and Thompson are unable to identify a specific month in which the acquisition program was adopted. For these firms, December of the program-adoption year is used as the announcement month. Four of the remaining 17 firms had multiple announcements of their programs, and the date of the last announcement is used for these firms.

---

[13] In the remaining seven observations, the unsuccessful bidders did not match the successful offer price even though the data suggest that the matching would have been a positive net present value investment. The average potential gain for these seven observations is $23 million ($t = 0.64$). The low t-value suggests that these "mistakes" are not statistically significant. However, as noted in Ruback (1983a), the measured potential gains are likely to underestimate the actual potential gains when the probability of success is less than one.

The difficulties in identifying the exact announcement date imply that the capitalized values of the acquisition program are impounded into stock prices prior to the Schipper and Thompson "announcement month." Consistent with the hypothesis that mergers are positive net present value investments for bidding firms, they find abnormal returns of 13.5 percent ($t = 2.26$) for their sample of 30 firms in the 12 months prior to and including the "event month." However, the imprecise announcement month, the resultant necessity for measuring abnormal returns over a 12-month interval, and contemporaneous changes in corporate policy make it difficult to determine with confidence the association between positive abnormal returns and initiation of the acquisition program. For example, suppose "good luck" provided bidder management with additional resources to try new projects such as mergers. As Schipper and Thompson discuss, in this case stock prices would show the pattern evidenced in their study even if the mergers have zero net present value.[14]

Asquith, Bruner, and Mullins (1983) also examine the profitability of merger programs. They focus on the abnormal returns associated with the first four bids after the initiation of a merger program, arguing that the earlier bids in a merger program should contain more information about the profitability of the program than later bids. This suggests that the price response associated with the first few bids should be greater than the price response associated with later bids. They analyze the abnormal returns for successive merger bids (up to four) of 156 firms that initiated merger programs in the period 1963–1979 after eight years without a bid. Their results indicate that merger bids (both successful and unsuccessful) are positive net present value investments, as evidenced by significant average bidder gains of 2.8 percent ($t = 5.20$) in the 20 days prior to and including the first public announcement. However, there is little evidence that the major gain to the acquisition program is capitalized into the bidder's stock price on announcement of the early mergers. The returns, sample size, and t-statistics by merger sequence number are

	Merger Sequence Number			
	1	**2**	**3**	**4**
Abnormal return	2.4%	3.7%	2.4%	2.8%
(*N*, *t*-statistic)	(70, 2.21)	(59, 3.13)	(47, 1.37)	(38, 2.38)

In addition to the problems caused by prior capitalization of the gains from takeover bids, measuring the gains to bidding firms is also difficult because bidders are generally much larger than target firms. Thus, even when the dollar gains from the takeover are split evenly between bidder and target firms, the dollar gains to the bidders translate into smaller percentage gains. Asquith, Bruner, and Mullins (1983) report that the abnormal returns of bidding firms depend on the relative size of the target. For 99 mergers in which the target's equity value is 10 percent or more of the bidder's equity value, the average abnormal return for *bidders* is 4.1 percent ($t = 4.42$) over the period 20 days before through the day of announcement. For the 115 remaining mergers in which the target's

---

[14] Schipper and Thompson conclude that negative abnormal stock price changes for their acquiring firms around times of restrictive regulatory changes help resolve this ambiguity and make the evidence that the programs were positive net present value projects for acquirers "more compelling." However, this conclusion cannot be drawn. Negative returns on the imposition of regulatory changes that impose higher future costs on bidders would also be observed if the original acquisition programs were negative net present value projects as long as the regulatory changes do not cause the bidders to abandon their acquisition programs.

equity value is less than 10 percent of the bidder's equity value, the average abnormal return for bidders is 1.7 percent ($t = 2.00$). Furthermore, the precision of the estimated gains is lower for bidders than for targets because the normal variation in equity value for the (larger) bidder is greater, relative to a given dollar gain, than it is for the target. Thus, even if the gains are split equally, the relative sizes of bidding and target firms imply that both the average abnormal return and its t-statistic will be smaller for bidding firms.

Returns to bidders also show evidence of other measurement problems. Several studies show indications of systematic reductions in the stock prices of bidding firms in the year following the event. These post-outcome negative abnormal returns are unsettling because they are consistent with market efficiency and suggest that changes in stock price during takeovers overestimate the future efficiency gains from mergers. Table 4 presents the cumulative abnormal returns in the year following takeovers in six different studies. One of the post-announcement abnormal returns in the two tender offer studies in Panel A of Table 4 is not significantly different from zero. In addition, the post-outcome abnormal returns for the merger studies reported in Panel B of Table 4 provide evidence of systematic reductions in stock price. Langetieg (1978) and Asquith (1983) report significant negative abnormal returns in the year following the outcome announcement. Malatesta (1983) finds insignificant negative abnormal returns in the year following the merger announcement for his entire sample, although he finds significant negative abnormal returns for bidders in mergers occurring after 1970 and for bidders with smaller equity value.

There are several potential explanations for the negative postoutcome abnormal returns. One hypothesis is that the studies impose ex post selection bias by using information that is not available at the announcement date to select samples. Alternatively, the negative drift could be caused by nonstationary parameters or other factors of model misspecification, but Langetieg (1978) finds these factors do not explain the negative post-outcome returns in his sample. Schipper and Thompson (1983a) argue that regulatory changes that reduced the profitability of mergers could explain the negative abnormal returns, but Malatesta (1983) finds significant negative abnormal post-outcome returns of −13.7 percent ($t = 2.88$) for mergers occurring after the regulatory changes. Explanation of these post-event negative abnormal returns is currently an unsettled issue.

Summary: The Returns to Bidders. The reported positive returns to *successful bidders* in *tender offers* and the generally negative returns to *unsuccessful bidders* in both *mergers* and *tender offers* are consistent with the hypothesis that mergers are positive net present value projects. The measurement of returns to bidders in mergers is difficult, and perhaps because of this the results are mixed. The evidence suggests, however, that returns to *successful bidding* firms in *mergers* are zero. Additional work on this problem is clearly warranted.

2.3. The Total Gains from Takeovers

The evidence indicates that shareholders of target firms realize large positive abnormal returns in completed takeovers. The evidence on the rewards to bidding firms is mixed, but the weight of the evidence suggests zero returns are earned by successful bidding firms in mergers and that statistically significant but small positive abnormal returns are realized by bidders in successful tender offers. Since targets gain and bidders do not appear to lose, the evidence suggests that takeovers create value. However, because bidding firms tend to be larger than target firms, the sum of the returns to

Table 4 Summary of Post-Outcome Abnormal Returns[a] for Tender Offers and Mergers (Sample Size and t-Statistic[b] Are Given in Parentheses)

Study	Sample Period	Event Period	Bidding Firms		Target Firms	
			Successful (Percent)	Unsuccessful (Percent)	Successful (Percent)	Unsuccessful (Percent)
Panel A. Tender Offers						
Dodd and Ruback (1977)	1958–1978	Month after through 12 months after the offer announcement	−1.32 (124, −0.41)	−1.60 (48, −0.52)	+7.95 (133, 0.85)	−3.25 (36, 0.90)
Bradley, Desai, and Kim (1983)	1962–1980	Month after through 12 months after the offer announcement	n.a.	−7.85[b] (94, −2.34)	n.a.	+3.04 (112, 0.90)
Panel B. Mergers						
Mandelker (1974)	1941–1962	Month after through 12 months after the effective date	+0.60 (241, 0.31)	n.a.	n.a.	n.a.
Langetieg (1978)	1929–1969	Month after through 12 months after the effective date	−6.59 (149, −2.96)	n.a.	n.a.	n.a.
Asquith (1983)	1962–1976	Day after through 240 days after the outcome announcement	−7.20 (196, −4.10)	−9.60 (89, −5.41)	n.a.	−8.7 (91, −2.11)
Malatesta (1983)	1969–1974	Month after through 12 months after approval for entire sample	−2.90 (121, −1.05)	n.a.	n.a.	n.a.
		Month after through 12 months after approval for mergers occurring after 1970	−13.7 (75, −2.88)	n.a.	n.a.	n.a.
		Month after through 12 months after approval for firms with equity value under $300 million	−7.70 (59, −1.51)	n.a.	n.a.	n.a.

[a]This abnormal return covers the period from the day after through 180 days after the offer.

[b]n.a. = not available.

The t-statistics either come directly from the cited study or were calculated from implied standard deviations available in the cited study, or come from an earlier draft of the study.

bidding and target returns do not measure the gains to the merging firms. The dollar value of small percentage losses for bidders could exceed the dollar value of large percentage gains to targets.

Malatesta (1983) and Bradley, Desai, and Kim (1982) measure the changes in total dollar value associated with completed takeovers. Malatesta examines a matched sample of targets and their bidders in 30 successful mergers and finds a significant average increase of $32.4 million ($t = 2.07$) in their combined equity value in the month before and month of outcome announcement. The acquired firms earned $18.6 million ($t = 5.41$) of the combined increase in equity value, and acquiring firms earned $13.8 million ($t = 0.91$). Bradley, Desai, and Kim (1982) report positive but statistically insignificant total dollar gains to bidders and targets in 162 tender offers of $17.2 million ($t = 1.26$). However, the average percentage change in total value of the combined target and bidder firms is a significant 10.5 percent ($t = 6.58$). This evidence indicates that changes in corporate control increase the combined market value of assets of the bidding and target firms.

3. Antitrust and the Source of Merger Gains

The evidence indicates that, on average, takeovers result in an upward revaluation of the target's equity, and that shareholders of target firms realize a substantial increase in wealth as a result of completed takeovers. Understanding the source of the gains to merging firms is important since acquisition attempts often meet strong opposition, sometimes from target management, sometimes from antitrust authorities. Target managers, for example, often argue that target shareholders are harmed by takeovers; indeed, the common use of the emotion-laden term "raider" to label the bidding firm suggests that the bidder's gains are coming at the expense of the target firm's shareholders. The evidence summarized above indicates that this argument is false, the bidder's gains (if any) do not appear to be simple wealth transfers from target shareholders.[15] Acquisition attempts are also opposed by target firms, competitors, and antitrust authorities, among others, who argue that mergers are undesirable because they reduce competition and create monopoly power.[16] Such opposition has delayed merger completion, caused merger cancellations, and resulted in court-ordered divestiture of previously completed acquisitions.[17] In addition, the evidence indicating positive net benefits to merging firms, together with the zero or positive abnormal returns to bidding firms, is inconsistent with the hypothesis that takeovers are motivated by non-value-maximizing behavior by the managers of bidding firms.

3.1. The Source of Takeover Gains

Various sources of gains to takeovers have been advanced. Potential reductions in production or distribution costs, often called synergies, could occur through realization of economies of scale, verti-

---

[15] See Bradley (1980) for an extended discussion of these issues in the context of tender offers.

[16] Arguments by target management that a takeover should be prohibited on antitrust grounds seems particularly self-interested and inconsistent with maximization of shareholder wealth.

[17] For example, the Justice Department's request for additional information from Mobil during the Conoco takeover prohibited Mobil from buying Conoco common stock and prevented Mobil from actively competing with DuPont and Seagram for control of Conoco, even though Mobil's offer was approximately one billion dollars higher. Ruback (1982) analyzes this takeover in detail.

cal integration, adoption of more efficient production or organizational technology,[18] increased utilization of the bidder's management team, and reduction of agency costs by bringing organization-specific assets under common ownership.[19] Financial motivations for acquisition include the use of underutilized tax shields, avoidance of bankruptcy costs, increased leverage, and other types of tax advantages.[20] Takeovers could increase market power in product markets. Finally, takeovers could eliminate inefficient target management. Each of these hypotheses predicts that the combined firm generates cash flows with a present value in excess of the sum of the market values of the bidding and target firms. But the abnormal returns do not identify which components of the present value of net cash flows have changed. Studies of the abnormal returns to takeover participants cannot, therefore, distinguish between these alternative sources of gains.

Two important exceptions are the studies by Stillman (1983) and Eckbo (1983), which use the equity price changes of firms that *compete* in product markets with the merged target to reject the hypothesis that takeovers create market power. The market power hypothesis implies that mergers increase product prices, thereby benefiting the merging firms and other competing firms in the industry. Higher prices allow competing firms to increase their own product prices and/or output, and therefore the equity values of competing firms should also rise on the offer announcement.

Stillman (1983) examines the abnormal returns for rival firms in 11 horizontal mergers. The small sample size arises from his sample selection criteria. Of all mergers challenged under Section 7 of the Clayton Act, these 11 are the merger complaints in unregulated industries whose rivals were identified in the proceedings and for which constraints in data availability were met. While this screening process creates a small sample, it reduces ambiguity about the applicability of the test and the identity of rivals. He finds no statistically significant abnormal returns for rival firms in nine of the mergers examined. Of the remaining two mergers, one exhibits ambiguous results, and the other is consistent with positive abnormal returns for rivals. Stillman's evidence, therefore, is inconsistent with the hypothesis that the gains from mergers are due to the acquisition of market power.

Eckbo (1983) uses the stock price reaction of rivals at the announcement of the antitrust challenge as well as at the announcement of the merger to test the market power hypothesis. Eckbo's final sample consists of 126 challenged horizontal mergers, and, using product line classifications rather than records of court and agency proceedings, he identifies an average of 15 rivals for each merger. He also identifies rivals for 65 unchallenged horizontal mergers and 58 vertical mergers.

Eckbo's results indicate that rival firms have positive abnormal returns around the time of the first public announcement of the *merger*. Rivals of unchallenged mergers realized abnormal returns of 1.1 percent ($t = 1.20$), and rivals of challenged mergers realized abnormal returns of 2.45 percent ($t = 3.02$) in the period 20 days prior to and 10 days following the first public announcement. These results are consistent with the market power hypothesis.

Eckbo uses the stock price reactions of *rivals* at announcement of the *antitrust challenge* to reject the market power hypothesis. The market power hypothesis predicts negative abnormal returns

---

[18] See Chandler (1962, 1977) and Williamson (1975, 1981) for discussion of advantages of the multidivisional form of organization which seems common to merged firms. Bradley, Desai, and Kim (1982) investigate the role of specialized resources in merger gains.

[19] See Klein, Crawford, and Alchian (1978) for discussion of the agency costs of outside ownership of organization-specific assets.

[20] See Benston (1980, p. 21).

for rival firms at the time the complaint is filed because the complaint reduces the probability of completion of the merger (which, it is assumed, would have generated market power), and the concomitant increase in output prices is then less probable. In the period 20 days before through 10 days after the antitrust challenge, the rivals to 55 challenged mergers realize statistically insignificant average abnormal returns of 1.78 percent ($t = 1.29$). This finding is inconsistent with the market power hypothesis, which implies the returns of rivals should be significantly negative at the complaint announcement. Furthermore, Eckbo reports that rivals with a positive market reaction to the initial merger announcement do not tend to have negative abnormal returns at the time of the complaint. Thus, Eckbo's evidence is inconsistent with the market power hypothesis.

Although the evidence in Eckbo (1983) and Stillman (1983) is inconsistent with the market power hypothesis, identification of the actual source of the gains in takeovers has not yet occurred. There is evidence in Asquith (1980, 1983), Malatesta (1983), Langetieg (1978), Ellert (1976), and Mandelker (1974) that target firms experience negative abnormal returns in the period prior to approximately six months before the acquisition.[21] This below normal performance is consistent with the hypothesis that inefficient target management caused target firms to perform badly, but there is currently no evidence that directly links these negative pre-merger returns to inefficiency. Eckbo's results, moreover, are inconsistent with the target inefficiency hypothesis. His evidence indicates that the gains are more general, extending to rivals in the industry as well as to the specific target firm, and removal of inefficient target management is unlikely to be an industry-wide phenomenon.

It would be surprising to find that all the gains reflected in Table 3 are due to a single phenomenon such as elimination of inefficient target management. Some of the gains are also likely to result from other synergies in combining two or more independent organizations, and discovery of the precise nature of these synergies is a complicated task. Ruback (1982), for example, examines the DuPont-Conoco merger to determine the source of the revaluation that occurred; the stockholders of the target, Conoco, realized gains of about $3.2 billion whereas stockholders of the bidder, DuPont, incurred losses of almost $800 million. The DuPont-Conoco merger, therefore, "created" about $2.4 billion of additional market value. Ruback explores a variety of different explanations for the revaluations, including synergy, the release of new information, undervalued oil reserves, replacement of inefficient target management, and departures from stockholder wealth maximization by the management of DuPont. None of these hypotheses provide an adequate explanation for the revaluation, although it is impossible to reject the hypothesis that DuPont had some special new information about Conoco's assets. These results suggest it is difficult to identify the source of the gains from takeovers—even in the context of a single takeover.

Information effects of various kinds might also play a role in explaining the behavior of stock prices at times of takeovers. For example, DeAngelo, DeAngelo, and Rice (1982) conjecture that information effects associated with bidder management's possession of inside information about its own value might help explain the difference in bidder returns in tender offers and merger proposals. The evidence indicates that bidders in successful tender offers earn small positive returns and that successful merger bidders earn approximately zero returns. Tender offers are frequently cash offers,[22] and mergers are usually stock and other security exchange offers. When bidder management's inside

---

[21] The declines reported by Asquith (1983), Malatesta (1983), Langetieg (1978), and Ellert (1976) are statistically significant.

[22] Bradley (1980), Jarrell and Bradley (1980), and Bradley, Desai, and Kim (1983) sample only cash offers; Dodd and Ruback (1977) and Ruback (1983a) sample both cash and security exchange tender offers.

information (unrelated to the acquisition) indicates its stock is undervalued, it will prefer a cash offer and vice versa for a stock offer.[23] Therefore, astute market participants will interpret a cash offer as good news and a stock offer as bad news about the bidder's value and incorporate this information into bidder stock prices along with the estimated value of the acquisition. This argument implies that returns to bidders in cash tender offers will be higher than in mergers, if other aspects of the deals are approximately equivalent.

The inside information argument is as yet untested. However, it implies that stock prices fall when new shares are sold and rise when shares are repurchased, and this implication is consistent with the price effects associated with intrafirm capital structure changes found by a growing number of authors. For exarnple, prices generally fall on the exchange of common and preferred stock for bonds (Masulis [1980a]), on the call and conversion of convertible bonds to stock (Mikkelson [1981, 1983]), on the issuance of convertible debt (Dann and Mikkelson [1982]), on the issuance of stock through rights offerings (Smith [1977]), and on the sale of common stock in secondary offering (Scholes [1972]), while prices generally rise on repurchases of common stock (Dann [1981], Vermaelen [1981], Masulis [1980b], and Rosenfeld [1982]). The only inconsistent evidence is the significant negative returns associated with targeted buybacks of large blocks of stock documented by DeAngelo and Rice (1983) and Bradley and Wakeman (1983). However, the targeted buyback evidence seems well explained by other factors, as discussed in Section 4.5 below.

3.2. The Costs of Antitrust Actions

The evidence indicates that merger gains do not come from the acquisition of market power, but rather from some source of efficiencies that also appears to be available to rival firms in the industry. Given this evidence, it is of interest to examine the effects of antitrust actions on merging firms.

In their studies of antitrust merger actions, Ellert (1976), Wier (1983), and Eckbo (1983) demonstrate that antitrust opposition to takeovers imposes substantial costs on target firm shareholders. Wier examines the abnormal returns for firms involved in mergers which were opposed by antitrust authorities under Section 7 of the Clayton Act. Her sample contains mergers involving 16 bidding firms and 17 target firms that were cancelled after antitrust complaints. The cumulative abnormal return from 30 days before through the proposal announcement is 9.25 percent. During the period *following* the proposal announcement through the complaint period and the cancellation day, all the previous target firm announcement gains are eliminated; the cumulative abnormal return is −12.43 percent. Bidding firms in her sample appear to show no abnormal returns at the time of proposal announcement or cancellation.

Wier (1983) also examines the abnormal returns associated with the announcement of antitrust complaints for 111 completed mergers, and her data reveal significant abnormal returns of −2.58 percent for the day before through the day after the complaint announcement. Ellert (1976) reports an abnormal return of −1.83 percent ($t = -3.24$) in the complaint month for 205 defendants in antitrust merger cases over the period 1950–1972. Similarly, Eckbo (1983) reports an average abnormal return of −9.27 percent ($t = -7.61$) for 17 target firms on the day before through the day after the announcement of an antitrust complaint. In addition, Wier finds that the abnormal return

---

[23] See Myers and Majluf (1981), who argue that sale of shares by a target through merger can reveal negative information about the target's value.

for 32 firms that completed their mergers and were later convicted of antitrust violations is −2.27 percent ($t = -4.11$) from the day before through the day after the conviction announcement. However, she finds no significant abnormal returns on announcement of the outcome for 30 firms whose antitrust suits were dismissed and for 66 firms that settled their antitrust suits. Dismissal or settlement of a suit, unless fully expected, would generally represent good news. As Wier points out, the absence of significant abnormal returns at these announcements is puzzling.

There is also evidence consistent with the hypothesis that Federal Trade Commission antitrust actions benefit rivals of merging firms by restricting competition. Eckbo (1983) finds that rivals of mergers challenged by the Federal Trade Commission earn essentially zero abnormal returns on the day of the merger announcement and significantly positive abnormal returns on the day of the complaint announcement. In contrast, rivals of mergers challenged by the Justice Department earn significantly positive abnormal returns on the merger announcement and essentially zero abnormal returns on the complaint announcement. Eckbo (1983) concludes: "This evidence strongly contradicts the [market power] hypothesis and gives some support to a 'rival producer protection' rationale for the behavior of the FTC towards these mergers."

In sum, the negative abnormal returns associated with antitrust complaints, Section 7 convictions, and cancellations of mergers induced by antitrust actions indicate that antitrust opposition to takeovers imposes substantial costs on the stockholders of merging firms. This finding is particularly interesting given that the evidence indicates merger gains do not arise from the creation of market power but rather from the acquisition of some form of efficiencies.

3.3. The Effects of Takeover Regulation

In addition to antitrust regulation, the imposition of security regulations governing takeovers appears to have reduced the profitability of takeovers. The effect of changes in tender offer regulations (such as the Williams Amendment and state tender offer laws) on the abnormal returns to bidding and target firms is examined in Smiley (1975) and Jarrell and Bradley (1980). Smiley finds that the Williams Amendment increased the abnormal returns to target firms by 13 percent. Jarrell and Bradley find that the target's average abnormal return increased after the Williams Amendment and the bidder's average abnormal return decreased. They find that average abnormal returns for 47 target firms prior to the Williams Amendment were 22 percent ($t = 12.9$) in the period 40 days before through five days after the first public announcement of the takeover. In comparison, the average abnormal return for 90 targets subject to regulation under the Williams Amendment is 40 percent ($t = 19.2$), and the returns to 20 targets subject to both the Williams Amendment and state tender offer laws are 35 percent ($t = 5.1$). For bidders, the average abnormal return in the period 40 days before through 20 days after the first public announcement is 9 percent ($t = 3.5$) for 28 unregulated offers, 6 percent, ($t = 2.1$) for 51 offers regulated by the Williams Amendment, and 4 percent ($t = 0.7$) for 9 offers regulated by the Williams Amendment and state tender offer laws. Asquith, Bruner, and Mullins (1983) provide similar evidence. For mergers prior to October 1, 1969, they report average abnormal returns to bidders of 4.40 percent over the period 20 days before through the first public announcement and average abnormal returns of 1.7 percent to bidders in mergers after October 1, 1969.

The evidence seems to indicate that the regulations increased the returns to the target's shareholders at the expense of the shareholders of bidding firms, but the tests are not sufficient to draw this conclusion from the data. Suppose the regulations have no effect whatsoever except to eliminate the low-value offers. By raising transactions costs and imposing restrictions on takeovers, the regulations could simply truncate the distribution of takeovers that would actually occur. This truncation of less profitable takeovers would reduce the returns to shareholders of firms that do not become targets and have no effect on the returns to those that do become targets, but it would increase the *measured* average abnormal returns for targets of completed takeovers. The effect of such truncation on the abnormal returns to bidding firms is less clear since no well-developed theory exists that determines the division of the net benefits between target and bidding firms.

Schipper and Thompson (1983a) examine the effect of four regulatory changes that occurred in 1968–1970: Accounting Principle Board Opinions 16 and 17, the 1969 Tax Reform Act, the 1968 Williams Amendment, and its 1970 extension. Each of these regulatory changes restricts bidders and thereby reduces the profitability of bidding firms. The abnormal return for bidders engaged in merger programs at the time of four regulatory changes is interesting because, in an efficient market, the effect of the regulatory changes is impounded in the bidder's stock price on announcement of the changes. They find an average abnormal return of −1.3 percent ($t = 4.5$) during the 15 months in which events related to regulatory change occurred between January 1967 and December 1970. Schipper and Thompson (1983b) use an alternative technique to estimate the effects of the regulatory changes. They report that the Williams Amendment reduced the equity values of acquiring firms by about 6 percent. The Schipper and Thompson event-type tests are more precise than the comparison of abnormal returns to bidder before and after regulation, and they indicate that the regulatory changes impose costs on bidding firms. Their approach cannot be used to assess the effect of the regulations on target firms because it is difficult, if not impossible, for the market to identify future target firms.[24] If market participants cannot identify targets prior to the bids, appreciable changes in stock price will not be observed for targets of future takeovers at times of regulatory changes.

4. Manager-Stockholder Conflicts of Interest

4.1. Corporate Control: The Issues

Takeovers serve as an external control mechanism that limits major managerial departures from maximization of stockholder wealth.[25] It is unlikely, however, that the threat of takeover ensures complete coherence of managerial actions and maximization of stockholder wealth. Because of the existence of other control mechanisms, the inability of the takeover market to eliminate all departures from maximization of stockholder wealth does not imply that these departures are prevalent in modern corporations.[26] The limitations of the takeover market also do not imply that the departures,

---

[24] Palepue (1983) uses a binary logit model to identify determinants of the probability of acquisition. While he finds several variables that are statistically significant, the overall explanatory power of the model is negligible.

[25] The average abnormal returns to target shareholders in Tables 1 and 3 are not measures of the extent of managerial departures from shareholder wealth maximization. For example, in addition to the gains from eliminating inefficient managers, they include the gains from efficiency innovations and synergies available to the combined firm.

[26] See Fama and Jensen (1983a, b, c) and Jensen (1983) for discussions of agency costs, control, and survival in a theory of organizations that views conflicts of interests in a general fashion.

when they occur, are costly to shareholders; some of the costs are borne by managers themselves through reductions in their salaries.[27]

Measurement of the costs of manager-stockholder conflict by direct examination of managerial decisions is difficult for reasons that include the difficulty in identifying the benefits to managers that emanate from particular decisions, the difficulty in determining the information base for the decision, errors in the stock market assessment of value, and the difficulty in ex post auditing of decisions. For example, suppose the announcement of a capital investment is associated with a decline in the firm's stock price, suggesting that the investment reduces shareholder wealth. There is no particular reason in this case to suspect that the decision benefits managers.[28] Furthermore, the price decline could be an error due to the market's lack of inside information possessed by managers. Alternatively, even if the investment is value-maximizing, the decline in price could result from an exogenous reduction in profitability that the investment reveals to the market. Finally, even when the investment proves to be a negative net present value investment, it is difficult, given uncertainty, to distinguish among managerial incompetence, managerial opportunism, or mere bad luck.

Some evidence on the costs of managerial departures from maximization of stockholder wealth can be obtained by focusing on changes in the rules that govern manager-stockholder interactions. Corporate charter changes that affect the probability of a future outside takeover are good examples. The evidence summarized in Section 2 indicates that shareholders in successful takeover targets realize substantial wealth increases. Managers of potential targets, however, can suffer welfare losses in takeovers—for example, through their displacement as managers and the resulting loss of organization-specific human capital. In such situations, managers have incentives to take actions that reduce the probability of an outside takeover and thereby benefit themselves at the expense of shareholders.

However, the conflict between shareholder interests and managerial opposition to takeovers is not clear-cut. Corporate charter changes that increase the ability of target managers to control the outcome of a takeover bid can enable managers to extract a higher offer price from the bidder or to solicit higher offers from other bidders. Jarrell and Bradley (1980) and DeAngelo and Rice (1983) argue that uncoordinated wealth-maximizing decisions by individual shareholders can result in takeovers that grant a larger share of the takeover gains to the shareholders in the bidding firm.

Suppose a firm has 100 shares of common stock with a market price of $9.50 per share and a total market value of $950. Economies with total value of $50 can be realized only if the firm is

---

[27] See Jensen and Meckling (1976, p. 328) and Fama (1980). However, unless the cost of perfectly enforcing managerial contracts is zero, the agency costs of managerial discretion will not be zero. Zero costs of managerial discretion imply zero costs of constructing a managerial performance measurement, evaluation, and compensation system that perfectly reflects in the manager's salary all deviations from shareholder wealth maximization. Contrary to Fama's (1980) argument, this implication holds even for the monitoring performed by the managerial labor market. Consider, for example, a case in which the value of a manager's human capital that is specific to this current organization is large relative to the value of his general human capital. (The value of general human capital means the value of human capital in its highest-value use outside the manager's current organization.) In this case, fluctuations in the value of his general human capital, even if they perfectly reflect the manager's deviations from maximization of shareholder wealth, will have no direct effect on his welfare. Therefore, the managerial labor market will not eliminate the agency costs between managers and stockholders in such situations.

[28] For example, the evidence presented by Mikkelson (1981, 1983) and Masulis (1980a) indicates that call and conversion of convertible bonds to common stock and exchange of common and preferred stock for bonds are associated with statistically significant stock price declines. Except for cases in which managerial compensation depends on earnings per share, it is difficult to see how managers benefit from such capital structure changes.

Table 5   Per Share Dollar Payoff to Individual Shareholder Who Either Tenders His Shares or Keeps His Shares

	Offer Outcome	
Individual Action	**Unsuccessful**	**Successful**
Tender	$12.00	$9.55
Don't tender	9.50	7.00

merged with firm A. Firm A makes a two-part takeover bid, offering $12 per share for up to 51 shares and $7 per share for the remaining 49 shares.[29] Note that if the offer is successful, the bidder obtains the target firm for $995—an amount only $5 over its market value. Shareholders of firm A therefore receive $45 of the $50 total takeover gain. As Table 5 illustrates, each shareholder faces the classic "prisoner's dilemma" problem. Acting independently, each shareholder maximizes his wealth by tendering, although all target shareholders are better off if nobody tenders until they receive a larger fraction of the takeover gains.[30] This problem is reduced by requiring bidders to get simultaneous approval of more target shareholders, and enabling management to act as agent for target shareholders can accomplish this. If antitakeover amendments increase the bargaining power of target managers to elicit a higher offer price, they could benefit target shareholders.[31]

It is worth noting that firm A in the example cannot take advantage of the target shareholder's prisoner's dilemma problems to acquire the target at less than its market value of $950 (perhaps by offering $12 for 51 shares and $5 for the rest for a total of $857). If firm A attempts this action, competition from other firms will drive the total offer to the target's current market value of $950 if there are no gains from merger. Thus as Bradley (1980) argues, competition prevents corporate raiding or corporate piracy.[32]

---

[29] Such two-part offers were used in the Conoco, Marathon, and Brunswick takeover attempts, perhaps to reduce minority shareholder blocking power. Dodd and Ruback (1977) present evidence that non-selling target shareholders receive positive abnormal returns of 17.4 percent ($t = 6.68$) in subsequent "cleanup" offers to outside minority interests. DeAngelo, DeAngelo, and Rice (1982) find abnormal returns of 30.4 percent to minority shareholders and indications of minority blocking power in going private transactions. (See Section 4.7 below.) Others have argued (see Grossman and Hart [1980]) that shareholders face free-rider problems when there is a holdout premium available. They argue that if holdout premiums exist, free-rider problems prevent takeovers from succeeding even when they are profitable for all parties. In such a situation shareholders as a group would be better off if two-part offers are made by potential bidders.

[30] If less than 51 percent of the shares are tendered and the offer is therefore unsuccessful, the tendering shareholder receives $12 per share as compared to the $9.50 market value if he does not tender. This assumes, for simplicity, that the bidder does not abandon the takeover effort. If abandonment occurs, the target firm could then become the bidder and use the same strategy to take over firm A. If the offer is successful and 100 percent of the shares are tendered, the shareholder expects to receive a minimum of $9.55 per share ($12 per share on 51 percent of his shares and $7 per share on 49 percent of his shares if he tenders immediately). If he does not tender immediately, he will receive only $7 per share. Since, independent of the outcome, immediate tendering has higher value, the optimal non-collusive decision is to tender.

[31] For simplicity we have assumed the $50 gain is independent of the takeover bargaining procedures. Easterbrook and Fischel (1982a) examine the implications of various gain-sharing rules for the creation of gains.

[32] The timing of the offer expiration is obviously important to the bidding process because it could limit competition and is worthy of additional analysis.

The remainder of this section discusses several studies that estimate the effects on stock price of managerial actions that can affect the probability that a firm will be a takeover target—including changes in the state of incorporation, adoption of antitakeover charter amendments, managerial opposition to takeovers, going private transactions, standstill agreements, and targeted large block repurchases. The results of the studies are mixed. On the one hand, there is little or no evidence of a decline in stock price that is associated with either changes in the state of incorporation or adoption of antitakeover charter amendments, and outside selling shareholders gain substantially in going private transactions. On the other hand, there is evidence that shareholders are harmed by targeted large block repurchases and standstill agreements. Overall, the evidence indicates that negative returns are associated with managerial actions regarding takeovers (1) if the action eliminates a takeover bid or causes a takeover failure, or (2) if the action does not require formal stockholder approval either through voting or tendering decisions.

4.2. Changes in State of Incorporation

Corporate charters specify the governance rules for corporations, including rules that establish conditions for mergers (such as the percentage of stockholders that must approve a takeover). Individual states specify constraints on charter rules that differ from state to state. This variation in state law means that changing the state of incorporation affects the contractual arrangement among shareholders effected through the corporate charter, and these changes can affect the probability that a firm will become a takeover target.

Dodd and Leftwich (1980) investigate changes in stockholder returns associated with changes in the state of incorporation for 140 firms during the period 1927–1977. Of these firms, 126 reincorporated in Delaware, a state that provides few constraints on charter rules and therefore provides greater contractual freedom for shareholders and managers. Delaware also provides a set of well-defined legal precedents that facilitate contracting and resolution of disputes. Only six firms left Delaware, and there were only eight changes in states of incorporation that did not involve Delaware.

One explanation for reincorporation in Delaware is that managers use Delaware's minimal restrictions on charter rules to exploit shareholders. An alternative explanation is that the more lenient Delaware code enables managers to take actions to increase shareholder wealth that are not possible (or are more costly) under the more restrictive charters in other states. For example, for a portion of the sample period Delaware required only simple majority stockholder approval for mergers, while many other states required greater than majority approval. Under these conditions, reincorporation in Delaware reduces the costs of merger approval and thereby raises the probability of becoming a bidder or a target in a takeover.

Dodd and Leftwich attempt to isolate the first public announcement of a change in the state of incorporation, but in many instances it is likely that the announcement date they identify is not the first public announcement of the reincorporation. Therefore, the market reaction to the change is likely to be incorporated in stock prices prior to the "event day," and this prior response reduces the power of their tests. They find abnormal returns to shareholders of firms that changed their state of incorporation of about 30 percent ($t = 7.90$) over the period 24 months prior to and including the announcement month—abnormal returns that seem too large to be caused solely by changes in the state of incorporation. Dodd and Leftwich use a variety of tests to determine the source of these gains, including examination of 50 firms for which precise *Wall Street Journal* announcement dates are obtainable, analysis of changes in systematic risk, and elimination of the largest positive abnormal return for each firm over the 25-month interval. These additional tests suggest that firms changed their state of incorporation after a period of superior performance and that the change itself is associated with small positive abnormal returns. Importantly, they find no evidence of a decline in stockholder wealth at times when the state of incorporation is changed—an observation inconsistent with the hypothesis that the changes are motivated by managerial exploitation of shareholders.

4.3. Antitakeover Amendments

Firms can amend their charters to make the conditions for shareholder approval of mergers more stringent. These antitakeover amendments include super-majority provisions and provisions for the staggered election of board members. By increasing the stringency of takeover conditions, such amendments can reduce the probability of being a takeover target and therefore reduce shareholder wealth. However, as explained above, by increasing the plurality required for takeover approval, the amendments could benefit shareholders by enabling target management to better represent their common interests in the merger negotiations.

DeAngelo and Rice (1983) and Linn and McConnell (1983) examine the effect of the adoption of antitakeover amendments on stock prices of the adopting firms. DeAngelo and Rice examine 100 firms that adopted super-majority, staggered board, fair price, and lock-up provisions over the period 1974–1978. Shareholders of these firms realized statistically insignificant abnormal returns of −0.16 percent ($t = -0.14$) on the day of and the day after the mailing date of the proxy containing the proposals. Over the period 10 days before through 11 days after the proxy mailing date the cumulative abnormal returns are an insignificant −0.90 percent ($t = -0.70$). These results suggest the adoption of antitakeover provisions does not reduce stockholder wealth, although DeAngelo and Rice point out that the results might be positively biased if the proposal of the amendment communicates to target shareholders an increased probability of a takeover attempt and its associated gains.

Linn and McConnell (1983) find no significant abnormal returns on the proxy mailing date for a sample of 388 firms that adopted antitakeover amendments over the period 1960–1980. They argue, however, that it is difficult to identify the precise date on which information about the antitakeover provisions is released. The information could be released on the date the board approves the amendments (which occurs prior to the proxy mailing date) or on the date of stockholder approval (which follows the proxy mailing date). Hence, they examine the abnormal stock returns throughout the amendment process. For 170 firms in which the day of board approval is available, the cumulative abnormal returns from the day of board approval through the day before the proxy mailing date is an insignificant 0.71 percent ($t = 1.20$). For 307 firms they find significant average abnormal returns of 1.43 percent ($t = 3.41$) over the period from the proxy mailing date through the day before the stockholders' meeting. In the 90-day period beginning with the stockholders' meeting, the cumulative abnormal returns are an insignificant 0.86 percent ($t = 1.65$). These results provide weak evidence in favor of the hypothesis that antitakeover amendments increase stockholder wealth. The results also suggest that the proxy mailing date is not the date when the information is incorporated in stock prices, a finding that is inconsistent with market efficiency.

Linn and McConnell also examine the abnormal returns of 49 firms that removed previously enacted antitakeover amendments. Over the period between board approval and proxy mailing, these firms experienced a statistically significant average abnormal return of -3.63 percent ($t = -2.33$). This result implies shareholders benefit from the presence of antitakeover amendments, but leaves a puzzle in understanding why they were removed in these 49 cases. In a related test, Linn and McConnell examine the abnormal stock returns of 120 firms incorporated in Delaware when the fraction of shareholders required to approve a merger was reduced by Delaware from two-thirds to a simple majority. The average abnormal return in the month of the change in the Delaware law is -1.66 percent ($t = -2.15$), and each of these 120 firms subsequently adopted antitakeover amendments. However, these 120 firms were selected because they adopted antitakeover amendments. This selection bias means that these returns are also consistent with the hypothesis that changes in the Delaware law on average had no effect on stockholder wealth.

Consistent with the DeAngelo and Rice results, the Linn and McConnell results imply that on average antitakeover amendments do not decrease stockholder wealth. In addition, the Linn and McConnell evidence is weakly supportive of the hypothesis that on the average such amendments increase shareholder wealth.[33]

4.4. Managerial Opposition to Takeovers

Target firm managers can make outside takeovers more difficult in ways other than through adoption of antitakeover corporate charter amendments. Since target shareholders benefit from takeovers, explicit managerial actions to prevent a takeover *independent of the price offered* appear to be an instance of managerial pursuit of self-interest at the expense of shareholders. Managerial opposition to a takeover in order to elicit a larger premium can increase the benefits of the takeover for shareholders. Such opposition can take the form of press releases and mailings that present the manager's position, the initiation of certain court actions, and the encouragement of competing bids.[34] However, it is difficult to argue that actions which *eliminate* a potential bidder are in the stockholder's best interests. Actions that can eliminate a takeover bid include cancellation of a merger proposal by target management without referral to shareholders, initiation of antitrust complaints, standstill agreements, or premium repurchases of the target's stock held by the bidder.

Kummer and Hoffmeister (1978) examine the abnormal returns associated with tender offers that are opposed and unopposed by target management. The average abnormal return of target shareholders in the announcement month is 16.45 percent ($t = 15.16$) for the 44 successful targets in which managers did not oppose the offer, versus 19.80 percent ($t = 13.62$) for 21 targets in which managers opposed the offer. Thus, managerial resistance is associated with higher premiums for offers that proved successful. However, 15 of the 21 targets in which managers opposed the offer were not acquired within ten months, and the shareholders of these firms incurred abnormal losses of 11.7 percent in the ten months following the initial offer. This pattern of abnormal returns is consistent with our earlier interpretation of the stock price behavior of unsuccessful targets and with the

---

[33] H. DeAngelo and E. Rice have suggested to us that when a super-majority provision grants acquisition blocking power to a manager or other stockholder (for example, a manager holding 21 percent of the stock when an 80 percent super-majority provision is implemented), the stock price effects will be more pronounced. This hypothesis has not been studied.

[34] See Easterbrook and Fischel (1981a, b, 1982a, b), Gilson (1981, 1982a, b), Bebchuk (1982a, b), and the references therein for discussion of various antitakeover tactics of target management and arguments regarding whether target management should remain passive in the presence of tender offers or whether they should take actions to help run an auction for the firm by encouraging competing bids. The effects of target management actions on the rewards to investment in takeover activities and therefore on the overall frequency of bids are an important aspect of this issue.

results of Bradley, Desai, and Kim (1983): Stock prices rise at the announcement of the initial bid and then decline if future takeover bids do not materialize. The Kummer and Hoffmeister results are consistent with the hypothesis that, on average, management opposition benefits target shareholders. The question remains, however, whether the shareholders of the targets of unsuccessful takeover bids could be made better off by less intensive managerial opposition—opposition that would allow their mergers to succeed without reducing the higher premiums in the otherwise successful offers. There appears to be an interesting free-rider problem here; although it might pay targets in general to establish a credible opposition threat, the costs to a particular target's shareholders imply they would not want a manager to let an above market offer fail.

The higher average return to targets with managerial opposition to takeovers is also consistent with the hypothesis that such opposition harms stockholders of target firms by reducing the frequency of takeover offers. For example, the higher returns could arise because only the more highly profitable takeovers are pursued when bidders believe managerial opposition will lower the probability of success and raise the expected costs.[35] If managerial opposition simply raises costs, bids will be lower than they would be otherwise and low profit takeovers would not occur. As explained earlier, this truncation of the distribution of takeovers would raise the measured average profitability of manager-opposed takeovers. Since the target's board and management must approve a merger offer before it can go to a shareholder vote, hostile takeovers must be accomplished by gaining control of the board either through tender offers or other accumulation of shares or proxies. The evidence in Tables 1 and 3 indicates that premiums to targets in tender offers are greater than premiums to targets in mergers. This could be due to the truncation phenomenon. Moreover, the truncation hypothesis is consistent with the evidence that the gains to *bidders* are also larger in tender offers.

Dodd's (1980) evidence indicates that managerial opposition harms stockholders. He partitions his sample into 26 mergers that appear to be terminated by targets and 54 mergers that are terminated by either bidders or an unidentified party. In the target-terminated subsample, the cumulative abnormal returns from ten days prior to the first public announcement of the offer through ten days after termination is about +11 percent for the target firms. In contrast, the abnormal return over the same period for the "bidder-terminated" subsample is an insignificant 0.2 percent. The average abnormal target return on the day before and day of termination announcement is a significant –5.57 percent for the cancellations by the target and a significant –9.75 percent for the cancellations by the bidder. If targets cancel mergers in anticipation of more profitable future takeover bids that will benefit stockholders, the abnormal returns to targets on announcement of cancellation would be positive rather than negative. The negative returns are consistent with the hypothesis that target managers who cancel such mergers are not acting in the stockholders' interest. In addition, the complete loss of gains to targets where bidders cancel indicates that when bidders back out (perhaps because they find they overestimated the value of the target), the target price returns to its pre-offer level.

4.5. Targeted Large Block Stock Repurchases

Currently available evidence suggests that managerial opposition to a takeover does not reduce shareholder wealth unless the resistance eliminates potential takeover bids. Two papers, Dann and

---

[35] The costs associated with making an unsuccessful takeover bid sometimes go far beyond the search costs and the administrative, legal, and other out of pocket expenses. See Ruback (1983b) for a discussion of the losses incurred by Gulf when they withdrew their bid for Cities Service.

DeAngelo (1983) and Bradley and Wakeman (1983), examine the effect on stockholder returns of privately negotiated or targeted stock repurchases. In a privately negotiated or targeted repurchase, a firm repurchases a block of its common stock from an individual holder, generally at a premium. These premiums can be interpreted as payments to potential bidders to cease takeover activity. The evidence indicates that such repurchases are associated with significantly negative abnormal stock returns for the shareholders of the repurchasing firm and significantly positive abnormal returns for the sellers. Dann and DeAngelo report an average premium over the market price of 16.4 percent on 41 negotiated repurchases involving a premium, and for these 41 repurchases they report an average abnormal return on the repurchasing firm's stock of -1.76 percent ($t = -3.59$) on the day before and day of announcement. For 17 instances of non-premium targeted large block repurchases in which the price was equal to or below the market price, Dann and DeAngelo report insignificant average abnormal returns of -0.34 percent ($t = -0.33$) on the day before and day of announcement. Bradley and Wakeman report abnormal returns of -2.85 percent ($t = -5.82$) for 61 firms that repurchased a single block of common stock and abnormal returns of 1.40 percent ($t = 2.24$) for 28 selling firms. They also present regression estimates indicating the total value of nonparticipating shareholders' stock declines dollar for dollar with increases in the premium paid to the seller, and that selling firm shareholders gain commensurately. The combined evidence presented by Dann-DeAngelo and Bradley-Wakeman indicates that premium targeted large block repurchases reduce the wealth of non-participating stockholders.

The reductions in shareholder wealth associated with targeted repurchases suggest that explicit managerial actions to eliminate takeover bidders are costly to non-participating stockholders. Bradley and Wakeman reinforce this interpretation by examining 21 firms whose targeted repurchases were associated with a takeover cancellation. For these firms the average abnormal return the day prior to through the day after announcement of the repurchase is -5.50 percent ($t = -7.14$). Over the same event period, 40 firms that made targeted repurchases unaccompanied by merger cancellations experienced average abnormal returns of -1.39 percent ($t = -1.97$). Thus, targeted repurchases are more costly to non-participating stockholders when they are used to thwart takeover attempts.

The evidence on the negative effect of targeted repurchases on shareholder wealth is especially interesting when contrasted with the large positive abnormal returns ranging from 12.4 percent to 18.9 percent from the day before to 30 days after the announcement of non-targeted repurchase tender offers documented by Masulis (1980), Dann (1981), Vermaelen (1981), and Rosenfeld (1982).[36] Moreover, Dann and Vermaelen document positive abnormal returns of 4.1 percent and 3.4 percent for 121 and 243 open-market repurchases over the same event interval. Bradley and Wakeman report abnormal returns of 1.9 percent for repurchases from insiders, 1.6 percent for repurchases of small shareholdings, and 0.6 percent for 40 targeted repurchases where no merger bid is involved (all over the same 32-day event period). All these estimates of repurchase effects are positive and are in striking contrast to the average abnormal returns of -12.5 percent over the same 32-day event interval for two targeted share repurchases which involve a merger bid. The evidence provides fairly strong indications that targeted large block repurchases at premiums over market price reduce the wealth of non-participating shareholders.

---

[36] Sample sizes range from 119 to 199.

4.6. Standstill Agreements

Dann and DeAngelo (1983) examine the effects of standstill agreements on stock prices. Standstill agreements are voluntary contracts in which a firm agrees to limit its holdings of another firm, and, therefore, not to mount a takeover attempt. The 30 firms in their sample that obtained standstill agreements earned average abnormal returns of −4.52 percent ($t = −5.72$) on the day before and day of announcement of the agreement. In addition, the 19 firms entering standstill agreements that were unaccompanied by repurchases earned average abnormal returns of −4.04 percent ($t = −4.49$) in the same event period. Bradley and Wakeman (1983) present regression evidence suggesting that the "news of the merger termination and the announcement of a standstill agreement have the same informational content." This evidence also supports the hypothesis that managerial opposition that thwarts takeover bids reduces the wealth of non-participating stockholders.

4.7. Going Private Transactions

DeAngelo, DeAngelo, and Rice (1982) examine returns to stockholders in 72 "going private" proposals for firms listed on the New York or American Stock Exchanges in the period 1973–1980. In pure going private proposals the public stock ownership is replaced by full equity ownership by an incumbent management group and the stock is delisted. In leveraged buyouts (also included in their sample) management shares the equity with private outside investors. They find abnormal returns for the public stockholders of 30.4 percent ($t = 12.4$) in the period 40 days before through the announcement of the going private proposal—gains that are virtually identical to the 29.1 percent weighted average returns in interfirm tender offers shown in Table 3, Panel A. They argue that the gains from going private are due to "savings of registration and other public ownership expenses, and improved incentives for corporate decision makers under private ownership." There is no evidence that outside stockholders are harmed in these transactions, which are commonly labeled "minority freezeouts." Moreover, the fact that stockholder litigation occurred in over 80 percent of the going private proposals that did not involve third parties provides a hint that these premiums are due to the blocking power typically accorded minority stockholders in going private transactions.

4.8. Direct Evidence on Stockholder Control

The evidence on takeovers and actions that affect the probability of takeovers suggests that takeovers serve to limit managerial departures from maximization of stockholder wealth. Conflicts of interest between owners and managers can, however, be limited in the absence of takeovers through mergers or tender offers. Stockholders elect the board of directors, and the board of directors directly monitors managers. Stockholders can change managers by electing a different board of directors, and voting rights and proxy contests are therefore important aspects of the general control process.

In this section we first examine the empirical evidence on internal transfers of control provided in the study by Dodd and Warner (1983) of the abnormal equity returns around the time of 96 proxy fights over the period 1962–1978. We then discuss the Lease, McConnell, and Mikkelson (1983) study of the value of voting rights.

Proxy Contests. In a proxy fight, dissident shareholders solicit votes to elect directors who differ from management's proposed slate. If the proxy fight results in dissidents obtaining a majority of seats on the board of directors, some change in corporate control occurs. Since both takeovers and proxy fights transfer control over assets, it is likely that the announcement of a proxy fight will be associated with an increase in equity value if the assets are to be put to superior uses. However, in a takeover the bidder offers a premium to target shareholders so that the stock price of the target can rise even if no higher value uses for the target's assets exists—the premium representing in this case a wealth transfer from bidding firm shareholders to target firm shareholders. Thus, examination of changes in equity value associated with proxy fights provides direct evidence on the gains resulting from changes in management and presumably, therefore, from changes in managerial decisions on resource utilization.

Dodd and Warner (1983) study a sample of 96 proxy contests in the period 1962–1978. They report that stockholders of firms realize a significant positive average abnormal return of 1.2 percent ($t = 2.52$) on the day before and day of the first *Wall Street Journal* announcement of a control contest. Furthermore, Dodd and Warner argue that information about the forthcoming proxy contest is available prior to the initial *Wall Street Journal* announcement and that 1.2 percent is therefore a downward-biased estimate of the abnormal stock price increase due to the contest. Over the period 59 days before through the initial announcement of the contest the abnormal return is 11.9 percent ($t = 5.09$). The significant positive abnormal return on the announcement day and the period prior to it suggests that proxy contests increase equity values and redirect the assets of the firm to more profitable uses. This implication is strengthened by the positive abnormal returns of 8.2 percent ($t = 2.78$) over the period 59 days prior to contest announcement through the day of the election outcome announcement in *The Wall Street Journal*.

If the gains to stockholders associated with a proxy fight are due solely to potential changes in management, equity prices should decline when dissidents do not obtain board representation. The results in Dodd and Warner indicate that the acquisition of even partial dissident representation on the board is associated with positive abnormal returns, and complete failure to obtain representation results in negative abnormal returns. In 56 contests in which dissidents obtained seats on the board of directors, the abnormal return on the day before and day of the outcome announcement is 1.1 percent ($t = 2.38$). Alternatively, in the 40 contests in which the dissidents failed to obtain seats, stock prices fell by 1.4 percent ($t = -1.67$) on the day before and day of the outcome announcement. However, the holding-period returns throughout the entire control contest indicate that the positive average effect of the contest is realized regardless of the outcome. Over the period sixty days prior to the initial announcement through the outcome announcement, the average abnormal return for contests in which dissidents win seats is virtually identical to that for contests in which dissidents win no seats. (These contest period estimates, of course, have much higher standard errors than the outcome announcement effects.)

Thus, while the relation between the revision in stock prices and announcement of the election outcome supports the importance of board representation, the magnitude of the revision is small relative to the total gains. The combined implication of the Dodd and Warner results is that, independent of the outcome, control contests increase equity values and the increase is larger when the dissidents win seats.

The Value of Control. We define corporate control as the rights to determine the management of corporate resources, and these rights are vested in the corporation's board of directors. Lease,

McConnell, and Mikkelson (1983) examine an important aspect of control, the value of rights to vote in elections to select the board of directors and to vote on other matters that require stockholder approval. They identify 30 firms that have two classes of common stock that differ only in their voting rights. Both classes have identical claims to dividends and are treated equally on liquidation. They calculate the ratio of month end prices for the two classes of stock over the time in which the two classes traded in the period 1940–1978. For 18 firms with voting and non-voting common stock and without voting preferred stock, the average premium for the voting stock is 3.79 percent. Of the 360 month end price ratios in their sample, 336 indicate that the voting stock traded at a premium. For the 9 firms without voting preferred stock that have two classes of voting common stock which differ only in voting rights, the common stock with superior voting rights traded at an average premium of 6.95 percent, and 393 of the 468 month end price ratios indicate a premium for the stock with superior voting rights. Finally, for four firms with voting preferred, the class of common stock with superior voting rights traded at an average discount of 1.17 percent.

While the discount for stock with superior voting rights in firms that have voting preferred remains an unexplained puzzle, the weight of the Lease, McConnell, and Mikkelson evidence indicates that voting rights are valuable. In addition, Dodd and Warner (1983) present evidence that voting rights are valuable. For 42 proxy contests with record dates that follow the initial announcement of the proxy contest, they report that stock prices fall on average by 1.4 percent ($t = -3.02$) on the day after the record date (the day the stock goes ex-vote).

5. Unsettled Issues and Directions for Future Research

Careful examination of the reaction of stock prices to various control-related events has greatly increased our understanding of the market for corporate control. Nevertheless, much remains to be learned, and the measurement of effects on stock prices will continue to play an important role in this research effort. We are, however, reaching the point of rapidly diminishing returns from efforts that focus *solely* on stock price effects. Further progress toward understanding the market for corporate control will be substantially aided by efforts that examine other organizational, technological, and legal aspects of the environment in addition to the effects of takeovers on stock prices. Of course, the relationship between these other factors and stock price effects will be of continuing importance to future research. This section is devoted to discussion of a number of unsettled issues and suggests some directions for future research.

5.1. Competition among Management Teams

In our view the takeover market is an arena in which alternative management teams compete for the rights to manage corporate resources.[37] In small takeovers management teams can consist of a single proprietor (with staff) or a partnership of managers. Competing management teams are also commonly organized in the corporate form, especially in large takeovers. In these cases the managerial team consists of the top-level internal managers and a board of directors. The board acts as the top-level control device and is the repository of the control rights acquired by the team. The

---

[37] This phenomenon is made particularly evident by the simultaneous mutual tender offers that have become common recently, the so-called "Pac Man" defense. See Herzel and Schmidt (1983) for a penetrating discussion of these offers.

competition among management teams is complex, and it is not yet fully described by theory or evidence. The following discussion, however, suggests an analytical approach and directions for future research.

The Contractual Setting. Analysis of the competition among management teams in the market for corporate control must begin with a specification of the analytically important aspects of the institutional and contractual environment.[38] In particular, the nature of the rights of each of the parties in the set of contracts that define the open corporation are important to the functioning of the market for corporate control. The corporation is a legal entity that serves as the nexus for a set of contracts among independent agents. One implication of this view is that the corporation has no owners. Instead, stockholders are agents in the nexus of contracts who specialize in riskbearing. Indeed, unrestricted common stock residual claims are the unique contractual aspect of the open corporate form that distinguishes it from all other forms of organization. Its residual claims are unrestricted in the sense that they are freely alienable and do not require the claimant to have any other role in the organization—in contrast, for example, to the residual claims of closed corporations that are generally restricted to agents with other roles in the organization. This unrestricted alienability enables separation of the riskbearing and management functions and therefore facilitates the realization of the benefits of specialization of these two functions. In this view, control of the agency problems of separation of residual riskbearing from management functions requires separation of the management function (initiation and implementation) from the control function (ratification and monitoring). Observation indicates this always occurs and that boards of directors or trustees are the common institutional device for accomplishing this separation.

The board of directors in the open corporation is elected by vote of the residual claimants who, while retaining the rights to ratify certain major decisions by shareholder vote, delegate most management and control rights to the board. The board in turn delegates most of its management and control rights to the internal managers while retaining the rights to ratify certain major decisions. Most importantly, the board of directors always retains the top-level control rights, that is, the rights to hire, fire, and set the compensation of the top-level managers. Board membership consists of internal managers and external agents with expertise of value to the organization. Moreover, the complex contractual arrangements that define the open corporation are embedded in a legal system that further defines the contracts and rights of the parties. For example, the legal system imposes fiduciary responsibility on board members and managers and delineates the legal rights and remedies available to shareholders who challenge the actions of the board members and managers.

The unrestricted alienability of the common stock residual claims of the open corporation is essential to the existence of the market for control. Unrestricted alienability allows the existence of a stock market that facilitates transfer and valuation of the claims at low cost. Low cost transferability makes it possible for competing outside managers to bypass the current management and board of directors to acquire the rights to manage the corporation's resources. These control rights can be acquired by direct solicitation of stockholders, either through tender offers or proxy solicitation. Outside management teams can also acquire the management rights by merger negotiations with the target's management and board, subject to ratification by vote of the stockholders.

---

[38] This discussion draws on the analysis in Jensen and Meckling (1976, 1979), Fama (1980), and especially Fama and Jensen (1983a, b).

The internal control system has its foundation in the corporate charter and is strengthened or weakened by day to day operating practices and procedures and by the quality of the individuals who hold board seats and positions in top management. Competition from alternative management teams in the market for corporate control serves as a source of external control on the internal control system of the corporation. Alternative institutional forms such as professional partnerships, non-profit organizations, and mutuals do not receive the benefits of competition from alternative management teams in an external control market.[39] Of course, internal competition in each of these organizations and the external regulatory environment (such as in banking) contributes to the control function. But the corporation alone receives the benefits of the private external control market in addition to the internal control mechanisms.

When a breakdown of the internal control system imposes large costs on shareholders from incompetent, lazy, or dishonest managers, takeover bids in the market for corporate control provide a vehicle for replacing the entire internal control system. Competing managers who perceive the opportunity to eliminate the inefficiencies can offer target shareholders a higher-valued alternative than current management while benefiting their own shareholders and themselves. Similar incentives come into play when the acquisition of substantial synergy gains requires displacement of an efficient current management team.

Management teams receive the assistance of legal and financial institutions with expertise in both offensive and defensive takeover strategies. Sometimes this assistance is acquired under direct contract (for example, legal services) and on other occasions the assistance is provided by independent agents acting in their own interest. Takeover specialists sometimes referred to as "raiders"— who acquire specialized expertise in takeover strategy and in ferreting out and amassing a controlling block of shares—perform an important function in facilitating transfers of control. Such agents may or may not take control of a firm. They can succeed solely by developing expertise in discovering companies where potential takeover gains exist and in amassing blocks of shares sufficient to enable other management teams to acquire the control rights. The takeover specialists' gains come from transferring their shares to these other acquirers at the takeover price. Arbitrageurs perform an important role by specializing in valuing the competing offers and providing a market that allows investors to delegate both the valuation and riskbearing function during the takeover period.

5.2. Directions for Future Research

Many interesting and important research issues are suggested by the managerial competition view of the market for corporate control. It also suggests new perspectives on a number of unresolved issues that promise significant advances in the development of a theory of organizations.[40]

Examination of the costs and benefits to competing management teams of success or failure in the takeover market will aid in understanding the forces that determine when and why takeovers are initiated, and why target managers oppose or acquiesce to such proposals. Factual knowledge about

---

[39] Fama and Jensen (1983a, b, c) provide detailed analyses of these alternative organizational forms and their survival properties. Mayers and Smith (1981, 1982) and Smith (1982) provide a discussion of conflict resolution, contracting practices, and the differences between mutual and corporate organizational forms in the insurance and banking industries.

[40] See Jensen (1983) for a discussion and overall perspective on organization theory and methodology and the emerging revolution in the science of organizations.

the career paths and compensation experience of bidder and target management personnel will be valuable in such efforts. For example: How does management turnover frequency in takeover situations compare with that in non-takeover conditions? Do target managers lose their jobs more frequently in unfriendly takeovers than in friendly or "white knight" acquisitions? What happens to the managers of targets who successfully avoid takeover? When target managers remain with the merged firm, how do they fare in compensation, rank, and rapidity of promotion in the merged firm? How do target managers who leave the merged entity fare in the external labor market? What happens to managers of successful and unsuccessful bidding firms, and how does their experience (compensation, promotion, etc.) relate to the stock price effects of the outcomes? What is the relative frequency with which takeovers are motivated by inefficient target management versus the acquisition of other economies or synergies? What are the synergies that contribute to takeover gains? How are takeover frequency and terms affected by (1) antitakeover amendments, (2) golden parachutes (that is, contractual employment guarantees and compensation in the event of control changes), and (3) various other managerial actions to oppose takeovers?

The definition of the market for corporate control as the arena in which managers compete for resources to manage raises a variety of questions regarding the form of the competition. Takeover strategies, both offensive and defensive, have received relatively little attention in the academic literature. The managerial competition model provides an interesting framework for the evaluation of alternative strategies. For example, bidders in hostile takeovers typically try to reduce the time that the offer is outstanding by keeping it secret prior to its announcement and by structuring offers (e.g., two-part offers) so that early tendering is beneficial to shareholders. Incumbent managers attempt to lengthen the time that an offer is outstanding. These opposing strategies are consistent with managerial competition, the bidder tries to reduce the incumbent management team's ability to compete, and targets want more time to respond to the bid or to seek out other bidders that offer better opportunities for themselves and their shareholders. This is consistent with the observation that potential targets prepare takeover defenses prior to the occurrence of a hostile bid.

The managerial competition perspective also helps explain the types of defensive strategies used by target firms. For example, suppose the incumbent management team has reliable information that its equity is underpriced. If this information cannot be made public, the managerial competition model predicts that incumbent managers will attempt to find a white knight. The information could be released to the white knight, perhaps through a confidential information center, and both the incumbent management team and the shareholders of the target would benefit. While this analysis is preliminary and speculative, the interactions between the incentives of competing management teams and the strategies they adopt is an interesting area for future research. Knowledge resulting from such research will allow us to understand better the determinants of the offer, such as structure (single or two part, cash or exchange of securities), timing, type of offer (tender, merger, or proxy contest), and tax effects. Understanding takeover strategy also requires more detailed knowledge of the effects of voting rules (see Easterbrook and Fischel [1983]), the determinants of effective control, the effects of institutional ownership, and the effects of specialized takeover agents and arbitrageurs (see Wyser-Pratte [1982]).

Detailed knowledge of the control market should also provide insights regarding the reasons for spinoffs and divestitures, and why joint ventures, which can be thought of as partial mergers, are used in some cases and not in others. Why, for example, are joint ventures often used for new ventures and not for ongoing operations, for example, by divestiture of a corporate division into a joint venture with outside partners? A thorough understanding of spinoffs, divestitures, takeovers, and joint ventures should also help us understand the discounts and premiums on closed-end funds and, in particular, why closed-end funds selling at substantial discounts are not either liquidated or turned into open-end funds (see Thompson [1978]).

Finally, a number of more familiar issues require substantial additional research to complete our knowledge. No one as yet has studied the prices paid by white knights in mergers; folklore holds that embattled target managers search out such friendly merger partners to rescue them from an unfriendly takeover. But if the takeover premiums paid by white knights are generally no lower than other offers, shareholders are not harmed. In addition, precise measurement of the returns to bidders in takeovers is still an unsettled issue. Finally, knowledge of the sources of takeover gains still eludes us.

5.3. Conclusions

Many controversial issues regarding the market for corporate control have yet to be settled, and many new issues have yet to be studied. It is clear, however, that much is now known about this market. Indeed, it is unlikely that any set of transactions has been studied in such detail. In brief, the evidence seems to indicate that corporate takeovers generate positive gains, that target firm shareholders benefit, and that bidding firm shareholders do not lose. Moreover, the gains created by corporate takeovers do not appear to come from the creation of market power. Finally, it is difficult to find managerial actions related to corporate control that harm stockholders; the exceptions are those actions that eliminate an actual or potential bidder, for example, through the use of targeted large block repurchases or standstill agreements.

While research on the market for corporate control has mushroomed, it is, in our opinion, a growth industry. Much exciting and valuable knowledge remains to be discovered, and there are valuable prospects for beneficial interdisciplinary exchange among lawyers, economists, accountants, and organization theorists. An important result of this research will be a greatly expanded set of knowledge about the functioning of this enormously productive social invention: the corporation.[41]

References

Asquith, Paul, 1980. A two-event study of merger bids, market uncertainty, and stockholder returns. Ph.D. dissertation (University of Chicago, Chicago, IL).

Asquith, Paul, 1983. Merger bids, uncertainty, and stockholder returns. *Journal of Financial Economics* 11, 51–83.

Asquith, Paul, Robert F. Bruner, and David W. Mullins, Jr., 1983. The gains to bidding firms from merger. *Journal of Financial Economics* 11, 121–40.

Asquith, Paul, and E. Han Kim, 1982. The impact of merger bids on the participating firms' security holders. *The Journal of Finance* 37, 1209–28.

Bebchuck, Lucian, 1982a. The case for facilitating competing tender offers: A reply and extension. *Stanford Law Review* 35, 23ff.

Bebchuck, Lucian, 1982b. The case for facilitating competing tender offers. *Harvard Law Review* 95, 1028ff.

Benston, George J., 1980. Conglomerate mergers: Causes, consequences, and remedies (American Enterprise Institute for Public Policy Research, Washington, DC).

[41] See also Meckling and Jensen (1982).

Bradley, Michael, 1980. Interfirm tender offers and the market for corporate control. *Journal of Business* 53, 345–76.

Bradley, Michael, Anand Desai, and E. Han Kim, 1982. Specialized resources and competition in the market for corporate control. Working paper (University of Michigan, Ann Arbor, MI).

Bradley, Michael, Anand Desai, and E. Han Kim, 1983. The rationale behind interfirm tender offers: Information or synergy? *Journal of Financial Economics* 11, 183–206.

Bradley, Michael, and L. MacDonald Wakeman, 1983. The wealth effects of targeted share repurchases. *Journal of Financial Economics* 11, 301–28.

Brown, Stephen J., and Jerold B. Warner, 1980. Measuring security price performance. *Journal of Financial Economics* 8, 205–58.

Brown, Stephen J., and Jerold B. Warner, 1983. Using daily stock returns in event studies. Unpublished manuscript (University of Rochester, Rochester, NY).

Chandler, Alfred, D., Jr., 1962. Strategy and structure (MIT Press, Cambridge, MA).

Chandler, Alfred, D., Jr., 1977. The visible hand: The managerial revolution (Belknapp Press, Cambridge, MA).

Dann, Larry Y., 1981. Common stock repurchases: An analysis of returns to bondholders and stockholders. *Journal of Financial Economics* 9, 113–38.

Dann, Larry Y., and Harry DeAngelo, 1983. Standstill agreements, privately negotiated stock repurchases, and the market for corporate control. *Journal of Financial Economics* 11, 275–300.

Dann, Larry Y., and Wayne H. Mikkelson, 1982. Convertible debt issuance, capital structure change, and leverage-related information: Some new evidence. Unpublished manuscript (Amos Tuck School of Business, Hanover, NH).

DeAngelo, Harry, Linda DeAngelo, and Edward M. Rice, 1982. Going private: Minority freezeouts and stockholder wealth. Managerial Economics Research Center working paper no. MERC 82–18 (Graduate School of Management, University of Rochester, Rochester, NY).

DeAngelo, Harry, and Edward M. Rice, 1983. Antitakeover charter amendments and stockholder wealth. *Journal of Financial Economics* 11, 329–60.

Dodd, Peter, 1980. Merger proposals, management discretion and stockholder wealth. *Journal of Financial Economics* 8, 105–38.

Dodd, Peter, and Richard Leftwich, 1980. The market for corporate charters: "Unhealthy competition" versus federal regulation. *Journal of Business* 53, 259–83.

Dodd, Peter, and Richard Ruback, 1977. Tender offers and stockholder returns: An empirical analysis. *Journal of Financial Economics* 5, 351–74.

Dodd, Peter, and Jerold B. Warner, 1983. On corporate governance: A study of proxy contests. *Journal of Financial Economics* 11, 401–38.

Easterbrook, Frank H., and Daniel R. Fischel, 1981a. The proper role of a target's management in responding to a tender offer. *Harvard Law Review* 94, 1161–1203.

Easterbrook, Frank H., and Daniel R. Fischel, 1981b. Takeover bids, defensive tactics, and shareholders' welfare. *The Business Lawyer* 36, 1733–50.

Easterbrook, Frank H., and Daniel R. Fischel, 1982a. Corporate control transactions. *Yale Law Journal* 91, 698–737.

Easterbrook, Frank H., and Daniel R. Fischel, 1982b. Auctions and sunk costs in tender offers. *Stanford Law Review* 35, 1–21.

Easterbrook, Frank H., and Daniel R. Fischel, 1983. Voting in corporate law. *Journal of Law and Economics* 26.

Eckbo, B. Espen, 1983. Horizontal mergers, collusion, and stockholder wealth. *Journal of Financial Economics* 11, 241–73.

Ellert, J. C., 1975. Antitrust enforcement and the behavior of stock prices. Unpublished dissertation (University of Chicago, Chicago, IL).

Ellert, J. C., 1976. Mergers, antitrust law enforcement and stockholder returns. *The Journal of Finance* 31, 715–32.

Fama, Eugene F., 1980. Agency problems and the theory of the firm. *Journal of Political Economy* 88, 288–307.

Fama, Eugene F., Larry Fisher, Michael C. Jensen, and Richard Roll, 1969. The adjustment of stock prices to new information. *International Economic Review* 10, 1–21.

Fama, Eugene F., and Michael C. Jensen, 1983a. Separation of ownership and control. *Journal of Law and Economics* 26.

Fama, Eugene F., and Michael C. Jensen, 1983b. Agency problems and residual claims. *Journal of Law and Economics* 26, June, forthcoming.

Fama, Eugene F., and Michael C. Jensen, 1983c. Organizational forms and investment decisions. Managerial Economics Research Center working paper no. MERC 83–03, April (Graduate School of Management, University of Rochester, Rochester, NY).

Gilson, Ronald J., 1981. A structural approach to corporations: The case against defensive tactics in tender offers. *Stanford Law Review* 33, 819–91.

Gilson, Ronald J., 1982a. The case against shark repellent amendments: Structural limitations on the enabling concept. *Stanford Law Review* 34, 775–836.

Gilson, Ronald J., 1982b. Seeking competitive bids versus pure passivity in tender offer defense. *Stanford Law Review* 35, 51–67.

Grossman, S., and O. Hart, 1980. Takeover bids, the free-rider problem, and the theory of the corporation. *Bell Journal of Economics*, Spring, 42–64.

Herzel, Leo, and John R. Schmidt, 1983. Simultaneous mutual tender offers. Unpublished manuscript, March (Mayer, Brown and Platt, Chicago, IL).

Jarrell, Gregg, and Michael Bradley, 1980. The economic effects of federal and state regulations of cash tender offers. *Journal of Law and Economics* 23, 371–407.

Jensen, Michael C., 1983. Organization theory and methodology. *Accounting Review* 58, 319–39.

Jensen, Michael C., and William H. Meckling, 1976. Theory of the firm: Managerial behavior, agency costs and ownership structure. *Journal of Financial Economics* 3, 305–60.

Jensen, Michael C., and William H. Meckling, 1979. Rights and production functions: An application to labor-managed firms and codetermination. *Journal of Business* 52, 469–506.

Keown, Arthur J., and John M. Pinkerton, 1981. Merger announcements and insider trading activity: An empirical investigation. *The Journal of Finance* 36, 855–69.

Kim, H., and J. McConnell, 1977. Corporate mergers and co-insurance of corporate debt. *The Journal of Finance* 32, 349–63.

Klein, Benjamin, Robert Crawford, and Armen A. Alchian, 1978. Vertical integration, appropriable rents, and the competitive contracting process. *Journal of Law and Economics* 21, 297–326.

Kummer, D., and R. Hoffmeister, 1978. Valuation consequences of cash tender offers. *The Journal of Finance* 33, 505–16.

Langetieg, T., 1978. An application of a three-factor performance index to measure stockholders' gains from merger. *Journal of Financial Economics* 6, 365–84.

Lease, Ronald C., John J. McConnell, and Wayne H. Mikkelson, 1983. The market value of control in publicly-traded corporations. *Journal of Financial Economics* 11, 439–72.

Linn, Scott C., and John J. McConnell, 1983. An empirical investigation of the impact of "antitakeover" amendments on common stock prices. *Journal of Financial Economics* 11, 361–99.

Malatesta, Paul H., 1981. Corporate mergers. Unpublished Ph.D dissertation (University of Rochester, Rochester, NY).

Malatesta, Paul H., 1983. The wealth effect of merger activity and the objective functions of merging firms. *Journal of Financial Economics* 11, 155–81.

the threat of liquidation would deter strategic defaults. As we discussed above, suboptimal liquidations can occur also following liquidity-induced defaults. Debt restructuring may be a solution. Mechanisms which facilitate debt restructuring (private or court-supervised) will reduce the costs of premature liquidation following liquidity defaults. However, the same mechanisms will reduce inefficiencies following a strategic default, encouraging such defaults. The ex ante efficiency of the debt restructuring mechanisms will depend on the relative importance of these two effects. Hart and Moore [60], Harris and Raviv [59], and Bolton and Scharfstein [28] develop related arguments.

In addition to incomplete contracting, asymmetric information between debtors and creditors about the value of the assets (ongoing firm value or liquidation value) can frustrate mutually beneficial debt renegotiation (see, e.g., Giammarino [52]). As Brown [30] points out, when there is symmetric information between management and creditors, a private workout is always successful. Many of the theoretical models in the area examine the consequences of incomplete contracting and asymmetric information on the efficiency of contracting and the mechanisms to manage financial distress arising from breach of the terms of the contract.

I will use the framework developed above to next organize the survey of the theory and evidence on asset restructuring (Section II), private debt restructuring (Section III), and the formal bankruptcy process (Section IV).

II. Asset Restructuring

As outlined in the general framework developed in Section I, one set of mechanisms to deal with financial distress involves restructuring the asset side of the balance sheet to generate sufficient cash to meet the requirements of the hard contracts. Assets can be sold (either piecemeal or in their entirety) to other firms or new management teams. Asset sales can be accomplished privately or through court-supervised stages either during bankruptcy reorganization (Chapter 11 of the Bankruptcy Code) or under the liquidation process (Chapter 7 of the Bankruptcy Code). Each of these alternatives has different costs attached to them. Whether asset restructuring is actually used to manage financial distress would depend on its costs relative to those of financial restructuring.[3]

Shleifer and Vishny [104] study the liquidity costs associated with interfirm asset sales prompted by financial distress.[4] In identifying the determinants of market liquidity, they focus on (i) fungibility (i.e., the number of distinct uses and users for a particular asset), (ii) participation restrictions (e.g., regulations on foreign acquisitions, antitrust restrictions), and (iii) credit constraints in the industry. They argue that the price received in a distress sale may have large liquidity discounts if the entire industry is in a downturn. In an illiquid secondary market, the costs of asset restructuring are likely to be high, and financial restructuring may provide the dominant mechanisms of dealing with financial distress.

---

[3] The role of asset restructuring in improving investment incentives when risky debt is outstanding has been analyzed by John [76] and John and John [77]. John [76] provides a theoretical rationale for value gains from spin-offs and asset sales and characterizes the optimal allocation of the pre-spin-off debt. John and John [77] demonstrate conditions for the optimality of limited recourse project financing arrangements.

[4] Asset sales in bankruptcy may have some advantages over those done privately outside formal bankruptcy proceedings. Purchasing assets from a financially distressed firm is less risky in Chapter 11 because asset sales are executed by a court order and are thus free from legal challenge. In addition, if the seller subsequently files for Chapter 11, the buyer may have to return the assets as "avoidable preference" or "fraudulent transfer." Given the material costs of being challenged or cancelled, asset sales in Chapter 11 may be preferred by potential buyers.

In an integrated model of asset and debt restructuring, John and Vasudevan [74] examine how the cost of asset sales, the current liquidity position of the firm, and the option value of its equity determine the choice between a private workout (with or without some asset sales) and filing for the formal Chapter 11 process, possibly seeking debtor-in-possession (DIP) financing. Since asset sales may extinguish some of the option value of equity, there is an endogenous cost of asset sales to equityholders (in addition to the costs of illiquidity discussed by Shleifer and Vishny [104]). When the combined costs of asset liquidations are high, the firm may file for Chapter 11 bankruptcy and seek new financing as DIP financing, which has priority over existing debt. To determine the expected payoffs to equity under the different alternatives, the reorganization process itself (both workouts and Chapter 11) is modelled as an alternating offer bargaining game with asymmetric information, where the equityholders are better informed than the bondholders or the judge (in Chapter 11). Based on the allocation of value in equilibrium, the outcomes include private restructuring with and without asset sales, and Chapter 11 filings with DIP financing. The time spent in the Chapter 11 reorganization is endogenous to the model, and one of the possible outcomes is a "pre-packaged" bankruptcy with a speedy reorganization.

John and Vasudevan [74] obtain several empirical implications:

(i) Successful completion of debt workouts should result in increased stock prices and increased combined firm value. Chapter 11 filings should produce a negative announcement effect. Firms which privately restructure their debt have higher going-concern value when compared to firms which file for Chapter 11. Average time spent by firms in Chapter 11 reorganizations is more than that in workouts. (Gilson, John, and Lang [55] document evidence consistent with these predictions.)

(ii) Asset sales by distressed firms to make debt payments have a positive effect on stock prices. This is consistent with the empirical evidence in Lang, Poulsen, and Stulz [87].

(iii) Deviations from absolute priority are higher in workouts than that in Chapter 11 reorganization. Write-downs are lower in workouts. This is consistent with Franks and Torous [48].

(iv) Write-downs in prepackaged bankruptcy filings will be lower than ordinary Chapter 11 reorganization.

(v) The payoffs to bondholders monotonically increase in the indirect costs of bankruptcy.

The framework of Section I, in characterizing financial distress as a mismatch between the currently available liquid assets and the current obligations of its "hard" financial contracts, suggests that after financial distress has occurred, managing it involves correcting the mismatch by either increasing the liquidity of the assets (through asset sales) or decreasing the "hardness" of the debt contracts (through debt renegotiation). However, before the firm is in financial distress it can design the structure and the form of its debt contracts and choose its leverage and liquidity policies such that its costs of financial distress are reduced. Opler [97] and John [75] study these issues empirically. Leveraged buyouts have been increasingly funded in ways which appear to reduce the risk and cost of financial distress. Leveraged buyout financing methods include the use of specialist sponsors, strip financing, covenants which require that excess cash flows be paid to debtholders, and debt provisions which allow deferral of interest payments in periods of financial distress. Opler [97] documents the prevalance of these innovative financing techniques and estimates their impact on the risk-adjusted cost of debt in 63 LBOs which occurred in 1987 and 1988. The results show that sponsorship by an LBO specialist lowers the weighted average cost of LBO debt and the imputed cost of capital by roughly 60 basis points. In addition, debt provisions which allow deferral of interest payments on junior debt and which maintain a minimum bond value are used in many of the LBOs in the sample. While these provisions do not lower financing costs, their use indicates that LBO capital structures are designed to avoid the need for debt workouts or Chapter 11 proceedings in periods of financial distress.

Given the above characterization of financial distress, a firm with high costs of financial distress will reduce its exposure in two ways: (*i*) increase the liquid component of its assets, and (*ii*) reduce the extent of its hard contracts (such as debt). Based on this argument, John [75] postulates (*i*) a positive relationship between corporate liquidity and distress costs, and (*ii*) a negative relationship between leverage and distress costs.[5] A major component of distress costs is the costs of illiquidity of assets. These costs include costs of distressed asset sales and loss of going-concern value in liquidations. Some new proxies are proposed for the costs of illiquidity and the indirect costs of financial distress. These include Tobin's *q*, R&D and advertising expenditures, an index of asset specificity, and an index of the probability of bankruptcy. The liquidity ratio is documented to be positively related to these proxies of financial distress costs. It is negatively related to proxies for alternate sources of anticipated liquidity such as intermediate cash flows, debt financing, length of cash cycle, and the collateral value of assets. Total debt is also negatively related to Tobin's *q* and asset specificity as well as measures of intermediate cash flows. Long-term debt is also negatively related to proxies for alternate sources of anticipated liquidity such as intermediate cash flows, debt financing, length of cash cycle, and the collateral value of assets. Total debt is also negatively related to Tobin's *q* and asset specificity as well as measures of intermediate cash flows. Long-term debt is also negatively related to Tobin's *q* and asset specificity. Overall, the evidence is strongly consistent with the hypothesized relationships between corporate liquidity and financial distress costs, and corporate leverage and financial distress costs.

Brown, James, and Mooradian [31], Asquith, Gertner, and Scharfstein [15], Lang, Poulsen, and Stulz [87], Hotchkiss [61], and Ofek [96] present evidence of asset restructuring by firms in distress. All of the above papers document that asset sales are frequently used by financially distressed firms in their sample. Brown, James, and Mooradian [31] find that firms which sell assets are distinguished by multiple division or multiple subsidiary operations. Conversely, most of the firms which do not sell assets operate only a single division. They also find that the announcement of asset sales elicits *insignificant* abnormal stock returns. However, the announcement effect is positive for the subset of seller firms which also subsequently avoid bankruptcy. Lang, Poulsen, and Stulz [87] document that the abnormal return is higher for sellers who use the proceeds from asset sales for retiring debt. Asquith, Gertner, and Scharfstein [15] conclude that asset sales are an important means of avoiding bankruptcy. They find that only three out of 21 companies that sell over 20 percent of their assets go bankrupt.

The overall evidence seems to suggest that although asset sales are used to deal with financial distress, in most cases they are used in conjunction with debt restructuring.

---

[5] The negative relationship between leverage and distress costs has been documented in several earlier studies, e.g., Titman and Wessels [105]. See John [75] for a summary of this research and a complete list of references.

III. Private Debt Restructuring

Informal reorganization of corporate financial structures through debt restructurings and private workouts can be used to "soften" the hard contracts which caused financial distress. Consistent with the model of Section I, to remedy financial distress the firm will reduce or defer payments on its debt contracts or replace debt with soft securities having residual rather than fixed payoffs. We can define a debt restructuring as a transaction in which an existing debt contract is replaced by a new contract with (*i*) a reduction in the required interest or principal payments, (*ii*) extension of maturity, or (*iii*) placement of equity securities (common stock or securities convertible into common stock) with creditors. Private debt restructuring is surveyed in this section, and debt reorganization in a court-adjudicated formal bankruptcy process is surveyed in Section IV.

Haugen and Senbet [61], [62] argue that capital market mechanisms could accomplish the restructuring of problematic hard contracts and replacing them with a softer mix. They argue that the transactions costs of these "private" mechanisms are small and should form an upper bound on the costs of managing financial distress. Jensen [67], [68] has also argued that since these private restructurings represent an alternative to formal bankruptcy proceedings, it pays to "privatize" bankruptcy if this informal mechanism is cost-efficient. Roe [100] has also made similar arguments in the legal literature.

A simple conceptual framework is developed in Gilson, John, and Lang [55] to determine the choice between private restructuring and formal bankruptcy process, which is based on two factors. Let ΔC be the cost saving by choosing the first alternative over the second. If ΔC is positive, by choosing the first alternative, the firm's claims can be restructured to leave each of the original claimants better off (they share the incremental value ΔC collectively). The larger is ΔC, the stronger are the claimholders' incentives to settle privately. However, the private alternative will be adopted only if there is unanimous agreement on how to share ΔC. Impediments to teaching a settlement on a private restructuring can be (*i*) holdout problems encountered when a firm's debt is held by a large number of diffuse creditors, (*ii*) informational asymmetries that can arise between poorly informed outside creditors and a better informed manager or insiders of the firm, and (*iii*) conflicts among different groups of creditors.

A. Holdout Problem

Achieving an agreement among creditors outside of the formal bankruptcy process will depend upon what type of debt is restructured, e.g., private debt or public debt. The restructuring of public debt is governed by the Trust Indenture Act of 1939, which requires *unanimous* consent of every bondholder to change the maturity, principal, or coupon rate of interest in the bond indenture. Such stringent voting rules preclude a debt restructuring in which the core terms of widely held public debt can be changed. Consequently, almost all restructurings of public debt take the form of an exchange offer.

An exchange offer and the resulting holdout problem can be understood based on the framework developed in Section I. In an exchange offer, the bondholders are given the option to exchange their old bonds for a package of new securities (often including some form of equity). The idea here is to swap the existing "hard" contract for a "softer" mix. Since participation is optional, individual